191

L. D. Holt

June 1974

# Studies in
# ISAIAH

*by*

## F. C. JENNINGS

## LOIZEAUX BROTHERS
*Neptune, New Jersey*

FIRST EDITION, 1935
FOURTH PRINTING, 1966

*Loizeaux Brothers, Inc.* • *Bible Truth Depot*

**A Nonprofit Organization, Devoted to the
Lord's Work and to the spread of His Truth**

PRINTED IN THE UNITED STATES OF AMERICA

# TABLE of CONTENTS

# CONTENTS

CONTENTS

# CONTENTS

8                            CONTENTS

## CHAPTER FIFTY-ONE

## CHAPTER FIFTY-TWO
### Verses 1 to 12

## CHAPTERS FIFTY-TWO (Verses 13 to 15)
### AND FIFTY-THREE

## CHAPTER FIFTY-FOUR

## CHAPTER FIFTY-FIVE

## CHAPTER FIFTY-SIX

## CHAPTER FIFTY-SEVEN

## CHAPTER FIFTY-EIGHT

## CHAPTER FIFTY-NINE

# FOREWORD

JEWISH tradition claims that Isaiah the prophet suffered martyrdom by having been sawn asunder. We do not know if this is true, but we know the book of Isaiah has suffered severely in the hands of the modern destructive critics. They have used the knife as the wicked Jewish king did when he cut the sacred scroll of Jeremiah and cast it into the fire. They claim to have discovered what was unknown to the ancient Jewish synagogue and its able scholars, and what the great giants of intellect and scholarship of Christendom never knew, that the book of Isaiah is not the inspired work of the man of God whose name it bears. They have invented an unknown writer who assumed the name of Isaiah, but was not the prophet at all. They call him a "Deutero-Isaiah"; they did not stop with this but speak of a "Trito-Isaiah." Thus the majestic book of Isaiah has been and still is the battlefield on which true faith and the most subtle infidelity clash.

The denial of the authenticity and unity, as well as the one authorship, is a serious matter. It impeaches the testimony of the Lord Jesus Christ, the infallible Teacher, and also the testimony of the Holy Spirit. We find in the New Testament Scriptures a number of quotations from Isaiah, taken from different parts of the book. They are prefaced by different phrases—"Spoken by the prophet Isaiah"..."Fulfilled which was spoken by Esaias" ..."As said the prophet Isaiah"..."Well spake the Holy Spirit by Esaias"..."The saying of Isaiah the prophet," and others.

The work of the author of the volume shows the unity of the book and that only one person could have written it. This fact alone disposes of the puerile theories of the destructive school.

Our beloved brother has rendered a real service to the Church of God in giving us such a scholarly, premillennial and, above everything else, spiritual interpretation of this great prophetic book. For about ten years thousands of lovers of the Word of God read these unfoldings month after month in the pages of "Our Hope" and many expressed a desire that these excellent expositions be brought out in a volume. And now after a careful revision we are happy that this has been made possible.

A real commentary, covering every verse in the book of Isaiah, has been for many years a real *desideratum*. While there are several most helpful expositions in existence written by German exegetes, very little has been available in the English language.

We know God will richly bless this volume in leading His people deeper into the vision of Isaiah, the prophet.

ARNO CLEMENS GAEBELEIN.
Editor of "Our Hope."

# INTRODUCTORY

**Prophecy, its value. Deep significance of both names and numbers in Scripture. The divisions of the book.**

OUR poet Cowper sang, and sang truthfully enough,

> "Sweet is the harp of prophecy; too sweet
> Not to be wronged by a mere mortal touch,"

for, ever sweet to the ear of faith, and especially to faith in a day of trial and chastening, is the music of prophecy. It was never sounded, and its worth is still rarely appreciated, save in days of depression and declension amid the Lord's people; and whilst it spares not their sins, but exposes them fully, it ever points to a tender grace that is ready to meet and welcome penitence, and to a wisdom that has made provision to do so righteously.

If this be true, how peculiarly attractive should dependent and diligent prophetic study be today—a day so clearly characterized, not merely by declension, but by an incipient and fast-coming apostasy, and filled in every sphere with gravest portents. We hear amid the nations, self-styled "Christian," boastings of emancipation from the foundation truths of Christianity, whilst we discern as the result of that emancipation that those nations are "distressed with perplexity at the sounding of the sea and the rolling surge" (Luke 21: 25).

Does it not behoove us then to humble ourselves under God's mighty hand, and to beseech Him for that light upon His holy Word that can alone come from Himself, the "Father of Lights," that we may cherish no false expectation, nor abandon any true one: but that in quiet peace amid the turmoil we may hold fast a divinely accredited confidence that shall never make us ashamed?

In the assurance, then, first that God's Word has never yet been exhausted—that there are, and ever will be, depths in it still unfathomed: and next, that we need today what no other books, written by human authors of the past can, in every detail, give us, since they were written in a different combination of events than that in which our lot is fallen, let us enter on our meditation on the prophet Isaiah.

ISAIAH! How little that word conveys to our minds! It is but a name given to an individual who lived nearly three thousand years ago, and as far as getting anything of real value from it, it might just as well have been anything else. But we are not wise in thus treating these Hebrew names in the divine Word as being valueless. It is an unworthy way of dealing with a book that itself insists on the profound significance of such names as Jesus, Melchizedek, Salem, and a host of others. Is it rational then to pass over Isaiah, and get nothing from it? To a Hebrew ear it would be quite as intelligible as Bunyan's "Worldly-wise-man" and "Valiant-for-truth" are to us, inpenetrably obscure as they would be to the Chinese if not also translated.

Similarly, if the names in Scripture give evidence of *divinely intended* significance, it is worse than folly, as having an element of indifference, to neglect them. I recognize how limited is our ability, and the danger that there is of seeking to make up for that limitation by giving rein to imagination, but, giving weight to both these objections, a multitude of names in the Scriptures will be found to be as clear evidence of divinely intended significance as those I have mentioned. Deepest New Testament truths are discernible in Old Testament names, and amongst these Isaiah, the son of Amoz, will serve as a timely illustration.

This name, Isaiah, then, is a compound, and means as clearly and simply as possible: *"The Salvation of Jehovah."* Who superintended the parents' choice when they gave that name to that infant, born approximately B. C. 780? Little we judge did either father or mother know of its future value to generations not even to be born for millenniums! Yet Isaiah himself, in his eighth chapter, really insists upon its significance:

Behold I and the children whom the Lord hath given me are for signs and for wonders in Israel from the Lord of Hosts that dwelleth in Mount Zion.

But in what do the signs consist? What, for instance, do we know of those children that would make them "signs?" Not one thing are we told of their doings or sayings; we know nothing about them but their *names*. The conclusion is inevitable that the whole "sign" must lie in those names. But this being the case with the children, then the name of the father must also be a sign, and can *"Jehovah's salvation"* fail to be that?

It is impossible! For in that one name is compressed the whole contents of the book! All through it, amid its thunderings of stern reprobation of the sin of Israel (the nation that is the representative morally of the race as a whole), the words "salvation" and "save" ring like joy-bells, all the more melodious because of the foil of the awe-filling thunderings of judgment that ever precede the sweet melody, as in our own book of prophecy, Revelation, the constantly recurring "lightnings and voices and thunderings" throw into clear relief the "new song," the "harpers harping with their harps," and the God-made tearless scene of endless peace.

But if the names of prophet and children be of such value, is there none in that of his progenitor? Are we told in vain that he was the son of "Amoz?" The meaning of that name is perfectly clear. The very word is to be found in Ps. 27: 14, "He shall strengthen," whilst in Deut. 31: 6, 7, 23, as in Josh. 1: 6, 7, 9, it is rendered, "good courage." Thus do these very names tell us that the courage or strength that is the evidence or expression of faith, for that is the connection in which the word is alone used, results in "The Salvation of Jehovah" (Isaiah). Those who put aside such significance in the names of Scripture give little honor to the microscopic beauty of the Word of God.

But further, filled with the same divine significance is the *number* that is imprinted upon the book by its clearly marked divisions. But in this, too, I am aware that many have an almost invincible distaste to attaching any significance, or deducing any teaching, from the numbers of Scripture. Both by temperament and by training, they are inclined rather to avoid and reprobate this line of study than pursue it. Nor may they lack some grounds for such an attitude in the extravagancies in which some who have followed it have indulged. But the existence of the spurious is no disproof of that of the genuine. On the contrary, a spurious coin is really proof of the existence of the genuine, and the only sensible course is to "prove all, and hold fast that which is good."

Again, what line of Scripture-truth would not have to be abandoned on the same principle? *Prophecy* certainly has been, and is today, the sphere of boundless extravagancies: shall we then turn a deaf ear to 2 Peter 1: 19, and say we do well *not* to take heed to it? Alas, many do just that, but it can only be to their loss. Acting on the same principle, we will not then refrain from seeking the significance of the numbers, and the numerical structure of Holy Writ. The more clearly we see the proof of this divine intent, the more will our hearts be led to burst into David's song, "Thou, Lord, hast made me glad through Thy works." For He who has imprinted on every minute detail of His works in nature the inimitable imprint of His Finger, so that

> "Not a flower
> But shows some touch in freckle, streak, or stain,
> Of His unrivalled pencil,"

has done exactly the same with His Word, and those who refuse it, do so at their own loss.

Nor are there lacking guards and limitations that will serve to keep us from error or extravagance. Nor shall we transcend those guards, or go beyond those limits in discerning the number clearly impressed on Isaiah.

The three main divisions are abundantly clear:

1: Chapters 1 to 35 in which *Assyria* and Jehovah's salvation hold the prominent place.
2: Chapters 36 to 39—the historic interlude.
3: Chapters 40 to 66 in which *Babylon* and Jehovah's salvation hold the prominent place.

But not only is the book as a whole a trilogy, but each of these parts has the same number, *three,* imprinted upon it in its own divisions. Let us first take what perhaps is the most evident. In the second part—chapters 36 to 39—a child could see that the first division consists of chapters 36 and 37, that tell of the

Assyrian invasion. The second deals with quite another theme, Hezekiah's sickness and recovery, chapter 38: whilst the last gives us the visit of the Babylonian ambassadors. Thus the whole forms a link between the relation of Israel with Assyria and with Babylon.

But the last or third division is, we may say, even divinely marked by the same endings—thus:

1: Chapters 40-48, the terminus marked by "no peace to the wicked."
2: Chapters 49-57, ended by "no peace to the wicked."
3: Chapters 58-66, in which we end with the penalty of "no peace to the wicked."

No one can question the threefold division there!

Turning back now to the first part, a similar structure is marked on chapters 1 to 35, thus:

1: Chapters 1-6, in which we find a *threefold* introduction.
2: Chapters 7-12: Immanuel and the Assyrian with three subdivisions.
    1: Chaps. 7 to 9: 7, Immanuel.
    2: Chaps. 9: 8 to 10, The outstretched Hand.
    3: Chaps. 11 and 12, Revival of Israel.
3: Chapters 13-35 clearly subdivided into "Burdens," "Woes," and ending in "Peace."

So that here we have a threefold division, each itself divided into three.

I might go further, but this will surely be enough to prove that there has been a divine intent in imprinting the number three on every part of the book in the fullest way.

Of course, the natural and inevitable question is as to what we must gather of practical edification from this admitted fact. Well, the simplest interpretation of the full significance of that number is without controversy to be found in the revelation of God as a *Trinity of Persons* in the one Godhead: Father, Son and Holy Ghost. Here God is *fully manifested!*

But in what way has God been fully manifested if not in the salvation of a sinful, lost, but beloved race of men? This, and only this, could tell out to all the universe all His Heart and

Mind: for none but God could conceive or carry out that salvation. Here, in this "Isaiah," the Salvation of Jehovah, is expressed in His manifold wisdom, the exceeding riches of His grace. Here *mercy* in all its sweetness, *truth* in all its purity are met together. Here *righteousness* as light unflecked and unsullied by the slightest film, and *peace* as a river unruffled by one adverse ripple, "kiss each other." In a word, God is fully manifested as Light and Love in the salvation of a fallen but beloved race. That is, we may again say, the *number* coincides with the *name* and tells precisely the same story, gives out the same melody as does "Isaiah," for "three," too, tells of "The Salvation of Jehovah!" Surely we are looking at the very Fingerprint of God!

Thus, too, the book is not sealed but lies open before us, or to employ another homely figure, the key of the structure hangs at the front door. Yet not one step can we (nor do we desire to) take to enter into it, nor tread its court, nor examine the furnishings of its chambers with profit, until we put our hand dependently and trustfully in His who has given His Spirit to "lead us into all truth," to "take of the things of Christ and show them to us," and "to show us," as in this prophetic book, "things to come."

# STUDIES IN ISAIAH

## CHAPTER ONE

**Jehovah's plea against His people. Invites them to come into court with Him. The court in which the trial is to be held. Their evil not found in their worst, but in their best. What is the City of Sodom in which our Lord was crucified?**

THE first verse differs from what follows in being written in prose, and forms the superscription of the whole book, itself being a complete "Vision." Through four reigns it extends: reigns in which Judah's path has lain through the sunshine of prosperity and the shadow of disaster; now happily along the uplands of an Uzziah, and now sorrowfully through the swamps of an Ahaz: and in these vicissitudes, that path of the nation forms a picture of that which most of us travel through life, "sometimes singingly and sometimes sighingly," like Bunyan's Pilgrim.

Judah and Jerusalem are the direct objects of the vision, but these form the centre of a circle, the radii of which stretch far out into the heathen world about, and the circumference of which, ever enlarging, finally includes all mankind.

In this how strikingly this "Salvation of Jehovah" corresponds with the "Gospel of God" in the New Testament, for that, too, begins at Jerusalem, but also does not end there. A heavenly vision of eternal blessedness ends the New Testament: an earthly vision of millennial blessedness ends Isaiah, and before the book closes we shall see not only the light of God's love resting on Jerusalem, but the Gentiles coming to that light, and invited to rejoice in the comforting warmth of its beams.

There is, too, a more spiritual correspondence between Isaiah and Romans, the "salvation of Jehovah" and "the gospel of God," for as in this chapter we have a solemn exposure of sin, so does the New Testament epistle begin with a similar indictment, by which "every mouth may be stopped, and all the world become guilty before God." To convict thus of guilt, seems a strange part of "good news," but it is a very essential part, for as only the sick send for a physician, so do those only who are convicted of sin care for salvation from its penalty and power. Nor indeed, is it anything but the best of news that God knows the very worst of us, and yet loves us. Apart from this, how often should we fear that after all, we must have exhausted the patience of our God. But no! He has known the worst long ago, and so faith in His everlasting love does not fail. But whilst we ever get this individual profit, we must remember that the Church, hidden entirely from all the Old Testament prophets, is not directly the subject to be found in the book. These reigns of Judah's kings forbid, at the outset, any such spiritualizing. But I attempt a free metrical rendering of the first part, for we are apt to forget that the text is really Hebrew poetry.

2: Hearken, O heavens, and listen, O earth;
    For 'tis Jehovah who's speaking.
    Children I've raised, to maturity brought,
    But they have revolted against Me.
3: The ox knows his owner, the ass knows the crib
    That his master for him hath provided;
    But Israel knoweth Me—no, not at all,
    My people doth not consider.
4: Woe to the nation so full of gross sin!
    Woe to the guilt-laden people,
    Who are of the worst of ill-doers the seed,
    Children e'er acting corruptly!
    They have forsaken Jehovah their Lord,
    And Israel's Holy One scoffed at.
    Estranged from Him, they've gone backward.
5: Why should ye be stricken, and stricken again,
    It will but increase your revoltings?
    Sick is the head, the whole heart is faint;
6: From the foot-sole to head's highest crowning,
    Nothing within it is healthy.
    Its wounds and its stripes and its festering sores
    Have neither been closed up nor bandaged,
    Nor with the smooth ointment been soothèd.
7: Your country is desert, your cities are burned,
    Your farm-land by foemen so harried
    It lies as a desert before you,
    Brought to its ruin by foemen.

8: And Salem, fair Salem, the daughter of Zion,
   Is left as a hut in a 'vineyard,
   As a lodge in a field of cucumbers,
   E'en as a city besiegèd.
9: Save that Jehovah—Jehovah of Hosts—
   Had left us a very small remnant,
   We had been like to Sodoma,
   We had been like to Gomorrah!

It is a grand setting: a Court is formed, and in it is a Complainant and a defendant. Jehovah Himself is the former, and, as it were, pleads His own case, whilst in the dock stands that nation which was alone, of all the nations of the earth, in a recognized relationship with Him. All the heavens to their furthest bounds, and all the earth beyond the limits of that guilty nation, are called upon to be the witnesses of the trial; for He never judges in a corner, but openly before all creation, so that every creature, whether elect angels, or opposing principalities or powers, with the Devil at their head, may witness and be compelled to confess to the inflexible righteousness of His government. Nor shall that malign accuser, impelled though he be by the strongest motives of self-exaltation, and the keenest in discernment of all creatures, be able to discover one film of injustice on the Throne that he was "set to cover" (Ezek. 28: 14), even though the chief of sinners be justified before that Throne. Yet when the accuser himself has been sent to his final doom, at the judgment of the Great White Throne, then earth and its heaven flee away, for the ages of time with their testings are forever past, and these sad witnesses of creature-failure are no longer needed.

We must note, too, that even the charge itself, far from having any of the malice of the great accuser in it, is full of the most tender affection. If God did not love, would He complain of not being known? That sigh, "How often would I have gathered thy children!" speaks the same language and tells of the same Speaker. Nor do the words, "a people *laden* with iniquity," form a completed sentence from that Speaker's heart, however it may do so from His lips, until they are supplemented by, "Come unto Me, all ye that are heavy *laden,* and I will give you rest."

The picture of Judah's condition is so distressing that the prophet appears to soliloquize: "Except the Lord of Hosts had left us a very small remnant, we should have been as Sodom, we should have been like unto Gomorrah;" and with that sigh, in which however there is hope, the first part closes.

10: Hark to the word of Jehovah, the Lord,
      O ye judges of Sodom!
      Give ear to the law of (Jehovah) our God,
      Ye people who are as Gomorrah.
11: What do I get in your offerings slain?
      They have nothing for Me, saith Jehovah.
      With the burnt off'rings of rams I am filled,
      With fat of the beasts that are well-fed.
      No pleasure have I in the blood of the bulls,
      Nor in that of the lambs, nor of he-goats.
12: When ye do come to appear before Me,
      Who this from your hand hath demanded—
      Simply to trample My courts?
13: Oh, bring nevermore an oblation,
      Empty and vain as they are.
      Sweet incense itself is to Me
      An abomination repulsive.
      The new-moons, the sabbaths, th' assembly-calls,
      Are to Me utterly noxious:
      The most solemn meeting is evil.
14: Your new-moons and feasts, doth My soul hate,
      A burden 'neath which I grow weary.
15: And when ye in them do stretch forth your hands,
      I will turn My eyes from beholding.
      Yea, when ye pray and make many prayers,
      To never a word will I listen—
      For your hands are reeking with bloodshed!
16: O wash ye, and washing, make yourselves clean,
      Put out of My sight your vile doings.
17: Cease to do evil, learn to do well;
      Seek judgment, and help the oppressèd;
      Let not the orphan be robbed of his rights,
      And plead ye the cause of the widow.

Now Jehovah takes up the words "Sodom and Gomorrah" and applies them even to Judah and Jerusalem; it is *they* who are "Sodom and Gomorrah"—*they*, the only people who are the Lord's

people on earth, with whom alone is His dwelling—*they*, who are
so faithfully observing all His ordinances as He had appointed—
*they*, who are offering all the sacrifices, from whom the sweet
incense is still ascending, by whom sabbaths and feasts are most
rigidly observed—it is *they* who are Sodom and Gomorrah! And
to substantiate this, the Lord goes over, not the terrible moral
corruption that characterized Sodom, but all the religious observances that might well be considered quite enough to *save* from
such a charge, rather than be the basis of it! Although He had
Himself instituted these feasts, He now repudiates them all with
disgust, for they are as empty of all that He intended in them
as Cana's empty water-pots that illustrated them so well (John
2). In a word, it was, as with their forefather Cain, not what
might be thought their *worst*, but their very *best*, that He utterly
repudiates as being only empty form; for withal, their "hands
are full of bloods."*

But of what practical value is it to us to learn His estimate
of Judah's offerings of three thousand years ago, unless it may
possibly be that, were our ears keen enough, we might hear Him
speaking in the same way to His *present* witness on earth? Is it
not possible that Christendom may be fast becoming, if it be not
already, "Sodom" to Him? Indeed, many of us are well assured
that it *is;* nor is this conviction lessened by the use of the words
in Rev. 11: 8: "Their dead bodies shall lie in the street of the
great city, which is spiritually called Sodom and Egypt, where
also our Lord was crucified." For what is this "great city?" Is
it the literal Jerusalem? Certainly it was there "our Lord was
crucified;" and it is also possible that this has been called
"Sodom," as in the scripture before us, yet even in this scripture
it has a wider application than to the *city*, for it includes Judah.
As far as I am aware, Jerusalem has never been called "Egypt,"
nor is it in accord with the profoundly spiritual character of
this book of "signs" (Revelation) to look for a literal city here.
No, we cannot thus easily put on one city the responsibility

---

*"Bloods," being in the plural, tells of life violently taken, for as
soon as shed every single drop utters its cry, as did that of Abel
in Gen. 4: 10.

for the Lord's death; "the great city" stands as a symbol of all that man, away from God, has ever built on the earth. Cain founded that, Nimrod added to it, and while Jerusalem was in its day of Christ-hating its most perfect expression, yet it may be discerned even now in all that is being built under the name of Christian, even where apostasy from Christ is daily increasing. It is "Christendom" that is now carrying on Cain's work of city-building, the whole edifice forming but one city, and it was in *that* city "our Lord was crucified." It shall be in its "street"* that this last competent testimony of God shall be slain (Rev. 11: 8)—it is *one* city (compare Matt. 23: 23-36 with Rev. 18: 24), as there is but *one* generation that crucified Him, *i.e.*, man in the flesh.

Well may we see to it, then, that we rest not in any ordinance, however certain it is that the Lord Himself may have instituted it; for in that way, even the Lord's Supper itself may be as hateful to Him today as those holy feasts of which He here says, "My soul hateth them; I am weary of them." It is all too possible to be most punctilious in all observances of ordinances, indeed, to give them an utterly disproportionate importance, and yet the "hands to reek with bloodshed" in God's holy sight, as neglecting the precious Blood of Christ as our only confidence; for in that case it is on us indeed, but in condemnation; for we are then guilty of the body and blood of the Lord (1 Cor. 11: 27). See *through* the ordinance the Lord Jesus alone, and all is a sweet savor. "Discern the Lord's Body," and for this it is well to use the best of lenses, *a contrite tear*, and great is the blessedness; but rest satisfied with the mere observance of the ordinance, and it becomes as loathsome as the manna kept over night; till, in Laodicean days, the present professed witness for Christ on the earth is "spued out of His mouth." Is it not of weightiest significance to us that *those are the very days in which we are living?*

---

*The word "street," as used in Rev. 11: 8, cannot be a literal thoroughfare, but stands for the internal relations of the different parts of the city, as the "wall" speaks of the external. Street and wall thus make up one city, as in Dan. 9: 25.

But let us listen to the counsel: "Wash you, make you clean, cease to do evil, learn to do well." It is the cry taken up by John the Baptist: "Repent and bring forth fruit meet for repentance." But new fruit means a new tree; the old tree can only bring forth the old fruit. Washing externally will not alter the spring from which all flows. Can good ever be brought out of evil? Can pure waters come from a mud-pit? Why then does the Lord tell us to do what He knows well we cannot do?

Yet this He ever does. It is the way of His righteous government, never relaxed, never modified, never changed; and what that government demands must be clearly expressed, and must be obeyed, too, in some way or other. For even the grace of the gospel does not set aside these just requirements; nay, it is this alone that permits their accomplishment. It is through "the grace that is in Christ Jesus" that we are washed "clean every whit;" it is by the Spirit's law of a new life in Him, that the righteous requirements of the law are fulfilled (Rom. 8: 4). Nor, I take it, is the principle different in relation to the Sermon on the Mount. This comes at the very beginning of the Gospels, and while it is thus an integral part of those Gospels, far from being in itself the *way* of salvation, it is but to prove the impossibility of salvation *in that way*. Although blended with the sweetest assurance of God's love, seen as it were from afar, it is Sinai intensified; the law piercing through all mere external morality, penetrating the inmost recesses of the heart, revealing the evil that is ever there, either dormant or active; and convincing us of our deep, deep need of the Lord Jesus, who alone saves from that evil.

18: Come now, and let us go into court,
    And there, saith the Lord, plead together.
    If your sins should even as scarlet be seen,
    They shall be as white as the snowflake.
    If they should be as crimson, so red,
    White as pure wool they shall come forth.
19: If ye be willing—submissively hear,
    Ye shall feed on the land's choicest dainties.
20: But if ye refuse—perversely rebel,
    Then upon you will the sword feed:
    For the mouth of Jehovah hath spoken.

21: How like a harlot she has become:
    The city that once was so faithful!
    Once filled with right, where righteousness lodged,
    But now do the murderers dwell there.

22: Thy silver, alas, has all become dross,
    Thy wine by water been marrèd.

23: Thy princes are rebels, companions of thieves,
    Lusting for gifts: bribes pursuing.
    They judge not the orphan, and little they care
    For the just cause of the widow.

24: Therefore is this the word of Adohn,
    Jehovah Tzebaoth, the Strong One!
    Ah, I will get relief from My foes,
    On Mine en'mies will be avengèd.

25: My hand once again I'll move over thee,
    Smelt out thy dross: tin removing,

26: I'll bring back thy judges as in the past,
    Thy counsellors as in the first time.
    Then ever after thou shalt be called
    City of Righteousness—faithful!

27: Zion through judgment shall be redeemed,
    And those that return, with strict justice.

28: But the destruction of those who transgress,
    And the sinners, shall be at the same time:
    Consumption awaits Jah's forsakers.

29: Ashamed shall they be of the oaks ye've desired,
    Ye shall blush for the gardens ye've chosen.

30: For ye shall be as an oak whose leaf fades,
    As a garden that's lacking all water.

31: The strong man shall then be likened to tow,
    His work, to the spark that consumes it;
    Both the worker and work together shall burn,
    Those flames there is none can extinguish.

Now comes a marvellous word of grace. Isaiah is indeed a "Seer," and can see far off to that day when his people in their cry, "His blood be on us and upon our children," accept the responsibility of that death. Aye, he sees further still, to another day in which they shall awaken to the guilt of that cry, to the terror of its consequences, and then shall they hear this word of invitation: "Come into court with Me; hide nothing, shrink not from having everything out; and even if your sins should there be seen as prominent as is scarlet to the eye—as they certainly would be in that case—I have a secret not yet fully told out, a divine alchemy, that shall make those sins invisibly white. But make no false plea. Accept the verdict of the Court (ver. 6, etc.), and not only will I forgive, but I will feed you on royal dainties. But should you refuse thus to plead 'guilty,' and rebel by maintaining your own righteousness, then instead of being fed, ye yourselves shall be food for the sword, for this is Jehovah's sentence."

How true all this has been proved! Israel did, notwithstanding that precious blood on her, go about to establish her own righteousness, and the "sword" of the Roman devoured her, whilst a remnant confessed to their guilt and were saved. Christendom has followed in precisely the same path, and as its privileges have been far higher, so its penalties will be proportionately severe! In these verses, this first introduction draws to a close, a close filled indeed with cheer for the penitent remnant, but with gloom and terror of judgment for the impenitent.

Jehovah looks back, with tender reminiscence, to the days when that city was faithful (as in the day of David), but now it must be likened to a common harlot, who owns to no holy relationship. It once was the lodge of right, but now murderers find a home within it; as when Stephen so charged the representatives of that nation (Acts 7: 5). So the sad contrasts go on, till (ver. 24) with a threefold accumulation of divine dignities, the Lord intervenes, and speaks. The common word for "saith" is not used here, but one of which Delitzsch writes: "The word signifies that which is spoken with significant secrecy and solemn softness." Then comes the "Hoi" (Ah), "the painfulness of pity being mingled with the determined outbreak of wrath!" Adversaries and foes are now swept away, whilst once again His Hand moves over the remnant of faith, which, passing through the time of deepest sorrow, shall come forth with dross purged out, alloy forever gone.

This will be enough to assure us that God still has purposes with that scattered people, and will express by them the righteousness of His government on the earth amid the nations. Beyond the earth, there are no nations, but individuals who are dealt with eternally.

The closing verses (27-31) give again a comprehensive view of "Judah and Jerusalem" at the end; "Zion shall be redeemed with judgment and her converts with righteousness;" *i.e.,* brought through a furnace of affliction, elsewhere called "the great tribulation." As to the apostate mass (the transgressors) and the lawless Gentiles (sinners), their destruction shall be together, and so, too, speaks the New Testament: "And the beast was taken, and with him the false prophet, and they were both cast alive into a lake of fire" (Rev. 19: 20). Nor shall the apostates find the slightest safety in the gods in whom they place their confidence: "For they shall be ashamed of the oaks which ye have desired, and ye shall be confounded for the gardens that ye have chosen." Oaks and gardens are here clearly used for the idolatrous worship that was conducted in them, and the latter come to have a deeper significance in later chapters. The abrupt change of pronouns is perplexing, as being so different from our manner of speech, but it has its value for, as Delitzsch writes: "The excited state of the prophet at the close of his prophecy is evinced by his abrupt leap from an exclamation to a direct address. He still continues in the same excitement," for their end shall show the vanity of their confidence. Do they trust in oaks? They, themselves, shall be as a withered oak, strong to outward appearance, because of their numbers, but with no real vitality, and they are set on fire by their own work ("his work a spark"), *i.e.,* their very confidence is their destruction, a constant principle of Scripture. So this introductory chapter gives a view of Judah's history from first to last, and, in so doing, gives the history of the whole race.

# CHAPTER TWO

The second vision. Jerusalem is not the Church. Jerusalem to become the metropolis of the earth. Peace impossible under human government. Man's day must end, and the Lord Jesus alone be exalted, for fallen man is nothing but frailty.

THIS second vision goes to the end of chapter five, and again gives a synopsis of the book, forming another introduction. The first verse, reading,

The word that Isaiah the son of Amoz saw concerning Judah and Jerusalem,

is a divinely given guard against that misdirection of the prophecy, that, notwithstanding that gracious care, has prevailed all through Christendom since it lost the hope of the imminent return of the Lord. It is difficult to see how any words could be selected to be less equivocal as to the subject of the prophecy. How can any presume to divert them from Judah and Jerusalem, of whose destiny the hearts of both prophet and his people were full, and apply them to the Church, of which neither he nor they knew, nor could know anything at all, for it was divinely hidden from them, "kept secret since the world began, but now (to the apostle) is made manifest" (Romans 16: 25). If that does not mean that all who press the Mystery into the Old Testament, are doing so without one letter of warrant, then it is difficult to see how words can convey any clear truth. But to paraphrase:

2: In the last days 'tis this shall occur:
The mount of the house of Jehovah
Shall firmly be set above other mounts,
And over the hills be exalted,
And all of the nations to it shall flow.
3: And peoples in numbers shall go there,
Saying, Let's up to the mount of the Lord,
To the house of the God who loves Jacob.

> For He will instruct us in His holy ways,
> In the paths that He leads we will follow;
> For then out of Zion shall go forth the law—
> From Salem the word of Jehovah.
>
> 4: 'Tis He that shall be of the nations the Judge;
> Reprover of numerous peoples.
> Swords into plowshares then shall they beat,
> And spears shall become hooks for pruning.
> Nation 'gainst nation shall never lift sword,
> Nor learn to wage warfare forever.
>
> 5: O come, house of Jacob, come, let us walk
> In the light of our God, our Jehovah!

Thus the vision begins with an outlook far beyond the present all-pervasive conditions of sin and suffering in the earth, to a day in which Judah and Jerusalem are not only restored, but shine with a far more exceeding and eternal weight of glory than ever of old, giving out the light of God to all the earth. But it is the earth, and not heaven that is in view. Apply this to Zion and the nations in the future day, and all is clear, sure and consistent; accommodate it to the Church, either now or in that day, and what contradiction ensues! What are the prospects of swords being beaten into ploughshares during the testimony of the Church?

In verse two we have the supremacy of that beloved people, Israel, when fully restored, in her Lord and Christ, to the favor of Jehovah. Jerusalem shall then be the center, spiritually and politically, as she is physically of all the earth. She shall have no rival in the capitals that now so far surpass her. All the other "mountains" or States, or their governments (for a mountain in prophetic symbolism is an excellent figure of a Government, and the Government, in turn, represents the whole State over which it governs, cf. Rev. 17: 10, 11), shall then willingly confess to the supremacy of Zion, whose government is perfect—being divine. For this is the time whereof our own apostle writes, wherein "all things are headed up in Christ, both which are in heaven, and which are on earth;" and when "every knee shall bow, and every tongue confess, that Jesus Christ is Lord to the glory of God the Father." For as now He, being in heaven, is

"Head over all things to the Church," so then when on earth will He identify Himself with penitent Israel, and be Head over all the nations of the earth to that beloved people. Up then, to the very head of the nations, goes down-trodden Jerusalem; up, nevermore to lose that place of supremacy, for she is established there in her Messiah. The "times of the Gentiles" are over; the day of man, the test of his ability to govern, is ended, and the Day of the Lord has begun.

But the Gentiles themselves shall then be no longer rebellious. Humbled and penitent, they too shall recognize that the Lord Jesus being there, Jerusalem presents a holy attraction after the storms of six thousand years, that makes them flow, as naturally, willingly, and peacefully, as rivers to the sea, to that center of light where the Lord reigneth.

Even the casting away of Israel has been the reconciling of the world; for since they have, for the time, rejected our "mercy" (Rom. 11: 31), or the gospel of His grace, God sends out His ambassadors beseeching men at large to be reconciled; but this being ended, that mercy returns to Israel and their reception shall be "life from the dead."

This is the day whereof the disciples asked: "Wilt Thou at this time restore again the kingdom to Israel?" (Acts 1: 6). That people—not Great Britain, nor Germany, nor France, nor any of the present "great powers"—shall be the dominant, the royal nation on the earth; for, as it is written, He will make it "high above all nations which He hath made, in praise, and in name and in honor" (Deut. 26: 19), that now being fulfilled to them in Christ which they failed to attain on the principle of law. These are those "kings of the rising again of the sun," as Rev. 16: 12 (when quite literally rendered) calls them, and when their Sun shall arise (Mal. 4: 2), the whole earth shall be flooded with its beams, and to that light all nations shall gravitate. It shines from Jerusalem.

Verse three gives details of the preceding: many peoples take counsel, and it is good counsel at last; very different from that in the day of Babel (Gen. 11: 4), or as in the day of the second Psalm, for they encourage one another to go to that center of light and there to learn. Oh, what evidence of divine intervention such an attitude presents! Think of New York or London confessing that they have anything to learn from Jerusalem! It speaks a very different state of affairs from that ruling today. Even among His people there is not too great a willingness to take the lowly place of "learner," and have we not largely forgotten the word that speaketh unto us, as unto brethren, "Be not many *teachers?*" (James 3: 1). But there is no warning against being many *learners*.

The outcome is universal peace, precious contrast to the ever-recurring wars and rumors of wars that have characterized the whole of the present time. These continue to speak, in the clearest way, of earth's true King rejected, and the usurping "prince of this world" still sitting upon His Throne. War, with all its horrible accompaniments, accords but too well with that usurpation. But in the day of Isaiah's vision, earth's true King has returned, and having with a strong hand put down all opposition, becomes in very deed the "Prince of Peace." All the implements of war, all the inventions of human ingenuity to destroy life, included in the "sword and spear" that figured them all, are turned into instruments for the peaceful service of man, and banished forever.

Beloved brethren, let us too, "see" this "word." The earth longs for peace. Men are war-weary. Various expedients have been, are being, and will be tried, but all in vain. Permanent peace can only be as the result of God's intervention—the return of the Lord Jesus Christ to reign. We admit that this is to the man of the world, whether a professor of religion or not, altogether chimerical; a conception only possible to religious extremists or foolish enthusiasts. Far more practical is peace maintained by the Nations leaguing together, and becoming "the United States of Christendom" with, possibly, the Pope accorded the place of arbiter, as the surest guarantee of an unbroken peace. These are the ways that fill the minds of men who have not learned that God's way is, always and alone, by the manifested exaltation of His own dear Son, after man's impotence has been fully exposed. It is He who shall "judge among the nations;" it is He who shall abolish West Point, Sandhurst, St. Cyr, and all the military academies for learning war, for when

He thus comes, nevermore shall war be learned at all; till then, war with intervals of armed truce will prevail.

It is refreshing then, thus to see beyond the dark present in vision, as the prophet himself entranced with it, turns to his own people and cries: "Does not that attract you?  O house of Jacob, come ye, and let us walk in the light of the Lord."

But he does not ignore the actual present conditions of his people so different from the "word that he had seen;" and, turning again to Jehovah, he mourns, "For Thou hast forsaken Thy people, the house of Jacob;" but not before they had forsaken Thee "because they are replenished from the east, and are soothsayers like the Philistines, and they go hand in hand with the children of foreigners" (ver. 6). East and west have both contributed to draw them away, wealth has come from the east (ver. 7), and brought with it that independence of God that ever accompanies trust in it, whilst from the opposite quarter the opposite evil has come—soothsaying, and idolatry (ver. 8)—and God's people have friendship with all these.

We, too, stand between that same East and West, which have involved us in the same guilt, only of a far more serious character, for ours is the substance of which that of old was but the shadow.  On Israel's eastern border dwelt the base-born brothers, the Ammonite and Moabite, who ever and again made inroads into Israel's land, bringing its people into humiliating bondage. Exactly corresponding to these, bordering on the Church of God, have long dwelt the modern Ammonite, "Rationalism," and its very close relation, the Moabite, "Worldliness," and all that is comprehended under that comprehensive word.  Have they not made sad inroads among the Lord's people, bringing so many of us into bondage?  Surely they have.  From the opposite quarter, opposite evils; so in Israel's west—not on the border at all, but in the very land which he claimed for himself, and to which he gave his own name—dwelt the Philistine,* just as his antitype, Ritualism, involving superstition, with its claim to magic art, and formality has, in Rome and her daughters (who are quite numerous, and the family is still increasing rapidly) taken up

---

*Philistine and Palestine are really the same words.

its dwelling in the very Church, and in the same way as her prototype claims it for herself; claims, indeed, to *be* the "Catholic," or the "whole Church"—there is no Church outside her border!—while still in close league with demon powers, for *these* are "the depths of Satan" (Rev. 2: 24). It is too, with these strangers, as they surely are, that the professing Church has "joined hands;" has it not? Are we not then deeply interested in this vision?

What then does the opened eye of the prophet see as impending over all the outward prosperity of his day? This:

9: The mean man abased shall be,
    The nobleman also be humbled;
    Forgive them? No, that Thou wilt not!

When that cloud discharges its terrors, all these—great and small:

10: Creep to the rock, and hide in the dust,
    Fore the face* of Jah's terror, His Majesty's splendor,
    When He rises to make the earth quiver with fear.

Then, like a chant, rising amid the scene, sounds out the refrain:

11: Lowered man's lofty looks!
    Humbled man's haughtiness!
    Exalted alone Jehovah shall be,
      In that day!

What day is meant? Verses 12 to 16 give the answer. Jehovah of Hosts has a day of judgment on every form of human pride, summed up in four pairs:

"Cedars and oaks," noblest of trees, apt figures of *men* highest up in the *social* scale.

"Mountains and hills," *i.e.*, all organized *Governments* and *States*.

"Tower and wall," everything of *military* preparedness.

"Ships and pleasant pictures,"—all forms of *commerce* and *art*, finishing again with the chant, only slightly varied,

---

*The word "face" is expressed in the original in all these verses, and is retained for the link it gives with Rev. 6: 16.

17: Brought down man's loftiness!
    Lowered man's haughtiness!
    Exalted alone Jehovah shall be,
        In that day!

In verses 18 and 19 the prophet turns to the root evil of that time—idolatry. Jehovah has been forsaken, idols have replaced Him. In a short verse of only three words (*i.e.*, in Hebrew), their future is declared as with a lightning flash, as if with terrible terseness he said: "Nothings to nothingness." Vanities as they are, to utter vanity they go. What then can those who put their confidence in them, do? And again in answer we get the solemn chant:

19: They creep to the rock-caves; to earth-cellars go,
    'Fore the face of Jah's terror, His Majesty's splendor,
    When He rises to make the earth quiver with fear.*

We might also give verse 20 somewhat of the rhythm of the original by a paraphrase:

20: Away go the idols of silver and gold,
    The work of the hands of their own devotees,
    To their kindred companions, the moles and the bats,
        In that day!

Then once again as to their worshippers:

21: They creep into rock-clefts; into rock-fissures go,
    'Fore the face of Jah's terror, His Majesty's splendor,
    When He rises to make the earth quiver with fear.

Let us now ask, Who is this King of Glory thus coming with terror-striking face? The Psalm answers: "The Lord of Hosts, He is the King of glory." But we venture to further ask, "Who is this Lord of Hosts, the King of Glory?" May we not "see this word"? It is a "Lamb as it had been slain." It is Jesus

---

*Here there is an untransferable paranomasia, the sound of the words giving the sense they would convey, but anyone can catch it, for in the words, "*la-arotz ha-aret*," the rolling of the "r"s give in their *sound* the idea of a trembling of terror.

of Nazareth, and His rejecters are but fulfilling His own words in calling to the mountains, "Fall on us, and to the hills, Cover us" (Luke 23: 30); for it is the Lord who thus "consumes the wicked one with the breath of His mouth, and destroys him with the splendor of His coming" (2 Thess. 2: 8).

Surely both New and Old Testaments lift up their voices in unison to proclaim our Lord Jesus to be Jehovah, the Lord of Hosts, the King of Glory. Are *we* then quite uninterested?

Impossible, for that day of terror still impends, and we see it by every portent swiftly approaching. Nothing in the past satisfies the prophecy at all. Man's boasting is still to be heard on all sides; it is still man's day. May *we* then hear and heed the Spirit's gracious counsel:

22: Cease ye from man whose breath's in his nose,
At what then is he to be valued?

Estimate man at his true worth as a reliance. He is, with all his boasting, with all his ingenuity, his marvellous inventions, but a poor, vain creature. His breath, which is his life, is at the very door of his being, ready to step out at any moment, and his united powers are but weakness.

It is not such an one that *we* need, but One whose breath is *not* in His nostrils, for He is Himself "a quickening Spirit" (1 Cor. 15: 45), and is "able to save to the uttermost them that come unto God by Him, seeing that He ever liveth to make intercession for them" (Heb. 7: 24, 25). Then may we justly have "no confidence in the flesh" at all—in ourselves least of all—but joy, rejoice, boast in Christ Jesus, for He is worthy. In His revelation alone the earth finds peace.

# CHAPTER THREE

**Divine chastening is to be seen in feeble governments. How miserable the condition when men even shun, instead of seeking the place of rule; those least qualified then come to the head. A woman's dress not beneath divine notice.**

THERE ever comes a time when God intervenes in human affairs. History repeats itself, and in what occurs here in "Judah and Jerusalem" we may see divinely-given forecasts of what shall occur in that sphere of the present witness for God upon the earth, *Christendom;* for it has walked in the same steps. Filled with His mercies, yet "Judah and Jerusalem" forgot Him. They continued not in His goodness and are cut off, and thus He intervenes:

1: For lo, the Adohn, Jehovah Tzebaoth,
    Takes from Jerusalem the stay and the staff,*
    All of the stay that she gets from the bread,
    All of the stay she gets from the water.
2: The hero, the fighter, the judge, and the prophet,
3: Diviner and elder, and captain of fifty:
    Him skilled in counsel, him skilled in work,
    With him who is skilled in magical muttering.†
4: Then for their princes I will give children,
    And childishly shall they rule o'er them.
5: Oppression shall govern the people,
    Each oppressing the other:
    The boy insulting the old man,
    The base insulting the noble.
6: Till a man shall seize hold of his brother,
    One of the house of his father;
    "Thou hast a coat and must rule,
    This ruin be under thy hand."
7: Aloud will he cry in that day,
    Nay, I will not be a healer,
    For not a loaf, nor a coat,

---

*Lit., "Supporter and supportress," *i.e.,* support of every kind.
†The word refers to the muttering of magical formulas.

Is to be found in my house;
I will not rule over this people,
Nor are ye able to make me.

8: Ah, Salem is ruined, and Judah is fallen!
For their word and their work are aye 'gainst the Lord,
Defying the eyes of His glory.

9: The look of their face doth witness against them;
They expose their own sin as did Sodom,
No shame do they show in concealing.
Woe to their soul, for they make themselves suffer!

So here He comes upon the scene under His names of warlike dignity, ADOHN, JEHOVAH TZEBAOTH, the despotic Lord of all, Jehovah of Hosts; and the first sign of that intervention is not desolation and captivity, but the taking away all that the body-politic has depended upon for support, likened here to those simplest necessities for the natural body, "bread and water." That these are not literally meant is evidenced by what follows, a list of those who are depended upon as the supports, "the stay and staff" of a nation; the valiant and wise, the skilful in work and word. But these are but men "whose breath is in their nostrils," and among them we get "the diviner" and "skilful mutterer." But whatever they are, they are taken away, and who takes their place? Children! But again, not literally that, but men who, as far as their qualifications for government go, are no better; as Solomon speaks of himself in lowly self-depreciation as a "little child" (1 Kings 3: 7). The result of a government that does not command respect is the subversion of all natural order. The oppression, however, in this case, is not from autocratic tyranny *above,* but from democratic tyranny *below*: the child is above the elder; the base above the honorable.

Is there *no* such tyranny today? Is there *no* oppression in those "unions" that were organized to resist it? Is the Soviet more merciful than the Czar? Nay, further, is not this the inevitable result, *reasonably* to be expected from such a condition? We enter not into earth's politics. We are submissive to the powers that be, whatever form they may take. We are quite willing to concede that the form of government under which we live may be the best under all the circumstances; but where the true Source of all authority is ignored, and the government derives its authority from the governed, where the votes of the mass confer the government, surely the governed are, in a sense, *above* the government, as he who confers authority must be above him who receives it. Only by the sincere (not merely formal) recognition of God from whom all authority legitimately proceeds, is true government maintained, and all is in order. Apart from this, the more conditions are levelled by the education of the mass the quicker are the steps toward that anarchy foretold here. It is the end to which democracy has been ever tending, and which it shall at last reach, when, with a mighty upheaval in the day of the fourth trumpet, all executors of authority in the world-empire, from the Emperor down, shall be overturned (Rev. 8: 12). It illustrates the blessing of an enlightened, strong, and at the same time, beneficent government, and the miseries resulting from weakness and incapacity of rule.

The wretchedness in Judah and Jerusalem comes to such a pass that the highest office goes begging, till a comparatively respectable coat is considered qualification enough for installing its wearer over what they now own is a "ruin." He, on the other hand, is as anxious to avoid the once-coveted office as they to press it on him, and he cries out in great excitement, "No, no; I will not attempt to heal this distracted State, for, if you only knew, in my house too there is neither food nor clothing. You shall not, I protest, make me ruler over this people."

In verses 8 and 9 both in word and work they have been "against Jehovah, to defy the eyes of His glory"—a striking expression that brings before the mind all the infinite excellencies of God, focussed, as it were, in His Eye: infinities of holiness, burning as a flame of fire (*cf.* Rev. 1: 14); and His people have cared nothing how their words and works have appeared in *those* Eyes—they have defied them! Indeed, so lost are they, not only to all reverence, but even to self-respect, that they make no effort at concealment, but are like the Sodomites, who proclaimed shamelessly their shame. The maintenance of external decency is at least some evidence of a conscience not altogether seared, while the flaunting of impurity in public, say, in the theatre, in the novel, in the moving picture resorts, is a symptom of very deep degradation. Has not Christendom followed the Jew?

Nowhere today does this earth afford evidence of the righteous government of God—on the contrary, it is rather the wicked who get the good things, and the righteous the evil things in this life. That is the very reason for proclaiming a day in which all shall be made right; when, by an exact retribution, it shall be seen that men have worked out their own penalties, and are reaping only what they have sown. So,

> 10: Say to the righteous, Well shall it be for him;
>     For they shall enjoy the fruit of their works.
> 11: Woe to the wicked, for it shall be ill for him,
>     Since his own hand doth work his reward.

In verse 12, Jehovah, deeply moved with sorrow at the inevitable judgment impending, utters a cry of tender affection:

> 12: My people! O My people!   Their tyrants are but boys,
>     And women now are over them in the place of rule!*
>     My people!   O My people!   Thy leaders do mislead thee,
>     The path for thy feet they have blotted out.

Cannot we recognize that voice?   Do we not know our Shepherd's voice?   Is it not the same exactly that cried in the same tender tone over the same city as He foresaw its fast-coming desolation.

O Jerusalem, Jerusalem, thou that killest the prophets and stonest them which are sent unto thee, how often would I have gathered thy children together, as even a hen gathereth her chickens under her wings, and ye would not! (Matt. 23: 37).

It is thus the identity of Jehovah and Jesus is constantly proclaimed in the Scriptures, not only by isolated texts that the agents of the enemy may tamper with, but in the very warp and woof of those Scriptures, where none who profess to believe them can touch it.

---

*With universal suffrage and women in the majority, the prophecy applies equally to Christendom.   Tennyson speaks the same truth,

"Tumble nature heel o'er head, and yelling with the yelling street,
  Set the feet above the brain, and swear the brain is in the feet."

May not that same Blessed One be equally sorrowing too, for Christendom on the verge of judgment?  Both in the civil and ecclesiastical sphere all is failure: in the former there is weakness where there should be strength; in the latter, darkness where there should be light.

Thus ever, in every case of human trial, things always come to so hopeless a pass that Jehovah must "stand up," *i.e.*, intervene and judge all the nations of the earth, and this ever begins at His own house.

13: Standeth up the Lord to plead,
    Yea, He stands to judge the nations.
14: With the elders of His people
    Doth Jehovah go to judgment,
    Bringing charge against the princes,
    Ye have eaten up the vineyard,
    Furnished house with spoils of poor.
15: What mean ye to crush My people—
    Grind the faces of the poor?
    Proclaimeth Adonai, Jehovah Tzebaoth!

In this charge against elders and princes we again recognize the Voice of the same Speaker who said, "Woe unto you, Scribes and Pharisees, hypocrites," who "bind heavy burdens and grievous to be borne on men's shoulders, but they themselves will not touch them with one of their fingers." These are as "the deeds of the Nicolaitanes" that He ever "hates," wherever they are.

In verses 16 to 24 Jehovah, Creator of all things visible, and invisible, turns to—woman's dress!  Such points as these have been taken as so unworthy of a divine revelation as to refute the claim of the Bible to being the Word of God.  The triviality is only in the shallow reasoning of miscalled Rationalism, and such criticism does not tell the limitation of God's mind, but the narrowness of the critic's.  For His perfection must surely be marked equally on *all* His works; therefore there must be interest in and care of the least as of the greatest.  Let the telescope reveal mighty worlds far beyond the range of the eye, and compared to which our earth is but as a grain of sand, each travelling its well-beaten path, without swerving a hair's breadth; then let the microscope reveal identically the same perfections in every part of the diatom, quite invisible as its whole body is to the unaided vision, and see if this does not equally proclaim the "power and Godhead" of Him who can imprint such perfections on such minute creatures.    Then listen to these critics with their arbitrary line, above which they may perhaps own to a God of some kind, but below it—no: *that* would not be consistent with Deity!   Is it not pitifully shallow?   But the Author of the *work* is the Author of the *Word,* and it would be strange indeed if this did not show the same "mark of His unrivalled pencil."   Thus it is a harmony, not a discord, that amid thought too high for the unaided human mind to grasp, He takes notice of a sparrow's fall (Luke 12: 6), a school-boy finding a bird's nest (Deut. 22: 6), or a woman's dress, when that woman is one of His people, or, as our New Testament speaks, one "professing godliness" (1 Tim. 2: 9, 10).   In that sphere of professed faith in His dear Son *nothing* is too high, *nothing* too low for His keenest interest.   So, here, every detail whereby the women of Jerusalem sought to attract attention is noted, and,

16: Jehovah thus speaks:
    Because the daughters of Zion are haughty,
    Walk with their neck outstretched in their pride,
    Winking their eyes and mincingly walking,
    Tinkling their ankle-bells aye as they walk,
17: The crown of the head of the daughters of Zion
    Jehovah will smite with a scab,
    By shameful exposure abase them.
18: In that day will the Lord take away
    The adornment of anklets, of frontlets, of crescents,
19: The ear-rings, and chains for the arm,
20: The veils, and the diadems,
    The stepping-links, and girdles,
    The scent-boxes, and amulets,
21: The finger-rings, and nose-rings,
22: The festal robes, and tunics,
    The mantles, and the wallets,
23: The mirrors, and the linens,
    The turbans, and the flowing veils.
24: Instead of a scent there shall be a stench;
    Instead of a sash, naught but a rope;

> Instead of a braided curl, no hair at all;
> Instead of a mantle, a smock made of sackcloth;
> Instead of a beauty, the brand of a slave.

If the same keen note is taken by God in this day, what defiance must He see in the shameless fashions current everywhere. How great a change in the few years since Victorian days, when modesty was esteemed a feminine attraction, and to wear the garb of the man, a shame only adopted by the shameless. Well may Christian women who fear God, and desire above all, His approval, be very careful as to their dress, for which the Spirit of God gives them counsel by the pens of both apostles, Paul in his letter to Timothy (chapter 2), and Peter (chapter 3:3). The last word has still to be said to the fashions of our day, but verse 24 hints its character.

> 25: Thy mortal men by sword are slain,
>      Thy men of might in battle.
> 26: And Zion's gates lament and mourn,
>      Whilst she in desolation sits
>      All humbled on the ground.

The gates of the cities once so thronged with the men who gathered there for counsel or for judgment are all abandoned now. Where are the men gone? Mortal though they be, it is not nature's mortality that has brought this condition. The sword has taken them away, and so we have a touching picture of poor Zion as a woman in heart-broken desolation sitting on the ground. It is surely striking that this is exactly the posture in which Judea is seen in the Roman medal struck to commemorate the destruction of Jerusalem by the armies of Titus: "A Roman warrior is standing in front of her, the inscription on the medal being *Judea capta*" (Delitzsch). So Jerusalem has remained captive through the centuries, the most unanswerable, if sorrowful, evidence of our Bible being in very truth the Word of God.

# CHAPTER FOUR

**The Hebrew's wealth was in children: the misery of being child-less. The first mention of the "Branch," with effect of His intervention.**

THE first verse of this chapter, whilst it has little or no relation to what follows, is vitally linked with what has preceded, for further misery awaits the daughters of Zion in that day.

> 1: Seven women shall urgently plead with one man:
>     We will eat our own bread,
>     We will wear our own clothes,
>     Only let us be called by thy name;
>     Take thou away our reproach.

Instead of that striking provision of God's goodness, "male and female created He them"—a numerical equality of sexes being maintained—desolating war has so done its work that there is but one man left to seven women; who, all feminine modesty extinguished, beg to be taken into his household, engaging to to be of no expense to him.

To die childless was to the Hebrew the acme of misery, for when God was directly governing the land, as in Israel, His promises and threats, while pregnant with *suggestions* of a scene beyond this life, were, in their *direct* expression, confined to it; so that to pass out of it leaving no children, was a most suggestive figure of that eternal reprobation fully revealed only in the New Testament. A Hebrew woman's desolation could go no further.

All this is but a black cloud to serve as a foil to the beauty and glory of our Lord, for now again we hear the same refrain, only no longer in the minor key of a solemn dirge; a joyous song begins with the seventh repetition of "In that day." God never rests short of the perfection of the number seven.

2: The Sprout of the Lord shall be beauty and glory,
    The Fruit of the land shall be pleasant and fair,
        For His redeemèd Israel.
3: And holy shall he be remaining in Zion,
    All in Jerusalem written alive—
4: When Jehovah hath washed the filth of her daughters,
    And atonement is made for the blood she has shed,
    By the spirit of judgment, the spirit of burning.
5: Then Jehovah creates on the dwellings of Zion,
    On all her assemblies, a cloud and a smoke;
    These shall provide a shade in the daytime
    That turns to a fire, bright-shining by night;
    For high over all shall hover the glory.
6: A booth it shall be from the heat of the day,
    A refuge, a covert from storm and from rain.

A most refreshing change! However uninteresting we may have found the third chapter, woe to us if we are indifferent to *this*. For who is this "Branch," or rather "Sprout,"* of Jehovah? The Jewish Targum saw their Messiah in this beautiful figure, and shall *we* be more blind to Him? Nay, here we see "Jesus only," alone in His glorious divinity, the *"Only* begotten Son" of God.

But He has another title, "Fruit of the land," and in this we see Him in His spotless humanity, sprouting forth amid all the death and desolation of Adam's race, "a root out of a dry ground," as we may see Him later, the *"First*-begotten" Son.

Amid all the ruin, here is one single Star of promise, hope and blessing, filled with the irresistible energy of a new life, and thrusting that life forth in lovely contrasts of beauty, and all is for His redeemed, His Israel. For there shall be a remnant of Israel left after the burning judgments of Jehovah have passed over her, and every one of this remnant shall be written in the book of life; not only be born again, but *glorified,* although on earth. Over every family dwelling, over the totality of the nation, shall be the same visible evidence of His love and care as in the

---

*There are eighteen words in Hebrew rendered "branch" in A. V. Here it is *"tzemach,"* the prime root meaning "to sprout forth," and gives the idea of the energy of life. This would be better conveyed by "sprout" than by "branch."

day of the deliverance from Egypt. Thus overshadowed, no heat shall strike, no storm nor tempest invade that happy spot: it is truly—we may say literally—heaven on earth.

But where is *our* dwelling, the *heavenly* Jerusalem, in all this? May we not see a suggestion of it in that very "glory" that hovers over the earthly city? This is in strict accord with the book so justly termed "Revelation." There, the heavenly city holds the centre of the stage, and the earthly city takes the inferior place of the "wall great and high" (Rev. 21: 12).

This then is the beginning of what is termed the Millennium, when Israel's Messiah, our Lord Jesus, shall reign over the earth. It is the dispensation of the fulness of times, when indeed all things shall "be headed up in Him, both which are in heaven and on earth" (Eph. 1: 10). In one spot there is "New Creation," both heavenly and earthly, these being closely identified: the "new heavens" being the "City, the Heavenly Jerusalem," the "new earth" being the Jerusalem on earth, and, as coming between the "City" and the saved nations, it is termed the "wall."

It is the "regeneration" of the earth, and corresponds to the regeneration of the individual Christian today, for in his case, too, it is not a perfect condition, the body still having that evil principle "sin" within, and so being under the sentence of death (Rom. 8: 10); but the spirit, as Israel in that day, is even now fully renewed by the Holy Spirit. Israel shall then be Jezreel, the Seed of God, and her condition is one of unending perfection. To *her* the Heavens are New—to *her* the Earth is New; but mankind as a whole still awaits one final test, when the great enemy shall be released from that abyss that has been his prison for the thousand years; then, but not till then, will He (our Lord) proclaim Himself as the One who makes *"all things new,"* and there is "neither adversary nor evil occurrent" (1 Kings 5: 4) in the whole universe of bliss, for so hath God greatly purposed.

Thus are there three epochs of new creation: Individual (2 Cor. 5: 17): Israel (Isa. 65: 17): All mankind (Rev. 21: 5).

# CHAPTER FIVE

**Song of the disappointing vineyard. Meaning of Sh'ohl.**

"THE fugitive rhythm, the musical euphony, the charming assonances in this appeal it is impossible to reproduce; they are perfectly inimitable."* So writes Delitzsch of verses 1 and 2 of this chapter; and he continues: "The prophet commenced the first address in chapter 1 as another Moses; the second with the text of an earlier prophecy, and now commences the third as a musician."

> 1: Now will I sing to my dearly Belovèd,
> A song of my dearest concerning His vine;
> For a vineyard belongs to my dearly Belovèd,
> On the side of a hill, most fertile of soil.
> 2: He fenced it, He dug it, He cleared it of stones;
> And planted within it the noblest of vines;
> Then, for its guarding, He builded a tower,
> And hewed from the rock a winepress within,
> Then waited, expectant of sweet luscious fruit,
> And lo, when He came, the grapes were—a stench!†

Now the Lord invites those to whom the parable applies to pass judgment between Himself and His vineyard, and in so doing, they will be condemned out of their own mouth. This is profoundly significant and characteristic of God's ways with men. I beg my reader to compare 2 Sam. 12: 1-7 and Matt. 21: 33-41, and he will again see, and in so doing, rejoice to see, that

---

*Perhaps, however, even our ear can catch a hint of the "lark-like trilling" in the Hebrew of verse 1:

> "Ashirah nah lididi,
> shirath doodi le-karmo,
> kerem hayah lididi,
> beqeren ben-shahmen."

†Our word "wild-grape" does not convey at all the repulsive idea that is in this word that comes as an anti-climax. In Hebrew *"bushim,"* from a root, "to have a bad smell." The same word is in chap. 34: 3 rendered "stench."

Jehovah and Jesus are One; for as Jehovah dealt with David, so did Jesus with the Pharisees.

Has any care been omitted? The judges are silent; every mouth is stopped. Then Jehovah pronounces sentence:

> 5, 6:   No more will I trim it, no more will I dig it;
>         The briars and thistles about it shall grow;
>         Never a cloud shall drop blessing upon it,
>         Fruitful alone in its shame and its woe;
>         The beasts of the field shall tread in the mire
>         The vineyard I loved, My "plant of desire."

Then in verse 7 comes the interpretation of the parable: the vineyard is the house of Israel; His pleasant plant, the men of Judah; from these He expected good fruit; "but, behold, instead of *mishpaht* (judgment), He found *mispach* (oppression); instead of *tzedahqah* (righteousness), He found *tzeahqah* (a cry)." "The poet here closely depicts by word-likeness, which yet conceals a totally different meaning, the deceptive appearance in the conduct of the Israelites, which at first looked like a good vine and then developed a wild vine. This may be imitated in English thus: 'He waited for *equity,* and lo, *iniquity*: for *right,* and lo, *riot.'* "*

This is followed by the cry of "Woe," six times repeated, foretelling thus by doleful forecasts the execution of judgment. Looking closer, we discern that whilst the woes are six, the penalties are three: first in verses 9, 10; second in verses 13 to 17; third in verses 24 to 30. We may then again note the Divine Fingerprint in the impression of the number "three," and its multiple "six," on this section.

I cannot here refrain from further noting this profound and deeply interesting truth:  Israel is but a little stage on which has been acted out in the Scriptures of the Old Testament, as we may say, a drama that reveals to us what is occurring in a far larger one in the race of mankind as a whole; and *that,* in its turn, is only a miniature of a still larger and universal sphere where corresponding wonders are being enacted, only in this all is eternal.  Exactly what is in our chapter, predicated of Israel

---

*From the American translator of Lange's "Commentary."

and Judah, His "plant of delight" (as it very literally is), has
occurred with man as a race, also His "plant of delight," for He
sang a song of love and joy over him, too, at his creation, Gen.
1: 27 being really a three-lined song:

> So Elohim created the man in His image,
> In Elohim's image created He him,
> Male and female created He them.

Alas, that song has also been turned to sorrow, for after four
"days" of testing, it may be said of him, too, that "he stinketh,
for he hath been dead four days." So much for poor Adam the
first; God may well be praised then for the Last Adam, "the
Amen, the Faithful and True Witness, the Beginning of the
creation of God." The song over *Him* never ceases, and (oh,
wonder of wonders!) we, in Him, have a part in it, and abiding
in Him who is the true Vine, we (even you and I, dear reader)
may bring forth such good fruit as shall be to the glory of the
Father, and give Him joy; but in no other way.

In verses 8 to 10 the first woe is directed against the lust of
the eye: the coveting of house or land: the people are never
satisfied. Having acquired one house or field that has been long
coveted, that coveting is only diverted to the adjoining, and this
goes on till there is nothing left on earth that they do not own,
and then what? Will the earth satisfy that ever-hungry heart?
Indeed not. Yet hungering ever, here is a curse on the very
hungering! Nor is this coveting recognized at all as "sin," till
the law comes with, "Thou shalt not covet" (Rom. 7: 7). Alas,
might not the injunction as well be, "Thou shalt not breathe,"
for who does *not* covet? Nor can the whole earth fill this hungry
heart of man.

But Jehovah has spoken into the ears of the prophet—so
clearly as to preclude the possibility of any misunderstanding
—the penalty that shall correspond to the offense. There shall
be many beautiful dwellings, but no dwellers in them: as to the
fields, so barren shall they become that a vineyard covering ten
acres shall yield only a few gallons, and if one sows about thirty
pecks of seed, he shall get back about three! Again let us turn
to our "Last Adam" and sing:

> "Satisfied with Thee, Lord Jesus,
>           I am blest."

In Him, too, we are not forbidden to covet, but indeed are urged to "covet earnestly the best gifts," that is, those that shall make *least* of ourselves, and shall most edify our brethren (1 Cor. 12: 31).

In verses 11 to 17, the second woe is directed against the lusts of the flesh, against those who from break of day till the cool of the evening pursue strong intoxicants, till wine pursues *them*, gets hold of them, inflames them. This is combined with the more refined form of sensuous pleasure, music; which, from the day of Jubal, has been one of the chief delights of the children of Cain. These—wine and music—are their feasts: body and soul are thus provided for, but what of that spirit that can never be satisfied with aught but God?

Alas, it is dead, for "the work of Jehovah they do not regard, the work of His hands they do not consider." What then is the consequence? Judgment would overtake them in this blind, dull, animal condition:

13:  Banished are My people, all taken unawares;*
     Their glory dies of famine,
     The mass dried up with thirst.

The gluttonous rich, or aristocracy, called here "their glory," would be famished; the drunken mass would perish of thirst. Note again the correspondence between the sin and the penalty.

14:  Wide hath Sh'ohl oped its jaws,
     Its mouth is outstretched without limit;
     And down therein their glory falls,
     Their mass, their pomp, their revellers!

History closely repeats itself: substitute Christendom for Judah, and again we see the mass "lovers of pleasure rather than lovers of God" (2 Tim. 3: 4); and these pleasures have so dead-

---

*That is, had they meditated on the way the Lord ever works, they would have foreseen what was coming, been intelligent as to the signs of the times (Luke 12: 58): it is not "because they had no knowledge."

ened all spiritual faculties that they discern not that the Judge is at the door. No college can impart such knowledge.

I leave the word *"sh'ohl"* untranslated, for it is very difficult to render accurately. It is from a root "to ask," or demand, and may either have originated in the idea expressed in Prov. 30: 16, *"sh'ohl,"* never satisfied, never crying "Enough;" it is always asking (*shahal, sh'ohl*). Or it may have a more spiritual and pathetic force, and point not to the demand for fresh victims, but to the enquiring attitude of the survivors. They follow their kinsman to the exit from this scene; *he* goes, they stay, and as they stand before that closed door through which he has gone, they ask, "Where?" Is not that an inevitable cry of anguished affection? According to a most ancient custom, they thrice solemnly invoked his name, but no answer came back. So Job sighs, "Man dieth and wasteth away, yea, man giveth up the ghost, and *where is he?"* Aye, "Where is he?" The very Hebrew *"vayyo"* has the sound of a sigh: "Where is he?" It is the question that has ever been asked but to which there is no answer at all through the Old Testament, till *He* comes who brings "life and incorruption to light."

As time went on, the idea of locality became more prominent in the term, and as God is always recognized as *above,* and with Him life is linked, so death became equally linked with the other direction, *below,* and distance from Him, till sh'ohl was *lower* than the grave that received the body and was found in the "heart of the earth." But we must not press the literalness of location too strongly, as many do. The occurrences of these terms will not permit such literalness, *e.g.,* "Thou, Capernaum, which art exalted to heaven," does not mean that the city was literally in the air, but the unique privileges she had enjoyed gave her a distinguishing place; so, "Thou shalt be cast down to *Hades"* (Greek equivalent of *Sh'ohl*), does not necessitate the literal descent into "the heart of the earth," but the loss of all these privileges, and the being left far away from God and Light. Strong moral ideas are attached to the terms of direction, "up" and "down," and these are of far more value than literalness.

Seeking to preserve something of the rhythm, we might render:

15: Brought low shall the peasant be, humbled be the noble;
     The lofty looks of all the proud be humbled to the dust:
16: Then shall Jehovah, Jehovah, Lord of all hosts,
     Show Himself in judgment exalted very high,
17: For lambs shall then be grazing, as if on their own pasture,
     And nomads shall be eating the wastings of the fat ones.

Over ancient Canaan, once so prosperous, nomad shepherds pasture their flocks: the lambs graze as if the place had never been intended for anything else than to afford them pasturage. But in all this severity of judgment the Lord is indeed sanctified, as He shall be in eternity by that infinitely "sorer punishment," the "lake of fire." Oh, adore *Him* who bore all that judgment for us!

While "all have sinned and come short of the glory of God," an I in this sense "there is no difference," the seeds of all evils lying within every heart, yet those seeds do not germinate equally in all; the form in which the evil expresses itself in action, or externally, differs; so in these six woes there are six different forms of evil recognized. The third woe reads:

Woe to the drawers of sin!
By the strong traces of lying,
As with the ropes of a wagon,
They haul their sin along.
Who say, Let Him speed up His work,
Let Him hasten that we may behold it;
Let the counsel of Israel's Holy One
Come closer and come to fulfilment,
That we may know it indeed.

This then, is clearly directed against those who, boasting of liberty, are really but yoked beasts of burden, and the wagon they are drawing is their own sin. To ease it in its going, they make use of words of falsehood: for instance, the evil in which they particularly delight may be the love of money, this the Word of God calls "covetousness, which is idolatry" (Col. 3: 5). But that would never do for a "trace" by which to drag it along; they therefore call it being "diligent in business."* This, being

---

*This is a very unfortunate rendering of Romans 12: 11. It very literally is, "In diligence not slothful."

actually in the Bible, eases the strain greatly, for, under the guise of obedience to the Bible, they can turn with added zest to covetousness. Error would make slow progress were it labeled truthfully, so it is given some attractive name. Call unbelief of what God has said "infidelity," and the "wagon" would drag as heavily as Egypt's chariots; but under the name of "free thought" or "rational religion," it makes far better progress. But these are "lying words," and the goal to which they are progressing is greater *judgment*. As to this, they are boldly defiant, and challenge Jehovah to carry out what He has so long threatened. "Let it come," they cry, "let this long-predicted judgment take place, for that alone would convince us of its reality." Are those who insist that prophecy cannot be comprehended till its fulfilment, far from the same speech?

It is a long-lived generation, and the rationalists of our day take up the same cry in, "Where is the promise of His coming?" We might paraphrase vers. 18, 19 thus:

18: Woe to those whose wickedness is helped by words of lying,
Who in their pride and unbelief, the wrath of God defying
19: Cry, Let Him speed and haste His work, and then we may receive it;
Until that wrath, long-threatened, comes, we cannot quite believe it.

Now follow three woes in quick succession, with no intervening comment, like the cry of that angel that John heard as he flew through mid-heaven: "Woe, woe, woe" (Rev. 8: 13). We may render the fourth freely, thus:

20: Woe to those who quite ignore the standards God has given,
Who call the evil very good, true good they term the evil:
They claim their darkness to be light, true light they term the darkness:
The bitter they pronounce the sweet, and call the sweet the bitter.

We must not suppose, however, that men ever call murder or drunkenness or stealing, good. No, quite the reverse; they will rather take credit for their sharp condemnation of that against which the natural conscience revolts.   But there is a sphere in which we are dependent on God Himself for a standard of right and wrong, where His Word alone pronounces as to this, and it is here that the servants of that same  subtle  one  who in Eden assured our mother Eve that it was not "evil," but "good" to eat of that forbidden tree, again deny the truth of the Word of God as an absolute and final standard.   The formation of natural character is, they say, good, as the true basis of salvation. "All our righteousnesses is as filthy rags," says the Scripture, and it is the calling of these filthy rags clean, that is calling evil good. The doctrine of substitution is evil, says a popular preacher, for "it is an evil thing to punish the innocent for the guilty." "Christ died for our sins," says the Scripture, and thus today apostates, and (it is to be feared) the mass of professing Christians call good, evil, and evil good.

The fifth woe is the necessary consequence of the fourth:

21: Woe to those who're very wise in their own estimation!
    Woe to those who prudent are in their own sight!

We fear that there are few, if any, who adopt the principles of the modern school of infidelity called "higher criticism" who do not come under this woe.   They are wiser than all who preceded them, and are thus the forerunners of that apostate of the last days, addressed with stinging irony, under the cognomen of "*Prince* (not the king) of Tyre;" "Behold, thou art wiser than Daniel" (Ezek. 28: 3).   Each considers himself quite competent to bow (for it is done with educated politeness) God out of His world, His works, and His Word.

The sixth is in the same line:

22: Woe to those who heroes are—to drink the wine!
    (Woe) to those who valiant are—to mix strong drink!*
23: Acquitting guilty criminals, won over by a bribe:
    While from the truly righteous they take away the right.

---

*Note the sarcastic anti-climax.   Very heroic and brave are these, but it is only in drinking!

This is not a repetition of the second woe, for these heavy drinkers are on the judgment-seat, and show their incompetency for the place they have assumed by reversing all justice; acquitting the guilty, and condemning the innocent.

That would interest us but little, were it only a record of what obtained in an obscure little country ages ago, but many of us are deeply convinced that all has been "written for our admonition, upon whom the ends of the ages have come" (1 Cor. 10: 11), and that these linked woes are actually impending over us in Christendom today; for all through the centuries down to this very day there are the same reversals that are so sternly condemned in these woes. Judgment has not yet returned to righteousness.

But, you ask, are the leaders of Christendom "strong to drink wine?" All these literal evils, even in the Old Testament, had their spiritual antitypes, as in the New. The idolatry of old figured then, and figures today, covetousness (Col. 3: 5). So fornication of old, worldliness today (James 4: 4). What then is the spiritual counterpart of being "strong to drink wine," with the consequent reversal of all justice? In the light of Ephesians 5: 18, it would appear to be the opposite of being "filled with the Spirit." This leads to a clear discrimination between what is of God and what not, and between who is of God, and who is not, and thus to "unfeigned love of the brethren." Then spiritual drunkenness is the excitement of the old Adam nature, leading to the satiating of that "carnal mind that is enmity with God," and all that is of God, with hatred of His truth and all that adheres to it. Babylon the Great, the mother of harlots as she is, is also a "drunkard," in this sense, but it is dreadful "wine" she drinks, for John sees her "drunken with the blood of the saints and of martyrs of Jesus" (Rev. 17: 6). She, too, from the righteous takes away the right; as she ever did, as she will again, when she regains her power.

But now in verses 24 to 30 the penalty is announced, and this the more terrible from the graphic poetical form in which it is clothed:

24: Therefore as fire-tongue licks up the stubble,*
    As grass that is dry doth shrivel in flame,
    So shall their root become utterly rotten,
    Their blossom fly up as the dust.
    For the law of Jehovah of Hosts they've despised,
    The word they've rejected with scorn
    Of Israel's One—the Most Holy.
25: Therefore the wrath of Jehovah doth burn,
    Against His people Isràel.
    Stretched forth is His hand still against them,
    And He smites till the mountains do quiver,
    Their corpses become as the dust of the streets.
    For all this His anger is not turned away,
    But His hand is ever outstretchèd.

It is a clear picture of divine severity, ending in what becomes an oft-repeated refrain.

26: He lifts up a standard to nations afar,
    Calls them with hisses from ends of the earth,
    And see how they come with speed swiftly.
27: Not one is a laggard!
    None stumbles among them!
    Not one is drowsy or sleeps!
    Never a girdle is loosed from their loins!
    Never a shoe-string is broken!
28: Their arrows are keen, their bows are all bent;
    The hoofs of their horses are flint-like,
    Their chariots drive as the whirlwind.

This is obviously a graphic description in poetical terms of an ideal army, with no weaknesses at all, and the prophet seems to see it advancing from afar. In verse 26, God calls it, and at once the seer is struck with the swift motion as it sweeps along, like the shadows of clouds over a sunlit landscape in a high wind; then, as it approaches nearer, he is able to distinguish the perfect equipment, "never a girdle loosed, never a shoe-string broken;" weapons all in readiness for action, "arrows sharpened, bows bent." Still closer, and he actually hears the ring of the hardened hoofs of the cavalry, the whirlwind-like roar of the

*In the multiplication of sibilants: *"quash leshon esh,"* we hear the "crackling sparks and sputtering flames."—*Delitzsch.*

rushing chariots. The very words—short, sharp, quick—give the idea of the scene they depict.

But this brings up another figure of terror. "For thus far the prophet's description has moved along as if by forced marches, in clauses of from two to four words each, now it changes into a heavy stealthy pace; and then, in a few clauses, springs as a lion on its prey."* The first lines then should be read slowly, with pauses between the words.

29: Its — roar — is — as — a — lioness;
    They — growl — as — do — the — young — lions.

Then quickly, as if the lion were springing:

    Roaring, they spring upon the prey,
    And bear it off unhindered.
30: Their roarings rumble over them,
    As the roaring of the sea,
        In that day.
    If the look is to landward,
    Lo, darkness there, and sorrow;
    Yea, the light is very dark,
    In the skies o'erclouded.

Note the words "in that day," linking this with the previous chapters, and justifying connecting them together. In utter misery poor Judah, in the lion's mouth, looks about for help; first, to the earth—but there is nothing there but hopeless anguish. Upwards, there are occasional gleams of hope, but these only add to the distress by deep disappointment, for these gleams soon become darkened. Most of us know the deepening of distress by the failure of hopes which lift up only to let fall again. The picture ends with gloom—thick, impenetrable—hanging over all!

Let us note that although nations may be influenced by all kinds of motives, yet, little as they recognize it, God controls, and is moving behind them. He called Assyria, Babylon, and Rome against His people Israel. He called Saracen and Turk in their day against those that had taken the place of these "natural

---

*Delitzsch.*

branches," and most surely it is He, and He only, whose mighty Hand should be seen in all the present chastenings of war and its aftermaths on the nations calling themselves by the Name of His dear Son.

# CHAPTER SIX

The third vision, corresponding with the third book, Leviticus. Isaiah beholds the glory of God; it is that of our Lord Jesus. The preparation of a "vessel to honor" for service in three stages. The commission to harden: how effected? By the presentation of Messiah.

WE now come to a portion of our prophecy greatly hallowed to us by the words of the Holy Spirit in the Gospel of John, chapter 12: 36-41:

These things spake Jesus, and departed, and did hide Himself from them. But though He had done so many miracles before them, yet they believed not on Him; that the saying of Esaias the prophet might be fulfilled which he spake: Lord, who hath believed our report, and to whom hath the arm of the Lord been revealed? Therefore they could not believe, because that Esaias said again, He hath blinded their eyes, and hardened their heart; that they should not see with their eyes, nor understand with their heart, and be converted, and I should heal them. These things said Esaias when he saw His glory and spake of Him.

Well may we approach with reverence, and with earnest desire that our eyes may be anointed with that eye-salve that He sells only to those who are so poor that they can pay Him nothing for it (Rev. 3: 17, 18), except the full confidence of their hearts in days of stress, which is to Him of more worth than gold. So peradventure may we, too, "see His glory," and in our limited way, "speak of Him."

It is the third vision, the third introduction to the main contents of the book, and as a third again bears prominently upon it the significance of that number; and more evidently so in this case, since it has been put in the third place out of its natural order. For thus far, Isaiah has received no formal commission; we have it here. One would, naturally, have expected it to begin the book, but had it done so, its position would no longer have told of His glory *fully manifested*—for that, we remember, is the very meaning of "three."

Just as the third book of the Bible, Leviticus, takes us into the Sanctuary where the glories of Christ pass before us in its

types, so in our book, we are now coming into the Sanctuary that
we may there "behold His glory."

The scene, then, is laid in the Sanctuary, "the holiest of all;"
but while the temple on earth may supply the figures, it would
not suffice, in its physical limitations, to exhaust the grandeur of
this scene.

The chapter is very strongly marked by three divisions which
are themselves thrice divided, thus:

1: Verses 1-4: The glory, and this too in three parts—(a)
the throne; (b) the seraphim; (c) their cry.
2: Verses 5-7: The vessel to honor, prepared by (a) confession; (b) provision; (c) remission.
3: Verses 8-13: The commission, (a) its terms; (b) its limitation; (c) the restoration.

Three is everywhere marked on this singularly glorious
scripture. God in Christ is in very deed *manifested*.

The time of the vision is "the year that King Uzziah died," a
significant epoch. For fifty-two years has this king reigned, and
the nation has been blessed with every token of divine favor.
Philistines, Arabians, Ammonites, have all been brought into subjection (2 Chron. 26), and now Uzziah is to die—and to die a
*leper!* "The national glory of Israel died out, too, with King
Uzziah, and has never recovered to this day,"* and thus we may
say that its king's death figured that of the nation; for the
nation, too, has died—a leper! There is, thus, a sad harmony
between the time of the vision and its burden.

Nor may we pass over the very name of this king as being
without value. Uzziah means "the power of Jehovah." The
power of Jehovah to approve, bless, save the nation, *under the
covenant of law,* has been evidenced as abortive, as the vision
shall show. In this typical sense, too, then Uzziah passes away,
and many centuries must run their course before we hear one
who had seen a brighter vision, joyfully crying, "I am not
ashamed of the gospel of Christ, for it is the *power of God*
(*i.e.,* 'Uzziah') unto salvation to every one that believeth," not

---

*Delitzsch.*

then confined to the Jew, for He is also the God of the Gentile, and by that power every one, leper though he may be, may be healed, and given a deathless life.

In this chapter the prophet drops all that is in the least artificial; now we hear no poetry, no rhythmic chant. The occasion is too solemn for any other than the simplest form of speech—it is simply prose.

He, like John in Patmos, becomes "in the Spirit," and sees Adohn (the name of God as the supreme Lord of all; and here, as in Romans 9: 5, "Christ who is *over all*, God, blessed forever") with every accompaniment of majestic splendor, sitting on a Throne, which is itself "high and exalted," for "His Throne ruleth over all;" yet, while sitting on this lofty Throne the hem of His raiment fills that glorious temple.

Seraphim hover on one pair of outstretched wings, while with another they cover their faces, as not able to see that dazzling glory, and with the third they cover their feet, as not desiring to be seen.

Incidentally we may note for our comfort, that there are never any personal introductions in heaven, or the sanctuary. In that light of God, Isaiah knows the seraphim at once, in so far as to give them that name; as, long after this, Peter knew Moses and Elias, in the same light, also without any introduction. So, I gather, we shall need no introduction even to those whom we have never known here, how much less to those whom we have! That clear and holy light fully reveals everyone, and they are well known: "Not one shall seem a stranger, though never seen before," as we sometimes happily sing.

We are not told the number of the seraphim—it is not of importance. Nor does the word seraphim, so applied, appear elsewhere in Scripture, but its force is quite clear from the frequent occurrence of the root, *saraph*, "to burn," but not to burn-as-incense, not as a sweet savor, not as expressive of acceptance and delight—the word for that is *kahtar*—but "to consume," as in holy judgment. The word *saraph* is never used for the offerings of sweet-savor, always of the offerings that speak of sin put away in judgment. Burnt-offering, peace-offering, meat-offering, are *kahtared*, or burnt-as-sweet-savor; but as soon as we come to the sin-offering, it is *sahraphed*, or consumed without the camp. This will give us the significance of these seraphim as far as the profit for us goes; they express symbolically the active, searching, burning holiness of God, and the writer of the epistle to the Hebrews tells out the truth that the seraphim express when he says, "Our God also is a *consuming fire.*" All can see the accord of such a term with this scene.

Cherubim are another order—similar, yet somewhat distinct; for a difference in name speaks a difference in order. These are expressive, in living forms, of the various perfections of the righteousness of God's government, ever protecting His Throne; for over it they bend with protecting wing (Exodus 25: 20), forbidding the approach or acceptance of any sinner unrighteously. It was the cherubim that kept the way of the tree of life, that sinful man might not return, and eating of that tree, live in sorrow and separation from God, the source of all blessedness, forever. If the cherub has wings, these are not for flight, as are the seraph's, but for protecting care.

For while the seraph searches, the cherub protects: the seraph speaks of burning holiness, the cherub of inflexible righteousness: the seraph active, the cherub passive; yet we find, both in Ezekiel and in Revelation, living creatures that combine the characteristics of both seraph and cherub. One is therefore inclined to believe that we get the intent of the Holy Spirit when in both we see symbolic personifications of divine qualities, rather than actual personalities.

3: And one cried to the other, and said (and here there does intervene a cadence, thus:)

> Holy, holy, holy, Jehovah Tzebaoth!
> Full is all the earth of His glory!

Thus may we learn that in that scene heart responds to heart. There is no discordant discussion, no difference, "All the mind in heaven is one." Nor are any of them occupied with each other's beauty, far less with their own; for, "In His temple doth everyone speak of *His* glory" (Psalm 29: 9). Oh, that we could learn that language here, for it is to be our mother-tongue forever.

In this threefold ascription we may again see "God manifested;" and as we remember the still clearer revelation of Matt.
28: 19, we hear in this antiphonal cry not a mere repetition for
emphasis, but the recognition of a trinity of Divine Persons, each
of whom is hymned as holy; and at the same time, in view of
John 12, we must remember that it is Jesus' glory on which
Isaiah looks, and this threefold ascription only says that "in Him
dwells all the fulness of the Godhead bodily" (Col. 2: 9).   Oh,
the depths of God in Christ! (1 Cor. 2: 10).

Further, let us note, and I trust not without some delight,
that the atmosphere of heaven is very clear.   As in our earth we
sometimes say, "How near in this clear light those far-off hills
appear, that yesterday in the mist, we could not see at all;" so,
in the sanctuary, so clear is the atmosphere, so bright the light,
that the happy dwellers there see afar.   Though weary ages may
intervene, and we poor short-sighted creatures who live in the
murky atmosphere of this sinful world, may not be able to see
that coming scene of glory at all, or very dimly "as through a
glass darkly," to these sanctuary-dwellers all intervening ages are
as though they were not, and to them the "glory" ever fills the
earth, as it eventually shall.

Let us at least learn that when God has purposed anything,
so sure is its accomplishment that those who hear and believe
speak of it as though it were so already, for so these seraphim
cry, "The whole earth is full of His glory."

But not yet!   No, not yet!   The groans of suffering, the tears
of the bereaved, the wails of the oppressed, the quivers of anxiety
—these still fill the earth; but these do *not* tell His glory; far,
far from it.   But the present conditions do not *end* His ways.
That end shall see the earth, in every part, witnessing to the perfections of its true King. "He shall judge the poor of the people,
He shall save the children of the needy, and shall break in pieces
the oppressor." *Then* shall "the whole earth be full of His
glory."

> 4: And the foundations of the thresholds shook at the voice
> of them that cried, and the house became full of smoke.

Everything was *moved*, for in contrast with this earth, nothing
is insensate in *that* scene.   To the prophet's awe-struck sight, the

very foundations are swaying in responsive awe to His glory. This was *their* antiphon to the uttered ascription of the Intelligences of Heaven. So praise ever spreads; it is beautifully contagious, as that later Seer heard the ever-widening circles, till "every creature which is in heaven, and on the earth, and under the earth, and such as are in the sea, and all that are in them, heard I saying, 'Blessing, and honor and glory and power be unto Him that sitteth upon the throne, and unto the Lamb for ever and ever.'" Again I say, Oh, that we were quicker students to learn and to communicate *that* language—our mother-tongue.

Now we turn to the second section, in which we shall see the Lord preparing a vessel unto honor for His use; and, as I believe it to be a pattern case, it will be well to mark the steps.

> 5: Then said I, Woe to me, for I am lost; for I am a man of
>      unclean lips, and I am dwelling among a people of unclean
>      lips; for mine eyes have seen the King, Jehovah Tzebaoth.

The first step, then, is that he is brought into that holy light in which he sees everything clearly, exactly *as it is;* and at once he cries out in dread alarm, "I am lost!" O unhappy man! do you say? No, for that is the path in which every one is led whom God intends to use. The light that He causes to shine ever reveals, in us all as at first, that all is a chaos, "waste and desolate" (Genesis 1: 2), yet that light is always "good." So it was with Job (chapter 42), so with Daniel (chapter 10), so with Saul of Tarsus (Acts 9), so with John in Patmos (Rev. 1), and so with Isaiah. Saint, sinner; Jew, Gentile; king, peasant—all humbled to the same level of the dust in that Light.

Isaiah instantly recognizes that it is his own lips that are unclean, not merely those of his neighbors. He is of the same "clay lump" as all the rest (Romans 9: 21). In the light of that glory there is "no difference, for all have sinned and come short" of it. He is no better, any more than that one thief on Calvary was better than the other, he was no less a thief. The publican in the temple was not "better" than the Pharisee. The only difference was that these *confessed* that there *was no* difference. But that is of so vast a difference as to bring a blessing instead of a curse, a kiss instead of a blow, heaven instead of hell. This is invariably, in greater or less degree, the necessary precursor to all blessing or usefulness.

> 6, 7: And one of the seraphim flew to me, and in his hand a glowing coal, taken with tongs from off the altar. And he touched my mouth with it and said, Lo, this hath touched thy lips, thine iniquity is gone—thy sin is expiated.

Here, if I err not, we may indeed, see "His glory," even in this "glowing coal," for look a little more carefully at it, as that Seraph, or "burning" one, brings it. It is also burning; the fire from which it is taken is active in it still. It is, we may say, still suffering the judgment of the fire. Let this touch the unclean lips ever so lightly, and at once all iniquity is taken away. We must bear in mind, however, that the very word used for "touched" forbids the thought of its being a casual, inoperative contact. The word conveys the same significance exactly as its Greek equivalent in Luke 8: 45, when the Lord felt that light finger-tip and asked, "Who touched Me?" In that touch there is always an effect—a communication of virtue.

The "glowing coal," then, is our Lord Jesus Christ, but not on the "Throne high and lifted up," but lifted up upon the cross. Here we see in one complete scene, what historically took place in two actions, on and after the final entry into Jerusalem in Luke 19. Then, too, He came to sit upon His Throne. "Behold, thy King cometh unto thee, meek and sitting upon an ass, and a colt the foal of an ass," but His people were not ready for Him as their King, but sorely needed Him in other guise. His love must meet this need. So He steps, as it were, from off the throne, and laying Himself on the altar, becomes the paschal Lamb—the "glowing coal."

In view of this, can there be any question as to which of the altars this coal came from? There are two: the *golden* altar, standing in the "Holy Place," called the altar of incense, and the *brazen* altar, standing at the very entrance of the court, and called the altar of burnt offering, and since the glowing coal clearly speaks of the means by which sin was put away, that fact is quite out of harmony with the altar of incense, which was provided for the worship of those whose sins had already been put away. The fire by which that coal glowed must then have been the fire, not of complacency and delight, of which the sweet incense speaks, but of judgment. The burning in that coal was *"sahraph,"* not *"kahtar,"* and the altar was the brazen, not the golden.

But this must be much more than on our "lips" today. It was quite in accord with the character of the dispensation, in which everything was external, that Isaiah's *lips* should be touched, for the lips are the external manifestation of what we really are (Matt. 12: 37), but it is the inner man that must now be affected or "touched" by that "coal," for it is our Lord Jesus suffering, burning, being consumed for our *heart*-uncleanness. Let that touch the *heart,* and sin is both taken away before God, and utterly abhorred by him thus affected, and then the lip may make joyful confession unto salvation, and be used for service.

It is not at all necessary to look upon the prophet Isaiah here as taking the place of an unforgiven sinner: far from it; he was surely a saint long before this. It is not his regeneration that is here figured, but his being made meet for the Master's use, in accord with the context that follows. Just as it is not an unregenerate sinner that we hear in Romans 7 also crying, "Woe is me!" or "Wretched man that I am!" but a saint learning a deeper lesson. Nor does it mean that you and I are unregenerate because we, too, are learning the same painful, humbling, yet wholesome lesson of holiness, in the utter corruption of all that is in us, that is, in our flesh. For it is thus that we, too, turn to Jesus our Lord, learn of His infinite grace in being made the "glowing coal," and we are made "meet for the Master's use" in the way of making that grace known.

However, we must not confuse two truths; there is a cleansing that is accomplished at once by divine grace, as with Isaiah here, and also one that is progressive, the responsibility of which is pressed upon us in 2 Timothy 2, "If a man purge himself from these" (that is, all that is "wood and earth"); but the same principle or Person is the Agent of holiness in both cases, it is the "glowing coal," Christ suffering for, and as, sin.

Again, see it in that "Seraph," or "burning one,"* lifted up by Moses in the wilderness, for the sin of a people who (we may well note) had not just come out of Egypt; but who were just about to enter their inheritance. This may lead some of my readers, who may also be drawing near the end of their pilgrimage, to question whether they may not have something to learn still from that brazen serpent. Let us "consider" these things, and the Lord shall give us "understanding in all things" (2 Tim. 2: 7).

Thus the vessel to honor is prepared for the Master's use; now follows the commission, every step in which is filled with interest and profit.

> 8: And I heard the voice of the Lord (Adonai) saying, Whom shall I send and who will go for Us? Then I said, Here am I; send me.

The question is not addressed to the hosts of unfallen creatures of heaven, or there would have been a chorus of volunteers from among those angelic ranks crying, "Send me! Send me!" But no; they are silent. No seraph now responds, no cherub offers himself, since there is a man who is not only "a vessel to honor," but who, being "purged," has been thus "sanctified" and is "meet for the Master's use." None of the "ministers who did His will" could now be sent on this mission to sinful men: a man whose lips have been unclean alone can go to a people of unclean lips. May not that be why you and I are left here?

> 9, 10: And He said, Go, say to this people, Hearing, hear, but understand not. Seeing, see, but perceive not. Make the heart of this people fat, and make their ears heavy, and their eyes plaster over, lest they see with their eyes, and hear with their ears, and understand with their heart, and they be converted and be healed.

---

*In Num. 21: 6 the word for "fiery serpents" is simply "seraphim," exactly as in Isaiah 6; while in verse 8 the reading is, "Make thee a saraph—a burning one," with no other word for serpent. Moses attained this by making the likeness of a serpent in brass, which glowed in the light of the sun as if it were being consumed. Just as Christ was made in the likeness of sinful flesh, and, when lifted up, sin in the flesh was consumed in Him.

It is a strange and sad errand on which the prophet is sent, to blind, to deafen, and to harden. Yet we may safely say at once that God never harden hearts that would otherwise be soft, and that owe their hardness to His interposition. He does not blind the eyes of those that would fain see, and apart from His interposition, would see. It is but the foolish blasphemy of men in their enmity to God that thus argues. Let us seek for illustrations both from nature and from Scripture that shall help us.

Have any of my readers ever carried a bright light into a dark barn on a dark night? At once all the unclean creatures of darkness, the rats and the mice to whom darkness is alone congenial, flee from the light and scatter to their kindred darkness, but the birds, the creatures that are of the light, fly *to* the light. The lantern comes into the darkness for judgment, and exposes the true state of all—what they really are, and what must be their natural place according to that nature. But the light of the lantern did not alter any of the creatures—it only revealed them. It did not turn what was otherwise clean into unclean. So the Gospel in the same way results in the same discrimination.

The same genial beam of the sun which *hardens* the clay *melts* the wax: so grace rejected is what hardens. It is not wrath now, but "the riches of His goodness, and forbearance, and long-suffering," that would fain lead to repentance; which, being despised by the heart, hardens that heart and results in increased "wrath in the day of wrath" (Rom. 2: 4, 5).

So, wherever Christ is proclaimed as filling all the need of sinful men, there is always a sweet savor unto God; but not only in those who receive it—it cannot be without effect on any who hear—for to those who reject, the savor of Christ is "of death unto death"—it hardens! (2 Cor. 2: 15).

It is Jesus who is the full display of all God's glory, "the glory of an only begotten with a father, full of"—what? Wrath? Nay, "full of grace and truth" (John 1: 14). It is He, who coming—the very Light—into this dark world simply manifests everyone; but by what means? By strokes of active judgment? Was it *thus* He made blind those who did see in John 9: 39? Far from it! It was by manifesting the works of God in mercy, "going about doing good, and healing all that were oppressed of the devil," and finally being lifted up on the cross of shame. When all such love is rejected, what *can* He do? He "hides Himself from them" (John 12: 36). He, Adonai, Lord of all, rejects the nation that has rejected Him; yet, even then, leaves it with a cry to every weary one to come to Him and He will give rest; nor will He by any means cast out a single one who does come.

The poor nation of Israel has been blinded as a nation now for "many days" (Hosea 3: 4); Jesus has "hidden Himself from them." They read Moses, but "a veil is over their heart unto this day." Nor until it shall turn to the Lord shall that veil be taken away (2 Cor. 3: 15).

But what has now hardened the nations of Christendom? Twenty centuries of longsuffering, and the grace of the gospel sounding through those centuries. It is *this* grace despised, *this* love rejected that has brought the hardened Gentile very near to the same place of utter rejection as the hardened Jew—both are hardened by the very warmth of the goodness they have despised. It is a fearful, yes, a fatal thing to trifle with divine Love.

11, 12: Then I said, O Adonai, how long? And He said: Until cities be wasted without inhabitant, and the houses are without a man (in them) and the ground be utterly wasted, and Jehovah shall put men far away, and great shall be the solitude in the midst of the land.

Here then is the future of Israel revealed to the prophet in answer to his submissive yet mournful inquiry: "How long?"— an inquiry, that in itself, speaks eloquently of faith, for it recognizes that there must be a limit to Jehovah's judgments on a people who have promises still unfulfilled. To leave them thus would be quite impossible; Jehovah hath spoken; the only question then is "how long" before His word is made good? We, too, may learn of the prophet, for we also have a promise still unfulfilled: "I will come again, and receive you unto Myself"—Lord, how long?

But that limit will only be reached by that beloved elect nation after its towns are in ruins, and utter desolation reigns in the land once called for its beauty "the glory of all lands" (Ezek. 20: 6).

So has Palestine lain for many days, but Jehovah, the covenant-keeping God, could never allow such an end as that. To leave what He once made fair thus "without form and void"— *that* were impossible, whether it be the original material creation of Genesis 1, or Palestine, or this earth as it is today, or these bodies of our humiliation: all must, at the end, be "full of His glory," and none of these do, as yet, witness to that glory in their present conditions. Lazarus *in the sepulchre* did not witness to the glory of God; but Lazarus *raised therefrom* did do so very clearly (John 11:40).

> 13: And yet in it shall be a tenth; and this shall return; this also again is given up to destruction; as the terebinth and as the oak, which, when they are felled, the rooted-stump remains, thus the holy seed is the rooted-stump.

Like their father Jacob, whose history foreshadows their own, a conflict awaits them too on their way back to "Bethel," the House of God, and this is called "the great tribulation," or "the time of Jacob's trouble" (Jer. 30: 7); or, in the words of our prophecy, "they shall be given up to destruction."

So as to "Judah and Jerusalem" a tenth part shall return; not, of course, an exact literal tenth, but a tithe, expressive of the claim that Jehovah still makes on the nation. Jehovah shall have His tithe, which shall come back from their burial among the nations, and thus be a nation raised from the dead, "some to everlasting life, and some to shame and everlasting contempt" (Daniel 12: 2). For even after their return to their land, their sorrows are not ended. In accord with the whole principle of divine prophecy there has already been a foreshadowing of that return, in the remnant that came back from Babylon in the day of Ezra; but the prophecy was by no means exhausted by that very partial and shadowy fulfilment. God gives a prophecy, and then, to make it the "more sure," that is, more clear (2 Peter 1: 19), He gives a preliminary fulfilment as an illustration, but this illustration must never be counted as exhausting the prophecy.

So "Judah" shall return, and every sign of that return is prominent today, for never shall Israel perish utterly, any more than a living seed perishes when buried in the earth; the life-germ within it causes it to survive the dissolution of its outward frame, and even through that dissolution—for it is "not quickened except it die"—there springs up a new plant in new life and beauty, Or, to keep to the figure of the scripture we are considering, any more than an oak that has been cut down perishes finally when it has life in its roots; a fresh sprout springs up, and in that sprout the tree continues to live. All depends upon the life-principle being still in the rooted-stump. So, other nations may pass away altogether, Philistine may cease, and Amorite may be forgotten, for they lack that divine life-germ, but as to Israel, "the holy seed" (that is, "the remnant according to the election of grace" and with which Christ identifies Himself) secures the perpetuity of the nation, and that in holy blessedness; for it is the life-germ of the rooted-stump.

Wonderful and beautiful shadow is all this of what is true in a wider, and yet a more personal, sphere. It is on exactly the same principle of divine grace that every believer in Jesus has eternal life, and the dissolution of the body—the cutting down of the tree—cannot destroy that life-germ, for it is "the holy seed," as it is written: "His seed remaineth in him" (1 John 3: 9), and makes sure a "resurrection of life."

These chapters then, give a foreview of Israel's course: in chapter 5, the people, "alienated and enemies by wicked *works*" which are specified, are given up to the Gentiles. In chapter 6 it is the appearing of the glory of Jehovah—that is, Christ—that results in the same rejection. For the people are not in a state to take in that glory, and its display at His coming, as of the only-begotten of the Father, proved that, not only by what they had *done*, but by *nature*, what they *were*, they were at enmity with God. Yet grace will still linger over them, and sends a message which they still, as a nation, reject; and, rejecting, are confirmed in hardening, till the return from their scattering to their land, where again they shall suffer; yet, through all, there shall be divine life, preserved in the holy seed, which becomes the new nation, nevermore to be separated from the love of God, which is in Christ Jesus their Messiah.

# CHAPTER SEVEN

The commission carried out. The intense significance of the spot at which the prophet is directed to stand. Meaning and significance of the name of his son. Strange double meaning of the words, the one suited to unbelief, the other to faith. The words "Virgin" and "Son" also considered: both admit a twofold fulfilment. The feeding that ever results in divine intelligence. The chapter closes in judgment.

OF measureless importance to the universe, to this world, to every individual of the human family, is the prophecy to which we have now come; nor must we permit the intrusion of the chapter to sever its vital relation with its predecessor. The commission has been given, in chapter 6, we shall see it carried out in chapter 7: but in such a way as is possible only to God, for it could never have been conceived by any mortal man that ever lived.

For we shall see the divinely-led prophet, in one breath "making the heart of this people heavy and blinding their eyes," and yet giving the sweetest of consolations and comfort to lowly faith. For here is the echo of that promise that was first heard in darkened Eden, "The Seed of the woman shall bruise the serpent's head," since here we shall find that very "Seed of the woman" in the promise of a virgin's Son. Nor is it too much to say that on the fulfilment of this prophecy all Christianity rests as a building on its foundation; destroy *that,* and the whole structure falls in ruin. No marvel is it that to this very day it is the object of the most venomous attacks of unbelief. Can we consider it too carefully?

The vision of the last chapter was given in the year that King Uzziah died, and therefore the year in which his son Jotham ascended the throne of Judah. This opens with Jotham's son, Ahaz, on that throne. Thus Jotham's reign of sixteen years is passed over in absolute silence, for it was a time of comparative calm. But with Ahaz, a young man of twenty, storms again begin to lower, for *he* "did not that which was right in the sight of the Lord as *David his father*" (2 Kings 16: 2), but whom he now represents.

When our chapter opens two enemies, who have hitherto been acting independently against Judah, and with much success (2 Kings 16: 6; 2 Chron. 28), unite their forces, and are advancing against Jerusalem. Tidings of this confederacy have been brought, not exactly to Ahaz personally, but to *"the house of David"* which he represents. Nor is this distinction valueless in the subsequent interpretation, for when "the house of David" is touched, Messiah (by whom "the sure mercies of David" are secured) is touched; and this always necessitates divine intervention, as we find here.

This is not an intervention induced by the piety or faith of the present representative of *"the house of David,"* for Ahaz bears little likeness to the founder of that house, who sang in a day of threatening trouble, *"God is our refuge and strength, a very present help in trouble"* (Ps. 46: 1). Here, "like prince, like people." All hearts are terror-stricken, tremble, flutter, and sway "as the trees of the forest are moved by the wind," "looking after those things that were coming on the land."

That was surely a sad condition, but it has its benefit for us too, since it sets forth the more prominently the rich sovereign grace that could intervene in such a faithless state; for the history in 2 Kings 16, as well as the context here, makes it abundantly clear that Ahaz has his mind set on another deliverance altogether. In heart he is even now crying to Assyria for help. He believes an Assyrian army would be of far more practical value than any pious but theoretical dependence on Providence, which is always apparently "on the side of the strongest battalions."

Isaiah is now told to go forth to meet Ahaz, taking with him Shear-Jashub, his son: and, with such detailed precision does Jehovah tell him *where* to take his stand, that no thoughtful person can doubt the deep significance there must be in that place, as well as in his being accompanied there by his son, who, we are distinctly told in chapter 8: 18, was a "sign."

As the lad neither did nor said anything, the whole significance of his presence *must* lie in his name. *Shear-Jashub* means "a remnant shall return," and is clearly a link with the last words of the previous chapter, "Yet in it shall be a tenth" (there is the remnant: *"Shear"*), "and it shall return" (which is the meaning of "*Jashub*"). So this son of the prophet is a sign of the fulfilment of Jehovah's word to the prophet sixteen years before!

By what "divers manners" did "God speak in times past unto the fathers through the prophets!" Not only "plainly," but by names that should at one and the same time make the ears of the careless heavy that they should not hear, and yet speak most clearly to the penitent, and those longing to hear. Thus many an Old Testament saint may have had clearer glimpses of the Lamb of God in some (to us) unintelligible names, than we have any idea of. Here let the pious Hebrew—let the impious king, Ahaz—ponder and consider why this lad is standing here. His name cries aloud, "A remnant only out of all Israel shall be saved."

This encourages us to look carefully at the exact spot to which Isaiah was to go, and to examine each word. Let those refuse to accompany us who are willing to hear without really hearing. Some of us simply *dare* not turn away, but gladly venture in dependence on a love of which we know something, to learn why this spot is defined so accurately by Jehovah to His servant, the prophet.

It is surely a place of good omen for faith, for it was exactly at the same spot, thirty years later, that the Ayssrian stood when he defied Jehovah and threatened Jerusalem, and was answered by 185,000 of his men being slain in one night!

If we turn to our commentaries we find long dissertations on the geographical situation of this "conduit." But, we ask, will *that* fulfil its divine intent? Will *that* "satisfy the longing soul, and fill the hungry soul with goodness?" This scripture is a part of all Scripture that is profitable, but what profit, either in "reproof, or correction, or instruction in righteousness," shall we receive by learning that the conduit was on the west of Jerusalem? No, indeed, we are quite sure, whether we are able to discern it or not, that spot so accurately described by Jehovah, and that exact description repeated *three times* in the inspired volume, has the deepest spiritual significance for us, "on whom the ends of the ages have come." Further, we shall discover such links between this place and the prophecy that we may say this

·very spot suggests, in a veiled way quite consistent with the commission, the key to the prophecy.

The description of the trysting-place divides into two parts: Isaiah is to go

First—*to the end of the conduit of the upper pool;*
Second—*to the highway of the fuller's field.*

What at once strikes us as most remarkable is that *many words are capable of a double meaning,* a phenomenon that changes a geographical location into a Messianic prophecy!  Let us then consider these two pregnant phrases.

*"To the end of the conduit of the upper pool."* Isaiah is to go to the very *end* of the aqueduct, to where it pours its life-giving waters into Jerusalem, bringing them down from the upper pool to quench the thirst of the needy.  We shall get the significance of this "end" when we consider the conduit.

The word for "pool" is *"berekah,"* and is familiar to many Christian ears as having also the meaning of "blessing."  This is really the first meaning of the root, but as water has ever been recognized as of the first necessity, its abundance, when it becomes a "pool," was termed *"berekah"* or a "blessing."  The very word rendered "pools" in Psalm 84: 6, "The rain also filleth the pools,"* is exactly the same as is everywhere else rendered "blessing," so that we are not straining at all in hearing the alternative meaning of "blessing" in the word "pool."

But it is the "upper" pool, and the word "upper" too has a significant alternative meaning.  It is the exact word rendered over thirty times in the Scriptures by "Most High," as, for instance, its first occurrence, "He was the priest of the *Most High* God" (Genesis 14: 18).  Surely, then, any pious Hebrew, hearing the two words, would discern a double meaning in them, the popular one that required no hearing ear, no faith in the goodness of Jehovah, "the upper pool," and the hidden one for faith to discern, "the blessing of the Most High!"

There remain the words rendered "end" and "conduit;" this last is simply the aqueduct that conducted the water from the

---

* "The early rain covereth it with blessings."—*Numerical Bible.*

pool to Jerusalem, or the *channel* whereby "the blessing of the Most High" comes in a stream of life to those who know their deep need of it.

We know well, that through all dispensations, Christ the Lord is alone the Conduit or Channel whereby the blessing of God can come to poor, sinful man. He was the "Conduit" at Sychar's well, and the waters of life flowed freely to that thirsting one, who, after drinking of this living water, thirsted, as once she did, nevermore.

Nor may we overlook that little word "end," for no one can drink of a *pipe* or conduit itself; there is but one spot where the waters that fill it can be communicated, and that is at the "end," and to that end all must go. So as to Him who is the antitype to this *"conduit:"* not in His incarnation as being born of the virgin; not whilst as the "corn of wheat, abiding alone" (John 12: 24), could He communicate the water of Eternal Life: not until raised from the dead, did He symbolically breathe that Life into His disciples (John 20: 22): so, to this day, it is only as having died and being raised that He is "the *End* of the Conduit of the Upper Pool;" for those sufferings have put away every obstacle to the free flow of these waters of Life that come from the blessing of the Most High—the true "Upper Pool." Blessed indeed are all they who take their stand expectant, at "the end of the conduit of the upper pool," hearing the meanings to faith (nothing for proud unbelief) there are in the very words, for floods of Life in Love and Light are ever flowing there.

If the divine intent were simply to let the prophet know exactly the literal spot where he was to take his stand, not another word would be necessary, for nothing could be more precise than the end of a particular aqueduct—it would appear impossible to misunderstand *that*. But as this was not all, it confirms our conviction that the merely literal interpretation does not exhaust the divine intent, for there is added, *"to the highway of the fuller's field,"* and this we must also consider.

"The highway" is a path clearly defined by being raised up above the surrounding land, in order that passengers may walk without soiling their feet, as this same prophet speaks: *"Lift up,* *lift up the highway"** (ch. 62: 10). Not only was it raised up, but characteristically it *led upward,* for in 1 Chron. 26: 16 it is called "the highway *of the ascent."* Thus, if the conduit is the way by which the waters of blessing came *down,* the highway is the clean, the holy path leading *up* to the Source of the blessing.

Proverbs 16: 17 gives us still more clearly the moral truth in the word, and the bearing of the whole sentence: *"The highway of the righteous is to depart from evil,"* that is, this highway is the way of holiness. So equally specifically speaks our prophet: *"A highway shall be there, and a way, and it shall be called the way of holiness"* (ch. 35: 8).

Thus to the open ear of faith, the very word "highway" would have spoken then, and should speak now, of that one single path in which God can meet with His people in blessing, and well may we take up the words of the Psalmist and say, *"Blessed is the man whose strength is in Thee, in whose heart are the highways."†* Nor is the plural form of the word, used here, without its value, for it suggests that although there is but one such holy highway, it leads through such diverse scenes as greatly to multiply the aspects it presents. At times it leads over highlands of peaceful joy; at times it passes through "the valley of Baca" (weeping), but it always leads to the one end, for everyone that walks it, *"appeareth before God."*

Further, this is the highway *"of the fuller's field,"* i.e., the field of him who *washes garments,‡* who makes soiled garments white and clean. Let there be the slightest touch of defilement, there could be no restoration to communion apart from washing the garments: *"If he wash them not, he shall bear his iniquity"* (Lev. 17: 16).

We need only ask: What are the garments? We have one word that gives both the figure and the thing figured: "habits." Just as we take these up day by day, so day by day we are

---

*Hebrew: *"Sollu, sollu ha-mesillah."*

† Same word, Ps. 84: 5.

‡ This is strictly justified by the Hebrew word used. Out of four which are rendered "wash," that which is here selected for "fuller," *always* refers to the cleansing of garments from ceremonial defilement, as Lev. 13: 6, etc.

making those garments that shall manifest us before God (see 2 Cor. 5: 10). Oh, woe to those who, like their father Adam, have only their own doings in which to stand there; for they, too, will find that they are really naked, or at best clothed only in filthy rags, for so this Spirit-taught prophet spoke of his very best (chap. 64: 6). Even that which God works in us by His Spirit—the holiest deeds, the most unselfish acts, our "righteousnesses"—while they are indeed the fine linen, pure and white (Rev. 19: 8), are only so because they have been cleansed from all the defilement inevitably contracted in coming through the human vessel, by being washed in "the blood of the Lamb" (Rev. 7: 14), and it is this washing that gives a right to any to "eat of the Tree of Life" (Rev. 22: 14, R. V.).

These "garments" then bear close relationship to the "feet" which, in their walk through this defiling scene, need the work of Him who took the place of "the fuller" of the Old Testament, and in a love that could go no further—for He loved "to the end"—washed the feet of His dear people, saying to Peter, "If I wash thee not, thou hast no part with Me" (John 13: 8).

No one washed *His* feet in that upper room; nothing could defile them. No one washed *His* garment, His "habits" in the double sense; for they were ever as they were seen for a brief moment on the holy mount, "white and glittering" "as the light," "so as no fuller on earth could white them" (Mark 9: 3). He Himself is the true Fuller, and His "field" is the world, in which defiling scene His beloved still are. How precious even thus to need Him, for we only know Him by our need!

Thus, in this most significant spot, we have once more, in the two parts, the linking of sovereign grace with human responsibility, and the responsibility casting us back on grace. The blessing of Life comes *down* in sovereign grace—it is the "Conduit." That Life received leads *upward* by the path of practical holiness. It is the highway, and our Lord is both Conduit and Highway as well as Fuller.

The spot, then, on which the "Sign-prophet" was to stand, told in that symbolic way of One who is the only medium or channel of blessing from the Most High, Himself bringing the water of life, Himself "the way" up to God. That is a clear reason for the thrice-repeated mention of that spot in the only Book in the universe of which He claims to be the Author. These "wondrous things" justify that claim.

We must throw the light of this significant spot where the sign was given on to the sign itself; and as that was marked by the double meaning of words, so is there a correspondence with this in the sign. There is a meaning that Ahaz might get, but which does not finish till he is seen distressed at the feet of that Assyrian in whom his heart is at that very time trusting. But there is also a sign to "The House of David," that is, to all who are of the faith of David, and that sign is pure blessing.

For this double purpose, at least two words used in the sign, must also have the same double meaning as was so clear in "the conduit of the upper pool, the highway of the fuller's field." The words for the mother and her child, the "virgin" and the "son," must each cover both the sign of unmingled love to faith, and the threatening one to unbelief!

The word then for "virgin" here is *"almah,"* and this, as well as the only other word capable of being so rendered, *"bethulah,"* could, to quote Delitzsch, "both be applied to persons who were betrothed, and even to such as were married." The truth of this as to *"bethulah"* is evidenced in Joel 1: 8: "Lament like a virgin (*bethulah*) girded with sackcloth for the *husband* of her youth," although the fact that simple betrothal was in the Scriptures quite equivalent to marriage, since it gave to the Virgin Mary the title of "wife" in Matt. 1: 20, opens the way for that possibility in this verse in Joel. Still it is enough to justify a double bearing of the word *"almah,"** "virgin," in verse 14: first, to *faith* it refers to the maiden who shall while still literally unmarried bring forth a son, Immanuel, and who must therefore be without *human* father; but also, to the *unbelief* of Ahaz, the reference must cover another young woman who may turn out to be the mother of a threatening sign-child, the offspring of natural generation.

As to the other word, "son," that, too, to the ear of faith speaks with absolute certainty of Immanuel, the virgin's Child.

---

*The Hebrew word for "virgin" here used, *"almah,"* is from *"ahlam,"* "to be hidden," suggestive of delicate modesty.

But as Immanuel was born seven centuries after this, He could be no sign to Ahaz personally, and therefore this must apply to that "lad" of whom we are told in verse 16, and in whose early childhood, disaster should fall on the two threatening enemies of Judah.  But that "lad," by his name of Maher-shalal-hash-baz, shall tell Ahaz that the sign will only find its full termination in his own utter humiliation at the hand of the very man that was his secret confidence, even then: the king of Assyria.  This anticipates a little, but it seemed necessary, and we now return to the earlier verses.

The prophet, with his son, both of whom are signs, are standing before the king at this significant spot, and "moved by the Holy Ghost," he thus speaks, and again in rhythm:

4: Take heed and be calm, yea, fear not;
        Nor let thine heart be faint;
    For these two smoking torch-ends:
    For the wrath of Rezin and Aram,
    For the wrath of Ben-Remaliah.
5: Since Aram hath counselled against thee
    With Ephraim: Ben-Remaliah:
6: We will march against Judah—
    Shake it with terror; smash through it:
    Break it and take it ourselves:
    Set a King over it: the son of Tabeal.
7: Thus saith Adonai Jehovah:
        NO!
    It shall not be done—it shall not be!
8: For the head of Aram: Damascus,
    And the head of Damascus: Rezin—
    Years threescore-and-five shall pass, and then
    'Tis Ephraim that shall be broken
    From (even) being a people.
9: Ephraim's head: Samaria:
    Samaria's: Ben-Remaliah—
    If ye (too) do not confide,
    Ye (too) then shall not abide.*

---

*The Hebrew shows the play on these words:
        *"im lo taaminu,*
        *ki lo teamenu."*

Delitzsch paraphrases: "If Judah did not hold fast to God, it would lose its fast hold of the land."

This short portion begins with a warning against fear, and ends with a warning against unbelief. The fear, then, is that which is also seen in Rev. 21: 8, as having the same bad relation, and as coming to a still worse end: *"But the fearful and unbelieving, and abominable and murderers . . . shall be cast into the lake of fire."* Danger threatens, the terror it inspires is in exact proportion to the lack of fear of God (Matt. 10: 28), and of confidence in His beloved Son. Is there One to whom all power is given? Has He loved me and given Himself for me? All power! All love! All for me! Is that indeed true? Look at the menace—my heart sinks. Look at the Cross where He hung for me, the Throne where He sits high, with "all power"—my spirit revives.

It was this test that confronted Ahaz that possibly may this very day confront us, and show where our hearts really are. Even false profession may pass as genuine faith in the sunshine of prosperity, but let everything seem to be against us, where are we then? The calm, or the fear, that fills us, gives the answer, and, if one may speak for others, well do we know in what sad revelations of our feeble state do these tests but too often result.

Ahaz sees two victorious armies advancing. Jehovah says, "No; they are really only two tails of torches that are on the point of being extinguished altogether; they are only smoking, no flame left." Will his eyes be opened by these words, or be the more fast-closed in unbelief? Will he see with Jehovah's far-sightedness? If so, he will need only to look forward sixty-five years, and one of his enemies will cease to be a people at all. "I know," says Jehovah, "I know their devices, they would put on the throne of David their own king. Who is he? The son of Tabeal."

Now in this name we again have an alternative as given in Ezra 4: 7. "Tabeel" means "the good God," but the very slight alteration, not even of a letter, but only of one vowel-point, turns it into "Tabeal," which means "the good-for-nothing!" *So* He speaks of any who would rival the Son of David. Oh, what good names religious pretension always assumes! It is always the same, for so spoke the same spirit long after this,

"One is our father, even God," that is, we are the "sons of the good God." "No," is again the answer; "ye are of your father the devil, ye are sons of the good-for-nothing" (John 8: 44).

Will Jehovah allow the House of David, the true Tabeel, the Son of God, to be set aside for the "son of a good-for-nothing?" The answer is, with thundering emphasis, a mighty "NO!"

The next verses to "open ears" might speak something like this, "You fear the confederacy; you consider it the source of strength; you are meditating in heart a counter-confederacy; well, then, look and learn its end.    See the confederates in their heads, for the head sums up all that they are.    Thus Syria is headed up in its capital city, Damascus; and *that* may be seen in *its* head, Rezin.    When, then, you see Rezin, you really see all Syria.    He is in league with Ephraim, shall he, *can* he, save his ally?    Nay, for in sixty-five years Ephraim shall be smashed to pieces.    So much for the value of this confederacy."

But exactly so, when you see this base man, unworthy even of a name, for he is only Remaliah's son, you see all Ephraim. And since Ephraim has accepted this man for his "head," nothing can save him from being carried away by Assyria (2 Kings 17).    That is the end of the path he is walking.    If ye, too, walk that same path, leaning on an arm of flesh, then ye, too, will come to the same end and be scattered.

> 10: Moreover Jehovah spake again to Ahaz, saying:
>     Ask thee a sign of Jehovah thy God;
>     Ask it in the lowest deep,
>     Or ask it in the height aboye thee.

This is the answer: "I will not ask, and I will not tempt Jehovah."    Now that is exactly how Satan and his subordinate spirits ever speak in men even to this day.    He never shows plainly the evil that he is pressing, but hides it under pious words, so that one would think that it was a very angel of light that was speaking.    Who so pious as Ahaz?    Ask a sign!    Far be it; for that would be to tempt Jehovah, even the Jehovah who had directed him to ask!    Nor does he say anything as to his heart's confidence fixed all the time on Assyria.    Ahaz has gone to his account long ago, but the spirit that governed Ahaz at that moment has lived on, and may often be heard today, saying, in effect: "I am far too humble to take God at His word, and to confess that He hath given us His beloved Son, whose atoning blood fully avails for all my sins. No, no; that would be too presumptuous altogether." So exactly spoke the Council of Trent, terming confidence in the blood of Christ the vain confidence of the heretics.

It is the same "religious" Satanic modesty of Ahaz, and it shows that these speakers, too, have some other confidence, their "Assyrian," that shall fail them in the final hour of their need.

But the Spirit of Christ in the prophet answers:

13: Hearken then, ye house of David,
      'Tis a trifle, men to weary—
      Mortal men as frail as ye are—
      Dare ye weary my God too?

There, in that weary God, we may see the same One, who, seven centuries later, was seated one noontide on the well-side at Sychar, *"weary* with His journey" (John 4: 6). Not merely was He weary with the distance travelled. He entered, I doubt not, in His grace, into that sinless infirmity, and His holy Body knew literal weariness; but in John's Gospel, where He is the divine One who "fainteth not, neither is weary," we must look deeper to get the truth. It was the same spurious religion, the same false Ahaz-like piety of Judaism, that at that time refused the love He longed to give it. It was His "journey" through such a scene that wearied Him; as it was the confidence of a poor outcast sinner (like some of us, my readers) that refreshed Him, giving Him meat that His disciples knew nothing of. One may be quite sure that He has very much of the same "weariness," and surely a little of the same refreshment too (God be praised), even today.

This brings us to Jehovah's answer, which is of incalculable importance. I attempt a paraphase, keeping as close to the literal as possible, while endeavoring to retain something of the rhythm.

14: Therefore Adonai* shall give you a sign:
    Lo, the pure virgin shall mother a son,
    Whose is the name—'tis His name alone—
        Immanuel!

15: Milk† and sweet honey shall the child eat,
    So shall he learn the evil to shun,
    So shall he learn the good to select.
16: But ere the lad shall this knowledge attain,
    The land of two kings—thine abhorrence and dread‡—
        Desolate shall be.
17: Then shall Jehovah on thee too bring down,
    On thee and thy people, the house of thy sires,
    Days of such sorrow as never have been
    Since the day that Ephraim shattered the tie
        That bound him to Judah.

    (Wouldest thou learn the invader's name?
    Who is the hope of thine heart?   'Tis the same:)
        Assyria's king!

We must still bear in mind that, in accord with the commission the prophet is carrying out, it was intended to give light and comfort alone to faith, leaving hard hearts the more hardened, closed eyes the closer shut. Thus it is not, nor was intended to be, understood by the careless, nor to be without difficulties. Nor does the Holy Spirit, when referring to this sign in the Gospel of Matthew, solve these difficulties at all, or unravel the knot, as we may say, but cuts it with one stroke in the word, "Now all this was done that it might be fulfilled which was spoken of the Lord by the prophet, saying,

Behold, a Virgin shall be with child, and bring forth a Son, and they shall call His name Emmanuel; which being interpreted is, God with us.

---

*That is, "The supreme Lord of all."

†Most literally, "curdled milk," but it is used in poetry for any milk.

‡The one word rendered in A. V. "abhorrest" has in it both ideas of "fear" and "hatred."

This is absolutely final for faith, as regards the prophecy of the virgin's Son. No room is left for question, or the slightest uncertainty. For faith, *the sign is Jesus, and Jesus alone.* But when we consider the context, that there was a sign offered to, and in spite of his refusal even forced upon, Ahaz himself; when we consider the apparent close connection between verses 14 and 16; then the prophecy reads on the surface, that before the very son of the "virgin" shall know how to refuse the evil and choose the good, that is, apparently, before Immanuel has arrived at years of discretion, both Syria and Ephraim would be devastated; and it is of this devastation that the supernatural birth of the child would be a sign. I say, this is the way a superficial reader would understand the scripture.

We are thus compelled to recognize once more what is frequently, if not invariably, the case in prophecy, a near-by shadowy, and a far-off final and definitive fulfilment. Thus in this case, there must have been a near-by historic fulfilment for Ahaz himself, which was yet by no means a strict fulfilment of the deeper divine intent (nor would it be taken for such by the "opened ear"), in which some child should be born who should indeed be a sign to Ahaz, and before this child of near-fulfilment should attain to years of discretion, the two countries, now in alliance against Judah, of whose two kings Ahaz stood in guilty terror, would be desolated. This leaves the true Sign of Immanuel, the definite fulfilment, for some future day, as we know.

For it is absolutely certain that both such events have actually occurred. In the next chapter, Isaiah becomes the father of a child, who is also a sign (as we are divinely told in chap. 8: 18, and the fact that God tells us that the child is a sign justifies this interpretation), the mother being an unmarried young woman, the prophetess. She conceives and bears a son, but he is not, nor is he called, Immanuel. Thus this near-by fulfilment by no means satisfies the requirements of verses 14, 15. The threatening name given to Isaiah's son of Maher-shalal-hash-baz ("speed to spoil; haste to booty") can not possibly be made into the comforting Immanuel; nor as far as we know has any child that was ever born been called *by divine direction,* Immanuel, so that there has never yet been, even to this day, apparently a literal fulfilment of this word, "And shall call His name Immanuel," unless indeed Jesus and Immanuel are precisely the same.

That is exactly what they are; and that little Child in Bethlehem's manger, being divinely called Jesus, did fulfil, in the most clear, simple, unstrained way, the prophecy, "His name shall be Immanuel."

While it is quite true that there were many children called Jesus—it was not and is not to this day an uncommon name: Joshua is but a form of it—*no child had ever been so called of God, as was this*, for it means Saviour; and of no child ever born did, or could God say, "Call *Him* Jesus, for He is Saviour." All were *sinners* by their very birth, from their descent from the one father, Adam, not saviours. But here is One of whom God Himself says He must be called Jesus, for He is not a sinner, but a Saviour!

Saviour is in itself a *divine* title, never to be taken by any less than God Himself, as it is written: "I am Jehovah, that is My Name, and My glory will I not give to another" (Isa. 43: 8). But in what does Jehovah's peculiar glory consist? Again it is written, "I, even I, am Jehovah, and *beside Me there is no Saviour*" (chap. 43: 11), that is, beside Jehovah there is no "Jesus," or there is *no* Jesus but Jehovah. So that little Child, since He is owned of God as "Jesus"-Saviour, is Himself none other than God, for to "save" is the glory that He will never give to another. But He gives this divine name to a *human* Child, for He is

> "......hushed to rest,
> Upon a lowly virgin's breast."

The virgin's breast, the swaddling-clothes, the manger, do they not all witness clearly that He is "with us?" Most surely they do. Then it follows that the Name Jesus is in itself precisely and literally "God with us," or "Immanuel!"

Evidently this "sign," so filled with truest comfort, was never intended for that unbelieving Ahaz at all: the threatening Mahershalal-hash-baz was alone suited to his condition. But to the open ear of penitent faith it would revive hope in the long-awaited fulfilment of that first promise that sounded in the opened ears of our first parents: that the woman's Seed should bruise the serpent's head; a promise on which the hope of the race had really depended, whether intelligently or not, for ages, a hope held by a few amid all discouragements. Now at last it is so far made clear *how* this is to be the Seed of the *woman,* not of the *man;* of Eve, not of Adam, by His being the Son of a virgin-mother, and so Immanuel.

Next we are told—strangely told, I think we may say—that the virgin's son shall feed on milk and honey. Let the closed ear hear only the superficial natural meaning of the words: this demands no exercise, no confession of dependence, no drawing near to Him whose joy it is to teach; but at once there is a necessity for finding some other reading than that the feeding on this food should *give* Him intelligence. So, many commentators turn it into, "Curdled milk and honey shall He eat, *at the time* that He knows." But turn it as you will, no literal fulfilment can be found of this prophecy in Him who "came eating and drinking," so that they said, "Behold a gluttonous man and a wine-bibber." *That* is not "curdled milk and honey" surely!

But let the ear of the inner man of the spirit be opened, and a deeper spiritual meaning than that on the surface is discerned. We see the Child Jesus ever feeding, in the truest sense, on that truest food, the "milk" of the Word, sweeter to Him than "honey" or the honeycomb; and, by that word learning, "morning by morning" with wakened ear, "to refuse the evil and to choose the good" (ch. 50: 4-6). Where else, save in the volume of the Book (Ps. 40: 7, 8), could it be learned that for Him the "good" would consist in giving "His back to the smiters, and His cheeks to them that plucked out the hair, to hide not His face from shame and spitting," and thus go on to the cross? (ch. 50). Peter judged this by no means "good" (Matt. 16: 23), for Peter had not as yet fed on that "milk and honey;" but He, Immanuel, was not disobedient, nor turned away back (Isa. 50: 4-6); to Him it was the "good."

Thus how perfectly appropriate is the most simple and exact reading of the text, "Milk and honey shall He eat *in order that*

He may know to refuse the evil and choose the good." By what He thus fed upon did this perfect human Child learn of the path laid out for Him—a path that indeed led to life, but only by the way of death and the cross (Ps. 16: 11), for so only could we, poor sinful men, share that life with Him.

Was then that path, so "uncheered by earthly smiles" that "led only to the cross," really good? Let the Voice that was heard whenever its earthly end was in view, answer. Twice the very heavens opened under the weight of God's delight. First, when He joined His poor sheep in the river of death, Jordan; and being baptized therein in figure fulfilled all righteousness (Matt. 3: 15-17). Then, on the holy mount, when they spoke of His decease that He should accomplish at Jerusalem, then God said, "This is My beloved Son, in whom I am well pleased" (Matt. 17: 5)—surely He had chosen the "good" in the very path of the Cross.

And how shall you and I acquire the same intelligence as to what is really good, and what is really evil, amid all the confusion of this day? Will it not be in the same way, by the same feeding, morning by morning, on the same "sincere *milk* of the Word?" Shall our "good" then be found in quite a different path, or will it be the same as His, in measure? Will it be merely in some religious profession—some Church association of the day, respectable, decent, religious—the Church in which less and less is ever made of that "beloved Son," the Church in which Christ is by no means "all," which is really indistinguishable from the world, and has become altogether "the camp," the Church where no shame shall meet us, no reproach be ours, but rather honor and praise of men? Has the Cross then at last become popular, and its offence ceased? Is it quite possible in these days to live godly in Christ Jesus and yet escape altogether the persecution so surely promised to all who even *desire* to do so? (2 Tim. 3: 12). Feeding on that same food, we, too, shall learn the same lesson. In going forth to Him outside the camp, bearing His reproach, we too shall find the "good" in seeing the "evil" of conformity to this "present evil world," even though it has put on a religious apparel.

Before leaving this part of the prophecy, there are two points that tend strongly to confirm the interpretation that verses 14, 15 alone refer to Immanuel; and then the reference in verse 16 is to some other child who is also yet to be born at the time the prophecy was uttered.

First, the address in the earlier verses is not to Ahaz personally, but to him only as a representative, unworthy indeed, of the "House of David" (ver. 13). Thus the mystic promise of the Virgin's Son is to "you," not to "thee," and will be fulfilled, not to Ahaz, but to the "House of David" at some indefinite time in the future. But verse 16 recurs unequivocally to Ahaz personally: "The land will be desolate, whose two kings *thou abhorrest*" (R. V.), and must be intended for him and no one else. It follows that the "child" of that verse must be some other than the Immanuel of the previous ones.

Next, a word is used for "child" in verse 16 that is never, as far as I am aware, applied to Immanuel. It lacks the dignity of "son," and is variously rendered in our Authorized Version "boy," "lad," "young man," "servant." It is the word, too, that we next meet in ch. 8: 4, where the reference is clearly to the son of the prophet, Maher-shalal-hash-baz, not to Immanuel. It refers equally to that same child of the prophet here, and who was also a sign.

After verse 16 the voice of comfort is heard no more; threat follows and altogether displaces it.

Let us stand for a moment with Ahaz, and remember that his secret heart-confidence is in the help of the Assyrian king; he hears with complacency that his enemies' lands will be laid waste, and he says in his heart that he knows how that devastation shall come about, it shall be by the Assyrian. Then suddenly the tone changes, and he is listening to a threat against his own country of such extreme distress that it has had no precedent. Do you not hear the unspoken question in the king's heart? Who shall be the agent of *that* distress? Like a thunderclap from a clear sky comes the answer: *Melek Asshur*, "the king of Assyria," the very man Ahaz was, at that minute, hiring for his help! Then the prophet continues:

18: Jehovah shall hiss for the fly that is swarming
    At the end of the Nile-arms of Egypt's low vales:
    For the bee in the hills of Assyria hiving
19: Till they settle on Judah's desolate dales.
    The rock-cleft, the thorn-hedge, the beautiful tree,
    All shall resound with the hum of the bee.

Jehovah has but to hiss toward Egypt, and the flies that swarm in her lowlands by the Nile-arms (these flies—the accompaniment of filth—are expressions of that internal "corruption" of which Egypt speaks) would respond. Then, turning eastward, He gives the same signal, and the bees, those persistent pursuers that ever "compass about" the object of their animosity (Ps. 118: 12), expressions of that cruelty and violence for which Assyria stands, these shall come and cover the land of Judah.

*Naked* shall Judah be in that day (ver. 20), for, as Ahaz is hiring the king of Assyria, Adonai shall hire him, too; for he lies at the Euphrates, only waiting to be hired, and shall use him as a razor to shave away everything that speaks of dignity and self-respect, from head to foot, even including the beard, till Judah is as naked and exposed as Samson after Delilah had done her work.

*Poor* indeed shall Judah be in that day, for the sum-total of a man's wealth shall consist in a calf and two sheep, or goats, yet so abundant shall be the pasture afforded by the uncultivated lands, that even these three creatures shall give him all the food he needs, or indeed can get.

*Wretched* shall Judah be in that day, for in the place of the vineyards having a thousand vines each worth a "silverling" (or about twenty-five cents), nature, unchecked, covers all with the tokens of the curse; briers and thorns taking the place of grapes. These briers and thorns afford a jungle for the wild beast, so that none dare enter them unarmed; and the hills, once so smiling with crops, are clothed with briers and thorns, through which cattle may tramp, but no plough nor spade shall cultivate them. The jungle of briers and thorns defeats the husbandman.

Thus again, like the toll of a funeral bell, or the refrain of a dirge, sounds out the repeated "in that day," and the prophecy concludes with a threefold reminder of the primal curse in the words, "thorns and briers." Closely too does the condition of the land correspond in its nakedness, its poverty, its misery, its wretchedness, with the church in Laodicea of *today*.*

I cannot refrain from noting the correspondence between the physical and moral spheres. Simply leave the soil alone, give it up to itself; nothing more is necessary; it will quickly witness to the curse resting still upon it. So let parents simply leave their children alone, let them refrain from bringing them up in the discipline and admonition of the Lord, it is all that is necessary—a wilderness of moral "thorn and briers" will all too quickly bear their witness to the fall of our first parents. So let God simply leave man alone, give him up, as He did the Gentiles (Rom. 1: 24-32), and we see the correspondence to the thorns and briers in the abominations that covered them, and, alas, covers the vast professing body of Christendom today (2 Tim. 3: 1-5). May we each learn our absolute dependence on Him for true fruit, and cry, "Leave, oh, leave me not alone," for that were the worst of fates.

--------

*The description is tautological and pleonastic, heavy and slow in movement to produce the impression of a waste heath, or tedious monotony" (*Delitzsch*). Thus the very construction pictures the meaning.

# CHAPTER EIGHT

**Hebrew names are divinely intended to teach truths: The refusal of Shiloah: Where those waters are still flowing: The invasion of Immanuel's Land: Counsel as to consulting the dead: The Rock of the Word: Sorrowful condition of the deluded.**

THE opening words, "Moreover the Lord said," mark a new subsection of the prophecy, which we may say began with the child Shear-Jashub in chapter 7, ascended to the Son, Immanuel; descends again to the lad Maher-shalal (ver. 1), and finally ends with the Child "Wonderful" in ch. 9: 6.

Now, Ahaz is no longer seen: Isaiah is addressed directly. He is to take a large tablet, such as could be hung up prominently for all to see, and is to write upon it "with a man's pen":* that is, in such plain letters that the most humble of mankind may be able to see and read it, one strange compound word, surely never before seen—"Maher-shalal-hash-baz."

Then, by divine direction, he selects two witnesses—the necessary number for a competent testimony—whose names are given us, and therefore we may be quite sure are significant: *Uriah,* meaning, "Jehovah is my light," and *Zechariah,* "Jehovah remembers," son of *Jeberechiah,* meaning, "Jehovah will bless." Thus the one witness says by his name: "Jehovah is my *light,*" and the other, Jehovah's purpose is to *bless,* and the offspring of that purpose of grace is that He will *never forget* His people. Both Light and Love may thus be said to witness to the genuineness of the writing as to Maher-shalal, as indeed they do to *all* He writes. Are not our Scriptures similarly confirmed?

Thus when the Assyrian armies are devastating Syria and Ephraim, the two witnesses shall testify what the prophet's tablet, which has been exposed for about twenty months, bearing that one strange enigmatical word, has meant: first, that a son should be born to him, who should bear this name that none would

---

*Literally, the stylus of a frail mortal man: *enosh.*

think of giving to any child; secondly, *that* name has foretold what they see taking place before their eyes; and thirdly, all this should occur while the child was still an infant, unable to speak the simplest words, "Abbi" or "Immi"; thus it is not the military prowess or statesmanship of Ahaz that has brought this devastation on their enemies, but the determinate counsel and foreknowledge of Jehovah.

All is enigmatical and parabolic; and whilst Maher-shalal can by no means be absolutely equivalent to Immanuel, yet one can discern a link between them. Immanuel is "God with us;" Maher-shalal-hash-baz is "Hasten booty, speed prey;" that really means, "God is against those against us;" for God evidences Himself *for* Israel by the destruction of their enemies, which of course is another form of "God for us."

Verses 5 to 8 form another step in the progress of this prophecy. It is a continuation of Jehovah's word to the prophet:

5: Again the Lord spake to me, and spake to me thus:
6: Forasmuch as this people refuseth Shiloah,
   Whose waters go rippling so softly along,
   Boast in their treaty with Syrian Rezin,
   And with Remalýah's (weak) son,
7: Jehovah brings on them the flood of the river,
   Its torrent of waters many and strong
   (Even Assyria, its king and his glory);
   O'er-rising its banks and leaving its bed,
8: Till, passing through Judah, 'tis still overflowing
   Till a man is submerged to all but his head.
   As a bird on its wings, so shall he hover,
   Aye, even the breadth of thy land he shall cover,
        IMMANUEL!

Here the waters of Shiloah ("sent") are clearly in antithesis to the flood of the river (which can be none other than the Euphrates); the one so gentle, the other so threatening, so clearly picturing *judgment;* and since this latter is interpreted for us as representing the power that comes from the river, the Assyrian, with all his military pomp and power, the other must be identified with the House of David.

Marvellous is the very topography of that "pleasant land;" its rivers, its brooks, its springs, its mountains, its values, all silently, but eloquently preach eternal verities.   Here there are indeed,

> "Tongues in trees, books in the running brooks,
> Sermons in stones, and good in everything."

Listen to Shiloah softly flowing* between Mounts Zion and Moriah; if you are listening with the *inward* ear, you will hear a voice sweeter than its own rippling music, for Zion ever tells of *grace,* as in contrast with Sinai, which stands for *law* (Heb. 12: 18, 22).   Moriah tells the same story, for it was here that the sword of judgment was stayed in David's day (2 Sam. 24; 2 Chron. 2: 1).   It was here that God provided Himself a Lamb (Gen. 22: 2, 8), so that He should not be debarred from exercising that grace to sinful man.   It was on Moriah that the temple was built, where those sacrifices, so ineffective in themselves, still pointed forward to that same Lamb of God.   Now Shiloah is at the base of both these mountains.   Could anything speak more clearly of Christ—the true Shiloah, the Sent One— being *at the base* of all God's goodness, grace and mercy?

We must inquire then who is meant by "this people" who refuse the gentle waters of Shiloah, put their boastful confidence in Rezin and Remaliah's son,† and consequently are overwhelmed by the torrent of the Euphrates.   Surely it cannot be Judah, for Judah, far from trusting in, was trembling with fear, *because* of Rezin and Remaliah's son; and now, as in the worst of times, cleaves to the House of David.   Its prime application then, it would appear clear, must be to the *ten* tribes, under the lead of Ephraim.   For the refusal must have been *before* this time, since the Assyrian invasion is now the threatened penalty

---

* The word carries with it the idea of a gentle sound, murmuring as waters, or sighing as winds.   Compare "Flow gently, sweet Afton."

† These names again have striking and divinely-given significance.   *"Remaliah"* is a compound word, made up of "Rem," "lofty," or "lifted up"; the preposition "l" or "to"; and the easily recognized "Jah" or Jehovah—the whole reading, *"Lifted up to Jehovah."*   The Scripture tells us of one who answers to that name; for whom being a creature, it was the worst of robberies to make himself "equal with God," yet did that very thing.

in consequence of that refusal. We are then driven to that first refusal of the "sure mercies" ever linked with that House—in Rehoboam's day. The Spirit of God always takes note of the *first* lapse from what has been divinely set up, quite irrespective, as here, of the unworthy character of the human representatives of that institution. All that is now seen is that the revolt under Jeroboam was the forsaking of all the divinely appointed channels of the goodness of Jehovah—the "waters of Shiloah"—in

---

In chapter 14 this same prophet tells us of him who said, "I will be like the Most High." But that is precisely *"Remaliah,"* or, *"lifted up to Jehovah."* Surely this is quite simple and unstrained. Remaliah then is a name that is intended to lead our thoughts to Lucifer, or Satan.

We are not dealing here with Remaliah himself but with his *son.* It is the son of Remaliah who is one of the confidences of the apostates. Has then the true Remaliah, or Lucifer, a "son" whom he leads in the same path of assumption of being "like the Most High," and who thus evidences his sonship? Indeed he has, in that "son of perdition who exalteth himself above all that is called God" (2 Thess. 2: 4). There is the true *"son* of Remaliah" of the future, acting exactly as his father, walking in the same path. He is to be also found under such names as "False prophet," "Beast from the land," "Antichrist," and many another of dreadful import that he bears in the Scriptures, as heading up the corrupt or religious form of evil, when all evil, in both its forms, comes to its head; and, as of old, he was found at the head of apostate Israel, so shall his future antitype be a Jew.

His allay is Rezin, king of Syria. The very word, rezin, in Gen. 49: 6, is rendered *"self-will."* Nor can the name of his kingdom be misunderstood when we leave the Hebrew, *Aram,* unchanged into the Greek, "Syria;" for *Aram* is from precisely the same root as the first syllable of Remaliah, and means again, "lifted up." It was, of course, thus applied to the highlands of Syria as expressive of their topography; but what weighty significance it has as expressive of the moral characteristic of the sphere of the rule of this king. He, the self-willed one, is king of Aram, of those "lifted up"—the children of pride.

Thus Rezin, king of Aram, is an excellent prototype of that "prince that shall come" (Dan. 9: 27), the Gentile head of the revived Roman Empire in its utter apostasy, and ever, to the end, the ally of Jewish Ben-Remaliah, the false prophet—for pride governs both, and in *pride* is the bond of relationship between all the discordant elements of evil.

those days. These the ten tribes valued not; these they relinquished with Esau-like profanity, to secure some present advantage. In 2 Chron. 13: 4-12, a son of David convicts Ephraim of refusing the waters of Shiloah by treading under foot the divinely-appointed priesthood, by counting the blood of the divinely-appointed sacrifices an unholy thing, by doing despite to the Spirit of God in fighting against the one *anointed* by the Lord God of their fathers. Many years have rolled their course since then. Another king, another set of people, are on the scene, but it has never been forgotten; and now after so long a time, it is on *this* account, combined with a course consistent with that beginning, that the Assyrian is coming to take away their place and nation.

Now again the historical outlines fade, as mere history, and become prophetic of a far more serious rejection of the true "waters of Shiloah" in Immanuel Himself, the virgin's Son.

In what gentle grace the "Sent One" (Shiloah) of the Father came. How softly flowed the stream of His goodness! Let one drink of those waters, and never more would that one thirst (John 4: 14). Let the blind wash therein, and straightway he "comes seeing" (John 9: 7); wherever they flowed there was life and healing. Yet the waters were refused by that people, and the Cross was the evidence and measure of that refusal, while the *Roman, who was, in that day, in the place of the Assyrian,* took away the place and nation, and it remains scattered even unto this present hour.

Where are the waters of Shiloah now?—for we must learn what and where they are, that we may not refuse them. They are still "flowing softly," but it is through the Scriptures vivified by the Holy Spirit, and through those who have themselves drunk thereof (John 7: 38), by whom the "love of the truth" is still proclaimed. Alas, the story is unvaried, still these "waters of Shiloah," of the gospel of the grace of God, are refused with ever-increasing repulsion, for one must *stoop* to drink them, and they bring no promise of wealth.

In verses 7, 8 we see that, not content with overflowing Syria and Ephraim and thus fulfilling his mission, the Assyrian passes into Judah, still like the mighty river whence he comes, till in intensity that river becomes so deep as to reach even to the neck of a man; while, in extent, it covers, as a ravening bird's wings, the whole breadth of "Thy land, O Immanuel!"

Here these last words seem like a cry, an astonished shout, on the part of the prophet himself: "An enemy's foot is on the soil that is Thine, O Immanuel!   Wilt Thou—*canst* Thou—permit such a dishonor?"   So today the throne of the Earth has Satan the usurper on it, and we cry: "It is Thine, O Lord Jesus, our Immanuel!"

Earnest as is this appealing cry, there appears to be no answer.

But is there not?   Whence then that sudden change in the prophet's note, from fear to the joyous, triumphant chant that is now heard?

Ah, God can answer a cry without any audible speech.   In a moment He can put "gladness into the heart more than in the time that their corn and wine increase."   Here that gladness finds expression in a defiant, triumphant chant, thus:

9: Rage, ye peoples, and ye shall be broken;
   Listen, ye dwellers on earth afar;
   Bind ye together, and ye shall be broken!
   Bind ye together, and ye shall be broken!
10: Consult ye in counsel, it cometh to naught:
   Utter the word, it shall not stand:
      For — IMMANUEL!!

Here the same word, the Name of the promised Son, is, as it were, the very answer to the appeal, and becomes Israel's battle-cry.   Was there ever one like it?   "The sword of the Lord and of Gideon" was inspiring; but it challenged not all the far-off nations.   Here is a feeble little remnant of a people, solely in the power of this Name uttering the strongest challenge in one word, "Immanuel," to all the mighty nations of the whole earth! Do your worst!   Make your military alliances!   Form your new World-Empire!   Let the federated nations consult together! (Note the emphasized taunt in the reiteration of the line.) Thus perfect their plans!   Then issue their orders!   It will all

amount to nothing, for "Immanuel"—God, is *with us,* in Jesus
our Messiah, and, if God be with us, who can be against us?

But now there comes a word from Jehovah to His servant
Isaiah, with such power as accords with its importance:

> 12: Cry not ye, Confederácy!
>      As this people all, are crying,
>      Neither fear what they are fearing.
>      Let not this, their dread, affright you.
> 13: Sanctify the Lord Tzebaoth:
>      For indeed 'tis well to fear Him—
>      Well before Him may ye tremble—
> 14: So He shall become to you a
>      (Refuge safe), a Sanctuary;
>      But to both of Israel's houses,
>      He shall be a stone of tripping,
>      Rock that causes them to stumble.
>      He shall be a snare and gin to
>      Jerusalem: for its dwellers
> 15: Striking foot 'gainst it shall stumble—
>      Falling, shall be dashed to pieces—
>      Being snared, shall so be taken.

We may well question, with some misgiving, what would be
the result today of some widespread threatening terror as is predicated in these verses, and well may we listen to the word of the
Spirit through the Old Testament prophet, "Fear not their fear,"
taken up and repeated for our special benefit by the same Spirit
through the New Testament apostle: "Be not afraid of their terror, neither be troubled: but sanctify the Lord God in your hearts"
(1 Peter 3: 15). Set *Him* apart above all, give *Him* His rightful place in your hearts, fear only to dishonor *Him,* and then *He*
shall be for a sanctuary. But *who* shall be for a sanctuary? The
same One who, as the Lord Jesus, is to unbelief a "Stone of
stumbling." Therefore it follows beyond all cavil that Jesus *is*
Himself the Lord God.

So here we have the first reference to our Lord as "the
Stone;" but so small, and lying so low on the ground, that Israel,
who expected Jehovah's intervention in quite another way, and
was looking for Him high *up* among the great ones of the earth,

overlooked altogether the Stone lying so low before them that they tripped over it, and *fell;* and by that fall, salvation is come to us Gentiles.  It is that very lowliness of the Lord of Glory who came "not to be ministered to, but to minister" (to our very feet, as it were, see John 13), that makes Him a very precious Stone to all whose faith sees the divine glory beneath the humiliation.

This brings us to a portion of our prophecy of the greatest value to every Christian heart, and needing careful attention, as the words intimate.

16:  Firmly bind the testimony,
    Seal the law to my disciples,
17:  Whilst I upon the Lord will wait
    Who hides His face from Jacob's house;
    Yea, on Him—on Him alone—
    Will I wait expectant.

In the preceding verses, the prophet foretells of One who is to be a sanctuary for faith, but a stumbling-stone for unbelief; now the prophecy goes on without interruption till in chapter 9: 7 we see that same One crowned as the final King, never to be dethroned.  Nor is there apparently, at first sight, one break from the day on which he wrote to that day of final consummation. The conditions continue unchanged: the same mass in rejection of the light, the same few termed "the remnant," cleaving to the written Word as the only stay and anchor to their souls, and always the reference is to the Jews.  Now here is a difficulty, for *we* know of a tremendous change in all God's dealings with man, by which the Jew has been left utterly neglected—a nation without a country—and God's direct work confined to drawing out from the Gentiles a heavenly people.  That was a "mystery" of which Isaiah knew nothing (Romans 16: 25); how then could he write on it?  There must be then somewhere an unnoticed parenthesis of over 1900 years that really breaks into the line of this prophecy, before the end in chapter 9: 7 is reached.  We must find that hidden parenthesis.

The prophet prays that the Word of God may be bound to his disciples, that they may rest upon it, be governed in all perplexing questions that may come up, not by what the mass about them are saying, or doing, but rather standing apart from the great majority, and governed solely by what is written. What divine authority is thus given to the Scriptures!

Nor will Isaiah, who stands here symbolically for our Lord Himself, fail to associate himself with the few rather than the many: *his* part will be to wait upon the Lord patiently; in full recognition that Jehovah's Face is hidden from the house of Jacob.

Let us note the significance of that name of Jacob just here. In the day of Jacob's trouble, the One who was wrestling with him, had said, "What is thy name?" and he *had* to answer, "Jacob," for he had no other then. "Crooked, supplanting Jacob is my name; that expresses my nature;" and at once, instead of a blow on such a character, as one might expect, there is love and blessing embracing the poor, crippled, self-confessed sinner, Jacob. So here, the prophet confesses that the nation still bears every trait of their father "Jacob." But Jacob had a Lord who never left him, never forsook him, and so will never leave nor forsake any of his "House;" and Isaiah will wait both patiently and hopefully for His intervention. His Face is hidden now, it is true, from the nation, but soon it will shine upon them, as it did on their father when he joyfully called the place "Peniel," the Face of God (Gen. 32: 30).

All this is very interesting; but for *us* the joy is in seeing the force of the next verse wherein Isaiah says as plainly as possible that both he and the children whom God hath given him "are for signs and for wonders in Israel from the Lord of hosts which dwelleth in Zion."

Throw the light of Hebrews 2: 13 on this, and we see in Isaiah a type of our Lord. The two children then must also be types. Where shall we find their antitypes? Not in the Church; nothing in her answers either to *Shear-Jashub* or to *Maher-shalal;* but in that recovered remnant of the Jews that return to their land we shall find perfect correspondence to both.

Yet, while this primary application is surely to the *Jew*, ponder the cheering correspondences that directly affect ourselves:

Isaiah had disciples: that is, those whom he had "taught."

Jesus had disciples whom He had taught.

Isaiah *prays* for these, his disciples, who may be identified with "the children God has given him."

Jesus prays for *His* disciples, who are the children whom God has given *Him* (Heb. 2: 13).

Isaiah prays that the word he has given his disciples may be sealed to them, and so they may be kept from the evil.

Jesus prays that His disciples may be sanctified by the Word He has given them, and by it be kept from the evil that is in the world (John 17: 17).

Isaiah is indeed a type of Jesus, yet he comes short as every type must, for while he could thus "make intercession," *he* could not "save to the uttermost," *that* is reserved for the blessed Antitype.

But as to the two children, they *must* be typical only in their significant names, and in their relationship to Isaiah.

In the latter point of view (as Israelites) they may be discerned in that "remnant according to the election of grace" (Romans 11: 5) that is always to be found among the Jews, even to the present day; of whom our Apostle Paul speaks of himself as one. In their names they tell us of that remnant that shall return to their land after centuries of banishment (Shear-Jashub). There and then shall they pass through their final sorrow in which they shall "turn to the Lord," and the veil that now hides Jesus from them is taken away forever (2 Cor. 3: 16). There and then, they begin to see a glory in Moses, *i.e.*, in his writings, never seen in all the long, dark night of their unbelief. There and then are they given to the Lord Jesus, and then He owns them, too, as His "children," as having the same divine nature as Himself.

In the present day the elect remnant of the Jews have lost their identity with Israel; but (with all believers) form the one Body, the Church, in which there is neither Jew nor Gentile, neither of whom have any part or place in the land or the earth at all. But in the day of trial lying ahead, they shall again be strictly Jews and return to all Israel's peculiar hopes and expectations. No longer shall they anticipate any rapture to heaven, but wait expectant for His salvation *on the earth*. So speaks the prophet Micah in his fifth chapter: "Then shall he give them up, until the time that she which travaileth hath brought forth; then shall *the remnant of his brethren return unto the children of Israel.*" That is, in the time of Zion's travail, the children that she brings forth, pictured in our prophet by *Shear-Jashub* and *Maher-shalal,* shall not be a heavenly people, with heavenly hopes, but Jehovah's beloved people, Israel, with hopes and fears confined to the earth and its government; which they—"the meek"—shall eventually inherit (Matt. 5: 5).

Nor does the threatening character of the name Maher-shalal-hash-baz conflict with this, although it does undoubtedly speak of severe judgment; but this judgment is not directed against the afflicted remnant of Israel, but against their foes. For this child is also the offspring of Isaiah (the salvation of Jehovah) and must necessarily therefore forecast some element of that salvation.  Israel is saved *by* judgment.

Now comes the counsel needed by that remnant in the future, but no less by us this very day.

> 19: When they shall say to you:
> Ask counsel of dead ones,
> Enquire of the wizards,
> Who chirp* and who mutter,
> (Thus shall ye answer)
> Should not a people
> Enquire of its God?
> Should those who are living
> Take counsel of dead ones?
> 20: To the law—to the word of
> (Divine) testimony—
> If with these they agree not,
> They shall never see dawning.†

---

*The word I have rendered "wizards" has in its root the idea of supernatural intelligence. It is, literally, "the much-knowing;" wise-ards.  These "chirp," Heb. *tzaphtzeph*: the sound of the word giving its meaning.  It was in this hardly articulate way, that the shades of Hades uttered their oracles.

† The last line is much debated as to its exact form, but its force is perfectly clear; no true light of a happier day shall ever dawn on these apostates.  This dawn we shall see in the next chapter.

By our very constitution, by the very fact that man has a spirit as well as soul and body, he must seek some support for that spirit in the day of mental strain and distress. Nor does the enemy of men allow that need to go without filling it in *his* way, and for his own ends. As dependence upon "God and the word of His grace" is loosened, the chains of "spiritism" are bound upon truth-rejecting men. All kinds of information is sought from those who have been introduced by death into a sphere where the future is assumed to be as clear to them as the past is to the living. The "mediums" of these communications are "wizards" (wise-ards), and if you want any secret revealed—from the whereabouts of a lost article to the eternal condition of a deceased relative—you have only to consult some "medium," and you will be put into communication with the spirit of the departed, who will tell you—*just what you wish to hear!*

Take heed, says Isaiah to his disciples, and the Lord Jesus to His, that you have nothing to do with them. Go not near to their séances. Touch not the defiling thing. It *is* truly supernatural, it is to be attributed to personalities in an unseen world, it is information given by those who were exposed, when the Light of the World was on earth, as "unclean spirits of demons." Nor were they exterminated *then* or confined to the bottomless pit, but still left on the earth. *Where, then, are they now?* Do you think they are passive? Do you suppose that they have forgotten, or forsaken their old successful devices for deluding poor, wretched men? Nay, they are to this very hour active in teaching all that is opposed to the claims of the Lord Jesus, the Son of God, in the three spheres of infidel-rationalism, politics, and superstition.* They have a sure footing in that church which has taken the place of being the witness for God on the earth, and it needs but the rapture from this earth of the true people of God, for the formation of Babylon, in the union of all pseudo-Christian profession, to be the "hold of every foul *spirit*" (Rev. 17). Well may we avoid, as deadly poison, all traffic with

---

*Compare Rev. 16: 13, 14, the three frog-demons from mouth of dragon (infidelity), beast (politics), and false prophet (superstition).

spiritism, for Christendom is full of it; there is far more than goes under that name.

On the other hand, what is the resource of faith in every dispensation? *The Word of God!* In this you will find no "muttering" voice, no foolish "chirp," but the living Voice of Him who indeed is without limit of understanding, who knows our deep needs, and who, without pandering to all our unhallowed curiosity, has met them all. Here we may learn, if we be "poor, and of a contrite spirit, and tremble at His Word," divine secrets indeed, secrets of love and wisdom beyond human fathoming. Here we may find a light on the dark problems of our day, here the purposes of God as to heaven and earth are revealed, here faith may find a solid rock on which her feet may stand, and hope may be so directed as never to be disappointed. Well may we bring, then, every claim to supernatural assumption to this divine Standard. If there is divergence from this, then we may put it down as certain that our counsellors have no true light, and that indeed on them shall never the light of morning dawn.

But what, then, is the inward condition of those deluded ones all through the time of their darkness?

> 21: They shall pass through it*
> Hard-pressed and hungry,
> Torn with convulsions;
> When faces look *upward*
> Then king and God curse they.
> 22: When they look *earthward*,
> Trouble and darkness,
> Dimness of anguish,
> Thick gloom wide-spreading.†

Could there be a more distressing picture of misery? Amid thick darkness *without*, with a never-satisfied longing *within*, these wander. Looking *up*, they curse all above them; nor can they find any comfort in anything *on the earth* around them. Without, within, above, below, nothing but darkness and anguish.

---

*That is, through the gloom.

† Note the reference to gloom and darkness in these last three lines.

It is a picture of the land at the due time of the Lord's first coming, and we may say that it is a picture of us all, for we all have wandered till One who loved us came with a Light that is dispelling gradually the darkness of nature.   But we will eliminate the division made by the intrusion of the chapter, and see this Light shining in the darkness.

# CHAPTER NINE

Light appears where least expected. Can these words be applied to Christmas Day? Peace at last! What is in the Name? Growth here suggests growth in heaven. Is Christ's kingdom everlasting if it be given up? The sad refrain.

**D**ENSE indeed was the darkness in which the last chapter closed, but as it is ever darkest before dawn, so we might expect the brightest dawning to follow such darkness. That expectation would not be unjustified by the scripture itself, for the last verse of chapter 8 tells us of some who prefer any source of assumed intelligence (even though it be diabolical) to the "Word and the Testimony," and who will suffer the consequences of that fatal choice—to them that dawning shall never rise. But the inference is inevitable that there are others, who do cleave to that "Word and Testimony," on whom that light shall break. In this chapter, then, we see that light rising where least expected.

> 1: Nor shall the gloom be
> As in her anguish,
> When in the first time
> He lightly afflicted
> The land of Zebùlon,
> The land of Naphthàli,
> And in the last time
> More gravely afflicted*
> The road of the sea:
> The land beyond Jordan,
> Galilee of the nations.
>
> 2: The people there walking
> In darkness (gross darkness)
> Have seen a great light.
> On people long dwelling
> In the land of Death's shadow
> Hath the light shined.

---

*Or, But in the last time hath made it glorious.

The exact translation of this passage has been much disputed. The question at issue hinges largely on the precise rendering of one single word which is capable of entirely opposite meanings; and, as the one or the other is given to it, so the rest of the verse is to be understood.

That word is translated in our A. V. "more grievously afflict," and, if this be the right sense here, the antithesis compels reading the preceding context, "At the first did lightly afflict." But the R. V. (with many others) translates the same word in quite the opposite sense: "Hath made it glorious," and then reads the whole verse in conformity with this: "In the former time He brought the land of Zebulon . . . into contempt; but in the latter time hath made it glorious."

Here is indeed a difference! Shall we say that in the latter time greater affliction, or greater honor, comes to this northern part of the land? Our confidence in "God and the Word of His grace" is not shaken by these apparent anomalies. We say either that the difference is of no importance whatever, or *the ambiguity itself has been divinely intended,* and that *both* readings have their place; that is, there is what we may term a "near-by," or historical fulfilment, and God did at first afflict the north-eastern portion of the land comparatively light, in the invasions of the Syrians (1 Kings 15: 20); and, in a later day, brought heavier suffering upon that same portion, in the carrying away of the people into captivity by the Assyrians (2 Kings 15: 29).

But the final intent in the mind of the Holy Spirit looks far beyond that history, for it is Christ who alone is the final fulfilment of this, as of all prophecies, for He did also "make glorious" that same despised district, which had been brought into such contempt that it had become proverbial*—made it glorious by the *Lord of Glory* coming as the Light to dwell there, for so the Spirit of God uses this passage in the Gospel of Matthew (4: 12-16).

"Jesus departed into Galilee, that it might be fulfilled which was spoken by Esaias the prophet, saying: The land of Zebulon, and the land of Naphthalim, the way of the sea, beyond Jordan, Galilee of the Gentiles, the people which sat in darkness saw great light, etc."

---

*"Out of Galilee ariseth no prophet" (John 7: 52).

But in quoting from this scripture, it will be noticed that Matthew omits the ambiguous word rendered, "more grievously afflict." Had he quoted it, that of course would have settled the question; but he leaves out just that part of the quotation entirely, and all we are certain about is that Jesus is the "great light," and that, refusing that center of religious pretension, Judea, He makes His dwelling in that confessedly dark land, sunken to the level of the Gentiles, and loaded with contempt, but, by doing so "loads it with honor," and even the Gentiles who share in the darkness share in the Light. That is quite enough for us to know.

Neither rendering transgresses any lexical or grammatical rule, neither is opposed to any scripture; both are in full harmony with *all* Scripture; so either, or both, may be adopted without loss or hurt, and the very ambiguity may be of divine intent.

Between verses 2 and 3, we clearly have one of those strange parentheses that are not uncommon in the holy Word of God, and that give room for that heavenly work that was in the mind of God *before* the foundation of the world, as Eph. 1: 4 speaks. In this case, nineteen centuries have passed since that great Light brought to highest honor the dark road by the sea, where Galilee itself is no longer Galilee of Israel, but Galilee of the Gentiles. They are all on one sea-level morally—"there is no difference."

In the next verse we see that nation (*as a nation*, mark), rejoicing with a joy that can only be illustrated by the peaceful thanksgiving of a harvest successfully garnered and by a victory in a battle that had been well-nigh lost.

If I ask: "Have you ever heard or read of the Jews, *as a nation*, thus rejoicing?" your answer will at once be: "Far from it; wherever I read or have heard of the Jews since Isaiah's day, they have been in oppression, and in the distress that accompanies that condition. No, the Jews in all those centuries have never been a joyous people." And yet here it is a jubilant nation.

This and similar difficulties have led to the application of this and other such prophecies to the Church. It is a basic mistake! The Church is not a nation at all, but a Body, taken *out of* the nations (Acts 15: 14), whilst Israel is indeed a nation that is like an individual who has died and has been buried, but it too shall have a national resurrection, as our book will in due course show. But between this day of their sorrow and that of their song, lie still deeper distresses, that will be ended forever when they find the rejected Jesus is their promised Messiah, as in verse 6. Though a little pious remnant were awaiting Him, and both angels above, and little children below, "perfected praise," let us be careful not to deduce that the *nation* itself welcomed Him: its representatives —rulers, scribes, Pharisees—were almost a unit in turning from the Light till they led the thoughtless mass to cry: "Crucify Him! Crucify Him!" No! The Jew is not being preserved, whilst scattered, for nothing. He must again travel through that "dimness of anguish," terrors still await poor "Jacob," but he shall be saved out of them. Then comes this song:

3: Thou hast enlargèd
The (once little) nation.
Joy to it given,
Ever increasing:
Rejoicing before Thee
As in full harvest,
As victors exultant,
Dividing the spoil.
4: For the yoke of its burden,
The staff of its shoulder,
The rod of its tyrant,
Thou hast broken to splinters,
As in Midian's day.
5: For the boot (of the soldier),
In war-tumult trampling:
The cloak (of the soldier),
In blood saturated,
Are now but for burning
And fuel for fire.

Verse three brings a most important question: "Thou hast multiplied the nation and increased its joy," cries the joyful prophet. What nation *can* that be but that one that alone is beloved *as a nation* "for the fathers' sakes?" As surely as the Jewish nation must be here in view, so not one letter of this is as yet fulfilled in Christendom at all! It is, it *must* be, still future. *We* are living then, between the second and third verses of this chapter of Isaiah, in that unnoticed, and (to every Old Testa-

ment writer) absolutely unknown parenthesis in the course of
time of which the Spirit of God frequently speaks in the New
Testament, as for example:

"Now to Him that is of power to establish you according to
my gospel and the preaching of Jesus Christ, according to the
revelation of the mystery, *which was kept secret since the world
began,* but now is made . . . known to *all nations* for the obedience of faith" (Rom. 16: 25, 26).

Here in Romans is a glad tidings, not for one nation, but for
"all nations." In Isaiah is a glad tidings, not for all nations, but
for *one!* Is not the distinction clear?

Oh, the joy of that hour to the poor, long-suffering, but ever-
beloved, and now redeemed nation! It is indeed "life from the
dead" (Rom. 11: 15). Israel has been, and is, even in this resurrection, a type for us (1 Cor. 10). Nothing could give us a
clearer figure of the individual resurrection of the dead than that
of this long-buried nation sleeping "in the dust of the earth." So,
as we listen to the joy of Israel, we get a feeble pattern of the
joy of that long-looked-for morn of resurrection, drawing, as we
fondly hope, so near now, and can consider the details with increased interest, for that joy foreshadows ours, when He comes
for us.

Two figures are employed to express that gladness. First,
"they joy before Thee according to the joy of harvest." Indeed,
it is Israel's great ingathering, the feast of tabernacles. Today
Israel's year lacks its completion. The feasts that we may call
ours, Passover, Unleavened Bread, Pentecost, are all fulfilled, but
Israel's feasts of Trumpets, Atonement and Tabernacles are all
still in the future. But at that future time, Jesus will not come
up to that feast as once He did, "as it were in secret" (John 7:
10), but very openly, with clouds and great glory, and every
eye sees Him. Jerusalem again will have been captured, and
suffered all the horrors of a captured city (Zech. 14). The little
remnant of faith that will hold the citadel against the armies of
the then world-power will be about to be exterminated; then He
will come for their deliverance. Well may they exult!

But in that joy there will be another element, of which
Christians *ought* to know nothing—it is victory over human foes.

Those foes, cries Messiah, identifying Himself with His earthly people as a nation, have "compassed Me about like bees, but in the name of the Lord will I destroy them" (Ps. 118: 11), so there will be not only the joy of peaceful harvest, but of victory in battle.

It is Jehovah's intervention again: once more the nation will be delivered from the taskmaster. Israel is likened to a poor beast of burden, the neck under the yoke, the shoulder pierced with goads, the back scored with the driver's rod; all these indignities are inflicted on Messiah's people till He interposes, and breaks all these to splinters. It is as in the day of Midian, when 300 men, without weapons, armed only with trumpets, lamps, and broken pitchers, defeated all the mighty host of Midian.

Now all the military equipments, all the munitions of war, even to the personal accoutrements of the soldiery, are burned as never to be needed more (ver. 5). *Israel's* wars are ended forever. Has anything of this kind ever taken place? There was *a* peace when Jesus was born in Bethlehem: it was the *"pax Romana,"* a peace maintained by the very weapons needed for it *to be* maintained. The last war was to lead to a universal, permanent peace. What a baseless dream! Why will men disappoint themselves? Nothing can be more sure than that no human diplomacy, no league of nations, no triumph of democracy—*nothing* can bring permanent peace to this war-distracted scene save the return of its rightful King to assume its government and oust the usurper, that evil spirit, who is even now enthroned in it. It is Jesus, and He alone, who shall break the arrow of the bow (Ps. 76: 13). He, and He alone, shall make wars to cease to the end of the earth (Ps. 46: 9); for He, and He alone, can consummate this work, made sure by His atoning death, and cast out Satan from his usurped throne. All Scripture, with convincing harmony, witnesses to this truth, so utterly ignored by all the statesmen of the earth, that as long as that rebellious and usurping spirit called Satan, or the Devil, has his throne where it is to this day, on and over the earth, and is not actually cast out into the bottomless pit, wars and wars of ever more violent intensity, will correctly, but sorrowfully enough, express that usurper's reign.

The explanation of all that precedes is given in verse 6. What, or who, has caused all these war-equipments to be destroyed? The answer is another grand chant or song:

6: For unto us a Child is born,
   Unto us a Son is given;
   With scepter on His shoulder,
   His name shall be called,
        Wonderful!
        Counsellor!
        El-Gibbohr!
        Avi-ad!
        Sar-Shalohm!*

7: Of the growth of His rule,
   Of the growth of His peace,
   There shall never be end.
   To establish and fix it
   Through judgment and justice
   From now and for aye.
   This shall the zeal of Jehovah effect.

Here again we come to a passage overflowing with blessing, yet inviting some prayerful scrutiny, for there are questions in connection with it that we may well ask. "Unto us a Child is born," sings the prophet. But who is meant by *"us?"* The common answer is, "All mankind." It is assumed to synchronize with that song of the angelic host, "of good tidings of great joy... for unto you is born this day in the city of David, a Saviour, which is Christ the Lord." But we must then repeat our question, Did *mankind* thus sing with joy at that birth? Did mankind as a race respond joyfully with, "Unto us a Child is born?" Far from it; the mass of men knew nothing of His birth, and when they saw Him they despised, rejected, and finally crucified Him as the lowest of criminals: Jew and Gentile uniting in spitting on His face, in loading Him with shame and reproach, and in casting Him out of the earth altogether! If that be true, not only is it impossible to see all mankind in the joyous speakers here, but it

---

* The mighty God! The Father of Eternity! Prince of Peace! The last three names are left in the Hebrew to maintain the three syllables.

most justly becomes all mankind (who are today but later repro-
ductions of the same generation who thus dealt with Him) to
make the assumed date of His birth to be anything but a day of
feasting and revelry. Let us consider this seriously; it by no
means lacks importance. Should what is so ignorantly called
"Christmas Day" be a day of revelry, or rather of penitence for
the world?*

But if we have in this sixth verse the immediate response of
that nation of Israel to the birth of its Messiah that took place in
Bethlehem, what room does that leave for verses 3-5? No such
consequences followed that historical birth. Nothing of the kind
has taken place since. The poor nation has continued scattered,
and Jerusalem has ever been trodden down of the Gentiles. There
can be but one possible solution: the whole intervening period of

-----

*I cannot leave this reference to "Christmas" without reminding
my readers that not one of the religious festivals that mark the
Christian year (so termed), has one letter of Scripture to justify
it. On the contrary, whatever notice *is* taken of similar observances that had crept into the Churches in Galatia, condemns
them utterly. Here Judaizing teachers would bring them back to
the round of feasts of the Jewish year (Lev. 23), and what does
the divine Spirit say to that? "I am afraid of you lest I have bestowed labor on you in vain." And what was the cause of so
extreme a fear? Nothing but that they "observed days and months
and times and years!" Would not the same Holy Spirit say to us
in this day: "You observe 'Christmas' *Day;* the *Season* of 'Lent,'
'Easter' *Time?* You have not merely retrograded to Jewish ground,
but even to heathen. For, traced to their prime source, it is
nothing but sober judgment that attributes such a feast, say, as
'Christmas,' to the devil." At the winter solstice, when days began
to lengthen, pagans instituted a festival called the "Saturnalia" in
honor of Saturn, the assumed father of the heathen deities, in
whom we see the prince of the demoniacal powers. Roman Cath-
olicism shows its parentage from the same source by simply adopting this festival, but baptizing it with a Christian name, and thus
sanctifying it by blasphemously calling it the "Mass of Christ," or
"Christmas," and we have accepted the change of name, without
any change in the revelry, save that it is mixed with religion,
and these verses in Isaiah 9 are read, as referring to the birth of
the Lord on the 25th of December, whilst it is about as sure as
anything can be when not divinely revealed, that that could not be
the day of His birth at all.

this dispensation is eliminated altogether.  It is one of the basic principles of prophetic interpretation, that since the "heavenlies" are not subject to those revolutions of the earth by which time is measured, being as it were far above them, so it is only when God is dealing with His earthly people, that time is reckoned at all. When they are out of communion with Him—when He is not so dealing—then we may say, His clock stops—there is no measurement of time.  My readers' thoughts will probably recur to that prophecy in Gabriel's communication to Daniel, in his ninth chapter, of 490 years that were to see all Israel's sins, troubles and sorrows ended.  There is no possible reasonable understanding of that prophetic period except by seeing the interval of the heavenly work being a parenthesis between verses 26 and 27.  So here the Messiah is met at His birth with songs of joy from a little remnant of faith in Luke's Gospel, Mary, Elizabeth, Zacharias, Anna and Simeon—all are singing.  Well, wipe out the whole of the present age, and again you hear a song in our prophet's verses 3-7: a song due to the same cause, the birth of Messiah.  It is as if Messiah was just then born to them as a nation, as indeed He is; and that the nation itself is also just born to welcome Him.  They know Him now for the first time. Their joy is great.

It anticipates somewhat, but for the sake of a clear understanding we must look forward to the last chapter of our book, for there we have two distinct births, quite contiguous in the book, but actually separated by that intervening unseen 2,000 years. In chap. 66: 7 it is the birth of *One*—a Man-child, in whom we have no difficulty in again discerning our Lord, but as the Messiah of Israel.  But, mark, He is born *before* Israel's travail-pains, as that time of distress, the Great Tribulation, is called (Matt. 24: 8).  But in the next verse, 8, a whole nation is born in a day, and that birth is the *fruit of the "travail-pains"* of the Great Tribulation, by which the remnant has been severed from the apostate mass, and is owned as the nation of Israel.  *That* is the nation that is speaking in verses 3-7 of this chapter.  When the nation is thus new-born it will be as if Messiah were but just then born to them *as a nation*, although the literal birth occurred 2,000 years before.  The birth they thus celebrate, is His birth *to them* at that time, and the song is, as it were, a continuance of those in Luke.

Thus it is not to the Church that He is born here—nor to the world of men at large.* But that does not nullify the truth that the purpose of His coming into the world is indeed an everlasting source of joy to faith, and that faith will adore the One who "so loved the world" as to send His Son, "not to condemn, but that the world through Him might be saved." That is both infinitely precious and true, but what we have before us now is the precise bearing of these verses 3-7 in Isaiah, and here it is the same Christ *born to Israel at that time*. Nor must we altogether ignore that our prophet is also a poet and is writing his divine truth in poetic terms. Thus the very bursting on the consciousness of that renewed nation of the tremendous truth that their Deliverer is the Jesus whom they had rejected is perfectly expressed in His *birth to them*.

So we conclude that the "unto us" refers beyond all question to the only nation ever elected *as a nation*—the only people among whom the prophet could put himself in saying "unto *us*." At this time of exalted joy they fully discern in their Deliverer the virgin's Son, Immanuel, promised as the sign in chapter seven.

As Israel's whole history, with all its recorded vicissitudes, gives types of the exercises of the individual Christian, so do the experiences through which the Christian passes, throw back their light on Israel. Thus the Christian may learn all about the birth of Christ at Bethlehem even as a child, but little does it mean, and nothing does he profit, until he awakens, by a divinely quickened faith, to his own personal possession or part in that One so born. But when he does awaken to this mighty truth, that the Lord is *his*, when for the first time he really knows that he—poor sinner as he is—is the object of His redeeming love, then it is, and not till then, that the Lord is born to him. Is that not true? Has it not been your experience? Then that is precisely what shall occur to that elect nation, when it is new-born in a day

---

*The words "Which shall be to all people" clearly convey the idea that the Gentiles are also included in these "good tidings of great joy;" but when these Gentiles are meant the word is in plural, "peoples," whilst an article has been omitted. Read *all the people* and there is no question but that "the Jewish people" alone are here in view.

(chap. 66: 8): long after the land of Zebulon and the land of Napthali saw that great Light (Matt. 4: 15, 16).

Now let us listen to the names of glory that the Spirit delights to adorn Him with. They are like the bells on the High-priest's garment, for they ring His praise: Wonderful! Counsellor! The Mighty God! The Father of Eternity! Prince of Peace! Grand and beautiful as they are, there is not one that is not included and enwrapped in the one we know best—"Jesus," for,

> "His name encircles every grace
> That God as Man could show."

This is unquestionable, for whilst none of these names was ever formally or literally given to Him, any more than that of Immanuel, yet as we have no difficulty in discerning in the Babe divinely named Jesus, the Immanuel of Isaiah, so does that same divine-human Name embrace and include all these five.

"WONDERFUL!" This is not an adjective here, nor is this the first time that we find it as a name. "Why askest thou after my name?" the Angel of the Lord (the Lord Himself in that form) had asked of Manoah, "seeing it is 'Wonderful'" (Judges 13: 18), precisely the same word as in our chapter, but in its adjectival form, and it both expresses and hides the Speaker as Incomprehensible. "Wonderful!" indeed then He is, not only in what He says or does, but in the unfathomable mysteries of His own Person, for "none knoweth the Son but the Father." None by searching can find Him out: and when He does come forth to the sight of men He has "a name written that no man knows but Himself" (Rev. 19: 21. Too many have attempted to fathom that Name, but in no case has it resulted in anything but humiliating failure.

See how He proved Himself "Wonderful" in that interview with our poor brother (I so speak of him because of his dim insight, so like our own in this day) Manoah, in Judges 13. That poor man would in kindliness and courtesy have given Him food; but see how it is declined, for he must discern someone far higher than a mere human guest. Would he offer, then it must be "to Jehovah." And this Manoah does. Poor enough was the kid in itself, but the "Wonderful One" made it of infinite value *by adding Himself to it!*

Closely corresponding with Manoah was that young man of Mark 10: 17 who also offered Him courtesy in the word "Good Master;" but again He refuses the courtesy, and says in effect, "Thou must offer it to Jehovah," for he must discern in Him the only one who is really "good," that is God, for He only has title to such a term.

Every word that He spoke, every act He did, tells of Him as Wonderful. That He should be both sinless and the Friend of sinners, is infinitely wonderful; yet that is involved in the very name, Jesus.

"COUNSELLOR." That He ever was to all, nor did He ever seek counsel from any. How often men, under the superior subtlety of their master, Satan, sought to put Him into such a dilemma that, no matter what He said, He must condemn Himself, or refute His own claims. Did He in such cases take counsel with any? Far from it! The challenge of the apostle can be applied to Him perfectly: "Who hath known the mind of the Lord, or who hath been His counsellor?" (Rom. 11: 34). Never was there one instant's hesitation, never a reversal, modification, or regret for anything He ever said. As we see the subtle attacks of Pharisees in league with Herodians and later of Sadducees (Matt. 22); and of scribes and Pharisees in John 8, in spirit we fall at His feet and cry adoringly, "In Thy fathomless wisdom Thou art well named Counsellor!"

"THE MIGHTY GOD." All the efforts of rationalists to take off this pivotal central Name by rendering *"El Gibbohr"* as "Hero of strength," or "Hero-God," come to nothing, since we have precisely the same name applied to Him to whom the remnant shall return in chap. 10: 21. It is as simple, clear, unequivocal a claim of supreme deity for Messiah as could be expressed in human language, yet not more so than in every word He said, every act He did. To give but two proofs of this: Who, but the Mighty God, could have said without instant reprobation, "If a man come to Me, and hate not his father, mother, wife and children, and brethren, and sisters, yea, and his own life also, he cannot be My disciple?" Only Incarnate Love who could give another love compared with which that of the dearest relationship on earth is but "hate,"—could give another Life, with which this brief death-shadowed existence could bear no comparison; could have so spoken without being either condemned as the most blasphemous of men, or compassionated as the most insane. Or who could say, "Before Abraham was I AM?" We discern Him but dimly, but even that dim discernment is enough again to make us fall at His feet as we worship Him as "The Mighty God."

"FATHER OF ETERNITY," to which He is entitled as being the only One who so makes "all things new" (Rev. 21: 5) as to justify their being eternal. Do you not often ask yourself, Is it possible for the present condition of things to be everlasting? Is Satan to be permitted to usurp the throne of this earth's true King for ever with all the consequent miseries? It is impossible. The "mystery of God," that is, the permission of evil by absolute Good, has about come to its end, for the seventh angel is about to sound (Rev. 10: 7), and our Lord, Christ, is the Father of conditions that shall never change.

"PRINCE OF PEACE." Precisely in the same way as He is Father of Eternity, so is He Prince of Peace. He is the Author of conditions that involve everlasting, unbroken peace. The waters of the past eternity were unruffled until he who is a sinner from the beginning broke their peace by his rebellion (1 John 3: 8), nor is there to this day anything to justify our poet's lines:

> .   .   .   .   .   .   "and what remains
> Of this tempestuous state of human things,
> Is merely as the working of a sea
> Before a calm that rocks itself to rest."

No, dear Cowper, no. Many a storm shall still break on this devoted earth, and the fiercest of all is still to come, when man's foe, the Devil, shall be cast out of heaven to the earth, and have great wrath because he knows that his time there is short. Till then all man's efforts are utterly vain, and serve only to evidence his incompetence to govern. When He is thus manifested as Prince of Peace, we shall also be manifested with Him in glory (Col. 3: 4), for having been first caught up to be with Him, we shall accompany Him on the final stage of His return (1 Thess. 4: 13-18).

Having seated Messiah upon His throne, our prophecy follows Him there. His kingdom ever grows: the peace that characterizes it ever extends. Indeed, being divine, this is inevitable, for nothing that is of God can possibly stagnate. Stagnation is the mark of death: growth is the surest evidence of life. Stagnant water we call "dead" water, while the running waters of a spring are termed "living." So with His kingdom there is never stagnation; of its increase there is no end. Note then that here it is the Throne of David, with the limitations of that throne to Israel and the land between the Nile and Euphrates. But it "increases," and that throne seen in Ps. 2 grows to the throne of Ps. 8, where we see everything on earth put under His feet as Son of Man. How greatly has His kingdom increased! All things are within the sway of that sceptre. In this rule the heavenly saints share. It is the distinct promise to the Church as seen in Thyatira; in Revelation 20 it is *fulfilment;* "the first resurrection" being completed by those who have suffered martyrdom under the two "Beasts" in the day of the "Great Tribulation" joining those who had preceded them (Rev. 20: 4). The boundaries of this kingdom is the earth. But still it "increases," and where can it now extend? There is to be "no end" to its increase, then it must have a boundless limitless sphere, as the kingdom of the Son of God. Earth is too small now. Even the rule as Son of Man is too limited. The universe without any bounds—an idea that no finite mind can compass—is finally, after the millennial reign, the ever-increasing kingdom of Him who for us died upon the tree! In that final rule no creature shares, for then God is all in all (1 Cor. 15: 28). But we have a place that is not less happy, even if it is not that of rule—we still shall *"serve."* Does that appeal to us less than ruling? Surely not, for it was in that lowly guise we first knew Him who came not to be ministered unto but to minister and to give His life a ransom for many. What a blessedness there is in the very thought of such an infinity of time! No weariness! Ever fresh unfoldings of divine attractions and glories that forbid all such weariness as is due to those ceaseless revolutions "under the sun," that caused the wisest of men to groan again and again,

"Vanity." Here there is "no new thing" (Eccl. 1: 10); there, "all things new" forever, to all eternity new.

All this surely means that there shall be no limit to His reign, either in its duration or in its extent. Yet, on the other hand, is not Scripture equally explicit that His reign *does* end? Is it not written, "Then cometh the end, when He shall have delivered up the kingdom to God, even the Father" (1 Cor. 15: 24)? How can He "deliver" it up, if it never ends? How can it never end if it be delivered up? Does not *that* end it?

Now this is esteemed a satisfactory proof by some that the word rendered "forever and ever" does not carry the unqualified force that we have connected with it; for, as Messiah's kingdom is "forever and ever" and yet is "delivered up" (and so, it is assumed, ended), so those conditions of the finally impenitent which are also said to be "forever and ever" will also come to an end: that is, Scripture does not teach the eternity of retribution; but that even Judas will be finally saved, and Satan fully restored.

Far too solemn are such themes to be the subjects of mere controversy, but they call the more insistently for examination as unbiased as is posible. Yet I must be very brief, and it will be enough to point out that there is a vast difference in Scripture between a kingdom coming to "an end" through the incompetence of its administrator, and being "given up" in perfection to the one from whom it had been received. In this latter case there is still "no end," for it is continued in Him to whom it has thus been given. All the kingdoms and empires of earth end because of their wickedness and incompetence. On the other hand, the replacing in God the Father's hands, in perfect order, with every evil eliminated, of the kingdom received from Him, is essentially different. For even after He *has* delivered up that perfect kingdom, the King, who has ruled in righteousness for a thousand years, still reigns forever and ever in, and as one with, God, who is all in all.

This is "the day of man" (1 Cor. 4: 3, *marg.*), government is in his hands; it is soon to come to its end, and be followed by "the day of the Lord." Will then *man's* rule have ceased entirely in that day in which the Lord alone is to be exalted? (Isaiah 2: 17).

Or do we see in that alone-exalted Lord, a *Man,* and One in whom *man* is still reigning, and man's rule has *not* come to an end; as it is written, "For unto the angels hath He not put in subjection the age to come, whereof we speak, but one in a certain place testified, What is man, that Thou art mindful of him? . . . Thou hast put all things in subjection under his feet," and this is directly applied to Jesus. So that while the rule of man in one sense ends, in another and equally true sense, it continues *in* the Son of Man, Christ Jesus, who is both Man and the Lord, and who is "alone exalted in that day."

But that "day of the Lord" is in its turn followed by that eternal day, called "the day of God" (2 Peter 3: 12). Does then that Lord of glory cease to reign, in every sense, or *continue* to reign, in God (as man continued to reign in Him), forever and ever? There can be but one answer.

The kingdom of the Son of Man—of Jesus, seen as the perfect representative *Man*—is surely limited in time. This kingdom He shares with His saints—"they live and reign with Him a thousand years"—and, interpret that as you will, literally or figuratively, it can hardly mean anything else than a certain limited time.

But He is not only Son of *Man,* He is Son of *God,* and of His kingdom, in that specific relationship, there is "no end," in the most literal and simple force of the words: *"Thy throne, O God, is forever and ever."*

But it is neither as Son of Man nor Son of God that we see Him in our verse, but rather as Son of David. Thus, we may say He has three thrones—three spheres of rule—first, over Israel as Son of *David;* then, over the whole earth as Son of *Man;* finally, over heaven and earth—all things visible and invisible, as Son of *God.*

"The zeal of Jehovah Tzebaoth will effect this." Through all dispensations God is burning with jealousy for just one object, the glory of His beloved Son, in whom is all His delight. Let that poor nation of Israel, so long under the rod for the crucifixion of His Son, but turn to Him, and at once the zeal of *wrath* becomes the zeal of *love,* and shall bring it to the head of the nations of the earth. Let one poor, sinful Gentile but give Him, the Lord

Jesus, the confidence of his heart, and at once wrath no longer abides on him (John 3: 36), but that same zeal of love enwraps him as embraces the Son Himself. But on the other hand, let the professed people of God, those nations that have taken the name of Christ, and call themselves the "Christian nations," turn from His Son, make little of Him (as, alas, they have done!), and the zeal of God burns against them; but all works to His final fixed purpose to bring Messiah to that throne, here foretold.

Thus the zeal of Jehovah burns to bring the once-despised Jesus to the rule of heaven and earth, till "every knee shall bow, and every tongue confess that Jesus Christ is Lord, to the glory of God, the Father." "Blessed are all they that put their trust in Him."

We must now return for a time, and, as in the pages of our own prophet John, listen to "thunderings, voices and lightnings," in threats of those judgments that must precede those days of joy. Yet may we remember for our comfort, that we are over 2,500 years beyond the time Isaiah wrote, and "our salvation is nearer than when we believed."

Thus, after this burst of joy caused by the revelation of Jesus as the true Messiah, we return to the line of the prophecy broken off from the fifth chapter. This is evidenced by the resumption of that sad cry in verse 25 of that chapter: "For all this, His anger is not turned away, but His hand is stretched out still," and making it a refrain by which this part is divided. But if chapter five began in song and ended in sorrow, this part, chaps. 9: 8-12, reversing this order, begins in sorrow and ends in song.

We come then to chaps. 9: 8 to 10: 4, in which the Assyrian is used as the rod of Jehovah, clearly divided for us into four strophes, each ending with the doleful refrain to which we have already alluded.

> 8: A word unto Jacob, Adonai hath sent,
>    On Israel hath that word fallen.
> 9: All Ephraim's people shall hear of that word,
>    And they in Samaria dwelling.
>    Who in heart's pride are thus boasting:
> 10: Bricks may fall down, but with hewn stones we'll build,
>    For sycamores cut we'll plant cedars.

11: 'Tis for such boasting Jehovah exalts
   The foes of king Rezin against him (*i.e.*, against Ephraim).
12: Syrians east, Philistines west,
   With open mouth Israel eat up.
   *For all this His anger is not turned away,*
   *But His hand is ever outstretchèd.*

A threatening word is sent to Jacob and reaches its intended
mark first in the ten northern tribes, but passes on to the whole
of Israel. The first droppings of the storm that shall sweep
Ephraim away have fallen; how are they met? Do they search
out and confess that the cause of the infliction is in their own
evil ways? Not at all. They are filled with that "superb courage" that is so highly esteemed among men. Not in the least
depressed, but despising all pessimism, they will make the very
disaster a benefit by replacing the inferior brick and sycamore
buildings with stone and cedar.

Rezin, the king of Syria, had also his foe, and that same foe,
the Assyrian, shall not only put an end to Ephraim, but shall
invade Judah and threaten Jerusalem, for the language here used
seems impossible to be confined to the northern kingdom. The
"word" goes on in its course, eventually involving Judah, as the
next chapter clearly evidences. That gives point to verse 12, for
the Philistines never troubled the northern kingdom: their attacks were ever against Judah.

Human nature is unchanged from that day to this! Nor are
there ever lacking, in such times of national chastening, plenty
of false prophets to silence the voice of conscience, and prophesy
the smooth things that the ear of man loves to hear. Even to this
day God's hand is the very last thing that is seen in calamities,
disasters, sufferings, sorrows, wars, earthquakes, desolations,
famines—the very last. If He be referred to at all, it is but too
often to throw on Him the arbitrary and causeless responsibility
for the infliction, and to charge Him with being the Unjust Cause
of the suffering—our sin has nothing to do with it!

This brings us to the second strophe contained in verses 13 to
17, in which that outstretched Hand of Jehovah falls again heavily
on the people, who, although stricken, turn not in genuine repentance to the Hand that has smitten, with confession that their

sin necessitated, and that love has prompted the blow; but they again harden their hearts and "despise the chastening of the Lord."

13: For not to their Smiter do this people turn,
    Jehovah Tzebaoth they seek not.
14: Therefore He doth from Israel lop
    The head and the tail: palm and mire-rush.
15: The man whose long years have brought him respect,
    Is the head; whilst the false-speaking prophet
    Is but the tail (to be humbled).
16: For this people's leaders but lead them astray,
    Whilst those that are led are devourèd.
17: This is the reason the Lord hath no joy—
    In their young men taketh no pleasure:
    No mercy hath He on their orphans bereaved,
    No pity even on widows.
    For all of them are but liars in heart,
    And all in their speech are blasphemers.
    *For all this His anger is not turned away,*
    *But His hand is ever outstretchèd.*

Thus the blow falls again, and this time on the leaders, those who on the one hand are most highly esteemed in *civil* life, and who have been accorded positions of honor on account of their age; and, on the other, on the *spiritual leaders,* called lying prophets: the two political divisions of mankind that will head up in the last days in the "Beast" and "False Prophet," or Antichrist. The former are likened to the majestic palm-branch, in a dignity that Jehovah Himself recognizes, in some sort, as really their due; but as to those who assume a position of spiritual superiority over the people, on these He throws utter contempt. They are but as the mire-rush or as the "tail;" for as a dog fawns on its master with wagging tail, so do these pretended prophets seek only to please their hearers by prophesying the smooth things their itching ears demand. There would appear nothing so despicable in the eye of God as that same religious pretension of which our Lord has said, "Which thing I hate" (Rev. 2: 15). But the leaders in both spheres, civil and spiritual, are *mis-leaders*: the blind are leading the blind, and both come to the same end.

There is something peculiarly terrible and perplexing in the Father of mercies denying Himself the property of mercy even

toward the innocent and helpless: looking on apparently unmoved
while little children and helpless widows are involved in some
universal calamity.   There is no discrimination, all suffer alike;
for all are component parts of the nation, and it is the *nation,*
as such, not the individual, that is in view when God is thus
dealing with the earth in government.   Of course, the nation is
composed of individuals, but the individual suffering is, in such
cases, no evidence of wrath or judgment upon that individual.
God is not making personal selections in that way.

So, today, Christendom is but Israel "writ large," as we may
say; and have we not heard on all sides the questions: "Why does
not God stop human misery?   If any mere man having the
slightest sentiment of humanity, had the power, would he not
put a stop to the suffering at least of the *innocent,* and let the
inflictions fall on those who deserved them?   What have widows
or little children done that *they* should be dealt with so merci-
lessly?"   It is an old, old question due to the utter absence apparently of all moral discrimination in the providential government of the earth.   The best of men, Job, in his bitter trial
wailed, "If the scourge slay suddenly"—that is, if some widespread calamity is sent on men, is there any discrimination? Nay.
"He mocks at the trial of the innocent" (Job 9: 23): there is no
discrimination, no pity for the guiltless.   There is, apparently,
when the soul is on the rack of suffering, only mockery in the
very shining of the sun, the rippling of the waters, the singing of
the birds; these very sounds that in other times would soothe
and cheer, only increase our grief by their discord with it.   Then
Job adds, *"The earth is given over into the hand of the wicked."*
Could any infidel speak more bitterly?   And yet how true it appears to be.   How many who are *not* infidels have repeated that
groan.   There is no evidence of a just Governor of the earth; it
is given over to wickedness.

The light of the *whole* revelation that God, in His goodness,
has given us must be patiently and prayerfully pondered, for it
solves the problem, in showing the relative positions of Jesus, the
Son of Man, the true King of this earth, on the one hand: and
on the other, that of him who is, by creation, the highest of all
created intelligences, yet now a rebel, and usurper of this earth's

government, the Devil. All earth's discords, injustices, inequalities and calamities are in perfect harmony with the true King rejected and Satan's throne being still here: while, to our unspeakable comfort, One who loves us *over*-rules all things, so that they "work together," notwithstanding all the confusion, for our truest good in conforming us to the image of His Son.

The next strophe—verses 18 to 21—takes us another step along that path of sorrow that Israel is treading at this time. She is left alone—given up! It is as if a fire were left to work as it would in a mass of inflammable matter, without hindrance.

18: For like a fire doth wickedness burn,
    Feeding on thorns and on briers.
    In thickets of woods it kindles its flames,
    In a column of smoke then it mounts up.
19: By the wrath of Jehovah—Jehovah of Hosts—
    The land is charrèd and blackened;
    That fire in the people now finds its food,
    For no one spareth his brother.
20: They hew on the right; but, hungry still,
    They devour on the left, still unsated;
    And each his own arm is gnawing.
21: Manasseh for Ephraim serveth for food,
    Whilst Ephraim feedeth Manasseh—
    United they fall upon Judah.
    *For all this His anger is not turned away,*
    *But His hand is ever outstretchèd.*

The word rendered "wickedness" has in it the idea of a wilful turning away from known truth. It is not applied to mere ignorant wrong-doing. Where truth is known and thus wilfully rejected, there, sooner or later, the rejecters are given up, and left to themselves. Then, unchecked and unhindered, that fire of the perverse human will burns, and, as it burns, provides its own fuel. In the pictorial language of prophecy, the "thorns and briers" that express so graphically man's fallen state, keep the fire ever burning.

This suggests to us a solution of another sad problem in the drama of the ages: the eternity of punishment. As long as ungodliness is in the lake of fire, so long shall that fire continue to burn. Eternity of character alone necessitates eternity of penalty.

This is not due to the sins committed during the few short years of life, as people sometimes allege.  It is indeed *life*, whether it come from Adam or from Christ, that determines the final abode, and the *seriousness* of the infliction, the many or the few stripes, depends upon privileges unavailed of, and, in this respect there are as many divergencies in heaven or hell as there are individuals; but the *continuance* of dwelling depends on the *continuance* of the life in accord with that dwelling.

But Jehovah leaves His people to themselves.  Thus given up, the conflagration rages.  The tie with Him being broken, none other is respected; brother spares not brother, man's sword is turned against his own kin, and the poor earth, answering to the miserable condition of the man upon it, becomes like a charred cinder.  No real victory is ever attained by fratricidal strife: there is nothing but poverty and loss in both defeat and victory. Famine follows, as the handmaid of such war.  If brethren do unite, it is not against a common enemy, but against a third brother, Judah.  Fratricidal strife is the surest evidence of divine penalty on all.

# CHAPTER TEN

**A corrupt judiciary means the destruction of the basis on which the social structure rests. Who is the Assyrian? Where shall he be found in the last days of Israel's history? His pride insures his doom. A picture drawn of an invasion in order that it may be averted.**

THIS chapter should not be severed from the foregoing, for again we must hear, but for the last time, that doleful refrain of His wrath not turned away, of His hand still outstretched in smiting.

1: Woe to decreers of evil decrees,
   To the scribes who inscribe heavy burdens;
2: To turn needy men from judgment aside,
   And rob of their right My poor people.
   Desolate widows they thus make their prey,
   Nor shrink they from plundering orphans.
3: Oh, what will ye do, when I visit for this,
   In the storm that comes from afar off?
   To whom will ye flee in that day for help?
   Where find for your wealth a safe-keeping?
4: Nothing's then left them save to bow down
   Amid the mass of the captives,
   Or lie 'mid the dead who have fallen.
   *For all this His anger is not turned away,*
   *But His hand is ever outstretchèd.*

This final strophe touches the fundamental evil of all, that which provoked the sternest words that ever fell from those gracious lips of our Lord. Here is the thing that He hates. Here are those, who having sat themselves down on Moses' seat, make laws solely for their own interests, binding "heavy burdens and grievous to be borne" on others which they themselves "touch not with one of their fingers." Here the very foundations are destroyed, for when lawmakers make unrighteous laws, the very fabric of society is torn to shreds. "If the foundations be destroyed, what can the righteous do?" Where can the oppressed now turn for relief?  To the courts of justice?  Nay, widows and orphans offer the best opportunities for the judges' rapacity.

The whole strophe reminds one forcibly of the Lord's condemnation of the governing classes in Israel in His day, scribes, Pharisees, lawyers, who, when they could, "devoured widows' houses."  Nor are excluded from His condemnation more modern instances of spiritual guides, "priests," as they falsely call themselves, fattening on the superstitions they foster, and reaping a revenue from such deceptions as the sale of "masses" for the delivery of the souls of the dead from purgatory!  Is it loyalty, or true love to those it deludes, to be in friendship, or even neutral towards such a system, such teaching of lies?  We may well grieve that both leaders and people in Christendom do not merely "let alone that woman Jezebel" of Rome (Rev. 2: 20), but in the fear of being termed "bigots," or counting the votes she controls, are turning to her embraces.

Our prophecy goes on: What must be the consequence?  Can such a condition of things be permitted to be permanent?  Surely, "He who is higher than the highest regardeth" (Eccl. 5: 8). "What will ye do then," when the inevitable storm bursts on you from afar?  Where will ye find refuge from it?  Where can ye deposit those accumulations of wealth in which you glory, so as to find them again when that storm has passed?  Nothing shall be left them then, but, if life be spared, to bend their back with the other prisoners; or, if not, to lie amid the heaps of slain.  The change of pronouns says that Jehovah is telling some assumed listeners of the fate of those directly addressed in ver. 3.

This is but a picture in Israel of that judgment that overhangs the earth today, but there is still another blow to fall from the "outstretched hand" on that devoted nation, the agent of which is to be the Assyrian, whom we have now to consider.

"The discourse (chap. 10: 5 to 12: 6) subdivides into three principal parts, and each of them into three subdivisions, so that three forms the underlying number"—this is taken from Nagelsbach, in *Lange,* whose testimony is the more valuable since he did not apparently attach any significance to what he thus noted.

In this "three by three," we may well expect again to find "God fully manifested," and how can that be save in the work of redemption of sinful man through His beloved Son?   Nor shall we be disappointed.   May we enjoy it together.

The first of these sub-sections may be divided and entitled thus:

1. Verses 5 to 11—The Assyrian sows the seed of his own doom.
2. Verses 12 to 15—By denying that he is merely an instrument in Jehovah's Hand.
3. Verses 16 to 19—His doom.

We will consider them briefly, and render:

5: Ho, Assyrian, the rod of Mine anger;
 My fury, the staff that they wield in their hand!
6: I'll send him against a nation polluted—
 I'll give him a charge 'gainst the folk of Mine ire.
   To spoil spoil,
   To prey prey,*
 To tread down the people under his feet:
 To make them to be as the mire of the street.
7: Ah, but that is not his intention:
 Nor is it the thought of his heart.
 That heart only thinks of his own exaltation:
 To destroy and to cut off nations not few.
8: For he saith: My princes, are they not royal?
 Is not Calno as (conquered) Carchemish?
9: Is not Hamath as Arvad (subdued)?
 Is not Samaria as (fallen) Damascus?
10: As my hand hath reached to these kingdoms of idols,
 Of idols whose number are far in excess
 Of those in the which Jerusalem trusteth,
 With those of Samaria added thereto,
11: What hinders my doing to Salem's few idols,
 As to Samaria, and hers, I have done?

This may not be the time or place for an extended examination as to the various individuals prominent in the last days of this age, but, for anything like a clear view of that most critical

---

*Literal rendering of the Hebrew.

epoch in human affairs, we must at least endeavor to discern this Assyrian.

Past history, though it provides, as is so often the case in both Old and New Testaments, most valuable forecasts of the final fulfilment of the prophecy, cannot possibly exhaust that prophecy. No one can surely claim that Jehovah's wrath against His people Israel forever ceased in the destruction of Sennacherib's army, although that destruction may have afforded a very graphic picture of the final one.  Nor did such a song as here follows, in chapter 12, follow that partial deliverance: for the real accomplishment of all this we must then look forward to a day still future.

Many of us have been accustomed for many years to find the "Assyrian" of that future in the power that makes the last assault on restored Israel in Ezekiel 38, evidently Russia, and such an interpretation has much to commend it.  For, in the first place, the geographical position of Russia and her allies corresponds closely in a large part of her extended domain with the ancient Assyria, as being to the north and east of Jerusalem.  Then again, the Assyrian is, as far as Isaiah tells us, the *last* enemy destroyed (ver. 25), and with this agrees Ezekiel, who says that after this the "house of Israel shall know that I am the Lord *from that day and forward.*" This has led us to conclude that Russia and the Assyrian are identical.

But this is by no means without its difficulties.  Gog is never *called* the Assyrian, nor have we, as far as I am aware, any hint anywhere else in Scripture of Russia being used of God in the last days for the chastening of the Jew.  She may have shared in persecuting them with all the other nations of Christendom, in the past; and that persecution may even have been more acute in Russia than elsewhere, but that is not what we have here in Isaiah.  It is an oppressor specifically used and sent of God to chastise His people *when in their own land,* while in Ezekiel, Jehovah is not only *not* sending, but from the very beginning of his "evil" thought of invasion of the land, is "against" him, and that could never be said while the instrument was being sent and used.  Gog, then, is *not* the Assyrian!

Again, in Ezekiel the incursion occurs after the return of all the people, and when they are living in apparent security; in a "land of unwalled villages," as it is called in chapter 38. In Isaiah, on the other hand, that final return of Israel to their land does not take place till *after* the incursion of the Assyrian (see chap. 11). This would seem to be quite enough to make us pause before identifying them. The world-power of Isaiah's day stands for the world-power of any day, and particularly of the last days, even though it be not then literally Assyria, but "the Beast from the sea" (Rev. 13), that is, the revived Roman Empire, which then holds the political place of Assyria.

This is not without the clearest justification from Scripture itself, for in 2 Kings 23: 29 we read:

"In his (Josiah's) days Pharaoh-nechoh, king of Egypt, went up against the king of *Assyria* to the river Euphrates."

But this "king of Assyria" was really the king of *Babylon,* who was in the same position politically—that is, at the head of the then World-empire—as was Assyria in the earlier day, for of the same campaign of Egypt, which began so favorably for Pharaoh by the defeat and death of Josiah, but ended disastrously by his own defeat at Carchemish, Jeremiah records,

"The word of the Lord came against Egypt, against the army of Pharaoh-necho, king of Egypt, which was by the river Euphrates in Carchemish, which Nebuchadrezzar king of *Babylon* smote" (Jer. 46: 2).

That is, the same man who is here called "king of Babylon" was also termed "king of Assyria."

Again, the empire that followed the Babylonian was the Persian, yet the title "king of Assyria" is in Ezra 6: 22 attached to Darius, king of Persia:

"For the Lord . . . had turned the heart of the king of *Assyria* unto them."

If, then, the title of Assyria is projected to the two following World-empires, of quite different geographical boundaries, it follows that we are compelled to find it also attached to the fourth or last imperial power, the Roman. So it is in the *"Beast from the sea"* that we have the "Assyrian" of the last days. The prophet naturally speaks (ever under the inspiration of the Holy Spirit) in a way that his readers understand: nor does he therefore say anything of a western empire that had *no existence* at all at the time. He looks out upon the world, sees it with one dominant power, and takes its head as representing the World-ruler of the last days to which his prophecy extends. Nor is it of vital importance whether it be the Babylonian, Assyrian or Roman; there is one—the real "prince of this world"—who is behind each and all these human pieces on the chessboard of time, and links them all together, even from the day of Nimrod, who founded both Babel and Asshur, and whose spirit pervades these World-powers to the very end. As Nimrod (meaning "rebel") is behind Babel and Asshur (Gen. 10: 10, 11), so that great Rebel is ever behind the World-power of the day.

Thus it seems to me to be beyond all question that the "Assyrian" of Isaiah's day must be found in the "Beast from the sea" of the day of the Apocalypse. This is further confirmed by this clear truth that when the Lord is revealed for the deliverance of the remnant of His people, He finds *the Assyrian* oppressing them in the Old Testament (Zech. 14: 1), and *the Beast* in the New (Rev. 19: 20); that is, the Assyrian of the Old Testament *is* "the Beast" of the New.

In Isaiah's day the Assyrian received a commission from Jehovah to inflict His judgments. Though he is an utterly ungodly man, a good representative of the proud "prince of this world," Jehovah makes use of him, for there is no creature who can escape being made to serve Him, in one way or another, either as a vessel to honor or to dishonor (2 Tim. 2: 20).

But it is a dangerous commission, for he who inflicts judgment must be very careful as to his own condition: he who casts the "first stone" must be himself "without sin" (John 8: 7): he who sees the mote in his brother's eye, must have his own examined first, to be sure that there is no beam in it (Matt. 7: 3): those who "put away the wicked person from among" themselves, must first humble themselves, and "purge out" the leaven of being "puffed up" (1 Cor. 5: 12, 2). It is the same principle all through, as in the simple word: "Judge not, that ye be not judged." The time shall come, when His people, Israel, being all

righteous, shall "execute vengeance upon the Gentiles, and punishment upon the peoples; bind their kings with chains, and their
nobles with fetters of iron," but that will be when it can be added
of that whole nation, "This honor have all His *saints*" (Ps.149:9).

The Assyrian is quite unconscious of being only an instrument
of Jehovah. He thinks he is simply carrying out his own plans
for his own glory. He will be Lord of lords and King of kings.
It is the lust for world dominion that has constantly been evidenced by world-conquerors, although no attempt has as yet been
successful. But one day, out of the tossing waters of some such
world-conflict as the last, will arise the Beast who shall in this
*political* position (I more than question if it corresponds geo-
graphically at all) occupy the place of Assyria of the prophet's
day.

Note that the Assyrian of old does not merely contend that
the *deities* of Assyria are superior to those of Calno or Carchemish, but that *he himself* has proved his personal superiority over
them all: "As *I* have done to Samaria and her idol-deities, shall *I*
not do to Jerusalem?" (ver. 10). In a word, he, too, "exalts himself above all that is called God" (2 Thess. 2: 4). In that trinity
of evil of the last days—Dragon, Beast, False Prophet—that
same family trait is in all three, and the spirit who at the first
would exalt his "throne above the stars of God, and be like the
Most High," is the Dragon controlling the other two.

The path from Calno to Jerusalem, in more senses than one,
is ever travelled by all the aspirants to World-empire: a series of
victories leads the conqueror to esteem himself invincible and then
—his downfall! Sooner or later every fallen man breaks down
under the strain of success.

Second section: The Assyrian denies being a mere instrument
of Jehovah, or of being dependent on any other man, or men; and
this disproves absolutely any identity with the "little horn" of
Daniel 8, instead of the "little horn" of chapter 7.*

---

*In the study of prophetic truth we must remember that it is
like knitting, each stich, however insignificant it may appear,
is important, for on all sides there are others hanging upon it.

12:  And it shall be when Adonai hath finished
      The whole of His work, that He brings upon Zion—
      Hath punished Jerusalem to its full limit,
      Then will I turn on the fruit of the stout heart
      Of the king of Assyria, the blows of My rod;
      So shall the pride of his high looks be lowered.

---

Thus with regard to the Assyrian and where he is to be found in the closing days of this age, many esteemed interpreters identify him with the King of the North, found in Daniel's closing prophecy. This I had also naturally accepted, but have since been compelled to abandon, for from every point of view, I have found it to be quite untenable. The characteristic of the Assyrian is independence of all help, and he knows well that none can deny that claim: "By the strength of my hand I have done it, and by my wisdom, for I am prudent: I have removed the bounds of the people and have robbed their treasures, I have put down the inhabitants as a valiant man," etc. That is not the language of one who owes, and knows that he owes, to another whatever power he has. On the other hand it fits perfectly the King of the North, whose "power shall be mighty, but *not by his own power*" (Dan. 8: 24). Again, instead of honoring the God of his fathers, he shall "*honor the god of munitions*" (Dan. 11: 38), that is, he acknowledges his dependence on another. He is easily found in the New Testament, bearing precisely the same mark of dependence: "*He* (the second Beast, from the land) *exerciseth all the power of the first Beast*" (Rev. 13: 12). Independence marks the one, dependence the other—they cannot be the same.

But as evidencing to what absurdities the mistake may lead the most able of commentators, Mr. Wm. Kelly, comments on Dan. 8 thus: "The Assyrian understands dark sentences. He will take the place of a great teacher, which will naturally have much influence over the Jewish mind, for they have always been a people given to research, and intellectual speculations of all kinds." One can only ask, where is there in all Scripture, a hint of that mighty fighter, the Assyrian, being a great teacher! Think of that external foe of the remnant having a great influence over his enemies by *teaching them dark sentences!* Was it by giving them such instruction that he overcame Calno and Carchemish and all the others? But these words are perfectly applicable to the King of the North of Dan. 8: a false king, a false priest, a false prophet —the veritable Antichrist who is, like Balaam, in league with the occult. The fullest expression of violence cannot be identified with the fullest expression of corruption—the Assyrian with the King of the North.

13: For he saith, By the strength of my hand have I done it!
'Tis my wisdom hath wrought it, for prudent am I.
'Tis I who've removed the bounds of the nations,
'Tis I who have plundered their stores at my will.
Yea, as a bull,* thrown down all their rulers.

14: As one might discover the nest of a bird,
My hand hath discovered the wealth of the nations,
And as he might sweep up the eggs thus forsaken,
So have I swept the wealth of the world,
Nor dared they move wing, or peck me, or chirp.

15: Shall the axe vaunt 'gainst him that hews with it?
Shall the saw make, 'gainst its wielder, a boast?
As though a mere rod should swing its uplifter!
Or a staff should lift up what is not wood!

Jehovah's judgment on His earthly people is not unlimited, it has its end: He "hath not cast away His people whom He foreknew" (Rom. 11: 2), and His mercies shall return to them. Here we have that return. Jerusalem shall "receive of the Lord's Hand" the full measure of her guilt, but she shall not be given over unto death (Ps. 118: 18). Just as it seems to be all over with her forever, her Lord shall interpose, the days of unparalleled tribulation be stopped, and as He looks at the instrument that He has been using for her chastening, He alters the direction of the strokes of His rod, and the fruit of the pride (*i.e.*, what the proud heart of the Assyrian produces) becomes the object of the blows. For thus that heart speaks: "I, even I have done it! My wisdom has swept the earth, and none has had a word to say, even as to their own dwelling. I have shuffled the nations as I chose: if they had anything of value, I made it mine. There is no one to whom I give account, and no one can any more withstand me than a little bird can defend its nest from the depredating schoolboy— it dare neither strike with wing, nor beak, nor even protest with one feeble chirp."

Then Jehovah in verse 15 answers in keen irony: "Here is an axe, boasting that *it* has cut down the tree, not the man who

---

*The Hebrew word *"abbir"* may mean either "a valiant one," as Judges 5: 22, or "bull," as Ps. 50: 13. As the speaker is the Assyrian, and as the emblem of Assyrian royalty was the bull, I have adopted the latter, although probably it is one of Isaiah's puns.

wields it! Here is a saw boasting that it has done the work by
its own clever swinging to and fro! One would suppose to listen
to this boaster that it is the rod that swings the man, not the
reverse; or that it is the wooden staff that lifts up something that
is *not* wood." A staff of wood surely needs something that is not
mere wood to move it, so if a staff *does* move, it is evidence of
something "not wood," far higher than wood, behind it. So if
this boastful Assyrian ever moves, and is of any effect, it is evidence of a power as much higher than himself behind him as a
man is higher than wood.

Third section: the doom of the Assyrian.

16:   Therefore Adonai Jehovah Tzebaoth
      Will send on his fat ones a wasting disease;
      Under his glory He'll kindle a burning,
      A burning as burneth a firebrand of fire.*
17:   So the Light of Isràel becometh a fire,
      So Israel's Holy One turns to a flame,
      And it burneth, yea, it burneth and devoureth
      Assyria's briers, Assyria's thorns,
          In a day!
18:   The glory of forest—the fruit of his garden,
      Shall all be destroyed, e'en body and soul;†
      So shall they be as a sick man that fainteth:
19:   Till the trees that remain in his forest are few,
      So few that a small child could count them.

Here is the final doom of the Assyrian; his host melts away.
He, with his host, are like a stately forest of beautiful trees, but
really he is but "thorns and briers" which Adonai (the supreme
Lord of all) Jehovah (that supremacy linked with Israel) Tzebaoth (for whom He takes up arms), the very Light of His beloved Israel, like that cloud that covered His people in the Red
Sea, becomes of quite opposite character toward their enemies—

---

*I have tried to give a correspondence to "Isaiah's masterly
painting in tones. The whole passage is so expressed that we
can hear the crackling, and sputtering and hissing of the fire, as
it seizes upon everything within its reach" (*Delitzsch*). The
Hebrew reads: *"v'tachat, k'bohdu yehqad yeqoad keqohd"*—note
the crackling sounds in the last three words.

†*Lit.* "both soul and flesh," utterly.

a very flame that consumes them utterly.  Thus the Assyrian becomes as a dying man that faints till the watchers think the end
has come.  But not quite, for still a few "trees" are left in his
"forest," that is, the men of his army, but so few that a little
child, whose powers of enumeration are limited, could number
them.

Was this fulfilled when the army of Sennacherib lost 185,000
men in a single night?  How is it then that even to this very day,
we see the Jew, far from being delivered from his Lord's wrath,
scattered all over the earth, and for whom that earth, purchased
at the price of Blood of infinite value, is but an "Aceldama," for
their national burial?  For our scripture distinctly tells us that
this final judgment on the mighty world-power shall be when the
"Lord hath performed His whole work on Mount Zion and
Jerusalem."  Who can possibly deny that that is, even to this
very day, still in the future, although it is indeed approaching
nearer and ever nearer, till, as I write, Christians are once more
awakened to a serious hope of *themselves* being alive and remaining alive till He come for them, end His heavenly work, and re-
commence that for the earth.

But now the comforting gospel continues to be preached to
the remnant of faith, standing for "all Israel" that "shall be
saved" (Rom. 11: 26) amid the apostate mass of the Jews:

20: Then, in that day, shall Israel's remnant,
    And those who of Jacob's house have escaped,
    Will never again put trust in their smiter,
    But (in deed and) in truth shall lean on their Lord,
        Who is, of Isràel, ever the Holy.
21: The remnant returns!—the remnant of Jacob—
    To God, the most Mighty One, shall it return!
22: For Israel's people though they're exceeding
    In numbers the sand lying by the sea-shore,
    Yet but a remnant alone shall return to Me;
    For the consumption decreed, and far back determined,
    In righteousness flows to the end.
23: Yea, for Jehovah Adonai Tzebaoth
    Long hath decreed a finishing stroke
    To be inflicted on all of the land.

In that very day, not a day of twenty-four hours, but the
time of which it is said: "Alas, for that day is great" (Jer. 30: 7),

the last three and one-half years of Daniel's seventy weeks, in that day, God shall eventually interpose in judgment on the Assyrian. Then the remnant of Israel, those who have not perished in terrible persecutions, shall change their confidence completely. The king of Assyria in whom Ahaz trusted, carried the ten tribes into captivity, over-ran Judea, besieged Jerusalem, and thus provided pictures of the day still future, in which, in the first half of that last week of Daniel's prophecy the whole of the returned nation puts its trust in the "Prince," the Emperor of the World-empire, with whom they make an alliance for seven years (Daniel 9: 27). The protection of this "Prince" with all the military resources of the world at his back, naturally gives them a perfect sense of security, under which sacrifice and offering are renewed. But in the midst of the week, the scene suddenly changes. The New Testament gives us the great cause of the change. Satan, who even up to that time has had full access to heaven, is cast out to the earth; then he causes all recognition of the true God to be stopped, and in the place of the morning and evening sacrifice, an image of the "Prince" is set up, "standing where it ought not" (Mark 13: 14). That changes everything. A Jewish remnant, hitherto not distinguished in any way from the mass of the nation, is forced into prominence by the fires of persecution, and that feeble remnant is henceforth in Jehovah's eyes *The Nation*. On whom, then, can this remnant lean? On the Holy One of Israel, Jehovah, and that with no feigned piety, no Pharisaic pretension, but in such sincere self-judgment, such genuine penitence, as shall in very truth tell of a divine work of grace in that hitherto cast-away Israel.

We must ever remember that Isaiah's children, as seen in chapter 8, were for signs, their names telling a story of mingled sorrow and joy. Shear-Jashub's name spoke of the apostasy of the mass of the people, since it makes mention of but a "remnant of them that shall return." But it also foretells the conversion of that remnant in their discovery in that day of the "Son given" in Jesus, and in Him, "the Mighty God." Thus shall they return to the Mighty God, discerning God in Christ, and own the true divinity of their Messiah. This is very refreshing.

For even though the children of Israel were as numerous as

the seaside sands, a remnant only shall be saved, as our Apostle Paul quotes in Romans 9: 27. That remnant is the result of the intervention of God in electing grace—it is *His* work. As regards the mass, Jehovah has decreed such a consumption as shall flow on in righteousness, like a tidal wave; carrying righteousness, as it were, upon its crest, the very judgments teaching righteousness to the inhabitants of the earth.

The last words of verse 22 are further emphasized in the next verse. Such a destruction has been surely determined by the Lord God of Hosts as shall embrace the whole land of Palestine in the first place, and then the whole prophetic earth. But our own apostle, Paul, quotes this, not from the Hebrew text, but from the Septuagint, which reads: "He will finish the work and cut it short in righteousness, because a short work will the Lord make in all the world." Here there is no question as to the sphere of the "short work in righteousness." It is the whole world, a word being used that makes it apply to the Roman Empire. Here a work is being done that God brings to a sudden stop by "righteousness." We shall come across this again in chapter 65 and will reserve comment.

For at this crisis those days are cut short by the appearing of the Lord Jesus in great power and glory. But what power does the Lord find when He cuts His work short? The literal "Assyrian?" Not at all, but "the Beast from the sea," in whom we recognize the "Prince" of Dan. 9: 26, the emperor of the then-revived Roman Empire, who has a "False Prophet" for his coadjutor.

24: Thus saith Adonai Jehovah Tzebaoth,
    Fear not, O My people now dwelling in Zion,
    Fear not the Assyrian though he may smite,
    Swinging his rod as once did (proud) Egypt.
25: For yet but a little, a little indeed,
    And My indignation shall come to its end—
    My wrath shall be finished, in their destruction.
26: For Jehovah Tzebaoth swings the whip over him,
    As once He smote Midian at the rock of the raven.*
    His staff He outstretches over the sea,
    Lifting it up as aforetime in Egypt.

---

*Oreb* meaning "raven."

27: Then shall his burden fall from thy shoulder,
   Then shall his yoke pass off from thy neck,
   Smashed shall the yoke be by the anointing.

With tenderness Jehovah speaks to the afflicted and almost exterminated remnant! The very mention of their being in Zion, that stronghold of Jerusalem, is full of promise, for Hebrews 12: 22 has made us acquainted with the deep, spiritual significance of that Mount, as in contrast with the Mount of law, Sinai. So the very fact of His saying, "Fear not, O My people, dwelling in Zion," is full of comfort. Let Asshur smite, let him treat you as did Egypt your fathers in the days of old, the same Jehovah is over you now as then. Fear not, for He will surely interpose for your relief. We, too are dwelling in the grace of Zion (Romans 5: 2). It is the place for joy, as Rev. 14: 1 proves.

Yes, in a very little while, His indignation with the Jews shall come to its end in the destruction of the one He has been using for their chastening. How perfect is the harmony of the prophetic Word. Daniel writes the words of Gabriel: "He shall make desolate, even until the consummation, and that determined, be poured upon the desolate" (chap. 9: 27), that is, there is a limit to this decreed outpouring. So again in chap. 11: 36. The wilful king, the true Antichrist heading the apostate mass of Jews, shall prosper "till the indignation be accomplished, for that that is determined shall be done." With one accordant voice all prophecy assures us that a long period of distress has been decreed for the Jew, but has an end; that end comes with the destruction of their persecutor, or persecutors. In this chapter, he is the "Assyrian;" in Daniel 11 he is "the king who does according to his will;" nor are these the same personages at all, but represent, respectively, the Beasts from the sea and land, united in opposition to the remnant. Proofs will be found in later references to these personages.

In verses 28 to 34 we have the path of a conqueror told out grandly. As Delitzsch writes: "Aesthetically considered, the description is one of the grandest, most magnificent, that human poetry has ever produced." But strictly speaking, it has never been fulfilled; nor is it necessary, for its purpose, that it ever *should* be, in these graphic details. Let us turn back to the mo-

ment when it was given.   Assyria threatens invasion, and the
Spirit of God would bring that danger graphically home to His
people.   How can that be better done than by an ideal description
of a conqueror's march *from* that quarter whence the Assyrian
would naturally come?   It is not intended to give such minute
details of future history as are here—that would be quite beside
the mark.   The one purpose, as in all pictorial parabolic teaching,
is to bring home one main point; and here it is the defeat of
Israel's enemy at the summit of his success.   Had it been the
divine intent to foretell the details, then the prophecy would
either have fitted only *one* event, had but one fulfilment, or every
detail would have to be repeated again and again, even to the
cries.   But in this ideal way, the prophecy may find a near fulfilment in Sennacherib, but a far-off, final one even still in the
future; for admittedly Jehovah's anger did not forever and finally
turn away from the nation of the Jews at the destruction of
Sennacherib.

Being well assured that this prophet of fire would never give
a cool, tame description of this rush of the Assyrian on his victim,
I have made the following attempt to reproduce the vivid lines—
the terrified shouts—of the original:

28: To Aiath he's come!   Through Migron he passes!
      Leaves baggage behind him at Michmash!
29: They're through the Pass!
      They're pitching their tents at Geba!
      Ramah is quivering!   Gibeah of Saul flees!
30: Scream! Scream! O daughter of Gallim!
      O hark, Laishah!
      O—poor Anathoth!
31: Madmenah's in flight!
      The dwellers in Gebim do gather their goods!
32: He halts for the day at Nob:
      Shakes fist at the mount of the daughter of Zion;
      The hill of Jerusalem!
33: But look!   See! Adonai Jehovah Tzebaoth
      Lops off the boughs with a terrible force:
      Cuts down the high ones!
      Humbles the lofty!
34: Fells He the shrubs of the forest with iron!
      And Lebanon falls by One mighty indeed!

The invader first puts his foot on Judah's land at Aiath, and was then about fifteen miles north of Jersualem, from which he was separated by a range of high hills.  But these prove no obstacle, for soon we hear the cry of terror: "He's through the pass!"—that pass that saw the victory of Jonathan and his armour-bearer (1 Sam. 14), two men defeating the entire army of the Philistines, and which surely might have been held indefinitely by a determined band of men. The loss of the Pass is noted with a cry of despair, and the towns that lie at the conqueror's mercy have the sympathy of the speaker.  We last see him standing on one of the hills north of Jerusalem, looking at the beautiful city and shaking his fist at it.  But he has to do with One who is not as the deities of Calno and Carchemish, and woe to any who defy *Him!*  All the lofty coronals go; branches fall; down crash the lofty trunks, the whole forest is levelled, and the enemy, so like to Lebanon in his pride, falls by One who is majestic indeed, and there is no need to specify further who that must be.

# CHAPTER ELEVEN

I N what we have just considered, we have seen the Imperial
World-power, here termed the Assyrian, in its pride and
doom (chap. 10: 5-19). Then an assumed picture of the
last attack of that World-power on Jerusalem (vers. 20-34),
which brings us to the third step, the resurrection or revival of
this nation in, and as identified with, their divine Messiah.

The chapter opens thus:

1: From Jesse's (live) stem there shall come forth a rod,
   From his roots a Branch shall there spring forth.
2: On Him then Jehovah's own Spirit shall rest,
   Of wisdom and clearest discernment:
   The spirit of counsel and limitless might,
   Of knowledge and fear of Jehovah.

Thus in contrast with the forest, to which the Assyrian in all
his pride was likened in our last chapter, poor Israel's broken
stump (and we must note the figure continued from chap. 6: 13)
now gives evidence of renewed vitality. Jesse's root is not dead.
A living Sprout appears, a fruit-bearing Branch springs from it.
But not from *David*, mark, but from *Jesse*, which tells us that
"the royal family has sunk down to the insignificance from which
it sprang." No royal throne does it enjoy, any more than when
Jesse, not David, was its representative. How feeble at first this
lovely Sprout appears to be, as Delitzsch again well says, "In the
historical fulfilment even the ring of the words of the prophecy
is noted: the *nehtzer* (Branch) at first so humble, was a poor
*Nazarene*" (Matt. 2: 23).

But we must still consider that living Branch, for upon Him
the Spirit of Jehovah shall find His only fitting resting-place,
which He, as Noah's dove, amid the waters of death, has sought
in vain amid the sons of men. Like the Lampstand in the Tabernacle, with its one central shaft and three pairs of branches, so
the Spirit upon Him, as the central shaft, shall give Him a dual

threefold qualification for perfection of government, which may it be our joy, by that same Spirit, to note:

1: The Spirit of wisdom and discernment.
2: The Spirit of counsel and might.
3: The Spirit of knowledge and fear of Jehovah.

The first pair may correspond with the lowest branch in the Lampstand, and tell of His *personal* qualifications, what He had, and shall ever have *in Himself*, irrespective of anything to draw them out.

The second pair correspond to the intermediate branches, and speak of His perfections *in relation to His people*, amid whom He takes His place.

The third, or uppermost, pair speaks as we should expect, of His relation Godward. The three being *Selfward, Manward, Godward,* as we may say.

1: "Wisdom and Discernment." Latent these ever lay in Him, only awaiting the occasion to evidence themselves. He ever was, and ever shall be the very personification of Wisdom. All who come before Him are instantly "discerned;" every hidden thought understood afar off; no word of the tongue but that He knows it altogether (Ps. 139: 1-4). He is the "Discerner of the thoughts and intents of the heart" (Heb. 4: 12). Let *Him* be the absolute Monarch, and who would not rejoice in the unlimited sway of One who could never err?

2: But we only learn of these qualities as they are called out, and so we next have "Counsel," that is the ability to advise, with unerring intelligence, in every situation, no matter how perplexing it may be. He is indeed, too, a very Boaz, for "in Him is strength." In His hands *autocratic* rule, so bitterly repudiated just now, would be perfection.

3: "Knowledge and fear of Jehovah." The connection of the two words shows what is meant by "knowledge." It is the capacity of the spirit for discerning God, and man's proper relation to Him. Thus it is linked here with that "fear of Jehovah" in which He, as perfect Man, abounded, never taking one step that was not ordered by God's Word. But this is very wonderful as coming as the *topstone,* the *climax,* the *acme* of the qualifications of "The Branch" for rule. Even on the throne of all the earth, the highest qualification will be "the fear of Jehovah!" One need hardly point out how directly this contravenes all the current thought of the day. The only "fear" that rulers have who owe all their authority to "the people," is *of* the people. Their fear is of those *beneath* them, on whose suffrages the continuance of their power depends; not of God above, who no longer exists for all these practical matters. The Holy Scriptures make it only too clear, that the world, rejoicing in the triumph of democracy, will shortly lament that triumph.

But these qualifications for rule of "The Branch" that we have looked at, do not answer the question as to His *benevolence.* He has all *wisdom,* all *power,* every quality of the Head and Hand; but how as to the Heart?—that is of all-importance. How will He use these powers?

The answer to this is included in the last, the topstone, of Spirit-qualifications—the fear of Jehovah—which is repeated, thus linking the verses together:

3: Fragrant* to Him is the fear of Jehovah;
   Nor doth He judge by what His eyes see,
   Nor doth He blame by what His ears hear;
4: But righteously judges the poor of His people,
   And justly rebukes for the poor of the earth:
   Smiting the earth with the rod of His mouth,
   Slaying the wicked one with His lip's breath.

This fear of Jehovah is very wonderful in its effect, it results in His looking at everything in the light of Jehovah's will. Not deceived will He ever be, in the future, as He never was in the past, by any mere external show (what His eyes see), however plausible it may appear to be, whether in the kiss of a false disciple, or (what His ears hear) in the superficially kindly words of a *true* one (Matt. 16: 23); but with a justice that is absolute, earth's government will be administered. When He thus comes in

---

*While there is doubt as to the exact bearing of the word, it undoubtedly has in it the sense of smelling with delight. See its use in Gen. 8: 21, etc.

great power, He finds His poor people, the Jewish remnant, at the point of extermination from "all the nations." He discerns the issues involved, delivers the poor, by smiting "the earth" in its ruler, whom we know as the "Beast from the sea," and, with one breath, destroying the other hostile chief, the "Wicked One."

But who is this individual here called the "Wicked One?" Can there be amid all the revolted race, not one of which has not sinned, one whom that title can distinguish as pre-eminently "the Wicked One?"

The apostle Paul quotes this very scripture in 2 Thess. 2: 8: "And then shall that Wicked One be revealed;" and this is enough to identify this "Wicked One" with him who, in that same epistle, is called "the Man of Sin, the son of perdition, who opposeth and exalteth himself above all that is called God or is worshipped;" and by *these words*, we discern him as "the king who does according to his will, and who shall exalt himself and magnify himself above every god . . . neither shall he regard the God of his fathers, nor the desire of women"—Christ (Dan. 11: 36, 37). But these last marks assure us that he, the Antichrist, will be a *Jew*, who thus denies the Father and the Son (1 John 2: 22), for never would they be so used of a Gentile. From this, it equally clearly follows that (turning to Rev. 13) we must discern him in the "Beast *from the land*," rather than the more powerful politically "Beast *from the sea*."

We may not, without loss, pass by verse 5, ignoring our own apostle's word to "consider Him" being thus faithful in judging on behalf of the meek of the earth, or that garment that fits Him for that dignity.

5: Girdled is He with strict righteousness,
   With faithfulness are His loins girded.

There is no part of the clothing of greater significance in Scripture than the girdle. The loose flowing robes, as worn by both sexes in the East, so interfered with movement, that whilst they gave dignity in repose they greatly impeded any form of activity, and for that needed to be gathered up, and firmly held by a girdle about the loins. Thus not only was the clothing kept in its place, but the girdle communicated its support to the person. In every case, when we are told of our Lord Jesus being girt, both the material of which that girdle was made, and the exact place that it had on the body, are filled with truth for our profit.

Three scenes will be sufficient for us to consider. First, look at Him on the same night in which He was betrayed, and see how "He takes a towel and girds Himself" (John 13: 4). By the lowliest of ministries He tells us there of a love that has no cessation in its activity as long as its objects have need of it. Thus does He make us know His present infinitely gracious service; and I suppose that only in eternity shall we fully learn how much we owe to it.

What a different picture Rev. 1: 14 gives us, and necessarily what a vast corresponding difference there is in the truth we are to derive from it. No longer are the robes gathered up, but flow to the feet! No longer are loins girt, but the breasts! No longer is there a linen towel, but a girdle of gold! It is no longer the activity of service, but the dignity of judging in the midst of the churches that is in view. But what might possibly impede that judgment? One sentiment—*the depth of His love!* So those affections which are symbolized by the breasts must be kept strictly within the limits of the glory of God, figured by the golden girdle.

Turning back to our prophet, we see that the Lord's loins are girt, for He is entering upon His government of the earth, and, *"He that ruleth* must rule *with diligence"* (Rom. 12: 8); the "girdle" that here communicates its strength is that vertebrate quality of government, *"righteousness,"* as dealing with the remnant's oppressors, and *"faithfulness,"* as fulfilling the promises made to that faithful remnant itself.

The long-hoped-for return of the Lord has at that time been fulfilled, and one of its blessed consequences is the restoration of the harmony that was in Eden, in that kingdom of which our father Adam was monarch. The Last Adam comes, and naturally the results of the sin of the first are nullified; the chain now being closely attached, by an irrefragable link, to God, all the other inferior links are re-established and,

> 6: Wolf with the lamb is now dwelling,
>     The leopard with kid is reposing,
>     The calf and the lion and fatling together—
>     Little the lad that doth lead them.

7: The cow with the bear finds its pasture,
   Their young ones are couching together,
   The lion on grass feeds as ox doth;
8: The infant now plays on the hole of the asp,
   The weanèd puts hand on the den of the viper,
   For nothing shall hurt nor destroy
   In all of My mountain—the holy.
9: For full of Jah's knowledge shall the land be,
   E'en as the waters cover the sea.

Verily a lovely picture! It is the creature now delivered from that bondage of corruption into which its ruler's sin brought it (Rom. 8: 21). But we are plainly told that this can only be when "the sons of God" are manifested; so that our prophet is telling us of the conditions on the earth, as our New Testament tells us of "the glory that shall be revealed in *us*." Thus we have our part in this lovely scene, and shall have our unselfish joy in seeing the peaceful happiness of the regenerated earth. No bloodshed shall then be needed by those creatures that are no longer carnivorous, but have returned to their original food (Gen. 1: 30), the green herb. As our poet Cowper sings,

> "No foe to man
> Lurks in the serpent now; the mother sees,
> And smiles to see, her infant's playful hand
> Stretched forth to dally with the crested worm,
> To stroke his azure neck, or to receive
> The lambent homage of his arrowy tongue.
> All creatures worship man, and all mankind
> One Lord, one Father."

It may possibly be questioned whether this perfect unbroken and everlasting joy, based on the knowledge of the Lord covering it, as the waters the sea, shall then obtain over all the *earth*. I have hesitated as to the rendering of the word that stands for both "land" and "earth," for if we let the light of Rev. 20: 8, 9 fall on our scripture, it would appear quite sure that there will, even at the end of the millennial reign, be an innumerable multitude in the four quarters of the *earth* who can have no true knowledge of the Lord at all; whilst, at its beginning, we gather that some shall yield only "feigned obedience," not consistent with knowing Him truly (Ps. 18: 44), so that a more correct rendering of the word *"eratz"* in verse 9, would be "land," confining this everlasting perfection to that one "pleasant land" of Israel, and the people that shall there and then be "all righteous."

> 10: Then shall there be of Jesse a Root,
>     Raised as a standard the nations to gather;
>     To it shall the Gentiles of all the earth seek,
>     And the place of His rest shall be glory.

If so, this would naturally lead to the question: Shall the *Gentiles* then have *no* share in that joy? The 10th verse answers this, for He who is "Jesse's Root," as well as Jesse's Branch, shall be manifested in such resplendent majesty as to be a "banner" that shall rally about itself all the saved Gentiles, as our own prophetic book clearly testifies. "And the city had no need of the sun, neither of the moon to shine in it; for the glory of God did lighten it, and the Lamb is the light thereof, and *the saved nations (i.e.,* Gentiles) *shall walk in the light of it, and the kings of the earth shall bring their glory and honor into it"* (Rev. 21: 23, 24). The whole earth then shares in the joy of Him who is there both Root and Offspring of David.

This scripture speaks, it is true, of the *"heavenly Jerusalem,"* but since it is lighted by the "glory" of God, that, too, is a city wherein He finds His rest, and it is *His* being there that makes it so infinitely attractive to the nations that have been saved through the time of great tribulation, and are still upon the millennial earth in that day. Nor should we fail to admire the harmony between the two prophets of the two Testaments: "God and the Lamb" are in the heavenly, while of that Jerusalem that shall then be on earth, it is said: "His rest shall be glory," that is He, Messiah of Israel, shall rest and only rest when and where God in all the infinite excellencies of His wisdom, power, love and grace—all included in the one word "glory"—are fully displayed. But thus, if I err not, the two Jerusalems shall be unified by this identity of "Glory," or by His presence, and be really *one.* We do not see the heavenly *city* at all in the Old Testament, for this has to do only with the earth, but in the New, the one city, with its "wall," includes both. "Jerusalem above" being the *"City"* itself, "having the glory of God," while Jerusalem on the earth forms, in the intensely symbolic language of the Apocalypse, the "Wall" of this heavenly city, so-called since separating it from, yet connecting it, by its twelve gates (representing the twelve tribes of Israel) with the saved nations of that millennial earth (Rev. 21: 12-14). Here then in that "glory" shall He find His resting-place, as indeed Ps. 132 teaches us.

11: Once again shall Jehovah recover His remnant,
From Egypt, Assyria, from Pathros and Cush,
From Elam, from Shinar, from Hamath and Islands
That afar off are laved by the sea.
12: A banner Jehovah shall raise for the nations,
And this shall Isr'el's outcasts draw home;
The scattered of Judah 'twill gather together
From the remotest four corners of earth.
13: Ephraim's envy shall then be no more,
The foemen of Judah shall all be cut off;
Ephra'm shall not be jealous of Judah,
Nor shall Judah e'er vex Ephraìm.

Verse 11 tells us, "in that day," *after* (mark carefully) the Lord is thus revealed in glory, shall Jehovah be active "a second time"* in gathering His people from every country to which they have been scattered. But this suggests two questions: (1) When did He gather them the *first* time? (2) Is this second gathering final, or will there be a third?

There can be but one answer to the first question. It was Jehovah's hand alone that recovered His people from Egypt the first time. With "a high hand" He brought them out, and this first deliverance is made a kind of pattern for the second future one when His *hand* shall again be active, only this second time it shall not be only from Egypt but from every country of the earth.

But then it follows that this second recovery of Israel will be as much the direct work of Jehovah as the first from Egypt. He alone, actively, will or can truly restore that "second time."

Suppose, then, that the Zionist movement results in the return of a large number of Jews to Palestine, eventually forming there an autonomous State. Would that fulfil, as seems to be the

---

*This is the more literal.

general idea, this scripture: "I will restore a second time?" Most assuredly not, for in the first place, in our prophecy Jehovah is gathering them to everlasting blessing; in the next, the second and true restoration takes place *after* the revelation of the Lord and not *before*. These two considerations taken together forbid absolutely the Zionist movement being a fulfilment of this, or any similar prophecies.

It is indeed true that all prophecy unites in telling us that the same nation must be in the same land as was there at the rejection and crucifixion of the Lord; its people, then, must return to that land, *in order that prophetic Scriptures may then begin to be fulfilled,* nor till they are there can any direct fulfilment begin. But Jehovah is not now active in gathering, although permitting it in a providential way, and they are now returning in the same unbelief in which they left it; and far from going back to never-ending blessedness, it will be, alas, to that time of unparalleled suffering called "the great tribulation."

The events that take place subsequent to that return, as told in Daniel 9: 27, 28, the present heavenly witness, the Church, will not see; for before the work of God with His earthly people is thus renewed, the gathering out a people of a "heavenly calling" will have ceased (Acts 15: 14-17).

So, in accord with all this, we conclude that verses 11 and 12 speak of the *final* gathering of both the two tribes (here called Judah), and of the ten (called Israel), and is not to be followed by a third. Here the rallying Center, the Ensign to which all shall joyfully flock, is God's beloved Son, Israel's true Messiah, our Saviour, Jesus Christ the Lord. Nor need we forget that the same blessed One is, this very day, the one rallying Center—the Ensign—for His scattered flock.

But further as to Israel's internal condition: the antagonism begun in the day of Rehoboam and continued ever since, between the ten and the two tribes, shall be annulled forever. Whether the lost ten tribes shall be restored at the same time as the two, may be a matter of question. They were not, as separate tribes, in the land at the time of the great tragedy of Calvary; they were not then, as distinct tribes, involved in that awful guilt directly, and therefore it is *possible* they will not be involved in the retribution of the great tribulation, and will be gathered separately and later than the remnant of the two.  But it must also be remembered that we are now listening to a prophecy that tells us, not of the Zionist movement, but of something that shall occur long after that.  It is the sweeping of all the earth by Jehovah Himself, so that *every one* of His earthly people shall be restored.

Shall they renew then, in that resurrection of the nation, the antipathies of the past?  Shall Ephraim envy Judah its surpassing privileges of temple and priesthood?  Shall Judah again vex and distress the less privileged Ephraim?  Nay, for at that time Ps. 133 shall be fulfilled, in that brotherly love so indicative of the Lord's gracious work of gathering together His people; as their scattering into sects, denominations, parties, and exclusive circles of various kinds is equally indicative of the activity of their common enemy, Satan, quite irrespective of the dispensation in which that scattering may occur.  I fear we may but too safely, if sadly, say that it will not be till the *literal* personal resurrection—as here of the national—that the whole universe shall be able to see in the divinely formed unity of the Church, that work of God.  At present, it is in fragments, as far as sight goes, and its testimony to the unity of all believers—ah, where is it?

Verse 14 returns to what, to our Christian ears, sounds like an intrusion, since it introduces a warlike element, so foreign to the spirit that should govern Christians today; but we must remember that the writer speaks not of *our* day, but the day of the Lord, and the government of the earth is in view.  So these prophecies as to Israel and the earth always close with the same martial note as here.  They deal with a time in which political dominance shall speak of Jehovah's favor, nor will the time of peace come until it is preceded by the time of triumph.  So we may paraphrase the verse thus:

> 14:  They fly on the shoulders* of Philistines westward;
>       Together they plunder the sons of the east:
>       They lay a strong hand on Edom and Moab;
>       And the children of Ammon are forced to obey.

---

*"*Catheph*: 'Shoulder,' was the peculiar name of the coast-land of Philistia which sloped off towards the sea" (*Delitzsch*).

Thus after striking victoriously east and west, three peoples are given as examples of willing submission: Edom, Moab, and the children of Ammon. Here I come to where all my readers may not follow. In the almost universal cry for the most elementary truths, the deeper things of God find little acceptance, and are apt to be slurred as being the result of "straining," or as fantastic. But there are still some who believe that the Bible, being the Word of God, must have depths of truth, not on the surface, but which are the portion given to patient industry and searching. These three peoples are illustrative of that. For note how strangely under divine protection Edom, Moab and the children of Ammon always appear to be. Why is that? When Israel, with pilgrimage nearly ended, approached their land, most strictly are they charged not to make any attack on Edom, Moab, or the children of Ammon (Deut. 2: 5, 9, 19). Then again, in the last prophecy in Daniel we read: "But these shall escape out of his hand, Edom, and Moab, and the chief of the children of Ammon" (Dan. 11: 41); nor is it necessary to discuss whose "hand" is here referred to, the one point is the Shield over this trio of peoples.

A few years more pass, and this 14th verse of our prophet finds its accomplishment, and again Edom, Moab and the children of Ammon are seen as submitting to restored Israel. Can any reasonable person who believes that the Spirit of God is the real Author of the book, put these repetitions on one side as meaningless?

One of the basic principles of interpretation of prophecy is this: What shall be true in Israel as a nation, identified with Christ, is true of every individual Christian in this day. That same principle of grace under which *Israel* can alone come into blessing is equally the principle under which any *individual* in this day can come into blessing. As an illustration of my meaning, take the apostle's use in Gal. 4: 27 of the 54th chapter of our prophet. Isaiah is clearly addressing Jerusalem on *earth*, for it cannot possibly be the Church, either as seen in its external profession, or as the true living Body of Christ, for the former is never restored, but "spewed out of His mouth," and the latter is never forsaken. But both the earthly and the heavenly Jerusalem are unified in this: *they are both brought into divine favor on the same principle of grace,* Israel as a nation in the millennial day, and every individual child of God today. The work of God will be with nations then as with individuals now.

Let us look then on Edom, Moab, and the children of Ammon in the light this has given us: the divine care over this trinity of peoples with their final submission to Christ, must speak of a corresponding care and the submission of a corresponding trinity now. If so, it can only be one of those inimitable finger-prints of God by which the Bible is distinguished from any other book in the world. The very composition of man's being will give us that correspondence, for that, too, is as Edom, Moab and Beni-Ammon, a trinity in body, soul and spirit.

But that is not sufficiently proved unless we can get details that shall show correspondences in the respective parts. Let us see.

Take the first, "Edom:" it is a word that, both in its derivation and significance, is identical with "Adam," both meaning "red" from the "adamah," or ground, whence Adam and all his race have been taken. But that source can only apply to the one part of man's being that was "of the earth, made of dust" (1 Cor. 15: 47), that is, the *body.* In that trinity of nations then, Edom represents the "body" in the trinity of man's being, nor can there be any strain charged in this.

But how inevitable is the next question: Is the body of the child of God today to be brought into the same subjection to Christ as the nation of Edom will be in the day approaching? That very question finds its definite answer in the words of our apostle, "I keep *under* my body, and bring it into *subjection*" (1 Cor. 9: 27). Further, it is our "bodies" that, belonging to our Lord, it is our intelligent service to offer as a living sacrifice, so placed submissively at His service (Rom. 12: 1). Of that submission Edom is the divinely given type.

But this leaves Moab and Ammon to be paralleled by soul and spirit: and no one can deny that there is at least *this* correspondence, that as Moab and Ammon were very closely related by the same fatherhood, so the human soul and the human spirit are in the same way both the *offspring* of the one "breath" of

God (Gen. 2: 7). Moab and Ammon were half-brothers, having the same father, and so have the *spirit* and *soul* of man, for so only was the apostle justified in quoting the heathen poet in the words: "For we also are His offspring" (Acts 17: 28). So closely is spirit related to soul that many confuse and confound them. The dividing Word alone can distinguish them, apportioning to each (Heb. 4: 12), as He did to Moab and Ammon, the allotted sphere and possession, so that we who have that Word know the discriminated qualities of these two immaterial parts of our being.

Thus, everything that we read of Moab leads us to conclude that, in her ease-filled plains, and the sensuous and sensual attractions whereby the pilgrims were induced to cease their pilgrimage, we get a clear correspondence with the sensuous (which has become in fallen man *sensual*) part of man's being. For by Scripture we are taught that the "soul" is the seat of human emotions and affections. In us naturally these are not subject to Christ, but in the new creation, they are. Thus Moab stands for the *soul* of man.

This leaves "the children of Ammon" to correspond with the higher reasoning faculty, having its seat in the human *spirit,* nor is there lacking much to make this correspondence perfectly assured, for the chief city of Heshbon, which was within the borders of the Ammonites (although they had no real title to it) has the clear, sure meaning of *"Reason,"* that divinely communicated faculty which in the strictest sense is confined to the *spirit* of man. In one word, "the children of Ammon," opponents of faith as they were, faithfully represented that *debased* and *fallen* "reason" that we term today Modernism, or that is self-termed, Rationalism.

From all this, we gather this practical truth that, as God Intends His beloved Son, Jesus, to reign during the millennial day over a submissive Edom, Moab and children of Ammon so, *this* day, every part of our tripartite being, body, soul and spirit, is to be brought into willing captivity to that same Lord. The correspondence is too perfect to be slurred as strained.

Verses 15 and 16 are to give their light and comfort to Israel, and they read:

15: Jehovah pronounces His ban on the sea-tongue,
    Even the tongue of Mizraim's sea.
    Over the river His hand He is swinging,
    Puffs with His glowing breath—lo, it is smitten,
    Divided to streamlets: so shallow the seven,
    That for His people they now form a shoepath.
16: Thus shall a highway be there for His people,
    (The remnant of Isr'el that shall be left)
    Out of Assyria, as once at the first time,
    When from the land of Mizràim he came.

The Israel that shall read this, will understand the figure of both sea and river again drying up as in the past. It would convey absolute truth to their minds, altogether apart from a literal repetition of those miracles. There shall be obstacles to the return, corresponding to the Red "sea" (as between Egypt and Arabia, called the "sea-tongue") and the "river" Jordan. His ban shall be on the one, the "sea"—that is, on what shall represent the sea of Egypt in that final deliverance, possibly the nations that otherwise would have retained His people. They shall interpose no obstacle, but, so thoroughly shall their opposition be destroyed, that they shall rather *further* that return. Over that other obstacle, the river—Euphrates, which is always meant when nothing is added—He swings His hand as if to smite it, at the same time a puff of His glowing breath, so graphically speaking of His wrath, divides it into seven easily fordable brooklets—in a word, there shall be nothing to impede their return.

It is impossible that the mind should not turn to Revelation 16, where again we have the Euphrates "dried up, that the way of the kings of the rising of the sun might be prepared;" and this drying up is by the pouring out of the last of those vials, in which is filled up the wrath of God. In the Old Testament, the hot breath of His wrath dries up the river; in the New, the vial of His wrath. Surely there is a strong similarity, even though the two scriptures may not refer to the same moment; for in Revelation the Lord's manifestation in glory *follows*—in Isaiah *precedes* this drying up. In neither would there appear to be any necessity for a *literal* accomplishment of these prophecies to be looked for, certainly not in that book of symbols, Revelation.

There can be no controversy, at least whether we esteem it merely a coincidence, or as evidencing a clear and divinely intended application of the prophecy, that the *Turk* has been the great obstacle to the Jews possessing their land. It is the foot of the *Turk* that has trodden down Jerusalem; it is he who has claimed ownership of the soil of Immanuel's land, and is figured by the river from which he came, just as the other conqueror, Assyria, was so figured of old (chap. 8: 7).

This surely testifies in harmony with the many portents that are passing before us, that the Lord's coming is near, although no one can say how near. Can we greatly err if we accept it as a solemn call to us, individually, to be practically ready by putting away everything inconsistent with seeing His face?

# CHAPTER TWELVE

**Israel's song when Jerusalem's walls become no longer wailing-places, but resound with joyful praise.**

IT will be noted that, in these later chapters, the past deliverance of Israel from Egypt has provided a pattern of the future and final deliverance from every yoke; and as then, as soon as they had crossed the sea, they burst into song, so here again we hear the same outburst of joy. That praise of old soon gave place to the unbelieving groan at the waters of Marah, but *this* song shall never cease, for its cause is everlasting, no "bitter waters" await restored Israel; that nation's trials will be then forever past.

Nor is it without added interest that again that significant number "three" is clearly impressed upon the song as upon all the book. For there are six verses (and we must remember that in Hebrew poetry the division into verses is not for human convenience, but of divine inspiration), unmistakably and intentionally divided into two parts of "three" each, by the words with which each begins, "And in that day." The first part (vers. 1-3) speaks of Israel's own abounding joy; then in the second (vers. 4-6), this joy runs over to all the nations of the earth.

We may well say that is ever both the natural and the divine order. The vessel that is placed beneath the flow of the spring must itself first be filled before the water can run over; but as soon as full, then every drop that falls *in*, inevitably forces a corresponding drop *out*. Israel's vessel is full in verses 1-3, and runs over in 4-6.

We may then interpret the numbers thus: the song, in its two parts, *witnesses* (for 2 is the number of sufficient testimony) that God has indeed manifested Himself, in His government of the earth, in the salvation of His people Israel. The song is a grand chant, and may be paraphrased, while still cleaving closely to the original, thus:

1: In that day shalt thou say: O Lord, I will praise Thee,
   For though Thou wast angry, Thy anger is gone,
   Thy comforts abound to me.

2: Behold, my salvation is God, the most mighty,*
   In Him will I trust, and not be afraid.
   For Jah, e'en Jehovah,† my strength and my song,
   Is now my salvation.
3: Therefore, with rapture shall ye draw water
   From founts‡ of salvation, never exhausted.

4: In that day shall ye say: Praise to Jehovah!
   His glorious Name—proclaim it abroad!
   His doings declare amid all the nations.
   Boast § that His Name be exalted!
5: Harp to Jehovah, for great are His doings;
   Make it be known all over the earth.
6: Shout and be jubilant, dweller in Zion,
   For He who of Isr'el is the One Holy
   Is great in the midst of thee!

The poor scattered nation has never, up to this very day, sung that, or any other song. The great foundation-stones of the temple have only thrown back the echo of its groans. "Wailing-places," they have indeed needed, but not orchestras of joy. It has then either been fulfilled in the joy that follows the present

---

*"El," that is, "the mighty God."

†"Jah" is assumed to be simply an abbreviated form of Jehovah, but when, as here, the two names come together it must have some special significance, and there would appear to be sound reason for Mr. Wm. Kelly's suggestion that as the name "Jehovah" always tells of God *in relation to His people, so Jah expresses His essential Deity,* and when together as here, adds in a human way of speaking, even to infinity.

‡There is much beauty in the Hebrew word rendered "well" in A. V., but much better "fountain." It is from a root meaning "to flow," having in it the idea of constancy. It is a perennial flow, and is the common word for the "eye," since that is the source of a never-ending flow. Alas, this flow now is in tears. But God intervenes with His salvation, and stops that sad flood by wiping away all tears of grief from every eye. The tears are then gone and the flow of the fountain is of joy alone, for the eye can shed tears of joy.

§The word I have rendered "boast" is "to make mention," but in the sense of "taking as a confidence." As in Psalm 71:16, "I will make mention of Thy righteousness, even of Thine only," that is, "I will not even speak of any other righteousness than Thine; this shall be all my confidence and boast." Compare Phil. 3:3.

Gospel of Christ, as in the city of Samaria (Acts 8: 8) or it remains still to be fulfilled. But all the context forbids absolutely that our prophecy should refer primarily, far less solely, to the present time, of which Isaiah, Scripture assures us, knew nothing. It remains to be sung in the future, for "that day" has not yet come, nor can it possibly be sung while the Jew is a wanderer in strange lands.

To this very day Jehovah is unmistakably "angry" with that nation, not now on account of its idolatry, for which it was originally banished to Babylon for 70 years, but far more for the crucifixion by "lawless hands" of His beloved Son, the Messiah, that infinitely heavier sin of those who returned from that captivity, and have again been banished for 1900 years, and are so still: thus may the over-abounding sin be measured. But even that anger has a limit, as chapter 10: 25 has already told us, and it shall be "turned away," for the Blood of that Messiah, which was shed for "that nation" (John 11: 51, 52), and by which it has been "sanctified" (Heb. 13: 12), shall yet speak *for*, not *against*, its afflicted and penitent remnant, which we may feel assured is the "treasure" that that precious Blood has purchased, and which has been so long hid in the field that He has also thus bought (Matt. 13: 44).

I do not see that the song even permits any extended exposition, it is too perfectly simple. The returned, the renewed nation first quenches its own thirst at the fountain of salvation, and then, the waters still flowing in undiminished volume, they long for all the peoples of the earth to share in those never-to-be-exhausted springs of happiness. Thus shall the "receiving of them be life from the dead" for the world (Rom. 11: 15). For now shall this ever-flowing fountain burst forth in missionary effort, as we shall see later. Blessed ministry! Striking it is to see that even our unfaithfulness in leaving, after 2,000 years, so large a proportion of the race ignorant of the Gospel, has been foreseen by the Spirit of God, and turned to His own purposes as thus providing a field for His restored people, Israel, to fill with their more faithful, but not happier service.

Ever blessed beyond all power of expression is it to see the "end of the Lord," whether with one single individual of His afflicted people, as Job (James 5: 11), or with an elect nation as a whole, as here. Always that end is joy. Blessed be God that this is so happily confirmed in that book of Psalms that tell out those ways, through human sighs and tears and songs. But the songs always prevail at the end, and when we come to the last psalms, the sighs have ceased, the tears have been wiped away, and Hallelujahs ring without the discord of a groan through them all, and the very last word is "Hallelujah!"

So shall it be for the feeblest of us whose heart's confidence is in the Lord Jesus. Many a sigh and tear may come first, but even by these we shall not be losers. Even now we shall learn by them of our Lord, as is possible in no other way, and in the future they will give God Himself a happiness that angels cannot afford Him, of wiping tears away, and then songs shall take their place to end nevermore.

The second subdivision of our book ends here. It began at chapter 7 with the birth of Immanuel, and traces His path till He is seen reigning as King in chapter 9. Here the section ends, and the second begins with the Assyrian (representative of Violence as he is) heard digging his own grave in his boastings, then seen threatening Jerusalem, which he does not capture, but is instead brought very low. Then the remnant of Israel finds new life in the "Sprout" from the broken stem (chap. 6: 12), and with *His* introduction as the "Branch," not Israel only, but creation resumes its primal harmony, and the section ends with a Hallelujah in which we may anticipatively share.

# CHAPTER THIRTEEN

**Burden of Babylon. Force of the word "sanctified." The strange creatures that take up abode in Babylon; why their names are not to be translated.**

A THOROUGH change now comes over the spirit of our book. Assyria is no longer the prominent oppressor. The stout heart of the Assyrian has been brought low and that punishment has induced Israel's song. But now the song dies away, and its place is taken by every terrible accompaniment of divine chastening. The whole earth, nation after nation, provides the object of the infliction, even the Jew having to take his place amid those nations, as we shall see. Yet all is but a shadow of what is still overhanging the world. He, by whose severity a whole race of men, with the exception of one family only, was swept away by the waters: He who in His severity sent His armies against Jerusalem, and the awful sufferings of that siege cause Jewish tears to flow to this day: He who still keeps before the eye of Christendom a "nation scattered and peeled;" He who by His severity has sent ever and anon the most fearful chastenings on Christendom, from the last of which the nations are still suffering—is He who has spoken in no uncertain terms of a "wrath" still to come, as far exceeding all that has preceded as clearer, greater light increases the guilt of sinning against it. From it there is but one deliverance, and one Deliverer, "even Jesus who delivered us from" it (1 Thess. 1: 10). May God write upon our hearts His holy fear as we read of these "burdens."

We here begin, then, the third division of the first main part of our book, and are again met with the number "three," so clearly upon it as to confirm our conviction of its divine intent, for there are

1: Ten "Burdens" Chapters 13-27.
2: Six "Woes" " 28-33.
3: The end of both—Peace and song
        after storm and sorrow " 34, 35.

Babylon comes first under the divine *sentence,* called "bur-
*den,*" a word that possibly may include the *weight* of the sentence
announced.   But although this comes first, we must not forget
that this was written when Babylon had not reached the foremost
place amid the nations of the earth.   Rationalism and its offspring, Infidelity, with that stern adhesion to "reason" so loudly
proclaimed, and so strangely evidenced, argue from this that
Isaiah could not possibly be the author of these chapters, since
"the standpoint of the writer is in the time of the captivity when
the Chaldean Empire was flourishing," and "Isaiah could not
transfer his position into that distant future, disregarding the
horizon of his own day."   In other words, Isaiah could only prove
himself a divinely accredited prophet by *not* foretelling events
*too* far in the future!   The limit of the prophet's outlook, or that
of the Spirit of God behind him, must correspond exactly with
that of these gentlemen!   Well does Delitzsch comment: *"Stat
pro ratione voluntas,"* which may be freely rendered, a desire to
reach a preconceived conclusion is all that is necessary for doing
so.

In verse 2 the burden begins in that intensely picturesque
and graphic style so characteristic of our prophet, with a threefold signal to some army thus ordered to approach:

2: Lift up an ensign on a bare hill,
   Lift up the voice and cry loudly:
   Beckon then, urgently waving the hand,
   That they enter the gates of the nobles.
3: 'Tis I who thus summon My sanctified ones—
   'Tis I who do thus call My heroes:
   Those who are thus as inflicting My wrath,—
   My warriors proudly rejoicing.

What could be more vivid than that threefold call!   First
find a mountain without a tree on it that would obstruct the view,
and then place on it the ensign; then the eye being thus attracted,
shout to some army to come quickly, and still further hasten
them by beckoning with the hand, for the gates that have hitherto
only admitted the nobles of Babylon shall now admit its conquerors.   It is Jehovah, and none other, who is thus summoning
the executors of His wrath, and actually calls the hosts of Persia

His "sanctified ones!" Nor does that mean here that these soldiers are essentially holy in character, any more than are the "sanctified" ones of Heb. 10: 26, who can have nothing but an awful judgment before them.   Nor is the "sanctified" food (1 Tim. 4: 5) changed in its character by the thanksgiving with which it is received; nor were the children of the Corinthian Christians, although "holy" and "clean" (1 Cor. 7: 14), essentially different in character from all other children.   The word "sanctified," in all such cases means that they were "set apart;" if the sanctification be on earth, by some *ordinance,* or *agency,* as the altar sanctifying the gift (Matt. 23: 19) for some specific purpose.   Here it is a divine pronouncement and thus they were, by this call from a bare hill, distinguished from others.   So filled are these Persian "sanctified ones" with the assurance of victory, that Jehovah calls them His "proudly rejoicing" ones!

Now comes the answer to this urgent call:

4: Hark to the rumble!   A crowd in the hills,
   As the noise of a numerous people.
   Hark, what a tumult!   Ah, 'tis the sound
   Of the gathering kingdoms of Gentiles.
   Jehovah of Hosts thus musters His force:
   His host for the soon-coming battle.
5: They come! They come from a far-off land,
   Aye, from the limits of heaven!
   'Tis Jehovah who comes with weapons of wrath,
   To bring the whole earth to destruction.
6: Wail, for the day of Jehovah is nigh.
   As destruction it comes from El-Shaddai.
7: 'Tis this that accounts for all hands hanging down,
   And the heart of each frail-man is melting.
8: Troubled—they're seized with anguish and pains,
   Aye, writhe as a woman in travail.
   Each looks at his neighbor—is filled with amaze,
   For as flashing of flames faces flicker!

Thus is pictured the effect in Babylon of hearing of the approach of this invading host.   No courage is left; hands hang feebly at the side; men are no longer "heroes," for the hearts of the bravest are melted like wax, as the dwellers in the doomed city hear a rumbling in the mountains.   The terrifying sound tells of an advancing host, but little do either the invaders or the invaded realize that GOD is coming with that host, for it is but the agency whereby He inflicts penalty upon the earth. Little did Titus and his Romans think that they were but the armies of the "King" carrying out God's decreed penalty on Jerusalem (Matt. 22: 7). A hostile army overwhelming in numbers and equipment is terrible in itself, but when God is with it the terror becomes limitless. And here the prophet takes that common example of extreme suffering—a parturient woman. Each looks with astonishment at the change that has taken place in his neighbor's appearance, for the face of each flushes and pales as the blood first flows from and then back to the heart, like the changing color of flames.

> 9: Lo, 'tis the day of Jehovah thus comes,
>     Cruel with wrath and fierce anger;
>     To turn once again the earth to a waste,
>     Sweeping the sinners out from it.

In connection with this last line, note its correspondence with Matt. 13: 40, where the "tares" are taken from the earth in judgment. Again similarly in Matt. 24: 40, 41, where one is taken away in judgment, and the other is left upon the earth in blessing. In all cases where the Jew is the subject, the earth is the place of blessing. Thus, the being forced out of it is penal, in sharpest contrast with the present heavenly calling of believers, and their rapture *out of* the earth to their everlasting abode with their Lord in heaven (1 Thess. 4: 17). All blessing depends on where God's beloved Son is. Is He in Paradise? Then "far better" it is to be there with Him. Is He reigning over the earth? Then woe to those who are then swept out of it!

But is it possible that any sober mind could be satisfied that it was the very "Day of the Lord," which is to be "on everyone that is proud" (chap. 2: 12), when Darius the Mede diverted the course of the Euphrates, so that, in its dried bed, his army could have entrance into Babylon? If there were no other reason, this would appear quite impossible in view of the assurance given long after, that that day has not even yet dawned (2 Thess. 2: 3). But that does not forbid that in every upheaval of the existent world-empire, there should be a grim pictorial foreshadowing of that final day of wrath; and to *one single city*—say Babylon—all the terror there should afford a perfect picture, in miniature, of the far more wide-spread terror of that coming day.

Nor can any form of catastrophe that seriously affects one country leave the others quite unaffected, for amid the nations of the earth it is also true, that if one suffer, all must suffer with it. When wealth or property, or lives, which are the basis of both, are destroyed, it matters little who effects that destruction, or the motive for it; it is the world of men as a whole—the whole race—that is thus rendered the poorer by the destruction. It is always true, irrespective of the sphere, that a biting and devouring of one another must eventually result in mutual destruction. Wars, then, become a divine judgment; not merely upon the loser, but upon both conqueror and conquered. The Word of doom goes on:

10: The stars of the heavens are darkened and dimmed,
    Lightless are now its Orìons:
    Dark e'en the sun as it rises at morn,
    And the moon refuses her shining.
11: On the world of earth-dwellers I'll visit the sin,
    And punish the guilt of the wicked.
    To silence I'll cause all their boastings to sink—
    The fear-striking proud ones will humble.
12: More rare than fine gold shall the frailest man be—
    A poor man than gold-wedge of Ophir.
13: Therefore I'll cause the heavens to shake—
    The earth from her place shall be movèd
    Because of the wrath of Jehovah of Hosts,
    In the day of His terrible anger.
14: Like a startled gazelle, or shepherdless sheep,
    Each man shall turn to his people,
    And flee to his own native country.
15: For all that are found by spear-thrust are slain,
    Or put to the sword when o'ertaken.
16: Even their infants to pieces are dashed
    Before the eyes of their parents:
    Their houses are plundered of all they contain:
    Their wives are the prey of the victors.

When the Day of the Lord does come, as coming it surely is, it will be in a judgment in which there is no pity, no tenderness. As unlimited sufferings were poured upon the belovèd Son, so those who turn their backs to Him become the objects of those same awe-inspiring sufferings! That day may even be termed "cruel"—a word the very sense of which is the exclusion of all pity—in its effects, for then the long-restrained wrath of God bursts forth so that the earth, the whole earth, not "the land" here, becomes desolate.

The heavens fall into accord with this infliction on their sister planet (ver. 10): they refuse to give cheer or modify distress by their light. For as light and joy are correlative, so are darkness and sorrow, and this is alone now in order. The brilliant Orions* keep back their glittering glories: the sun when about to rise, "alters its mind" (*Delitzsch*) and the moon is invisible. When the wrath of God is active, the heavens ever refuse sympathy with the objects of that wrath, and darkness adds (oh, how greatly!) to the terrors.

The whole round globe, wherever men dwell, comes under this visitation. The lesser provides a picture of the greater slaughter, till even a frail mortal man ("Enosh") becomes precious as gold, and earth-born "adam" more valuable than Ophir.

Shaking heavens are a constant accompaniment of God's awakening to judgment. So our Lord tells of *"the powers of heaven being shaken,"* which is not to be dissevered from men's hearts failing them for fear. As when we see waves mountain high we do not attribute that convulsion to the water, but to the invisible wind, so these "powers of heaven" share in the terrific agitation of that Day of the Lord, and must not be identified with the visible stars.

As a timid gazelle starts in instant flight when alarmed, or as a flock of sheep scatter in fright, so the foreigners living in Babylon scatter each to their native land. For there is nothing but death for any who are caught.

That terrible cry for a strictly retributive penalty, which is nothing less than repulsive to a Christian, is yet in perfect keep-

---

*It is the word so rendered in Job 9: 9; 38: 31, and Amos 5: 8. The word "Orion" comes from one meaning "a fool," and is assumed to speak of the presumptuous folly of Nimrod, who is assumed to be bound to the sky, for his pride. Here it is simply a name inclusive of all constellations.

ing with the Jewish spirit found in Psalm 137, *"Happy shall he
be that taketh and dasheth thy little ones against the stones,"* and
is now accomplished.  These cruelties had been practised, and
must therefore be suffered according to that law which demanded
"a tooth for a tooth, an eye for an eye."  But the natural question comes up: Would not such practices necessarily bring the
same retribution on those who in their turn did them?  That is,
if the Medes dashed Babylon's babes to death as the Babylonians
had dashed Jerusalem's, why should not the Medes themselves
similarly suffer in their turn, and so endlessly?  Would not strictest righteousness demand this?  Most surely; unless, themselves
self-judged penitents, the Medes only acted, even in this, as execu-
tioners of God's stern justice, in His fear, and not at all as satis-
fying their own cruelty and vindictiveness, which would be no
less wicked than that which was being avenged.  This would be
exactly in the spirit of those who were bound to stone without
pity—it might be a young lad (Deut. 21: 18-21), or one to whom
one might be attached by strong ties of nature (Deut. 13: 6-10).
It is the awful judgment of God, which never can be safely exercised in man's hand without a continuation of the very evil that
is sought to be put away, till it is in His that are not stained, but
"without sin;" to Him alone is finally committed all judgment,
for He is the only one who *can* judge (John 5: 22).  Empire after
empire, each as guilty as its predecessor, has been, and shall be
overthrown, "till He comes whose right it is."  One must ever
bear in mind, too, that in all these inflictions, connected with the
government of the earth, there is no question of eternity; no
eternal penalty follows these little ones, but they come under the
shelter of that same atoning work that is effective for Babylonian
and Median, as well as for Israelite babes, for He has come to
"save that which was lost" (Matt. 18: 11).

17: Behold, I raise up against them the Medes,
    Who care not for gold nor for silver.
18: Their bows send forth arrows that dash to the ground;
    On the fruit of the womb they've no mercy,
    Their eye doth not spare even children.
19: And Babel, that is of all kingdoms the pride,
    The boast of all the Chaldeans,
    Shall be as the terrible overthrow wrought
    By Jehovah on Sodom-Gomorrah.

20: Inhabited never again shall it be,
    No dweller shall ever be in it,
    From age unto age everlasting.
    No wandering Arab shall there pitch his tent,
    No shepherd shall e'er fold his flock there,
21: But there the *tziim* of desert shall couch,
    And filled shall their house be with *ochim*.
    The *benoth yaanah* shall there seek a rest,
    The restless *seirim* shall jump there.*
22: *Iim* shall there in her palaces howl,
    And *tannim,* in places of pleasure:
    Near is the time of Babylon's fall,
    Nor shall its days be prolongèd.

The overmastering motive of the conquerors, now plainly named Medes, is not booty, although that they shall have. It is their own sufferings from Babylon that they are now intent to redress.

That there has been a striking fulfilment of this prophecy is beyond all controversy. Can any Rationalist bring our faith to confusion, by pointing to a city of Babylon and say, "There is a living refutation of all the claims to divine inspiration that you make for your Bible." How quickly, how vociferously, how constantly, should we be reminded of such a failure of fulfilment, could it be brought! How silent the opponents of faith are as they look on the mounds of earth that cover the temple of Belus, to the glory of which Xerxes gave the last thrust. Alexander the Great thought to rebuild, in spite of the prophecy, and to make it the metropolis of his empire. He was carried off by an early death, and Strabo (60 B. C.) applies to the ruins of the mighty city the words of the poet: "The great desert was the great city." Why should Arab pitch tent where nothing but scant vegetation offered food for his flocks?

But further, is it possible that any sober mind could insist that this prophecy has been finally and exhaustively fulfilled in

---

*The evident spirit of misery that pervades these verses, has led me to replace the word "dance," so constantly identified with pleasure, by "jump:" the prime meaning of the root is "to leap," "to skip," so it is the more literal. Even the Latin poet Virgil calls unclean spirits "Jumping Satyrs."

the past? That "Day," this prophet tells us, was to be "on everyone that is proud" (chap. 2: 12). Were there no "proud" then outside those walls of Babylon? Many centuries pass, and still the Spirit of Christ assured those who were then living that the Day of the Lord had not yet come (2 Thess 2: 3). Nor, as I write, nineteen centuries after the Lord Jesus took His seat at the right hand of the Majesty on high, has that "Day" even yet come, although we see its approach to be very near indeed.

Turning to the last two verses, strange and mysterious enough are those outlandish Hebrew words, yet in that very strangeness and mystery, they may, and I believe do, fulfil the intent of the divine Author of the book; for this, and this alone, is consistent with the Old Testament that has the visible alone for its sphere, and those visible things afford pictures of the invisible with which the New Testament has to do. But suppose—and surely that is not difficult—that there is nothing in this visible creation that will serve as a symbol of the invisible, so as to typify the varying characteristics of the "unclean spirits" of the heavenlies, how could that difficulty be met better than by just such words of mystery as we have here?

Now we have a Babylon in the New Testament of which the Babylon of old is but a symbol, and these creatures that none can identify with assurance (for not one of them is really *known**) afford the most perfect picture, as nothing else that was familiar to us could do, of those demons, unclean spirits, and "hateful birds" that are finding their congenial dwelling in that future Babylon, the unified apostate Christendom (Rev. 18: 2). The modern "Confusion" of Christendom is full of them even today.

The one main idea running through all, if etymology is to be considered—as surely it is, for it is absolutely all we have to give us any light on the use of the words—is of mournful, doleful wails that add their horrors to the desolation of the scene.

The first is *tziim*, from a root, "to be dry," hence "desert;" and thus the A. V. renders the one word, "wild beasts of the desert." These *tziim* find their "own place," their congenial home,

---

*Our commentators are sorely puzzled, and Delitzsch confesses that "it is impossible to determine what are the animals referred to "

in "a dry and thirsty land, where no water is," but find no rest there (Matt. 12: 43). In just such a scene exactly shall the Babylon of the future be found; for in order to see her, John has also to be carried into the "desert" (Rev. 17: 3). These *tzüm* then simply represent "desert-dwellers" whose abode is away from the love and light of God.

"*Ochim,*" from a word whose sound tells its meaning: *oh-ach* whence "*ach,*" an interjection of sorrow (Ezek. 6:11), and constantly rendered, "Alas!" So these "*ochim*" are "ever-lamenting ones," "mournfully howling ones," whose only cry is "Alas!"

"*Benoth yaanah,*" literally, "daughters of a doleful cry," is found in Micah 1: 8, "I will wail and howl; I will make a mourning as the *benoth yaanah,*" which the translators have rendered "owls," but there are other words for that, and it is but a conjecture: it is again an unknown wailing creature.

"*Seirim*" is probably the most interesting to us of them all, for while the word is rendered in Lev. 4: 24 by "goat," that would be quite impossible in Lev. 17: 7: "And they shall no more offer their sacrifices unto *seirim:*" so here the A. V., following the Septuagint, has "devils," or "demons." So, in 2 Chron. 11: 15: "He ordained priests for the high places, and for the *seirim* (demons) and for the calves which he had made." So we may fairly take the word as referring to those unclean spirits termed in the New Testament "demons," so closely identified with idols that the apostle can say, "The things that the Gentiles sacrifice, they sacrifice to demons, and not to God" (1 Cor. 10: 20), and this word thus governs the rendering of all these.

"*Iim,*" rendered "wild-beasts-of-the-islands," is a contraction of "*ohee,*" another interjection of lament, and evidently carries on the same idea of "dolefully howling ones," as so perfectly fits the context here: for these shall howl in palaces whose walls once resounded only to songs of revelry. Where Belshazzar feasted a thousand of his lords, and shouts of merriment were on all sides, *iim* shall howl dolefully. Well may all this throw its gloomy light on "there shall be weeping and gnashing of teeth." Note the corresponding picture of that one who, under the power of a legion of these same fallen creatures in Mark 5, amid the tombs, was *crying* and *cutting himself with stones!* Who can estimate the

spirit-anguish of a spirit's separation from God! Every name
here tells of *that*.

So the last, *tannim*, is usually supposed to be "jackals;" but
we do well to leave this word with the mystery that is also involved in the word "dragon," as our A. V. renders it.  For how
could it be said that Pharaoh was a "jackal" in the "midst of the
seas" (Ezek. 32: 2)—*that* would be no place for jackals, so the
A. V. renders it "whale;" but in Ezek. 29: 3 the same word is
rendered "dragon:"  "I am against thee, Pharaoh, king of Egypt,
the great *dragon* that lieth in the midst of his rivers;" while in
Exod. 7: 9 Moses' rod becomes a *"serpent."*  In that grand call
to universal praise to Jehovah (Ps. 148), which begins with the
highest of His creatures, and gradually comes down, the earthly
chorus is to be led by *"dragons,* and all deeps" (ver. 7), where
this last word is simply a synonym for "the abyss" or "bottomless pit," in which the devil is to be cast bound for a thousand
years.  I can but see in this mysterious creature, then, coming
here as the climax of doleful spirits, a clear symbol of him who is
"the great dragon, the devil."

We cannot greatly err then, in considering the acknowledged
mystery enveloping these words as being divinely intended, for it
is in this very way that they speak, as otherwise they could not,
of what is beyond human ken, what we call the occult, or hidden.

One point may occasion some surprise, for while in Isaiah we
have the world-empire Babylon before us, we find in the New
Testament that name borne, not by the political or civil government, but by "the harlot sitting on many waters," in whom we
discern the spurious imitation of the Bride of Christ—apostate
religious Christendom headed up in Rome.  But political world-
power is what this apostate claimant of being the "Catholic," or
Universal, Church, has ever aimed at.  Her Popes have claimed,
and do still claim—since it was acknowledged by Pepin (himself
a usurper) in the eighth century—not only spiritual, but temporal
authority over the whole earth, as their God-given right.  All the
promises made to the Lord Jesus Himself have logically to be
claimed by him who assumes to be His "vicar:"  "all kings should
fall down before *him,* all nations should serve *him,"* "his (i.e., the
Pope's) enemies must lick the dust;" and never, for one moment,

no matter what individual was in "the chair of St. Peter," has he
abandoned that claim, or given his consent to that abnegation
which Italian bayonets under Garibaldi forced upon him.   With
keen eyes made the more hungry by abstinence, has he watched
the politics of earth, biding his time, yet neglecting no opportunity of thrusting himself into prominence, as the true Arbiter of
the earth: a prominence that the civil powers are apparently becoming more and more inclined to restore to him, as they have in
principle, in his dominance in the Vatican City, already.   Nor
among these are any more yielding and complacent than those
who, but a comparatively short time ago, were in sternest out-
spoken opposition to all these claims of the Papacy.   But that is
a thing of the past: no longer do we hear the old cry, "No
Popery," but rather, "No Protestantism,"* for any protest against
these assumptions is frowned upon as being "bigoted."   Bigoted!
As if the very basic principles of Rome do not compel her to exercise the most uncompromising bigotry wherever she has the
power of racking and burning, as her whole history tells.

One thing alone hinders the full fruition of Rome's desire: the
presence of the Holy Spirit in His Church!   Let that divine

------

*It is not without significance that as the power of the United
States amid the nations has increased, so, proportionately, have
Rome's efforts to control that power, and to make Romanism the
recognized national religion, increased. The success of these efforts
may be gauged by the last step, which has been to advertise
throughout the country for $5,000,000 with which to erect a Cath-
edral in the national Capital, "To the glory of Almighty God, who
hath given us Victory, and in honor of Mary Immaculate, *Patroness of the United States!*"

We are not told who it was who requested that "highly favored"
woman to accept this dignity of "Patroness of the United States,"
or who installed her into it; or whether her own consent to this
use of her name has been obtained at all (as is usually esteemed
an indispensable pre-requisite in all such cases); or, if so, how
that was accomplished. "The end sanctifies" all that—for that end
is the erecting such a building at Washington as may give the
appearance, at least, of the whole country being "Roman."   Altogether the most suggestive part of the matter is the absence of
any protest against it.   Think of how it would have been met a
hundred years ago!

Hinderer depart, and quickly shall this compromise be effected, by which the unified harlot-church shall be supported by the unified empire, and then shall the *tziim*, the *ochim*, the *iim*, the *seirim*, find their congenial home in that Babylon, ruin as she will be, and fill her with their hopeless lamentations of despair. Oh, listen to the voice of the Lord addressed to His people who may even now be in what is Babylon in embryo: "Come out of her, My people, that ye be not partakers of her sins, and that ye receive not of her plagues." For whilst we hear from Heaven "harpers harping with their harps," there is, alas, no music in hell, but weeping and gnashing of teeth!

## CHAPTER FOURTEEN

**A complete revolution; the slave becomes the master, issuing in a song of triumph over Babylon. Sh'ohl and its shades. Lucifer; for whom does that word stand? The problem of the existence of evil in the world: whence could it come, the one Creator being absolute Good? Our foe's first appellation now borne by the Lord Jesus. Significance of the points of the compass. Philistia; its teachings. Who is the "flying serpent" here?**

ISRAEL expects no "rapture." No deliverance shall there be for her save by "the revelation of the righteous judgment of God" in the destruction, from the earth, of her oppressors. What wonder, then, that her prayer is for the execution of that sentence, whilst ours, who expect to leave the world to *our* oppressors, is for mercy upon them. It is with Israel we have to do, and I paraphrase, keeping as close to the literal as I can, to give the sense:

> 1: The Lord shall have mercy on Jacob,
> And again shall make choice of Isràel—
> Shall settle them in their own land; .
> Where the stranger shall join himself to them,
> And cleave to the people of Jacob.
> 2: Back to their own place (and homeland)
> Shall they be brought by the Gentiles,
> Who then become servants of Isr'el,
> And held as bondmen and handmaids
>      In the land of Jehovah.
> Thus shall they take them as captives,
> Whose captives they themselves had been;
> Thus shall they rule o'er their rulers.

A little remnant of a few thousand Jews *did* return from Babylon in the day of Ezra and Nehemiah, but it is absolutely impossible to be satisfied with that as a final fulfilment of this promise, for, far from leading their captors into captivity, they confessed themselves to be servants still: "For we are bondmen," says Ezra (chap. 9: 9, R. V.), and, "Behold, we are servants this day," says Nehemiah (chap. 9: 36). Who then can possibly claim that the promise that they should *not* be bondmen was fulfilled, when they were? Nor can any time be found, between that and this, that has seen any fulfilment at all. It *must* await this then in the future; surely it must, for neither Jew nor Christian can be finally blest save by the very Presence of the Lord Jesus.

> 3: And in the day when Jehovah shall rest thee,
>     Give ease from thy sorrow, thy fear and thy toil,
>     In the which, a poor slave, thine oppressors have made thee,
> 4: This is the song thou shalt raise over Babel:
>     Chanting in triumph over her king:
>     How hath th' oppressor ceased (from oppressing)
>     The place of extortion come to its end!
> 5: Jehovah hath broken the rod of the wicked!
>     (Jehovah hath broken) the sceptre that ruled!
> 6: He that smote peoples with scourgings relentless,
>     He that ruled over the nations in wrath,
>     With such persecution that none did restrain
>             (Jehovah hath broken).
> 7: The whole of the earth is at rest and is quiet,
>     Breaks forth into jubilant singing.
> 8: Even the cypresses joy at thy fall,
>     Lebanon's cedars now are all singing:
>     Since *thou* art laid low, in safety we stand,
>     No woodman his axe lifts against us.

Thus will Israel's joy at the fall of her enemy be celebrated. Their oppressor comes to a sudden end: the place in which they have been tortured has ceased to exist, and now the whole earth is flooded with genuine peace. The poet follows the fallen oppressor into the Underworld:

> 9: Sh'ohl beneath thee shakes with excitement—
>     Springs at thy coming to welcome thee there!
>     The Shades* are thrown into tumult—
>     All who on earth were its leaders—
>     From their thrones do they spring:
>     All the kings of the nations.

---

*Shades, from a word meaning "to be weak," "since the life of the Shades is only the shadow of a life."—*Delitzsch*.

10: All of them (scoffingly) cry to thee,
       Art even thou become feeble as we—
       Art even thou become like unto us?

We must most surely not assume with some, that we have here a simple prosaic revelation of the world of the dead, any more than that in the previous verse we are told with prosaic literalness that the trees talk. In both cases the language is intensely poetical, and yet nothing could more graphically bring before our minds the height from which this king of Babylon had fallen, and the depth to which that fall had taken him. The poet-prophet pictures his entry into the unseen world of disembodied spirits, called "Sh'ohl."* As he enters, the whole concourse of those who have preceded him are pictured as thrilled with excitement, the royal shades (for they are assumed to retain the same dignity as they enjoyed on earth) spring from their thrones with a cry of astonishment—"What! Is it possible that *thou* art become as weak and powerless as we? It is incredible!"

Then the original chorus resumes the taunting chant:

11: Low, low to Sh'ohl thy pomp!
       Low now the notes of thy harp-strings!
       Maggots beneath thee alone for thy couch,
       And worms must suffice for thy cov'ring!
12: O thou bright star, thou son of the dawn,†
       From heaven how low hast thou fallen!
       Down to the very ground art thou hurled—
       Thou who didst hurl down the nations.
13: Thou who hast said to thyself in thine heart,
       I will mount up to the heavens.
       My throne shall there be exalted on high,
       Far above the stars of Elohim.

---

*Usually taken to be from *shahal* "to ask," either because that place is constantly demanding fresh victims, being one of the four things that never say, "Enough!" (Prov. 30: 15, 16) ; or because it takes from those who still live, all knowledge of their deceased friends, and it is they who ask, and ask, and ever ask in vain, as to *where* those who have thus gone are—as Job 14: 10: "Man dies and wastes away, he giveth up the ghost, and *where is he?*" or it may well cover both ideas, as I have assumed in the text.

†This term "son of the dawn" is but a poetical expression for "star of the morning."

On the highest bound of the gathering-mount,
On the verge* of the dark northern quarter,
14: Far o'er the heights of the clouds will I rise,
Will make myself equal the Highest.
15: Nay, but to Sh'ohl depths* shalt thou go,
To the depth of the pit of perdition.

No one could surely suppose that the entry of weak, dissolute Belshazzar could be pictured as causing any such commotion as this anywhere. Be as literal as you will, one is at least compelled to lose sight of the person, and see only *the king*, the ruler of the world. But if Belshazzar must thus disappear in person, and be seen only as the representative world-ruler, may not that world-ruler himself be "the prince of this world," upon whose person and dignity our New Testament Scriptures throw their clearer light? As in the mysterious *tziim* and *ochim* of the previous chapter we discerned those unclean demons that shall be inhabitants of fallen Babylon, so in the fallen king of that fallen Babylon we are compelled to discern the *prince* of those demons, whom we know as the devil, the king of all the children of pride, and who, far from *reigning* in hell, shall be brought to the lowest depth of all!

But so important is this, so closely linked even by the most striking contrasts with the path of our divine Lord, that we cannot pass over it without considering the very words used, patiently and carefully. While I am well aware of the need of the utmost caution, lest the working of the mind take the place of the teaching of the Spirit, yet caution may go too far, and become refusal to be led of that Spirit.

In verse 11 I have felt compelled to leave the word *Sh'ohl* untranslated, for I know of no exact English equivalent. Its etymology I have given in a footnote to ver. 9, and this tells us that it is a word that recognizes both the intuitive knowledge in man, that there is a continuance of being after death, and at the same time his ignorance of the place and condition of that continuance —an ignorance that itself cries with agony for light. Of one thing

---

*The word rendered in our A.V., in both these verses, "sides," carries with it the idea of "extremity" in whatever direction it may be. Here, this proud one aimed upward at the *extreme* of self-exaltation; his doom is to be cast down to the *extreme* of humiliation. See Phil. 2: 5-10.

he is sure; death is, for him, *not the end*. The grave takes the
body; but the body is not the whole of man. There is something that the grave does not take. His reason, apart from any
divine revelation, rebels against the thought of there being no
radical distinction between himself and his dog. But where, then,
does that immaterial, that responsible, part of himself (for insensate matter cannot be responsible), that survives the dissolution
of his body, go? Where? To the place that gives no answer to
this agonized question of human affections, yet is ever demanding
fresh victims! It is the place on which no clear light of revelation
had dawned in the Old Testament, and thus even to the most
upright of men it was "the land of darkness and shadow of
death, a land of darkness as of darkness itself and where even
the light is as darkness" (Job 10: 22). This is sh'ohl, the under-
world, the region of the unclothed spirits of the departed, irrespective altogether of their character, of their relation to God, or
of their final destiny. God be praised that the resurrection of
Jesus has thrown so clear a beam of light on that darkness, that
for the believer in Him, it has been dispelled, and sh'ohl, or
hades, is no longer the "undiscovered country from whose bourne
no traveller returns," for one Traveller has returned, filled its once
dark chambers with the warmth of the Love that took Him there;
with the light of a sure hope, for it could not retain Him, and in
that light we see death to be the introduction to "Paradise,"
"with Christ"—"at home"—"far better!" The everlasting question, "Man dies, and where is he?" of Job 14, is thus answered
now for the penitent believer in the Lord Jesus.

In verse 12, this "King of *Babylon*," King over "Confusion,"
and so a representative of the "prince of this world," has a distinct name given him which is very literally rendered: "Bright-
shining one, son of the dawn," and the last is simply a poetical
term for the morning star, and thus the whole is a very close
parallel to "Bright Morning Star."

Here then is a name at least worthy of being given as expressing the person of him who "sealed up the sum" of creature-
perfection, "full of wisdom, perfect in beauty" (Ezek. 28: 12).
When bearing this name he does not *"transform* himself into an
angel of light," for he *is* that by creation. When he has lost the

name of Bright Morning Star and become Satan, then he does transform himself, in assuming still to be an angel of light.

As surely then as students of Scripture have seen him who now is called Satan, behind the King of Tyre in Ezek. 28: 11, etc., there is equal reason for discerning the same personage behind this "king of Babylon." Tyre was the representative exponent of *Commerce*, as Babylon was of the *Religion* of this world; Tyre represents the *material* side of this fallen one's activity, ever desiring to possess the earth; Babylon the *spiritual*, that would aim at heaven, and as in those primal days when rebellious man would build both "a *city* and a *tower*," Tyre would correspond with the city that was to cover the earth, and Babylon with the tower that was to reach heaven. Both the king of Tyre and of Babylon evidence the same sin of pride, and whilst this is not, alas, distinguishing, being the common heritage of all of us as fallen from God, yet the superhuman character of this aspirant that would ascend "above the stars of God," can but suggest an idea far beyond poetical rhetoric in the mouth of any mere man, and that these two are one, and *that* one he who is now called Satan.

What questions have ever been asked as to the source of the evil, the sin, suffering and sorrow, so universal in this poor earth. Whence did all this moral and physical disorder and confusion come, if the one Creator of all is only good? Can God then be the Author of the confusion that *is not* good? Can good produce evil? It would be an equally intelligent question to ask: "Can the sun give out darkness?" If we take, then, simply as a working hypothesis, that as God is the Source of all that is good, so the devil is the source of all evil, we have narrowed the question down to, "Whence then that devil?" Scripture, God be thanked, is at least clear that as "God created man upright, but he sought out many inventions"(Eccl. 7: 29), so God created one, long before man, "perfect in his ways," and the very top-stone of His spirit-creation: and that being the case, necessarily having absolute liberty in his equipoise, to go in any direction—not *compelled* (since a creature, and not divine; innocent, but not holy) even to keep aright, but with power of free choice of, and to walk in, any direction, moral as well as physical. Thus launched from his

Creator's Hand, what name could be given him? It must at least express what he *then* was, not what he afterwards made himself to be. No "Devil" was he then—no "Satan" could or did God make, but a brilliantly shining one, the very "Star of the Morning" amid the hosts of heaven. To so name Belshazzar, or any poor mortal man, would be hyperbole gone mad and carried to an absurdity.

This, then, is very clear, that as it would be absurd to trace *sin* and all its evil consequences in this world up to the Source of all *good* and of good alone, God, so it is reasonable in the light of Scripture to trace it to him who was the first sinner (1 John 3: 8), once the "Bright Star of the Morning," but now called Satan.

If freedom of will, liberty of choice, was the most exalted attribute of the highest and erstwhile noblest of God's creatures, if that liberty necessarily predicated the *possibility* of that free unbound will arising opposed even to his Creator, what follows as to our Lord Jesus? Do we not believe that *He could not err*, was impeccable? Does not then that apparent lack of the very power of choice rather detract from, than add to the dignity of His Person?

Far be it. On the contrary, He, though impeccable, by no means lacked freedom of choice, yet *could* only walk in a path that was not relatively, but absolutely *good*. It may well be that into these higher mysteries of His Person, no finite mind can penetrate, for "No man knoweth the Son but the Father" (Matt. 11: 27). But this I am bold to say, that in this He transcends all creatures. In Him there was and ever will be freedom of choice, yet a freedom—paradoxical as it may sound to some (and there will ever be paradoxes in these infinitely holy mysteries)—that it was impossible for Him to exercise in an evil way, for that was forbidden by the law of His holy Being. It is written even of the poor failing and often sinning children of God, that, *as so born of God*, they cannot sin (1 John 3: 9). If He so speaks of those to whom the Word of God came, and the Scripture cannot be broken, can anything *less* than that be true of the *Son of God* Himself? It is the difference between Innocence and Holiness. Innocence has not done, but *can* do wrong; holiness *cannot*, any more than a sheep *can willingly roll* in filth, even though it has perfect freedom of choice to do so, or than the lily *can* be tainted with the mud amid which it lives its own pure life, ever repelling all its defilements. So our Lord, in virtue of His own inherent immaculateness (not that of His mother, as the Papacy blasphemously teaches), both before and after birth, repelled all the evil by which He was surrounded here; and this so adds to the superhuman dignity of His Person that every believer veils his face in spirit, and adores Him as God manifest in flesh.

But, our enquirer may say, that only pushes back the difficulty as to the presence of evil in the creation of a God only good, and gives rise to another question: whence could that evil suggestion come to him here called king of Babylon, when there was no evil occurrent in all the universe? It certainly could not have come from anywhere *external* to himself, for there was none there.

True; but our Bible suggests a clear answer in the words, "Thine heart was lifted up because of thy beauty; thou hast corrupted thy wisdom by reason of thy brightness" (Ezek. 28: 17). It was *self-born;* it came from *self*-occupation with his own creature beauty, ignoring his dependence on his Creator for all. You and I, my reader, may learn much from this. Complacent self-occupation even with what God may work in us, is filled with grave danger, and only in occupation in our thoughts with the Lord Jesus Himself, *His* beauty, *His* perfections, *His* love, lies our safety, joy, blessing—yes, our true holiness. For, to be attracted to Him, where He is, out of this defiling scene, as strangers and pilgrims, *is* practical holiness.

But the name of the Bright Morning Star being given to him whom we have known as the very antithesis of light and hopefulness, may give rise to a certain sense of resentment, since we know it as justly belonging to Another, who now claims it, and in whom alone all light and hope for our race is focussed—Jesus. He is for us alone, the Bright Morning Star.

Aye, true enough; but, let me ask, do not all His *acquired* (mark) glories come to Him by the way of creature sin and failure? First, the creature fails, and then He lifts up that which has thus been bemired by that fall. What greater dignity has He than in that name which is above every name—Jesus, Saviour?

But could that highest Name ever have been given Him had there been no poor sinners, as we, to save? (Phil. 2: 9). The eater has indeed thus been made to yield meat, the strong, sweetness, to our great joy. God planted a vine, His people Israel, and that vine brought forth vile grapes (Isa. 5); then He comes, the true Vine, in whom alone sweet fruit is found (John 15). Do we joy in Him less, because every other source of fruit has been found vain? Not till the Church has utterly failed as a witness, as it has in our day, does He present Himself as "The faithful and true Witness," who alone shall never fail (Rev. 3: 14), to our great consolation—our shameful failure is the dark foil that sets off His perfection. So here, that name of Bright Morning Star has been dragged into utter ruin by the mighty creature to whom it was first given, but is lifted therefrom by One who is indeed the true Bright Morning Star, the Herald of a day that knows no night, as cloudless as clear shining after rain. Surely there is no sound reason for questioning that Lucifer, Son of the Morning, "The bright Morning Star," was the original and worthy name, expressing the creature-dignity, of him who was afterwards named, as expressing his self-acquired character, the Devil, Satan, that old serpent, and the dragon! Thus there is no rivalry, for he to whom that name was first applied has lost it forever, and gained these others which tell out most clearly his antagonism to our poor race. But that race has been so loved by Him who now bears it, that He has Himself borne the sins of His people, and now lives (in contrast with him who *accuses* day and night), to make *intercession* for them.

Let us trace the ambitious path of this "Lucifer" further. He who reads all hearts has read this in *his*: "I will exalt my throne above the stars of God," that is, above the other angelic powers, for the term "stars of God," as that other, "the host of heaven," covers both the material and spiritual, both the visible and invisible. This Bright Star of the Morning aims to place *his* throne above all other stars. "I will also sit upon the mount of the assembly, in the extremity of the north."

The term "Mount of the Assembly" is strikingly suggestive of that other mount, Har-Mageddon, for that also means when translated from the Hebrew tongue, "mount of assembly, or gathering;" but the last part of the word (*maggedon*) has in it the idea of a *military* gathering of troops, in undisguised warfare, and speaks of the final gathering of all the children of pride in open conflict with "Him that sits on the horse" (Rev. 19: 19), in whom we recognize our Lord Himself. But this idea of a military gathering is quite lacking in the word rendered "congregation" (ver. 13). *That* is the peaceful word used for those appointed feasts in Israel's day, when Jehovah gathered His people around Himself; and we can see how perfectly consistent is this peaceful word with the time in which the proud king is speaking in his heart. No rebellion had as yet broken the calm waters of that sinless past, and introduced the storm that is even to this day raging. All angelic "assemblies" then were in willing submission to the Throne of God. It is with *this* assembly in mind, that this Bright Morning Star aims to place *his* throne, in the "extremity of the north," the highest possible elevation.

Scripture itself affords the clearest evidence that even the cardinal points of the compass have deep spiritual teaching. Thus "east" in the light of Gen. 41: 6 and Exodus 14: 21 is beyond all question the quarter that speaks of sharp distress, and indeed divine judgment—a teaching with which that of nature is in perfect accord, for everywhere the east wind is esteemed as opposed to man's good. The "west" must, as the opposite quarter, speak of *prosperity* and *blessing*. Scripture fully confirms this, for when Moses blessed the tribes, Naphtali is given the "west and the south;" but far from that being literally true of that tribe, its lot fell rather to the north and east, bordering the Sea of Galilee and extending north of it. But let the clear, typical meaning be heard, and in the bright sunny south we have no difficulty in reading of the love, warmth and light of God. So Naphtali's possession of "west and south" means the enjoyment of the divine light and love that those points figure.

Then the north, being the direct opposite to the south, must speak as clearly of the opposite, "darkness"—it is the dark, obscure quarter,* as the word itself proves. But in our prophet, "the extremities of the north" seems to be less in contrast with

---

*North: Heb., *tzahphohn;* properly, "hidden, obscure."

"south" than with "the pit" of the next verse; it is the most
exalted situation possible, as the pit is the lowest (*cf*. Matt. 11:
23). We must then combine these two ideas of exaltation and
impenetrableness, and learn that Lucifer's proud ambition did not
stop short of sitting enthroned at a height far above the power
of any other creature to penetrate.

But this is essentially a position that belongs to the Creator
alone. In human affairs it is what we call Providence, that ambiguous word with all its impenetrable mystery of suffering and
calamity, knowing no intelligent discrimination; for as the rain
falls indifferently on the just and unjust, so everything in this
disordered scene is apparently under the guidance of blind
chance. So the wisest of all men wailed as he looked upon these
inequalities and confessed his inability to pierce this "north"
quarter:

"For the race is not to the swift, nor the battle to the strong
. . . but *time and chance* happeneth to them all. For man also
knoweth not his time; as the fishes that are taken in an evil net,
and as the birds that are caught in the snare, so are the sons of
men snared in an evil time when it falleth suddenly upon them"
(Eccl. 9: 11, 12).

Who of us has not echoed that groan? For still we, too, even
to this present hour, have the same "north" to perplex us, in the
same providences so impossible of interpretation. As Israel's foes
ever came from the literal north, so do the attacks on our faith
come from these dark, obscure providences that answer to that
quarter, till like Job we hardly know to whom to attribute the
afflictions from which all are indiscriminately suffering. Is not
*our* enemy in them? Has he not some power, however limited it
may be, over these providences, as we are told he had in Job's
day? But, blessed be God, we have at least learned two comforting truths: first, that our God *over*-rules all for the real good of
His people (Rom. 8: 28), and that all the present discords of
providences shall eventuate for them in the sweet harmonies of
eternity. Secondly, that the "seventh angel" shall soon sound,
and then this "mystery of God"—that is, a God of infinite benevolence, infinite wisdom, and infinite power, permitting the apparent triumphing of evil—"shall be finished" (Rev. 10: 7).

Let us note that as this extremity of the north was and is the only limit to the proud ambition of the first Bright Morning Star, so shall that very dignity be *His* who has now the only true claim to that name, for so speaks Ps. 48: 23: "Beautiful for situation, the joy of the whole earth, is Mount Zion, on the sides (or extremities) *of the north,* the city of the great King.  God is known in her palaces for a refuge."  No doubt the reference here is to that millennial scene wherein the literal down-trodden Jerusalem has indeed become the city of the great King, our Lord Jesus, so that a topographical interpretation is not to be rejected.  In this divinely designed topography, we may discern spiritual verities by which we see the true Bright Morning Star actually occupying the place desired by the first.  Then nevermore shall the "north" be dark, for He, the Lamb, is there, and shall enlighten it, as He does all.  The seventh angel will then have sounded, and in the complete expulsion of him who had been permitted so wide a sway over providences, the "mystery of God is finished."  It is refreshing to hail that scene, and salute it, surrounded as we still are, by all the darkenings of the "north quarter."

The rest of the chapter, as far as it refers to the King of Babylon, would appear to need but little comment, and I will only paraphrase as closely as possible.  It frequently seems to return to the earthly monarch, as will be seen.

16: They that now see thee look at thee narrowly,
    Consider thee carefully, saying:
    Can *this* be he that made the earth shake:
    Its (mighty) kingdoms to tremble?
17: Who made the earth-dwelling a desert;
    Destroyed its (populous) cities;
    Nor e'er let his prisoners homeward.
18: All kings of the nations are buried with honor;
    Each in his sepulchre lying.
19: But *thou* art cast out afar from thy grave,
    Like a sucker-sprig deemed worse than worthless.
    Like the garments of those slain in battle,
    Ruined by tearing and sword-thrust,
    Going down to the stones of the pit;
    Aye, like a carcass down-trodden.

In sharp contrast with the ordinary custom of following with

honor the very corpses of deceased kings, *this* king, in his death,
is likened to three shameful and worthless things: a sucker-sprig
that although still *living* is ever ruthlessly thrown away, its life
is valueless; ruined garments that by their condition tell of discord and conflict with *men;* and a carcass left to be trampled in
the dust; again, it is not difficult to see a reference to man's
tripartite being, spirit, soul, and body.

20: Thou shalt not be joined unto them in the grave
    For thou hast destroyèd thy land,
    Thou hast murdered thy people,
    The seed of the wicked shall ne'er be renowned.
21: Sow for the seed of the sinner the slaughter,
    Because of the sin of their sires!
    For never again shall they rise,
    As conquerors over the earth,
    Nor fill the world's face with their cities.
22: For I will rise up against them,
    Saith Jehovah Tzebaoth:
    From Babel the name and the remnant—
    Both issue and offering—root out,
    Saith Jehovah.
23: I'll make it the home of the bittern;
    Turn it to marshes of water:
    With the broom of destruction will sweep it,
    So saith Jehovah Tzebaoth.

Here in this threefold sentence "the true sayings of God,"
ends the "burden" of Babylon; what follows returns to the
Assyrian, but in a very peculiar way. We are in what we may
call the "burdens," in which every separate object of the divine
judgment is introduced by the word "burden." But here, as if to
assure us that although the names differ, there is some form of
identity in the object of this infliction with the one we have just
considered, there is no word to indicate any break at all. The
burden flows on in uninterrupted continuity, most surely suggest-
ing at least, as so much else does, that there is a close link between the king of Babylon and the Assyrian, for they come under
one and the same "burden."

As a matter of history, the Assyrian came to his end as the
dominant world-power *before* the Babylonian, who succeeded him

in that supremacy, while here, it is after we have heard of the doom of the Babylonian that we are told of that of the Assyrian.

In all these prophetic details the oldest of us are but beginners, as it were, in this school of God, but, as already written, I have become increasingly assured that this "Assyrian" of Isaiah must be found in the holder of the same place of world-power in the time of the end, and called in the book of Revelation "the Beast from the *Sea*," even although the empire over which he rules is then Roman and not literally Assyrian. The identity consists in the same position of world-power he enjoys, not in the geographical boundaries, or the name given his empire.

The striking way in which the Assyrian is introduced here serves to confirm such an interpretation. The most simple deduction would be that in the last days there will be two individuals so governed by the same spirit, the same aims, as to be united in both sin and doom.

If we look at the matter in the light of the New Testament, all becomes plain. Just as in the prophet Daniel we have two "horns," western in chapter 7, eastern in chapter 8, and have no difficulty in discerning the antitypes of these in the two prominent personages of evil, the two "Beasts" of Rev. 13, so here we have the same two evil personalities in Assyrian and Babylonian, again foreshadowing, respectively, the same two expressions of creature wickedness, "the Beast from the sea" and "the Beast from the land," in such evil accord with one another, in being possessed and governed by that one fallen spirit, Satan (of whose *primal* fall from heaven we have just heard in our prophet, and of whose *final* fall and literal expulsion from heaven we have been similarly told in Rev. 12) as to make together a trinity of super-human pride and rebellion. Here, too, both the human dupes shall come to one awful end at the same time (Rev. 19: 20) and by the same divine judgment, as is suggested in the unification of the two under one "burden," or divine sentence, in the prophecy of Isaiah.*

---

*I find it impossible to accord with Mr. Wm. Kelly in his comment here. He writes: "The King of Babylon sets forth no other than the last head of the Beast" (*Exp. of Isaiah*, p. 194). That would be the head of the revived Roman Empire of Dan. 2, but

This burden closes with the following solemn assurance of its fulfilment, and to that we are rapidly approaching.

24: Jehovah Tzebaoth hath uttered His oath,
    And thus doth He speak: Without question
    As I have thought, so shall it be—
    As I have purposed, so shall it stand;
25: Th' Assyrian will I smash in My land,
    Underfoot on My mountains will tread him.
    Then from off them his yoke shall depart,
    His burden be rolled from their shoulder.
26: This is the purpose that has been determined
    To come upon all of the earth—
    This is the hand outstretched
    Over all of the nations!

continuing on the same subject, he finds the same personage "under the symbol of the harlot riding the Beast" (p. 195)—that would mean that Babylon symbolized both the Beast and the woman riding upon that Beast! This is surely self-refuting.

We must, I believe, exclude any reference to Babylon *as the woman of Rev.* 17 in our interpretation of Isaiah; for, though she is utterly rejected by the Lord—spewed out of His mouth, and so left on earth in the day of the fulfilment of 1 Thess. 4:13-18, she will still claim that high-sounding title, "Historic Church;" and *as such* the vision of the prophet could not include what was "kept secret" from him (Rom. 16:25).

If we then eliminate that religious harlot of Christendom, the secular or civic opposition to Christ must be found in the Gentile whom Isaiah terms "Assyrian," and who shall be found in Immanuel's land when the Lord returns and shall be "broken upon its mountains," as is also told in Zech. 14. The *religious* opponent will then be seen in a Jew, that False Prophet, the "Beast from the land," but who, Scripture tells us, is also a king (as Dan. 11: 36), of whom our prophet speaks as the king of Babylon, and who is the true Antichrist—both being completely united under the control of Satan. In Isaiah, the Assyrian shares the "burden" of Babylon. In Revelation (the woman Babylon, having previously been "eaten and burnt with fire by the ten kings and the Beast, as Rev. 17:16 should read) the *religious* form of antichristian antagonism passes from apostate Christendom to the apostate mass of the Jews, and specifically to their head, the False Prophet. In Revelation 19:20 we see the infliction of what is in Isaiah called the "burden:" "And the Beast was taken and with him the False Prophet . . . these were both cast alive into a lake of fire, burning with brimstone"—a burden indeed!

27: For Jehovah Tzebaoth hath purposed
    And who can bring it to naught?
    His hand is still outstretched
    And who shall turn it aback?

Does this not remind us of Acts 17: 31: "God hath appointed
a day in which He will judge the world by that Man whom He
hath appointed; whereof He hath given assurance unto all, in that
He hath raised Him from the dead?"

Our chapter closes with a return to the word that is characteristic of this part of the book, "burden"—"In the year that King
Ahaz died was this burden" (ver. 28); but the construction of
what follows makes it by no means easy of understanding by
those accustomed to the more prosaic, and less spiritual form of
Gentile speech. To gather the intent of the inspired writer, we
had better forget, to some extent at least, the rather tame rendering of our venerated Authorized Version, and remember that we
are listening to the most emotional, the most lofty, in poetic
flights, of all the prophets of Israel.

It is, of course, of great significance that we are again told
the very year in which the "burden" was given, that in which
"king Ahaz died." Very low indeed at that time had fallen the
fortunes of the House of David, and consequently of the whole
nation. Blow after blow from Syria, and from the northern
kingdom of Ephraim, had apparently brought that elect House
very near its end; and in such case, it was but natural that the
Philistines, those hereditary foes of God's chastened people,
should rejoice at their sad condition. *That* is the setting of the
"burden" which runs thus:

29: Rejoice not so fully, thou land of Philistia,
    Because that the rod that once smote thee lies low;
    For out of the serpent's root springs forth an adder,
    Whose fruit to a burning winged serpent shall grow.
30: The poorest of poor shall pasture in peace then,
    In peace shall the needy lie down once again.
    But to thy root I'll destroy thee by famine,
    Thy remnant, Philistia, by him shall be slain.

The above is the first of the two strophes into which the
"burden" is divided, and surely not without practical value and

interest can it be for us, since it tells of that turning-point in God's ways with His people when His chastening of them, bringing them very low, has provoked the mirth of their enemies. But that turning-point can never be severed altogether from Him through whom alone all blessing can come, and we must find Him here. It is true that we naturally shrink from thus applying the intensely figurative language used, and from seeing even in that "burning and flying one" the Messiah of Israel, the Christ of God. But that was the unprejudiced explanation given even by the Jewish Targum, and we must see if it has not at least some good foundation.

The "serpent" here, then, is the elect House of David, brought low indeed, but its root remains, and from that root springs an adder, or basilisk, a far more terrible creature than the ordinary serpent, but which in this case would represent the good King Hezekiah. The moral character of the figure must then not be pressed, but only the severity of the judgment it inflicts. In this way, Hezekiah was indeed as a "basilisk" to Philistia; for "he smote the Philistines even to Gaza, and the borders thereof." Still more intense is the next agent of divine judgment: the "fiery flying one." Here, too, as in the case of both the House of David and of Hezekiah, we must see a good agent, and none can so well answer to this as Messiah. He comes, and Philistia is destroyed to the very roots; nothing can spring from them, as there shall in the case of Israel, and we see the Lord's people, like a well-protected flock basking in peace in the divine favor. Much do we need in these democratic days, to bear in mind the severity as well as the goodness of God; it is denied, but is quite unaffected by the denial.

The second strophe opens with the most lively poetic language:

> 31: Howl then, O gate!  Cry aloud then, O city!
> All melted must thou be, Philistia's land!
> For see, from the north a smoke is advancing;
> No straggler is there, 'tis a well-ordered band.
> 32: What shall we say to the messengers coming
> Afar from the Gentile?  Oh, speak of His care;
> And tell them Jehovah hath founded Mount Zion,
> And the poor of His flock have found covert there.

In verse 31, so futile will be the resistance of the defences of the Philistine to the invading host from the north, that the cities are bidden to howl, rather than rejoice, for as wax melts in the sun's heat, so shall they melt away in the fierce heat of that coming trial. But what is that trial? Look northward, and see that cloud of smoke. It tells of the burning of towns wasted by the devastating march of a large army from whose ranks there are no stragglers.

This may or may not have some degree of interest for us, but of how little practical value it is if it has no kind of application to our present time and to the living issues that face us. Have we any foe such as the Philistine was to Israel? Have we, too, a covert answering to Zion? Surely these questions can have but one answer. Every enemy that oppressed Israel in her last days oppresses us in its spirit-counterpart in ours. None is more fatal than the Philistine, and it becomes us to ask where he may, in this very day, be found.

He came of the house and lineage of Ham (Gen. 10: 6-14), and "wandering" (the word "Philistine" has in it the meaning of "wanderer") from Egypt, found his way, but not as a pilgrim, into Immanuel's land, to which he attached his own name, Palestine. He enters that land by an easy way—it is the "other way" of John 10: 1, by which the blood of the Lamb is not sprinkled, the Red Sea and the Jordan are avoided. Thus no blood and no cross in its true power (the Philistine has plenty of crucifixes) serve to mark him to this very hour. He depends on dead works, rather than grace; on form rather than power, on Church rather than on Christ, and practically does away with the perfect efficacy of the one Sacrifice, once and forever offered on the Cross. In his conflict with the armies of the living God, he ever takes his stand in Ephes-dammim (1 Sam. 17: 1), which literally means "without the shedding of blood,"* for his strong

---

*The word *"ephes"* is translated for us in Dan. 8: 25: *"without hand;"* while *"dammin"* is the plural form of *"dam,"* "blood." As long as this is in the body, the word is used in the singular, but as soon as it is out of the body, every separate drop speaks, and so the plural form, *"dammim,"* is always used. So "Ephes-dammim" must mean, "Without the shedding of blood."

strategic position to this day is in that "unbloody sacrifice of the mass," as his chief exponent calls it. In a word, he represents the spirit of Ritualism, for as the Philistine dwelt on quite the opposite side of the land from the Ammonite, so does his spirit-representative, Ritualism, and cold, heartless Formalism, live at quite the opposite extreme from the Rationalism of which this son of Lot speaks.

Easy enough is it to discern him in his clearest expression, Papal Rome. Here, from first to last, from the sacrament of baptism, whereby a little child is not merely introduced into the external sphere of Christian profession, but is supposedly actually made a "member of Christ, and a child of God," down to the very last, when that same poor soul is launched into eternity under the futile shield of the sacrament of "extreme unction"— all reliance is on religious form and ecclesiastical sacraments. Oh, there, most assuredly, is the Philistine, in very truth.

But has he no close relations? Has "Rome," that veritable Jezebel, no "children?" (Rev. 2: 23). Where is not the Philistine? Have you never been in Protestant churches, where all is as cold as ice, and as formal as arithmetic—where all the external forms are correctly gone through, but love and power are conspicuous by their absence? Well, there, too, is the spirit of the Philistine.

Have you never been in a gathering, professedly to the Name of Jesus, that once was characterized by a hunger for the Word of God, and by the warmth of Christian love that pervaded it and met you at the very threshold; but now it has become very "rich, and has need of nothing." With calm, courteous indifference they will listen to the sweet truths that no longer affect them —they are. tired of that "light food." There, too, none other than the Philistine has become the lord of that meeting or assembly. Who among us dare say that he has nothing to fear from the Philistine? He is our most terrible and dominant foe this very day.

But is there no deliverance from that dominance? Most surely there is. If the Philistine figures the spirit of self-sufficient formalism, then Samson, his hereditary foe, is the spirit of Nazarite separation to the Lord. But this must ever be distinguished carefully from all that pharisaic separation from fellow-believers that is not altogether unknown in this day just before He comes again, as it was when He came at first.  The Philistine and the Pharisee are very close relations, as father and son; so Samson and the spirit that finds every loveliness, beauty, power and grace in the Lord Jesus are related in the same way.  As Samson at the close of his stormy life was "poor" (what could a captive really possess?), "blind" (for they had put out his eyes), "naked" (they had even cut off his hair!), and thus "wretched and miserable;" so He who cannot lie, tells us that this is the precise condition of the last phase of the professing church (Rev. 3: 17). It is true that the great mass of professing Christians "wist it not," but are filled with foolish boasting; but wherever this is confessed in heart, there, in that individual, "the hair begins to grow again" (Judges 16: 22), and once again there comes the power that is ever connected with being hidden and dependent, for of this the veil of the long hair ever speaks (1 Cor. 11: 15).  To let the same narrative throw its light on that fast-coming future, as Samson was more fatal to the Philistines by his death than he had been in his life (Judges 16: 30), so when the true heavenly testimony is "caught up," the spurious pretender to being that—the professing Church of the day— shall be "spewed out of His mouth," a nullity.

Have we in this gone far away from "Isaiah?"  Indeed, no; if there be any significance in his name, "the salvation of Jehovah."  For in that day of shadows that salvation consisted in a literal deliverance from an earthly and literal foe—all well enough for those who *then* lived.  But our lot is cast in the end of the age, and we need another kind of salvation of which that was but a type, and *Isaiah* must speak to us of that, or it will lack its practical value.

How sweetly the closing words sound even to us who hear them from afar.  "Jehovah hath founded Zion" speaks of grace, and it is in the ceaseless flow of that grace that His people have found their "covert" even to this day.

Oh, blessed, blessed end of all His ways with us!  After permitting all kinds of chastenings and sorrows, "Zion," well and firmly "founded" in the atoning death, the precious Blood of the Lamb, is the security of all who cast themselves upon that grace, and not one of them shall ever be confounded.  Thank God! Thank God!

# CHAPTER FIFTEEN

**The Burden of Moab. A picture of the sorrow that worketh death. One song amid earth's groans glorifies God who alone gives songs in the night. A balance to this.**

THIS chapter continues the "burdens," and also continues the intensely animated style of its predecessor. We are tempted to pass them by, as having little that is of interest or profit to us Christians of the Gentiles, so far separated as we are by time, space and conditions from the actors in those far-off scenes. What have *we* to do with Moab? How can the temporary distress of that obscure people affect us who but lately saw all Europe deluged in blood? Of what practical value now, is the history of a people that can have no influence whatever on the world-politics of the day, nor any part in any League of Nations, for they have long ceased to exist as a nation? The waves of the centuries that have intervened have swept them away. How can it then affect us, that they, too, experienced the common lot, in this devil-ruled world, and suffered from the ravages of war?

Nor is our interest increased, or our difficulties lessened, by questions as to the text, and still more as to the correct renderings of the text, as to which the most competent of scholars, the most spiritually-minded of students, differ. Shall we then say that here is a portion of the Word of God that can have no part in making "the man of God perfect?" Dare we say that? Or shall we the more earnestly and helplessly cast ourselves on the love that has never failed His people yet, and hope to discern at least *some* feature of "the salvation of Jehovah" in this portion of "Isaiah?" Nor should we expect to find the experiences of the Psalms, nor the simplicity of the Gospels, nor the revelations of the Epistles, but if we are hungry, we shall not be sent altogether empty away even from "the burden of Moab." The first four verses are rendered thus:

1: For in a night, AR-Moab is wasted—
   Brought down into silence!
   For in a night KIR-Moab is wasted—
   Brought down into silence!
2: They haste to the Temple,* rush unto Dibon,
   Up to the heights that they may weep there;
   On Nebo is wailing; yea, on Medeba:
   Shorn are their heads, their beards are torn,
3: E'en in their highways they gird them with sackcloth—
   Hark to the wailing on house-top and street!
   Everyone's wailing—drowned in their tears!†
4: Heshbon is crying, and so Elealeh;
   So piercing their cry, to Jahaz 'tis heard!
   Even the soldiers of Moab are wailing!
   The soul of the nation doth tremble within!

Note how the text opens with a "for," which attached to the word "burden" tells the readers that this burden on Moab is a "burden" indeed, *for* a single night suffices to replace the song with the wail. Then follows a most graphic picture of Moab's night of distress; and no "song in the night" can poor Moab raise, for *that* comes from a secret that no Moabite ever learns. As is always the case in times of serious calamity people fly to "religion," so here, crowds of wailing fugitives run to the house of their god. All dignity and self-respect are laid aside; the bare head and torn beard vividly expressing the depth of the distress. Sorrow fills the whole scene! Temples and highways, housetops and public squares, are all resounding with lamentation. The larger cities raise such a wail that it is heard afar. The very soldiery, hardened men as such are, are not unaffected! Yea, the soul of the whole nation is quivering with terror, for this I believe is the sense of this last line. If that is not a picture of the effect of a sudden and heavy calamity on this world, so well symbolized by Moab, then it would be difficult to find any. Now suppose that amid all those sounds of sorrow, one voice should be heard lifted up in joyous song, would not that be a striking testimony to the intervention of God? Indeed it would.

---

*I have thus translated the word *Bajith* which means "house," and here refers to the Temple of Chemosh.

†Lit. "To descend," and thus "sinking," and so the not unusual expression, "drowned in tears."

It is easy to praise in the sunshine, but it takes God Himself
to give us "songs in the night!" Do we not in this light see
what is meant by: "He that offereth praise *glorifieth Me?*" Of
course he does, for songs in suffering express God. But ever the
sunshine of His love falls on the tear-dimmed eyes of the
penitent, and those tears in that light make a rainbow that tells
of the everlasting covenant of the Cross.

Note then, that even that man of God, Isaiah, who in a way
represents Jehovah Himself, is not callous to the sorrow of Moab,
for he apparently forgets the national enmity and expresses his
own forced sympathy in the following verses, and as we listen,
let us gather that God has no pleasure in the pain of any of
His creatures, that not one is lost that does not make Him
lament.

> 5: My heart for Moab is crying.
>      Her nobles flee unto Zoar,
>      (To Zoar that) three-year-old heifer:
>      Weeping they climb the hill-sides of Luhith:
>      With all that the foe may have spared.
> 6: Where sparkled the waters of Nimrim,
>      All dry are the waste-places now;
>      The grass is all withered!
>      The sward is all parched!
>      The green is all gone!
> 7: All they can save, they gather together,
>      With all that the foe may have spared.
>      This bear to the brook of the willows.
> 8: For to its uttermost borders
>      The cry of Moab has gone.
>      Its wailing has reached to Eglaim,
>      Beer-elim its howling has heard.
> 9: The waters of Dimon are blood-filled.
>      Yet more will I bring upon Dimon;
>      On th' escaped of Moab a lion.
>      And on the rest of the land.

Little Zoar, for which Lot successfully pleaded in the day of
his flight from the doomed cities of the plain, is again the refuge
of Lot's children, but now likened to a fair heifer in her prime;
yet as never having been yoked, suggestive of a city that has
never been captured; while doubtless the tradition of its security

in the day of Sodom and Gomorrah had given it the reputation of being a sanctuary. But now all is in vain; the whole land becomes as bare as if fire-swept. The fugitives gather together what they can, and wade across the willow-brook into Edom, the air filled with the screams of the women, and deeper groanings of the men. The Arnon runs blood; nor even yet is the limit reached, for a "lion" (symbol of Judah) awaits the fugitives and the few that may have been spared at home.

Thus place after place joins in the cry of anguish till it reaches Beer-elim, "the well of the strong ones," or leaders, and our minds go back to the digging of that well, when far different music attended its springing waters. "Spring up, O well," Israel then sang, for "the princes digged the well, the nobles of the people digged it, by the direction of the lawgiver with their staves" (Numbers 21: 17, 18). Now the *well* is the same, the *waters* may be springing as pure and sweet as ever, but Moab gets no refreshment from them now. How the darkness of unbelief that so often accompanies our days of sorrow, prevents our getting any comfort from those same springs that in brighter days afforded us such joy! The well is the same, the Word of God and its living streams are the same, it tells ever the same story of a Sun that still shines behind all clouds, but the dark, bitter waves of sorrow have gone over our heads, and we have no "song in the night." O happy people that can echo, however feebly, the song that first was heard in the dark groan-filled dungeon of Philippi! But the modern Moabite or world-lover is not much of a singer, save in the sunshine of prosperity.

CHAPTER SIXTEEN

The Burden of Moab, continued.   Pride the cause of sorrow.

THE burden of Moab is continued, and the chapter, a continuation of its predecessor, begins with the Spirit's counsel to Moab by the pen of the prophet thus:

1: Send ye the lambs to the Lord of the land,
    Send them from Sela through desert,
    To the mount of the daughter of Zion.
2: As little birds flutter when frighted from nests,
    So shall the daughters of Moab
    Tremble at fords of the Arnon.
3: Take counsel, and come to decision,
    Make thy shade as the darkness of midnight,
    Dark in the midst of the noonday,
    Then in that shade hide the outcasts,
    Nor betray to pursuers those fleeing.
4: Let My outcasts find dwelling with thee,
    O Moab, be for them a covert
    From the spoiler that would devastate them.
    For th' extortioner comes to his end,
    The spoiler shall not be forever,
    And earth shall be freed from oppressors.
5: A Throne shall be set up in mercy,
    And on it shall one sit in truth,
    In the tent of (King) David there judging,
    Zealous for right and swift justice.

If the first verse is as "a long-drawn trumpet blast," as Delitzsch says, the trumpet certainly here gives no uncertain sound. All divine counsel to our proud race is precisely of this same character, and demands attention, as here. "Humble thy proud heart, bow thy stiff neck, and own to the supremacy of Zion, for that very name tells of the *grace* thou needest. It is pride that ever denies submission to grace. Divert then that tribute of lambs from Samaria (2 Kings 3: 4) to Zion, for there is still trouble ahead for Moab, and her daughters shall be at Arnon like little birds that flutter over their nests when they are shaken. Learn then by thy trouble to have compassion on others; and when Israel My people shall be outcasts, as darkness hides, so be for them a haven, hiding them from their persecutors. For although David's throne may seem forever abased, it shall yet be restored, and then shall the tables be turned on the oppressor, and the earth be freed from them forever."

Now let later light be thrown on this prophecy which without that light may appear meaningless as far as we are concerned. That there is to be a time of grievous trouble for the Jews on their return to their land is as clear as words can make it. When this is at its height, the Lord Jesus will be manifested for their deliverance. Then, sitting on the throne of His glory, all nations shall be gathered before Him, and He shall discriminate between them solely in view of their treatment of those He terms His "brethren" in the day of their distress (Matt. 25: 32). Thus this becomes the way of salvation for the nations living on the earth at His appearing, and this begins to throw its light on this counsel to Moab.

But further, precisely at that same time, called "the great tribulation," Satan, cast out of heaven to the earth, will seek to stop every confession of the rights of Jehovah to that earth, and to destroy the confessors of that right. Such he finds in those Jews who will not acknowledge the "Beast" as the only rightful object of worship, in his image set up at Jerusalem. Many are slain; many flee. In the pictorial language of prophecy, he then sends forth a flood out of his mouth to swallow these fugitives up, but "the earth opened her mouth and swallowed up the flood which the dragon cast out of his mouth" (Rev. 12: 16); or to interpret the sign-language of prophecy into our plain speech: the Devil stirs up the nations of the earth to follow in dire persecution the scattered remnant of the Jews: but these find favor with those whose hearts God touches, and they evidence "new birth" by feeding them when hungry, giving them drink when thirsty, hospitably receiving them when sick, and when in prison coming to them (Matt. 25: 31-46).

I cannot refrain from one practical word for ourselves from this counsel to Moab. God never permits any form of distress to come upon His people simply in order to deliver them from it.

Whether a man is rich or poor, well or sick, is comparatively a small matter now.  For the work of God in this day when His Son is rejected on earth, and the Spirit is here, is not with men's *bodies,* as it was when Jesus was here before His crucifixion; *that* has made a difference in God's work among men as radical as that solemn fact.  Now that work is with the spirit, which shall still abide when the body may have gone to its kindred dust. That "good" to which "all things now work together" is no form of earthly prosperity, but the being "conformed to the image of His Son." I beseech you, then, in the day of distress, do not simply long for deliverance from it—although that is not to be condemned—but that the distress may yield that which the Father's love sees shall be for your truest good, "the peaceable fruit of righteousness," and one form of this shall show itself in tender sympathy with others who are suffering too.  But to continue our paraphrase:

6: We have heard of his pride: proud Moab's pride,
And that is pride beyond measure.
(We have heard) of his pride, his arrogance, wrath,
But all in vain are his vauntings.
7: Therefore shall Moab for Moab lament,
Yea, everyone shall be wailing;
For the grape-cakes of Kir-hares shall mourn,
Stricken—utterly stricken!
8: The fruit-fields of Heshbon have faded away,
And faded the choice vine of Sibmah.
For the lords of the heathen have broken its sprouts,
The branches that reached unto Jazer;
All through the desert those branches have trailed,
And spread till the sea they passed over.
9: So for the vine of Sibmah I'll mourn,
And weep with the weeping of Jazer.
O Heshbon, I'll water (thy fields) with my tears,
And flood with my tears Elealeh.
For on thy fruits and fair harvest-fields
The shout of the battle has fallen.
10: The harvest now reaped from the once fruitful field
Is the gladness and cheer taken from them!
From the vineyards there sounds no jubilant song,
No shout of joyous exulting;
The treader treads out no wine from the press,
The song of the vintage is ended.

11: Wherefore my bowels for Moab shall sound,
    My inward parts mourn for Kir-hares.
12: Then it shall hap, when weary with tears,
    And Moab climbs to the hill-tops,
    Would enter his temple to pour out his prayer,
    That prayer shall be unavailing.
13: This is the word that Jehovah did speak
    From far away back, touching Moab.
14: But now hath Jehovah spoken and said:
    In the space of three years as a hireling,
    The glory of Moab shall give place to shame,
    Together with all that great number,
    And only a poor little remnant be left,
    And that contemptibly feeble.

I need add little to the above in the way of comment. Moab seems to stand as the very symbol, not merely of pride, but of a peculiar degree and character of pride, as that repetition in the second line suggests. Would you see how lofty worldly pride can be? Look at Moab: there is pride indeed! But the higher the poor proud one climbs in self-exaltation, the heavier his fall. Every step upward increases his degradation when it comes. Would you see the misery of that fall, then listen! No longer do cheerful songs sound from the grape-gatherers, but those wailings that have taken their place are Moab's, for such a storm of desolation has swept over the land that the meadows of Heshbon, trampled by the invaders, look as if sun-parched, and the pleasant vine of Sibmah, the national emblem of Moab, droops.

Then, verse 9, "the circumstantiality of the vision is here swallowed up again by the sympathy of the prophet, and the prophecy which is throughout as truly human as it is divine, becomes soft, and flowing like an elegy" (*Delitzsch*). Can anything be more affecting than to see the prophet himself (Oh, how like unto our Lord he is in this!) foreseeing without one shade of doubt the sorrows that he is foretelling, actually anticipating them with his tears. That seems to be not only the faith that substantiates what as yet has no existence, but sends a ray of tender gracious light onto the very Heart of God. He takes no pleasure in the sorrows of any creature! Could anything witness more strongly to that than His taking up a lamentation, not merely for Jerusalem, but even for Satan! (Ezek. 28: 11). I am not sure that there is not a hint of this in the line: "I'll weep with the weeping of *Jazer*," for that word means: *"The one in whom is help,"* and who can that be but our Lord?   Isaiah is, in a very deep sense, "a man of God!"   So we go back to verse 11, and find in the prophet no paid mourner, but his innermost being resounds with the mournful desolation that he foresees.

But the climax of Moab's misery is that they can get no help from Chemosh.   Natural religion may suffice for men in the day of prosperity, but it fails utterly in the day of trouble.   In such times, darkness may enshroud the mind of the Christian temporarily, but Christ is ever most real, most precious, to His own people in the night of their sorrows.

The burden concludes with Jehovah's fixed decree, told when everything was outwardly smiling, "In three years, as the years of a hireling," that is, one who will not work one minute beyond the time that has been agreed upon, so at an equally fixed moment all the glory of Moab shall only emphasize his shame!

This is, indeed, very ancient history, yet, I again say, being in that Word that is ever "living," Moab too, must be living, even to this day, and be as great a foe to faith as was his prototype of old.   We will consider three clear and simple features that characterized him: his origin, geographical position, and the line of his opposition to God's people, for these will help us in discerning him.

1: His origin.   He was the offspring of horrible incest.   So today, it is the worldliness of true Christians, the uniting of the Lord's people with the world, that produces in the next generation positive opposition to the path of pilgrimage.   How many Christian parents are bewailing the worldliness of their children!   Has their own worldliness nothing to do with it?   Demas was an early dweller in Moab, but this was so rare a case in those happy days, as to make this worthy of notice.   Today the land of Moab is so crowded as to forbid a comment on *one!*

2: Moab's inheritance lay on the east of Jordan, and so we may say today, the modern Moabite will always be found on the easy earthward side of the Cross, as the two-tribes-and-a-half loved those fertile fields so well adapted to their own wealth of flocks and settled there.   Moab's land was on the opposite side to that of the Philistines, nor was it, as theirs, directly within the borders of Israel's true possession, so that if the Philistine must be found in the religious formalism *in* the Church, the Moabite must be found in the dead worldliness that *borders* the Church, and has a spurious relation to it. The Philistine had his counterpart, in our Lord's day, in the Pharisee; the Moabite, in the Herodian. Today the Philistine is the formal Ritualist; the Moabite, the mere worldly professor.

3: As to the nature of his opposition to faith, the clearest light is given in the Lord's letter to Pergamos, that Church that was settling down in the world where Satan's throne was, and is, and in which there were "those who held the doctrine of Balaam who taught Balac, king of Moab, to cast a stumbling-block before the children of Israel, to eat things sacrificed to idols, and to commit fornication." It was the false prophet then, who taught how to entangle the feet of pilgrims in that day, and precisely the same spirit of false prophecy in the Church today soothes the conscience with the lie that this world, being now Christian, if not the final resting-place of the Christian (for death is an awkward fact that cannot be ignored), is very attractive, and far pleasanter to settle down in whilst living, than to turn one's back in spirit on all, and keep the heart fixed on the future when He, earth's true King, shall reign, and we shall reign with Him.

All is in perfect accord, and all points to "religious worldliness" being the Moabite of today, and ever the pilgrim's worst enemy. The increase of wealth, with all the luxury that accompanies it, fosters pride, dulls all affection for Christ and His people, and induces short-sightedness, whereby nothing is recognized as of any practical value, save the transient attractions of this fleeting scene.

What shall Isaiah ("the salvation of Jehovah") counsel? "Send the Lamb of the tribute to the Ruler." Give the willing submission of thine heart to that God who is high over all, and (whilst not the intent of the prophet) may we not say it is by means of the Lamb of redemption? For it is His love that has provided that Lamb and awaits thy return to welcome thee with His kiss. Leave Moab; for know, O world-loving Christian, that the glories, the inventions, the wealth of the world, all lie, this very instant, under the doom of which we have a shadow in these two chapters.  May the Lord make us to fear, for that is one of the elements of faith.

# CHAPTER SEVENTEEN

**The Burden of Damascus.   History ever repeats itself.**

ONCE more the rod of the Lord falls, and now it strikes Damascus, the representative city of Syria.  But as the ten tribes have joined themselves to Syria, entering into an offensive alliance with it against Judah and the House of David (chaps. 7 and 8), they too must share in the infliction, for such a communion always means a "partaking of the evil deeds," and so necessarily of their punishment (2 John 11).  In looking back, we are really looking forward at a scene that will be reproduced in the future, for this history will be repeated, only, of course, with different actors, in a day fast approaching. Once more, as Ephraim joined Syria, so shall the mass of the Jewish nation, again restored to its own land, put its confidence in the military resources of the Gentiles (Daniel 11: 38), with whom a covenant will be made for seven years.  This shall again bring on them, both Jew and Gentile, as here on Damascus and Ephraim, a very heavy "burden."

  1: Consider Damascus!—'tis taken away,
     No longer a city is counted,
     'Tis naught but a heap of bare ruins.
  2: Flocks are now lying in pastoral peace,
     In the towns of Aroer all emptied,
     Reposing with none to affright them.
  3: Ephraim's stronghold existeth no more:
     Gone, too, the realm of Damascus:
     Gone the remnant of Aram!
     Thus shall their glory as transient be
     As that of the sons of Isràel—
        So saith Jehovah Tzebaoth!

As far as the past history is concerned, this dual judgment on Syria and Ephraim was fulfilled by Tiglath-Pileser (2 Kings 15: 29).  But the value of the record for us consists in underlying principles that always hold good, and in that history repeating itself in a day still future. Another Gentile shall be found in the revived Roman Empire, and another Ephraim (Jewish, as it ever was) shall be found in an apostate mass of Jews: the alliance between these shall again bring down the divine judgment here foretold. But in both scenes there is a remnant of faith, and to this our prophecy now turns. That remnant is described.

4: Then shall the glory of Jacob too shrink,
   The fat of his flesh become leanness.
5: Then shall it be as when reapers do grasp
   The stalks of the wheat, and then cut off
   The ears with a sweep of the sickle.
   Or in what time a gleaner doth pick
   Ears in the vale of Rephàim.
6: So a small gleaning shall still be left there,
   As when an olive tree's shaken:
   Two or three berries on loftiest boughs,
   Four or five on the branches most fruitful,
        Saith Jehovah, the God of Isràel.
7: Then to his Maker shall a man look,
   Turn his eye to Israel's "Holy;"
8: No count will he make of the altars he built,
   Nor care for the fruit of his labor:
   Neither Ashèrim nor Sun-gods.

Little do we think of the vital interest that the whole race of men has in such an apparently negligible passage as this. In that afflicted remnant low indeed shall Jacob be brought, yet shall not be utterly destroyed. As there was a stump left to the cut-down tree in chapter 6, from which a fresh sprig shoots, so here the glory of Jacob shrinks, till nothing is left of those who can still be owned as belonging to Jacob, save so few that they may be likened to two or three olives that may be left on the tree after it has been shaken. These stand for that pious remnant of faith from whose hearts, when turning to the Lord, the veil is removed. For each component of this remnant gives up all other confidence and looks expectantly alone to his Maker. The Asherahs and Sun-gods correspond with the Venus and Jupiter of the Greeks: the Moon and the Sun in the heavens: the female and the male principles identified respectively with those two forms of evil: "Corruption" and "Violence."      This pious, penitent remnant becomes the "all Israel" of Romans 11, and this settles it that the prophecy has had no final fulfilment yet, and that God still has much use for that people.

> 9: In that day his strong cities shall be as a tract,
>    In forest or hill-top, forsaken,
>    What time  'fore the sons of Isràel they fled—
>    So shall there be desolation.

That is, the same desolation should come to "Jacob" as came to the original possessors of the land in the day of Joshua.    Then those inhabitants fled before the victorious hosts of Israel, and the ruins of their cities might still be seen deep in the forests that have covered them, or standing on the bleak hills as monuments of the transient character of mere human glory apart from God.

> 10: For thou hast forgotten thy Saviour, thy God,
>     Nor the rock of thy strength hast remembered;
>     'Tis this that hath led thee fine gardens to plant,
>     And to set the strange vine-slips within them.
> 11: In the day thou didst plant, thou didst put up a fence,
>     With the morn made thy sowing to blossom;
>     But the harvest shall be a heap pilèd up,
>     In the day of sad grief and dread sorrow.

In the reminders of the past, seen in verse 9, the future may be seen, for the same cause brings out the same consequence. But what was that cause?   They had simply forgotten who it was to whom they owed everything, and in place of following the faith of their fathers they had devised a plan that was in their esteem as beautiful as a garden filled with choice plants.   Aye, but these were "strange plants," as their policies were foreign to that principle of faith in God that resulted in their fathers' victories.   It is true that all looked favorable at first.   Like the garden, they have hedged it about, and for a time all has apparently gone well.   It is but a deceptive prosperity.   The wind may blow softly just outside Fair Havens, and they may suppose that they have gained their purpose, but Euroclydon is not far off, and the end of all policies that leave God out was, is, and ever will be "grief and dread sorrow."

12: Woe to the roaring of nations—a mass,*
　　Like the roaring of seas is their roaring!
　　Woe to the surging of peoples that surge
　　Like the surging of ocean's vast waters!
13: The peoples may surge as the surging of seas,
　　He rebukes, and lo, they are far off:
　　Are chased by the gale as the chaff of the hills,
　　Like the whirling of dust 'fore the whirlwind.
14: As evening shades fall, lo, the terror is great,
　　But when morning dawns, lo, they are not!
　　Of them that would spoil us, this is the doom:
　　The fate of all who would rob us.

It is a grand picture of the onward sweep of a victorious army. "It spreads, and stretches out as if it would never cease to roll and surge and sweep onward in its course" (*Drechsler*). It would be strange, if remembering this, we did not call to mind the similar picture that our Lord drew of those same days, which are yet so much like those in which we live that he is insensible indeed who fails to heed them. There shall be, just before the end of these days, "Upon the earth, distress of nations in perplexity at the roaring of the sea, and the rolling surge" (Luke 21: 25); for even now, although the great war has ended at least for a time, the nations continue in tumult, and are as a troubled sea that still tosses its waves in a restlessness that foretells a renewal of the storm.

In the past, the Assyrian host came on; and it was thus the evening saw them encamped in enveloping folds all around the city that seemed inevitably doomed to fall. But ere the morning broke, that host had melted away, its thousands sunk in the sleep that knows no waking here, and His people were free! So again shall it be in a day yet before us. Once more the nations shall envelope a doomed city. This time it will be Jerusalem, and then dark will be the night that appears as if about to settle over poor Israel in that sole remaining remnant of the Jews. But says another prophet, "At evening time it shall be light" (Zech. 14: 7).

---

*"The destruction of Asshur is predicted here, but not of Asshur as Asshur, but of Asshur as the imperial kingdom, which embraced a multitude of nations" (*Delitzsch*)—that is precisely the conclusion that has been repeatedly expressed in these pages.

The night shall not fall, the threatening darkness shall flee before Him whose feet shall stand upon that mountain they left long ago, and Israel's everlasting light shall have broken upon her, as the sun rose upon their forefather Jacob after *his* time of "great tribulation" (Gen. 32: 31).

Our lot is cast neither with the Assyrian of the past, nor with the Assyrian of the future, yet all these actors may be found as energetic and active as ever they were or will be. We must find "Ephraim" in that proneness of the flesh to lean on what is esteemed tangible and real. "Syria" may be discerned in the various false confidences, as, for instance, our material resources as a defence against poverty, and thus this poverty itself may well stand today as an illustration of our "Assyrian," or anything that displaces dependence on a Father's care ever shielding those whose hearts' confidence is in Him as revealed in Christ our Lord. May His grace make us so to trust.

## CHAPTER EIGHTEEN

**What people are designated as "scattered and peeled?" Which is the "land that shadows?" What are the vessels of bulrushes? How can rivers spoil a land?**

WE HAVE now come to a chapter, short indeed, but full of thrilling interest to every lover of the Word of God, and especially to all to whom the study of Prophecy is a delight, as indeed it should be to every Christian in these portentous days. I say of thrilling interest, since it deals with events which, although future, seem to be so imminent as to bring them within the possibility of many now living seeing their actual accomplishment. I refer to the establishment, under Gentile protection, of a Jewish State in Palestine, with the people as a whole still rejecting their Messiah; but this State becoming disrupted by a return of the most Satanic idolatry, there will be the manifestation of a faithful remnant, and then finally a divinely ordered and everlasting restoration of every Israelite from the uttermost parts of the earth. That Jewish autonomy is not yet effected, but how near it appears to be!

Fully in accord with this, we note that we are still under the "burden of Damascus," and that another "burden" only begins with the next chapter. We have in the preceding chapter noted the significance of Damascus as a representative Gentile, in alliance with that part of the Jewish nation that had revolted from "David's House." In the past this was the ten tribes, headed by Ephraim, and often so designated. Now, in our chapter, we leap over a long period of already more than 2,500 years, and find a prophecy that can only be understood in the light of a repetition of just such a state of affairs: Jew and Gentile united in a political alliance, and this ended by the revelation of the Lord Jesus, the restoration of the House of David, and the regathering of the still-scattered Israelites.

Thus the one root question that will govern our understanding, and so translations, wherever two or more different renderings are admissible (as is so frequently the case in the Hebrew Scriptures), is of what people is the prophet speaking as "terrible from their beginning hitherto?" Let *that* be settled, and all becomes comparatively simple. Beyond all controversy the Lord's *direct* interest among the nations of the earth, is in one people only, and that one is the nation ever and still beloved for the fathers' sakes; for does He not say, "You only have I known of all the families of the earth" (Amos 3: 2)? Is not that sufficient to identify that people here?

The chapter again bears on it the number "three" in its divisions, and the significance of that number is with equal clearness marked upon it, for it tells of "God manifested in the salvation" of Israel. Do you think that the human writer, Isaiah, himself could have intended, or indeed have been cognizant of all these wonderful numerical markings, indelibly interwoven into the texture of his prophecy, yet not pointed out, or to be discerned by a superficial reader? It is just such points that the apostle Peter refers to in his first Epistle, chapter 1: 10, 11.

The three divisions of the chapter are:

1: Verses 1-3. The divine call demanding the attention of the whole earth.
2: Verses 4-6. Man's political plan; its initial success and final failure.
3: Verse 7.   The final and divine recovery of Israel.

We will again attempt a rendering as faithful to the original as we can make it, endeavoring at the same time to make the sense clear.

1: Ho! Land shadowing with wings, beyond the rivers of Cush,
   Ambassadors sending by sea, in vessels water-absorbing,
2: Saying, Swift messengers go to a nation scattered and ravaged,
   To a people terrible ever, from their beginning and onward,
   A nation forever under the line, and so forever downtrodden,
   Whose land the rivers have spoiled!
3: All ye inhabitants of the whole world,
   All ye dwellers on the whole earth,
   When a banner is raised on the mountain-top, look!
   When a blast is blown on the trumpet, hark!

It will be necessary to examine with such care as we can, the very words that are here used.

The first may rendered either "Woe," or "Ho!" or "Ah." It is an interjection, either conveying a threat, as in chapter 10: 1, or a call demanding prompt attention, as in chapter 55: 1; or a sigh, as in chapter 1: 4, where it is rendered "Ah!" The second rendering is decidedly preferable here, as introducing an urgent call.

But now comes a most interesting question. What "land" is here addressed? Is it one single country, as if the word "land" were synonomous with "people" or "nation?" Or is it a wide district of undefined boundaries, but including *many* nations and peoples? As it is the ordinary word for "earth," covering our whole globe, or that part of it that is before the Mind of the Spirit, there would not seem to be the slightest reason why it should *not* be understood in this sense here, if the correspondence with other scriptures justifies it. As to its geographical position, we are only told that it is "beyond the rivers of Ethiopia, or Cush." But there was not only an African Cush (Isa. 20: 3-5), but another in Asia (Gen. 2: 13, these rivers are all Asiatic; Num. 12: 1, *cf.* Exod. 2: 15-21, Midian was Asiatic); so these two rivers may here be confidently assumed to be the Euphrates in Asia, and the Nile in Africa, which formed the very boundaries of the Land of promise, as given to Abraham in Gen. 15: 18, from the river of Egypt, the Nile, the African boundary, unto the great river, the river Euphrates, the Asiatic. As far as this goes, then, *all* the land outside of Palestine, might here be called with this "Ho!"

But the sphere from which we may select the "Land" becomes rather more contracted by the next words, "shadowing with wings," which is a perfectly correct rendering, and which speaks of this "land" taking under its protection dependent nations, or *one* dependent nation, and that one possibly lying in the only other sphere mentioned, that is *within* the bounds already given, the rivers of Cush or Ethiopia. All such possible alternatives must be settled by other scriptures.

The phrase, "beyond the rivers of Cush," occurs in one, and only one, other place in Scripture, and this must lend us its aid:

*"From beyond the rivers of Cush shall they bring My suppliant,
even the daughter of My dispersed to Me as an offering"* (Zeph.
3: 10). As this evidently deals with the final gathering of Israel
from *all* lands outside of those boundaries (as, among others, in
verse 7 here and in chap. 43: 5 and Jer. 29: 14: "I will gather
you from all nations"), we are justified in seeing those same
lands here. Only here, in Isaiah, the Jewish State is not under
the protecting wing of Jehovah; but (if other scriptures justify
such a thought) of a League of Nations unified under one head,
be it Emperor or President. That the Roman Empire which ruled
the known world for about 500 years, and is now non-existent,
shall again be revived, is as sure as that the *Jew* shall be restored;
for so speak many sure foretellings of that revival, as Rev. 17:
8, "The Beast was, and is not, and shall come" (R. V.), and
Daniel's prophecy. Thus we may finally conclude that the "land"
addressed in our first verse is that revived Empire covering *all
Christendom,* and so, of course, this western hemisphere. But it
is not the place here to follow this further, other than to repeat
that the scene opens with the stage filled by two actors, Gentile
and Jew, the former outside the boundaries of the latter's land,
but protecting it.

It is surely striking that we are assumed to be interested in
knowing in what kind of conveyances the ambassadors carried out
their mission! Nearly all translators render it practically as our
A. V., "vessels of bulrushes;" but that does not forbid further
inquiry. Ships made of literal bulrushes would surely be ill-
adapted to travel the seas in safety—to outlive a storm on the
Atlantic, or such as brought shipwreck to Paul on the Mediter-
ranean. But dig out the root of the word rendered "bulrushes,"
*gomah,* and we find that its first meaning is "to drink," to
"absorb" water, and from this root comes the word for bulrush
(*gomeh*), because that mire-loving plant does "drink up water"
(see Job 8: 11) and thus naturally the word was assumed to refer
to "vessels of bulrushes," as in A. V. But why should we not
render it quite literally, *"in vessels that drink up water?"* That
is, as the bulrush lives by drinking up water, so do these vessels
carry out the purpose of their formation in precisely the same
way.

The word for "vessels" strengthens this literal rendering, for it is one that is never used in Scripture for either wind-propelled sailing ship, or oared galley propelled by human strength. There are specific words for these, so that the "vessels" referred to here must have another agent for propulsion. This word for "vessel" always tells of careful construction and delicate adjustment fitting for a specific purpose. As the "vessels" (the same word) of the Tabernacle, were each most carefully prepared for a specific work, so these carefully constructed "vessels" are propelled by "drinking up water!"

In short, no combination of words could be found better calculated to express the modern steamboat! Of course this could not be discerned before the coming of the steam-propelled ship, but now that it has come, it is surely legitimate, and within the limits of sober exegesis, to recognize that in these remarkable words, God had foreseen that invention of man's ingenuity. Nor again, is this other than greatly strengthened by the call to them: "Go, ye *swift* messengers."

Many have concluded that since the "land shadowing with wings" must send its ambassadors by sea, that it must be insular, and the position of Great Britain, with its marked characteristic of assuming the protection of other peoples, pointed to *that* being the country intended here. This view I have shared; but of late I have been compelled to abandon it, for the two very simple reasons that there is no other word of Scripture to support it, and that there is another interpretation that *has* this support.

In the day fast approaching, when once more there is an autonomous Jewish State, Daniel 9: 27 tells us that the "Prince" of the revived Roman Empire (the same people that destroyed Jerusalem) shall make a covenant with that State for seven years, thus taking it under its "wing." The "land shadowing with wings" is, therefore, as we have seen, that revived Roman Empire, and the incident here referred to is the *making that "covenant"* or treaty.

So much for the *sender* of the embassy. As to the people to whom they are sent, they have ever been marked out "from their very beginning," by portents, prodigies and such interpositions of divine guardianship as has ever made them objects of fear to all others (comp. Gen. 35: 5). Yet it is a nation of "line, line" (as it is literally written), that is, constantly under the measuring line of Jehovah, who since they fail to come up to that measure, thus chastens them, as it is written: "I will stretch over Jerusalem the line of Samaria," and if we ask what that means, the words following will answer, "I will wipe Jerusalem as a man wipeth a dish" (2 Kings 21: 13). That gives the idea in the word "line" very clearly, and then attach to this the word in Amos 3: 2: "You only have I known of all the nations of the earth: therefore I will punish you for your iniquities." We can have no uncertainty as to the force of this "line, line" here: that nation has ever been under the line of divine chastening.

The other mark is, "Whose land the rivers have spoiled." In the clear light of Scripture, the meaning of this is as sure as it is valuable for the correct understanding of other prophecies in which we ourselves have a more direct interest, as for example Rev. 16: 12, where we have again the Euphrates used in a symbolic way. Note, then, the divine interpretation of a "river" when thus used in chap. 8: 7. There it is "the Assyrian and all his glory," because he and his army, as a river breaking over its banks in irresistible flood, invades Palestine. In the light this gives, there can be no difficulty in seeing in these "spoiling rivers," those nations which have from time immemorial spoiled, by their constant ebb and flow, the land of Israel.

It is surely nothing less than an absurdity to think of literal rivers as spoiling that land. It had but one, the Jordan, and that one, far from being destructive, was really a guard along its eastern frontier. But let Egypt (symbolically the Nile) attack Assyria, or let Assyria (the Euphrates) attack Egypt, in either case, the land lying between them, Palestine, must be overrun and so "spoiled" by those rivers.

Yet spoiled as it ever has been, here are its own people back again in it, but not yet in believing dependence on the God of Jacob; their trust is not in the shadow of His wing. Their return has been simply a matter of world-politics; and instead of honoring the God of their fathers, they, under their leader, honor the god of fortresses or munitions (Dan. 11: 38), thus relying on that protection of the "land shadowing with wings" that we are told of here, making a treaty, as Daniel tells us (9: 27), for seven years.

The next verse opens with some very striking event that should command the keenest interest of all who dwell within the bounds of the prophetic earth. This is likened to a double call, first to the eye: a banner, high and lifted up on a bare mountain-top where no trees can impede the vision, and so within sight of all. Then the ear is appealed to by the sound of the trumpet. Again how impossible it is to take these as being literal, for how few could see a literal banner even on the highest mountain. How few could hear the loudest trumpet-blast! But some event has happened, or is happening, that, as a banner or trumpet, should rivet the attention of everyone on earth who hears of it. In these days how short is the time needed to disseminate any news of interest all over the civilized world. To ear and even to eye, in television, distance is annihilated.

What, then, can that event be, but just what we have been told in the previous verses? The Jews are once more in their land, forming an autonomous State—*that* is a "banner" worth looking at! Israel is once more making a treaty as a fully re-stored nation—*that* is a trumpet-blast that one must be deaf indeed not to hear. But in these is involved another sign, super-seding in its significance all others, for then, and not till then, shall the long-broken thread of Old Testament prophecy be taken up again. Then, and not till then, shall time begin again to be noted; for at this very juncture, the last week of seven years of those "seventy weeks" of Daniel's vision, is beginning, and the nation, so accurately described in verse 2, so marvellously pre-served through all the centuries, comes again into God's plan. It is this that is the "banner" lifted up, the "trumpet-blast," so loud that all should heed it.

This is so important that I would linger a little. Those of my readers who are familiar with Daniel's prophecy of "seventy weeks," in his ninth chapter, will remember that that period was divided into three unequal parts, thus: 7-62-1. I cannot now attempt any detailed interpretation of this most interesting of prophecies, save that I would ask, "Why that first pause at the end of *seven* weeks, or forty-nine prophetic years?" A very little study of the angel's words will show that the starting point of the whole period is the twentieth year of Artaxerxes (Neh. 2: 1), or B. C. 445: that forty-nine prophetic years (or forty-eight calendar years) from that date would bring us down to B. C. 397. Now if we turn to the last of the Old Testament prophets, Malachi, and possess a Bible that gives the dates of the book, we shall see that the voice of prophecy ceased in B. C. 397, or exactly "seven weeks of years" after the commission to restore Jerusalem.   From the beginning of that silence until Messiah presented Himself to Jerusalem as Prince there were precisely sixty-two weeks of years to a day (Luke 19: 42).   The consequence of His rejection was, as we know, the destruction of their city, and to the very end the "desolations determined."   But during all this present parenthetical time, not one word of Old Testament prophecy is being directly fulfilled, for God is doing quite another character of work altogether, in taking "out of the nations, a people for His Name" (Acts 15: 14).   But when those ambassadors of whom our chapter speaks, go to the "nation scattered and peeled," then shall the last verse of Daniel 9 be fulfilled, which says, "And he, the prince of the revived empire, shall confirm a covenant with the many for one week."   Such a resumption of Old Testament prophecy is then, I take it, a "banner and a trumpet-blast" of unspeakable significance.

When, or by what means, that people is restored to their land, we are not told here, nor am I aware of any prophecy that does tell us a word of the *actual returning* of the Jews *in unbelief* to their land.   Prophecy takes them up just where it left them, that is, already in their land, and making a treaty there with the one other actor on that stage in the past.   How long they may have been there before this, we are not told.   One would suppose that the formation of a settled government, capable of executing a treaty, and the rebuilding of the temple, as evidently must be the case, since again the morning and evening sacrifice shall be offered (Dan. 9: 27), must have taken an appreciable length of time; but how long, we are not told.

From this it may be deduced that the heavenly witness, the Church, *may* (not must) be still upon the earth, when that State is formed and that Temple built, *since these are not the subjects*

*of Old Testament prophecy.* If they were, if we had been told
in the Old Testament of the actual transport of the Jews to Palestine in their present unbelief, then the catching up to the Lord
of all "in Christ" would, if I err not, necessarily take place before
such return, but not as it is, nor can we be on earth when this
treaty of which we are here told is made.

The way is now clear to consider the second part of the
prophecy:

4: For thus hath Jehovah spoken to me,
   I will retire to My dwelling and rest,
   There to be still, but closely observant:
   As the clear heat of the sunshine,
   As the cloud of the dew in the harvest.
5: For ere the harvest when finished the blooming,
   The blossom becoming a ripening grape.
   Then shall the branches be cut off and prunèd,
   Then shall the tendrils be taken away.
6: Forsaken to carrion-birds of the mountains,
   Left to be trodden by beasts of the field,
   The carrion-birds shall summer upon them,
   The beasts of the field shall tread them all down.

Verse 4 speaks of Jehovah's attitude toward this arrangement,
or "covenant." He has nothing to do with it directly. His will
has not been sought. It has simply been the outcome of human
politics, and He is not active in the movement. He retires from
the earth, as it were, to His own dwelling; leaves the "earth-
dwellers" to pursue their own ends. His providences indeed seem
to favor the scheme, and just as clear warm days and dewy
nights favor the ripening of grape and corn, so do all events
seem to further the plan, with which all goes well for a time. The
temple is rebuilt; morning and evening sacrifices are smoking
once more on Israel's altars; the whole mass of returned Jews
go up to worship there, without any discrimination marking out
the true from the false; all is about to come to full fruition,
nothing could be more promising.

Can we not put ourselves beside some pious Jews of that day?
We hearken to the praises that go up for this marvellous recovery
after two thousand years of wandering. Surely all Israel's former
glory is about to be restored—when: crash! A thunderbolt falls

out of a clear sky. In an hour everything is changed, and from that time that pious faithful remnant is left a prey to carrion-birds, by which I take it are meant their *spirit* foes, and beasts, their *human* political enemies.

What is it that has happened? It is not the way of the Spirit to tell us every detail in one prophecy, or diligence in searching the whole of Scripture would not be needed. Isaiah, and his readers of that day, must wait many centuries to learn what that event is that in a moment will change the whole aspect of the scene. Three years and a half have elapsed since those ambassadors came in their swift vessels to make the covenant. It is "the midst of the week," of Daniel 9: 27, and during that time, while things have gone thus on earth, in heaven there has been war; and now the conquered in that war, under the leadership of the Devil, are cast out to the earth, nevermore to defile the realms above it with their presence. Short shall their stay be even here; they are but on their way, *via* the abyss, to their final abode in that Lake of Fire prepared for them; and a malignancy beyond all that is merely human characterizes that short stay, for the Devil has great wrath, for "he knoweth that he hath but a short time" (Rev. 12: 12).

Is that not enough to account for this change? The "abomination of desolation" is now set up in the holy place of that re-built temple. Seven spirits, more wicked than that spirit of idolatry that has been so long cast out of Israel, have now returned, and the last state of that apostate mass is worse than the first. But it is not the mass that we see in verse 5, but rather that afflicted desolate remnant with whom the Spirit of God is concerned, in whose sorrows the heart of our Lord has a part. It is these—not the mass, still in covenant with the (then) Satan-possessed Prince of the Roman Empire—that are here downtrodden and desolate. These are the desolate who refuse to worship that image, and desolate they must be "till the consummation, and that determined be poured upon" them (Dan. 9: 27).

But not forever does this condition of things last. The days are shortened, and the last verse, in the significant third place, gives us the happy scene of a divine restoration. God appears. God manifests Himself for His poor people. The Feet of the

Lord have, between these verses 6 and 7, stood upon the Mount of Olives.  Let us listen:

> 7:Then to Jehovah Tzebaoth shall there be brought as a present
> A people scattered and ravaged—terrible ever and always:
> A nation forever under the line; and so forever downtrodden:
> Whose land the rivers have spoiled,
> To the place of the name of Jehovah of Hosts, the mountain of Zion!

Mark the difference in this return from the Zionism of the present day.  Jehovah takes no direct interest in this present movement; but here and now the very recovery of the scattered Jews is welcomed and accepted by Jehovah (*i.e., Israel's* God) as a holy offering, a "gift-offering."  It is the time more fully referred to by this same prophet in chapter 66: 20, where we shall hope to consider it.  It is the time referred to by all the prophets that so clearly foretell the final recovery of all Israel.  It is the time referred to by our Lord when He said the Son of Man "shall send His angels with a great sound of a trumpet; and they shall gather His elect from the four winds, from one end of heaven to the other" (Matt. 24: 31).  The fruition of the hopes of the Zionist may possibly be seen by the Church still upon earth, but this joyous recovery shall be witnessed indeed by the heavenly redeemed, only as accompanying the Lord on His triumphant return.  May our God win our hearts to Himself by the love this speaks to us as to *friends* (John 15: 14, 15).

# CHAPTER NINETEEN

The burden of Egypt. Who is the "cruel lord?" The conversion of Egypt. The blow that heals. Jehovah's threefold blessing.

WE HAVE found, I trust, something of a "living issue," as it is termed, in each of the "burdens" that have preceded the one to which we have come, and this surely should lead us confidently to expect no less from that most ancient seat of civilization, Egypt. How often is the inspired Word of God treated as if it were nothing more than a profane and very imperfect history, a kind of companion to Herodotus; and if these two authorities are not in exact accord in any detail, the writer who makes *no* claim to divine enlightenment and control, is considered more trustworthy than the one who *does*. Yet, our learned professors fear to assert plainly that the claim is fraudulent, for, like their fathers, they too "fear the people, for all (Christian) men count" Isaiah to be a prophet.

Unless, then, we can see something beyond a mere account of the doings of a people whose bones have long been mingled with their kindred dust, something that is of living importance to ourselves in this very day, we might well say that these Scriptures were not worthy of being called a divine revelation at all, and deny that their human authors "spake as moved by the Holy Spirit." So long then as we are assured that this claim to divine inspiration is not false, but well-founded, so long are we bound to seek the deeper truths, not seen on the surface, for superficial details, like those bones in Ezekiel's valley, may be *"very dry"* (Ezek. 37: 2). May the Spirit of God then breathe on these dry bones of historical detail and geographical situation and make them "live."

If any land bears a share in providing types for us, "on whom the ends of the ages are come," it is Egypt. As the taskmaster of God's Israel, it speaks of those *fleshly lusts,* to the hard bondage of which the child of God is first awakened, and groans. Then, in another point of view, it is, as here, the *world,* in its complete

independence of God.  All Egypt's wealth is in her Nile; and she
cries, "My river is my own!"  Every year its swollen flood bears
down a rich alluvial deposit, which covers her desert sand with
that fertile soil on which her very life depends.  Strange river of
blessing!  Of its *source,* those who enjoyed the blessings it
brought were quite ignorant, precisely as the world has ever accepted, and does still accept, the providential blessings that "fill
hearts with food and gladness," as a matter of course, without
any thought of whence, or from whom, they really come.  But the
correspondence goes further, and comes to our own present day,
for as explorers have discovered the sources of the blessings of
Egypt's river in a chain of lakes, so of late explorers in the field
of science have discovered the *natural* source of everything that
comes to men in their life here.  But might it not be asked: Are
those lakes, Albert and Victoria Nyanza, after all the *final* source
of supply?  Let the heavens withhold their rain, and how long
would it be before those lakes themselves had to acknowledge
that they too were dependent on the heavens?  And should God
withhold His mercies in providence, how long would it be before
the world would have to own that no science that excludes God
as the great First Cause can be anything than "falsely so-called?"
It is not "science," or what is *known,* at all.  In this chapter we
see that lesson taught and learned.

In a still more spiritual sense, let the professing Church, let
any individual practically, in conduct or in doctrine, neglect or
reject the Lord Jesus, the Head, whence all nourishment proceeds, then in proportion to that neglect, the fountains and rivers
of refreshment will dry up and eventually send forth only the
"blood" that speaks of death.  Alas, that it must be added that
is already the character of the outflow from many a pulpit, from
many a seminary, from many a college even today.

So again we may read the future even in the past, remembering that Isaiah is not a historian, but a prophet, and while he
speaks of an Egypt of the *past,* we must discern one of the *future,*
nor can we close our eyes to *present* conditions in Christendom,
so nearly approaching those that shall then obtain.

The chapter divides as under, and I would beg my readers to
note the beauty and order of these clearly marked, and, I can but

believe, divinely intended divisions.  Note, too, once more the prominence of "three;" for it is "God manifesting" Himself.

> First triad: verses 1-15, Jehovah's intervention in judgment and its result.

1: Verses 1-4: in *internal* discord.
2: Verses 5-10: in failure of *material* resources.
3: Verses 11-15: in failure of *spiritual* resources.

> Second triad: verses 16-20, Jehovah's intervention in grace, and its result.

1: Verses 16, 17: Egypt *fears* Jehovah.
2: Verse 18: Egypt *turns* to Jehovah.
3: Verses 19, 20: Egypt *worships* Jehovah.

> Third triad: verses 21-25, Jehovah responds in grace.

1: Verses 21, 22: The healing of *internal* discord.
2: Verse 23: *Material* blessing through Jerusalem, the Center of the earth.
3: Verses 24, 25: Final *spiritual* blessing of the millennial earth, including representative peoples.

The first strophe opens grandly with Jehovah entering Egypt on His swift-rolling chariot, a cloud. At once false gods flee, and there is universal internal disruption. Mutual distrust and animosity between those who, by their common interests, should be united, is ever the evidence of God's activity in judgment; as the opposite, love and confidence and the dwelling together in unity, is the "good and pleasant" evidence of His intervention in grace.  We shall see both in our chapter.

Let me attempt a free paraphrase of the grand original, at least seeking to give the true sense:

1: See Jehovah swiftly riding into Egypt on a cloud:
From His presence Egypt's idols take their flight (a troubled crowd).
Then the trembling heart of Egypt melts within her at the sight:
2: While the maddened hosts of Egypt 'gainst Egypt's hosts are waging fight.
Every man attacks his brother: neighbors now are neighbor's foes:
City against city warring: kingdoms interchanging blows.

3: Well may Egypt's courage fail her: I her counsel bring to
      naught:
   Idols, mutterers, necromancers, wizards, all with folly
      fraught.
4: Thus Egyptians I abandon to the hand of a hard lord,
   And a fierce king reigning o'er them doth their punish-
      ment afford.
   'Tis Jehovah Tzebaoth who proclaimeth this His word.

Most solemnly does this apply even to our own day. In a
scene that has turned from Him, a necessary preliminary to divine
intervention in *grace,* is divine intervention in *judgment.* Mark
then, the consequences of that intervention. The "religion" that
held the people together fails to do so longer; and as if they had
lost all powers of self-control and were bitterly insensate, those
with common interests destroy one another!

This may have occurred more than once in the antitype of
ancient "Egypt," the "world" of Christendom, but never has it
been so sadly emphasized as during recent years, in that unfaithful witness.

As to that "hard lord" of verse 4, history tells us that he
was not an external conqueror, but a native despot, and "kingdom
against kingdom" exactly suits the twelve small kingdoms into
which Egypt was split up after the Ethiopian dynasty was overthrown in B. C. 695, until Psammetichus brought all under a
single monarchy, and *he* is "the hard lord." So much for the
history, but history here is divine prophecy, and we, as the last
verse most clearly shows, are looking to what is still before us.
We find in that Psammetichus merely one of several types of that
internal oppressor of whom we hear in Dan. 8: 23, "a king of
fierce countenance," and in whom is to be seen (not the Assyrian,
who is never represented in Scripture as dependent on another,
but) the veritable Antichrist, the second Beast, from the land, a
"hard lord" indeed, to the little remnant of faith whom he perse-
cutes (Rev. 13: 11-17). Note the well-known trinity here too;
*internal* in this strophe, *external* in the next, and *eternal* in verses
21-25. It is a Fingerprint.

But now we see the severity of Jehovah's intervention in the
failure of all *material* resources:

5: Waters fail from Egypt's sea: Egypt's Nile is parched and dried.

6: The river's arms, once beautiful, now become a noxious tide; *

The streams of Egypt now are minished; parched is all the countryside.

7: Reed and rush by drought are shriveled; grassy tracts by river's shore:

All the sowing by the river, scattered now, is seen no more.

8: Mourning are the fisher-people, all who angle now lament; Those that cast the net on waters languish through empoverishment.

9: Workers in fine flax and weavers of white fabrics all despair.

10: Pillars of the State are broken, toilers faint with hopeless care.

Egypt's wealth, as already said, practically consists in her river, because of its volume here called a sea. When that is dried all her prosperity is shriveled and disappears. The rainfall on the land of lower Egypt is utterly insignificant and insufficient, as Deut. 11: 10 and Zech. 14: 18 tell us, so the Nile becomes the only source of Egypt's prosperity. We may, without much uncertainty, see how terribly there has been the correspondence to the loss of that wealth in the present condition of the civilized world. It cannot be insisted upon that this prophecy has been, or is being, literally fulfilled in this day, or ever will be, in the literal, complete drying up of the Nile; but that there is a most remarkable, clear and significant correspondence in the spiritual sphere, will be denied by no man who is in the least thoughtful.

The rain, or blessing, from the heavens has stopped, and the result is a drying up of the source of prosperity; the natural consequences of that are told in a depression affecting all classes, from the highest (pillars of the State) to the discouraged and even despairing laborer. Let Christendom turn away from Christ, and the description of Egypt with a dried river will apply.

---

*By referring to the Revised Version, my readers will see that I have accepted most of its readings as far nearer the original. Here the dried channels emit a stench from the decomposing matter.

But further, when God intervenes in judgment, how all human wisdom is proved to be but folly!   This the next strophe emphasizes:

11:  Fools are all of Zoan's* princes!   Fools are Pharaoh's men
          most wise!
      Foolish is their senseless counsel!   Counsel theirs of
          foolish lies!
      Still they dare to say to Pharaoh: Son of wisest men am I:
      I'm the son of ancient kings, whose times in far-off distance
          lie.
12:  Where are then thy trusted wise men?   Let them wisely
          make thee know
      What Jehovah hath determined; warn thee of His coming
          blow.
13:  Fools are all of Zoan's princes!  Noph's† proud princes are
          deceived.
      Egypt they have made to err, though corner-stones by all
          believed.
14:  'Tis Jehovah mixed within her a spirit of wild discontent,
      A spirit of perversity, and that is an ingredient
      Causing Egypt far to wander in all work her hand may
          find,
      As when staggers in his vomit one strong-drink has robbed
          of mind.
15:  Neither shall there be for Egypt any work that she may
          do,
      Whether done by head or tail: by palm or rush, by high
          or low.

Again I say there is not a reader of these lines but will recognize what a true, if sad parallel our own very day presents to this picture in the utter inadequacy of all the wisdom of Christendom. The very "corner-stones" (as Egypt's princes) of the nations, their wisest and best, are seeking some plan that shall serve to ward off another such holocaust of death as that of the late war.‡ How vain the effort!   They desire to attain permanent peace while the

---

*Zoan, the Tunis of profane history.

†Noph, *i.e.*, Memphis.

‡Never has this world seen such a sight as the representatives of over sixty nations sending the wisest men that they possess to take counsel together as to economics at London.   It has been

Prince of Peace is rejected!  They would dispense with the return of Him to whom this earth belongs, and from which we have banished Him.  Not one single idea have these great men of earth that the universal peace for which they long can never be brought about save by His return to assume the Sceptre which is most justly His by the double title of creation and redemption.  The *motive* for peace in itself cannot be stigmatized as evil.  It would be nothing but senseless fanaticism to condemn the desire to prevent the bloodshed and unutterable misery that ever accompanies war; it is not *that* which is "wicked."  But how evil is the refusal to own the claims of the Son of God, or more correctly, in this connection as having this title to the earth, of the Son of Man!  How evil to close the eye to the universal *sin* that has alone brought the universal *suffering!*  How foolish to deny the root, the sin; while deprecating the fruit, the misery and bloodshed!

The disgusting, repellent picture of a drunken man staggering in his vomit, is not far astray from that picture presented by the bewildered counsels of all from the best to basest; the noble palm and the mean rush, *i.e.*, the wise statesman and the ignorant proletariat, all are evidently equally incompetent to guide the ship of Christendom, laboring against contrary winds and heavy seas, to the quiet harbor of established Peace where they would be.  Let the King come, the King of the kingdom of the heavens, let Him return in power and great glory, and lo, as in the early morning of His coming to the disciples as they toiled on stormy Gennesaret, then immediately winds were hushed, waves subsided, and at once "the ship was at the land whither they went;" so, and only so, shall the present storm cease, and this poor distracted earth shall be where it desires, basking in unbroken peace in the healing rays of the Sun of Righteousness. But our hope shall be fulfilled long before that, in His coming as the Bright Morning-Star.

-----

an utter failure.  At Geneva the course taken by Japan has exposed the impotency of the League of Nations politically.  A new religion is promised at Chicago that shall unite all the race.  How these repeated failures cry for the return of The King!

Now we come to what must always precede the manifestation of the Lord for any deliverance, whether of the individual, or as here, for that of the earth.

16: In that day shall boastful Egypt be like women in their fear,
   Terror-stricken; for Jehovah's threatening Hand is drawing near;
   Ever swinging close above them is that awe-inspiring Hand;
17: Fear takes hold of trembling Egypt at each thought of Judah's land,
   As often as this word is spoken, then upon them like a pall,
   The terrors of the Lord of Hosts over Egypt's spirit fall;
   For they know that in His counsels, He is threatening them all.
18: In that day in Egypt's land there shall be of cities five,
   Yet their language shall be one, which from Canaan they derive.
   All of them shall to Jehovah, Lord of Hosts, together swear;
   *"Ir-ha-Heres"* shall the *name* be, that one city then shall bear.
19: In that day shall be an altar in the midst of Egypt's land,
   And a pillar to Jehovah on the margin of her strand:
20: This shall be a sign and witness, e'en in Egypt to the Lord,
   When oppressed they cry unto Him, ever faithful to His word;
   Then He shall a Saviour send them: aye, and that a great one, too.
21: Jehovah then is known to Egypt, Egyptians then Jehovah know;
   And with sacrifice and off'ring, they shall vow and pay their vow.
22: Then Jehovah shall smite Egypt: yet heal them with the very blow;
   And they shall return to Him, propitious now He grants their prayer,
   For He'll be entreated for them, and shall heal them even there.
23: In that day shall be a highway linking those two age-long foes,
   So Assyria goes to Egypt, Egypt to Assyria goes:
   Both united in one service—that which to Jehovah flows.

24: In that day with Egypt, Asshur, Israel shall be a third:
    The three united sounding music such as earth has never
      heard,
25: Responsive to Jehovah's blessing, for this shall be His
    blessèd word:
    Blest be Egypt, My dear people; My work, Asshur,
      blessèd be:
    Blest My heritage, Isràel—blest this human trinity!

In verses 16 and 17 we have Egypt's terror at the evident favoring of the cause of the faithful remnant of Jews by Jehovah: a strange people, "ever terrible from their beginning hitherto." Her resources dried, her wealth dissipated, and during all the time of her increasing impoverishment, the Jews coming more and more into their own; Egypt, standing for the Gentiles, at length connects cause and effect. She sees that it is not mere "chance," but Jehovah's Hand that is swinging over them, and whether it be national, or in the secret place of the individual conscience, there is trembling.

That one section of the Jewish people has often been a factor in the revolutionary movements of the day, wherever they may have occurred, cannot be denied, any more than that it was a Jew who assassinated, with all his family, the former Autocrat of all the Russias; or than that Jews formed a large proportion of the earliest Bolshevist Government in Moscow; while along other lines in the assembly of the League of Nations, the Jew's voice is heard, and it is by no means a plaintive, timid, or uninfluential one. The Jew is the coming man. Have we not just been reminded that he is "terrible from his beginning?"

But this is not alluded to here in this chapter. Jehovah is not shaking His Hand over Christendom in favor of Bolshevism. When He does thus shake His Hand, it shall be manifestly in behalf of a poor penitent and lowly people who are themselves suffering from persecution of the most virulent type. Egypt is recovering, and that recovery is in six successive steps, each marked by the words, *"In that day."*

The second recurrence, in verse 18, tells us that this repentance on the part of Egypt is genuine, as it shall be on the part of that innumerable mass of Gentiles whom we see in vision peopling the new earth in Revelation 7: 9-17, for here, too, we begin to be introduced into a millennial scene. "Egypt" shall not then fear and *flee from,* but fear and *turn to* Jehovah.

Verse 18 is difficult, nor is the difficulty lessened by the uncertainty as to even the correct text of the last line. But after considering all the alterations suggested, they appear to be so arbitrary, that I can but conclude that the safest thing is to accept it as it reads in our A. V. Then the verse amounts to this: out of six cities in that regenerated Egypt, five shall speak the language of Canaan, and thus evidence that they have indeed turned to Jehovah. Have we not, too, learned to speak in a tongue that has become to us our "mother-tongue?" It has a vocabulary of its own to express those holy truths that "Egypt" knows nothing of, and so has no words for. How many words has a Christian ceased to use since he turned to God? How many words never used before are now in his mouth? He looks with profound distrust on the modern claim to "tongues" that edify no one, but only make the speakers prominent, and greatly fears that while they are admittedly under the influence of some *spirit,* that spirit is not holy. The speech for which he longs is that which is "alway with grace seasoned with salt," and that shall be "good to the use of edifying" (Col. 4: 6; Eph. 4: 29) —*that* is *our* language of Canaan, and these five cities adopt that tongue.

One city in that renewed "Egypt" still speaks the old tongue, and it gets a name to correspond therewith, for it is called "Ir-ha-Heres,"* or "The City of Destruction." This at least would perfectly harmonize with this being a millennial scene, for

---

*"*Ir-ha-Heres*"—This name has been the theme of any amount of discussion. I simply quote Delitzsch's conclusion, which is so consistent with the genius of Isaiah's writings that it commends itself. "Ir-ha-heres" (meaning "City of Destruction") is simply used with a play upon the name, "*Ir-ha-cheres.*" This is the explanation of the Targum: "Heliopolis, whose future name will be destruction," the difference in the writing of *Heres* ("destruction") and *Cheres* ("the sun") is almost infinitesimal: the city now called in pride "the city of the sun" shall in the future be termed "the city of destruction," as representing that evil that shall still be in the world even in the millennial day.

that is never represented as a perfect one, any more than the Christian's present condition is a perfect one.  He, too, has still some of the dwellers of that doomed "city of destruction" within him, and will have, as long as he is in the body.  They give him a good deal of trouble at times, as the beloved Peter found on one occasion when he returned to the old language, and was still able to speak it all too fluently; see Matthew 26: 74.  So in the millennial day, there will be an evil element still in the earth; the children of pride, "the city of the sun," yield but feigned obedience (Ps. 18: 44, *marg.*), and are really "of destruction."

In verse 19 we have a further "sign" of the genuineness of "Egypt's" conversion, for an altar is built to Jehovah, and a pillar for witness.  But have there never been altars in Egypt till that day?  Surely; plenty of them.  Are there not plenty of altars throughout the professing sphere of Christendom?  Surely there are.  Rome has her altars on which she offers her bloodless sacrifice of the Mass that can never take away sins, but the Lord ignores them.  Here, however, is one that at length He does own.  It is not a Jewish altar in the temple at Jerusalem, but Gentile; and while of course it is literal, yet I believe there is a correspondence with that "altar" that is measured in Revelation 11.  *That* is a Jewish altar by which the afflicted remnant of pious Jews is symbolized in the very beginning of the day of the great tribulation.  It is not on earth, for all sacrifice and oblation has been made to cease; but God, their God, owns them now as He has not done for 2,000 years.  So, here in our book, too, is the *Gentile* remnant, and here too is *their* altar, equally owned of God, and a clear sign it is of conversion.  But whether Jewish or Gentile, we can but discern in the pillar a correspondence to that pillar that poor Jacob set up on the night of his distress, and welcome one more figure of our Lord Jesus Christ.  There shall surely be, not only a Jewish remnant, but an innumerable host of saved Gentiles in that millennial day to which both this prophecy and Rev. 7 point.*

------

*A modern school assures us that this "altar and pillar" must be found in one object, the great Pyramid; and it must be confessed that such a scheme is attractive enough to that nature that is still in us all, since it gives such mathematically explicit light

Now for the fourth recurrence of the term, "In that day." It is the first of the third series, and so full of sweet anticipation that I beg of you to note its strong antithesis to verses 1 to 4. It is the healing of that *internal* discord there foretold.

Though "Egypt" is thus converted, it does not follow that there is no more need of discipline, any more than in your own case or mine; but whereas in that far-off day in the past, when Israel was in bondage there, Jehovah smote them with no gracious healing following; in that *future* day it shall be as it is now with us; in the very blow that smites there is a tenderly gracious purpose of healing. No sorrow that He sends but has in it that gracious intent for His child, and each individual evidences his birth by the spirit in which he accepts the stroke of the paternal rod. If he accepts it as the chastening of love, he is a true child; if he resents and rebels, it proves him to be a "bastard" and not a son. Egypt here has begun to know Jehovah, as it has never yet done, and owning the justice in the stroke of the rod, seeks mercy, and finds it in healing.

In the second of this series we get the penalty of verses 5 to 10 removed, and the recovery of *material* prosperity through unrestricted commerce.

In these strange and unexpected words of verses 23-25 (for who would expect divine blessing to be attached to such names as Egypt and Assyria?) a new earth lies spread out before our eyes. No barriers hinder the free intercourse of nations hitherto hostile and filled with mutual jealousies. No tariffs limit commerce; no "protection to home industries," for all industries are for all. There is no enmity; the road is quite free to all between those extremes, Egypt and Assyria. But these two names stand

---

on the future—so much so as to tell us that the length of the main passage of the pyramid makes certain that this era will come to its final conclusion in 1936. All such fixing of dates (and they are many) is both self-confuting and denied by the Scripture that tells us, "of that day and hour knoweth no man." This cult, too, is in close relation with the unscriptural doctrine that the "ten lost tribes" are found in the Anglo-Saxon race, which in itself is enough to empty this teaching of all real value or credence. The pyramid is *now;* the altar shall only be "in that day."

as representatives of the Gentiles in that whole happy millennial scene. Egypt, that ancient captor of the Lord's people, would be the human representative of "corruption," as Assyria of the opposite evil, "violence." No longer do these Satanic principles characterize these nations, but rather Light and Love, the dual characteristics of good.

As it is impossible even to think of the blessing of God resting on wickedness, such as we have been compelled to identify with both Assyria and Egypt, so are we compelled to see in this Egypt and Assyria symbolic representatives of all the Gentiles, Israel completing that trinity which shall in that blessed millennial scene compose the whole of mankind. Nor, I take it, is this in the least strained or without the simplest and clearest proof from Scripture.* Egypt is an apt figure of the characteristic evil linked with *weakness,* "corruption." Assyria is ever that *strong* one who represents that evil of the strong, "violence." There was a day when all mankind was found of God to be divided between these:

"The earth also was *corrupt* (i.e., Egypt) before God, and the earth was filled with *violence*" (*i.e.,* Assyria).

Thus the two forms of evil included all the earth, which of course is a word that speaks of its dwellers; the family of Noah then representing the third component of the human trinity here, Israel.

We shall not greatly err if we go a little further, and as in Genesis 6 God makes man's incorrigible evil the ground of the infliction of that dire penalty, the deluge, so when He smells the sweet savor of Christ's sacrifice for that evil, He makes poor man's hopelessness in evil the field for the display of His grace. "I will not curse the ground any more for man's sake, for the imagination of man's heart is evil from his youth" (Gen. 8: 21). So here in Isaiah the curse is removed, the blessing takes its place, for the sweet savor of Christ has intervened; and although the names remain the same, it is a penitent, converted Egypt, a

---

*Let me quote from Delitzsch, "If Israel relied upon Egypt, it *deceived* itself, and was deceived; if on Assyria, it became the *slave* of Assyria." Note the two forms of evil.

self-judged and lowly Assyria, that now make up the inhabitants of that fair scene.

No longer, too, do "all roads lead to Rome," but rather to Jerusalem, or through Israel's land that lies directly in the path between Egypt and Assyria. Was not this the ancient gospel preached to Abraham: "In thee shall all the nations of the earth be blessed," and again after the offering of Isaac: "In thy seed shall all the nations of the earth be blessed?"

But that "Seed" is not on earth yet; He is at the right hand of the Father, and His presence "adorns the heavenly throne;" hence the blessing that comes forth to us Gentiles now makes us to correspond with the heavenly host, the stars; for, "So shall thy seed be," was God's promise to Abraham as he looked at the star-spangled sky. But the Lord Jesus shall return to the earth, and when He is here, then Israel shall be as the sand by the sea-shore, the center of blessing for the earth.

Never then shall there be rivalry of armies, fleets of sea or air. In vain shall be the search then for Protestant or Romanist, for Democrat or Republican, for Monarchist or Anarchist, for Aristocrat or Proletariat, for Jesus, Lord of all, has caused the earth to bask in universal peace and concord; and He, the Melchizedek Priest, is here seen spreading His hands in blessing over the whole scene. Egypt, those of the Gentiles once expressive of corruption, are now His "people;" Assyria, those of the Gentiles once expressive of violence, are now "the work of His hands," and quite a different handiwork will they be then; while Israel, the long-wandering one, the once unfaithful wife, the disowned, and for a time castaway, is now the precious treasure that has long been "hid in the field" of this earth, and now is owned as His "inheritance." Christ, who now alone binds the Church in unity, as every saint confesses that He alone meets all his need, shall then bind the whole earth in unity of blessing.

# CHAPTER TWENTY

Egypt a symbolic nation of vain-confidence. The three years'
sign. The nakedness not the extreme as with us. The discord of
evil.

IN conformity with a plan that frequently governs the prophetic writing, after having taken us down to the end of
the ways of God with the earth, as far as to millennial
blessedness, we are, in this very short chapter, taken back that
Israel, seeing the complete humiliation of Egypt, may be warned
against putting confidence in a nation that cannot even maintain
its own liberty, much less throw an effective shield over others.
But as it is a warning not alone needed by that Israel after the
flesh, we too may listen with genuine personal interest.

There is one point that is only incidental, but not without its
value, as evidencing the absolute accuracy of Scripture. Sargon
is a name that does not occur elsewhere in the Bible, and not
once in classical writers, so that it is not surprising that Christian
commentators concluded that this must be another name for
Shalmanezer, of whom we read in 2 Kings 18. "The monuments,
however, removed this doubt, and made Sargon a successor, but
not a son, of Shalmanezer, and the father of Sennacherib."* Now
if my reader will turn to 2 Kings 18: 10, he will note that the
capture of Samaria is *not* attributed to Shalmanezer himself, but
it is written: "And at the end of three years *they took it*
(Samaria), even in the sixth year of Hezekiah Samaria was
taken." That is, *the army* captured the besieged city, but it was
not at that time under the leadership of Shalmanezer. As we
learn from our chapter, and as recently the monuments have
also shown, the general of the victorious army was the hitherto
unknown Sargon. This time, at least, the "monuments" have
proved their own correctness by being in accord with the divinely
inspired Word of God.

--------

*Birks* on "Isaiah."

2: Go, loosen the sackcloth from off of thy loins,
   From thy foot, too, put off thy sandal.
   And he did so, walking naked and barefoot.
3: As My servant Isaiah walked shamefully thus,
   Naked, and foot without sandal,
   A sign and a wonder of three years in length,
   'Gainst Cush and the crafty Mizraim,
4: So shall the king of Assyria lead
   Egyptians and Cushites all captives,
   With buttocks uncovered to shame them.
5: And all who have placed in the Cushite their trust,
   And based their vain boastings on Egypt,
   With terror and shame shall be stricken.
6: And this island's dweller shall say in that day,
   Behold now what has befallen
   Those up to whom we did trustfully look
   To be our salvation from Asshur!
   Oh, how then can *we* be delivered?

Thus the prophet Isaiah is commanded to make of himself a symbolic prophecy that shall tell, in that most graphic and appealing way, the fate in store for the nation that is Israel's confidence. He is to go "naked and barefoot." Of course, we must not force into this the literalness that the words convey to us. I again quote Delitzsch, with whom are associated in this all sober commentators: "With the great importance attached to clothing in the East, where the feelings on this point are peculiarly sensitive and modest, a person was looked upon as stripped and naked if he had only taken off his upper garment. What Isaiah was therefore directed to do, was simply opposed to common custom and not to moral decency. He was to lay aside the dress of a mourner, a preacher of repentance, and to have nothing on but his tunic; and in this, as well as bare-footed, he was to show himself in public." Could anything arouse attention and call for explanation more tellingly than that?

Nor is it necessary to read the third verse as in our Authorized Version; as if the prophet must thus walk about the city for three literal years; but thus: "And Jehovah said, As My servant Isaiah goeth naked and barefoot, a *three years' sign* and wonder against Egypt and against Ethiopia, so shall the king of Assyria lead away the Egyptians prisoners, etc.;" that is according to a principle well understood, if Isaiah had thus walked three *days*, it would have been a "three years' sign," and denoted the period of Egypt's humiliation for three years, as will be clearly seen by a reference to Num. 14: 33, 34; Ezek. 4: 1-8.

The result of this humiliation of Egypt, is given in verses 5, 6, on those who have put their trust in her as being too well established, too strong to be defeated. And the inhabitants of this isle, or coast-land (that is, all Palestine) "shall say in that day, Behold, thus it happens to those to whom we looked, whither we fled for help to deliver us from the king of Assyria; and how should we escape?" (*Delitzsch*).

Whatever near-by fulfilment of this prophecy there may have been, it can but have foreshadowed a far-off one that lies still, even now, in the future. Does not our prophetic book of Revelation tell us of a crisis that corresponds very closely (although in a spiritual sphere, as in accord with the spirit of that book) with this strife between two powers, both of which are equally hostile to God and His people?

As there is harmony and accord in the kingdom of God, so there is antagonism and discord amid the components of the kingdom of the powers of darkness. "Every kingdom divided against itself is brought to desolation, and every city or house divided against itself shall not stand; and if Satan cast out Satan, he is divided against himself; how then shall his kingdom stand?" These words of our Lord must not be forced into denying this, nor in teaching that there is harmony and accord in that kingdom of Satan. In the poor men who are in, and compose, that kingdom on earth, who are not only hateful, but *hate one another*, we get a sad picture of the discordant conditions that characterize it. It is said that "misery loves company," but even this negative comfort will not be enjoyed by those who refuse the grace of Christ in the gospel, and finally share the penalty prepared only for the devil and his angels. When the devil has derived all the service he can from one instrument, he has no hesitation in abandoning it and destroying it by another. Egypt may have served him well on occasion, when the Lord's people were captives within its borders, but Egypt having thus served his turn, the inherent discord of his kingdom is told out by the destruction of that abandoned instrument by another, Egypt by Assyria. So we read in Rev. 17: 16: "And the ten horns which thou sawest, and the Beast, these shall hate the whore, and shall make her desolate and naked, and shall eat her flesh and burn her utterly with fire."

That filthy "woman," this world's Church, which still assumes to be the bride of Christ, has long served, and is still serving her master, Satan, well; but let him cast away his pretension to being an angel of light, and come out in his own true character of Dragon, and he will give that Church short shrift, and use another of his instruments to bring her to her end. God over all, and overruling all, even in permitting him to do this, will carry out His own profound purposes.

Just as Assyria (representative of violence) conquers Egypt (representative of corruption) so shall the Beast and ten horns destroy the woman (religion). That is, the political State (the then "League of Nations" embracing all Christendom) that has supported that woman (the whole religious profession after the rapture), under the devil's control shall utterly destroy every vestige of profession of faith in the Name of Christ, however false it may have been.

Thus this short chapter springs into life, as it were, and historic details in which apparently we can have no possible interest, personally or directly, become, in the light of other scriptures, themselves filled with prophetic light on our own day, path and future.

# CHAPTER TWENTY-ONE

**The Burdens of countries, known by emblems. Babylon first; why emblemed by "desert of the sea." The prophet's grief at the vision. The watchman and what he sees. Significance of the roar of a lion. The second scene, the return of the expedition. Babylon fallen. Burden of Dumah: the source and meaning of that word. God hears the cry of a condition. Burden of Arabia.**

I N the next two chapters we have four "burdens," linked together by each of their subjects being expressed, not in a plain word or name, but by an emblem. Thus in the first, "Desert of the Sea;" next "Dumah and Sęir," meaning "Silence and Storm," and in the last, "Valley of Vision," we have respectively and with tolerable clearness Babylon, Edom and Jerusalem expressed; whilst in the one remaining—the third in the order given in the text—while it is not quite as clear, yet the one word *"ehreb,"* or *"ahrab,"* with only a difference in pointing, covers in its double meaning both "Arabia," and, in view of Arabia's approaching night, "evening."

Verses 1 to 10, then, deal with Babylon (as is evident from verse 9) under the emblematic phrase "Desert of the Sea," and may be rendered thus:

1: As sweep the whirlwinds through the south
So comes it from the desert,
From the land that strikes with terror.
2: Oh, cruel is the vision that is shown me!
The spoiler, he is spoiling still!
The waster, he is wasting!
Up then, Elam, up! Besiege, O Mede, besiege!
So will I make all those sighings to cease.
3: For this are my loins with anguish filled!
Pangs of affliction have seized me,
As the pangs of a woman in travail!
I writhe at the hearing!
Am amazed at the seeing!
4: Wildly my heart beats!
Horrors affright me!
Even the calm of the twilight I love
Hath he turned for me into quaking!*

---

*These lines, it will be noted, differ from the A. V., but the above rendering is not far from the Revised, and gives the sense intended.

First, we must ask, Why is Babylon called "Desert of the Sea?" No doubt a natural reason might be found in the topographical situation of that most ancient city, in a vast plain or desert, and yet with its precise location amid marshes, broad sheets of water, and intersected by the great river Euphrates. Jeremiah's description (chap. 52: 13) as "dwelling upon many waters," would appear literally more correct, and so nullify Isaiah's "Desert."

We who have a more spiritual light from the completed volume in our hands, can throw that light on the strange paradoxical term that unites dry desert with a sea of waters, and can interpret it with deeper significance, and more value to ourselves than that derived from a mere geographical position. She is "desert," because God is not "known in her palaces for a refuge;" and wherever that is the case, though all the glories of the world, all its wealth, learning, honors and refinements, be there, yet it is really a "dry and thirsty land where no water is," or, in one word, "desert." So, in order that he may see the antitypical Babylon, our Seer, John, must be taken into the desert (Rev. 17: 3), for there only will she ever be found, there only can she find an environment in any degree congenial to her own proud, vain boastings. This desert-world well suits that harlot church which will soon include and unify all the denominations of Christendom. Even in that vast multitude itself, we may discern the *many waters* on which she is sitting, as indeed Rev. 17: 15 necessitates our saying.

Thus nothing could give a better idea of Babylon, whether ancient or still future, than that conveyed by the double emblem of "Desert" and "Sea," that is, "without God" as desert, and ever restlessly chafing in unsatisfied discontent, as sea.

This city, then, which it is again well to remember had not yet attained, when Isaiah wrote, to the place of imperial dominance over the whole earth, is the subject of this burden, and a very heavy burden it evidently is. The prophet's eye is caught by the march of an invading army, sweeping swiftly along, reminding him of a storm-wind in the southern desert where there is no obstruction to its full powers. Then he gives the cause of the visitation. The doomed city is seen sending out its spoilers and devastating armies, till moved by an overwhelming indignation the prophet cries, and in so crying, gives voice to the command of God, "Go up, O Elam (*i.e.*, Persia). Besiege, O Media, for thus will I make those sighs, that are ever sounding in My ears from Babylon's oppressed prisoners, to cease," that is, those who have hung their harps on Babylon's willows shall cease their weeping (Ps. 137: 1, 2). Then he gives us to enter into what is passing before his eyes by telling us of its effect on himself, the most graphic way of speaking.

So swift, so sharp, so terribly severe is the blow, that the prophet, while he knows well that Babylon is to be the oppressor of his own people, yet cannot repress the most profound emotions of humanity that such a sight naturally produces. His heart throbs violently, horrors affect every part of his being, till he trembles in every limb. Perhaps the still hour of twilight that so often communicates its own calm to man's spirit, will afford him some relief. No, not now; even that quiet hour only brings with it further terrors that increase those tremblings.

Let us still listen, and we shall learn what is passing before his far-seeing eyes. He is looking at a scene that, at that day, was still nearly two centuries in the future,* and he sees a banqueting hall wherein is revelry by night; a watch has been set, giving the revellers such a sense of security as permits them to enjoy their feast without fear, for the words he hears are:

> 5: Set the table!   Watch in the watch-tower!
>    Eat!   Drink!

When, lo, in the very midst of the revelry there is the startling shout from the watchmen that tells of a thorough surprise:

> "Up, princes, up! The shield anoint!"

Another prophet, Daniel, who shall actually live among those scenes, shall give us in his fifth chapter as history what is here prophecy, and add the divine sentence on Babylon's plaster walls, but nothing of the surprise attack itself. This shall be supplied

---

*Assuming that the accepted chronology is at least approximately correct, Isaiah prophesied B. C. 714; Babylon was taken by the Medes, B. C. 538.

by still another, Jeremiah, who tells us of couriers running to tell the king of Babylon of the capture of the city (Jer. 51).

Here Isaiah, in the very way that he uses words, tells us the same thing—the crisis is so imminent that the watch seems to *bark* out a few short, sharp words; there is no time for more. Princes who should have been at the head of their companies are reclining at their ease. "Up, princes!" the watch shouts. Their shields, which should have been ready for instant use, are hard and dry, without the necessary oiling that shall divert the strokes they may receive. "Anoint shield!" is enough to tell what is threatening.

Then that vision fades, and its place is taken by another. Jehovah directs him:

> 6: Go, set a watchman on the walls,
> What he sees there, let him tell.

This being done, Isaiah, himself the watchman, again tells us what is passing before him:

> 7: A cavalcade of cavalry—they are going two by two—
> A cavalcade of asses—a cavalcade of camels.*

That is all. It is evidently some military expeditionary force, which the prophet-watchman would not have been thus shown did it not have vital reference to his own people. Not only cavalry, but in those wars even asses and camels were used, not only for carrying the necessary *impedimenta,* but were also taken into the fighting line, and by throwing the enemy into confusion, more than once turned the tide of battle. But the swiftly moving army passes out of sight, leaving him to ask on what errand they are being sent. Against what power can they be moving? What will be the outcome of the expedition?

For the answers to these unspoken, yet surely to be supplied questions, for only by something of this character can the proper connection be seen, he listens intently.

---

*The word rendered in A. V. "chariot" is given not only for the occupants of one chariot (*Gesenius*), but for the whole of the horsemen of an army.

8: Then he cried as a lion:
   High on the watch-tower,
   My Lord, I am standing:
   Watch and ward keeping, day after day—
   Yea, my watch keeping, night after night.

If commentators, like Delitzsch and others, are to be followed, this must be interpreted thus: Weary with watching day after day and night after night, with nothing occurring, no tidings, nothing to be seen, his overstrained nerves at length succumb, and he breaks out in irritable complaint. "He loses all patience and growls as if he were a lion, with the same long deep breath out of full lungs, complaining to God that he has to stand so long at his post without seeing anything, except that inexplicable procession that has vanished away."*

We are not compelled to accept this: feeble, tame and pointless as it is. Is such impatience altogether consistent with the submissive obedience of the prophet? Is this an adequately and scripturally sustained reason for that lion-like roar? Will it not be safer to let Scripture interpret for us?—and doing so, we gather that the lion's roar is a cause of terror to those who hear, and *never* the expression of irritable discontent. On the contrary, "Shall the lion roar *when he hath no prey?* Will the young lion cry *when he hath taken nothing?*" (Amos 3: 4). These questions surely demand a negative answer, and must mean that whenever the lion does roar, he is not at all discontented, but well satisfied, for his prey is within his power. He roars—springs—kills! The roar foretells the death of the quarry.

So in Revelation 10, in that cloud-clad personage with sun-like visage, we discern our Lord, the Lion of the tribe of Judah, who Himself "cries as when a lion roareth," and immediately seven thunders utter their voices, echoing, as it were, that roar, and apparently putting it into articulate phrase—for John, you remember, understood what the thunders said, and would have recorded it had he not been forbidden. But what follows? A most solemn oath that there shall be no longer any delay, but that the "mystery of God," the long inexplicable permission of, and the triumph of evil, shall end in the sounding of the seventh

---

*Delitzsch.*

trumpet. But that trumpet, since itself going down to the very end, must include in the final fulfilment, the seven vials; and if we trace these to *their* end, we find the wrath of God filled up, and falling on apostate Christendom, and finally ending, as here, in His visitation on Great Babylon and her utter fall (Rev. 16). The lion's roar then in Rev. 10 spoke clearly, as it does in nature, of the doom of the quarry, of swift-coming judgment *on Babylon*.

Precisely so here. The lion's roar does not speak of the impatience of the watchman; but as in Revelation, the prophet's lion-like roar is really interpreted for us in what follows, in articulate phrase. After watching day and night, at length his vigil is rewarded, he does see something. It is the reappearance of that cavalcade of cavalry, but this time not merely crossing the line of vision on the horizon, but *approaching* him. As soon as near enough to be heard, the riders call out their tidings, and in *their* report the lion's roar has its interpretation and significance. It is a kind of triumphant chant:

> "Babylon is fallen!   Babylon is fallen!
> And all her graven images lie broken on the ground!"

We hear the same triumphant song in Revelation (14: 8), and still again in chap. 18: 2; not the literal city this time, but its spiritual antitype, all that which proud religious man is, even up to this very day, building on the earth, till "Rome" shall put her headstone on that proud "tower," and give her vile character to it all. So shall end all that, under the name of Christ, has been utterly anti-Christian, and has made that Name which of all names is dear to God, to be a symbol of all that is crafty and false in her Jesuits.

Alas, that we have to see such sorrow still in the future for our poor insensate race, and that over the future, and ever drawing nearer, there still hangs a thick cloud of divine judgment! Alas, that the false prophets from so many pseudo-Christian pulpits still prophesy smooth things for hire, knowing well what the itching ears of those who hire them demand, and are soothing consciences with their false forecasts of prosperity and peace, which they gild with the pleasant word "optimism," as might have done those ancient "optimists" of whom we read in 2 Chron.

18: 5-11, that they led Ahab to shame and defeat with their optimistic promise, "Go and prosper!"

But well for us, since all the present ecclesiastical profession shall soon merge into "Babylon the Great," to be thus forewarned; for this gives a present application to the command, "Come out of her, My people, that ye be not partakers of her sins, and that ye receive not of her plagues."

One more verse remains to complete this burden on Babylon, but it is, as it were, the consequence of that "burden" as it affects Israel, and thus a word of comfort to that beloved remnant who shall pass through their destined time of suffering, called the "Great Tribulation."

> 10: O thou, My threshing, and the child of My threshing-floor!
>     What I have heard from Jehovah of Hosts, the God of
>         Isràel,
>     I have declared unto you.

Here the prophet, who expresses the emotions and tender sentiments of Him who has sent him, turns to his own nation, and speaking as the very representative of Jehovah, he addresses it with all the tenderness of a parent who has been chastising his child, and has himself suffered in so doing. All fathers, worthy of the name, can surely enter into *that*. O child of My threshing-floor whom, by these various world-powers, I have stricken as wheat is threshed on the threshing-floor; I have now shown thee in this last vision what I am about to do to the "flail" that I have used in thy chastisement, and when I so deal with the instrument, thou mayest be quite sure that I need it no longer. It has done its work, it has brought thee back to My embrace in penitence, and I can cast it away.

All this most surely points forward to a still future day, when the place of that world-power that oppressed the Jew in the past shall be taken by another, the "Beast from the sea" of Revelation, and which in its final form shall be so identified with the great enemy of mankind, the devil, as to bring the poor remnant of Israel into a time of sorrow, which, for its intensity, can only be likened to the threshing-floor of our prophet. But when the Lord does intervene on Israel's behalf, the "threshed" becomes at once the "thresher," as Micah distinctly assures us (chap. 4: 13): "Arise, thresh, O daughter of Zion!" It is like the two buckets of a well: one being up, the other must be down: Babylon, up, Israel down. So that chant, "Babylon is fallen," though a *dirge* for Babylon, is a *triumph song* for Israel.

This justifies our saying that the judgment on the spiritual Babylon, the harlot-church, equally involves the full and final deliverance of the true bride of Christ, by her rapture to be with Him forever. In other words, that seventh vial, that sees the final judgment on "Babylon the Great" and that follows the recent world conflict called (however mistakenly) Armageddon, must really be introduced by that rapture since it is poured upon "the *Air*," which is as apt a symbol of the *spiritual* witness, the Church, as "the *Land*" is of the Jew, or "the *Sea*" of the Gentile. If so, then the Lord's coming for us must be near indeed, the very next event foretold by our own prophetic book of Revelation!

The next burden is that of Dumah, which by an Isaiahan play on words is a form of the word "Edom," only with the removal of the vowel sound "E" from the beginning to the end of the word, in order to give it that double meaning so characteristic of Isaiah's use of words, and introducing into it that of "deep silence," for that is the English equivalent of "Dumah." Thus the *name* Edom is turned into an emblem of the future *fate* of Edom. It becomes the land of death-like silence;* nor can we afford to be indifferent to this strange, short "burden," since we hear in it that oft-repeated inquiry that so many weary spirits have uttered throughout the centuries, and never with more earnestness than today; for the crowding of portents into the last few years has both awakened hope, and certainly deepened this longing. The whole "burden" consists of just this one question and its answer:

11: A cry comes to me from Seir:
    Watchman, what of the night?
    O watchman, what of the night?

---

*See the very word thus used in Ps. 94: 17: "My soul had almost dwelt in *silence*" (*dumah*).

12: The watchman says:
   Morning comes; but also night.
   If ye will enquire, enquire!
   Return!   Come!

It is certainly cryptic enough, but not the less eloquent on that
very account.  The cry comes from no specified person, but from
"Seir."   Nor can it be without any significance that again the
name is changed; the same country is no longer either Edom or
Dumah, but *Seir*.   That very name, then, will suggest to us the
reason for, or significance of, the cry.  What is Seir?  The word
means "rough, hairy," precisely as is said of Esau, the first
settler in this land (Gen. 25: 25); he was the hairy (*seir*) man,
and as is not uncommon in Scripture, the man and his land are
identified by some striking characteristic that they have in common.  Here the rough, hairy man Esau, "goes to his own place,"
finds his suited dwelling in a rough, mountainous, forest-covered
and storm-swept country.*  It is not without interest that, as the
topography of Babylon corresponded to the *spiritual* significance
of the emblem used, so here; all travellers report that the land
of Edom has indeed become "Dumah," a silence of death ever
brooding over its desolate and storm-swept mountains.   Thus we
again have precisely the same anomaly as in the apparently incongruous terms of "Desert" and "Sea," in this "Dumah" and
"Seir;" Silence and Storm.

Again, as in that earlier burden, we will not stop at superficial
topography, but let the light of the New Testament put its deeper
and truer meaning into these words.  How strikingly, then, does
the present condition of the present prophetic earth answer to
both "Dumah" and "Seir;" it is silent Godward, as Babylon was
"desert" from that same point of view.   No songs of adoring
praise are rising to God from its masses of lifeless professors, for
they have neither felt the burden of their guilt, the terrors of a
coming judgment, nor seen that guilt borne by Another.   In this
respect it is also "silent" as Dumah.  Yet from the *manward*

---

*This added idea of "storm-swept" is fully justified; the root
"*sahar*" has for its prime meaning "to bristle up," hence the
derived noun "hair;" and then "to shudder," and so it is used of
the commotion of a storm; hence "to sweep away in a storm"–
*Gesenius*.

side, how filled is that same scene today with tumult, how tossed with storm it is!  What a tumult!  It is *Seir*.

Again I say, how true is this to the actual condition of the antitype of Dumah and Seir today!  The very condition of this prophetic earth, the sphere in the consideration of the Spirit of prophecy, cries for intervention.  A cry is ever coming from it, from its tumult, from its restlessness, from the evident failure of the last experiment in the form of human government, Democracy, from its death-shadowed silence Godward, from the storm-swept earth, a pathetic longing cry comes, not only from a few human lips, but *from that very condition*.  It comes "out of Seir," and this is the burden of the cry: "Watchman, what of the night?  O watchman, what of the night?"

Nor is this simply a repeated question.  There is a very slight difference in the way it is put that leads Delitzsch to say: "The more winged form of the second question is expressive of heightened anxious urgency and haste,"* just as a sick man, who has tossed through many weary hours, longs for the night to end, and ever and again asks, "What time is it? Oh, tell me, is it not nearly daybreak?"

Whether it be a legitimate deduction or not, there has arisen within the last hundred years an extraordinary, ever-spreading interest in, and a longing expectation for, the ending of the night, or, in other words, the return of the Lord.  This, if one considers it thoughtfully, is such a remarkable—or one may say, super-natural—phenomenon as to assure its own fulfilment!  I mean that when we think of One who, to external sight, was during the greater part of His short life only a poor mechanic, living in a conquered country, and in a peculiarly despised region of that country, who apparently achieved nothing in the way of political or economic reform, or military achievement, was not what we call a successful man in business, for He was always poor, and ended that brief and apparently (from the world's point of view) inglorious career by being executed amid criminals, as being

---

*What he means by "the more winged form" consists in the word for "night," *"milailah,"* being shortened to *"mileil,"* the last merely paragogic syllable being cut off.  This heightened urgency I have retained by introducing the exclamatory "O."

Himself a criminal, and yet here today are thousands upon thousands of the most sober and thoughtful of the race, not ashamed to say that they are confidently expecting that Galilean carpenter, in whom they have discerned the very Son of God, by whom the worlds came into being, and by whom alone the whole universe subsists, to return and take possession of the earth, to "hush its groan," and to awaken its joyful song, by Himself reigning over it! That undeniable phenomenon can only be accounted for in one of two ways. Either it is an unprecedented, and (one must surely say) unaccountable miraculous delusion, affecting not the thoughtless, the fanatical, the unintelligent, or the careless, as delusions have done and still do, but those who are the very reverse of these! Or, on the other hand, it is a divine *certainty*— one or the other. The first is so utterly unreasonable, that it becomes impossible to any reasonable person, and then the last becomes a clear and sure foreshadowing of its own fulfilment.

It is not in the least difficult to trace the path of the Church through the watches of that night, as to which the cry comes, for these we are not only told are four, but their significant characteristics are given us by the very lips of our Lord Himself in Mark 13: 35. Nor is he very clear-sighted who cannot discern "the *evening* watch" in the gradual loss of the light of truth, the shades that began to veil the Church in the first centuries. Deeper the darkness thickened, till, in the sway of Rome and her efforts to quench the Light altogether, the "*midnight* watch" came slowly on, in what are significantly called "the *dark* ages," and passed slowly off. At length the Nazarite spirit, like Samson in Gaza, awoke, and burst the gates and bars of that Philistine Rome in the Reformation, and in this who will deny that we have the re-awakening or *cock-crowing*, watch? We come down to our own time in which, in the recovery of many a long-lost truth, the light that faded in the first centuries is returning, another day is breaking, and we are in the fourth, the last, or *morning* watch; so that we, too, join the sweet singer in crying that we "wait for the Lord more than they that watch for the morning (Ps. 130: 6).

Thus, and it is of unspeakable value, we can get such an answer to that cry out of Seir as was then impossible; *we* know, with an intelligence that even the beloved Apostle who wrote the words could *not* know, that "the night is far spent;" three of its watches are already past and gone altogether, and since we are in the fourth, or last, "the day is at hand." Thus it is really most fitting for us to embrace the hope that *we*, even *we*, may be "alive and remain" till the Morning Star, that first herald of the new day, shall arise, and all the prophecies that refer to the waiting Church and her rapture to be with the Lord have their fulfilment in our own brief day of life. Do you not long for it, dear reader?

At all events, the prophet Isaiah, though writing seven hundred years before the Christian era, is in perfect harmony with the apostle of the first century of this era, for he, too, in his response to the cry, cheers with the hopeful word: "The morning comes!" We can see that,

> "The summer morn we've sighed for,
> The fair, sweet morn awakes"

for Israel (and it is Israel that is always primarily in view in these prophecies relating to the earth), a morning, as her poet speaks, "without clouds, as clear shining after rain." All her storms shall then be as yesterday, as a tale that is told; all her future shall then be one long bright morrow, in which the sun, her own Sun of Righteousness, shall flood the happy scene with His beams.

"The morning comes," says the prophet; "The day is at hand," says the apostle, and so far they are in perfect accord. But here our apostle stops, and rightfully and happily stops, for there shall never be night to that day whereof *he* is speaking. Not so with the prophet; the morning comes indeed, but "also the night." That is, in full accord with the cryptic oracular character of the whole "burden," the same moment that ushers in the perfect day, ushers in the night too! That should present no difficulty to us who have the light of 2 Thess. 1: 6, 7 upon it. It is "the day of the revelation of the righteous judgment of God;" "seeing it is a righteous thing with God to recompense tribulation to them that trouble you, and to you who are troubled, rest." There we get both the night and the day, as another prophet writes: "Woe unto you that desire the day of the Lord! To what end is it for you? The day of the Lord is darkness and not light" (Amos 5: 18). That must mean that even when that longed-for day does break in blessing on the *penitent* Jew and Gentile, it is "night" still, and (alas) forever for the impenitent. Thus interpreted, the "morning" and the "night" are in absolute harmony with the other apparent anomalies of Desert and Sea, of Silence and Tumult.

Is there still perplexity in your mind? Are you still uncertain as to the meaning of this strange combination of "day" and "night?" Then inquire. No honest inquirer is ever denied. Only be careful to inquire at the right source; for today there be many who assume to be able to answer every prophetic question, till the very air is filled with wild speculations and hypotheses that are asserted with all the assurance of being directly inspired of God (discordant and mutually destructive as they are), to be *answers*, till the simple inquirer is bewildered, discouraged, and tempted to drop the whole matter as being beyond the possibility of solution. That is not wise. Far better is it to wait patiently on the Lord. His Spirit is still with us to lead into all truth. Nor does that mean that we shall acquire everything in a moment, leaving no more to be learned, but by slow degrees, testing our faith and patience, ever leaving much still unsolved that shall serve to maintain our dependence, and which shall also be communicated as we are fitted to receive it; not refusing, in what is spiritual pride, light from others who may have been taught of the Lord before us; yet, on the other hand, whilst not accepting quickly every new thing, yet not hastily abandoning what we have long believed; ever testing all, not by some fragments, but by the *whole* of the written Word.

The oracle ends with two words, "Return! Come!" The first can only refer to those who *need* to return, that is, who have wandered away, and we must surely assume from God. That strange "day" of both light and darkness is near. Let us make very sure that for *us* it shall be light, not the darkness; the morning, not the night. So this answer to the "cry out of Seir" ends with that gospel word of invitation as to the weary and heavy-laden: "Come." Oh, come to an embrace that will hold thee safe amid all the storms that are lowering on our horizon, and have still to beat on this earth!

Verse 13 begins "The burden against Arabia," which may also be read, "The oracle *in* the evening," for in this case, as if to guide us into seeing an emblematic designation where we might possibly question it, there is added what is entirely lacking in the others, the preposition "in," so that just as we have in *"Dumah"* a word with two meanings, and itself thus telling of the over-hanging penalty, so here. The very word "Arabia," with only a difference in the vowel-points, means "evening," telling surely of Arabia's day drawing to an end, and the night approaching. This is in perfect accord with our prophet's love of a play on words, over-ruled by the inspiring Spirit for His own ends.

> 13: In the forest in Arabia (or, in the evening)
>     Must ye pass the night,
>     O ye caravans of Dedanim.
> 14: Bring water for the thirsty,
>     Th' inhabitants of Tema
>     With their loaves of bread are coming
>     To feed the famished fugitives.
> 15: For these are all a-flying from before the swords—
>     Flying from before the flashing sword, unsheathed,
>     Flying from before the bow, ready bent,
>     Flying from before all the miseries of war!

Here, then, we have an evening picture. Caravans of Dedanim, those people who are so mysteriously connected both with Ham (Gen. 10: 7) and Shem, through Abraham and Keturah (Gen. 25: 1-3), and who here represent Arabia, are first seen travelling their accustomed route, but are being driven out of it by a powerful military expedition, from which they can only hope for safety by flight and concealment. The picture in verse 15 is intensely graphic with its fourfold repetition of the expression, "flying from." From swords they flee, aye, from drawn flashing swords ready for use, and bows all strung and ready to follow even those at a distance, and the last line sums up all, comprehensive enough to all who know what war is, with its widespread miseries. So these Dedanim hide wherever thickets promise shelter.

The prophet's sympathies are again wakened, and he cries for water to be brought, whilst those who live in Tema recognize

their blood-relation to the fugitives (Gen. 25: 13-15) by stealing
to them with bread.  But the burden goes on:

16: For thus hath Jehovah said unto me:
  Let but a year pass, as the year of one hired,
  Then all shall be over with Kedar's display.
17: And few shall the remnant be
  Of the bows of the mighty, of Kedar,
  For Jehovah, the God of Israel, hath spoken.

Kedar stands here as representative of all the Arabians, and
again the very word speaks in its mournful meaning of the
gloomy cloud that overhangs them, for it means "black" as the
sign of sorrow and mourning.  But gloom never ends God's ways
with men. We turn over a few pages of our prophet and we hear
Kedar even bidden to sing with joyful exultation (chap. 42: 11),
"Let the wilderness and the cities thereof lift up their voice, the
villages that Kedar doth inhabit: let the inhabitants of the rocks
sing, let them shout from the top of the mountains."  What has
caused such a difference?  Jehovah's Servant has been manifested,
and joy ever comes with *His* coming.  So mournful Kedar echoes
rough Seir's cry for the Morning.  I am able to say little more
as to this "burden," but we may all be very thankful that the
"evening" never ends God's ways.  Always is it, as at first, "the
evening *and the morning*" that make up the days; every evening
being but a new beginning, the morning of another day.

# CHAPTER TWENTY-TWO

The burden of the Valley of Vision: the meaning of that term. The merriment of the doomed; preparations for resistance; the vision told in order that penitence may avert it. Whom does Shebna represent? His deposition; his place taken by Eliakim. Who is thus named? The difficulty of the last verse.

THE chapter to which we have now come clearly divides into two parts: the earlier, verses 1 to 14, following in regular course the "burdens" of the previous chapter, on some place emblemed by the title "Valley of Vision;" and then, in verses 15 to 25, apparently an illustrative appendix, breaking into the regular order, which we may call the "burden" of the highest court official in Jerusalem.

As Delitzsch notes, the idea in the grouping of the four burdens is not chronological as to dates of composition, but suggests a storm coming from a distance, first rising in far-away Babylon, and approaching by way of Edom and Arabia till it bursts over Jerusalem in awful fury. That Jerusalem is here the object of the "burden" is assured by the fourth verse.

1: What aileth thee that to the housetops
   All of thy people are going?
2: Thou that art full of commotions,
   Thou city of constant clamor,
   City of merriment baseless:
   Thy slain are not slain by the sword,
   Nor killed on the field of the battle.
3: Thy rulers, caught in their flight,
   Are all of them bound up together;
   With no foeman's bow being bent,*
   All found within thee are fettered,
   Caught when fleeing afar.
4: Therefore I cried: Oh, leave me alone,
   That I may weep bitterly.
   Press not thy comforts upon me,
   For the city, dear as a daughter,
   Is brought to the depth of destruction.

---

*Literally, "with bow bent," "without any need of the bow being drawn" (*Delitzsch*).

5: For 'tis a day of confusion,
   A day of abusing, a day of delusion,*
   From Adohn, Jehovah Tzebaoth,
   In the dark valley of vision;
   A day of the crashing of walls,
   With cries of despair thrown back by the mountains.
6: Elam has taken the quiver,
   With fully-manned chariots and horsemen;
   Kir hath uncovered the shield:
7: Thus it cometh to pass,
   That (all) thy choicest of vales
   Are filled with the enemy's hosts:
   His chariots and his cavalry
   E'en threaten a dash at the gates.

We must first ask what is meant by the cryptic title: "Valley of Vision." The context gives a clear answer, for just as in the preceding emblems there have been clear paradoxes in the terms used, as Desert and Sea, Silence and Tumult, so here Valley and Vision are equally paradoxical. If it had been "Mount of Vision" there would have been congruity; but who would expect to get a clear vision of what was far off when in a valley, and that a gloomy one? For the word for "valley," while there are several in Hebrew, is that one used when a *threatening* idea is to be conveyed. It is *Geh,* and is found in "The valley of slaughter" (Jer. 19: 6), "valley of salt" (2 Sam. 8: 13), "valley of death-shade" (Ps. 23: 4) and is particularly clear in the awful *Geh*enna, the "Valley of Hinnom," the word used for the place of everlasting punishment. In verse 7 the word for "valley" is quite another, and has no such gloomy association. We gather, then, from the two contrasted terms, valley and vision, that the object on which this burden falls is characterized by a corresponding contrast; that is, while morally dark and low, as this word for "valley" suggests, there is a claim to high privileges and great intelligence, suggested by "vision." It is that city that well represents the religion of man, Jerusalem as seen in her Pharisaic rulers in the Gospels, and as the prophet foresees in his vision.

---

*A characteristic play on words that I have tried to transfer. All can discern it in the Hebrew *mehumah, mebusah, mebucah.* "Confusion," "abusing," "delusion," have at least a similar assonance.

There are points in the chapter that must not be passed over without note, as may be for our edification in Christ; yet, as a whole, it calls, as far as my light goes, for no extended comment. The free paraphrase will be enough to give its general bearing.

The scene opens with a city that had been filled with activity, and all those sounds that accompany the daily pursuit of business and pleasure; but the prophet is apparently astonished to see all the populace rushing up to their flat-roofed houses, and asks the question as to the cause. Is it to get a clear view of an advancing army? Or do they hope thus to escape it? It would be a vain hope, for, says the prophet, "My vision goes further, and I see many slain who have not lost their lives in honorable conflict, but have been slain as prisoners. I see rulers taken captive and fettered, while the common people, who have endeavored to flee afar, are ignominiously chained together.

Now note the effect, not of the fact, but of this vision on the spirit of the Seer, and learn from it what the same Spirit of Christ ever works in His people who see, in that Word that gives us the only "vision" that we now have, the coming wrath.

"Therefore I said: Oh, leave me alone! Hinder me not in my bitter weeping! Press me not with comforts! For how can I see unmoved, the destruction of the daughter of my people?" A tender way of speaking of his beloved nation as seen in the fate of its chief city, Jerusalem; and particularly significant in this connection in which his own lips are announcing the judgment he thus bewails. Well may we learn that God takes no pleasure in inflicting judgment on the creatures He has made, whoever they may be. Judgment is indeed His work; but it is His *strange* work (Isa. 28: 21); and the same Spirit by which our prophet sees the coming suffering, leads him to weep over it. So did He who was in Himself the very "outshining of God's glory, the exact expression of His substance," shed tears, as He, too, foresaw and announced that same judgment on Jerusalem, and in utter tenderness bewailed the hardness of heart that refused to be sheltered by His wing. Well may we learn then, again I say, that none even to this day, if under the control of the same Spirit, will speak of the awful penalty awaiting the finally impenitent, with a cold heart or a tearless eye. He who is in communion with God, loves with Him, rejoices with Him, and weeps with Him.

It is to be feared that any who speak callously or harshly of Hell cannot have entered into the compassionate spirit which should mark the servant of Him who wept.

We may discern in this very day a correspondence to that scene of excitement in the doomed city. Even now there is a strange sense of some imminent danger, leading to the ever-recurring question that men pass one to another: "What's coming?" In that unrest we have a parallel to the rushing up to the housetops in Jerusalem. Alas, too, the parallel may be seen still further as we continue.

"For a day of tumult, of treading down, and of confusion, is on the way from Jehovah, and in the Valley of Vision I can see it clearly, and even hear the crash of falling walls, and the cry of despair that beats against the mountains as they fall. For Elam has taken quiver, with chariots and horsemen. Kir has uncovered the shield, and thus it is that thy choicest valleys are full of chariots, and that horsemen threaten thy gates."

Thus in the prophetic vision, in verse 5, Isaiah foresees the chastening of Jerusalem and bringing on her double for all her sins; for while the sins of no *individual* can be eternally forgiven without the shedding of Blood of such value that God can accept it in expiation; yet the sins of a nation, *as such,* as an entity with a *national* responsibility, can be met only upon the earth.* For there are no *nations* in eternity, and they must, as evidencing the inflexible righteousness of the divine government of the earth, pass through retributive suffering which they bring upon themselves by those sins; and this is inflicted by mutual antagonisms. Thus God used the Assyrian in his day, and later, the Babylonian in his; still later, Persia is used in the punishment of Babylon, and then Greece in that of Persia; finally Rome displaces in the same way the World-empire of Greece; and Rome, broken up by the Goth, Huns, etc., brings the series to an end for a time, till that fourth empire is again revived, and of this we seem to be on the threshold. But this, too, shall come to its end, not by the sub-

---

*The reader's thoughts will probably go to John 11: 50-53, but there the Spirit of God adopts the words of Caiaphas, altering his use of them and enlarging their scope. The nation undoubtedly has profited, and will profit, by that atonement, but everlasting forgiveness of sins is by personal individual faith.

stitution of another merely human power—for in democracy fully displayed this form of man's testing comes to an end—but by the smiting by the Stone cut out without hands; that is, the revelation of the Lord Jesus Christ and the setting up of His kingdom that shall never be removed.

8: He takes off the cover that covereth Judah.
   With eye thus clear-seeing, thou didst direct look
   In that day to th' armor in House of the Forest.
9: Also ye have seen that the breaches are many
   In the (royal) city of David.
   Into the city ye've gathered the waters
   That flow from the lower pool.*
10: Jerusalem's houses ye've carefully counted,
   And houses demolished to strengthen the wall.
11: A cistern ye've built between the two walls,
   The water of th' old pool to store up.
   But naught have regarded the One who hath wrought it,
   Nor considered who formed it afar back.
12: Then did Adonai Jehovah Tzebaoth
   Sound a loud call for the penitent tear,
   For baldness of head and sackcloth begirding:
13: And lo, there was gladness and much merry-making,
   The slaying of oxen, and killing of sheep,
   Eating of flesh and drinking of wine—
   Let's eat and let's drink, for tomorrow we die!
14: Jehovah Tzebaoth hath revealed in my ear:
   Not till ye die shall this sin be purged from you,
   So saith Adonai Jehovah Tzebaoth.

In verse 8 and following there is an admixture of the historical with the prophetic; for much of what is here foretold was actually done by Hezekiah (2 Chron. 32), but the history eventuated in the *deliverance* of Jerusalem, the prophecy in its *capture;* therefore the history does not fulfil it.

The people awaken to the seriousness of the threatening danger and take every precaution within their power, save only that they quite overlook Him in whom alone is there any hope of their deliverance; they "neglect the great salvation" in that they look not to Him alone who is the one effective Defender, whose decree long ago determined this visitation that now threatens them.

--------

*See 2 Kings 20: 20; 2 Chron. 32: 30.

In our A. V. the last clause of verse 11 would read as if Jehovah were reproaching the people for not considering him who long ago had made the "pool," the antecedent of "thereof" being a work merely of human engineering.  That is, of course, impossible, and is an example of the need of care in finding the antecedent to pronouns in Scripture.  The reference is to the calamity that is overhanging it; it is this that has been "fashioned long ago."  But, although this has been formed in Jehovah's mind, the very telling it forth thus as by the prophet was that it might not eventuate, but be averted by a timely repentance, as was really the case when a similar threatening was proclaimed to Nineveh by Jonah (Jonah 3).

Yes, the very foretelling the calamity was really a call from Jehovah for that repentance that should avert it; but instead of the weeping, mourning, disheveled hair and sackcloth garments of humiliation that should express the inward sorrow, what does He find?  Mirth, pleasure, feasting, and revelry, through the whole scene; saying thus, in deeds if not in words, "Let us eat and drink, for tomorrow we die."  This life is all we have, there is nothing either to be feared or hoped beyond it; so let us get all the pleasure from it that we can. The apostle takes up (1 Cor. 15) the same words, and admits that they might be defended if there were no resurrection.  "How foolish I myself have been," he says; "if there be no resurrection, like those foolish men who throw away their lives fighting with wild beasts, so have I thrown away my life without the slightest compensation.  If it be really true that the dead rise not, then the only path of wisdom is in that wild counsel of despair: 'Let us eat and drink, for tomorrow we die.' "

This brings us, in verse 14, to a very solemn word that verges on the full revelation of truth in the New Testament. "Listen," says the prophet, "for Jehovah hath whispered this solemn sentence into my ears: 'This iniquity shall not be expiated till ye do certainly die.' "  That must mean far more than the execution of that primal sentence passed upon all men, and to which all are so inevitably going that it is called, "The way of all the earth;" it means that you shall go out of this life with that iniquity still upon you, and awaiting another death than that which all suffer. It is precisely what the Lord said to the most religious men of

His day: "If ye believe not that I am He, *ye shall die in your sins.*" The first death will not exhaust the penalty.

Ever may we, ever should we, rejoice and make our boast in the Lord—always, always. He, and He alone, is a fount of joy that is perennial, never becoming dried, in fine weather or foul. When we consider the one Witness for God upon the earth, the Church, and the utter, complete and most shameful failure that we have all made of that testimony, we may well hear our God calling us to weeping rather than merriment; to repentance rather than boasting; to humiliation rather than pride.

Verses 15 to 25 are almost universally accepted as foreshadowing in Shebna and Eliakim, the future Antichrist replaced by the true Christ, and the use that the Spirit makes of verse 22 in Revelation 3: 7 tends to confirm such an application. The one difficulty is that the chapter appears to close with a threat even against Eliakim, who would figure Christ Himself. This impossibility compels us, in this application of the prophecy at least, to see here a return to Shebna.

> 15: Thus saith Jehovah Tzebaoth: Now go
> And say to that steward there, Shebna,
> The man who is over the house:

This is Jehovah's commission to the prophet: "Go, get thee to that steward there" ( a contemptuous form of speech), to Shebna, who is over the house, and say to him:

> 16: What hast thou here?  And whom hast thou here?
> That thou makest a tomb for thyself here?
> He is hewing him out a sepulchre high!
> He is cutting himself a home in the rock!
> 17: Take it to heart, for Jehovah will hurl thee,
> Hurling thee with a strong man's throw:
> Grasping, He graspeth thee ever so tightly:
> 18: Coiling, He coileth thee into a coil,
> Then as a ball to a broad land tosses thee.
> There shalt thou die, thy chariots of glory there,
> Thou shame of the house of thy lord!
> 19: Down will I thrust thee, down from thy post,
> Down from thy station He plucks thee.

The word rendered above by "steward" (A. V., treasurer) was used for the most important office in an eastern court. Its occu-

pant, who was said to be "over the house," was in closest intimacy
with the king; nor was it beneath the dignity even of the heir to
the throne to fill this high position as did Jotham (2 Chron. 26:
21); all of which strengthens its applicability to our Lord, the
Son of Him sitting on the Throne, and Heir of all things. But
the present holder, Shebna, is referred to contemptuously.

Note the threefold recurrence of the word "here" in verse 16.
It is strongly emphatic: "Here, here, here; what right hast thou
*here?*" Then in supreme indignation, Jehovah turns from the
direct address to Shebna, to tell, as it were, to some imagined on-
lookers: "Why, he has actually hewn out his sepulchre high
among kings, and thus provided a permanent position of proud
superiority for himself even after death!"

Then, once again, directly facing Shebna, Jehovah says:
"Behold, take this to heart, for Jehovah will first twist thee into
a ball, and then throw thee as a strong man throws it, into a
wide far-off country where nothing shall impede thy shameful
rolling. Not *'here,'* but *there* shalt thou die; and all these
chariots of glory, these trappings that thou hast acquired for thy
glory, shall come to an end with thee there, O thou shame of thy
lord's house!"

If we pass on without noting the extreme significance attached in that dispensation to the disposal of the body after decease,
we shall altogether miss the point of this threat to Shebna. It
was not mere sentiment or natural affection that led to an honored tomb being given, or that feared any dishonor to that which
was inevitably soon to mingle with, and be lost as a body in its
kindred dust.

The disposal of the body after death, inanimate and unconscious as it was, was evidently regarded as a kind of visible reflex
of the condition of the departed spirit. Thus, as Jehovah permitted the dust either to be honored or dishonored, so did that
express the condition, in the unseen world, of the *person* who had
worn that vestment; and also, in the case of burial, a living hope
of the recovery of a clothing of the spirit (which alone completes,
and indeed constitutes, a *"man"*) in resurrection.

With such a significance, how could it be a matter of indifference to the Hebrew as to what became of his own body, or the
bodies of those he loved? In Israel what strange disproportionate

anxiety there seems to have been as to the disposal of the unconscious dust! Could this be due to mere sentiment? Impossible. They that do such things declare plainly their convictions that death does not end the person, and that their God will both care for them in their unclothed condition and also intervene, and not permit that sin-ruined condition of His redeemed to deny the efficacy of the redemption wrought by His beloved Son. These spirits of "just men" must be "made perfect" (Heb. 11: 40); and spirit, soul and body, once more united in an eternal association, shall witness forever to the infinite and eternal efficacy of the atoning death of His dear Son. Would, beloved, that we all had more joy in these bright hopes!

Before leaving Shebna, there are two points that are worthy of consideration: the first is the light that the inspired history throws on his subsequent position in the court of Hezekiah. In 2 Kings 18: 37 we find him no longer "over the house," but in the comparatively inferior position of "scribe," or secretary. But while this is a fall, it is certainly by no means an adequate fulfilment of the threat we have been considering, nor does any scripture give us such fulfilment. Surely this indicates that the divine Spirit is occupied far less with the historical, than with the prophetic Shebna, the Antichrist yet to come. Just as it is not the historical Eliakim but the prophetic Christ who is the real subject of the prophecy.

The next is of similar import; for wherever the name of Shebna occurs, in marked contrast to all others, nothing is said of his parentage, and he, too, is without father, without mother, without descent, and is thus a kind of imitation Melchizedek (but always in a contrasted way), who was also a figure of Christ. This affords another assurance that we must still look forward and not backward to find the *true* Shebna.

Shebna's doom is, alas, not a solitary one. What myriads go out of life, as they have lived, "without God and without hope" as to what comes after death. Hearken to that solemn threat in Jer. 25: 32, 33: "Thus saith the Lord of Hosts, Behold, evil shall go from nation to nation, and a great whirlwind shall be raised up from the coasts of the earth; and the slain of the Lord shall be at that day, from one end of the earth even unto the other end of the earth; they shall not be *lamented*, neither *gathered*, nor *buried;* they shall be dung upon the ground." Note how the solemn threat stays absolutely with the earth. There is not a whisper of a heaven lost, or a hell gained, nor even of the fate of a soul being involved at all; yet, in that distinction between being "gathered" and "buried" (although still without the clear teaching of the New Testament), who could refrain from asking: "If it is the *body* that is affected by the *burial,* what is affected by the *gathering?*" And then we see that this word "gather" is always one of tender consolation to His people, that God gave His saints all through that long period of waiting, and we feel assured that, as certainly as the *body* is buried, so it is the person, as identified with his *spirit,* who is *gathered.* Further, there are three different threats here: the *body* is affected by the refusal of "burial;" the *soul,* the seat of the affections, by the refusal of "lamentation;" and what then is left for the *spirit,* but the refusal of "gathering?" All three speak of complete divine reprobation, and the denial of burial becomes terribly suggestive.

In our day of the bright light of revelation, burial has no longer the significance that it had; and while piety will still confess to the truth of God's Word, and tender human affection will reverently care for the beloved form in committing it to its kindred dust, yet faith no longer lingers over that dust, but rather follows the spirit to its temporary rest in Paradise "with Christ," to await in His company that long-looked-for resurrection morn, when the person shall be clothed with an eternal house that shall fit him for his heavenly environment, as did the body of earth for the earth; *that* depends on our link with Him whom Eliakim figures.

In this light as to the significance of burial in those days, this threat to Shebna has a solemnity that would otherwise be lacking. It does not speak *clearly,* it is true, of an awful future awaiting him after death, but it certainly *suggests* it; and as this magnificent sepulchre, placed high up in the rock amid those of kings, expressed his pride, so was the superhuman nature of that pride evidenced by an ambition that went beyond this life, scene and sphere, and that was distinctly like that of Satan.

Thus, while in Shebna we may see a figure of the future Antichrist, yet *behind* even him, the servant, we may discern (dimly perhaps through the gloom, yet assuredly, too) his master, the Devil; and, in the doom of the servant, see a foreshadowing of the master's shameful end; for he, too, is "the shame of his lord's house," as our Lord Jesus is its glory.

Now the prophecy turns from Shebna to Eliakim, who shall take his place by divine appointment:

20: In that day will I call to My servant,
     Eliakim, son of Hilkiah.
21: With thy robe will I invest him,
     With thy girdle will I empower him,
     And the sceptre of thy government will I place within his
          hand.
     To the dwellers in Jerusalem
     And to all the house of Judah
     He shall be a father truly on whom they shall rely.
22: When he opens none shall shut,
     When he shuts then none shall open.
     Upon his shoulder will I place the Key of David's House.
23: As a nail will I thus fasten him,
     Within a place securely;
     Till a very throne of glory to his father's House he be.
24: Then on him shall depend all the glory of that dwelling,
     The offsprings and the offshoots,
     And all the vessels small:
     From the little cups of gold to the flagons made of skin.

This reference to the Key of David provides what the Spirit of God shall need as a figure in the day of Revelation 3, when another Eliakim, the only One really true to that name that means, "Whom God establishes," shall present Himself to one of that group of churches that may be discerned in one condition of the Lord's people even this very day. Surely we should be interested in such a theme.

He is writing to the church in Philadelphia, or to interpret the name, "Brotherly-love," so that we may justly conclude that this letter is addressed to all among us who are *really* "brethren," and as being that, are held closely bound together in "love" by a common divine life and nature. Thus He speaks: "These things saith He that is holy, He that is true, He *that hath the key of David, He that openeth and no man shutteth; and shutteth and no man openeth.*" Aye, many to this hour rejoice to own that He, the Man of Nazareth, is Lord of all, and "over the house," "whose house are we." Nor does He use that "Key" to shut doors against the dweller in Philadelphia, but sets before him an open door of feeding, of fellowship, and of service, that none can shut. Happy dweller in Philadelphia then! More happy dweller in true "brotherly love" now, to whom He is the one attractive Object, being "holy," amid all earth's defilement; "true," amid all earth's falsehoods; and who thus draws His people to Himself as a gathering Center. Those thus drawn have the whole dear family of God as the only circumference of the circle of their affections and fellowship; that, and only that, bears the character of "Philadelphia" today.

We still have to consider the last verse, the application of which has been disputed:

> 25: In that day, saith Jehovah Tzebaoth,
> Shall the nail that was fastened securely
> Be removed and be cut down and fall.
> Then the burden that upon it depends
> Shall also be cut off and fall.
> Jehovah hath spoken!

All in these later verses seems quite simple and clear until we get to this. On Jesus, the true Eliakim, does indeed hang all the glory of His Father's House, and all the vessels, *i.e.*, His servants, whether they be small or great, as important as the apostles, or as insignificant as ourselves. All alike do surely hang upon Him, and as long as He is "established of God" they are equally secure. Thus it is impossible to apply this verse and its threat to our Lord. Never shall any that depend on Him fall. Fastened in a very sure place, His are "the sure mercies of David." His is the Key of David too; He shall never, never fall.

Then the verse must apply to Shebna; and we may discern in the very phrase by which it is introduced, "In that day," a suggestion to go back to him; for in that day in which the true Eliakim shall be thus exalted, all connected with and depending on Shebna shall fall with him. This is perfectly true, as we see in Revelation 19: 19-21 with regard to the antitype of Shebna, whether Antichrist, or his master, the Devil: absolutely untrue with regard to the Antitype of Eliakim and those who are His.

# CHAPTER TWENTY-THREE

**The Burden of Tyre. What Tyre symbolizes. Significance of Tyre distributing crowns. The strange recovery of Tyre, as still a harlot and yet her hire to be "holiness to the Lord;" explanation of the apparent anomaly.**

W E ARE now brought to the last "burden" of the series of five. The first was on Babylon, and the last on Tyre. Both have far more than a superficial interest for us, since the one as here seen is the representative of the last imperial world-power, attaining and maintaining its position by military force; and the other, Tyre, the great merchant city of the past, shall also find here its representative in the future in the alternative to the military spirit, that of commerce. Behind both is our terrible foe, Satan.

The fall of any mercantile center necessarily causes widespread distress. In a very true and real sense we can say that no nation today "liveth to itself, or dieth to itself." With the prosperity of each one, that of all is so intertwined, that if one suffer —quite irrespective of the *cause* of the suffering—all suffer with it. Forcibly has this been brought home to us all recently. Grant, if only for the sake of argument, that the guilt of initiating war rests on one nation, the *sad effects* of that war cannot be confined to that guilty one. Thus in the book of Revelation that gives a prophetic picture of the last days of this age, we hear both the kings and the merchants of the earth bewailing the fall of the spiritual Babylon, which is not to be understood there as a military, but rather a spiritual empire, that is weaving together, by the threads of commerce, the nations of apostate Christendom.

Thus the Tyre of our chapter represents the commercial glory of the world, and in the graphic picture given in *her* fall, we may see, as in a mirror, some utter disruption of the world's commerce in the future.

I have accepted the divisions of the chapter as in the Hebrew Bible, which is both true to the characteristic "three" of Isaiah, and is confirmed by its correspondence with the value of the numbers, thus:

1: Verses 1 to   9: Tyre's fall the consequence of Jehovah's
counsel.
2: Verses 10 to 14: The hostile human agent of Tyre's fall.
3: Verses 15 to 18: The recovery, or resurrection of Tyre; at
first in unbelief, then final acceptance.


1: Howl, ye ships of Tarshish, howl!
For wasted lies your home-port.
Every house is broken down,
And ye are barred from ent'ring.
These the tidings they receive
From the land of Chittim.
2: Silence! dwellers of the isle,
Filled with wealth from Zidon,
Brought by sailors over-seas;
Sea-wealth thus has filled thee.
3: By many waters comes the seed
That has been raised on Sichor.
The harvest of that river Nile,
Not only doth enrich her,
But gives wealth to the nations.
4: Be 'shamed, O Zidon, be ashamed,
For list, the sea is speaking—
List, thy daughter—the strong one
Of the sea is speaking:
I'm as though I'd travailed not,
Nor bore, nor trained my young men:
Nor had brought up my maidens!
5: When this report to Egypt comes,
The news from Tyre makes trembling.


Thus this "burden" opens with the picture of Tyrian vessels
sailing home from Tarshish, and being met with the news that
their city has fallen before some invader who has utterly destroyed it, so that its dwellings are levelled, and its very harbor so
blocked that entrance is impossible. The news may well be
credited, for it comes from the island lying across the sea from
Tyre, Chittim, or Cyprus.

Then the Tyrians, here termed "dwellers on an island," on
which their city was partly built, are bid to be silent in their
desolation and shame, as they remember their past and now lost
wealth that came to them by mariners belonging to their mother-
city, Zidon.

Next, Egypt comes into the picture, for Sichor, meaning the "Black" river, is a name for the Upper Nile, the black slime of which gave such fertility to all the land of Egypt. Thus fertile Egypt pours her wealth into Tyre. It is the harvest of her river, and all her crops come through Tyre to the nations of the earth thus enriched.

Tyre was the daughter of Zidon, and now the "mother" comes to see how fares her daughter, and what does she hear? The wailing alone of the empty sea! Nay, more, the ruin of that once strong fortress, Tyre, mourns to her mother thus: "I am as a barren woman, my sons and my daughters are all gone! I am bereft of all my children; thus indeed I am as a barren woman in my shame and sorrow."

When Egypt hears of the disaster that has befallen Tyre, she, too, trembles at the report, for Tyre is her customer, and the ruin of one's customer sometimes comes very near to being one's own ruin. In a word, this fall of Tyre causes widespread distress, so the lament continues:

6: As ye flee to Tarshish, howl!
   Ye dwellers on the island.
7: Can *this* your joyous city be
   In far-off ages founded?
   Her feet must carry her afar
   To dwell in alien countries.
8: Who hath taken against Tyre
   Such an evil counsel?
   Tyre, distributor of crowns,
   Whose merchants were as princes;
   Whose traffickers were in the earth
   As very chiefs of glory!
9: 'Tis the purpose of the Lord,
   Of Jehovah Tzebaoth,
   The pride of beauty all to stain,
   Thus to make earth's chief ones
   Contemptible, dishonored!

The people of Tyre are counselled to flee as far away as they possibly can; not to stay at Cyprus, but to go on to Tarshish; for what a change has come over that once joyous city, a city that was founded so far back that human history gives no record of it. Now she must flee afar for safety.

Then we hear someone asking a question: Who has purposed this on Tyre—on Tyre, the giver of crowns? The answer comes at once: "The Lord of Hosts." And why? "To stain the pride of all beauty"—that is, the pride that comes from self-occupation with one's natural endowments. Pride, pride, pride, is that basic sin to which God is ever opposed, and man is ever expressing.

Can we be satisfied with simply stopping at the little *comparatively* insignificant seaport? Is it straining beyond the intent of the divine Author of the Scriptures to discern *behind* Tyre some expression of that all-pervasive creature-pride. As we hear her called the "distributor of crowns" can we keep our minds from going to that chief of the children of pride who did, and does indeed, distribute the crowns of earth? As surely as the "King of Tyre" in Ezek. 28 stands for that grand, yet fallen creature, Satan (as practically all Bible students agree), so surely, in this term here applied to that city, do we see him who claimed to be able to give, even to the Lord Himself, the "crown" of all the earth. He showed the Lord all the kingdoms of the world, and said: "All this power will I give Thee, and the glory of them: for that is delivered unto me." Think not to say that it was simply a great liar who there spoke, and therefore his word must not be credited. While that is indeed the case, we must bear in mind that *his* lies are not those of a fool; on the surface, easily seen and refuted; but covered up most skilfully with truth. The lie here is in the tense. Had he said, "All this *was* delivered me, but I have forfeited it all by my rebellion, even as my human type, King Saul, did later," that would have been quite true; but (also like Saul) he cleaves to what he has lost in title, and still he claims the glory of the world. Surely, then, Tyre as "the distributor of crowns" is in this a very fitting representative of that once glorious creature; nor is that correspondence lessened by the revealed truth that *he, too,* was created (as was Tyre) in those far-off days before human history began. A third correspondence is in his fall being due to the pride in his own beauty, for that is precisely what is charged against him: "Thine heart was lifted up *because of thy beauty*" (Ezek. 28: 17).

Thus is our chapter lifted out of a dull record of long-past events in which we can have no direct interest, and made worthy of Him who, in inspiring these records, had even *us* in His mind, "on whom the ends of the ages have come" (1 Cor. 10: 11). Nor will it be written in vain if we learn the grave danger there is in contemplating with complacency any form of *our* endowment, whether physical, mental or spiritual, for that is following the path of Satan and of this world. Our own path is marked out for us in Phil. 2: 5-8; shall we not ponder it?

But mark that the Lord does not *Himself* directly touch the corrupt form of evil in the earth, but commissions the other, the "violent," to do that. Thus Chaldea must destroy the unchaste Tyre; and so must "the ten kings and the Beast" hate the "harlot" (now about fo come into being by the unification of the religious sects of Christendom) and "burn her with fire," for thus in both cases do they unconsciously carry out the counsel of "the Lord God strong to judge" (Rev. 17).

> 10: Freely flow o'er all thy land
>     As the Nile, O daughter
>     Of Tarshish, now no girdle binds.*
> 11: His Hand is stretched upon the sea,
>     Kingdoms hath He shaken.
>     The Lord hath issued His command
>     Against the merchant-city†
>     To destroy its stronghold.
> 12: And He said: That nevermore
>     Shall ye have rejoicings,
>     O Zidon's virgin-daughter,
>     So humiliated!
>     Rise and pass to Chittim, pass,
>     Though there no rest awaits thee.

Tyre continues to be the subject. Jehovah has again stretched His hand over the sea (*cf.* Exod. 14: 21), putting it into fear and commotion. Kingdoms, too, has He stirred up; but why? That they may carry out His purposes, and it is to destroy the mer-

---

*This verse is admittedly obscure, but the above rendering gives the accepted interpretation. As the Nile (simply called "the river") is free to overflow its banks, so Tarshish, which stands here for colonies which, having no longer to account to Tyre, may do as they will; they are no longer under restraint.

†In the Hebrew text, "*Canaan.*"

chant-city of Tyre, here called "Canaan," which means "merchant."

Then He again addresses Tyre direct: "O thou disgraced virgin, thou daughter of Zidon, thy rejoicings have come to their end; go, cross the sea to Cyprus; but if thou thinkest there to find rest, thou shalt only find fresh disappointment."

13: See the land of Casidim,
    This a people were not;
    (Asshur founded it of old
    For the desert-dwellers).
    Towers they set up for its siege;
    They destroyed its mansions,
    He brought it down to ruin!
14: Howl, ye ships of Tarshish, howl!
    For wasted is your fortress.

The prophet directs attention to a power that is to figure large in connection both with the whole earth, and specially his own people, "Chaldea," or, as the word is written, the Casidim. Now while this people must certainly have been in existence in the days of Nimrod, for he was the founder of Babel, yet Chaldea did not come within the vision of the Spirit of Prophecy until after Assyria had passed out of it, but this Chaldea is to be important in relation to the future fortunes of Israel, so the verse begins by directing the attention to Chaldea in the word "See," for here is a future World-conqueror.

Then the prophecy is rounded off, so to speak, by a return to its first line; again bidding the crews of the ships coming home from Tarshish to Tyre, to howl, for the Chaldean has brought it to ruin.

The third and last part of this prophecy tells, as one would expect from its numerical place, of the *recovery* of Tyre, but in a very strange way:

15: In that day it comes to pass
    Tyre shall be forgotten
    For seventy years, as the days
    Of a single monarch,
    But at close of seventy years
    Shall Tyre renew her singing,
    Singing as a harlot.

16: Take the harp; go round the town,
    O harlot long-forgotten:
    Play sweetly and, with many a song,
    Seek to be remembered.
17: At the end of seventy years
    Jehovah visits Tyre:
    To her hire she then returns;
    Committing fornication
    With the kingdoms of the earth,
    On the globe's broad surface.
18: But her traffic and her gain,
    Holy to Jehovah,
    Shall not treasured be nor stored;
    But for people dwelling
    In the presence of the Lord;
    And shall suffice their eating,
    And for their stately clothing.

Difficulties abound here!  Grant that Tyre was captured by Nebuchadnezzar; grant that the time of her humiliation corresponded with that of Jerusalem, seventy years; grant that she may have had some measure of commercial revival after that; but granting all this, it could only have been, as verse 17 assures us, like those resurrections of which we are told in the Gospels, a return to a natural life with all its old sin and sorrow resumed, only to pass out of it again by death.  For the condition of Tyre today corresponds rather with Ezek. 26: 14; it is "like the top of a rock," so bare that it is only fit for the fishermen to spread upon it their nets, and "shall be built no more."  It is again as dead as is, at this date, Lazarus, or Jairus' little daughter, or, to give a national parallel, Israel.

But we care little for the political history of ancient Tyre. Our souls hunger, not to know when it was captured by Babylonian, Saracen, Mameluke or Turk—*that* will not satisfy our deep soul-needs.  We want to learn what *God* would teach, and, whether we can discern it or not, we know well that His teaching will result in abasing all our pride that comes from mere knowledge (1 Cor. 8: 1), and exalting before us His beloved Son and His interests, wherever they may lie.  We will, then, drop the literal Tyre, and accept her only as a symbol of the commercial glory of this world.

That, however, does not dispel all our difficulties, for in this restoration Tyre is morally unchanged; she is still likened to a thoroughly depraved woman, and yet, precisely what was never, under any circumstances, to be offered to the Lord is here said to be "holiness unto" Him, even the very words inscribed on the High-priest's mitre (Exod. 28: 36)!   For thus reads Deut. 23: 18: "Thou shalt not bring the hire of a whore, or the price of a dog into the house of the Lord thy God for any vow: for even both these are abomination unto the Lord thy God."   Yet here is that very hire, "holiness to the Lord!"   Is that not indeed a difficulty?

Are we not compelled to see here another of those strange parentheses, not pointed out, but left for us to discover, as necessitated by the context, and by the light of all Scripture?   I need hardly remind my readers of Daniel 9, and that between the contiguous verses 26, 27, whilst the narrative apparently continues in unbroken sequence, we are forced to see an unnoticed interval that has now lasted nearly two thousand years. So, again in Isaiah 61: 2, when, in the synagogue at Nazareth, the Lord read this prophecy, He stopped in the middle of the verse, and again we have the same long parenthetical time exactly, even between the words!

Thus there is no reason why, in precisely the same way, there should not be that same unnoticed interval between verses 17, 18, leaving room for precisely the same interval.   In verse 17 the commercial wealth of the Gentiles is still unholy and defiled, as being the gain of departure from God and friendship with the world (James 4: 4), and thus must refer to a time *prior* to the Lord's return to the earth; while in verse 18 we have a fulfilment of those prophecies that speak of the wealth of the Gentiles poured into the holy and beloved city Jerusalem in its millennial glory after that return.   For thus it is written: "The daughter of Tyre shall be there with a gift" (Ps. 45: 12); and again: "The wealth of the Gentiles shall come unto thee" (Isa. 60: 5), and other scriptures might be added.   That is, the wealth of the Gentiles due to commerce, is no longer stored for selfish aggrandizement, but is "holiness to the Lord," it is no longer a harlot's hire.

This brings the verses into perfect harmony with all Scripture, provides us with truth that edifies, and yet gives, as I venture to apprehend, a satisfactory explanation of this difficult part of Holy Writ.   It exalts the Lord Jesus in telling the gracious wonders that must await His return to this poor sin-defiled earth, when even that which has been most filthy becomes "Holiness to the Lord."   Well may we say in view of it, "What hath God wrought!"

# CHAPTER TWENTY-FOUR

**The whole world comes into judgment. What is the everlasting covenant? The city that becomes "tohu." The pessimism of prophecy. The song turned to a groan. The earth's regeneration, preceded by judgment on both heavens and earth.**

SO interesting and valuable have I found the writing of Delitzsch on this section, that I could wish that space permitted the transcription of most of it; but as it is, I must give a word or two that shall pass on some measure of that interest to my readers, although it will necessarily greatly suffer by the contraction.

He begins by noting that the section is thoroughly eschatological, dealing with the closing days of this age, and apocalyptic, that is, a divine revelation; certain historic events being taken, but "which vanish, like will-o'-the-wisps, as soon as you attempt to follow and seize them; the prophet only using them as emblems of far-off events of the last days, and not to be assumed to be final fulfilments of the prophecies, for in so doing, you will find yourself where will-o'-the-wisps ever lead, in swamps of obscurities and difficulties.

"The particular judgments that we have been following in the preceding 'Burdens' all flow into this last judgment as into a sea; and all the salvation that formed the shining edge of the oracle against the nations is here concentrated in the glory of a midday sun. These chapters form the 'finale' to chapters 13 to 23, and that in a strictly musical sense: what the 'finale' should do in a piece of music, namely, gather up the scattered changes into a grand impressive whole, is done here by this closing cycle. Song follows song 'mid the crashing of judgments, and these songs contain every variety, from the most elevated heavenly hymn to the most tender popular song. Moreover, we do not find so much real music anywhere else in the ring of the words, for Isaiah is fond of painting for the ear, and the reason he does it here more than anywhere else is that these chapters are in-

tended to form a 'finale'—intended to surpass all that had gone
before. The whole is a grand 'Hallelujah,' hymnic in character
and musical in form." There was no other than Isaiah who was
so incomparable a master of language.

Now it is surely good to see that this Christian, competent
as he was by his knowledge of the idiom of the language of the
Old Testament, was in perfect accord with what we have previously gathered as to the *final* fulfilment of these prophecies being entirely in the future; nor does it lessen our pleasure to read
of this accord in his own choice words and poetical figures that
are worthy of forming a commentary on this "prophet of fire."

Further, it serves to confirm the conviction that many of us
have long held that our own prophetic book of Revelation is governed by the same principle, and can only be rightly understood
by a twofold interpretation: the one referring to near-by, the
other to far-off events, distinguished by the words "historical"
and "futurist."

Let us turn to our chapter and throw a free translation into
a slightly rhythmical form that shall at least give the reader both
the sense and some idea of the poetical character of the original.

1: Behold, the earth is emptied
   By Jehovah who maketh it waste;
   Yea, He turneth it upside down
   And scatters its dwellers abroad.
2: People and priest; mistress and maid; buyer and seller as
      one;
   Lender, borrower; debtor, creditor; to all it happens alike.
3: The earth is utterly emptied,
   The earth is utterly spoiled,
   For Jehovah hath spoken this word!

In the preceding burdens we have had torrents of judgment,
each dashing fiercely along in its own channel, directed against
nation after nation. But here we have them all joined together
in so swollen a river that it sweeps everything before it in one
awful cataclysmic catastrophe, which, while it may begin with
apostate Israel, as the word "priest" in the second verse suggests,
certainly does not end till the whole world is affected.

There is nothing in the past that can possibly be considered

as anything like a fulfilment of this prophecy, and so, according
to the short and easy method of infidelity, called Modernism, it is
calmly swept aside as being spurious, and not written by Isaiah
at all! In this way all prophecy is disposed of. If the fulfilment
in the *past* is too evident to be denied, *that* proves that it was
written after the event. If, on the other hand, no fulfilment can
be found in the past, then it is evidently spurious! Well, to us
there is not the slightest difficulty in recognizing that this "holy
man of God" is here being "moved to speak" by that Spirit to
whom the future is as clear as the past, and depicting the terrors
of that day in which "God will judge the world by that Man
whom He hath appointed." It is true that from a human point
of view, it was very far off in the day the prophet wrote; but it
has come very near now, for that very same Spirit has taught us
to "see the day approaching." Does not the book of Revelation
also tell the Churches of that "hour of trial that is to come on all
the world to try the earth-dwellers," precisely as does Isaiah?
Only there we have the comfort of a gracious promise of some
who have kept the Word of His patience, not heard in the Old
Testament at all. Here, *in* the hour, there is no discrimination
whatever: the whole earth is like a vessel turned upside down;
and thus emptied, all classes and conditions are involved in one
sweeping overthrow, and the reference to priest as well as people,
assures us that it must refer to a time of complete and universal
religious apostasy, in which the leaders of religious thought have
led the people away from the truth. Now while this must, I believe, refer primarily to the Jewish apostasy, yet the New Testament speaks exactly of the same thing: "For that day shall not
come except there come *the* apostasy first," and every falsely
called "Christian" pulpit shall ring with open attacks on the Person and Work of the Son of God. I can leave my readers to decide as to there being any such indications this very day. Even
the confession of the fact, sorrowful as it is, turns to a testimony
of the truth of the Word of God, and to a brighter hope of our
Lord's speedy return. But to go on with Isaiah:

4: The earth doth mourn and fadeth away,
   The whole world droops and fades,
   The proud of the earth are drooping!

5: Under its dwellers the earth is defiled;
   For the laws have they wilfully broken;
   Have changed the decree, and have broken
   The covenant everlasting!
6: Therefore the curse hath devoured the earth,
   For guilty are all that dwell on it.
   'Tis for this the dwellers .on earth
   Are consumed almost to extinction,
   And few are the mortals remaining!
7: Mourneth the new wine:* withered the vine.
   The once merry-hearted are sighing:
8: Ceased is the mirth of the tabrets;
   Ended the revellers' tumult;
   Ceased is the joy of the harping:
9: No wine with a song are they drinking:
   Strong drink to the drinkers is bitter.
10: Shattered the city of Tohu,
    Its houses are closed, none may enter.
11: Instead of the wine there is wailing;
    Darkened is now all its gladness:
    The mirth of the earth is all banished:
12: What remains of the city is desert:
    Its gate is shattered to ruins!

There are several things that may make this obscure to us
Gentiles, not accustomed to the Hebrew forms of expression, but
we shall be losers should we therefore neglect it, for it is "profitable" as well as other parts of God's Word. It would appear
clear that the prophecy of judgment begins with a center, Israel,
and from that center sweeps in ever-widening circumference till it
includes the whole earth. Thus, while in the first verse there is
some degree of uncertainty as to whether the Hebrew word
*ehretz* should be rendered "land" or "earth," the word "priest,"
on the one hand, compelling us to think of Israel alone, where
alone was a divinely appointed class of priesthood; on the other,
we have a word in verse 4 that can only refer to the whole prophetic earth; and by the time we reach the end of the chapter,

---

*This term, "new wine," must not be taken as corresponding
with our grape-juice, which has neither exhilarating nor (even if
taken in large quantities) intoxicating powers as has this *"tirosh,"*
or "new wine," to which the Apostle refers at Pentecost: "These
are not full of new wine, as ye suppose."

all uncertainty disappears, and "earth" is the only equivalent possible. It is, then, the whole prophetic earth that is coming under divine visitation; and in the light of other scriptures, we see in this chapter those fearful preliminary judgments that lead up to and introduce the "day of the Lord," heralding and including His actual appearing.

Our poor earth! It shares in the vicissitudes of that race which, by the body, springs from and is still related to it. It actually suffers for the sin of its dweller, man. In Eden all was unmingled loveliness, for all was well with man; but with the entrance of sin its beauty was sadly defaced, and not till the manifestation of the Son of God, the second Man (and with Him the fruit of His redemption, the sons of God, Rom. 8: 19), shall the earth regain its perfection of Edenic loveliness; but that will only be through the birth-pangs of which we are here reading. Thus, we here see the earth like a fading plant, and the "high ones" among men are likened to the blossom at the head of that plant; but that blossom hangs down drooping! But why is this? Because they have all defied God the Creator, by setting at naught all His laws, whether given to the Jew at Sinai, or to the Gentile in conscience and nature, or the professing Christian as to Christ. Is it not true, my reader? Is it not true? As far as it lies within the power of people even the laws of nature are ignored or reversed, and that with a smile of amusement that they had ever been regarded! The apostle could appeal confidently in his day to the teaching of nature, as to the long hair of women being their glory. How little point would that have now! God strictly forbade the changing the distinctive garments of the sexes. Are these things so small that He cares nothing for them? So might it have been said as to simply taking a fruit from a tree. Which shows the direction of the wind better—a stone or a feather?

We have another expression that is full of interest: What is that "everlasting covenant" which the inhabitants of the earth are charged with breaking?

In Genesis 9: 8-17, after and closely connected with that sacrifice of a sweet savor that Noah offered (chap. 8: 20, 21) within the compass of those few verses, we have exactly a sevenfold recurrence of that word "covenant," which, in itself, is a clear mark of the divine importance attached to it, and among the terms applied to that covenant which God then made with the *earth*, it is called "everlasting" (ver. 16). Here, then, we clearly have an "everlasting covenant," of which at that time the rainbow was the token, nor need we question that it is to this that the reference is made here. What was the basic principle of that covenant that made it everlasting? It could be nothing but grace, well-founded on absolute justice. This, in a figure, Noah's sweet-smelling sacrifice provided, but the substance of that figure is alone found in the Cross. This "everlasting covenant" of grace, through righteousness, is alone that on which at any time, through all dispensations, God can ever bear with the earth, or any true blessing can come to sinful man, however penitent he may be.

But then has God, in giving that "everlasting covenant" of grace founded on atonement, deprived Himself of all powers of vindicating His government? Must conditions that flout that government, and set at naught the very basis of the covenant, be also borne everlastingly? Far from it, as our chapter evidences.

In verse 10 I have left the word "*tohu*" untranslated. It is always used of that chaotic condition, the result of sin when visited by God. In Genesis 1: 2 it is rendered "without form." I take it that no specific city is intended by the City of Confusion, but as in Rev. 16: 19, where it is termed "the great city," not a literal city (for that would not accord with the intensely spiritual and symbolic character of that book), but what man has been building as in united opposition to God, as Babel of old, expressive of their pride.

Nothing could exceed the gloom of the whole picture, and as the central city Jerusalem is really the representative of all Israel, as Babel was the representative of the whole earth, so here there is again a symbolic city that represents the proud building of the whole earth, and it is a desert, its gate in ruins—it is chaos returned.

No one can read these divinely inspired prophecies without being struck with the sharp contrast they present to the prevailing teachers of our day. According to *this*, Isaiah, with all the prophets of the Old Testament, and the writers of the New, yea, even our Lord Himself, would be branded as "pessimists," for they give but one consistent expectation as to the character of the closing days of this age, and it is one of ever-increasing evil and gloom. Yet in the next verses of our chapter we have indeed a break in the heavy clouds, and a streak of heavenly blue appears for a moment. How welcome that is in times of storm, we all know. Thus Isaiah sings:

13: In the midst of the land, 'mid its peoples,
    Shall there be as the beating of olives;
    As the gleaning when vintage is finished.
14: These lift up their voices exulting,
    For Jehovah's revealed in His glory,
    And they shout with joy from the sea.
15: Glorify ye now therefore Jehovah,
    In the lands of the light (of the east);
    To the Name of Jehovah, the God of Israel,
    Give glory in th' isles of the west.
16: From the end of the earth have we heard
    Songs that delight in ascribing
    Glory unto the righteous.

Here we again discern that remnant of Israel, preserved by divine grace, and as long as there is one single true Israelite living (not merely a "Jew outwardly" but "inwardly," as in Romans 2: 29), neither "all flesh" nor the earth itself can be utterly destroyed; for Christ, the Messiah of Israel, is to be identified with that remnant. Thus its preservation, and with it, that of the earth and "all flesh" (Matt. 24: 22), is assured. Precisely in the same way, and for the same reason, as long as there is one single member of the Body of Christ on the earth, one single true Christian (not merely one outwardly, but in truth), the "great tribulation" of which our chapter speaks, cannot possibly come; for the Church, composed of all these would still be here, and dwelling therein, that effective "Hinderer" to the working of man's assumption, the Holy Spirit.

Here, then, we see a faithful remnant, few indeed, so few that they can only be likened to the olives that may fall when the tree is beaten after the picking; or, after the vintage, when the grapes having been gathered, a bunch or a solitary grape may be seen here and there that has been overlooked. These few are filled with holy joy, and that because Jehovah has at length intervened "to avenge these, His elect, who have cried day and night unto Him." From the east to the west, faith anticipating that day, substantiating those long-hoped-for conditions, hears joyous songs resound. And now the Gentiles "catch the flying joy" and the earth, being likened to a spread-out garment, from its very fringe (lit., "wing") they join in that song with the words: "Glory to the righteous;" that is, the Gentiles shall at that time unselfishly delight in the glory given to that elect remnant of Israel that shall then be recognized as the one absolutely "righteous nation that keepeth truth."

But the song ceases almost as soon as it has begun, and as is so often the case in times of unsettled weather, the clouds again cover the whole scene, as we hear the prophet himself uttering this lament:

16b: My misery! My misery! O woe is me!
　　　Robbers do rob, and are robbing, as robbers indeed do
　　　　　they rob.
17: The Horror, the Pit, and the Snare*
　　　Are upon thee, O thou earth-dweller.
18: When the tidings of horror are heard
　　　They flee, but their flight is in vain,
　　　For into the pit do they fall;
　　　Or if they escape from the pit,
　　　Then are they caught in the snare;
　　　For the floodgates of heaven are opened,
　　　And earth's foundations do rock.

---

*Verse 16b, and the first line of verse 17 form a striking illustration of Isaiah's characteristic play on words. It is next to impossible to transfer this to English, but anyone can see it in the language the prophet himself used, which reads thus:

　　　Rahzi-li! Rahzi-li! Ohi-li!
　　　Bogdim, bahgadu v'beged bohgdim bahgadu,
17: Pachad vahpachath vahpach.

*Rahzi* is from a root "to make thin," so "impoverish," hence "to make miserable," which justifies the rendering "My misery!" The next line has the same word in slightly different forms five times. Its root meaning is "cover," hence "treachery," but the parallelism of chapter 21: 2 and 33: 1 clearly tells us that this treachery is in

This sudden change from song to groan, the one verse, as it were, swallowing them both, can but remind us of the effect of that little "opened book" that John took from the hand of the mighty "cloud-clothed angel" in Revelation 10, for when in obedience to his command, he had eaten it, it was in his mouth sweet as honey, but as soon as he had eaten it his belly was bitter. That "little book" tells of Israel's final recovery and perfect blessedness, and consequent blessing to this sin-racked earth. It is very sweet, and this is paralleled by these songs of joy that we have heard in verses 14-16. But after the book is swallowed, and it begins to be digested, it is very bitter, for it then tells of that time of unparalleled tribulation that must come first; and *that* bitterness can be discerned in these groans that we are now listening to from our prophet. The end is sweet, but the path to it is bitter.

We must not fail to note that however true it may be that this great tribulation begins with the pious Israelite in the land, it does not end there. The very terms, "the floodgates of *heaven*" and "*earth's* foundations," indicate a far wider sphere, for the heavens do not cover Palestine only, nor are the earth's foundations beneath that land alone. That, too, is in strict accord with the New Testament prophecy, for after we have seen, in Rev. 7, the sealed 144,000 of *Israel's* tribes, we behold an innumerable company of *Gentiles* who have also come out of "the great tribulation," having "washed their robes and made them white in the blood of the Lamb," which is, incidentally, a strong testimony to the truth that human suffering does not in itself cleanse human sin as to individuals; the retribution of nations, as such, is different. But to return: I render the next verse very literally thus, for it is graphic and terrible:

19: Torn, torn asunder, the earth!
    Burst, burst in pieces, the earth!
    Shakes, shakes and totters, the earth!

---

robbing, which I have adopted. Whilst very poor English it preserves some idea of the original. The play in verse 17 on the one sound *pach* is clear enough, but I have found it impossible to transfer.

20: Like to a sot the earth is all reeling,
Like to a hammock to and fro swinging,
Its sin lies upon it so heavy a burden
That it falleth and riseth no more!

That lies still before us, and not far ahead. Do we not need —living as we do in the very atmosphere of unbelief in the Scriptures—to challenge our own hearts and repeat to ourselves that word so frequently pressed upon us amid those corresponding terrific scenes of the Apocalypse: "These are the true sayings of God?" This is particularly needful for us, living in the comparative quiet which the merciful providence of God has up to this time granted to this land; for it becomes most difficult to realize even the possibility of so awful a calamity falling on New York, Boston or Philadelphia, and sweeping over the whole country. But can we not well understand how a dweller in a devastated, war-torn, famine-stricken, pestilence-filled country could do so easily enough?

The whole creation, which has been groaning and travailing in pain even until now, is here suffering the climactic anguish of its new birth, by which Christ "the Child" is about to be born, the Son is about to be given to Israel,* and when He comes and identifies Himself with that beloved, though long-rejected people, when "she which travaileth hath brought forth," when "the remnant of His brethren shall return unto the children of Israel" (Micah 5: 3), then the new birth of the earth is accomplished, its regeneration has come.

How graphically, with what inimitable strokes, does this master of words picture its agonies and bewilderment; it is first rent by fissures, then these spread wider into chasms, then it reels, totters, sways aimlessly to and fro, as a man overcome with intoxicants, or as a hammock slung between supports; till at last, weighted down with the heavy load of sin that its dweller, man, has put upon it, it falls never to rise again. Its place is taken by a "new earth" wherein righteousness is in the place of government, although not yet *"dwelling"* there—for *that*, it must await its perfected condition (Rev. 21).†

---

*See chapter 9 and comments thereon.

†This picture of an imperfect, or rather partial, New Creation condition of the earth may perplex some, but the scene is un-

We have one final and terrible act still to be fulfilled in the great drama, and this time it involves not only the earth and its dwellers, but the heavens and *their* dwellers. I am sure that it will have been noted that there have been ever-widening circumferences of judgment in the chapter: first Israel, and the apostate mass, with a little remnant saved; then the whole earth also, with a remnant brought through; but finally the very heavens become involved, as we now see:

21: And it cometh to pass that
  Jehovah shall punish
  The host of the high ones
  Dwelling on high.
  With them he will punish
  The kings of the earth-realms
  Who 'dwell on the earth.
22: Together they're gathered,
  As captives are gathered
  Into the pit.
  They're shut up in prison,
  Till many a day pass,
  Then visited.
23: Then the moon blushes;
  The sun turneth pale;
  For royally reigns
  Jehovah Tzebaoth
  In Salem on Zion,
  'Fore His elders in glory.

This is indeed a remarkable prophecy, and affords a striking proof of the word in 2 Peter 1: 20: "No prophecy of the Scripture is of any private interpretation," that is, certainly not that it is intended to be so obscure that the readers are not themselves to interpret it at all, and therefore this must be left to "the Church," as the Papacy teaches; but the very first meaning of the word rendered "private" is "its own;" no prophecy is of

---

deniably millennial, not eternal, and corresponds with the present condition of everyone in Christ. There, too, "is a new creation;" there, too, "old things are passed away;" there, too "all things are become new, and all things are of God" (2 Cor. 5: 17, 18), and yet how far from perfect in us each, we all know, and thus will it be in the millennial earth. For further comment see chapter 65.

its own interpretation, is to be interpreted *by itself*. Prophecy, more than any other line of truth, needs the light of *all* Scripture thrown upon it. So here, no man, apart from the inspiration of God, could have foretold the punishment of a *heavenly* host as well as earthly kings. Do other scriptures confirm or deny this?

It is exactly what we see in Revelation 19: 19, 20; 20: 1-3:

"And I saw the Beast and the kings of the earth, and their armies gathered together to make war against Him that sat on the horse and with His army. And the Beast was taken, and with him the False Prophet...These both were cast alive into the lake of fire...He laid hold on the Dragon, that old serpent, which is the Devil and Satan, and bound him a thousand years, and cast him into the bottomless pit."

We must then place the two prophecies together in order to correctly understand either. Then we learn that while that fallen star, Satan, is the leading actor in that last scene, yet his host of subordinate spirits are with him, and that as he was not cast alone out of heaven (Rev. 12: 9), so he is not cast alone out of the earth, but in both cases, his angels with him; for Isaiah tells us that it is the host of the high-ones on high* (and that is surely the angelic powers that have followed him in his rebellion) that are shut up in the pit.

Our prophet has before him a picture of a defeated army, from which the prisoners are confined in a pit to prevent escape, and for their final disposition, are "visited" later. In the Old Testament prophet all is upon the earth; but Revelation, true to its name, *reveals* to us a pit that is "bottomless," and therefore not on earth at all, and there Satan, and (as we should gather from what Isaiah tells us) his host with him, are cast, and there earthly kings accompany them.

The epoch at which all this occurs is clearly the revelation of our Lord, or as it is termed in 2 Thess. 2: 8, "the brightness of His coming," and see how perfectly the poetic language of our prophet accords with this, for such is the radiancy of the Lord's appearing that the moon blushes with shame, the ardent sun be-

---

*See Job 16: 19; Ps. 68: 18; Isa. 57: 15 for the term "on high," referring to heaven.

comes pale as a lamp at noonday, while prominently exalted before the eyes of His elders is the Lord of glory, in glory.

No hint have we of a "Church" here, no new Jerusalem coming down from God out of heaven, no ranks of heavenly redeemed on white horses; all this has to be filled in by other scriptures. Yet that word "elders" may have a wider bearing than even the prophet himself conceived, and may not only refer to those who shall be owned as elders upon the earth. In that connection we may see in the word a correspondence with Matt. 19: 28: "Ye who have followed Me in the regeneration" (and that is the time of which this prophecy speaks), "when the Son of Man shall sit on the throne of His glory" (as here), "ye also shall sit on twelve thrones, judging the twelve tribes of Israel"—*that* must surely be on earth. We have other elders in Revelation, chapters 4 and 5, who are symbolically *twenty-four* in number, also seated each on his throne, and in them we may discern a completion of that scene in the heavenly redeemed. Among these, you whose eye may now be reading these lines, and I, the writer of them (by still greater grace) shall have our part.

But I can easily conceive some saying: "Are not the twelve apostles members of the Church as the Body of Christ, and will not *their* part be also in the heavens, and not earth? How then can they judge the twelve tribes of Israel *on earth,* and yet be *in heaven?*" That is surely somewhat of a difficulty, but in the first place, let us remember that this was said in answer to a bargaining question of Peter: "We have forsaken all, what shall *we* have therefore?" Nor is the Lord's answer to it complete without that parable of the householder and the laborers, wherein those who make a bargain get exactly what they bargained for, and not a fraction more. If therefore Peter and the rest were to maintain that self-seeking bargaining spirit, they would lose the heavenly place, with its far higher dignities of judging, not twelve tribes merely, but the world, yes, even angels (1 Cor. 6: 2, 3). But may we not be assured that those dear men repented of that spirit of their father Jacob (Gen. 28: 20-22), and other representative elders of Israel will be seated on those inferior thrones on the earth, while the apostles will have the higher blessings of the heavenly portion? That is assuming, what is not necessarily the case, that they will not, in some way fill both dignities.  Further, we may at least be quite sure that neither Peter, James, John, nor you and I, will then esteem any "throne" as giving opportunity for self-exaltation in that day, for we shall have none of that "flesh" that troubles us so much now, but for *worship*, as giving us more to cast at His feet, and for *service*, as giving us greater opportunities for that.

How perfectly it all accords with that picture of the kingdom given us on the holy mount!  In Him whose very garments radiated a glory that was inherent in His ineffable Person, we see the "Lord Jehovah Tzebaoth reigning gloriously;" in Peter, James and John, as representatives of the earthly saints brought through the sorrows of the great tribulation, we see those "elders" before whom He thus reigns: while the heavenly people have their representatives in the same scene in Moses and Elias, also elders who have reached the goal by the different paths—the one by the resurrection and the other by the rapture.  There can be no millennium without those four preceding essentials: 1, Christ in all His personal glory; 2, Raised saints; 3, Raptured saints; and 4, Israel restored to the favor of Jehovah and singing in her joy. The next chapter gives us her song.

# CHAPTER TWENTY-FIVE

Song of Israel forgiven and restored. What are the "wines on the lees?" The veil over all flesh. Moab; who is meant?

NOW we consider, and I trust with some true delight, a wondrously beautiful chapter. The strains of those ancient prophets are for the most part sad rather than joyous, and any burst of singing, amid their confessions, tears and stern denunciations, is like that song in the prison at Philippi, a striking witness to the intervention of the blessed God in grace. We heard a little trill of singing in the previous chapter, but this soon died away, awaiting some long-expected event before being continuous; that event was the revelation of the Lord Jesus as the Redeemer of Israel. Our songs will never be unmixed with sighs till we see Him.

At the close of the chapter moon confounded and sun ashamed tell that He has come. Long hidden, as was the High Priest on the day of atonement, He has been revealed at last in all His glory and the holy angels with Him (Matt. 25: 31). While songs did attend His first coming, they were but from a feeble remnant, and soon died away; nor has there been any singing from that poor nation since: it has been silent Godward, and uttered its wails alone to the stones of its ruined temple. But now the whole nation—few in number, it is true, but as a unit—has been learning to sing these songs that have been provided for them in Psalms 95 to 100, and with great joy do they cry: "O sing unto the Lord a new song, for He hath done marvellous things: His right hand and His holy arm hath gotten Him the victory."

Let us, then, listen to the song:

1: Thou art my God, O Jehovah!
   I will exalt Thee: Thy Name will I praise!
   For Thou hast wrought wonders.
   Thy counsels of old: Faithfulness!   Truth!
2: For 'tis Thou who hast made
   Of a city a stone-heap!
   Of a fortress a ruin!
   The palace of foemen, no longer a city,
   To be built nevermore.

3: 'Tis for this the strong people
　　Shall give Thee all honor.
　　'Tis for this the great city
　　Of terrible nations
　　Shall yield Thee its fear.
4: For to the poor Thou hast been as a stronghold—
　　A stronghold to needy ones sunk in distress:
　　A refuge from rain-storm:
　　A shade from the scorching,
　　When the blast of the fierce ones
　　As storm 'gainst a wall, beat.*
5: As the heat in the desert, the noise of our foemen
　　Thou didst subdue.
　　As a cloud's shadow doth temper the noon heat,
　　So was the triumph song of our foemen,
　　Our terrible foemen, brought very low!

Joyous as is the song, it certainly is not, to our ears, as sweet as that we hear in heaven. We miss one note that is the very ground of our own singing, nor are we altogether in accord with what we do hear. There is no clear avowal of redemption by the blood of God's spotless Lamb; while, on the other hand, it rather grates against our spirits to rejoice over ruined cities, fallen fortresses, and desolated palaces. We are not of that "manner of spirit." But that is the way of God's dealing with the earth, and its government; judgments great and terrible can alone usher in that fair morning which is like the "clear shining *after rain*" (2 Sam. 23: 4); the rain-storm, with accompanying lightning and thunder, must first clear the murky atmosphere.

The "city" here referred to is not necessarily literal; this is rather another reference to that "city" of which the previous

*In this I follow the mass of translations, but am by no means convinced that it is the exact rendering. The very important word "against" has to be inserted, while not explicit in the original. The word for "storm" comes from a root, "to overflow, to inundate," and evidently carries with it the idea of a rushing mass of waters, so I have thought that the two words, "storm," "wall," might be intended to suggest what is known as a tidal wave, or bore, that sweeps all before it: "When the blast of the fierce ones was as a wall of a rushing flood." Lowth renders it, "Rages like a winter storm;" but the meaning is not greatly affected.

chapter (ver. 10) spoke as "The city of confusion," the full expression of all that man, in the pride of his heart, is building on the earth. While this is, if I err not, the direct reference, it is not of course at all impossible that the unified civilized nations— again forming an imperial world-power—may build or adopt a central metropolis to which they may attach some high-sounding name, yet God may call it (since it is only another Babel), "the city of confusion," for that word is, as we know, but another form of "Babylon."

Be that as it may, here we have Jehovah celebrated as having brought down to ruin all the proud building of man. The foundation of *that* city is being laid and its walls are being built this very day. Whenever or wherever you hear the sound of boasting, you will, if your spiritual senses are at all keen, discern the same materials that were used in building the Babel of long ago: the "slime" of self-exaltation and self-seeking that still poor men substitute for the "mortar" of divine love and self-forgetfulness; and the dead dry "bricks," manufactured by ordinances quite powerless in themselves to give the life needed, in the place of the "living stones" that make the whole building to be filled with divine Life. Let us have nothing to do with it. It looks fair; it shall soon be a ruin. It looks strong; it shall soon be fallen to the ground. It looks as grand as any palace in its lofty pride; soon shall it all be in the dust, and be rebuilt nevermore! This, and only this, is in accord with these divine counsels determined very long ago, and now declared in this fulfilment to be even more than faithful and true, for they are "faithfulness," "truth," in very essence.*  May every one of us have full confidence in them.

In verse 3 we have indeed the "conversion of the world." This intervention of Jehovah has so awakened its inhabitants that the cry is no longer heard: "Since the fathers fell asleep, all things continue as from the creation of the world," for there has been a terrific break in the ordinary course of nature and providence, the result of which is that the "strong people," *i.e.*, the Gentiles,

---

*Both the Hebrew words are forms of the well-known "Amen."

in genuine fear and holy reverence, join with the restored Jew in giving honor to Israel's Jehovah. Happy earth, in such a case!

How sweet the memory of such a deliverance will be to that little flock! How beautiful the figures used in verse 4 to express that tender care during the day of awful stress! In the hour of storm there may have been moments when they (it would not be very unlike many of us) had said: "Hath the Lord forgotten to be gracious? Is His mercy clean gone forever?"(Ps.77:7-9). Now, with clearer eye, no longer dimmed with, but rather cleansed by, past tears; with mind no longer darkened; with heart no longer weighted with pressing distress; they look back and see that all through He has been a stronghold against the attack which, nevertheless, He had permitted to so far succeed as to capture their city (Zech. 14: 1). Even this was a rain-storm beating vainly against a wall.* In the scorching heat of that persecution, when all who refused to worship the image of the Beast were under sentence of death, even then Jehovah, now discerned as being the long-rejected Jesus, was to them as a gracious cloud modifying the burning heat of a summer day.

So when the shout of victory that the enemies of Israel's remnant raised as they captured the city, and the words, "Peace and Safety," resounded all through the earth—for, say they, we have finally disposed of the only Witness to God upon it, henceforth the earth is ours—it was then, at that moment, that He, His feet standing on the Mount of Olives, has made that proud boast sink to a whisper, and finally to silence. It is intensely significant that within the last few years we have heard precisely that awful character of defiance against God, not merely as the fool, saying that there is no God, but admitting that truth, and then uttering the most blasphemous defiances and obscene insults. God has shown us in Moscow what shall be all over the earth, before our Lord is revealed. How loud will be the cry of the earth in that day!

This brings us to the first division of the second part of the song, verses 6 to 8, and it is here that we find our special direct interest.

---

*See footnote to ver. 4.

6: For in this mountain Jehovah Tzebaoth
   Doth make for all peoples a feast of rich dainties,
   A feast of old wines on the lees,
   Of fat things rich in their marrow,
   Of wines on the lees well refined.
7: Yea, in this mountain doth He destroy
   The cover that shadows the face of all peoples,
   The veil that has spread its shade o'er the nations.
8: He swallows up death, and that, too, forever!
   Jehovah Adonai wipes tears from all faces.
   His people's reproach He taketh away
   From all over the earth—
   Jehovah hath spoken!

Judgment being over, the pride of man humbled, the Lord alone exalted, Satan bound, Jehovah becomes the world's Host, and while He makes the whole earth "laugh with abundance," yet, in one spot, He spreads a table loaded with such dainties for eating, and such wines for drinking, as our poor race has never yet enjoyed. One need hardly say that these must not be understood as literal, even although there can be no question as to the literal abundance, but we must most surely discern *spiritual* dainties and refreshments, of which these material things are the figures.

If this is justified, then these material things, these "fat things" and "wines," stand for some real corresponding spiritual feast in which we, even *we*, have our divinely given part. At this table we can sit, and the spiritual dainties that Israel shall enjoy in the millennial day we may enjoy in the same spiritual way and by the same grace, even now. Those "fat things, rich in marrow," speak of those rich blessings that we have in Christ— the "unsearchable riches of Christ" that are made ours, and on which we can feed, through the Holy Spirit making them realities to our souls. They thus become as much part of our spirits as literal food of our bodies. Do we never enjoy a taste of these "rich things" at His bountiful table?

No one can thus feed on Christ without corresponding *joy*, and that is figured by the "wines." The one single word in Hebrew for the four in English, "wines-on-the-lees," is from a root meaning "to keep, to preserve," and is thus used to speak of wines that have been *kept* on those *lees,* or the dregs, that have been eliminated from the grape-juice, and have sunk to the bottom during the process of fermentation. The clear wine is not drawn off at once, but *kept* on those dregs; and by that keeping, it is improved in strength, color and bouquet. Before being put away for use, it must be drawn off, and in the last line of verse 6, the pure clear liquid has thus been decanted, and is now well-refined from the dregs that have done their work.

Who could resist the conviction that where all is so filled with symbolic significance, *this* cannot be an exception? Jehovah has been dealing with His elect nation Israel, but Israel is but a representative of the whole race, and in those dealings we can trace, as taking place in an open way on the earth, what *has* taken place, what *is* taking place in a spiritual way and individually in His elect heavenly people, not of the Jews only, but of the Gentiles also.

He does leave the lees, the dregs, of our old Adam nature within us; does He not? The wine that is above them is that life in Christ that is indeed joy-filled, and which every child of God, from the youngest to the oldest, has by his new birth. But it is still "on the lees" of the old nature derived from Adam; for thus, and from those very "lees," it shall gather what shall increase the *strength* of its joy, add fragrance of humility to its adoring worship, and yield a lovelier *hue* to the eye of God in that day when there shall be no lees at all, but it shall be "well-refined," even the dregs, the "lees," having done their work, and under the grace of God our Father, done it well. Does not this give a worthy reason for our present condition with the old nature within us still?

Delitzsch again writes here of Isaiah's wonderful word-painting—the very words used bringing the picture of the scene that they portray. "The ring of the verse 6," he says, "is inimitably pictorial. It is like joyful music to the heavenly feast. It is as if we heard stringed instruments, played with the most rapid movement of the bow." That my reader may test this, let him quickly pronounce the Hebrew of the lines, beginning at the words, "A feast of fat things" (verse 6), and see if his ear can catch the sounds, and his eye see the rapid movement of the bows of the violins: *"mishteh shemahnim mishteh shemahrim shemahnim memuchim shemahrim mizuqahqim."*

Can you not see the arms of the musicians working their bows rapidly over the strings?

Oh, how good it is to note the strong words the Lord uses when speaking of death! As a feeble folk might rejoice to see their oppressor abased and overcome by a strong ally, so we joy that our terrible pitiless oppressor that has caused rivers of tears to flow from human eyes, and tempests of anguish to sweep over human hearts, is swallowed up in victory. The Septuagint reads, "Death has prevailed and swallowed up." That has been true enough; but now the tables are turned, and it is death that is swallowed up, and not a single tear-drop will be left on human eye to bring the griefs of the past to remembrance. Of all the wonderful visions that prophecy brings before our eyes, can any greatly exceed that of seeing God—God infinite in every attribute, the Creator of all—actually wiping away tears from the face of His poor creature, man! Are we not reminded of that symbolic picture of a poor blind man, and the disciples' question: Who did sin, this man or his parents, that he was born blind? No, no, says the Lord; that was permitted that the works of God should be made manifest in him. And so the sorrows, the tears, of life are permitted that God may manifest His beloved work in wiping them away. Is it not a blessed vision of God? These are the cords that draw and bind us to Him.

As to Israel, the Jew, the despised, hated, baited Jew, whose national name has been a reproach throughout the earth, that reproach shall be taken away (can we not well afford to joy in that joy?), and then the Jew shall be the glory of mankind; and this, "Jehovah hath spoken!"

The seventh verse continues and deepens the interest, yet has its difficulties which, in the danger that we feel of erring in so infinitely important a matter, may well cast us on the grace of Him who loves us, by whose Spirit we trust we may not only be kept from error but led "into all truth." Let us then take the context as being the divinely given, and so the safest, key. That context says with the clearest precision that it is the "earth" (verse 8) and not heaven that is in the prophet's Spirit-taught mind. It follows from this that "this mountain" necessarily refers to a mountain on the earth, and not to the heavenly Church. The specific mountain must be Zion, as we have seen was meant by "mountain" in chapter 2. But, as we have also seen, Zion is but the representative of Israel when restored and established solely by the grace of which, as Hebrews 12 tells us, Zion speaks. Do not, I beg of you, divert this from Israel, as the first prime recipient of this joy. She has had darkness and sorrow enough, but her God, even Jehovah, has never forgotten nor ceased to love her for the fathers' sakes. That very name for God, "Jehovah," speaks of this as clearly as all else, for it is by that Name that He is directly in relation with Israel, as by the dear name of "Father" with us. We can well afford to let Israel find her part in this lovely scene, for as we shall see, we can find ours too.

What a clear suggestion lies in these words of some strange spiritual power that has succeeded in weaving a veil by which our poor race has been kept in the *dark,* from the light of God's truth, and in the *cold,* from the warmth of His love. Alas! alas! Dark are all our minds by nature, dubious as to the disposition of our Maker towards us, while conscience gives justification for those doubts; nay, tends rather to assure us of the certainty of His wrath (Ps. 90: 7-11), and that awful end, death, confirms all these fears. In this condition someone weaves a veil of contrasted attractions, such as this present scene and transitory life can give; pleasures, wealth with its luxuries, the boasting of pseudo-science, the marvels of man's inventive genius, with a decent amount of "religion," so long as it does not involve a heart-confession of *sin.* Out of such materials the same unseen enemy weaves so thick a veil that it hides all the radiant glory of God shining forth in the gift of His Beloved Son for the very sins that we have committed against Him! In a comparative few, that veil has been rent even now; and they have seen through that torn veil, the glory of God—all the perfections of His love and wisdom, grace and justice, shining with beauteous radiancy in the Face of Christ Jesus (2 Cor. 4: 4), as we sometimes sing with chastened joy:

"In that Face, once marred and smitten,
All His glory now we read."

Our scripture speaks of a day in which that veil shall be torn
away from all faces. Well may we cry, "Oh, haste that day of
cloudless ray!" How many hearts will utter a silent "Amen."

Verse 8 is explicit, and it is this very verse that the Spirit of
God quotes, telling us that when "this corruptible shall have put
on incorruption, and this mortal shall have put on immortality,
then shall be brought to pass the saying that is written, Death is
swallowed up in victory" (1 Cor. 15: 54). The epoch thus defined as "the corruptible putting on incorruption" must refer to
the resurrection of those who have departed from this life, and
whose bodies therefore have been subject to corruption. We must
remember that there was ever a spanless difference between that
"Holy Thing," the Lord's body, and ours. *That* was never subject to corruption; for while real flesh and blood, yet it was only
the "likeness of sinful flesh" (Rom. 8: 3), and so differed from
all others in that it had not the slightest taint of that ingredient
that involves corruption, sin. As long as the life-principle is in
the body of every sinful man, it prevents the action of corruption,
but as soon as death intervenes and the soul departs, then the
offspring of sin, corruption, has its way unhindered at once. The
holy body of our Lord was never subject to corruption, for He
knew no sin, and we refuse to enter into any unhallowed analy-
sis, or speculation as to it. Our bodies are then in that full sense
corruptible only after death, and the word "corruptible" has in
view those who have departed this life.

Even as living, the children of Adam are not only capable of
dying as was our Lord, but are *subject* to death, as He was not;
and so with the living in view, the writer adds, "When . . . this
mortal shall have put on immortality." That also is at the coming of our Saviour for us, for then He shall change this body of
humiliation, and make it like His own body of glory (Phil. 3:
21).

Note carefully the exact term used. It is not, "Then shall
be *fulfilled*," but, "Then shall be *brought to pass* the saying that
is written." Do you say there is no difference? Ponder it a
moment. If the saying had been *fulfilled*, that would have meant

that at that specific moment of the Lord's coming for us, when His shout is heard, and we are caught up to be with Him forever, this scripture would be so finally and completely satisfied as to leave nothing more to be expected, either for Israel or for the rest of mankind.  But since the words are, "Then shall it come to pass," it leaves room for others later to share in the infinite blessings of that death being swallowed up in victory when it shall come to pass for *them.*

We have a very simple yet clear illustration in the advancing tide.  It comes to a certain marked spot, the tide "has come to pass" thus far, but it still advances and rises to a higher mark, and again we may say "it has come to pass" so far; finally it reaches its high-water mark, and then we may say the rising tide is "fulfilled" and will go no further.

Here the tide is the new-creation life, given not only to the spirit, as indeed it is already, but to the whole man, spirit, soul and body.  Paul in writing to the Christians at Corinth tells them, and us, that the rising tide of this "Life" will reach them, so as to affect their whole being when the last trumpet shall sound; that trumpet which is to give no "alarm," God be thanked, nor is it sounded, as it was in the day of Israel, to gather all the assembly to Moses, "to the door of the tent of meeting," but to gather all the redeemed to Himself, to the door of His Father's House, to which His gracious promise pledges Him to take us (see Num. 10: 3, 7).  It is what we call "the rapture," the very next critical and long-hoped-for event for which we look.

Isaiah, however, cannot possibly refer to that of which he knew, nor was intended to know, nothing whatever. *His* interest, and the interest here of the Spirit of God, lies with his nation, Israel; and when the Lord shall come for us, and we shall be caught up into that deathless scene, and death shall be forever destroyed, *as far as it affects us,* the poor Jew has the time of his greatest sorrow still before him; for in the time of persecution that shall arise concerning the worship of the "image of the Beast" (Rev. 13: 25), death shall put his hand on many a Jewish saint, and prove that he is not yet destroyed.  But let some years pass from the time of the rapture (at least seven, and how many more I am not aware that Scripture specifically

tells us), and then our Lord shall be revealed to all flesh; every
eye shall then see Him; and at that day, the saying that is written in our chapter "comes to pass" for that elect nation.  From
that time it would appear that there would be no death in Israel,
for they "shall be all righteous" (Isa. 60: 21).

Even then the victory over death will not be final, for Scripture tells us that even in the millennial day some will only yield
"feigned obedience" (Ps. 18: 44, *marg.*); and of such it is written: "The child shall die an hundred years old, but the sinner
being an hundred years old shall be accursed" (chap. 65: 20).
So that even during the millennium the saying is not "fulfilled"
for all.  But at its end, when for the third time that one word
"Finished," or "Done," sounds through the universe, then shall
be the final fulfilment of this saying: "Death is swallowed up in
victory."  For Death and Hades have had their long day, have
fulfilled their needed but mournful ministry, and being no longer
needed, shall be cast into the lake of fire which is the second
death; the first thus passing into the second, which retains all the
finally impenitent forevermore!

Alas, these impenitent are at that time, the "lees," the dregs
of the universe, and the "wine" of that New-Creation scene must
be well refined from them.  Can we live for ourselves with such
a prospect?  Who does not feel the force of the apostle's, "Knowing the terror of the Lord, we persuade men."

How we all love to linger on such joyous themes as the end
of death for men, and leave them with reluctance.  We feel with
Peter when on the holy mount that "it is good to be here," and
with him we rather shrink from again descending from this holy
elevation into scenes of judgment that still lie before us.  But
our chapter itself carries us down, and we must follow.  Here it
is well worthy of our calling to keep in mind that in all the
melody which the harp of prophecy gives, telling of the blessedness that divine Love has provided for penitence and faith, there
is ever at the close a solemn note of judgment as still active.  In
the Old Testament we get pictures of this in the government of
the earth.  Take the prophetic blessing of the tribes by Jacob
(Gen. 49); it ends with, "Benjamin shall ravin as a wolf; in the
morning he shall devour the prey, and at night shall divide the

spoil." So, in the same way, in the closing blessing of the tribes by Moses (Deut. 32: 41, 42), "I will make my arrows drunk with blood." Though having to do solely with the earth, they form pictures of eternal verities; and when we turn to those eternal verities themselves in the New Testament the witness is the same. Look at that chapter to which many a weary human heart has turned for refreshment (Rev. 21). Even there in that eternal scene the last word is: "But the fearful, and unbelieving, and abominable, and murderers, and whoremongers, and sorcerers, and idolators, and all liars, shall have their part in the lake which burneth with fire and brimstone, which is the second death." So in the last chapter of our Bible, the close is filled with solemn warnings. We do not well, my beloved reader, we do not well to avoid or pass these by because they may not be agreeable to us, and perhaps especially we who live in an atmosphere by no means favorable to holy fear, filial reverence or creature awe. So we address ourselves to what Delitzsch calls "the second echo," reaching to the close of the chapter.

9: In that day shall they say:
  Lo, 'tis our God; for Him we've long waited,
  And now hath He saved us.
  This is Jehovah, for Him we've long waited,
  And in His salvation we'll joy and rejoice.
10: For in this mountain the hand of Jehovah resteth in peace;
  But down it thrusts Moab to Moab's own place,
  As straw is downtrodden in water of dunghill.
11: Yea, in their midst His hands He's outspreading
  As the hands of a swimmer sweep round in his swimming:
  Thus abases his pride with the craft* that his hands
    wrought.
12: Aye, the steep walls so towering and lofty—
  These He abases—these He down-forces,
  Casts them to earth e'en down to the dust-heap.

In the day in which the prophecy in these verses shall become history, the Jews shall not only be back in their land, as a good many of them are even today, but they shall be there as they

---

*The word rendered in A. V. "spoils," occurring nowhere else, is from a root meaning "to lie in wait," and so it becomes "cunning," or "craft," as adopted in the text.

are not today, in that dignity that is expressed in the term, "the kings of the rising of the Sun" (Rev. 16: 12). That "Sun" shall at that time have risen upon them with healing in His wings, and the people whose very name of "Jew" has been a term of reproach in all the earth, insomuch as it has added to the colloquialisms of Christendom a verb meaning "to drive a keen, hard bargain," shall then be a royal nation set high above all the nations of the earth. The promise of this as given in Deut. 28: 1 was conditioned on their obedience to the Law, but when did any obtain promise on such ground? Far from it. Centuries of shame and sorrow have been their portion, through which they have had to await the salvation of Jehovah: it is a long waiting, and who of us does not know the difficulty of "waiting?"

Have any ever really waited for Him in vain? Most assuredly not. Here that salvation has come; and Isaiah, by his name, is a most appropriate announcer of it. Surely if our ears are a little opened we can hear, in the words of our ninth verse, their mutual and joyful congratulations. "Long have we waited," they say, "for this intervention of our God. Long has He borne with us, apparently not heeding our cry at all. But all through that weary time of waiting, we have been preserved amid all the nations of the earth, and now at last His Kingdom has come, and now His will shall be done on earth as it is in heaven. Joyfully do we fulfil His own word that we should not see Him henceforth till we should say, Blessed is He that cometh in the name of the Lord. Yea, blessed is He!"

Verse 10 is admittedly difficult, as the many different renderings of commentators evidence. The main question is: Who is the subject, Jehovah or Moab? Many, naturally offended by Jehovah being assumed to be in such a place, have adopted the latter. But against this is the simple fact that the natural predicate of the verb "spread out" is Jehovah and not Moab. Nor does there appear to be any necessity for carrying on the figure of the dung-pond into the next verse. There we only see Jehovah's arms sweeping in a wide circle within which everything is brought low.

Thus the Hand of the Lord rests in benediction, for this is involved in the word used, on Mount Zion; but across the river there is still fleshly pride to be dealt with, and there it rests in different fashion. On Moab it falls heavily. Moab, I take it, is not to be interpreted as applying, at least exclusively, to the people literally so called, but to the sphere of this earth that is here in the mind of the Spirit of prophecy that is best pictured by Moab.

This necessitates our recurring to Moab and to what that name applies today. We must recall his shameful origin forever expressed in his shameful name, "Moab," that is, "seed of a father"—he is the son, by incest, of Abraham's nephew, Lot, the world-loving, "righteous man" (2 Peter 2: 7, 8).

Since Moab owes his very being to shame, since he himself loves the filthiness of the flesh, he shall have a corresponding penalty. Reaping as he sowed, he shall be pressed down, ever down, lower and lower into a vile, noxious filth for which he has fitted himself. The pleasures in which he delighted have become filth, their true character. Thus he goes to his own place, as shall every individual—even you and I, my dear fellow-believer—but as in Christ, how different the place that He has prepared for us, and for which He has made us meet (Col. 1: 12).

# CHAPTER TWENTY-SIX

**The Tale of Two Cities. Is Jehovah the Name that is intended for Christians? The resurrection of the nation of the Jews a figure of the personal resurrection.**

IN chapters 25 and 26, as in our prophecy called "Revelation," we have what might be termed The Tale of Two Cities; the one representing that proud city which man is building, contemptuously called (chap. 24: 10) "the city of *tohu,*" or confusion; the other, the building of God. When one is up, the other is down. When Jerusalem is trodden down of the Gentiles then that "great city" of the nations flourishes. When Jerusalem is lifted up, then *that* falls. This is the burden of the song.

We now come to the third division of this song—the separation by the chapter being simply a human unjustified intrusion. This "third" brings its constant significance of Jehovah fully revealed, and here in the resurrection of the long buried nation of Israel. As God was fully revealed as Father in the resurrection of His Son (and then He too sings, as in Ps. 22: 22), and our Father by our resurrection with Him (Eph. 2: 1), so we too may sing, for we "rejoice in the Lord always." We listen sympathetically to Israel here:

1: Then in that day this song shall be sung
In the country of Judah:
Strong is our city: its walls and its bulwarks,
Jehovah's salvation.

2: Fling open the gates that a nation all righteous,
The people that keepeth the truth, may go in.

3: Thou keepest in peace, yea, a peace that is perfect,
The mind of the one leaning hard upon Thee,
For in Thee he confideth.

4: Trust in Jehovah forever and aye,
For in Jah, our Jehovah, is strength everlasting.

5: And low hath He hurled the dwellers on high:
Low hath abased the proud city exalted—
E'en to the ground hath Jehovah abased it.
Cast it down low, yea, to the dust-heap.

6:  Low 'neath the foot of the trampler 'tis trodden,
    'Neath the feet of the lowly, the tread of the poor.

The last verse of the previous chapter has told us of the great
world-city, represented by Moab, brought down to the dust; but
in contrast therewith, Israel, brought through the time of trouble,
cries: "We have a strong city;" yet not strong in walls of huge
stones  as in that day when the disciples said: "See what manner
of stones!" for little did they avail to save the city from destruction—they must have a much stronger wall than that.  They
find it in "Jehovah's salvation."  His tender favor makes it
impregnable.

Incidentally let us apply it to present conditions.  Let the
feeblest of churches unfeignedly confide in all that the Name of
Jesus tells, and that church, or assembly, also becomes impregnable to every form of danger by precisely the same "bulwark;"
for that Name means "Salvation," and it is a strong tower indeed.
The assembly bulwarked by our Lord alone is impregnable to all
the assaults of every foe.

The city of which our prophet writes is evidently on earth,
yet corresponds very closely to its counterpart, the *heavenly*
Jerusalem, since its gates also admit nothing that defileth, or
works abomination, or a lie, but open wide to admit the righteous
nation.  Should it be asked who compose that righteous nation
and where can they be found, let us turn to Zech. 12: 11, and
find the "righteous" there, for among the children of Adam, those
only are righteous who confess to their unrighteousness and
gratefully accept God's provision for it.

This brings us to that lovely verse that has been the stay of
many a stricken heart: "Thou keepest in peace, a peace that is
perfect, without one ripple of anxiety, the mind of the one leaning hard upon Thee."  We must note the emphatic individuality
here pressed.  Though everyone about you is trusting the Lord
Jesus, and you are not, the companionship and atmosphere will
profit you nothing.  On the other hand, if you are in an atmosphere of mistrust, let your own heart be firmly confiding, you
shall not be affected at all.  This individuality characterizes the
last days, as evidenced in the letter to Laodicea: "If any *one*,"
etc.

The word for "mind" here is *yehtzar,* "that which is formed."
It is the *formed* outcome of thought, as that, in its turn, comes
from the "heart" whose depths are beyond the human power of
fathoming. The Lord alone knows it. The three words are together in Gen. 6: 5: "Every *imagination* of the *thoughts* of the
*heart.*" The *heart* is thus the womb whence emerge, and that
without the impulse or consent of the will, *thoughts* which are
still shadowy, undefined as a fog from a marsh. These *thoughts*
are formed into *imaginations,* of which we can discern the character, and the *will* can then repress them, or see that they are
properly directed. *That* proper direction for all of all ages is to
have them stayed on the Lord. We too may find our "everlasting
strength," or, as our old hymn has made so happily familiar, our
"Rock of Ages" in our God as revealed in Christ. But this is in
the next verse.

We have an outburst of exultant exhortation in ver. 4: "O
trust in Jehovah forever and aye, for in Jah our Jehovah is
strength everlasting." The reduplication of the name has its
significance, and to get it we must remember the meaning of the
name Jehovah. It is truly a divine word, for, like Him of whom
it speaks, it is impossible for finite minds to compass its infinite
significance. Its most simple English equivalent would be, "He
Who Is," answering precisely to Exod. 3: 14, "I AM"—that is,
He who is ever existent, ever present, ever immutable, who,
therefore, if He enter into any covenant, will surely maintain it.
But this being true, then the Name must cover all tenses. "He
who is," is always the I AM, must ever *have been,* and ever *will
be.* Thus we have in the one sacred name, the full equivalent of
"The Same, yesterday, today and forever," written to Hebrews
who would understand the reference as we might at first fail to
do. Again, in Revelation 1, we note a similar reference in the
greeting from Him, "who is and who was, and who is to come,"
for that is a translation of Jehovah for us. In the day when restored Israel has learned again to sing, she is not content with
the one Name, but must intensify her comprehension and delight
in the covenant-keeping faithfulness thus expressed by redupli-
cating it "Jah, Jehovah," the Jah speaking of simple Personality,
of what He is in Himself, apart from any relation; the latter of

His relation with men and especially Israel. I need hardly say that in Christ we have a far dearer Name of relationship, that of Father; nor does that debar us in the least from accepting this exhortation to put unwavering confidence in our "Rock of Ages."

In strong contrast to this sweet peace of the penitent, are God's dealings with pride (vers. 5, 6). All such boastings shall be silenced, all its "city" that forms the basis of that boasting shall be cast down to the dust.

7: Footprints of uprightness ever do mark
    The path of the just.
    Thou, the One Upright, dost level* aright
    The path of the righteous.
8: Yea, in the way of Thy judgments, O Lord,
    Have we waited for Thee.
    To Thy holy Name, and remembrance of Thee,
    Is our soul's strong desire.
9: For Thee my soul thirsted in the night of my sorrow,
    My spirit-depths in me were thirsting for Thee.
    I long for the dawning Thy presence will bring.†
    For when on the earth Thy judgments are striking,
    Then only its dwellers will righteousness learn.
10: Yea, let Thy favor be shown to the wicked,
    Righteousness still he never will learn.
    In the land of uprightness he'll still deal unjustly,
    Nor own to Thy glory, Jehovah!
11: Jehovah, Thy hand was uplifted—they saw not!
    But they see and are shamed by Thy zeal for Thy people,
    And the fire for Thy foes shall feed on them.
12: Jehovah, Thy peace is our portion,
    For Thou hast ordained it;
    For Thou too hast wrought all our works for us.
13: O Jehovah, our God, other lords have enslaved us,
    But by Thee, and Thee only, Thy name will we praise.

---

*The prime meaning of the word rendered "weigh" (A. V.) is "to make level," and as in weighing the scales must be made level, the word "weigh" became a derived meaning; but the original is better here.

†"The dawning of the morning after a night of suffering—by God manifesting Himself—was the object for which he longed" —*Delitzsch.*

Is there one feature of life in which we are more deficient than in discerning the right path in which we should walk? What perplexities! What exercises! What waverings! What fears arising from our many errors in the past! How often have we not longed for that promised Voice that should speak to us, when two divergent ways lay open, and much depended on our decision! *"This* is the way; walk ye in it." Well, says our verse, look at the footprints of the flock, and while the blood-marks tell you plainly enough that it has not been an easy one, yet it has been marked by uprightness of intent; and He who is the very Source of uprightness has levelled it as they walked. Mountains of difficulties, that looked too formidable to be crossed, have sunk as they approached. Thus the way, although it led through the Great Tribulation, has been levelled aright. It is not without interest that we note that the word rendered "uprightness" is very literally "uprightnesses" (comp. Rev. 19: 8, R. V.), indicating that this level path is made up of successive steps—step after step—of which we can only see one at a time, and as we take that one, the next becomes clear. Distress and poverty, sickness and bereavement, extreme need, and even death, are no evidences of the path being a wrong one—very far from it, it is in all these things that we are more than conquerors.

The Jew never looks for divine intervention on his behalf by being caught up to meet his Messiah in the air; but he waits for that Messiah in the way of judgment on his oppressors on the earth. Dear to their thoughts, through the dark night of their sorrows, has been the Name of Jehovah, for their salvation lies imbedded in that Name, as ours does in the same God, but under the Name of Jesus. The Jew's night will cease when his Sun shall arise. Then shall it be a morning without clouds for him, as verse 9 intimates.

Favor has long been shown to the earth-dwellers, in the gospel of the grace of God. Have they learned either the righteousness on which that gospel is based, in the judgments overflowing on the Holy One, or the practical righteousness in self-judgment that ever follows such comprehension? Far from it; there are those even dwelling in the "land of uprightness" (a reference to the apostate mass living in their fatherland of promise), who yet even there deal unjustly.

Long·has Jehovah's arm been uplifted ready to strike.  Many a portent, many an infliction, like the few large drops that herald a rain-storm, have given warning of coming wrath, but, blinded by pride and by confidence in a false Science that excludes God from His creation, they have accounted for all by natural causes, and they will not see.  Now the Lord is revealed in flaming fire. That cannot be attributed to nature, and *see they must*.  He has come in His zeal for the remnant of His people, and that fire of wrath which has been prepared for other foes, even the devil and his angels, shall feed also on their enemies.  This is the just portion of those who afflict His people, but Thou hast ordained peace for us after all our storms, for Thou hast never forsaken us. Indeed, as we review the past we now see that Thou hast worked in us and for us; never should we naturally have loved Thy ways: it is not due to our goodness that the veil has been withdrawn from our hearts (2 Cor. 3: 16); these are Thy works.

"Other lords, O Jehovah our God (note the tenderness of this appeal), beside Thee have had dominion over us."  We have served Baalim and Ashtoreth, and what resulted?  Bondage to Babylon, Persia, Greece and Rome!  These are not our rightful lords, and now we will take none other Name on our lips, and the very liberty that we enjoy shall make that Name to be praised.

We can but note one important principle that verse 13 emphasizes; each individual of the nation identifies himself with the common sin of the nation.  So the remnant of this day, as of that, is not manifested by denouncing the wickedness of others, although that may have its place, but in confessing their part in it all, for that alone is the spirit that brought the words, "O man greatly beloved," to Daniel.  It needs far less grace to condemn others—that may feed pride—than to confess our own part in the common sin.

So unspeakably precious to us all is the hope of a personal resurrection of the dead, that we are inclined to resent any word that appears to bear upon it being applied to anything else than the literal, physical resurrection of the deceased.  The words that we are now to consider are constantly applied to that blessed hope.  But we need have no fear of this being weakened, far less lost, by a true and faithful interpretation of Scripture, nor does truth ever need the diverting of any scripture from its clear application to sustain it.

14: Dead are they now, nor ever shall live,
 Shadows are they, nor e'er shall they rise:
 For Thou hast visited, so hast destroyed them—
 Made all their memory forever to cease.

15: Thou hast enlargèd the nation, Jehovah,
 Enlargèd the nation and gotten Thee praise;
 Hast stretched out afar the bounds of the land.*

16: In their affliction, Jehovah, they've sought Thee,
 Poured out their prayer in whispering words,†
 When Thy chastisement was on them.

17: As a woman in travail—the birth-hour approaching—
 Writhes in her pangs: in her anguish doth cry,
 So have we been in Thy sight, O Jehovah!

18: We too have travailed, have writhed in our anguish;
 We have, as it were, given birth to—the wind!
 Nought of salvation have we wrought for the land,
 Nor have the world-dwellers by us been brought low.

Verse 14 must be interpreted by its context. Who are these dead who shall never revive? These shades who shall never again rise? To say that they were individuals who shall have no personal resurrection would contradict the plainest scripture that there shall be "a resurrection both of the just and unjust" (Acts 24: 15). Who then can these be? They can only be those "lords" who have had dominion over Israel—Gentile world-powers that have successively lorded it over her. These shall pass away and never return.

Nations die; empires crumble, and others take their place; but *they* never recover; and this is the fate of the dominant world-powers that are here referred to as "lords" in verse 13. But in strongest contrast here is a little nation, long dead and

---

*This line might also read: "Thou hast moved it far away to the ends of the earth," but the context favors that given above, for it is recovery here.

†The first meaning of the word rendered in A. V. by "prayer," is a "whispering," indicative of the timid humility of the suppliant.

buried in the dust of the earth (that is, long scattered amid other peoples), now revived and restored to their homeland. It is growing fast, and its borders need ever enlarging. That national resurrection shall speak of Jehovah's work, tell out the glory of God as did that of Lazarus, or as shall that brighter day for which we wait.

The prophet soliloquizes in verse 16 and his memory lingers over that time of sorrow and suffering through which they have been so recently brought, and in which that penitent little remnant, gradually turning to the Lord, express their repentance in timid whispering appeals, now admitting that their sorrows have been the chastening of His love.

Still musing, the prophet likens that time of anguish to travail-pangs,* and the word suits so well the character of that "Great Tribulation" that he dwells upon it. The anguish has increased in its intensity as the hour of the delivery draws near; but there the parallel stops, for all the sufferings of Israel have been absolutely resultless. There has been no deliverance to her land, nor have her earth-dwelling oppressors been brought down. But now another Voice is heard:

> 19: Thy dead men shall live, My dead bodies arise.
> Awake and rejoice, ye dwellers in dust;
> For thy dew is the dew of the dawning,
> And earth shall cast out the dead.

Here the voice of the prophet is lost in that of Jehovah Himself who cries: "Thy dead shall live!" Whose dead? There can be no other answer to this than Israel—with which the whole chapter and the whole prophecy is primarily occupied. It is in this reviving that she is in contrast with all other Powers of earth. *"Thy* dead shall live:" *other* dead shall not. The final hegemony of this earth shall belong—not to Babylon nor Rome, to no modern nation nor League of Nations, but—to Israel. It is this little people identified with its Head, Christ, who even speaks of her buried members as "My dead bodies," that is here invited to sing with joy; for is she not that Treasure of the par-

---

*In Matt. 24: 8 the word "sorrows" is literally "travail-pains."

able (Matt. 13: 44) to obtain which He bought the whole earth with His blood, and had hidden it there, with this very day of resurrection in view?

Yet this must not be altogether divorced from *our* blessed morning when "the dead shall be raised incorruptible and we (the living) shall be changed;" for as each of the six formative days of Gen. 1 was a kind of prophecy of the first Adam, for whom all this beauty was being arranged, so each dispensation carries with it a prophecy as to the "Second Man, the Last Adam," to whom the age to come is to be subject, and for whom all is being prepared. The earth shall be filled with the glory of the Lord, through the resurrection of Israel, as foretold in our chapter. But the heavens too must be filled with the same glory, and that shall be by the resurrection of all the redeemed for heaven; for all things, both in heaven and in earth, are to be headed up in Christ.

But some may still question whether such a word as, "Thy dead shall live," must not refer exclusively to individuals, so let us see how clearly a national resurrection is taught in other prophetic scriptures. Ezekiel 37 deals with a figure: a valley of dry bones becomes, under prophesying, "an exceeding great army." The interpretation tells us that these bones represent "the whole house of Israel," but certainly not literally individuals who are dead and buried, for they complain (which the literally dead do not): "Our bones are dried and our hope is lost," yet the Lord promises that He "will cause them to come out of their graves and bring them into their land." It is Israel as a nation that is buried among the nations of the earth, and each of these nations that contain them is here termed their "grave," from which their restoration is certain.

Daniel 12: 2 has been almost universally accepted as referring to a personal resurrection, and whilst it is of great value as a figure and prophecy of this, it cannot be its direct application. For (and I beg you consider it) in all the proofs of the resurrection of the dead given in the New Testament, not a single speaker or writer ever refers to this, or any other of these scriptures as such proofs. How could they be thus ignored if they plainly asserted what was desired to be proved? In the chapter devoted to this very subject (1 Cor. 15), not one word of proof is drawn from this or any of these passages! Yet the resurrection of the dead, in perfection of spirit, soul and body, is triumphantly proved altogether apart from it, so that we may rest assured that *that* truth is not in the least affected by this interpretation whereby we recognize that the Jewish nation is to be divinely restored to its nationality in its homeland.

Consider how impossible it is that Dan. 12 should speak either of a general or discriminative resurrection. It cannot be the former, for only "many," not all, are awakened. Nor can it be the latter, for *at the same time* some "awake to shame and everlasting contempt" as well as "some to everlasting life." Thus it can be neither the one nor the other. Then what is it? It can only be national, and they err greatly who teach that God has no further use for the Jew. Verse 19 declares, "For thy dew is as the dew of the dawning." The long-buried Israel is called to awake and sing for joy, for she awakens to a morning without clouds. The night has been cold, the moisture of the atmosphere has been pressed by condensation out of it, and now the rising sun causes this to sparkle as dew-drops in their purity and beauty. So after Israel's long, cold, dark night—that *"night"* referred to in verse 9—in the last hour of which the remnant of faith has been *pressed out* from the mass, the Sun of Righteousness arises. His beams manifest that beloved Remnant in radiant beauty as the "dew." Another scripture also makes use of the same beautiful figure: "In the beauty of holiness, from the womb of the morning, thou hast the dew of thy youth" (Ps. 110: 3). This, if I err not, refers to the Jewish youth flocking in holy devotion to Him, their Messiah, who are likened to dew-drops on a bright cloudless morning, glittering like diamonds in the sunbeams. Nature affords Revelation some lovely illustrations.

One sentence remains: "And the earth shall cast out the dead." Someone says, "Surely that *can* only refer to a literal resurrection, when all that are in the graves shall hear His voice and come forth." No; it is a mistake thus to connect those two scriptures. They refer to quite different events. The Old Testament gives us in this, as ever, the *shadow*—not the very "image" —of the New. Here is rather a companion picture of that given by another Old Testament prophet, Jonah, who himself representing his nation, was cast into the sea, but remained unassimilated by the great fish, as the Jews by the Gentiles, till he was "cast forth" as here foretold. Again we must remember that there is in the New Testament a scripture directly giving divine light on this vital theme, as John 5: 28 does *not*, and that plainly tells us that the resurrection bodies of glory come, not from earth, but in a sense, to be determined from the context, from heaven (2 Cor. 5: 1).

Now the standpoint of the prophecy changes and returns to a time *before* the divine intervention. "Indignation" is still to come, and Jehovah counsels His people to come, as it were, like Noah, into the Ark, whilst the storms of that indignation sweep over the earth.

20: Come then, My people, and enter thy chambers,
    Shut fast thy portals that close thee around:
    Hide thyself thus—'tis but for a moment,*
    Till the storm of His anger forever be past.
21: For, lo, from His place Jehovah is coming,
    To punish the people that dwell on the earth,
    For the iniquity they are committing:
    The earth too exposes the blood shed upon her,
    No longer her dust shall cover her slain.

All prophetic Scripture unites in a harmony that is convincing, that, while martyr blood shall flow freely during that awful time still awaiting the returned Jew, there shall be a saved as well as a slain remnant. Here that remnant is seen hidden as in secret chambers. (How they will enjoy Ps. 27: 5: "For in the time of trouble He shall keep me secretly in His pavilion; in the covert of His tabernacle shall He hide me.") In Matt. 13 it is the "barn." In Rev. 12, "the earth" is used as a figure of its preservation by the well-disposed Gentiles as seen in Matt. 25: 40. Under these various figures, is clearly told that Jacob shall be saved through his time of trouble, as was his type Noah; whilst Christ's Church, like Enoch, shall be kept out of it altogether.

---

*"A moment," literally, "a little wink," or, "a twinkling of the eye."

Long has God been apparently indifferent to the violence and corruption of the dwellers upon earth. Blood, by rivers, has sunk into its soil, and been forgotten. No, never forgotten, for in our prophecy the time has come. Jehovah arouses, and in that Jehovah we already discern, as will Israel, "That Man whom He hath ordained to judge the world in righteousness" (Acts 17: 31), even Jesus, before whose Eye the earth exposes all the innocent blood that has been shed, and the murdered hosts arise to justify His awful intervention.

# CHAPTER TWENTY-SEVEN

*Leviathan; its meaning and application. What the close scales stand for. Rome's scales; Rationalism's scales. Israel as the fruit-bearing vine of the future. The nation, but not the same individuals, restored.*

THIS is the closing chapter of this part of Isaiah; the next evidently introduces another sub-division. Whilst the strange mystic language of the first verse evidently has direct reference to Israel's literal enemies, we should really miss much of the divine intent were we to stop there, and not discern in this Leviathan that mighty fallen angel, who is as surely the deadly foe of our whole race as the malignant world-powers, which he uses, have been, and shall be again, of God's beloved Israel on earth. It is thus that a value—we might say a *glory*—becomes attached to the events of earth as recorded in the Scriptures, when they are recognized as a part of that "enigma" (1 Cor. 13: 12, *marg.*) through which we may discern, dimly indeed, but not doubtfully, eternal spiritual verities—the seen providing us with pictures of the unseen, the temporal of the eternal. But let us consider the chapter.

Again it clearly divides into the significant *three* parts thus:

1: Verses 1 to 6: The song of the vineyard expressing God's care.
2: Verses 7 to 11: Contrast between the chastening of Israel and the punishment of their oppressors.
3: Verses 12, 13: The final change and resurrection of Israel for eternal blessing.

The first verse appears to complete the previous chapter, for it is not a part of the song. This is a martial chant, and may be rendered thus:

1: In that day shall Jehovah, with His sharp, great and strong sword,
Punish Leviathan, the swift-fleeing serpent;
Even Leviathan, the all-crookèd serpent;
And slay the fierce dragon that lurks in the sea.

"In that day" must refer to that day in which Jehovah comes forth to deal with the evils of the earth, and sends forth His angels to gather out of His kingdom all things that offend.  But that involves not only rebellious men, who are but the pawns on the great chess-board, but that mighty spirit who is behind and who moves them; and who is plainly called "the Old Serpent" and "Dragon" in chap. 12 of that book which is the "Revelation" of what is behind the veil of the visible.  Here another name is added—Leviathan.

This strange word must surely have some significance worthy of its being found in a divine revelation. Let us seek to discern what it is.  It is a compound, made up of *"levi,"* "joined," and *"than"* a "dragon," or "serpent," so the whole would be, "The joined dragon." But that is not very intelligible, and we must seek further.  Turning then to Job 41, we get a description of a leviathan—a description that has universally been recognized as applying to the creature we know as the crocodile—and verses 15-17 will throw much light on the word itself:

> "His scales are his pride, shut up together as with a close seal!  One is so near to another that no air can come in between them. *They are joined one to another,* stick close, and cannot be sundered."

In these words we see the basis of the word "leviathan." It is the monster with joined scales, which are the expression of his pride and by which he defies every weapon formed against him. The description closes with the suggestive sentence, "He is a king over all the children of pride!" (Job 41: 34).  With the light thus given by Job let us again turn to Isaiah, and we shall see who it is that the Spirit of God designates by the word *leviathan.* That it is used emblematically cannot be questioned, for Jehovah does not contend with literal crocodiles.  But of whom, or of what is it thus used?  Let us grant that Delitzsch is correct, and that the "swift-flowing serpent" is Assyria, represented by the swift Tigris; and that "the crooked serpent" is Babylon, represented by the winding Euphrates; and that the "dragon in the sea" is Egypt, represented by the Nile, termed a "sea," as any expanse of water was; yet we have "leviathan" as an addition to all these, or rather as uniting them, for this leviathan is both the swift and the crooked serpent.  Can there be a doubt as to who is meant?

Have we not learned that every beautiful, majestic, useful creature has been made with the ultimate purpose of expressing some corresponding loveliness in our Lord Jesus?—for thus God would ever attract us to Him, and awaken our thirst to know Him well.  Thus in the *lion* is pictured His royal dignity; in the *ox,* His patient, gracious ministry; in the *dove,* His holy purity; so we must discern in every noxious creature, with offensive characteristic, some corresponding repellent evil in him who is the enemy and moral antithesis of that blessed One.  What then can be so apt an emblem of that creature who introduced that primal sin of pride (for that was the "crime—*Gr., krima*—of the devil," 1 Tim. 3: 6), a sin that is still all-pervasive among the race brought under his sway, as that *leviathan* that can be called "king of all the children of pride?"

It is the antitypical leviathan behind the systems that express, in opposite ways, the antagonism of the devil to Christ, and His claims to man's earth and to man's heart, as based on His atoning sufferings.  It is this leviathan who is behind "Modernism," which, in its developed form, denies those very foundation truths on which Christian faith rests.  Can you find any space between the scales of the pride of any form of Rationalism that will admit the arrow of conviction of error?  Error!  Why, it is the very leader of science, or knowledge, and it would need to be a new creation before it could possibly confess that after all it did *not* "know."

It is leviathan too that can be discerned behind that opposite wickedness, headed up in Jezebel—"Rome," the Papacy.  How is it possible for one who claims infallibility to confess to being fallible?  "She *wills not* to repent," says our Lord of her in Rev. 2: 21 (R. V.).  Do not such close-set scales of pride resist all conviction of truth that humbles?  Indeed, she is the true daughter of Eth-Baal (1 Kings 16: 31), that is, "the very Baal;" but Baal is but one of the many names by which the king of all the children of pride is known—the prince of the demons, the devil.

It is he too who is behind the world-empires that have oppressed Israel, and it is he who shall at the last unify all the discordant characters of evil into one spirit of hostility to all that is of God on the earth. He, the devil, is leviathan, the dragon or serpent of the joined scales!

The sword that Jehovah uses has three stern qualities; it is "sharp," *i.e.*, keen, incisive; "great," as able to overcome all forms of evil; it is "strong," as being effective and thorough in its work. Our book of Revelation gives us its name as proceeding out of His mouth; it is the Word of God.

But now for a more cheery note in another song. It begins with the repetition of the words "In that day," and then, at once, in intensely dramatic form, bursts out with a joyous lilt:

2: A pleasant vineyard—sing it!*
3: I, Jehovah, keep it!
   Every moment water it!
   Lest anything should harm it
   I will watch it night and day.
4: Wrath have I none.
   Who will set against Me,
   Thorns and briars in battle?
   I would march upon them,
   And burn them up together.
5: Or else let him hang dependent on My strength—
   Make peace with Me! Peace make with Me!
6: In coming days shall Jacob root,
   Shall blossom, bud and fill with fruit
   The face of all the earth.

Leviathan being slain, or, as the clearer light of the New Testament tells us, the devil being shut up in the bottomless pit, we naturally have joy expressed in song. But here it is the Lord Himself who sings, and celebrates the attractions He now finds in His vine, Israel. And how blessed a contrast it is to the song of chapter 5 of our book. There it soon lost all its joy, and turned into the minor note of disappointment, for that vine brought forth only repulsive grapes. Here Israel is a new crea-

---

*One letter in the text is doubtful; the alternative would be, "A vineyard of red wine—sing to it."

tion, identified with her true Messiah; and solely because of this, there is nothing but delight in the vineyard.

It is a lovely vineyard, giving even to God its wine of joy. Oh, celebrate it in song! It shall have no meaner Husbandman than Jehovah Himself, who will refresh it constantly with the waters of His blessing; and lest any unwelcome visitor should threaten it, He will keep constant watch over it night and day. His wrath is all gone now, and He defends those with whom He was once angry. That righteousness which was once against, is now *for* them. As a mail-clad warrior presses through obstacles, so here Jehovah even invites opposition that He may press through it. But what can oppose these purposes of His love? Thorns and briars would do that, for they are the tokens of the curse on the earth that followed man's sin, and ever resist man's blessing. Resist Him now! He marches through them as if non-existent, as indeed they are, for He has put away the sin that brought the curse.

Do we not see this very story retold in Rev. 5? Who can open that fast-closed book, completely and effectively sealed with seven seals? In other words, who can bring Israel to her place of blessing? Search heaven, earth, and the underworld. Nowhere in the universe is one found who is able to open that book. Dost thou too grieve at all creature-helplessness? Weep not! The Lion of the tribe of Judah has prevailed! See, He marches through thorns and briars of interposing sin, and breaks seal after seal, for He has put away the sin, for He is "a Lamb as it had been slain!"

But is this blessing to be for that one favored nation alone? Not at all. If there be anyone, anywhere, at any time, who feels and confesses his guilt and need, let such give full honor to the strength, the ability of God to save now; hang dependent entirely on God in Christ, and at once there is peace.

What a beauteous, harmonious, and still clearer ray of light does our New Testament throw on this: *"He hath made peace by the blood of His cross."* And we, poor sinners as we are, take hold of His strength, His power to save, and under the shelter of His blood we too "have peace with God through our Lord Jesus Christ."

Note too the deep emotion under which God speaks that is told in that repetition: *"Make peace with Me! Peace make with Me!"** God (with reverent joy let us take it), thus repeats, to express the depth of His Heart's longing with which He would press this, the only way of Peace, on us all.

Thus ends the song, but verse 6 is still attached to it as a far outlook on the future of Israel. The whole earth shall be blessed through her. The gracious favor of Jehovah, although focussed on herself as identified with her Lord, shall yet radiate to earth's remotest bounds, and fill it with the fruit that is sweet to the taste of God. Then Love shall abolish all armaments of war. Joy shall displace all present groanings of sufferings that Discord engenders, while Peace shall reign over the whole scene with a very sabbath-calm.

> 7: Hath He smote him as his smiters He smote?
>    Or slain him as slew He his slayers?
> 8: Nay, 'twas in measure that Thou didst contend;
>    E'en in the day Thou didst banish her far;
>    In the day when the east wind blew keenly,
>    And rough was His blast that did take her away.
> 9: For 'twas even by this Jacob's sin was all purged—
>    This fruit sprang from that expiation.
>    Now He doth make his altar's firm stones
>    To crumble as if they were chalkstones:
>    Ashtoreth's images—those of the sun—
>         Rise again never!

Jehovah's dealings with Israel have not been as those with her oppressors. They have indeed been sharp and long, but they have been in the way of chastening, as she indeed sings: "The Lord hath chastened me sore, but He hath not given me over unto death" (Ps. 118: 18). Nay, more, He has most carefully measured and limited that chastening. Rough was the wind that scattered her from her Homeland, for it was the day of the east wind, which ever tells of suffering: but what was the final aim of that rough wind? It was that the iniquity of that nation, termed

---

*The words and the order are precisely as thus rendered into English.

"Jacob," might be purged. The fruit of that severity was its sin taken away!

It is a strange thought that "Jacob's" sin could be expiated by Jacob's own suffering. To understand this we must bear in mind the peculiar place that people has amid the nations of the earth. It is the only one with which He has entered into a blood-based covenant relationship, as He says: "You only have I known of all the families of earth, therefore I will punish you for all your iniquities" (Amos 3: 2); that is, I will chasten you because I take a tender interest in you as a father in the child he punishes. Jacob has already been redeemed by the blood of the Lamb in and from Egypt, but that does not take him out from, but puts him under, the government of God. Just as we believers in the Lord Jesus, in the same external way are sanctified by that precious blood (Heb. 10: 29), and are not taken from, but introduced to the divine government. This is directly the teaching of 1 Cor. 11: 32: "We are chastened of the Lord that we should not be condemned with the world."

Thus today, it is in virtue of the blood of Christ that Israel is preserved, and after His heavenly work is accomplished, the same grace will bring the Jewish nation through waters of deep sorrow to repentance; the sincerity of which will be evidenced by casting down all forms of idolatry, never to be set up again (ver. 9). This will show that the severe chastisement has brought forth its expected fruit, the furnace of affliction has done its work.

I beg my readers not to pass this over hastily: it is a principle that will aid in many a difficulty. Sin is put away forever *from before* God, not by any *amount of suffering here on the part of the sinner,* but alone by the value of the atoning blood of divine Lord, who alone is "the propitiation for our sins, and not for ours only, but also for the sins of the whole world" (1 John 2: 2). But under the government of God *upon the earth,* unrepented sin brings the chastening of love, as He says: "As many *as I love I rebuke and chasten*" (Rev. 3: 19); and when this has led to penitence, as it always does in every *true* child of God sooner or later, it has then borne its fruit, and sin is "expiated" under that government.

> 10: For the fenced city all desolate lies—
>     A dwelling forsaken, a desert abandoned;
>     There doth the calf feed, there doth it couch,
>     And browse on its outgrowth of herbage.
> 11: When its branches are withered, they're broken;
>     The women then come and consume them;
>     For 'tis a people of no understanding;
>     Therefore their Maker hath no mercy on them,
>     And He that has formed them shall show them no favor.

Ever and again the prophecy returns to the city-building of men upon the earth, but here the builders are the Jews, and their banishment from their city, with its consequent desolate condition, is told in the picture drawn in these verses. In the place of a busy throng of men, herbage grows amid its ruins. There the calf feeds on the sprouts that nature ever throws quickly to cover the disfiguring ruins. There women come and gather the dry sticks for kindling-wood. In that condition it tells as clearly of Jehovah's attitude toward it, as did the fig-tree that was thus cursed in the day of Mark 11. But it also witnessed to the folly of the people; they were foolish enough to turn from the true Source of all their wealth, and what could be expected but this real poverty? It is to be feared that we too in our day have lacked understanding and have been very foolish, for we are very poor (Rev. 3: 17). But wait! Let penitence displace pride and He will respond quickly, as the closing verses show, and as all His blessed ways with penitent men ever disclose:

> 12: And it cometh to pass in that day,
>     That Jehovah shall winnow His corn,
>     From the flood of the river Euphrates
>     To the torrent of Egypt's Nile;
>     And ye shall be gathered, one after one,
>     O ye sons of Isràel.
> 13: And it cometh to pass in that day,
>     A blast shall be blown on the trumpet;
>     And the lost in the land of Asshùr,
>     And those who in Egypt were outcasts,
>     Shall come and worship Jehovah,
>     In the holy mountain of Salem.

Jehovah has a threshing-floor on which, by the blows of His flail, He will separate the wheat from the chaff. It lies between those boundaries that marked the land promised to Abraham (Gen. 15: 18), the flood of the river Euphrates on the northeast, and the torrent of Egypt, that is, the Nile or one of its mouths, on the south-west. This is Jehovah's threshing-floor, and it is here that He winnows* Israel, for that beloved people shall not be swept into everlasting blessedness in a mass, not by fifties, nor even five in a rank, as from Egypt, but "one by one." Thus is here pictured as the blows of a flail that Tribulation that is termed "the great one." God is making use even of the devil then upon the earth, through the persecution of Beast and False Prophet to manifest His true people. That "one by one" means that each individual evidences personal penitence and personal faith, and is personally embraced in the tender acceptance of Jehovah.

Again I say, let us not rob Israel, the Jew, of his portion. We have a lovely spiritual counterpart to this, for our land (for us, our Lord) lies between those two enemies, Corruption and Superstition (Egypt) on the one side, and Violence, Infidelity, Atheism (Assyria) on the other; and we too are led individually to constant repentance, and individually do we receive the Father's kiss.

Verse 13 records what follows chronologically. After the separation is effected between the false and the true in the land, then those who are still outside those bounds are remembered who remain among the Gentiles. Are they to be left there? Far from it, for now we hear of a trumpet-blast which recalls them all from every quarter of the earth. It is true that only two countries are here named, Assyria and Egypt, but all through this part of our book these represent by characteristic moral qualities all the lands outside Israel's borders, as we shall see more clearly later.

A "trumpet" is spoken of frequently in the Scriptures. What does it refer to here? Let us first eliminate what it is *not*. It is

---

*"Winnow," that is the force of the word rendered "beat off;" it is used of a threshing by which the grain is separated from the husks (see Ruth 2: 17; Judges 6: 11). Thus it is not the waters of these rivers that are here being driven back, but Jehovah is doing the work of a Thresher in the land.

not that "trump of God" that awakens all the dead in Christ (1 Thess. 4: 16) at the Lord's return; nor is it that "last trump" of 1 Cor. 15: 52. These two (if they be not the same) are the antitypes of those in Num. 10: 1-7. Nor is it that trumpet that introduced the seventh month, for that *precedes* the day of "affliction of souls," the "great tribulation;" nor can it be found in that series of seven trumpets of judgment that we hear in Revelation, for they all shall precede the one that we have in view in Isaiah. This then is Israel's trumpet, calling her outcasts home, and we may find it in Matt. 24: 31: "And He shall send forth His angels with a great sound of a trumpet, and they shall gather together His elect from the four winds, and from one end of heaven to the other." That is the trumpet of verse 13.

This, then we may say, completes the resurrection of long-buried Israel. First, there is the return in unbelief, which even our eyes are permitted to witness; amongst those returning there will develop a remnant, manifested by the "winnowing" of that great tribulation. To these He comes in the hour of their direst need (Zech. 14); then those still buried among the Gentiles are gathered by this "trump" of angelic ministry, and the resurrection of that beloved people is complete! They worship the Lord in His holy temple in Salem, for The Holy of Holies is anointed (Dan. 9: 24).

Is it not sure? Is it not as clearly taught as words can make it? Is not the past history and present position of the Jew a seal of its certain accomplishment? Unquestionably it is. Then in that sure and certain hope of Israel's resurrection, we may see our own. For as God will not rest till this *earth* sees the one nation that He has redeemed express the righteousness of His government in being recovered from the dust of death in answer to the Blood of the Lamb, so will He not rest till the *heavenlies* see His heavenly saints recovered to a still more glorious, a more joyous, resurrection than that of Israel.

This of course does not mean that the same individuals that were buried in captivity in the day of the Roman conquest shall return to the land; it is the *nation* as such, that ever maintains its identity on the earth, *as belonging to Christ*, who, having found that "treasure" (Matt. 13: 44), has bought the "field" (the "earth") in which it was, and hiding it there till His return as still belonging to Him; for He calls it, as we have seen, "My dead body." It is His always, and although the components change, the identity is secured by what is divine. The same *nation*, Israel, shall be raised effulgent with divine glory, the identical Israel that was buried. So shall every one in Christ be "made perfect" in spirit, soul, and body, in every part of his being, in resurrection-glory; that body of glory having a real true identity with his present one as the future Israel shall have with the past.

The parallel is perfect and shows how valuable these Old Testament parables are—not as teaching, but illustrating, the doctrines of the New. In her millennial glory Israel shall be a worthy witness to the value of Christ's atoning work, and every member of Christ shall also be (in the glory that shall be revealed in their very bodies, heavenly in their source, 2 Cor. 5: 1) worthy witnesses to the value of the same precious Blood. This will be "the adoption, even the redemption of our body" (Rom. 8: 23), for which we wait.

# CHAPTER TWENTY-EIGHT

Samaria's woe. Moral evils not merely literal. Jehovah's anger brings down the beauty of Samaria. Figure of a first-ripe fig; but Jehovah takes the place of that which He destroys. The simplicity of divine truth not to be abandoned to suit men's desires. The apostle's use of this scripture. What is the "overflowing scourge?" It is a morally discriminative judgment, which a literal army never is. A false confidence used as a penalty. A personal word.

WE HAVE now been brought by divine goodness to the closing section of the first part of our prophet, and may recall, for our encouragement, the path already trodden and the many difficulties that have been smoothed for our feet. How often what seemed, on approaching it, impenetrably obscure, has glowed with light, even as we pondered it, and we may confidently trust that the same goodness will still be with us for difficulties that still lie ahead.

There are again three main divisions in the chapter:

1: Verses 1-4: Jehovah's threat against Samaria.
2: Verses 5-22: The contrast; confusion of apostates, mercy on penitents.
3: Verses 23-29: The end of God's ways told in parable.

The text may be put in metrical form, thus:

1: Woe to the pride-crown of Ephraim's drunkards,
   To the fading flower of his splendid adornment,
   That blooms on the head of the valley luxuriant
   Of those prostrated by wine.
2: Behold, to Jehovah a mighty, a strong one,
   Like a tempest of hail, a storm of destruction,
   Like a tempest of waters, of fountains o'erflowing,
   It casts to the earth by its power.
3: The crown of the pride of the drunkards of Ephraim
   Shall under the feet be downtrodden.
4: The fading flower of his splendid adornment,
   Which lies at the head of the valley luxuriant,
   Shall be as a fig that is ripe before summer,
   Which whoever may see, looks at it with longing,
   And no sooner plucks than he swallows.

The "woe" is on Samaria, the chief city of Ephraim, which was so beautifully situated that the poet can only liken it to a crown, as it stood on its hill above the fertile valleys that surrounded it. When Isaiah wrote all was fair enough to outward appearance, but a deeper insight, given alone by the Spirit of God, discerned that the moral condition of that kingdom was crying aloud for divine intervention; its prime was past. It was a flower still, but only a "fading flower." For its people were so given up to worldly luxury and fleshly pleasures, that, in the spiritual paralysis that these always produce, they could only be likened to drunkards who, stupefied by excess, are lying prostrate in their shame!

It is ever the characteristic mark of the "last days;" so today, under cover of a formal religion called "church-membership," the mass of Christian professors are "lovers of pleasure, rather than lovers of God" (2 Tim. 3: 4), and there is again, alas, that same spiritual torpor as wine produces on the brain. But Jehovah has an agent for the infliction of chastening that shall overflow the country like an irresistible flood; and the very beauty of Samaria's rich valleys, and of the city that crowned them, shall only whet the appetite of this conqueror, as the sight of a ripe fig in June, before the time of figs, first fixes the eye, is then plucked, and instantly swallowed. This doom has long been fulfilled on Samaria. Assyria longed for it, Shalmanezer captured it B. C. 721, and its people were led away into captivity. But this does not complete the prophecy in its deeper meaning. But in all judgment on apostasy God knows how to deliver those who confide in Him, and so the prophet continues, Jehovah Himself replacing the beauty of Samaria:

> 5: In that day Jehovah Tzebaoth shall be
> A crown of adorning: a diadem splendid
> Unto His people, the remnant beloved.
> 6: The spirit of judgment to him who is judging,
> The spirit of courage to warrior turning
> The tide of the war to the gate.

Seven years after the fall of Samaria, the Assyrian armies invaded Judah, and threatened Jerusalem, but Hezekiah, who

was then reigning, took Jehovah for all his glorying, and placed
the matter unreservedly in His hand, with the result that the
city was completely delivered (2 Kings 19).   But this too cannot
be considered the final settlement of the above consoling prophecy; for after Hezekiah's death and the true condition of the
people was again evidenced, judgment again overhung Jerusalem,
and quite another character of deliverance is foretold than the one
which came through the piety of one man.   It will not be the
hand of God sweeping 185,000 Assyrians off the earth, but both
civic and military leaders, judges and generals, will then be divinely equipped to execute the judgment.   A defeated foe will
be pursued to the gates of his own cities.   This, I repeat, has
had no satisfactory fulfilment in the past; it can be found nowhere in history, and we must still look to the future for the
final fufilment of these verses.

> 7:  These also through wine have erred, reeling!
>      Through strong drink have, staggering, strayed!
>      Through strong drink have erred both priest and the
>           prophet,
>      The wine they have swallowed has swallowed up them!
>      Through strong drink they've strayed as they staggered,
>      Have reeled e'en when seeing a vision!
>      Have staggered, pronouncing a judgment!
> 8:  All tables are filled with their vomit—vile filth!
>      Not a spot can be found that is cleanly.

These verses refer to Judah, where the people have walked in
the same path of uncontrolled self-pleasing, termed "drunkenness," as in Samaria, and with even more disastrous results, for
their privileges have been greater; for the depth of the fall is always determined by the height of privilege.   But even the
"priests and prophets" are swallowed up of the very wine that
they have swallowed—for thus it literally reads.   This we may
interpret as, intoxicated with the falsehood they preach, they have
imbibed baseless hopes, and the false merriment these hopes give
is like that due to excess of wine.   They have even received their
inspiration for visions as prophets, or for giving judicial decisions
that demanded the most sober discrimination from this intoxica-
tion; not a spot can be found not defiled with their filth!   But
again this must most assuredly not be confined to literalism, **even**

if it be taken as literal at all. Rather does it bring before a proud self-satisfied people, what they are really like in the eye of God. They are as repulsive in their senseless pride, in their ill-timed pleasures, as drunkards who foul their own food! Alas, are we, as the present responsible witness for God upon the earth, any better? How repellent must it be to the Lord when He says of it, because of lukewarm self-complacency, "I will spue thee out of My mouth" (Rev. 3: 16).

But again we are turned to the compassionate dealing of God with His people, and here get a word that links these lines with our well-beloved 53rd chapter. Our A. V. renders it by "doctrine;" it is really what is "heard," *i.e.*, a report of tidings, and it is a question as to who will receive it. If people do not, their refusal shall not be attributed to its obscurity; it shall be adapted even to those who have just been weaned. Let us hear the prophet:

9: To whom shall He knowledge impart?
    To whom shall He give understanding as to the tidings?
    To those who've been weaned from the milk:
    To those who from breasts have been taken.
10: For charge to charge, charge to charge;
    Line to line, line to line;
    Here a bit, there a bit.*

The prophet on the part of Jehovah asks to whom shall the knowledge of His ways be imparted? It shall be so simple that even infants with nothing but the ability of listening shall be able to understand it; yet that very simplicity will stumble the wise and prudent who in their pride will be blind to its perfections. Patiently too will He work, precept adding to precept, line to line; giving a little here, and then a little more there, till the words become so familiar as to be monotonous. But if thus revealed to babes it is hidden from the leaders of the nation who

---

*As will be seen, I have at the expense of all elegance endeavored to transfer the monosyllabic simplicity of the original; for this is really the point emphasized. For "precept" I have used the monosyllable "charge," to correspond with the Hebrew "tzav."

conceive of themselves as the "wise and prudent."   Then another
form of speech will be sent them:

11: For with lips that are stammering,
    With speech that is foreign,
    Will He speak with this people:
12: To whom He hath said:
    This is true rest, giving rest to the weary,
    And this is the way of refreshment.
    But to this they refused to give ear.
13: But still shall the word of Jehovah be to them:
    Charge on charge, charge on charge;
    Line on line, line on line;
    Here a bit, there a bit,
    That they might go, and fall backward,
    Be broken, be snared and be taken.

Here we get a forecast that the proud will reject the "report;"
then He will speak to them in quite a different way, even in the
foreign speech of a conqueror.  The burden of the speech in their
own tongue was "rest for the weary," a tender message of grace.
They would have none of it, and thus having refused the love of
the truth, they must bear its severe side in judgment.

Does not this accord perfectly with our Lord's words in Matt.
11? He, the true "Isaiah," rejoices that God had hid these things
from the wise and prudent, and had revealed them to babes.  But
no baseless arbitrary selection is this; it is only because the
proud *will not* receive these words of grace, for He cries to all:
"Come unto Me, all ye that labor and are heavy laden, and I
will give you rest." That was, is, and ever will be, a word of refreshment for the weary.  Nor is it without painful interest that
in close connection with this blessed invitation to rest, we immediately hear those scornful men that were rulers, claiming to
have perfect ability to attain to rest, in their keeping the sabbath
(which word means "rest;" Matt. 12).

But that anticipates a little.  We must first let the light of 1
Cor. 14: 20 fall on this scripture, for it is there quoted; and
mark, we have there, too, the same reference to "children" and
"babes" as here: "Brethren, be not children in understanding:
howbeit in malice be children, but in understanding be men.  In

the law it is written, With men of other tongues and with other lips, will I speak unto this people; and yet, for all that, they will not hear Me, saith the Lord. So that tongues are for a sign, not to them that believe, but to them that believe not." But when the Spirit of God says, "In the law," He would warn us that we must not interpret the gracious gift of tongues in the gospel exactly by the prophet Isaiah. The law and the grace of the gospel are quite in opposition, and while, in the former, the strange foreign speech would be a divinely sent penalty, in the latter, the only point of contact is that it is intended to awaken interest, enquiry and so blessing to those who have not yet believed. Nor is it necessary to infer that they have finally and definitely rejected the report of the gospel, as those "in the law" of whom Isaiah writes.

Jehovah will not alter the style of His proclamation; it shall still be as simple as "precept on precept, line upon line;" only now it shall result in their going on in their own way, and that in their being broken up, snared and made captive. Precisely so, the simplicity of the preaching of the Cross is not to be altered. It may be, and is, "a stumbling-block to the Jew, and to the Greek foolishness;" but change it not, attempt not to replace that simplicity with human learning, oratory or wisdom. Still, to the end, preach Christ and Him crucified to the proud professors of this day, even though it shall, in its very grace, prove God's way of hardening; for it will be to them, alas, a "savor of death unto death." For mark it well, He never makes a heart, that would be otherwise tender, to be hard, for that would surely put the responsibility of that "hardness" upon Him. Nothing can be more hardening than to listen to the gospel, the "tidings" of grace, unmoved. It is nothing but a blasphemous calumny, by an over-weighting of one side of truth, to make God the Author of man's evil. Thus, Jehovah will continue to speak in the simplest, clearest words; but that will be in order that all responsibility for their rejection can only be charged, not to the obscurity of the message, but to those who reject it.

14: So hark to the word of Jehovah,
Ye scornful men that are rulers
Of people dwelling in Salem.

15: For ye have said:
    With death have we made an alliance,
    With Sh'ohl we are in agreement;
    The threatening scourge overflowing,
    When passing shall not come a-nigh us;
    For we have appointed a lie for our shelter,
    And hidden ourselves under falsehood.

16: Therefore thus saith Adonai Jehovah:
    Behold, for a base a Stone laid in Zion—
    A Stone well-tried, a Corner-stone precious,
    A Foundation securely well-founded;
    And he that in *Him* puts his trust
    Shall never make haste as in terror.

17: And justice I'll take for the line,
    And right shall be for the plummet;
    The hail shall sweep the lie-shelter away;
    The hiding-place, waters o'erflow.

18: Your treaty with death shall be cancelled,
    Your agreement with Sh'ohl be annulled.
    When th' overflowing scourge shall pass through
    Ye shall ever by it be downtrodden.

19: As oft as it passes it grips you;
    For morning by morning it passes,
    Both by day and by night,
    Whilst only to learn the report,
    Causes the hearers to shudder;

20: For the bed is too short for the stretching,
    The cover too narrow for wrapping.

21: For again Jehovah will rise up,
    As once in the mount of Perazim:
    As at the valley of Gibeon,
    Again will be moved by His anger,
    To work His work that is strange—
    To do His deed so unwonted.

22: Therefore be ye not scoffers,
    Lest your fetters be strengthened,
    For I've heard from Adonai Jehovah Tzebaoth,
    That He hath decreed a finishing stroke
    Upon the whole of the earth.

These verses have always been of deep interest to all prophetic students; but whilst clear and simple in one respect they are by no means equally so in another. For instance, we have no difficulty in discerning who is meant by the "Stone," for it can be no other than that Holy One who forms the very Foundation of all God's ways, whether in government or grace. But what or who is meant by "the overflowing scourge" is by no means so simple, and we must give it patient attention.

In the first place, it would appear clear that this scourge is some threatened danger, against which the proud men who rule the Jews believe that their covenant gives them security, and it follows that this "covenant" is in direct antithesis to the "Stone." But as this is a symbol of our Lord Jesus, the covenant, or its object, must stand for someone or something in direct opposition to Him; and at once our minds turn to His great foe, the devil, or one of his human representatives.

Next, the rulers of Jerusalem, the representatives of the nation, are addressed; and these put their strongest confidence in the "covenant." Not of course that their lips actually utter plain words of complicity with the Satanic wickedness that is here attributed to them; *that* men never do, but always attach fairest words to foulest deeds. In this case the covenant was really with "death and sh'ohl;" the former taking man out of life, the latter receiving his soul after death. Some treaty then has been made by the governors of Jerusalem with the human representative (for no covenant could be made with literal death) of these normally terrifying and irresistible foes, whose own place is outside the sphere of life and light. But if these, their trusted allies, are in the sphere of the spirit, then the foe must also be found in the same sphere. If "death" and "sh'ohl" speak of some *spirit wickedness* then the "overflowing scourge" must be something of that same nature, even although having also a human representative.

Has this prophecy ever been fulfilled in the past? If not, in what way shall it be in the future? As to the past, it is impossible to find in Scripture anything that can be taken as a fulfilment. In 2 Kings 17: 4 we do indeed find an appeal to Egypt for help against Assyria, but that was not by Judah, or the "rulers of Jerusalem," at all, but by Hoshea, the king of the northern kingdom; so *that* must be abandoned, for this prophecy refers entirely to Jerusalem, or the southern kingdom.

When we do read of Judah in relation to Egypt, we find Josiah actually fighting against it, and losing his life in the valley of Megiddo (2 Chron. 25: 22); *that* assuredly does not admit of an alliance with, or confidence in, Egypt. Nor can it be with Assyria either, for it was against Babylon, not Assyria, that Pharaoh-Necho was on his way when Josiah sought to stop him.

The prophecy therefore must find its definite fulfilment in the future, when there shall again be a Jewish State so organized that it can make an alliance, or covenant; and whilst such a condition may be seen as approaching, it certainly has not yet fully developed.

All Old Testament prophecy converges and focuses on one supreme moment, the revelation of the Lord Jesus, and it is by comparing scripture with scripture, and bringing together the various prophecies that must refer to that same crisis, that we get a connected vision of the whole. Thus Micah (ch. 5: 5) writes: "And this Man (the Lord Jesus) shall be Peace when the Assyrian shall come into our land, and when he shall tread in our palaces." Here, then, we have someone called "the Assyrian," in the land of Palestine at that critical moment when the Lord is revealed. Compare with that another scripture which assuredly deals with precisely the same moment of the Lord's revelation: "Behold, the day of the Lord cometh, and thy spoil shall be divided in the midst of thee. For I will gather all nations against Jerusalem to battle: and the city shall be taken. . . . Then shall the Lord go forth, and fight against those nations, as when He fought in the day of battle. And His feet shall stand in that day upon the mount of Olives" (Zech. 14: 1-4). Micah has told us that "the Assyrian" will be "in the land" when the Lord shall intervene, and now Zechariah tells us that "all nations" will also be there at the same time. Naturally, we should conclude (as others have concluded), *were this all that we had,* that the nations must be the eastern nations under the leadership of the literal Assyrian, who certainly came from the east. But we must go further, and turn to the New Testament to a scripture that again refers to precisely the same moment: "And I saw heaven opened, and behold, a white horse, and He that sat on him was called Faithful and True, and in righteousness doth He judge and make war (beyond controversy, that is the same Lord, the 'Stone' of Isaiah, who is 'Peace,' as Micah speaks, and whose

Feet shall stand upon the mount of Olives, as Zechariah tells us) .... and the Beast was taken and with him the False Prophet ... , and the remnant were slain with the sword of Him that sat upon the horse" (Rev. 19: 11, 20, 21). Here, then, it is unmistakably clear that it is "the Beast" who is destroyed at the Lord's return in glory, whilst the hostile Assyrian is also in the land. What, then, is the inevitable deduction? Either that there will be two world-imperial powers—that is, two powers both possessing the rule over the whole prophetic earth (which, in itself, is impossible)—or that under these two names of the Assyrian and the Beast is the one hostile world-power that has the faithful remnant of Israel under its foot at that precise moment of the revelation of the Lord. Nor would there appear to be, as we have already seen, any difficulty in this identification of the Assyrian and the Beast; for when the Old Testament prophets wrote, the Assyrian was the world-power hostile to Israel, and thus is to be taken as the representative of that world-power at any time, irrespective of who might exercise it; that is, *the Assyrian of the past must be seen in "the Beast from the sea,"* the future head of the revived fourth empire of Daniel's second chapter.

This raises the next question: Can the "Beast," thus identified with the Assyrian, be the "overflowing scourge?" That would appear altogether impossible; for the covenant will be between the imperial Gentile world-power (the Beast) and the apostate mass of Jewry, as Dan. 9: 27 tells us; and the same object cannot be, at the same time, to the same people, both dreaded as a scourge, and boasted in as an ally. We have thus eliminated both the "Assyrian" and the "Beast" (even assuming them not to be identical) as being this "scourge"—what then is left?

To answer this, let us recur to a similar condition in chap. 8. There too the people had refused the gracious word giving "refreshment to the weary," and this refusal is followed by the waters of the river Euphrates overflowing them, and the covenant that was then between Ephraim and Syria was of no avail. But when considering that chapter we could but see in the history of the past a foreshadowing of what even to this day lies in the future; and *in that point of view* we took the "Assyrian" not to be a nation at all, but, in the final fulfilment, the false confidence itself! Thus God ever causes men to work out their own destiny, reaping what they themselves have sown. If Ahaz places his confidence in Assyria, then that confidence, Assyria, is sent against Judah as a punishment (ch. 7: 17). Hezekiah reveals all the precious things, the gifts of God's grace, to Babylon, thus making Babylon his confidant; and so to Babylon the Jews go in captivity. *That which was the confidence becomes the source of the infliction.* So here the word "lies" speaks as clearly of some "strong delusion" as of any literal nation of conquerors, for thus again *the confidence becomes the penalty.* No doubt, in the day to come, the mass of the Jews who have returned to their land in unbelief, as we see them doing as I write, will make some provision against a literal threatening danger, say of Russia, or Turkey, or both, but God sends them a scourge of another character altogether from which there is no possible escape.

But here, in sharp contrast with the "lies," One is introduced whom we know as "The Amen, the Faithful and True Witness," who ever intervenes in the extremity of man's failure, when every mouth is stopped. Then it is that He lays in Zion, the very mount (note) that speaks of His intervention in grace, a Stone that has these three basic qualities, "tested" (Godward), "precious" (manward), "solid" (selfward), precisely as we read of the huge stones that formed the base of the temple (1 Kings 5: 17), "Great stones, costly stones, hewed stones," the same qualities but in reverse order. So the apostle Peter directs our eyes away from himself to his Lord, applying the same virtues, "elect," "precious," a "corner-stone," again Godward, manward, selfward, and none trusting in Him can ever be confounded; he shall be as safe and immovable as the Stone on which he rests.

Here, then, we have the contrasted confidences; the divine in the Stone, the Satanic in the alliance. Then in verse 17, hail and floods, symbols of some divine judgment, sweep over the scene, and all save what answers to righteousness—all that is false; and only that—is swept away! Again, then, we must carefully note the strictly discriminative nature of the infliction. But that is never the effect of an invasion of a literal hostile human army; whether it be Assyrian or Babylonian, Russian or Turk; none of them care in the least for such moral distinctions in those they conquer. *They* do not slay all those who have no confidence in God, and spare all who have. *They* do not lead captive the proud and impenitent, leaving the lowly and penitent to liberty. Thus it would seem quite certain that this "overflowing scourge" cannot be a nation of invaders, morally discriminating, but a purely discriminative and spiritual judgment, afflicting some but having no effect upon others. "Every morning it comes by day and by night." That is precisely the way in which one would describe an ever-recurring spiritual terror. No sooner are the eyes reopened, whether in the night or in the morning light, than the terrors that were lost in sleep return. All truth is gone; a gloomy darkness prevails everywhere, and out of that darkness come the scorpion-locusts, the sting of which causes such intense suffering that men who have received the mark of the Beast (the sign of the covenant) seek death, but seek it in vain (Rev. 9: 6).

But if spiritual, what "spirit" do other scriptures tell us will at this time be especially active in malignity? Revelation 12 and 13 clearly teach that in midst of the last seven years of Israel's sorrows, Satan (under the fifth trumpet) is cast out of heaven to the earth, finds there one of the "heads" of the "Beast" (and the Beast being the world-power, the Assyrian of that day, its head would be the particular form of government that was then in force) "wounded to death." That is, some revolutionary convulsion has occurred that overthrows all government, of which the previous "trumpet," the fourth, had told us. Satan restores the emperor to his throne (Rev. 13: 3, 4); from that day the government of the earth becomes distinctly Satanic, and evidences the "dragon" character by fierce persecution of everything and every one that would acknowledge "the God of the earth" (Rev. 11: 4).

The God-fearing remnant of the Jews now begins to "turn to the Lord," and consequently the veil begins to fall from their hearts (2 Cor. 3: 16); and in the rejected Jesus they begin to discern God's "Stone." The grossest spiritual darkness covers that sphere that had enjoyed the blessed light of truth. Men, now judicially blinded, are under strong delusion, and "believe a lie." The lie is Satan's deception, the false confidence, sustained by "lying wonders;" and God turns it into an awful penalty—not merely, or alone, at least, material or physical, but pre-eminently spiritual, to conform to the whole character of the divine dealings in those last days.

Thus do the prophetic scriptures throw their light on each other; and as we have literal foreshadowings of that final heading up of the ways of God with Israel in the Old Testament, so in the New we may see in the overflowing inroads of Christendom by Saracen and Turk in the fifth and sixth trumpet, respectively, similar *foreshadowing* of the same crisis; but the crisis itself still lies before us.

Finally, a *spiritual* terror would be in much closer harmony with Luke 21: 26 ("men's hearts failing them for fear, and for looking after those things that are coming on the earth"—do not the very words suggest that the fear comes from a sphere above the earth?) than a visible human hostile army on the earth; for there would be no difficulty in discerning what was coming in such case.

To sum up: In those bitter closing days, when Satan is confined to the earth, and throwing away every mask, he evidences his draconic hatred of all that is of God thereon by a persecution of His people, transcending even anything that has gone before, since it affects *spirit* as well as body; God works in grace with, and for, a pious remnant of the Jews; and they (not instantaneously, but as the light dawns on the earth) put their confidence in The Stone, while the mass put theirs in the covenant with the imperial world-power. The result is that the devil (by divine permission) sends that bitter literal persecution on the God-fearing Jews called, "The Great Tribulation," while God sends a spiritual anguish, the inevitable consequence of the rejection of truth, on the wretched, but willing dupes of the great enemy of God and man. Thus all are tried (Rev. 3: 10).

Verses 20 and 21 speak of the utter inadequacy of all human schemes when God intervenes. The apostates had made a comfortable bed for themselves, as they assumed; it is too short to permit them to stretch themselves upon it. They had provided a covering that shall preserve them in comfort, and lo, it is too narrow to envelop them! For Jehovah is now active in (what we may rejoice that He Himself calls) His strange work. It *is* His work, necessary and inevitable, but He loves it not. He is not, as we may reverently say, "at home" in it. Two instances in Israel's past history may serve as examples of that "strange work" in the future. When David became established in his kingdom, as is David's greater Son at the crisis of which the prophet speaks, the Philistines "spread themselves in the valley of Rephaim,"* and then Jehovah burst forth upon them as the *breaking forth of waters*. At a much earlier day, after Joshua's victory at Gibeon, He cast great *hailstones* on the fleeing foe. Those judgments shall be repeated, although it does not follow that they will be literal or material. On the contrary, we are told in our own prophetic book of Revelation that among the

---

*The word *"Rephaim"* is well worth considering. It has in it a clear suggestion of applying, not merely to a literal people on earth, but to a counterpart of these in the spirit-world, and this gives it peculiar adaptability here. Further, it comprehends in itself the opposite meanings of "strength" and weakness." Thus it is frequently rendered "giants," as in Deut. 2: 11: "The Emims were also accounted giants (*rephaim*)," that is, people of super-human height and strength, and so inspiring terror. Yet precisely the same word stands for the spirits of the dead, as in Psalm 88: 10: "Shall the dead (*rephaim*) praise Thee?" Here this meaning is attached for the very opposite cause; because the spirits of the departed are weak, as devoid of body. This gives some suggestion, at least, as to the reason for the strange keen desire of the un-clean spirits, in the Gospels, for some material body to indwell, even that of swine being preferred to none, although un-clean men are far more in harmony with themselves. They are unclothed, uncovered and unclean; and it is this exposé and weak-ness that may bring the great distress. All is surely intensively sug-gestive that in those last quick-coming days, Satan and his hosts will be in very close relation with rebellious man, and when "the silence of God" ends, and He intervenes, it will be in judgment on both. We can see too how the body being the agent for the carrying out of the desires of the immaterial part of our being, the unclothed state is also comparatively undesirable for us (2 Cor. 5: 4).

divine judgments on men at the pouring out of the seventh vial there will fall a great hail out of heaven, every stone about the weight of a talent. This would mean, if literal, certain death for every living thing. No roof could protect, no building could stand. Such an awful storm would level everything on earth, and utterly exterminate all within its sphere. But that sphere is as universal as "the heaven" whence it comes. Not a man then could be left alive. But the subsequent context shows that men *are* still upon the earth, for they blaspheme; and this, as indeed all else, compels us to see the *symbolic* force of this hail-storm. The literal in the day of Joshua, provides a symbol of an awful judgment that shall fall on the nations and apostate Jews in the day of wrath to come. For whilst the soft and gentle rain distilling on the earth is a beautiful figure of God's blessing, let the warmth be withdrawn, and nothing but the cold left, and there's no longer blessing in rain, but infliction in hail. So let the love be withdrawn, and nothing but wrath left, what was a blessing becomes an awful judgment, as in our prophecy, of a weight corresponding to the responsibility (see Matt. 25: 14-30).

In verse 22 we have the Spirit's counsel: "O do not scoff at these threatening forecasts, for as surely as you do, the fetters that even now bind you will be strengthened; for the Lord God has irrevocably determined a finishing stroke on all the earth." Scoffing is the most hardened form of impiety. The first Psalm gives us three progressive steps in that evil path: first, "the counsel of the *ungodly*," who maintain a form of respectable religion; next, "the way of *sinners*," a more active character of evil; and, finally, as here, "the seat of the *scornful*," confirmed and contemptuous opposition to divine truth.

The prophecy closes with quite a different character of communication—a proverb illustrating Jehovah's ways with His people:

23: Lend me your ear, and list to my voice,
    To my speech be attentive and hearken.
24: Day after day plows the plowman to sow,
    Op'ning and breaking his earth-clods?
25: Nay, when the surface is level and plain,
    Doth he not then sow the fennel?

Doth he not then cast the cummin abroad,
And sow the wheat in its order?
The barley he puts in its own rightful place,
With the rye that is sown in its border?

26: For his God doth give him instruction aright,
And furnish him duly with knowledge.

27: For the fennel is not with a corn-drag threshed,
Nor cart-wheel rolled over the cummin;
But 'tis with a flail that the fennel is threshed,
With a staff is beaten the cummin.

28: Is bread-corn crushed?  He crushes it not;
Nor will he forever be threshing;
Nor will he suffer his cart-wheel to bruise,
Nor the hoofs of his horses stamp on it.

29: This from Jehovah Tzebaoth doth come.
Oh, wonderful is He in counsel,
And great indeed is His wisdom!

Once more the Lord is teaching here by parables, and, as later, by the sea of Galilee, He spoke of a "sower who went forth to sow," so here He uses the ways of a husbandman to illustrate His own.   First, he breaks up his ground by cutting into it, and upheaving it ,with his forceful share: exactly so does God by His Word; but does he do that interminably?   Nay, that is not the end desired, and so the farmer further breaks up by harrow the clods into finer pieces; breaks and breaks, for it is by this that his land is made fertile, as you and I, by a corresponding and painful process, ever making us smaller in our own eyes, and more submissive, and so, fruitful.   Then on the levelled surface, he scatters the various seeds from which he desires his harvest: first the inferior fennel,* then cummin,* then the wheat, noblest of the grains, carefully sown in rows, and not scattered broadcast: then the barley, and finally the coarse spelt, or rye. A good definition of man is that he is an "animal who sows seeds"—no other animal does—so it is *God* who has taught him this (ver. 26) and the wheat at least grows nowhere without human care, never spontaneously; left alone, it dies out.

But the solicitous care continues to the end.   The agriculturalist will never spoil by too rough usage.   Rods and staves

---

*Both of the parsley family.

he must use as flails to separate the grain from the worthless husks; but he never ruins it by excessive crushing. Is man wiser than his Maker? If he thus acts with such intelligence, in dealing with the fruit of his own work, shall not God who gave him that intelligence equally so act? Indeed He will; for He is the real Source of all true intelligence, wonderful in counsel, excellent in wisdom. So He prepares the ground of man's heart by trouble, conviction of sin, and sorrow, and then the good seed falls and fruit follows. But then follows the threshing—the *tribulum*, or flail, has to be used, and that is what is termed "tribulation," through which alone any can enter the kingdom of God. But in this the wise saint rejoices (Rom. 5: 3), for he knows that the end that his divine Husbandman has in view is that he may bring forth much fruit (John 15), and the flail of chastening has that effect on those exercised thereby (Heb. 12: 11). How good it would be were we more skilled to read the parables that are about us on every side!

# CHAPTER TWENTY-NINE

JEHOVAH now looks at a city that has ever been, and will ever be peculiarly dear to Him, for there dwelt David, the man after His own heart. He calls it Ariel, evidently a symbolic name, which lends itself to that play on words with which we have become familiar as a characteristic of our prophet. The Scriptures give us two different renderings of the word: first in 2 Sam. 23: 20: "Benaiah . . . slew two lion-like (*ariel*) men of Moab," the margin reading, "lions of God." This gives the simplest and most direct meaning of Ariel—"the lion of God." But in Ezek. 43: 16 the first part of the compound word, *"ari"* is rendered "altar;" and the whole may also be translated, "altar of God," as the place upon which the *fire* of God will be kindled and maintained. The chapter divides thus:

Verses 1 to 8: The Voice of Jehovah against Jerusalem.
Verses 9 to 14: The Voice of Jehovah against the apostate mass.
Verses 15 to 24: The recovery of the Remnant.

1: Woe unto Ariel—even unto Ariel!
The city in the which King David pitched his tent!
Add ye year to year, and let the feasts revolve about,
2: Yet Ariel shall suffer a very sore distress;
And there shall be within it a groaning and a moaning—
Aye, it shall be to Me as an Ariel indeed.
3: Yes, I will against thee on all sides round about encamp,
With military outposts will surround thee as in siege,*
Fortresses against thee also will I build up;

---

*This is a paraphrase of a difficult line. The word rendered "mount" in A. V. refers to the military outposts around a beleagured city.

4: And low shalt thou be brought till thou speak from off the
        ground;
    Low, yes, so low, that from dust shall be thine utterance,
    Thy voice shall come up from the ground as of one that
        is possessed;
    Thy speech from out the dust shall come, even as a
        whisper.

One may discern intense earnestness, emotion, and possibly
a kind of pathos, in the repetition of the "Ariel," for it reminds
us of a similar repetition when the same divine Speaker foresaw
and announced a similar judgment on the same devoted and beloved city—it was spoken in tears that were evident there, and
may possibly be discerned here.   The Lord was weeping when
He cried, "O Jerusalem, Jerusalem!"   Nor is it without tenderness that He here cries, "O Ariel, Ariel," for the interjection will
bear equally well the rendering "O" as "Woe."   Thus we ought
to be well prepared to see judgment and mercy mingled in what
follows.

What cheerful hope lies in the very word "Ariel" when applied as here to Jerusalem!   What memories of that far-off
prophecy of Jacob when he thus blessed his sons: "Judah is a
*lion's whelp;* from the prey, my son, thou art gone up; he stooped
down, he couched as a *lion,* and as an *old lion;* who shall rouse
him up?   The scepter shall not depart from Judah, nor a lawgiver from between his feet until Shiloh come; and unto Him
shall the gathering of the peoples be" (Gen. 49: 9, 10).   What
hope, again I say, when God recalls this faithful promise to mind
in the very word Ariel, "God's Lion."   Many centuries must
pass, but then we shall hear a still clearer voice carrying on the
same blessed hope in the Lion of the tribe of Judah, but now
"as a Lamb that had been slain," and as such having ability—
lacking to all in heaven, earth and under the earth—to open the
book of God's counsels as to this earth and bring them into effect
(Rev. 5).

It was here that warlike David camped, and here has David's
greater Son pitched tent, and shall do again, first sending His
armies against it, but eventually showing Himself for it.   Oh,
how like to His ways with us that is!   Trials of various kinds

come upon us, and they all cry, as it were, "God is against thee! God is against thee!" But as soon as they have done their intended work in breaking down all our pride, the clouds part, the blue of heaven appears, and the sunshine of His face says what the Cross of Christ has never ceased to say, "Nay, He is *for* us, and who shall be against us?"

But first, that most dangerous, widespread, and most subtle of all Satan's devices, a formal, conscience-soothing "religion," must be dealt with; and thus the closing words of the first verse are really a strong irony: "Go on, year after year, with your feasts, they will not avert the chastening stroke." Moans and groans are soon to be heard in Ariel, and that beloved city shall be to her Lord as Ariel in another sense, no longer a lion, but a *hearth* on which may burn His fire of judgment, as on the altar of brass.

That "fire of God," ever burning on that altar, being thus brought to mind, it shall come on Ariel, not as an exterminating flame but as a cleansing fire of chastening love; till low, very low is poor Ariel brought; and, in the place of the song of pleasure and the loud boast, her voice comes as a penitent whisper even from the very dust where she lies in her self-abasement; yes, like those who have a familiar spirit, in a faint whisper, so that it is difficult to catch what is said.

But, when at this extremity, the whole scene changes in a moment, what but the revelation of the Lord from heaven could effect that? This intervention must lie still before us, for nothing of what is described in the following verses has yet been seen or heard on earth:

5: But then shall be as powdered dust the legions of thy
    foemen,
  And as the chaff that flies away, the crowd that thee
    affrighted;
  And this shall come to pass in an instant suddenly.
6: From Jehovah Lord of Hosts there shall come a visitation,
  With thunder-clap and earthquake, and with a mighty
    voice,
  With tempest, and with blazing of an all-devouring flame.
7: And the legions of the nations that fight against Ariel,
  All that fight against her, her stronghold and distress,
  Shall even pass away as a vision dreamed at night.

8: For then shall it be as though a hungry man were dream-
 ing,
And, hungry as he is, he dreameth that he eats;
But he awakens, and he finds his soul is still a-hungered.
Or it shall be as though a thirsty one were dreaming,
And thirsty as he is, he dreameth that he drinks;
But waking, he is faint, and his soul is parched with
 thirsting.
So shall it be with the legions of the nations
That have gathered there to fight against the mount of
 Zion.

No single city on earth has stood as many sieges as Jerusalem, but it has at least one more still before it, and it is in the
harmony of the various prophecies that foretell that siege and
its issue, that we arrive at a clear assurance that we have not
erred in our interpretation of all.   Many today are, and not
without much ingenuity, pointing to the fulfilment of Old Testament prophecies in the events that are now taking place.   It is,
however, a fundamental axiom of interpretation that as long as
God is dealing with a heavenly, He is not dealing also with an
earthly people.   The "spirits" of the two dispensations are so
absolutely opposed as to make this impossible (Luke 9: 55);
and so not one single prophecy of the Old Testament is or can
be definitively and finally fulfilled today.   By this it is not meant
that conditions therein foretold are not in existence today—surely
they are.   To give but one instance: The Lord is sitting at the
right hand of God, precisely as Ps. 110 speaks: "The Lord said
to my Lord, Sit Thou at My right hand;" but what follows?
*"Until I make Thy enemies Thy footstool."*   It takes some strain
to force the gospel of grace into that threatening word, and follow the psalm a little further: "The Lord (same word as the
second "Lord" in ver. 1, *Adohn, i.e.*, Messiah, Jesus) at Thy
right hand shall strike through kings in the day of His wrath.
He shall judge among the heathen, He shall fill (the places) with
the dead bodies; He shall wound the heads over many countries."
Surely our Lord is not doing that today, although still seated at
God's right hand—this is not the day of His wrath.

Thus, too, there is a prophecy in Hosea (3: 4) that depicts
the Jews' condition during this present time: "For the children

of Israel shall abide many days without a king, and without a prince, and without a sacrifice, and without an image, and without an ephod and teraphim." None can deny that this describes their present condition with exactness; but when did that condition begin? When Jerusalem began to be trodden down of the Gentiles in B. C. 606; when the "Times of the Gentiles" began. It began, then, before this parenthetical time of the heavenly calling; it shall continue after that is ended: therefore the prophecy is not having a direct, exclusive or final fulfilment today.

When, then, was this prophecy in these verses 5-8 fulfilled? Or when shall it be? We have two answers, and I quote from Birks on this chapter: "The idea that this has no express reference to Sennacherib's campaign, but is only 'a figurative expression of the truth that the Church shall suffer, but not perish,' (as Alexander), exchanges a clear and definite sense, confirmed by the whole series and order of the visions, for one which is wholly vague, misty and undefined." If that were the only alternative—if the prophecy must find its fulfilment either in the Assyrian invasion of the past in Hezekiah's day, or in the Church of the present day, our difficulties would appear insurmountable; for how can anyone even think that this foretold siege in which Jerusalem is surrounded, towers set against her, and she brought low, can have fulfilment at a time when the same Scripture assures us that this did not take place? As it is written: "Therefore thus saith the Lord concerning the king of Assyria, He shall not come into this city, nor shoot an arrow there, nor come before it with a shield, nor cast a bank against it" (2 Kings 19: 32). A strange fulfilment truly! But, on the other hand, that God should "besiege" the Church, we must agree with Mr. Birks, is "vague, misty and indefinite" enough; nay, worse, for we ask, was it the Lord Jesus who distressed and persecuted His Church even to strange cities, or the human persecutor, Saul? Such interpretations of prohpecy are certainly enough to cause all sober minds to reject them.

But the moment that we see that Israel's history is not finished, but shall continue in the future, all difficulty disappears. Every prophecy with one harmonious voice tells us that at the

revelation of the Lord Jesus, Israel—represented by the poor
remnant of faith—shall indeed be at her last gasp, a humiliation
that is so graphically depicted in verse 4. With this, too, compare Ps. 126: 1, 2: "When the Lord turned again the captivity of
Zion we were like them that dream. Then was our mouth filled
with laughter." But here in our book the dreamers are not
Israel, but the victorious enemy who have taken the city (Zech.
14), and in that capture, "dream" that they have at last attained
their desire, and made a final end of all claim of God to the
earth, since those troublesome witnesses are now silenced, and
they are assured of naught but "peace and safety" (comp. Rev.
11: 7).

They dream that their longings are fulfilled and Israel is
annihilated. They awake, and lo, Israel is conqueror! Her moans
and groans, her sighs and cries, are suddenly turned to the
laughter of joy, and now the "dreamers" are addressed:

9: Stand, and astounded be!
  Blind ye, and blind be!*
  Aye, they are drunken, but 'tis not with wine!
  They stagger indeed, but not with strong drink!
10: Jehovah hath poured the spirit of stupor;
  He hath completely bandaged your eyes!
  The prophets, your rulers, the Seers He's veilèd.
11: All of the vision now has become to you
  E'en as the words of a book that is sealed:
  Which, given a reader, with—Read this, I pray thee:
  But he answers, I cannot, for the book it is sealèd.
12: The book is then given to one that's not learnèd
  With—Read this, I pray thee; but he answers, I cannot,
  For I'm lacking all learning!
13: Adonai hath spoken!
  Forasmuch as this people draw near with their mouth,
  And with their lips give Me honor,
  But their heart they do keep far from Me away,
  And their fear of Me's taught by the precepts of men,

---

*A difficult line, as the varying renderings evidence. The He-
brew word is quite capable of being rendered "cry" as A. V., but
it may also be derived from a root "to close up," and as applied
to the eye, "blind," as it is used of Isaiah's commission in ch.
6: 10; and as that would seem clearly in line with the immediate
context, I have adopted it, as the Revisers in the margin.

14: Therefore, behold, I will add to the wonderful
Things I have done with this people of yore,
A wonderful work—aye, the most wonderful,
So that the wisdom of wisest shall perish,
The prudence of prudent shall vanish away.

There seems a kind of paradox in verse 9, as so often in Isaiah. The people are bidden to stop as if suddenly struck with some astounding portent. But clear and striking as it is, they are unable to interpret it: for they have both blinded themselves and are blinded. The vision is there, plain for anyone who desires to see, and who is not self-blinded; but these are sunken in a stupor, not due either to wine or strong drink: they are judicially blinded. Having refused truth, having hardened their heart, God has left them to their infatuation.

So here Jehovah cries, "Blind yourselves in your insensate folly, and ye shall indeed be blinded." The vision itself is plain; but how can those sunken in pleasure enter into the thoughts of God? Israel is divided between learned and unlearned: between those who claim that they are quite able to read anything that can be read at all, and those who admit their inability. If, then, the first cannot read this, the fault must lie with the writing, not with their powers—it is a sealed book, that cannot be opened. Thus speak the prophets and priests, the "Seers" among them. But the mass by their admission of their inability expect to escape all responsibility for remaining in ignorance of its contents.

There is surely a very striking correspondence with just that condition of things today. We have a book answering to that "vision," for it is divinely called "Revelation," but, alas, many who claim to be teachers and leaders insist that it is utterly incomprehensible; or are not afraid to term it "dream-literature." Learned as they are, it is a sealed book to them. On the other hand, the great mass of professing Christians care nothing about it, cheerfully admit their incapacity, pay their pastor to read it for them, and if he cannot, who can? Yet God Himself in the Old Testament tells us that it is a vision, something to be seen, and in the New that it is a Revelation, and that must be something revealed.

Now with great strength comes the announcement, Adonai, the supreme Lord, hath spoken; and He Himself, although in human guise, takes up these very words and applies them to that people that represents us all.  There, man's heart is seen as the very mother of all ungodliness.  Yet that is quite consistent with a form of piety.  Head may bow, knee may bend, lip may speak fair and pious words, but that uncontrollable heart will not draw near to God in guileless confidence.  And the most serious charge is that people set aside the revelation that God has given, and substitute for the revealed will of God their own precepts.  The very Word that He has given set aside!  What *can* God do under such conditions?

He will interpose once more. He will add to all His marvelous works by another still more marvelous.  So wonderful is this— so superhumanly wonderful—that when it comes, it shall destroy all man's boasted wisdom, and so eclipse his prudence as to render it invisible, as the noon-day sun extinguishes the light of a taper.  That marvel is in God giving His own Son for a rebel race!

Our apostle Paul, while quoting directly from Habakkuk 1: 5, yet refers to this in the synagogue at Antioch of Pisidia as a solemn warning to his hearers not to trifle with the marvelous glad tidings he was bringing them.  This, then, is God's way of hardening judicially: sending such a flood of light and love in the gift of His beloved Son, as only wilfully closed eyes could possibly ignore; such a warmth of love in His atoning death, as only a heart that *will* not melt, could resist; and when that is the case, that hard heart is hardened indeed.


15: Woe unto them who seek to hide deep
    And far from Jehovah their scheming;
    And their works are done in the dark,
    Whilst saying, Who sees us?  Who knows us?
16: Oh—your—perversity!
    Shall the potter be counted as clay,
    That the work should say of its maker,
    He did not make me?
    Or that which is formed of its former,
    He knoweth nothing?

17: Is it not yet a very short while,
   That Lebanon's turned to a fruitful field,
   And *that* esteemed as a forest?

18: Then in that day the deaf man shall hear
   The words in the book that are written;
   And out of obscurity, out of the dark,
   The eyes of the blind shall see clearly.

19: The lowly shall add to their joy in the Lord;
   The poor among men of humblest degree
   In Israel's Holy One boast then.

20: For then shall the terrible one be brought low.
   'Tis all over then with the scoffer;
   And all who are watching for evil in men
   Shall then themselves be (all) cut off.

21: Those who condemn a man for a word,
   Lay snare by which they'd entrap him
   Who justly reproves in the gate,
   By accusations all baseless.

22: Therefore thus speaketh Jehovah—
   Abraham's Redeemer thus speaks—
   Concerning the household of Jacob;
   Never again shall Jacob be shamed,
   Never again shall his face be turned pale.

23: For when his offspring shall see in their midst,
   All that My hands have effected,
   Then shall they sanctify My Holy Name,
   Jacob's most Holy One hallow,
   And Israel's God shall revere.

24: And those who in spirit have erred
   Shall then attain to true knowledge;
   And those once filled with complaint
   Shall accept (with meekness) correction.

Another "woe" is here pronounced against—the Jew only?
Surely not; for the mournful text on which this part of the
prophecy hangs is supplied by what is common to Gentile and
Jew, the *heart*, and therefore all come under the same woe, for
"as in water face answers to face, so the *heart* of man to man."
What the Scriptures reveal as to the heart of man is in itself
quite enough to prove their divine inspiration, for no mere human
writer would give such a humbling picture. The heart is the
organ placed in the center of man's physical frame; it propels,
by its constant, unceasing rhythmic beatings, the vivifying blood
into every part of that complex organism so fearfully and won-

derfully made—the body. Thus physically placed, well does it
stand also for the very innermost citadel of our psychical, moral
and spiritual being. The "heart" is in the New Testament "the
inner man," that is, what one really *is*, underneath all external
veneer, as distinct and in contrast with what one may *appear* to
be outwardly. It is the birthplace of thought (Matt. 15: 19),
and so deep is it that no human mind is able to sound its profound depths. It is above all things deceitful; it will convince
us of the truth of the veriest lies, and forever does it seek to
justify to us every word we say, every act we do. One, and only
One, can pierce through all the endless layers of deception that
underlie each other, and He has given us the terrible result of His
knowledge that it is not only "deceitful above all things," but
"desperately wicked." Is there a man who would of himself
have so written, including himself in this universal condemnation?
Do men so write today? Most assuredly not. It is superhuman,
it "is not after man" (Gal. 1: 11), and the very opposite of
Satan's lie. *It is divine!*

So here the lips are piety itself, but the heart is not with
them; it is far away; planning, scheming in those dark recesses,
and hoping (how vainly!) that the fair speech will hide from
Jehovah the motives that are beneath it. Oh, the folly of it!
What a turning of things upside down! Verse 16 gives us an
exclamation of astonishment, the wonder being expressed in the
long-drawn-out words. What perversity! Can you claim to
have fashioned *yourselves?* Surely not. You are just like the
clay that the potter has fashioned into a vessel. The potter and
his clay are surely not on the same level: and that powerless
inert vessel of clay might just as well assure the potter that it
does not owe its existence to him; or the statue, so beautifully
fashioned, declare that the artist really knows nothing about it,
as for you to assume that your Maker does not know you to the
very depths of your heart with all its secret motives. The
Psalmist gives expression to a far more reasonable conclusion
when he says: "Thou understandest my thought afar off" (Ps.
139: 2).

Verse 17 shows, I apprehend, the close relation between man
and his earth, and particularly between Israel and Palestine.

Today Israel is a desolate, scattered people, and the land in its desolate condition harmonizes with that sorrowful fact. But that shall not be forever. Israel shall again be in the sunshine of God's smile, and then with corresponding beauty and fertility the land shall accord with that recovery. The wild forest of Lebanon shall become a Carmel, *i.e.*, a very vineyard or fruitful field of God, and what shall then be a fruitful field shall be comparatively despised as wild wood.

This happy change in the sphere of matter shall be paralleled by a still happier correspondence in the sphere of the spirit; joy shall flood the souls of the meek; and that book, so long a sealed book, shall be opened (*cf.* Rev. 10: 1, "a little book opened"— one that had been sealed); and those, once deaf to its voice, shall hear its words, and the eyes of the hitherto blind shall discern their true meaning. For in view of divine wisdom how pitiful is all human pretension, it becomes invisible. Finally, as the climax of these steps of blessing, the Lord Himself shall be the Source of purest, deepest joy—not indeed to the great or wealthy, but to the poor and needy.

How perfect and ever consistent are the ways of God, and how willingly, gladly, does even human reason, when not warped, bow to them! Ever does He hide from the wise and prudent; ever does He reveal to babes. But that never means that all are not equally welcome to all the light and love that is freely offered to all; but as the lowly valleys accept and profit by the rains of heaven that have been rejected and thrown off by the proud and lofty mountains, but which have fallen with absolute impartiality on both, so the self-complacent, and those wise in their own conceit, reject the precious truth that the lowly penitents most gladly accept.

The oppressor and the scoffer have long been in the ascendancy; in that day of which our prophet speaks, they will be looked for in vain. But again, mark the divine hatred and repulsion of all Pharisaic claims to superior holiness. Ever have there been those who think to establish their own superiority by really searching for evil like the carrion birds, and rejoicing if they can but find one ill-considered word, not up to the level of their own supposed correctness; it is enough to call the speaker of it a "sinner." So in verse 20 we have the *external* foe (the oppressor); then the internal *scoffer*, and, finally, the *Pharisee*, distinguished by spiritual pride—all are cut off.

But what as to the little remnant of His people, now called "Jacob," that "Jacob"* who has, in them, passed through his time of trouble (Jer. 30: 7)? This is answered by God: I am the same Jehovah who appeared unto Abraham, and poor Jacob is still Abraham's son, and I am Abraham's Redeemer; and as I redeemed the father, so will I redeem the son—for My Name is Jehovah—the ever-faithful, never-changing God, and Jacob shall nevermore be ashamed and show that shame by blanched face. For shame at having no Deliverer would be closely connected with fear. For then Jacob's children shall see how I have intervened in his behalf, and from that day they shall sanctify My Name, reverence Me alone. In the place of murmuring at My ways with them they shall humbly learn the lessons that those ways are intended to teach for their blessing.

Happy picture of Israel's future, and well, indeed, for us if we can personally appropriate its precious lesson, and trust our God who weaves our web of time with intermingling of mercy and of judgment. In this way there is an unfathomable depth of comfort in the title "God of Jacob."

---

*This name "Jacob" forbids any application to the Church.

# CHAPTER THIRTY

**False confidence condemned. The names Zoan and Hanes significant. Why told Hebron was seven years before Zoan. What God calls Egypt, and what Egypt stands for. The insistence on smooth preaching. Error can rob, but never give. What are the "hidden teachers?" Impossible to take what is said of sun and moon literally. Force of the coming of the Name. The sieve of vanity. What is Tophet? Who is "the king" here? A word as to Gehenna.**

THE chapter again divides into the same significant three parts, thus:

1: Verses 1 to 5: Jehovah's proclamation.
2: Verses 6 to 26: Discriminative judgment.
3: Verses 27 to 33: The end, in songs and groans.

The first part may be rendered thus:

1: Jehovah proclaimeth:
   Woe to the children rebellious,
   To them who take counsel together,
   But not with Me (do they counsel),
   To those who do make an alliance,
   A covenant not of My Spirit,
   Thus to heap sin upon sin.
2: Travelling down into Egypt,
   But no word sought from My mouth!
   Flying for shelter to Pharaoh,
   Trusting in Egypt's vain shadow;
3: To you shall the shelter of Pharaoh be shame,
   And the trust in the shadow of Egypt, disgrace!

4: His princes have come unto Zoan:
   His messengers come unto Hanes.
5: Shamed shall they be of a profitless people;
   For nothing of help or of profit is in them,
   Nothing but shame and reproach.

We search in vain for any strict fulfilment of this prophecy in the past, since the woe is distinctly pronounced against "Judah and Jerusalem" (verse 19). Ephraim, the northern kingdom, did indeed bring their own doom upon them by an appeal to Egypt (2 Kings 17: 4); but Ephraim is not Judah; and *this* Judah never did—Sennacherib's vain taunt notwithstanding (ch. 36: 6), for his word against that of the pious Hezekiah is worth nothing. It follows that in "Egypt" we must see another symbol of that false fleshly confidence that shall characterize the apostate part of the Jews in the day approaching. This chapter, then, in direct accord with its predecessors, refers to that same false confidence that in chapter 28 is termed "the covenant with death," although here seen in another light, and so having a different symbol: Egypt.

In his vision the prophet sees the progress of these ambassadors. First, they are at Zoan, and then they have reached Hanes —names that surely must have some teaching for us, either in their meaning, or in something that other scriptures may tell us concerning them. Zoan is significant enough, for it comes from a root meaning "to strike tent," as do nomadic tribes; and so tells of the opposite of a permanent rest or abode, as Jerusalem shall yet be. For the very word *Zoan* is found in chap. 33: 20, where it is rendered a tabernacle that "shall be taken down." What a perfect name for this poor world, characterized by constant "removals" where men must ever own that "here have we no abiding city," and that their very bodies are but tabernacles sooner or later to be taken down! "Zoan" is written on everything here. But beautiful indeed is the light that this throws by its very contrast on our Lord's words: "In My Father's house are many *mansions*"—abiding homes. Egypt and Zoan are in strict correspondence, as are our Father's house and the body which is the "building of God, a house not made with hands, eternal in the heavens" (2 Cor. 5: 1).

And even the old Hebrew names give a clear suggestion of this precious truth, for of Hebron it is written that it "was built seven years before Zoan in Egypt" (Num. 13: 22). How little would the simple knowledge that one city was a few years more ancient than another profit us! What do we care which was built first? How will that serve in the awful problems of time and eternity that we have to meet? But to Jewish ears these names would tell a weighty truth, and so they may to ours when we learn that Hebron is the very opposite of Zoan and means "communion"—that harmony of sentiment and affection, combined with perfect intimacy, that really makes *"Home."*

Thus Joseph was sent by his father out of "the vale of Hebron" to serve his brethren; a picture of our Lord sent by His Father away from the joys and intimacies of the bosom of that Father to His brethren who refused Him. Whilst in 1 John 1: 3 our Lord is bringing *us* back with Him to that "vale of Hebron," for "our fellowship is with the Father and with His Son Jesus Christ." We dwell in Hebron.

Now with these meanings in view, is it not something far more refreshing than merely saying which was the most ancient of two old cities, that "Hebron was built seven years before Zoan in Egypt?" The first would serve us little, but that "seven years"—symbol of a complete age—before this restless, homeless scene of constant "removals" was built, the purpose of God was to have all His redeemed *home* with Himself; or in other words, in grace incalculable, that we were "chosen in Him *before the foundation of the world* (that is, of Zoan), that we should be holy and without blame before Him in love" (Eph. 1: 3). Thank God that Hebron was built before Zoan!

These "messengers" of foolish Israel leave beautiful Hebron and go to Zoan. Then they are seen having made still further "progress" (?) to Hanes, a word that occurs nowhere else in Scripture; I take it to be a compound of *Han*, "grace," and *nes*, from a root "to flee," which is at least suggestive of the path the messengers were taking away from that grace that should have been Israel's surest confidence, as it is where we, too, alone can "stand," as Rom. 5: 2 tells us. Is it strange that the outcome of such a course should be shame and dishonor?

These things were not written for our entertainment, nor even for our enlightenment with that knowledge that puffeth up; they were given by One who knows our dangers and who cares for our profit. Who of those whose eyes may scan these lines, but is in the same peril of cherishing some false shame-bearing confdence? Always, through all dispensations, there are the same alternatives, Egypt or Jehovah, self or Christ, flesh or Spirit, sight or faith. Nor is it wise for us to mount the judgment-seat in order to condemn others, but rather challenge ourselves as to where our own hearts' true confidence is placed. Well for us, if we can in any measure sing, "Satisfied with *Thee*, Lord Jesus, I am blest."

The Seer is looking on this symbolic picture:

> 6: The burden of the beasts of the southland:
> Through a land of trouble and anguish,
> (Lion and lioness thence,
> Viper and burning winged-one).
> Their riches they carry on backs of young asses,
> Their treasure on bunches of camels,
> To give to a people that profit them nothing!
> 7: And Egypt!   Vain, hollow, her help!
> Therefore I give her this name,
> Boaster, who does nothing else!*

The prophet sees his people making a very poor bargain. They are giving much, but receiving nothing. In the Spirit, Isaiah is looking at a train of burden-bearing beasts going southward loaded with riches; nor do the perils of the desert hinder them. They will run many risks and suffer much in order to—What? *To give away their wealth!* What infatuation! And as for Egypt, what will Egypt do for them? Promise them much, and that is all. She will give them nothing; so Jehovah names her "Rahab,"* or "Boaster, who does nothing!"

But this involves a truth so weighty, so constant and so characteristic of fallen man through all time that Jehovah commands a permanent record to be taken of it:

> 8: Go now, and write it for them on a tablet:
> In a book make a (permanent) note;
> And let it be there for the day that is coming:
> For aye, and forever and aye.†

---

*Another play on words; for Rahab is the very word for Egypt in chap. 51: 9, while in Job 26: 12, it stands for "the proud;" thus the one word covers the double meaning of Egypt and pride—they are synonomous. The last line is very similar to the Latin proverb, "*Vox et praeterea nihil*," "a voice and nothing else."

†The idea of eternity is very strongly impressed on this line in a threefold repetition which Delitzsch paraphrases: "for futurity, for the most remote future, for the future without end."

9: For this is a people rebellious,
   Children who lie, children not willing
   To list to the law of Jehovah;
10: Who say to the seers: O see not!
    And to those having visions:
    For us, have no vision of right things,
    See visions that are but illusions;
11: Depart from the way,
    Err from the highway,
    Remove from being ever before us
    The Holy One of Israel.

Here the only One who really knows the human heart tells us in the most clear and emphatic speech, that any thought of evolution in the character of that heart is hopeless nonsense. The lines could not have been drawn clearer, and much as it may sadden and humble us, it can but strengthen our conviction that only One who could thus see from afar, is the real Author of the Scriptures. For both professing Jew of 2,700 years ago and professing Christian of today are alike. The former hated the faithful Word, it was unwelcome. He would rather be comfortably deceived in listening to a soothing lie, than be rendered uncomfortable by an unpalatable truth; smooth and only smooth things would he listen to.

Looking forward to this very day in which our lot is cast, another holy man of God, speaking by the same Spirit, wrote: "For the time will come that they will not endure sound doctrine, but after their own lusts will heap to themselves teachers, having itching ears, and they shall turn away their ears from the truth, and be turned unto fables" (2 Tim. 4: 3, 4). The time was when the ministers of Christ our Lord had no sense of being dependent for their livelihood on those to whom they preached. They were thus free from any temptation arising from that cause to suit their message to the wishes of those hearers. They served *God*, and Him only they feared, and of Him they sought approval; or, if they called themselves "your servants," it was only "for Jesus' sake" that they were that. But now, in that universal spirit of democracy that has taken possession, not only of the political field, but of the Church, the people select their own "pastors" (as they term them, as if that were the only gift of Christ to

His Church, or as if each assembly was to have but one!), call them, hire them, pay them, and since the preachers are thus their hearers' paid servants, they must see to it (poor men!) that they preach what shall suit their employers, and not witness too strongly against either their pleasures, their worldliness, or their false expectations. Let them beware of anything approaching "pessimism," or of throwing the slightest doubt on the spiritual prosperity of the day: never let them suggest that "as it was in the days of Noah," or "of Lot," so shall it be at the end of the present time; and that a black cloud of threatening judgment overhangs the scene, ready to burst in a storm at any time. Nay, let them prophesy smooth things and only smooth things, that can bring even Christ and Belial into sweet accord, and still gently treat these itching ears with assurances that all is going well. These preachings may indeed prove to be fatal illusions and awful deceits, but that is better than unwelcome truth. So let the seers of this day—millenniums after Isaiah wrote—see that they utter no heart-searching word that shall bring their hearers into the presence of the Holy One, for they still desire Him to be far away!

Is it not true? Is it not awfully, sadly true? Has there been any evolution or advance? And have you and I no part, nor interest, nor responsibility in it? Think, my dear brother or sister, think! There is the gravest danger in simply denouncing as if we were not connected at all with that faithless witness, and can congratulate ourselves on this superiority—it is fatally evil!

Could there be a truer word spoken of both forms of error that are oppressing us today than that they will take everything from us and give nothing? We are invited to give up our "treasure," all that we have on which to rest for time and eternity; and what do they give us in exchange? Can Rationalism, that takes from us His birth of a virgin, His literal, personal and physical resurrection from the dead, His coming again as He went, can Rationalism, I say, give us one single hope? It is only "Egypt" again; the "Rahab, Boaster who does nothing else." Nor is the other form of error any more able to *give*, although equally ready to *take*. Superstition, or Ritualism, is today the "seer" that gives only illusions that shall eventually make ashamed.

12: Therefore thus Israel's Holy One saith,
　　Because ye despise this word (I have spoken),
　　And trust in oppression—perverted self-will—
　　Making these to be your reliance,
13: Therefore shall this sin be to you
　　As when a wall lofty
　　First slowly out-bulges,
　　Then suddenly crashes
　　To ruin instanter!
14: The breaking shall be as the smash
　　Of a vessel made by the potter.
　　He smashes it all to small pieces;
　　Nor will he be hindered by pity;
　　Nor can there be found in the fragments,
　　A sherd to take fire from the hearth-stone
　　Or skim from the cistern the water!

No one is likely to feel very kindly to him who knocks away the one prop on which he is leaning; that always awakens resentment, as here. The mass of Jews will turn away with loathing from the word that rebukes their vain hope in the Gentile protector, whether he be symbolized by Assyria or Egypt. It is true that this puts them in fellowship with those who oppress their brethren—that matters not. Then the prophet will show them the value of their protector. You have seen a wall in which there was a horizontal breach; it is bending outward, slowly, slowly, till in one terrific crash down it comes. And, since it was only a poor thing made of mud and straw, so small are the fragments that one would search in vain for a piece large enough for the simplest service.

Do you, my reader, know of anything that awakens resentment like witnessing to those whose hopes for eternity are in a bloodless, Christless "religion," that it is a vain hope? Oh, the heart changes not. It was not the publican or harlot that "hated Him" (John 7: 7) because He thus witnessed against their evil deeds. It was the most religious men of that day. And we shall experience the same hatred in this, if we give a similar testimony. Yet would true care and love for them lead to any other? Are smooth things evidence of true charity? What parent knows not that the love that is always shown by an embrace is spurious, for ever are there times that demand rebuke, warning and stern destruction of false props.

Denounce murder, adultery, and theft, and who will not chime in with that denunciation?—if only to show how free they claim to be from such crimes that revolt the natural conscience. But denounce respectable "religion," which denies or ignores the need of the precious blood of the Lamb, that has in it no seeking of mercy and forgiveness with contrition, that makes membership of a "church" do duty for membership of Christ, and, as surely as this sweeps away all false confidence and baseless hopes, so surely is the word loathed, and he who speaks it hated. But while Egypt takes all and gives nothing, God gives the true in the place of the false, thus:

> 15: For thus saith Adonai Jehovah,
>     The Holy One of Isràel:
>     In returning and restfulness shall ye be saved;
>     In quiet and trustfulness shall ye find strength.
>     But this ye would not!
> 16: But ye said, No, for we'll flee upon horses—
>     Therefore (indeed) ye shall flee.
>     And, We will ride on the swift—
>     Then shall those who pursue you be swift.
> 17: A thousand shall flee at the threat of but one,
>     At the threat of but five shall ye all flee,
>     Till ye be left as a pine, alone on a mount-crag,
>     Like a lone flagstaff set on a hill.

If there has been no improvement in man's spiritual sickness, neither has there been any variation in God's remedy, and although it has since been expressed in clearer terms, yet it is essentially the same. Instead of departure *from*, a returning *to* God; instead of weary labor, rest; instead of perturbation of spirit, calm and peace; instead of quaking mistrust, confidence. But still, this is ever too humbling, and men "will not." Far more manly, virile, red-blooded is it to mount horse and away, swiftly escaping all danger, with no one to thank for it but ourselves!

They shall indeed in the truest sense of the word, *flee;* but those who pursue them shall be swifter. Nor will this flight be due to the overwhelming numbers of their enemies, for the promise to themselves, that "one should chase a thousand, and two put ten thousand to flight" (Deut. 32: 30), shall be reversed, and *they* shall be the fugitives from the few. Till, like one lone

pine on a mountain-top, all the world wonders at their being so
reduced, yet preserved.   But now our prophecy turns to a more
gracious strain.

No dispensational distinctions affect the heart of God; ever
swift is He to hear the cry of true penitence, ever does He run
to meet the returning prodigal seen afar, and only waits for the
first heart-confession to show the mercy sought:

18: Therefore will Jehovah wait,
    That He may be gracious to you;
    Therefore will He be raised up,*
    That He may have mercy on you:
    For a righteous God is Jah,
    Blessed all who wait on Him.
19: For in Zion dwells a people
    Having now their home in Salem.
    Never shalt thou weep again:
    Most gracious He'll be at the sound of thy prayer,
    As soon as He hears it, His answer is there!

20: And though the Lord feed you with bread of distress,
    And give you the water of sorrow to drink,
    Yet shall thy teachers be hidden no more;
    But thine eyes on thy teachers shall look.
21: Thine ears then shall list to a word that's behind thee,
    Which says to thee, This is the way, walk therein,
    When to the right or left ye are turning.
22: Then shall ye stain the beautiful cov'rings
    Of thine idols all graven of silver;
    And the adornments that are overlaying
    Those that are molten of gold:
    Thou wilt cast them away as a vile filthy thing,
    With a cry of: Away!   Get ye gone!†

Verse 18 is the pivot on which the spirit of prophecy turns
from threatenings to consolations that begin with a promise of a
settled home.   Babylon shall never be rebuilt (chap. 13); Nineveh may be a desolation (Zeph. 2); the city of the nations be

---

*The word is precisely as in chapter 52: 13, on which see notes.

†In the Hebrew there is but one short word, that, by its very
sound, expresses the four that I have used in the text: *"tzeh!"*

no city (chap. 25); yet the Jew shall have in Zion, even in Jerusalem, an everlasting dwelling.

In that millennial earth the metropolis shall surely be an earthly city; and although closely united with, yet not the *"heavenly"* Jerusalem that the Book of Revelation shows us as coming down from heaven. Israel shall take the place of the "wall" of the city, between it and the Gentiles, or nations.

It is this beautiful and everlasting city on earth that is here addressed. He waits that He may be gracious; that is both His desire and, in view of the Cross, His ability. But still He must wait till penitent faith in those atoning sufferings shall permit the righteous exercise of that grace. Then, in the next couplet, Jehovah must be exalted, or lifted up, that He may have mercy on His people. This has raised much discussion among commentators, but at least it is not unusual for the Lord's exaltation and man's salvation to be thus linked. In Ps. 108: 5, 6, we find an illustration of it. The power to have mercy is dependent on the being lifted up, and I can but see an indirect suggestion of that which lies at the base of all scriptural revelation. If the first lines speak of the essentials on the part of Israel (and of us all), repentance and faith; these speak of the divine prerequisite, that "lifting up" or *resurrection* of which we get a direct view in chap. 52: 13. There we see One, who a few hours before hung as a malefactor on a cross of shame, now exalted, raised, lifted up from the tomb, and in that resurrection lies the evidence of His power to have mercy. Then the last couplet of verse 18 gives the final reason for both the waiting and the lifting up, that "Jehovah is a righteous God," and can only act in righteousness, and that depends on faith on man's part and complete atonement on God's.

Israel's destiny, like ours, is to have a restful Home. Jerusalem shall be their rest from all their wanderings in alien lands, and there every token of divine love awaits them.

Jehovah then lets His people know that He has been neither ignorant of, nor indifferent to the sorrows through which they have passed. He has indeed fed them with the bread of affliction; but now that chastisement has done its work, their teachers shall no more be hidden. Up to that time He had been teaching them indeed, but in a veiled way, and by sorrows and adverse providences hard to understand. Thus, I take it, the "hidden teachers" *are* the bread and water of affliction. But from now on He will guide in a very different way, as in that book which "reveals" what this only hints, "The Lamb which is in the midst of the throne shall feed them, and shall lead them to living fountains of waters," so that at every branching of roads, they shall not be in the slightest perplexity, but shall hear a voice behind them plainly telling them which is the *right* way. Would that you and I, reader, walked so closely with the same Lord that, in those many perplexities as to which path to take, that constantly arise in life, we too might hear that gracious directing voice; for surely if "all the promises of God" are "yea" in Christ, this one, being of a spiritual character, must be included.

The genuineness of Israel's conversion is indicated in verse 22, what they had honored and loved, they now loathed, as once they had loathed the divine Word. Such a complete reversal of loves and hatreds always accompanies a divine work in the soul of fallen man, whether for the first or hundredth conversion.

The land of Palestine, now so barren, under the fertilizing rains that Jehovah shall send it, shall then support more than it ever did; while the very beasts that serve it by their labor shall be fed with choicest fodder, as thus told:

23: And then shall He give thee rain for thy seeding,*
    With which thou sowest the land;
    And bread for thine eating the land shall produce
    In full abundance and plenty.
24: Then shall the oxen, too, and young asses
    Serving the land, feed on provender clean,
    Winnowed by fan and by fork.
25: And then shall there be on every high mountain,
    And every hill that's exalted,
    Springs and fountains of waters,
    In the day when the slaughter is great,
    (In the day) of the falling of towers.

---

*Lit.*, "seed;" but the promise refers to the early rain of about our October, preparing the land for the seed.

26: And the moonlight shall be as the sunlight,
    And sevenfold bright shall the light of the sun be,
    As seven days' light (seen in one),
    In the day that Jehovah
    Binds the hurt of His people,
    And healeth the bruise of their wound.

For a people whose national promises and hopes are limited to this earth, their blessings must also be of the earth, and the only heavens that they know are those formed on the second day and garnished on the fourth. That earth and those heavens shall in that millennial day unite in expressing Jehovah's favor to His Israel. But I am not at all sure that we must take all that is here said of them as being necessarily literal, or conditions of life would have to be radically different from what now obtain. Were, for instance, our sun to shine with sevenfold intensity, we should not esteem that a true benefit; for it would render present life insupportable, and we should long for a return to its gracious modified radiance. Or were our moon literally to shine with all the brightness of the sun, we should soon esteem that a very doubtful blessing, and more likely mourn the loss of the drooping eyelid of night, and the chaste silvery beams that do not prevent, but aid, the needed sleep. These verses simply make a perfect picture of abundance below, and an increase of every gracious and beneficial effect of the heavenly luminaries, whilst Truth corresponding to the Light shall flood the scene.

But in the very midst of all this picture of peace and plenty, we have a few words that speak of quite a different condition; for this is to be "in the day of the great slaughter, and of the falling of towers." Israel's redemption by power is always thus linked with "the day of vengeance" on her enemies; when the "Lord goes forth and fights against those nations" that have captured Jerusalem, as Zech. 14; Rev. 14: 20; 19: 17-21, etc., and it is this that this crashing expresses.

27: Behold the Name: JEHOVAH!
    It cometh from afar;
    His lips are flecked with wrathful foam,
    His tongue like flame devouring!

28: His breath is like a stream o'erflowing,
Reaching half-way up the neck,
To sift the nations in a sieve
That shall reveal their vanity;
And be a bridle on the jaws
That leads the peoples all astray.

These two verses give Jehovah's indignant intervention for His poor Israel. Note He does not say that He Himself comes, but it is His *Name* that comes; for that Name, Jehovah, embodies in itself all that He is, in His relation to Israel. That Name, then, is, as it were, outraged by the condition of His people at their last gasp: such a condition for His redeemed contradicts His very Name, so now He will show that He is indeed Jehovah, the covenant-keeping, ever-living God of Israel.

What a contrast is the promised Presence with us in Matt. 18: 20, to that in which He here intervenes for Israel. Burning with anger He comes: lips, tongue, breath, aflame with awful indignation. His lips are flecked with foam, His tongue flashes as lightning, His very breathing is the snorting of irrepressible wrath. Then, in a change of figure, that breath becomes as a torrent of molten lava by which the people who are in its path are swept away, for it reaches half-way up the neck, the head alone appearing above it.

What is the purpose of Jehovah in this? It is "to sift the nations in the sieve of vanity." A sieve is used for separating between the chaff and the wheat, between the false and the true. Then there must be something at this crisis that must have just this effect; and to determine what this is, we must bring the light of other prophetic scriptures to bear. After the heavenly redeemed have been caught up out of this earth to be "forever with the Lord," Scripture tells of a time of testing that is "coming on all the earth, to try them that dwell on the earth" (Rev. 3: 10), and *that* test shall sever between the apostate mass and the God-fearing remnant of the Jews, between the goats and the sheep of the Gentiles. It is "the image of the Beast," that last expression of man's idolatry that shall be set up at Jerusalem at the direction of the other "wicked one," the "Beast from the *land,*" to represent, in the then metropolis of the religious earth, the imperial world-power, seen in its head, and called in Revelation "the Beast from the sea" (see Rev. 13).

But would such an idol-image be called "vanity?" One clear scripture will be enough to answer: "I have hated them that regard lying *vanities;* but I trust in Jehovah" (Ps. 31: 6); the contrast with the true God says that "vanities" are the false. That idol-image is the sieve that separates the true from the false, and with regard to the latter is "the bridle leading astray."

Could any illustration speak more clearly of that "strong delusion" so near at hand, by which the mass of men, religious men, in order to be "up-to-date," will "believe a lie." Perhaps it would be as well for us even now not to be over-anxious to be "up-to-date;" we may well be warned.

But how refreshing the contrast:

29:  To you shall be the song,
      As in the night of hallowed feasting,
      To you shall be the joy
      Of those who march with flutings,
      To go up to Jehovah's mount,
      The Rock of Israèl!

The foe may threaten, it shall not affect those whose mind is stayed on Jah: or on the Stone, tried, great and precious. These shall sing, as in the night of that feast, when the very remembrance of the delivery from Egypt led to the going to the House of God with a multitude that kept holiday, keeping joyful step with the sweet strains of music.

Now again, and for the last time, the prophecy turns to one of the great adversaries of the Jewish remnant, here termed "Asshur;" nor can the stroke that slew 185,000 in one night be anything more than a shadow of the final fulfilment of this prophecy. There was nothing, in that quiet single blow, in the silence of the night, to correspond with the terrific words here used; and this becomes more clear as the prophecy draws to a close:

30: Jehovah shall cause to be heard
    His voice ever majestic!
    Shall cause His arm to be seen
    In blows heavily falling,
    With snortings of His wrath
    The blaze of a fire devouring:
    The bursting of a cloud,
    Rain and hailstones outpouring.

31: For by Jehovah's voice,
    When with a rod He's smiting,
    Th' Assyrian shall be down-stricken.

32: At every stroke of the rod of doom,
    Jehovah shall cause to fall on him,
    'Twill be with the sound of timbrel and harp;
    With blows of an arm ever-swinging,
    Shall He do battle against him.

33: For Tophet hath long been ordained,
    For the king too hath been made ready:
    Deep and wide (hath He made it)*
    Its pile is of fire and much wood,
    Whilst, like a brimstone-stream,
    Jehovah's hot breath sets its flaming!

Let us bear in mind the warning of the Apostle Peter: "No prophecy of scripture is of its own interpretation," but needs for that interpretation to be justified, the accord of all other scriptures. Following that safe counsel here, we learn from Rev. 19 that when the Lord does intervene for Israel, He will cast the Beast and the False Prophet into the lake of fire. *Where, then, is "Asshur," if one of these be not he under another, yet fully justified, name?*

The joy of Israel (of course here confined to the faithful remnant) is in exact proportion to the terror of "Asshur." Every blow of Jehovah's rod has an accompaniment of timbrels and harps (ver. 32); whilst Jehovah beats time, as it were, to that music with swingings of His arm in battle-strokes against Asshur.

This brings us to the last verse, and a very solemn and important verse it is; nor can the least ray of divine light that it has pleased God in His mercy to give us as to the eternal condi-

---

*There are but two words in the Hebrew, "Depth!" "Width!" as exclamations of astonishment.

tion of our race—whether penitent, or impenitent—be without the most profound interest, and worthy of the most dependent consideration. It is holy, a solemn theme, and I dare not approach it without a prayer to be kept from a mistaken interpretation: will not my reader join me?

What then is meant by "Tophet?" It is first found in 2 Kings 23: 10. Josiah "defiled Tophet, which is in the valley of the sons of Hinnom, that no man might make his son or his daughter to pass through the fire to Molech."

As the "garden" was to Eden, as "Paradise" to the "Third Heaven," so Tophet to Gehenna. The first was planted *in* Eden, specifically for man's abode. The second, we are told, is *in* that highest heaven, and the present dwelling of the saints who have fallen asleep; thus, apart from further revealings, we should expect Tophet to be *in* Gehenna (as 2 Kings 23: 10 plainly tells us that it is), and prepared for some specific abode. Nor should we err in this expectation, for this word in 2 Kings tells us that Tophet, as it literally existed on the earth, was the scene of the most abominable idolatries, even to the sacrificing of little children as an offering to "Molech," the tribal deity of the Ammonites. But behind that Molech, 1 Cor. 10: 20 shows us another awful figure, the great enemy of our race, the very prince of demons, Satan. Thus the deep depression in the earth's surface in which Tophet was, becomes the dread symbol of the deepest depression in that Lake of Fire where "the worm dieth not and the fire is not quenched" (Mark 9).

As to the word *"Tophet,"* we find it elsewhere in just one place, Job 17: 6; and there it has been completely misunderstood by the translators of the Authorized Version, who render it "tabret," and thus alter the force of the verse entirely, reading it: "And aforetime I was as a tabret." The Revised gives the opposite, the correct, meaning: "And I became an open abhoring," and in the margin, "One on whose face they spit." It thus bears in it the sense of vomiting, or abhorring as the vilest of the vile. Thus the very word *"Tophet"* speaks that awful truth that what answers to this Tophet will contain only that which is so utterly abhorrent to God that He speaks of it as "vomit." But that is precisely the repellent figure that our Lord used in His letter to the Church in Laodicea, in which many of us recognize the professing Church of our very day: "I will spue thee out of My mouth." Could anything speak more strongly of utter abhorrence? It is the perfect parallel to "Tophet."

Mark another significant correspondence: this Tophet had been prepared "long ago"—a word that is strongly suggestive of what had taken place before the day of man altogether. Before man had come upon the scene, before he fell in disobedience and so came under the penalty of the first death, Tophet had been "prepared." But that inevitably suggests that there had been a prior fall—a prior sin in a pre-Adamite era; and this, the word of our Lord distinctly confirms: "Then shall He say to them on the left hand, Depart from Me, ye cursed, into everlasting fire, *prepared for the devil and his angels*" (Matt. 25: 41). Mark, that this fire is "prepared" for one direct purpose; and this very word "prepared" forbids that we conclude that it is literally the same as that element with which we are well acquainted, and that has its effect upon matter. But just as this literal fire has been prepared to affect matter, so that other fire has been prepared to affect *spirit;* the one being a perfect symbol of the other.

Further note in our scripture, it is "the breath of Jehovah" that sets on fire the pile in Tophet. Nor is the word for "breath" to be passed over without care. It is a word that speaks of *action,* what we call "breathing." As when deep emotion is aroused the breath comes quickly, and increases with the strength of the excitement, so here Jehovah's wrath has been stirred; His quick breathings express that wrath, and thus become the fire that kindles the flames of Tophet.

This, then, is the fire adapted to spirits such as are "the devil and his angels;" and which even now abides on all who "believe not the Son" (John 3: 36). Alas, as long as in the material body, how unconscious men are of that abiding wrath till awakened by the Spirit of God; but when man himself is stripped of all covering, and, a naked spirit, departs, then he shares in the uncovered condition of the devil and his angels, and as he has taken the same path of rebellion, he shares the same "fire."

Thus I conclude we have here in "Asshur" and "the king,"

the same two evil personages with whom other prophecies make us familiar. In Daniel 7 and 8 we see them under the figures of two "little horns," and in Revelation 13 as two "wild Beasts," one coming up from the "sea" and heading up the "violent" form of wickedness, and the other from the "land" and heading up the "corrupt" form of wickedness. In our prophecy, "Asshur," or the Assyrian, is the first, and "the king" is the second; and both come to the same doom, as Rev. 19: 20 assures us.

Some have taken the *anti* in the word Antichrist as meaning that whatever the true Christ was, the false will *not* be. Hence that he will *not* be a king. But that is altogether indefensible, for the preposition carries the idea of opposing, the false is opposed to the true Christ. But Satan's most effective way of opposing is ever, as it was in the day of "Jannes and Jambres," by imitation. Thus as our Lord was and is a true Prophet, Priest and King, so in quite a false way shall Antichrist be all these.

Although the word "Gehenna" is not in this form at all in the Old Testament, yet our consideration of the subject would be altogether incomplete did we not notice it: for it stands for that awe-inspiring Saxon word "hell." It is a compound word made up of *Geh,* meaning "valley," and *henna,* the Greek form of Hinnom, so that the whole word means "The valley of Hinnom," as it occurs in Josh. 15: 8, "The mountain that lieth before the valley of Hinnom" (*Gehinnom*).

The word used for "valley" is by no means the one used for a pleasant vale, watered by running brooks; but has in it the idea of stagnation, since there is no outlet. Thus it bears a close relation to that "Salt Sea" that affords another figure of the Lake of Fire, from which there is also no outlet.

As to the other part of the word *Hinnom,* it is, I believe, a part of the verb *noom,* "to sleep," and may be found in Ps. 76: 5, "The stouthearted are spoiled, they *have slept* their sleep." Here it speaks of that "sleep" from which there is no waking—it is death. The very word Gehenna thus suggests that awful Lake, which is the second death, as Rev. 20: 14 should read: "And death (that is, the first death) and hades were cast into the lake of fire. This is the second death, the lake of fire."

But all this, while quite literal in that millennial earth, is also a figure of all the moral filth and refuse which must be outside the universe of bliss: it could be nowhere else from its very nature. As with the human body, which, in rejecting all that is refuse, and that cannot be assimilated, "makes all meats clean" (Mark 7: 19), so, in the same way alone, can all be made eternally clean, for nothing that defiles can be in that eternal scene of bliss of which the millennial earth and the human body are shadows.

It is not a pleasant theme: yet do our holy Scriptures speak of it clearly and strongly, and we should greatly err did we avoid it. Nay, my beloved in Christ, let us not leave it without drawing one soul-stirring truth from it—that vile thing is what we, by nature, were! *That* vile, horrible, repellent, moral filth (thus figured by dung*), *that* is called SIN, is what our Lord, the Holy One of God, in His immeasurable love to us, was judicially made in God's sight, with all the awful consequences! Do you wonder at the holy shrinking of Gethsemane? Do you wonder at the agony that was shown by the sweat, as it were drops of blood? Would He have been the Holy One that He was, had He not shrunk with strong cries and tears from such a cup of suffering? Oh, beloved, add your stronger, sweeter praise to my too feeble song, and together let us repeat: "To Him that loved us, and washed us from our sins in His own blood, and hath made us kings and priests unto God and His Father; to Him be glory and dominion forever and ever. Amen."

---

*This word is never applied to any offering save those for sin or tresspass, Lev. 4: 11, etc.

CHAPTER THIRTY-ONE

The fifth woe.    A continuation of warning against false confidence.    A picture-parable.    Jehovah a "lion" and "bird."    Further clear proof as to the identity of the Assyrian.

SO deep-seated in every heart is the tendency to false confidence, that in this short chapter we have a strong reiteration of the warning with even a "woe" pronounced upon it.    Alas, it is inherent in everyone of us, and as long as that blood we have derived from our first father, Adam, flows in our veins, we each have the danger of that "woe" being on us, for we each have our "Egypt."    Dependence on this results, first, in evidencing that we know very little of our God as revealed in Christ, and then complete disappointment.    This really characterizes Christendom today.    To our statesmen, infantry and cavalry are tangible and practical, their power and effect can be estimated, but "God" is little more than a word, and those who place any confidence in an intangible word, are surely unpractical visionaries!    So speaks the confider in Egypt.

In our chapter, mark, it is not primarily against Egypt itself that this woe is pronounced, but against the Hebrews for depending on that "Egypt."    You will note too that the road to Egypt is always a "going *down*," a descent, a lowering of moral standing and dignity, for man's place of trust is the Heart of God as revealed in His beloved Son, and of course, to leave that must be a descent.    But we must also remember that no one can "believe in God" in that trustful way apart from the Lamb, as that excellent scholar in the school of God, Peter, tells us: "Who *by Him* do believe in God;" *i.e.*, apart from Christ as the Lamb of God, there can be no *nestling* faith in God.    But let us look at our chapter:

1: Woe unto them who to Egypt go down
   For help, on its horses relying;
   Putting in chariots all of their trust
   Because they see them so many;
   Confiding in horsemen because they are strong,
   But to Israel's Holy One look not,
   Nor do they seek for Jehovah.

2: But He too is wise, and evil doth bring,
   Nor will He His words ever take back.
   'Gainst the house of the wicked He will arise,
   'Gainst those who ill-workers are helping.
3: Egyptians, remember, are men and not God,
   Their horses are flesh and not spirit.
   The Hand of Jehovah shall still be outstretched;
   Then shall the vain helpers stumble;
   He that is helped also shall fall,
   And all of them perish together.
4: For thus hath Jehovah said unto me,
   As lion and young lion growleth,
   What time he's attacked when over his prey,
   By the crowd of the shepherds against him;
   He is not alarmed at the noise of their shouts,
   Nor will he give way to their numbers;
   So will Jehovah Tzebaoth come down
   To fight on the hill of Mount Zion.
5: As little birds fluttering over their nests,
   So will Jehovah Tzebaoth
   Hover o'er Salem, protect with His wing;
   Protecting, He will deliver;
   Passing over He'll make her quite free.
6: Oh, turn ye to Him 'against whom ye've rebelled,
   O ye sons of Isràel!
7: For in that day each man shall abhor
   His idols of gold and of silver;
   The sin which your own hands have made you.
8: Then Asshur shall fall pierced by the sword,
   But not by the sword of a noble,
   Nor shall the sword of a base man devour,
   Yet from a sword shall he hasten,
   His choicest young men shall pay tribute.
9: His rock in sheer terror shall hasten in flight,*
   His chiefs be alarmed at the standard.
   'Tis Jehovah's own saying—He speaketh thus,
   Whose fire is a-kindled in Zion,
   Whose furnace is burning in Salem.

Valuable indeed are all these Old Testament prophecies even
in throwing light on the symbols of our book of Revelation. In
the fifth trumpet the locusts that came out of the smoke from
the bottomless pit were in shape as horses, while in the following

---

*See Job 30: 15; here, *lit.*, "shall pass."

trumpet we see a host of horses (Rev. 9: 7, 16). Beyond all controversy, in the Old Testament these "horses" speak clearly of a
false confidence, as in Psalm 20: 7. Why then should not the.
same figure tell the same story and be so interpreted in the prophetic book of symbols in the New? "Some trust in chariots and
some in horses," will be the bold cry of the Remnant of Israel
in a day near at hand, "but we will remember the name of the
Lord our God" (Ps. 20: 7).

Note the strong irony in the first line of verse 2. Jehovah
says that He too is not altogether without wisdom, nor fears comparison with Egypt. Thus He will be against both the helped
and the helpers, or both the apostate mass of false profession,
and that in which they trust; or specifically against "False
Prophet" as well as "Beast," for there is an alliance between
them, and the former honors the latter as the god of forces (Dan.
11: 38). This throws light on ver. 4, where we have a parabolic
picture. We see a young lion growling over its prey;* a company of shepherds are approaching with the evident purpose of
taking away his food. Neither their numbers nor noise affright
him, and in this picture Jehovah places Himself. The scene is
perfectly clear, but the application can hardly be so called. Let
us then go on the safe principle of discerning what is certain,
and then make anything as to which there may be a question to
conform to this. First, there can be no question as to its being
a *parable,* and as such we must be careful not to stretch it beyond
its intent, which may lie in one single feature, and to go further
than that may lead to serious mistake. It would next appear
equally sure that the fearless lion pictures Jehovah Himself, who
has "come down" to contend with some foe. These two points,
the parable and the identity of the fearless lion, are, I believe,
the certainties. Then the question comes up: Against whom
does Jehovah fight? Never against faith, never against the penitent remnant of His people, but here against "the helpers and the
helped" of ver. 3, in whom we can discern the allied forces made
up of Gentiles and apostate Jews, against whom the Lord "comes
down," as in Zech. 14: 2, and whose numbers and noise no more

---

*The word usually rendered "prey" is at times simply "food,"
as in Prov. 31: 15; Mal. 3: 10, and so here.

affect Him than, in the parable, they do the lion. This is in full accord with other scriptures and with the following context.

If the figure of Jehovah as a young lion is suitable in view of Jerusalem's foes, that of a bird guarding her nest with fluttering wings suits His action toward the beloved city. This contrast of stern strength with tender gentleness is very lovely. The mothering bird gives a beautiful figure of tender solicitude, and raises the question whether, since it is precisely the word used for "passover," we ought not to understand *that* word to refer to Jehovah Himself sheltering with His wing every house on which He saw the blood; for thus our Lord Christ becomes "our passover." He is both the Defender *and* the Lamb. How impossible to express all His atoning work by one figure. By His own *Blood* He is set forth as *Mercy-Seat*—by His death as the Paschal Lamb He passes over in protecting love and righteousness.

We listen to a call so tender and appealing in verse 6 that we hear it as the oft-echoed appeal of God to His poor creature man, and not to Israel only. Now, incontestably our Lord Jesus proves Himself to be the very Jehovah of old, when He too cries, "Come unto Me, all ye that labor and are heavy laden, and I will give you rest," but there is no note of reproach, or even reminder of our wandering, as here. A weary spirit and a burdened conscience are all that is needed. But the gracious call shall be heard, and that Remnant of faith shall penitently "turn to the Lord." Then, when Moses is read, with no veil of unbelief over their hearts, they, too, shall see Him whom you and I have been refreshed by seeing, even Christ, in all that Moses wrote, in every lamb slain, in every clean beast offered. Then they shall so turn that they shall actually loathe what once may have been their confidence; and it is this that the holy Scriptures hold out to us too, as the revival that we should look for and expect in this very day, a deepening self-judgment and repentance, and the humbling ourselves under His chastening hand, whilst we confess how profoundly we too have sinned as the present witness for Him on the earth, and how far we have revolted or wandered.

But now once again in verses 8 and 9 the prophecy turns to Asshur. He shall fall by a sword in no human hand, be it noble or base. That sword shall proceed out of the mouth of Him whom we see in Rev. 19 coming on the white horse; or, in another figure, it is the breath of His mouth, whereby He destroys the wicked one.

Jehovah's indignation against His people Israel closes with the destruction of the Assyrian—that is sure—for so we have seen in chap. 10: 25: "For yet a very little while, and the indignation shall cease in their destruction." Note carefully the plural word "*their*." If only one person were in view, the Assyrian, what need of a plural word? But if the reference is to both the "Beast" (Assyrian) and "False Prophet" (or, King of the north), in alliance against the remnant, this would be accounted for.

Let us then *assume*, for the sake of argument, that the "Assyrian" is quite distinct from the Gentile opponent of the remnant of Israel, called in the New Testament "the Beast," and is an *Eastern* enemy, as many teach. Let us next ask, Is he destroyed *before* the Beast and False Prophet, or after? If before, and he no longer exists on earth, then it follows that both the Beast and False Prophet continue to prosper in their antagonism to Israel *after* the divine indignation against Israel has ceased (chap. 10: 25). That is, the great tribulation and God's hand being stretched out still, goes on *after* the "indignation" has ceased in the previous destruction of the Assyrian! That surely is self-refuting. The destruction of the Assyrian therefore cannot possibly occur *before* that of the Beast and False Prophet.

On the other hand, if the Assyrian is only destroyed *after* the Beast and False Prophet have come to their end, that would necessitate the divine indignation continuing (for it only ceases with the Assyrian's destruction) after the Lord Jesus has appeared for the deliverance of His people and the destruction of their enemies, the Beast and False Prophet—the divine indignation continuing after the divine deliverance! That surely is equally impossible. Recognize that the Assyrian *is* the "Beast from the sea" of the Gentiles, and all difficulty disappears; and when that one Imperial world-power meets its end in its head—the Beast—the indignation against poor Israel ceases forever.

The "rock" in verse 9 is the Assyrian, or the head of the world-power, the Beast, who has been looked upon as a rock by the apostate mass of the Jews. "Look at your *rock*," says the Holy

Spirit; "he is in flight—a poor rock!" His princes that have been confederated with him, and in whom we may discern the "ten horns" of the Beast (Dan. 7: 24; Rev. 17: 16), share his terror and his attempt to escape. But of what are they in such fear? It is of the "ensign." Chapter 11 of our prophet will be enough to tell us who is thus symbolized. It is Messiah! It is Christ whose Feet are now again on Olivet. Well may even the victorious besiegers of Jerusalem flee!

The chapter closes with the assurance that it is Jehovah who speaks; and therefore, quite irrespective of apparent delay in fulfilment, that fulfilment is sure. He has taken His place in Zion with burning wrath against her foes; in Jerusalem, as a furnace, hot against her conquerors.

# CHAPTER THIRTY-TWO

**The King shall take His Throne. The consequences of that day of revelation. Democracy not the last form of human government. The preceding distresses. The precise correspondence between the land and its people; both today in desolation. The limit. Is there any basis for the Pentecostal Movement in this outpouring of the Spirit?**

THE three clear divisions in this chapter are:

    1: Verses 1-8: The King reigns.
    2: Verses 9-14: The desolations that must precede
                   that reign.
    3: Verses 15-20: The latter rain on Israel.

We must not allow the artificial division of the prophecy into chapters to sever the connection of this with what has preceded it. There has been an awe-inspiring interposition of Jehovah on the part of Israel. Her Messiah has appeared as a Lion against her foes, as a bird fluttering over her nest toward the beloved city. The world-power of that day, called "the Assyrian," and by the apostates esteemed to be a "rock," has disappeared, as Revelation 19 tells us (although there the same world-power is called "the Beast from the sea"), in the most awful doom, and the princes of the Assyrian have been terrified. Now *his* place is taken by another King, and *theirs* by other princes.

How widespread is the conviction throughout Christendom, that Democracy is to be the final form of earth's government. President Lincoln's speech on the field of Gettysburg has given a world-accepted expression to the conviction that "government of the people, by the people, for the people, shall never perish from the face of the earth." It is a clear, evident and serious mistake, leading Christendom to an utterly false outlook. We say nothing as to whether it may not be the best practicable form under present conditions—that is outside the Christian's province. Monarchy, absolute in the first case, and then by ever-increasing constitutional limitations, modified in its powers, has been tried

and found woefully wanting.  Is that failure due to a defect in
the form, or to its being in the first man's feeble hands?  Scripture is perfectly clear in its answer.  We are living in a day in
which that last form to be tested, Democracy, is having its trial.
It is doomed to speedy and terrible failure, and from the same
cause as previous ones.  Man, as a race, is still in rebellion
against God; and as long as that is the case, whether the government be in the hand of the one or the many, the outcome will be
inevitably the same.  No great powers of discernment are needed
to foresee the terrific cataclysm that shall evidence sooner or
later that complete and final failure, to be followed by a brief
restoration of a tyranny that shall be the outcome of the Devil's
final banishment from the heavenlies and temporary confinement
to this earth.  Fierce indeed will his wrath then be against every
individual composing that witness symbolized by "the two olive
trees and the two lampstands standing before the God of the
earth" (Rev. 11: 4).  He claims the earth as his—*he* is its king,
*he* is its god, and *he* will extinguish all rivalry!  But his usurpation is short for,

> 1: Behold, a King shall in righteousness reign,
> And princes shall rule in just judgment.
> 2: A man as a shelter from storm-blast shall be,
> A shelter that hides from the tempest;
> As water-brooks flowing through a dry land,
> Or as a mighty rock's shadow,
> Cast o'er a land that's heat-weary.

The "Assyrian" has fallen; nor has it been the hand of any
man that has thus brought him to his end.  God has done it.
Shall that same One leave the throne of the earth thus vacant?
Far from it; He will set upon that Throne the One to whom it
justly belongs.  It is His by every claim of righteousness, and
in righteousness shall He carry out its government.  The King is
on His own throne at last!  The King, so long expected, so long
sighed for, is here; and when He takes the sceptre in His Hand,
judgment at last returns to the righteousness (Ps. 94: 15) from
which it has so long been divorced.  The rod, which out of its
owner's hand became a serpent (Satanic), again assumes its normal form when its rightful owner re-takes it (Exod. 4).  As to

the identity of the King there can be no question; nor do I think
that we err in seeing in these "princes," those twelve who
are to sit on twelve thrones judging the twelve tribes of Israel
(Matt. 19: 28).   To whom could the lovely figures of verse 2
apply but to One!   We instinctively feel that such figures of salvation, in its various gracious forms, could not be attributed to
any lesser personality than our Lord Himself.   Who but He
could shelter from the storm-blasts that sweep over our lives
here?   Who but He in this dry and thirsty land could give refreshing waters to the weary?—as He once did to our poor fellow-
sinner at Sychar's well, and as He has since done to myriads,
ourselves amongst them.   Who but He could afford as grateful a
shade from trouble as a huge "Rock" through which no scorching rays could penetrate?   None but our risen, living Lord could
ever answer to those lovely figures.   I am well assured that every
Christian heart will say, "That is true!"   Our keen delight in
the prospect is not lessened that "a *Man* shall be" all this, thus
forcing us to remember, "For unto *angels* hath He not put in
subjection the age to come."   Is it not infinitely good, fellow-
believer, that we know Him even now as ours?   May we grow in
that knowledge.

3: The eyes of the seers shall no more be dim;
   The ears of the hearers shall hearken,
4: The heart of the hasty shall ponder and know,
   The tongue of the stammerers, loosened,
   Shall speak with ease and refinement.*
5: The fool shall no longer be counted a lord,
   The churl shall not be called gentle.
6: For the fool shall proclaim his folly in speech,
   His heart shall still work at its evil,
   To practice indeed all impious work,
   Speak error regarding Jehovah;
   Thus leaving the soul of the hungry all void,
   Withholding the drink from the thirsty.
7: Craft is the tool that the crafty will use,
   Devising his wicked devices,
   By which to destroy the poor by his lies,
   E'en when the meek speaks but justice.

---

*"Refinement," *lit.*, "clear" (as chap. 18: 4), and, as applied to
speech, both intelligible and refined.

8: But the true noble man will noble things plan,
   And, noble, will cleave to them closely.


Here we have a picture of the day of revelation, as we may
term it. All the veneer that covers the ugly deformities of modern society is removed and everything is "out" and revealed at
its true worth, for it is the hour in which the beloved remnant of
Israel has turned to the Lord, and no longer is there a veil over
their hearts. Truth shall in that day permeate the whole social
fabric—everything shall be as it appears. What a change that
involves! But if all is exposed, another word from our prophet
will come into activity, and "the sinner" though "being a hundred years old shall be accursed" (chap. 60: 20).

One of the difficulties in these verses is their apparent tameness; in some cases they appear to be the veriest platitudes, little
in accord with the fiery style of Isaiah; for if anything is foreign
to him it is tameness. To tell us that "the craft of a crafty man
is evil," as Delitzsch renders verse 7, would appear hardly necessary or worthy of any, let alone an inspired, writer. The key to
all lies in "the King" being revealed, and as *He* is thus revealed,
so is everything in His kingdom exposed in its true colors. Those
eyes that were in the prophet's commission to be closed (chap.
6), shall then discern that truth to which they have been so long
dark, that "God was in Christ," and that Christ was and is to be
found only in Jesus of Nazareth. "He that hath ears to hear" shall
then hear a Voice never heard by the impenitent and unbelieving;
whilst, thus hearing, the lips no longer stammer with uncertainty,
but pour out from that fulness of heart true eloquence, the outcome of simplicity, sincerity and deep conviction.

The "rash" or "hasty," of verse 4, are those who think it
waste of time to meditate, ponder, consider; but rush to conclusions justified only by their ignorance, prejudice and conceit.
In that day even these shall "consider," and as by a divine law,
this leads to true intelligence as our apostle's counsel to Timothy:
"*Consider* these things, and the Lord shall give thee *understanding* in all things" (2 Tim. 2: 7).

The accident of mere social position shall then no longer com-

mand deference; so that one who is but a fool,* if born in that
position, is called what he is not, noble, for many a present-day
nobleman is anything but a noble man. No longer shall wealth,
whether inherited or acquired (too often by the shadiest meth-
ods), be able to purchase honors, but everything then shall be
seen to be exactly what it is.

Verses 7 and 8 in sharp contrast throw their light on one
another. The earlier one deals with the man who is termed a
"success" in this world, for he attains his end, although by very
evil means. But what does that matter? He has, it is true,
crushed the poor who stood in his way, but he has attained to the
wealth that has been his magnet; now the ruin of those poorer
rivals is forgotten, and by the very wealth that he has thus obtained he is able to purchase the name of "philanthropist" or
"noble."

By a subtle change of ideas this spurious noble becomes a
symbol of the one in another sphere, who would also rob the
*spiritually* poor of truth, and bring *him* to ruin by speaking falsely against the Lord, denying His essential deity, or the value of
His blood, and in so doing take away true food from the hungry,
and true refreshment from those perishing with thirst. Have we
not seen all this in our day?

In that happy day the "noble" man will be truly that, and as
regenerate will be ever devising noble, unselfish deeds, in accord
with his divine begetting. Nor will he stay with planning, but
will carry those plans into effect, as a poet has expressed it, will
"do noble deeds, not dream them all day long."

The foreview of the King and His kingdom is finished at
verse 8. With verse 9 we are taken back chronologically to the
sorrows that precede that scene, and even while the joyous notes
of an earth at peace under the sceptre of its true King are linger-
ing in our ears, we hear a very different note, even such a solemn
swell telling still of judgment that it appears to overcome the
sweet music that has just refreshed us.

───────

*The word "fool" does not here predicate the lack of mental
powers, but a misuse of them, as in in 1 Cor. 15: 36.

9: Rise up, ye women who are at your ease,
   To my voice give careful attention;
   Ye daughters who're living without any care,
   To my speech attentively hearken:
10: In a year and few days shall ye troubled be,
   Ye women carelessly living;
   For the fruit of the vine shall utterly fail,
   The harvest shall too come to nothing.
11: Tremble, ye women that are at your ease,
   Quake, ye falsely confiding,
   Strip ye, and make ye all naked and bare,
   Your loins with sackcloth be girded;
12: Be mourners, in sorrow beating the breasts,
   Lamenting the fields once delightful,
   Lamenting the choice vine so fruitful.
13: On the land of My people thorns, briers, shall grow,
   E'en the houses of merriment cov'ring,
   In all of the jubilant city!
14: Emptied the palace!   Silent the noise
   Of the city, once filled with its tumult!
   Its forts and its towers forever are dens,
   The wild-asses' joy and flocks' pasture.
15: Until that upon us the Spirit be poured
   From on high, and the desert be changèd,
   Becoming a field all covered with fruit,
   And the now fruitful field counted forest.
16: Then in the desert shall judgment abide,
   And righteousness dwell in the garden,
17: The outcome of righteousness then shall be peace,
   With rest and assurance forever!
18: My people shall dwell in a dwelling of peace,
   Their very abode shall be safety,
   Their resting-place never disturbèd.
19: But hail is outpoured—the forest falls down,
   And brought very low is the city.
20: Blessed are ye who by all waters sow,
   Whose ox and whose ass roam in freedom.

The women are here addressed because of the peculiar sensitiveness of the feminine temperament, quick to catch the first sight of coming danger and to take alarm. Even these see no cause for anything but confidence and pleasure. Soon they shall be mourning for the lack of all those bountiful supplies that nature gives from her breasts, which are here found in the fertile field and the fruitful vine. Desolation shall take the place of the abundance that marked the land of Israel, for the condition of that land must always be in accord with the condition of its people. Desolate still is the nation and desolate still is the land. But there is a limit, as we shall see.

Verse 15 tells of the limit to that desolation, and that shows there is also a limit to Israel's scattering. As the Land flourished under a twofold blessing of rain, the early and the latter, so there shall be a corresponding twofold pouring-out of the Holy Spirit upon its people. The first, or the early, rain fell at Pentecost. This had a double character, being first a sample of what Joel had foretold, and Peter so used it in his address that day, saying, "This is that which hath been spoken by the prophet Joel." It portended "the great and notable day of the Lord," with but one way of escape from its wrath, the "calling on the Name of the Lord" (Acts 2: 16-21). That "early rain" at Pentecost resulted in 3,000 souls turning to the Lord, but the representatives of the nation were far from so doing, and so "wrath has come upon them to the uttermost" (1 Thess. 2: 16). This still awaits its climax when they have returned to the land; it shall cease with the outpouring of the Spirit as the "latter rain." During that long time the land is as desolate as its people.

Poor Israel awaits that "latter rain," they alone are its object. God, the Holy Spirit, came to this earth at Pentecost, nor has He ever returned to the Heaven whence He came, nor will He return till, the mystic Body of Christ completed by its last member, He no longer shall hinder the heading up of wickedness, but go with all the heavenly redeemed to the Heaven whence He came. There *can* therefore be no second effusion during this dispensation, for He is already here. Thus, if this be justified, then what is termed the Pentecostal Movement can only be a delusion, nor is it needful to specify its true author. The Spirit cannot be poured out from on high as long as He is here. He cannot be poured out on Israel whilst they are scattered. When Israel is restored to her land, and her remnant to her Jehovah, then shall there be a second effusion of the Spirit as here told, and the land shall bloom in accord with it: "The barren shall become the beautiful, and the beautiful the majestic" (*Birks*).

I cannot leave this subject of the condition of their land ever changing to accord with that of its people, without enjoying its application to ourselves. What is our Land? What is our Inheritance? It is Christ and His unsearchable riches! Does the condition of that Land of ours ever change? Is His condition as variable as was that of Canaan? Far from it. It varies not one shade. The sun of God's smile is ever upon it and the very poorest and feeblest of us—aye, even the chief of sinners—are, as in that dear Land, accepted without the slightest variation forever. Does not Scripture assure us that we are "accepted in the Beloved?" Our *state*, alas, varies constantly and greatly, but look above, and in His unchanging acceptance see with unspeakable joy that since there is no variation in that of our Lord, so is there none with ours. This is the second result of that first—that early rain. It was the birthday of that greatest of all marvels, that hidden mystery, *the Church.*

In verses 16 and 17 we have another feature of beauty to be seen in the cross. *There* was the full expression of inflexible righteousness. *There* on our Lord fell the full penalty of our guilt, and "righteousness" was seen in its perfection in the sufferings He voluntarily bore. But for such service shall "righteousness" have no reward? Surely it shall. Who shall enjoy that reward? *The very people whose many sins He bore!* And what is that reward that they enjoy? Peace and assured rest forever (verses 18, 19).

The last verse is so constantly used of the sowing of the word of the gospel, that it is difficult to admit any other thought. Yet Isaiah's Jewish readers would understand a sowing in the land, as literal as the land itself in which the literal sowing would take place. What in that day will be material in accord with the character of that age, is spiritual today, in accord with the spiritual character of this; but we must not deny the direct and primary application to Israel. Their land shall "laugh with abundance," and careless shall they be as to their asses or oxen straying into cultivated fields; the extreme fertility of the well-watered land shall take away all such care. O happy earth with such a King! O wretched earth without Him!

# CHAPTER THIRTY-THREE

**The sixth woe. Spoiler and crafty are not the same individual. The kings of the four points of the compass. The weeping ambassadors. The broken covenant. Jehovah takes the place of a broad river.**

THIS brings us to the sixth and last "woe," which, being directed against some power hostile to the Remnant of Israel, is virtually the redemption of that Remnant, and the very "woe" being thus directed, includes many strains of joy which swell in volume till they reach the complete triumph of chapter 35. The first main division of the book thus closes with the note with which all God's ways with penitent man end—with perfect blessing!

Here we have again the "Salvation of Jehovah," or, as we may say in very truth, the one word "Isaiah," and the three chapters, 33, 34, 35, give precisely the characteristic divisions thus:

Chapter 33: The woe coming on the foes in the land.
Chapter 34: Extending to the whole earth.
Chapter 35: Its full effect in millennial blessing.

The first verse of chapter 33 stands by itself, as majestic a pronouncement of woes as by the same Speaker in Matthew 23:

1: Woe to thee, spoiler, for thou wast not spoiled!
   Woe to thee, crafty,* for none did deceive* thee!
   Ceasing to spoil, then thou shalt be spoiled!
   Ending deceit, thou shalt be deceived!

Commentators have seen in this verse, with practical unanimity, a reference to Sennacherib, his raid into Judah in Hezekiah's fourteenth year, and Jehovah's intervention. But whilst this gives the substratum, it will assuredly not account for the way the prophecy continues; and still less for its final outcome, as can be easily seen from chapter 35—that has never yet been ful-

---

*The word rendered in A. V. "deal treacherously" is primarily "to cover," hence, to "act covertly." If one individual be addressed, he is distinguished by both rapacity and craft; if two, then these two are thus distinguished from each other.

filled. The definitive final fulfilment of the prophecy is necessarily future; and we must discern, if possible, who shall then be addressed as "spoiler" and "crafty." But the question at once comes up: is it one person here? Are the "spoiler" and the "crafty" one individual? Or, is it possible that, while these evil qualities may have been united in Sennacherib of old, they may still characterize two distinct individuals in the future? Naturally we are inclined to refuse this at once, and assume that the whole verse is addressed to one and the same individual.

But the godly remnant of Israel shall have *two* enemies in that last terrible day called the Great Tribulation: the one external, and head of the revived world-empire, the man of violence, or the "spoiler;" the other, internal, coming up from the nation, who gains his ends by *craft*, as Daniel 8: 25 tells us. So our chapter must be considered as a whole before we can decide as to this.

That the "Assyrian" of the future must take the place of Sennacherib of the past is sure, and therefore we are quite safe in asking, Where is he to be found? As we have seen, Assyria simply stands for whatever power may be in that same place of political authority in the future and which inherits, with that place, the responsibilities and threatenings directed against it in the far-seeing eye of divine prophecy.

That this Assyrian "spoiler" is to be found in the "Gog" of Ezekiel 38 is more than questionable. In the first place Gog is never called the "Assyrian"—that is assumed—but he is plainly termed "Prince of Rosh" (R. V.), or Russia; nor, whilst the motive of powerful military chiefs is always to "spoil," Gog seems to have no success whatever in Ezekiel, as this one has here. Again, Gog comes up against "the land of unwalled villages;" that does not harmonize at all with the clear prophecy of a future successful siege of Jerusalem immediately preceding the revelation and millennial reign of our Lord, up to which these three chapters directly lead. We may be fully assured that Gog comes upon the scene long after this Spoiler, and therefore the Spoiler being the Assyrian, Gog is *not*.

This may possibly turn us from following a wrong clue, but does not necessarily give us a right one. Let us then go a step further and seek for that.

If our consideration of this book has done nothing else, it has shown us Jehovah's profound interest in His earthly people Israel, an interest that goes down to the very end, and does not leave them until they are, as a nation, fully restored to His forgiving favor. Jerusalem becomes the very centre of His dealings, and that is especially the case in the final few years. Let us then in thought transport ourselves to that city, and thus throwing ourselves forward to those last days, we hear of a foe at every point of the compass. There is a "King of the South," in whom we have no difficulty in discerning Egypt, but in the light of Daniel 11: 40-43, we note that he becomes of comparatively little importance after his utter defeat by the "King of the North." Further explanation would take me too far from Isaiah. It must suffice to say that Daniel 11: 40 reads: "And at the time of the end shall the King of the South push at him." At whom? Who but the same one who has been the object of every "pushing" of the southern king all through the chapter, *i.e.*, "the King of the North." It is as inadmissible as it is unnecessary to drag in here, as many do, a king of whom nothing whatever has been said. "And the King of the North shall come against him" (that is, not against this mythical third king, but against his old opponent, the King of the South) "like a whirlwind." They do not push at an unknown third, but at each other.

Turning from the south to the west, we find a mighty empire, inclusive of all that is now termed Christendom, inclusive of the Americas. With this western power the mass of the Jews are in alliance, but the remnant is not. That accounts for two points of the compass, south and west. Going to the opposite quarter, the east, we have already considered Gog, who is found there. Thus we have accounted for three out of the four cardinal points of the compass, leaving the quarter of ominous darkness, the north, still open to some prominent personage. Where shall we find him?

There is one who takes up a very large place in those terrible closing days of this era; and, for a time at least, he even forms a link with the apostasy from Christianity, as in 2 Thess. 2: 3, where he is called "the son of perdition," but in Revelation bears the title of "False Prophet," and, as being a Jew, the "Beast from the land." He is *the* Antichrist, and as such makes his claim to all the offices belonging to the true Christ, of Prophet, Priest and King. It is he who at the head of the large majority of the returned Jews—the mass—leads them to ally with the mighty power to the West.

We have then a vacant space, the North, unfilled, and there is no one sufficiently prominent in evil to fill it but this man of many evil titles, whose pre-eminent name is the Antichrist. So, as with our illustration of a modern picture-puzzle, we ask, Will this, the only piece that we have remaining, fit into the space that is left, for our piece is a "prophet," whilst the space demands a "king?" Can one person be both prophet and king? Beyond a question he can, for as the true Messiah is both Prophet and King, so will the false Messiah make a claim to be both—he will be both "King of the North" and the False Prophet.

As a strong confirmation of this, I note that the inspired writer of the Epistle to the Hebrews does not hesitate to use an incident in chapter 11: 35 that is only recorded in the apocryphal 2 Maccabees, chapter 7, which justifies our making use of the same authority, and find in Antiochus Epiphanes a striking prototype of the future Antichrist. He was then the "King of the North," and "aided by the apostate Jews" he set up "an abomination of desolation"—a statue of Jupiter—in the Holy Place, to which he compelled worship. Were it not for the Lord's words in Matt. 24, one might easily assume that this Epiphanes had fulfilled all that could be expected from any extreme hater of the truth of Jehovah. But it would seem inexplicable that we should not make use of him and these his acts, at least, in finding the final future Antichrist in the *"King of the North"* of the future, for he would thus fill the last point of the compass, the north!

Turning back to our chapter, we have then, in the "spoiler" and the "crafty" of the first verse, the two allied leaders found at the end in Satanic antagonism to Jerusalem (Zech. 14) and to the Lamb (Rev. 19); the second filling perfectly the space left vacant for him in the north quarter—both King of the North, Antichrist, False Prophet and other titles that express his pre-eminence in crafty religious wickedness.

2: Jehovah, be gracious; for Thee have we waited.
   Be a strong arm for them morning by morning;
   Yea, our salvation in time of sore trouble.
3: At the noise of the tumult the peoples do flee:
   At Thine uprising the nations are scattered.
4: Your spoil shall be gathered as when caterpillars
   Do make a clean riddance:
   As the leaping of locusts they leap (on their prey).
5: Jehovah's exalted, for, dwelling on high,
   Zion He filleth with judgment and justice.
6: By wisdom and knowledge thy times are made stable,
   (And these shall be to thee) the wealth of salvation:
   The fear of Jehovah's the treasure (of Judah).

This little section records the pleading of Israel's remnant, voiced by the prophet; but behind him, by the Spirit of Christ Himself, who identifies Himself with this oppressed people. It is He who says, "Be Thou a strong arm for *them*," etc. It is for Jehovah, and for Jehovah alone, that they have waited. If *He* should refuse to hear, then they will turn nowhere else. If *He* leaves them, then they will be left—they will have no other salvation.

Morning by morning the danger may threaten; then morning by morning Jehovah must be the strength of His people in the renewed conflict. Is that not vitally true today, only substituting God in Christ, for Israel's Jehovah?

Through all dispensations the new nature is ever Godward in its confidences and hopes, and we may well thus learn this way of beginning every day, and so doing we, too, shall find that, "His compassions fail not; they, also, are new every morning." "Oh, be *our* arm," let us cry, "this morning, for we too will expect help from no other or inferior source!"

Verse 3 anticipates the answer. Jehovah rises, and with a terrifying commotion, as the sound of many waters, strikes fear to the hearts of the hostile nations, and they scatter in flight. At once the tables are turned; the spoilers become spoiled. With the thoroughness of a host of caterpillars, that soon strip bushes of every leaf, and with the quickness of the locusts, those who were but just now captives and spoiled, spring on the spoil of their foes.

Verses 5 and 6 show there is a moral change in Israel now. No longer does even the Jew count material prosperity to be his real wealth, for it is Jehovah dwelling in Zion—the Holy of holies again anointed, as Daniel 9: 24 speaks—who has filled that ancient city with judgment and justice which make her times stable at last, after all the viccissitudes of the ages; and she has learned that the fear of the Lord is her true wealth.

In accord with the characteristic of prophecy, which ever goes swiftly to the end, and then returns to take up some special thread, the prophet goes back to the stress of his people, before the deliverance he has just foreseen.  The past history affords a pattern, which must, if we would profit by it, be used *as* a pattern, and not the end and substance of the prophecy.  Hezekiah had sent ambassadors to the threatening Assyrian who put him under a fine of 300 talents of gold.  This the king raised with difficulty, impoverishing the Lord's house, even to cutting off the gold from the doors and pillars.  Notwithstanding this, Sennacherib did not retire, but treacherously sent his generals to assault the cities of Judah, and the effect of this breach of faith is now told:

7: Listen, O list, for their heroes are crying:
   Those who were sent on an errand of peace
   Are bitterly weeping!
8: The highways are desolate: no trav'ler passes!
   He hath broken the covenant!
   He hath made light of cities!
   He hath counted frail men* as nothing of worth!
9: The land is all mourning, and sadly doth languish!
   Lebanon stands all parched in its shame!
   Sharon is now as the desert all barren!
   Bashan and Carmel both shake off their leaves!

10: Now will I rise! saith Jehovah:
    Now will I lift Myself up!
    Now will be highly exalted!
11: Ye are pregnant with chaff, shall give birth to stubble!
    Your own breath of anger, the fire that shall eat you.

---

*Heb., *Enosh*: frail, mortal man.

12: And the peoples shall be as lime-burnings,
   As brambles cut down they are kindled in fire.

In verse 7 we hear the wails of the ambassadors returning from their unsuccessful mission to Sennacherib, who, in spite of the "covenant" that he had made, takes the gold, but continues his march on Jerusalem, capturing city after city on the way, and making very little of human life. What wonder that the highways become desolate without a passenger! The very land itself reflects the misery of its inhabitants; the cedars of Lebanon droop as if weeping; the flowers of Sharon wither in shame, and the falling leaves of Carmel and Bashan are in perfect, if sad, accord with the people's falling tears.

But "now"—three times repeated—the due time has come; not one moment behind the "day appointed" doth Jehovah rise. He has borne long with the evil conditions, but He comes at last, always as it seems when His people are *in extremis*. The sisters must weep, and Lazarus die, but at the precise moment of His purpose He is there!

Note too the orderly progression in these three "nows." First, like a sleeper awakened, Jehovah rises from the couch; then He takes His place in the tumult, and it is ever a commanding one; and finally He is alone dominant, exalted above all.

Nor is this description of Israel's evil case an incorrect foreshadowing of the condition of His Church at the moment of His coming for her! *Her* glories, too, are lying waste! *Her* walls of separation from the world are all broken down; shame and confusion of face is also her portion. But the *"now"* approaches, when He shall arise, and till that happy moment, we can but "hold fast," and let "no one take our crown," which is our very dependence on, and glorying in, the Lord, as the Holy and the True!

Note the cutting sarcasm of verse 11. The enemy has conceived great purposes! They are but chaff! When these magnificent purposes have come to fruition, or when what has been conceived is brought forth—what is it? Stubble! That is well adapted for burning, and for nothing else. The enemy's own hot breath of wrath shall start the flame; for had he not burned with wrath against God's saints, he would not have suffered himself.  Again we have two figures, corresponding to the cater-pillar and the locusts of verse 4, in lime and thorns; lime sug-gesting the completeness, thorns the speed of the infliction.

One word as to the "broken covenant."  In the day near ap-proaching there will also be a covenant between the revived fourth world-power on the one side, and the mass of Jews re-turned to their land on the other (Dan. 9: 27).  Its term will be as beneficent as the spirit of Christendom is today towards Zionism,* and this is reflected in the restoration of the temple-worship in Jerusalem.  But in the "midst of the week," or three and one-half years after the signatures have been affixed to the treaty, it is broken; sacrifice and oblation cease, and a violent persecution rages to the end.  But (and this is what we must bear in mind) the accord between the forces of evil, whether on the side of Jew or Gentile, is not broken, for we see them still united at the end (Rev. 19: 20).  Another covenant is made, which from its extreme God-defying, Satanic character is said to be "with death and hell" (chap. 28); *this* binds together the evil forces of earth, but it is the "covenant" that protected the rem-nant that is broken.

13: List ye, that are far off, to what I have done;
    Learn, ye that are near, My limitless might.
14: The sinners in Zion are shaking with terror.
    Hypocrites (now) with trembling are seized.
    Who 'mong us shall dwell with fire so devouring?
    Who 'mong us shall dwell with burnings ne'er ending?
15: The doer of right!
    The speaker of truth!
    The loather of gain from oppression,
    Who shakes from his fingers the bribes that would stick
        there,
    Who stoppeth his ears from the counsel of murder,
    And closes his eyes from looking at evil.
16: 'Tis *he* who shall dwell in places exalted,
    The fortress of rocks his strong castle (shall be),
    His bread shall be given, his water be sure.

---

*Written before the Anti-Semitism of Hitler in Germany, but that is due solely to the internal prominence that the Jews have won in Germany, but would not follow them when there was no such reason.

Let us note here again that the call is to both those *afar off* (that is, the Gentiles) and those who are near (the *Jews* in the land), and this double form of address confirms the conviction that the whole prophecy from verse 1 has the same double application to Jew and Gentile. The next verse is further confirmation of this, for whilst the Gentile enemy is distinctly recognized in the Spoiler, typified by Sennacherib, "sinners *in Zion*" could never refer to any but apostate Jews.

Then comes a question and its answer that recalls Psalm 15, where the same question has the same reply. Who can estimate the importance of heeding what is thus reiterated in the Old Testament and renewed in the New, for the Epistle to the Hebrews reminds Christians that "Our God is a consuming fire." Who can dwell with such a God?

Let us not turn away wearied with reiteration, from a word that is thus surely marked as of the weightiest importance. The reiterated words "among us" (ver. 14) surely suggest a mass of profession among which is the true. How are the few to be discerned? By much intelligence in the Scriptures? No. By much activity in "church-work?" No. By much denouncing of the evil in others? Not at all; but by lowly penitence (Isa. 57: 15; 66: 1, 2), and being led of the Spirit in paths of love and holiness. Let us not be deceived in this day of much high knowledge and low conduct. It is still true that only those "among us" who are "led by the Spirit of God are the sons of God."

Such shall be well guarded, and even though some of them shall be put to death, yet not a hair of their heads shall perish (Luke 21: 16-18). So the apostle Paul was ready to be offered up, yet he too knew that the "Lord would deliver him from every evil work;" strange paradoxes apart from having a life that no tyrant can touch.

Another promise follows:

17: Thine eyes shall behold the King in His beauty,
The land of far distances they surely shall see.

For this last line does not mean, as our Authorized Version intimates, that the land is far away; but when in it, the boundaries shall not be contracted, but as far as their eye can see or foot can carry, shall be theirs: as it was said to their father Abraham, "Lift·up now thine eyes, for all the land that thou seest, to thee I will give it" (Gen. 15: 14, 15).

We may have no personal part in that land; *that* is not our country; but this promise is of the deepest interest to us, for we too shall see the King.   He is ours by more than one indissoluble tie.  He has literally loved us, bought us with His blood: we are infinitely precious to Him as the dear purchase of those sufferings: to Him we are united by the Holy Spirit; identified with Him by sharing His very life, we are thus the members of His Body.   Ours too is His present position, cast out by this world, whilst all the love of God the Father in which He is enwrapped, enwraps us too in Him.   His future too we fully share.   And, to come back to our scripture, our own very eyes shall see Him in His beauty, with eyes adapted to that glory, as are these to the inferior beauties of this scene.   We shall see Him in His perfect loveliness, and greatly shall we desire Him, a desire that He will be there to fill.   This was patterned for us in the holy mount, where, although Peter, James and John might then fear, Moses and Elias did not; and our place shall be that of those heavenly visitants.

He, the King, was then to be the Object of every eye; every ear was to be attent to His lips; so ever today, do we not get at times (but so rarely, alas, if one may speak for others), foretastes of that time when we shall see with our eyes without a cloud, the beauty of the King, and hear the music of that Voice whose faintest whisper gives us here joy for many days.

In our prophet we have to do with Israel and the earth, and in that day of deliverance this is foretold of the dweller in Zion:

18: Thine heart shall muse on past terror.
    Where is the scribe?
    Where the collector?
    Where the counter of towers?
19: The insolent folk thou shalt never see more—
    A folk of strange lip thou canst not interpret;
    Of barbarous* tongue thou canst not understand.

*First meaning "stammering," but it comes to mean "ridiculous," and so "barbarous" seems the closest to its intent.

The terror is gone forever, and is now but such a matter of memory as gives sweetness to the present peace. Those happy dwellers in that future Jerusalem muse on the time when they were trembling with fear, and ask, "What has become of the man who took stock of our goods? Where is he who followed him in taking those goods in the way of taxes? And as to the enemy who rode around our city counting its defensive towers before the attack—where has he gone? All have departed never to return."

The Holy Spirit uses this same language in 1 Cor. 1: 20, but in quite a different bearing; nor is the quotation precise, for the word "wise" is substituted for "scribe," "scribe" for "collector," and "disputer of this world" for "counter of towers." But as peaceful Salem shall say: "Where are all my foes?" so in view of Christ, *our* foes, no longer flesh and blood, but our own proud thoughts that exalt themselves against the knowledge of that same Lord Christ, are forever abased and annihilated. But we must ever remember that we still have that same old nature derived from Adam the first, to keep us watchful and dependent, and the very first evidence of its activity is proud self-esteem.

20: Look now upon Zion, our city all festal;
    Thine eyes shall see Salem, a dwelling all restful;
    A tent nevermore to be struck,
    Whose stakes shall never be drawn,
    Whose cords shall never be loosed.
21: For there, all-majestic, Jehovah is for us;
    A place of broad rivers; of streams deep and wide,
    Whereon never galley, propelled by oar, ventures,
    Nor strong man-of-war can ever pass by.
22: For Jehovah our Judge is!
    Jehovah our War-prince!
    Jehovah our King!
    'Tis He who will save us!*

---

*Note rhyme, rhythm, and the swing of the last verse in the original:

*"Jehovah shephtehnu!*
*Jehovah m'choqehnu!*
*Jehovah malkehnu!*
  *Hoo yoshiehnu!"*

Here we are called to use the eye of faith, forget the poverty of "Jerusalem that now is and is in bondage with her children," and see her in quite another guise, as made beautiful, the joy of the whole earth, with solemn feasts again held, each in its appointed time as the year revolves.  She will be well worth looking at, and many a long journey will be taken to see her.  There was a time when she was the scoff of the tourist, who only brought back word of her squalor.  No joy did any derive from seeing her in that day; but now in her beauty, she shows what divine grace can do with a city on earth; and, as principalities and powers shall be invited to consider, in the glories of the Church, what God can do in heaven, so shall the nations and powers of earth be invited to regard Jerusalem.

Nor shall she (identified with her people) ever wander more. Never again shall her stakes be pulled up, nor cords be loosened. The "wandering Jew" has finished his Cain-like vagabondage forever, and restful peace has taken her abode in Zion.  Long has that been desired, for we know Him who hath said: "Here will I dwell, this is My rest" (Ps. 132).

But more.  Let Babylon boast her Euphrates; let Egypt boast her Nile; it is true that Jerusalem has no river at all—what of it? Jehovah shall be to us in the place of the broad river of the one, and the broad floods of the other.  He, and He only, shall be all the defence that a river would be.  Nor on that "river" of ours dare any galley attempt invasion, no hostile battleship pass over.

Then in verse 22 there is a triumphant chant of anticipative faith, with its divine fingerprint of "three;" Jehovah our Bishop,* or ecclesiastical Head; Jehovah our Commander, or military Head; Jehovah our Monarch, or political Head; He, and none other, shall be our salvation!

23: How loosely thy ropes hang!
    Thy mast they support not!
    The flag cannot wave,
    Nor can the sail spread!
    Then is the prey of a great spoil divided:
    Even the lame take part in the spoiling.

---

*"Judge," very much as in the word "overseer;" one who sees that all is in order, as is the force in our word "Bishop."

24: He who abides there ne'er wails, I am sick!
The people there dwelling from guilt are all freed!

There is a divergence among commentators as to the bearing
of these verses. Many, as Delitzsch, insist that Jerusalem is addressed in verse 23; but others, with whom I must agree, see the
*enemy* of Jerusalem. The prophet has just said that while the
beloved city is defended by no literal broad river, Jehovah Himself takes that place, and then what vessel dare attack? One
does: it is the mighty world-power, the Assyrian, "the prince that
shall come" (Dan. 9: 26), with all the munitions of that revived
Empire at his back, and in league with the False Prophet; these
have dared to attempt to cross that "river" and in their attack
on Jerusalem, really make war against our Lord (Rev. 19: 19).
Look at that presumptuous vessel now! "Torn cordage, shattered
deck," its mast unshipped, all the ropes attached to it hang loosely down, its colors are fallen and droop in shame; its sails flap
idle and useless—a wreck! The cargo is at the mercy of others,
and is so abundant that even he who on account of being lame
only arrives long after the others, still finds plenty of booty.
Turn now to the "holy city;" can the ear catch one complaint of
sickness? No, not one single wail; for the very *bodies* of the
dwellers in Zion evidence redemption by power. And what is the
basic blessing on which all others are built? All iniquity is forgiven!

## CHAPTER THIRTY-FOUR

**The day appointed. A universal crash. The relation between Edom and Adam. The heavens share in the infliction, for there rebellion began. Military terms not literal. Distinction between the Millennial day and the Sabbath of God. Truth in words because they cannot be translated.**

JUST as the "burdens" that affected various nations in chapters 12 to 23 were followed by a general crash in chapter 24—the "finale," as Delitzsch calls it, borrowing the figure from an orchestra—and this was succeeded by the joyous strains of chapter 25; so here, we have had this nation and that, threatened by woe after woe, till (in the previous chapter) both Gentile and Jew are apostate, and now comes the crashing finale in divine judgment on *all* the earth. That too we shall find followed in chapter 35 by the sweetest strains of promise.

Again I must call Delitzsch to my aid. He well points out that it cannot be possible to misunderstand this chapter as having reference to past history. He says: "We feel that we are carried away from the stage of history, and are transported into the midst of the last things," and these chapters are the "last steps whereby our prophet rises to the height at which he soars in chapters 40 to the end. After the fall of Assyria, and when darkness began to gather on the horizon again, Isaiah broke away from his own times—'the end of all things' became more and more his home. . . . It was the revelation of the mystery of the incarnation of God, for which all this was to prepare the way." Of this, these chapters "are, as it were, the first preparatory chords," and Edom, the traditional hater of his brother Jacob, now becomes the representative "of the sum-total of all the enemies and persecutors of the church of Jehovah."

I have quoted this as written, nor is the word "church," as so applied, without Scriptural warrant (Acts 8: 38); but we must guard this in our minds, and avoid confusing it with that entirely unique and divinely formed "Body" of which the risen Christ is

the Head, and with which no nation, as such—Jew or Gentile—
has anything to do.  But to our chapter:

1: Come near, ye nations, to hear;
   Hearken attentive, ye peoples;
   Listen, O world, and all that's therein;
   Hearken, O earth, and all that springs from it.
2: For the wrath of Jehovah doth fall on all nations:
   His fury, all burning, is on all of their hosts:
   His ban is laid on them, they're delivered to slaughter;
3: Their slain are all cast away,
   From their dust a stench rises,
   And mountains do melt with their blood.
4: The heavenly host is dissolved,
   As a scroll the heavens are rolled up;
   And all of their hosts do wilt,
   As withered leaf falls from the vine,
   As blighted (fruit) falls from the fig tree.

Thus the chapter opens with a call to all the nations of the
earth.  No longer is the threatening directed to Assyria or Egypt;
and yet, before the close, we shall see another single symbolic
representative of all those nations in Edom, which, by its close
relation to "Adam," fits perfectly as a symbolic name for *all*
the nations.  It is a fearful picture of bodies unburied, scattered
in such numbers that the air is rendered fetid with the stench;
and the very mountains are melted by the blood.  It is evidently
intended to impress the mind with the awful "severity of God,"
when He thus arises to judge the earth.  For Isaiah is now
speaking of that same day as did the apostle on Mars' Hill.  The
"appointed day" has come, the "appointed Man" is there, and
the awful scene follows.

It is the whole prophetic earth that is in view, and by that is
meant that part of it upon which the light of revelation has
shone; for the infliction is ever proportioned to the privileges enjoyed and despised.  Reader, are these mere empty words that
shall never have fulfilment?  Who really believes them now?
And yet are we so bewitched that we cannot discern how fast
the nations of Christendom—that highly-favored sphere where
God's love in the gift of His Son has been for nearly two millenniums proclaimed—are ripening for just such an infliction?

That very condition witnesses to the certainty of this coming judgment. It will be a fearful thing to be on earth at that time!

Many modern pulpits preach now that God is too loving to be severe, and that the moral Governor of the universe is so weak that He will permit His own laws to be defied with impunity forever! But who can deny that He has given evidence of His power in the past? Did He not sweep the whole race away by the flood, with the sole exception of one family? Is the siege of Jerusalem, His beloved Jerusalem, with all its awful sufferings, altogether forgotten? Or if memories are too feeble for that stretch, is it not a fact, too recent for time to have wiped from memory, that the larger sphere of Christian profession has not even yet fully emerged from its blood-bath? Is there such universal repentance and humiliation as shall avert any further manifestations of wrath? *You know that there is not!* On the contrary, pride rules our nations Godward, while mistrust and fear are largely their counsellors in dealing with each other. The whole scene is solemnly prophetic of further inflictions. This judgment then lies in the future, and we believe, *near* future. Verse 4 gives an oft-repeated picture of a universal catastrophe affecting the visible heavens. The stars fall like the leaves in autumn, or the wilted figs that any breeze sends to the ground. This is repeated in Matt. 24: 29, and apparently points to a literal and universal convulsion amid the heavenly bodies, that shall immediately follow the "time of Jacob's trouble" (Jer. 30: 7) and announce the Lord's return in power and great glory. The visible fall of the stars thus speaks to the *eye* of the fall of the invisible "host of heaven," as the next verse in prophetic language explains.

5: For My sword shall be bathèd in heaven;
   Behold, it comes down upon Edom,
   For judgment on those of My curse.
6: The sword of Jehovah is glutted with blood,
   'Tis fattened with fat:
   With blood of (both) lambs and of he-goats,
   With the fat of the kidneys of rams.
   For Jehovah in Bozrah a sacrifice holdeth;
   Aye, a great slaughter in (proud) Edom's land.

7: And down fall the buffaloes with them,
   And bullocks together with bulls,
   Till their land becomes glutted with blood,
   And their dust is fattened with fatness.
8: For 'tis the day of Jehovah's avenging,
   'Tis the year that doth recompense Zion's (long) strivings.

Under the figure of a sword "intoxicated with blood" (as Delitzsch renders it) we have again that truth, so strange to us, of Heaven itself being the scene of the infliction of penalty; but, strange as it is, it is the consistent testimony of all Scripture. Chapter 24 has spoken of the punishing of "the host of the high ones on high," and our own prophetic book harmonizes with this, in that war in heaven, resulting in the final expulsion of "the dragon and his angels." Sin began in heaven, and its stain is in those courts so that even *they* "are not clean in His sight," and need the same precious blood to "reconcile" them as do we (Col. 1: 20). But that blood was not shed for "angels," He passed them by; and the penalty falls on them first. Then the same sword (which is here, I take it, a figure of "death," involving eternal separation from God) comes down on man; the people of the ban, who have rejected the light and love of the gospel. Divine judgment ever begins on what is nearest—has enjoyed the greatest advantage, and because of neglect or abuse of that advantage is "under the curse."

In verses 6 and 7 we have two series of offerings of three each; the first composed of the smaller animals devoted to sacrifice, lambs, goats and rams, representing the masses, or the common people; but, with these, the larger, buffaloes, young bulls and strong bulls, representing the nobles of the same "people of the ban." All suffer death, for it is the Lord's sacrifice that He holdeth in Bozrah,* the sacrifice that now alone can satisfy the righteousness of His own government. This poor earth, ever soaked with blood and tears, has still this awful baptism to go through, prior to its deliverance. Self-judgment, penitence, a shut mouth, and humble confidence in God's one all-sufficient sacrifice for sin, in His own beloved One—His Son, His Lamb—

---

*Bozrah, meaning a "defence" (Job 22: 25), protection, object of confidence.

is the sure, but absolutely the only, way of escape; for it is only Jesus who delivers us "from the wrath to come," of which this is the picture.

It is not necessary to insist that this picture should be literally carried out in every detail, as, for instance, the mountains being "melted with blood," or blood being literally shed in heaven; yet the truth brought to the mind is a literal judgment of intense severity; just as in Revelation 14 we have an impossible picture, if taken literally, of a vast sea of blood reaching in depth up to the horses' bridles "by the space of 1,600 furlongs." How could the intense severity of God's judgment be more impressively brought to our minds, when He thus "arises to judge the earth?"

Verse 8 gives the explanation of this severity. It is the end of Jehovah's controversy with Israel; and that end comes, not by catching them up to meet their Messiah in the air, but by *His* coming to the earth, His feet again standing on the Mount of Olives, and destroying their enemies. Thus the day of the Lord's vengeance on the nations is the year of deliverance for Zion.

Towards the nations of Christendom it is "the day of avenging;" toward Israel, as represented by the pious remnant, it is the "year of recompense for the controversies of Zion." Long has He borne with the unfaithful witness called "Christian," long has He had controversy with His people whom He foreknew, and so has not finally cast away. The end to both comes when Jerusalem, here held and defended by the pious remnant, is captured by the confederated forces of the nations (Zech. 14), aiding the Jewish apostasy, and the power of the holy people seems to be forever scattered (Dan. 12). Then comes the revelation of the Lord for their deliverance, their sorrows are forever past, and that long unfulfilled prophecy, which Gabriel was sent to give Daniel, is finally accomplished. Israel's transgression is forever ended; the atoning work, actually effected so long before, is now applied to them in their penitence and faith, and their "House" so long desolate, is anointed, and thus becomes again and forever a fitting abode for Jehovah.

9: And Edom's brooks are turned to pitch,
    Its dust is turned to brimstone,
    Till its very land becometh
    Pitch that is aflame!
10: By day and night 'tis quenchèd not,
    Its smoke ascendeth ever,
    Forever doth it lie all waste
    From — age — to — age!
    No one passeth through it more
    Forever and forever.

A gloomy picture of Edom's land, that seems to tell of its condition during the whole millennial day, is given in verses 9, 10. The brooks that murmured so restfully with their rippling waters now flow sluggishly and sullenly in gloomy silence, filled with that most combustible of matter, pitch, and they go through a dry land ever covered with clouds of smoke that arise from them—what a picture!

All Scripture agrees in its witness that the millennial day is not the perfect eternal one; it is not "the rest of God," the final Sabbath, the seventh day, but the sixth, in which the government of the earth is in the hand of the Second Man, the Last Adam with His Bride, with all evil kept in control, although present. Just as in our personal regeneration, there is still the old nature within, which must not be permitted to "reign" (Rom. 6: 12), so in that time called the "regeneration" of the earth, its very topography shall witness to God's judgment on evil. The Jews' land, Palestine, will have its witness of that judgment in its "miry places, and the marshes" bordering the salt sea (Ezek. 47: 11). The land of Edom will give the same witness to the severity of God, in the Gentile's earth; and the lake of fire will add its solemn voice to the same awe-inspiring testimony in the eternal scene. All three spheres combine to witness to what is so largely denied today, that side of God's holy nature, "Light," the necessary expression of the inflexible righteousness of His government of the universe in its every sphere in view of rebellion and sin. Thus all are made to serve that basic purpose of the Creator in His creation, of fully expressing Himself as both Love and Light. In this, even the "vessels to dishonor," as the devil and his angels, and all impenitent from among men, must have their part.

11: The pelican and hedgehog* now take it in possession,
The night-owl and the raven there take up their abode;
And He doth stretch upon it
The measuring-line of—waste!
And for a plummet—chaos!
12: Its nobles, none are there now
T' announce the kingdom 'stablished,
Its princes all have come to naught.
13: Her palaces break out with thorns,
Her forts with weeds and thistles,
A dwelling for the wild-dog,*
A pasture for the ostrich.*
14: And she is now the meeting-place
Of tzim,* and of iim;*
And there doth hairy satyr* make
A howling to his fellow;
And there doth rest the bird of night,*
And find congenial nesting.
15: There, too, doth the arrow-snake*
Make nest, lay eggs and hatch them,
And gather her foul brood beneath
The shade that doth protect them.
There the vultures gather too,
Each mating with its kindred.
16: Search ye in Jehovah's book,
And read there.  None shall fail,
Or be lacking in its mate;
For My mouth, it hath commanded,
His Spirit, it hath gathered them.
17: 'Tis He hath cast for them the lot,
His hand by line hath measured,
And they possess it evermore;
From generation there they dwell
Unto generation!

The words in verse 11 rendered in the Authorized Version "confusion" and "emptiness," and in Genesis 1: 2, "without form and void," speak of a condition of ruin, as is evident here and in Jer. 4: 23.  So that Jehovah pictures Himself as working as a Builder indeed, with "line and plummet," but not for the purpose of building up, but of bringing Edom's land, that is, *Adam's*

---

*These words are all of uncertain application, there is much controversy as to their true meaning.  See pp. 171-173.

*earth,* back to the chaotic condition in which we first see it in Gen. 1: 2, "And the earth was without form and void." Let these scriptures throw their light on each other, and as there later ones in Isaiah and Jeremiah tell us unequivocally that this scene of utter desolation is due to *sin,* so must the earlier one in Genesis make us assured that that condition was the result of the same cause. As man had not at that time been created, that sin could not have been his: the deduction is as certain as a direct and plain statement could make it, that some pre-adamite creation had been ruined by the sin of a pre-adamite race. The only other alternative that God created the earth in this ruined condition is inconceivable: God does not create ruins. Everything comes from His hand in the perfection of its being, although He does, by permission, bring the inevitable consequences of sin on that which He had created in perfection. Here the "line and plummet" tell us that He will not stay the progress of ruin till it conforms to that primal chaos.

These words, *"tohu va' bohu,"* taking us thus back to a time preceding Adam, and to a race of beings that were spirits, with other scriptures telling us clearly that among these was one who "sinned from the beginning" (1 John 3: 8), prepare us again to find in the mysteriously named creatures of the following verses divinely intended suggestions of those very spirit-powers that were the primal sinners of the universe.

Little edification can be obtained by following the guesses that have been made as to their literal identity; and the divergence of opinions shows that they are but guesses. Far better is it to see in the very mysteriousness a divine purpose to suggest something also mysterious in the world of evil spirits. We cannot believe that God has simply put meaningless words into that revelation on which all our light and hope depend; but would have us examine them with such care as we can, and we may find, in even these, truths of eternal value, for may they not have been thus recorded for us on whom the ends of the ages have come?

We have already noted some of these same strange words in chap. 13: 21, 22, merely adding as to those that do not occur there, which in A.V. are rendered "screech-owl" and "great owl," that the Hebrew of the former, "*lilith*," literally means "night-creature," one that finds its congenial home in darkness, and the latter is a close relation to the serpent, the arrow-snake. It is striking, too, that in the first three of verse 14, *tziim, iim, satyr,* we have the three spheres—land, water and air, respectively—which are typically the symbols for Jew, Gentile and the Church of God (by profession). Each of these becomes in its turn apostate, and thus demon-possessed, and the object of divine judgment.

This interpretation then of these mysterious words of our prophet must not, let me repeat, be considered the outcome of superstition—it is far removed from that—and is only a sober recognition of a sphere of the occult filled with evil intelligencies whose existence is impossible to be denied by any to whom the Scriptures are the very Word of God.

Now for two practical applications of what we have learned: First, as the prophetic book of Revelation shows us what the professing Church shall become, when all that is of God has been taken from it, do we not see the nearing approach of that very condition in the "doctrines of *demons*" that are rapidly taking possession of its pulpits? This very day those who cleave to the foundation truths of Christianity are in a minority, and the current is flowing with ever-increasing rapidity in that direction of apostasy.

In the next place we must carefully note that all these creatures make their *voluntary* choice of the scenes of death, darkness, desolation and ruin for their abode; so will all eventually go to their "own place," that is, the place that they themselves would choose as alone in any way corresponding to the nature that inevitably expresses the only life they have. For sooner would the birds of night fly with blinded eye in noonday, than unreconciled spirits—whether of angels or of men—desire, or be at home in, the courts of God's radiant light. As that poor man in Mark 5, in whom a legion of demons had taken up their dwelling, found no congenial place save the tombs, and there no rest, so every unforgiven child of man, who has refused the life (with its new nature of light and love) offered in Christ will find, alas, a more congenial abode in the "second death" and the "outer darkness" than he could in the heavenly courts of life and light. You and I, my dear reader, will eventually go to our own place; and that place, if we have life in Christ, can be none other than where *He* is.

Note, too, the power of evil to propagate itself. We know well that the angels neither marry nor are given in marriage; but in another sense, as in nature, the downy seed wafted by the wind bears within it reproductive life, so the seed of the Word, wafted by the divine Spirit, bears with it life eternal. But so, too, does evil not cease with itself, but carries its pernicious effects wherever it goes as suggested by verse 16: "None shall want his mate."

Jehovah's book has the interpretation of all these (ver. 16). Search and learn; for not one word that has come from His lips can fail. The prophet was only the mouth-piece, the Speaker was, and is, God. As He apportioned Israel her land of brooks of water, flowing from mountain and hill, so He appointed Edom's barren rocks for that people who should be symbolic of the natural man, and whose land should in its desolation picture the everlasting abode both of the natural man, as well as that of lost spirits.

# CHAPTER THIRTY-FIVE

HOW refreshing to turn from the storm of judgment to the calm of blessing! But the very storm affords a foil that increases the sweetness of that calm. Little do they know of the delights of spring who have never felt the pinch of winter; little do they value the "time of the singing of birds" who have never lacked their melody; little should we care for the promise, "God shall wipe away all tears," had we never wept. So this lovely little chapter is doubly refreshing from its sharp contrast to its predecessor. It has a lilt of joy and is almost metrical in our A.V., without much change.

1: Then shall the desert-places and all the wastes rejoice;
Then too e'en the wilderness shall blossom as the rose;
2: Blossoms then shall cover it, rippling it with laughter,
Till in its flowery gladness, it bursts into a song.
The majesty of Lebanon shall then be given to it,
The splendor too of Carmel and Sharon's lovely plain;
Then there shall be clearly seen the glory of Jehovah,
The splendor of our God!

This is very clearly the first division of the chapter; and with some joy we note again upon it the divine Fingerprint that we have so frequently discerned in the clear mark of "three" (God fully manifest). In these verses we have the effect of God manifesting Himself, first, on the *material* world; then in verses 3 to 7 we have the effect of the same manifestation on redeemed Israel, or as we may say, the *soul* of man; and, lastly, its effect in bringing that wandering *spirit* of man, in Israel, back to Jehovah her God. Thus the very Earth's body, soul and spirit give witness to that "manifestation of God."

Nothing could be sharper than the contrast to the dark picture of the previous chapter. Death and darkness, gloom and mourning reigned there; but now the very desert "laughs with abundance," for fertility and beauty of the earth are poetically its laughter of joy; and the greater its fertility the greater the joy of which it speaks. Every word that can express delight is called on for its contribution; and when these may be exhausted, Lebanon must add its majestic glory, Carmel its beauty, and the flowery plain of Sharon its loveliness. But these are but attendants on Jehovah, whose glory and beauty outshine all. With such a prospect what more fitting than the word of cheerful encouragement that now follows:

> 3: Strengthen then the feeble hands, confirm the knees that
> totter;
> 4: Say to them of trembling heart, Be ye strong and fear not!
> Behold, your God as Vengeance comes, as Recompense
> He's coming;
> And in His coming thus will be unto you Salvation.
> 5: The eyes of those who once were blind shall then be fully
> opened;
> The ears of those who once were deaf shall then be quite
> unstopped;
> 6: The lame shall then spring as the hart, the tongue long
> dumb shall carol;
> For waters in the desert flow, and torrents in dry places.
> 7: The glowing-sand* shall be a pool, the thirsty land be
> fountains;
> Whilst in the place where jackals couched grass grows
> with reeds and rushes.

There is a very delightful truth in verse 3. God does not even strengthen His weak people directly; He seems in the depth of His grace to make Himself dependent, as it were, upon them. Let us suppose that we have a very weak Christian—it is not a difficult supposition—God could of course lift up those downhanging hands and strengthen those tottering knees by Himself alone; but no, He admits others to share that gracious ministry with Him, and thus He makes us "workers together" with Himself, spreading thus His blessing, not merely over the one direct object of it, but over the many others who seek to strengthen the

---

*"Glowing-sand," literally, "desert-shine," probably what is termed "mirage."

feeble one; is not this a very much better way? There have always been, and never more than today, real, true Christians whose hands are hanging down, who are relatives of "Little-faith and Despondency, his daughter," as John Bunyan speaks. We have precisely the same cheering basis for encouraging each other as in our prophecy: "Say to the trembling heart, Be strong, for your God comes." The hope of that coming was to give strength to the fainting Israelite, and it is the hope of His coming that shall today strengthen the faint heart of the Christian. But note a striking difference: Isaiah gives the character in which Israel's God will come for her relief, as "Vengeance," for there is no word in the Hebrew between "God" and "Vengeance" in verse 4; nor in the following line, with its parallel thought; both tell the character in which He comes: "Vengeance" and "Retribution" characterize that coming.

But no threatening word like this do we find in the New Testament writer. How utterly inconsistent it would be! Our Lord is not coming in that character for us at all, but quite the reverse; we look for the Lord Jesus Christ, not as Vengeance but as Saviour, as Phil. 3: 20 literally reads. We have no human foes on whom we would desire vengeance or retribution. But not so with Israel. The salvation of that remnant of faith, that shall then be the nucleus of the new nation, awaits, as we have so frequently seen, the strong Hand of her God coming down on her mighty human foes, under whose feet she is lying helpless.

Reader, do you feel that you are one of the "weak?" Then before leaving this subject of heartening one another, let a fellow-weak one take thy hand; and together let us learn this strange truth that only they who know their real helplessness *are the strong!* Peter thought that he was the strongest of all the twelve, for he said: "Though all shall be offended, yet will not I." Poor Peter had to learn by a terrible fall, by bitter tears and many a sigh, another lesson altogether; and then when that was learned, and he "converted" from a false to a true confidence, then, and not till then, might he "strengthen his brethren," by telling them of that only Source of any true strength that he had found at heavy cost. It was in that day, it has ever been, it is today, that Strength that is alone "made perfect in *weakness.*"

At that most happy epoch of the coming of their God, all those sad consequences of sin suffered by man's body, will be removed. So at the proclamation of the Kingdom of Heaven as having drawn near (as it surely had in the Person of its King), samples, as we may term them, of this blessed condition were given, and wherever He came this prophecy (vers. 5-7) was illustrated, for did not the blind see, the deaf hear, and the lame leap as the hart? Surely they did. These are now the "powers of the age to come" (Heb. 6: 5), and it is in that age that our prophet's feet are standing, for God the Holy Spirit can carry His servants forward any length of time, as He does our prophet John in the book that he has given us.

It is a delightful scene. Everything that sin has turned upside down shall be turned back to normal, but yet not even precisely as it was; it shall over-abound in blessings. God never merely mends what Satan and sin have marred. The Paradise of God (Rev. 2: 7) is not a mere Paradise recovered as it was in Eden. Only the Tree of Life will be there; for its dwellers will be under no trial of that kind. No longer in that day shall the mirage deceive the traveller, and mock his parched lips by disappearing as he approaches, but it shall be found a springing fountain—"water, water everywhere and every drop" life-filled! Beautiful, external figure of the internal flood of blessing, in the Spirit springing up in every heart.

Our chapter is a very "song of degrees," for the following verses, 8 to 10, lead us another step higher. Here we are drawing very near to God Himself, and it is well for us to look at the path to that one goal for true joy:

> 8: A highway shall be there, a way that's called of all, The Holy,
>     For none unclean shall walk therein; but 'tis for those appointed;
>   Whoever walks that holy path, though simple, need not wander.
> 9: No lion shall be there to fright, no ravening beast approach it;
>     Aye, e'en if sought, not found thereon. The ransomed walk it safely.

10: Thus return the Lord's redeemed, to Zion come with
        singing;
    Endless joy doth crown their heads, and gladness is their
        portion,
    Whilst sorrow takes its final flight, and sighing flees
        forever!

We justly blame those who take all the promises of the Old
Testament, and leave only the threatenings for the poor Jew,
for in this they do greatly err; yet there is an element of truth
in their contention, since "all the promises of God are Yea and
Amen in Christ Jesus." Their error is in saying that since God
has no further use for Israel, these comforting forecasts apply,
and only apply, to Christians, not to Israel as a nation at all!
God be thanked that whatever is of a spiritual character does so
apply: the material blessings that Israel shall enter into on the
basis of the new covenant of grace are, in a spiritual sense, ours
by that same grace. But that does not *fulfil* these promises that
were given directly to Israel as identified with her Messiah,
Jesus, and given her long before the Church of God was revealed
at all.

How lovely the road to Zion! But even for Israel such terms
must also have a moral bearing. It is a *high* way: a path raised
above the surrounding land on either side, and keeping the feet
of its wayfarers from mud and defilement, as we have already
seen it in our seventh chapter. Along that road none unclean
can walk; it has no attraction for them; it is for those who have
been themselves sanctified (which is the very reverse of meaning
those who are conscious of being better than others), and for
them alone. They may be very ignorant and simple; but the
road is so clearly defined: it is such a high way, so far above
low self-seeking paths, that even these simple ones shall have no
need to stray from it. Nor can any beast of prey invade it and
terrify its travellers; absolute security characterizes it. Why is
that? Because those passengers Zionward have all been bought
at a great price, and are well-guarded by Him who has thus purchased them.

Surely nothing could exceed the beauty of the picture drawn
in the last verses. What sorrows have ever been sweeping across

what is called "The Christian world" during the centuries! What rivers of tears and blood have drenched its soil, and what sighs have burdened its air!

For Israel this is the end of their long journey. Like Jacob, their father, they have wandered far, and few and evil have been their days, as were his, for no time is worth anything at all that is spent out of communion with God. But here they are at last back again at "Bethel," the very House of God, and in that House they shall dwell forever, as Ps. 23 foresees.

For us too there is a Highway of holiness. High? Yes, high above the ambitions, the lusts, the Christless, bloodless religion of the world. Nor is it less secure than Israel's, for "neither death, nor life, nor angels, nor principalities, nor powers, nor height, nor depth, nor things present, nor things to come, nor any other creature, shall be able to sever us from the love of God which is in Christ Jesus our Lord," *for He Himself is that Highway!*

This brings us to the ending of the first main division of our book. Blessed, oh, how blessed, for us that the end of all His ways with His people is, as here, always one of blessing. To Him—three Persons, one God—be glory now and forever.

DIVISION TWO

Chapters 36 to 39

# The Historic Interlude

## CHAPTER THIRTY-SIX

**Difference between divine and secular history. Threefold way of using Scripture. Assyria is removed. Babylon takes its place. Importance of the change. Sennacherib's successful invasion of ten tribes; crosses border of Judah. Humiliation of Hezekiah. Silence the best answer to abuse. The return of the intermediaries.**

IN chapters 36 to 39 we now come to the historic interlude, forming a clearly marked second main division in our book, radically differing in its form from (although forming a link between) what precedes no less than from what follows. It will not detain us long; but we must not dishonor it by indifference or neglect, for since it is all profitable that would surely be to our loss. Divine history is never *merely* history, never simply a true account of past events. If we are enabled to profit by the *moral* lessons that we can deduce from it, we have not exhausted its profit; there are deeper truths still, of a *spiritual* character, that are only spiritually discerned, and for that discernment we are dependent on the Spirit of God. Do we not need to own that dependence by prayerfully waiting on the Lord? By that "Comforter" alone can we be led into all truth.

As we have already seen, the recognition of these chapters as a separate division serves to make the whole book a trilogy —that is, it gives the book the significance of that number (3) that speaks of the full manifestation of God.*

A comparison of these chapters with 2 Kings 18: 13-20, inclusive, gives every evidence of either both accounts being taken from some common source, or one from the other. Nor, if that be the case, does it seem possible to determine which is the original and which the copy. One commentator assures us that

---

*See Introductory Chapter.

"no impartial reader can doubt that Kings is the older;" and another that "it is inconceivable that the author of Kings should have written it!" With such irreconcilable divergencies, we may feel very thankful that it does not matter at all, and leaving the question as to what human hand first traced these accounts for the commentators to settle between themselves, we will stand firmly for the one Author, the real Source of both being God, the Holy Ghost.

We must, however, judge from the *repetition* (which we may call threefold, for 2 Chron. 32 also gives its addition) that there is vast importance to be attached to the events thus narrated— that they have a place in the ways of God with Israel His people, and so with men as a race, that is of the deepest significance. Nor does the importance of the drama depend upon the size of the stage on which it is acted. Human histories would give far greater space to wars that appear to affect the destinies of the race; but they would esteem a raid into a little country about the size of Wales as little worthy of notice. Yet the destinies of man, as a "dweller upon the earth," are far more dependent on the Jew than on any other nationality. *Spiritually* the "casting away of them" (Israel) has been "the reconciling of the world;" "the receiving of them shall be life from the dead" (Rom. 11: 15). Now Jehovah begins to sever the ties that bind His people Israel to Himself, ties that their iniquities have long since loosened, and this progressive severance has continued till the final capture of their city by the Romans has evidenced it, as for the time, complete.

Hitherto He has been dwelling at Jerusalem, "between the cherubim," having thus His Throne on earth, and giving in that one little country a sample of His government. As long as that condition prevails no hostile foot can tread that beloved city; and thus the Assyrian never captures it. But now we have come to the time when Assyria is to be eclipsed by Babylon; and Jehovah gives up the direct government of Israel, and commits earth's government to the Gentiles. Nebuchadnezzar then may capture the city, and in so doing begin those "times of the Gentiles" that are characterized, during their whole course, as our Lord tells us, by "Jerusalem being trodden down of the Gentiles" as it is to this very day, and will be until those "times" are fulfilled.

One can therefore see the immense importance that must be attached to the transfer of world-power from Assyria to Babylon, and in this we discern the ground for the repetition of the events of these chapters.

Now too, we must note that the writing is in prose. We shall have poetry again directly; but not here.

The account in Kings gives one detail at least, omitted by Isaiah, that explains the opening sentence of Rabshakeh's speech: "What confidence is this wherein thou trustest?" The course of Sennacherib's campaign had been one of unbroken successes. He had "despised cities," for one after another they had fallen before him, till Hezekiah felt the uselessness of further resistance, and sent an "ambassage desiring conditions of peace," as the Lord Jesus seemed to say was the wisest thing to do under such circumstances (Luke 14: 32). But suppose for a moment that Hezekiah had reckoned in *this* way: "The Assyrian has 20,000 men while I have but 10,000; but in addition I have Jehovah, the Creator of all, whose power and wisdom know no limit; while that poor feeble Assyrian has only a conquered Satanic power at his back, and cannot go one step further than my God shall see it well for us, His people, that he shall go. I will wait then upon Him alone, and leave all in His hands." That would have been common sense if God *is*, and must be reckoned with. But he "desired conditions," and got them. The consequence was that the Lord's treasury was emptied, and the very doors and pillars of His House were stripped of their covering of gold. That clothing of honor was taken and Jehovah's dwelling left to shame and reproach!

Poor Hezekiah! How weak was he to give up his Lord's honor in the vain hope of peace! But how easy it is for us all to discern others' weakness! It was in vain; even this failed to fill the sum needed for the tribute, or else the Assyrian, having no honor to care for, cared nothing for his own terms, and demanded more. Why not? Treaties among men are of little value when greed and power are combined against them, and are but "scraps of paper" when there is no fear of a Power above all

to whom account must be given.   Does not recent history tell us
that that marvellously strange worker, Evolution (who reminds
us greatly of Egypt in being a *"boaster who does nothing"*), has
not effected the slightest difference in the heart of man?   If in
2,500 years Evolution has made *no* difference, how long will it
take to effect a complete change?   That would be rather a difficult sum to work out.

Further demands Hezekiah could not, or would not fulfil, and
so Sennacherib diverted an army-corps under three officers,
Tartan, Rabshakeh and Rabsaris, to besiege Jerusalem itself.
Isaiah mentions but one of these three, Rabshakeh, a word that
tells of the office the bearer of it filled—he was the "Chief cup-
bearer," and a bitter cup he bears now.   He takes his stand at
a spot with which the seventh chapter has made us familiar:
*"The conduit of the upper pool, in the highway of the fuller's
field."*   This is enough to introduce us to the narrative as told
in our prophet, and gives the setting of the drama, which is
divided into two Acts.   Act 1 and Scene 1 opens with this de-
tachment of Assyrian soldiers about the walls of Jerusalem, and
its General standing in a spot where a few years before a King
of Judah had preferred the help of Assyria to reliance on Jehovah,
where yet the tender grace of that God had given the most wonderful promise on which the hope of all mankind has been made
to rest.   It was the coming of a Virgin-born Child, who is, and
ever will be in Himself, "the conduit of the upper pool," or,
as we have seen, the same Hebrew words with equal correctness
may be rendered: "The channel (conduit) of blessing (pool) from
the Most High (upper)."*   Surely that must a bad strategic spot
for an enemy to take, notwithstanding the weak faith of the
House of David.

But there he is, and three representatives of the King come
out of the city to meet him.   Haughtily, as a conqueror, he
addresses them, wondering at the temerity that dare refuse anything to "the great King."   What can have given Hezekiah so
vain a confidence?   It must, Rabshakeh thinks, consist in one of
three things, all equally baseless.   First, and the most probable,
he hopes for help from Egypt.   Egypt, that reed that splinters

---

*See notes on chapter 7.

with the least weight put upon it, and pierces the hand that expected its aid!  What a reliance!

But possibly—for it is a common report that Hezekiah is a religious fanatic—he may say that he is trusting in Jehovah, his God.  How can that be possible?  For whose high places has Hezekiah removed but those dedicated to that very Jehovah, insisting on so strict a conformity to his own narrow-minded bigotry, that people must only worship just what, where, and as *he* thinks right!

Or it is barely possible that he still retains some remnant of dependence on his own army.  Let him give hostages then, so that he shall not take advantage of Assyrian liberality, and Rabshakeh will let him have 2,000 horses if he can mount them with riders.  He cannot do it.  How then can he resist the youngest subaltern in the Assyrian forces?

Rabshakeh has covered the field well.  Hezekiah's hopes must be either on the world (Egypt), or on Jehovah, or on his own resources; the spheres of soul, spirit and body—every part of his personality—correspond with these respectively, and the Assyrian has covered them all.

The second is peculiarly interesting, for it shows how utterly incapable an unregenerate man is to discern the motives that govern him who is led of the Spirit.  So today: opposition to anything that is called religious is interpreted in precisely the same way.  When the reformers opposed the worship of the Virgin Mary they were charged with blasphemy!  It was (and is still) esteemed to be an impious thing not to bow down in adoration at the elevation of the "Host," and how many have been burned at the stake for denying the real presence of the Lord in the bread and wine of the eucharist!

Has there been any change in man's heart today?  Not one whit.  Speak of God, or religion in any of its externals, and you will be approved.  Speak of Jesus, tell of the virtue of His blood as alone able to cleanse from all sin, and it requires no divinely inspired prophet to tell what will happen; you are at once condemned as a fanatic.  Point out how severely God's holy Word condemns our divisions in that Church which is the one Body of Christ, gives no countenance to a humanly-ordained clergy,

or a hired ministry, resulting in many a pulpit being filled with
an unregenerate man, and you are not likely to be popular.
Press further that the Scriptures know nothing of any "Church"
made of stone, brick or wood, that the very use of such a tongue
obliterates the truth as to the *living* stones that alone compose
the Church of Scripture, and religious people are immeasurably
shocked; for are *we* not taking away the venerable high places?

We sincerely believe that as Israel's place of worship was
where *her* High-priest was, so ours is only where *our* High-priest
is: that is, in the Holiest where (feeble, poor and erring as we
are) we have boldness to enter because of the unchanging value
and efficacy of the precious Blood of Christ. It is not pleasant
to be misunderstood, but we are not losers by returning in self-
judgment to the path so clearly marked out for us in the Scriptures; to lose by obedience is impossible.

Egypt and the forces of Hezekiah he can understand, estimate
and despise, but Rabshakeh seems a little uneasy as to *Jehovah;*
he knows that He is venerated as the God of the Jews, so he
boldly cries that he himself is by no means an irreligious man,
but is really serving that same Jehovah even in his present attack,
for it is He who has commanded him to make it.

That same mysterious deity, Evolution, has not succeeded at
all in eliminating these Rabshakehs — they are as plentiful and
prominent as ever, and we know them well. What can
exceed their claims to reverencing the very Scriptures that they
tear to pieces? With what "piety" do they tread under foot
the Son of God, making Him less than a *true-born* child of human
parents! They are amazed and grieved that we should think
them lacking in reverence even though they count that precious
Blood of less value than human character. They are clever, these
modern Rabshakehs, as was their ancestor, as is their father
(John 8: 44).

Rabshakeh's speech cuts deep, and the three plenipotentiaries
fear the effect of it on the people who are listening to the colloquy
as they sit on the walls, and they beg that Rabshakeh will speak
in Aramaic, with which they, as educated men, were familiar,
while it had not as yet become (as it did later) the vernacular
of the people.

The Assyrian, first insulting in the coarsest way the Committee, steps nearer, raises his voice, and addresses directly the very people, thus: "Do not be deceived by Hezekiah—I will not call him king, there is but one worthy of the title, and that The Great King, the King of Assyria—he can not deliver you, nor can your Jehovah.  Let me give you some advice: make terms with me, and then you will be at ease till I transfer you to another land of equal fertility and beauty to your own, so that you shall suffer nothing.  But on no account let Hezekiah deceive you with such vain hope as that Jehovah will deliver you.  That is an old story due to superstition; let history speak, let experience be heard.  Where are all the gods who have opposed our march? —Hamath, Arpad, Sepharvaim?  Nearer and nearer as we approached they fell one after another.  These gods all failed to protect their votaries; and now look at your sister state to the north, Samaria!  Of how much avail was Jehovah there?  Shall He then deliver *you* out of my hand?"

This is received in absolute silence, and how often that is the very best answer to malignant reproach in the day of sorrow and humiliation.  Shimei must curse unrebuked as long as the Hand of God is on the King.  The very shame attached to our scattering is evidence of the same Hand being also upon us today, and we can only endure the reproach in silence, awaiting the intervention in grace of Him who says: "As many as I love I rebuke and chasten," and remember that that is not addressed primarily to an individual, but to the very last condition of the Church as a witness on earth, in which we all have a part.

The first Act then closes with the Jewish representatives seen returning to the city with every external mark of sorrow and of shame.  Clothing is not only for warmth but for honor, as the grass is *"clothed"* with its glory in the flower (Luke 12: 28), and so inconsistent is such humiliation with that, that they tear their clothes to express it.  Many of us are fully persuaded that the present conditions are so filled with shame, so utterly in contrast with that early day when "great grace was on them all," that to pretend to the same honor as then in works of power is as unfitting as would have been the return of that embassage with laughter and dancing.

# CHAPTER THIRTY-SEVEN

Hezekiah's second step: he sends to the prophet. Jehovah's encouragement. The letter. Hezekiah's growth. The song, the sign.

THE deputation of three, in telling the result of their mission, communicate their distress to the King; their torn clothes, and sorrowful faces speak clearly enough, but they do not give him the words of Rabshakeh in full. Hezekiah may have weakened through fear, and stripped Jehovah's House, but now, at the end of his own resources, he turns at once, as the quivering needle to the pole, to his true confidence, not to Egypt, but to the House of the Lord, not to take away its gold but to cast himself and the whole nation on the Lord of the House.

In addition to this, he sends to the prophet Isaiah the same deputation, except that the place of the son of Asaph the Recorder is taken by "the elders of the priests," as if in confession that this priestly, or ecclesiastical, link with Jehovah, as well as the personal and political, had failed, and that all depended on that which the grace of Jehovah alone still maintained through His prophet.

They bring a most pathetic appeal: "Oh, in what a day of distress is our lot cast!" Constant internal affliction (here is Eliakim, over the household, to speak of that), constant external opposition from foes too strong for us (here is Shebna, the scribe, to tell of that), and constant blasphemy against our God (the priests will tell of that), for the three words used in verse 3, "trouble, rebuke, blasphemy,"* cover these three spheres—self-ward, earth-ward, God-ward—as represented by the three orders of the deputation. How closely this resembles the condition of things of this day; failure *personally*, failure of the Church, as a witness in a hostile world, and failure (aye, far worse) God-

---

*The literal meaning lying at the root of this word is "to deride," "to despise," "to reject with contempt." Its correspondence to the New Testament may be found in Heb. 10:29, "Counted the blood ...an unholy thing."

ward. All now depends on that one link, "The Amen, the faithful and true Witness, the beginning of the creation of God"—that can never fail or be broken, but all else has.

And what resources, says Hezekiah, have we to meet all these? We are in such weakness as can only be illustrated by a metaphor that is "expressive of extreme pain, imminent danger, critical emergency, utter weakness, and entire dependence on the aid of others."* "The children are come to the birth and there is not strength to bring forth."

There is no escape, no going back, no going forward! "It may be," it is possible (note the humble timidity of true, but feeble faith) that Rabshakeh's proud words have entered the ear of the living God (as they had, see verse 29), and that He will rebuke the defiance that is really directed against Him. So we come to thee, O Isaiah, to beg thy intercession for the remnant that may still be found.† Isaiah is commissioned to answer at once with a reassuring message, "Fear not the words which thou hast heard, wherewith the servants‡ of the King of Assyria have insulted *Me*. And since it is Me that they have insulted it is I who will act, and so affect his spirit that he shall give heed to a rumor, go back to his own country, and there fall by the sword."

This scene then closes with the deputation again returning, but with much more cheerful countenances, and they pass on the courage that the word "Fear not" has given them to the afflicted King and to his people who, we may be sure, are also strengthened and cheered, although the narrative now leaves them and takes us to the main body of the Assyrian army.

To this Rabshakeh returns, and finds the King decamped from Lachish, and besieging Libnah. A rumor had come to him that Tirhakah, king of Ethiopia (as Egypt is here called), was on his way to give him battle. Stung with a sense of his impotence in being compelled thus to desist from his attack on Jerusalem,

---

*Alexander.

†Note the force of the word. It says that amid all the mass of apostates one would have to *seek* in order to *find* those who were true; is there not again similarity today?

‡Heb. *"naar,"* when thus used, is a term of contempt; it is often rendered "lad," as in Gen. 21: 12, etc.

he feels it necessary to "save his face" and vent his spleen by a letter assuring Hezekiah that his retirement was but temporary, and so destroy any hope Hezekiah might have derived from it. The writing of that letter was a bad day's work for himself as the sequel proved.

It contained little more than a repetition of what Rabshakeh had said, a series of boastings of victories over nations and cities, each of which had been under the protection of some local god, and again the enemy cries: "Where are they all?" Sennacherib, however, goes further back than Rabshakeh in recounting first the earlier victories of his ancestors (verse 12) before coming to the more recent ones of his own arms.*

Hezekiah lets the letter itself speak. He spreads it out before the Lord, and then adds to its silent call for intervention one of the most beautiful outpourings of an afflicted heart of which we have any record, so short and to the point, perfect too in its pure reasonings, for note even the form of the address: "O Jehovah of Hosts, God of Israel, dwelling (between) the cherubim."

"Thou, O Jehovah, art not a tribal deity, but Lord of all hosts, and therefore irresistible; but one people amid all the nations of the earth are Thine, and that is Israel. There Thou art dwelling between the cherubim, those personifications of Thy righteous government, supporting Thy Throne on either side. With such a

---

*Mark the significance of these names: "Gozan" from "*gooz*," "to pass away;" "Haran" from "*hoor*," "to burn;" "Rezeph," which is the very word used for "coal," and so speaking of the same action of fire, expressive of wrath. So "Hamath" is cognate with "*hamah*," "burning wrath." Sin and its penalty are suggested by the very names, and thus account for the inability of the places bearing them to stand; the fire of judgment is over them all. It is both interesting and instructive to note too how rapidly Hezekiah grew in grace and the knowledge of the Lord through these severe trials. Note the three steps. First he despoils the House of Jehovah to placate the Assyrian. That proving quite ineffectual, he sends to Isaiah, Jehovah's prophet: but at last he goes straight to Jehovah Himself. At no time do we so grow in that same grace and in our knowledge of the Lord Jesus Christ as in times of distress and trial. The king's growth illustrates his name which means "strengthened by Jehovah."

title, on such a Throne, canst Thou endure the insult of that letter, admit its charges, and endorse injustice and wrong? Surely not; all that is needed is for Thee to take notice of it, and for that I pray. Open Thine eyes and consider its presumption. Let Thine ears be attent to its insults. What it says as to those false gods is true enough; but wilt Thou be placed on a level with such? No, no; save us from his hand; and so shall all the kingdoms of the earth know that there can be no rival to our Jehovah; He, and He only, is Lord."

There are two points in this prayer that I cannot pass over without noting: first Hezekiah *admits what is true* in the accuser's charge. Now that is surely true wisdom. So there is always truth in the accusations that Satan brings against us, and we shall never overcome him by denying that. But not only admit the truth, make it the very ground of appeal: "Yes, I have sinned; the accuser speaks truth in that; had I not, were that not true, I should have no claim on that precious Blood shed only for sinners like myself. I plead no innocency; but the atoning value of that Blood that always cleanses from all sin." Thus and thus alone will anyone, anywhere, at any time, "overcome him by the blood of the Lamb, and the word of their testimony" as to the value of that Blood.

But again note that Hezekiah intimates that it is alone by the salvation of Israel that "the knowledge of the Lord will cover the earth as the waters cover the sea," as he pleads "that all the kingdoms of the earth may know that Thou art the Lord, Thou only."

Jehovah sends an answer through that prophet whose very name tells the nature of his message, Isaiah, "the salvation of Jehovah," and now again we have a magnificent chant, that "proceeds in rhythmic strides on the style of Deborah's song" (*Delitzsch*). I render it then as literally as possible, attempting to repeat its rhythmic character in English:

22: Despises and laughs thee to scorn,
　　Doth the virgin daughter of Zion;
　　Shakes her head after thee, fleeing,
　　Doth the daughter of Salem.

23: Whom hast insulted? whom hast blasphemed?
    'Gainst whom hast thou raisèd the voice
    And lifted thine eyes up on high?
    The Holy One of Isràel!
24: By the hand of thy servants
    Thou hast railed at Adonai,
    And thus hast thou said:
    With my chariots countless,
    Have I climbed to the summits,
    To the heights of the mountains,
    And Lebanon's sides;
    There will I fell its tall cedars,
    The choice of its fir-trees shall fall;
    And entrance I'll force to its borders,
    To its forest of Carmel.*
25: I have digged and drunk waters,
    And dried with my foot-sole
    All the rivers of Egypt.†

This is the first of the three parts into which this answer of Jehovah divides, and it is so clear and simple that it calls for no extended comment.

It begins by bringing before us Jerusalem as a gentle maiden, little adapted for conflict, yet she is seen actually laughing at her proud foe; and as he flees (for that is involved in the word) she shakes her head after him, mockingly. What gives her that courage? This: he, her enemy, has insulted and defied the Holy One of Israel, and thus has sealed his own doom.

And now Jehovah takes up His indictment, and reads the boasts that that proud heart has been making: "Mountains have proved no barrier. My countless chariots have scaled that natural defence of Palestine, the mountain-lands of Lebanon; nor will

---

*The word Carmel is a compound, *Cerem-El*, "the vineyard of God;" expressive of extreme beauty and worth.

†The fighting between Assyria and Egypt was hereditary. They were natural opponents, but *both* hostile to Israel, whose land lay between them and suffered, irrespective of which was uppermost. After the death of Alexander the Great, that antagonism was carried on by Greece with Syria on the north and Egypt on the south; and will, we believe, be again renewed in a day not far distant.

aught stop me till I have penetrated to the extreme limit of its border, and captured the gem of the country, the forest of its Carmel," which is probably a figure of Jerusalem itself.

But the campaign in Palestine is only an incident, not the main purpose. The Assyrian aims at Egypt, involving the passage through that waterless tract that lies between Asia and Africa. "What of that?" he cries, and he now speaks as if he were a very god, and that what lies before is so sure that he can speak of it as past, "I have dug, and found all the water that I needed, and when I have come to that land of many waters, the mouths of the Nile, I have but placed my foot upon them, and, lo, they have been dried!"*

But now Jehovah comes closer, and replies to that boastful heart in the second part, verses 26 to 29:

> 26: Hast thou not heard, I did it afar,
>     From times that are ancient I formèd the plan,
>     And have brought it to pass,
>     That thou shouldst lay waste, and bring down to ruin
>     Cities strong-fortressed?
> 27: Their dwellers were helpless, dismayed and confounded;
>     Became as the field-grass, or the green herbage:
>     As grass on the house-top, or corn that is blighted
>     Before it be grown up.
> 28: Thy sitting and going, and coming I know:
>     Thy raging against Me.
> 29: Because of thy raging, thy self-trust so haughty
>     Has grown till it reaches My ears.
>     Therefore I'll place My hook in thy nostril,
>     And make thee return by the way that thou camest.

Thus Jehovah accounts for the victories of evil, and there can be no doubt but that behind this proud Assyrian we may discern the "king of the children of pride," and in this scene may get, in a small sphere, what is taking place in the larger one of

---

*The word rendered in the Authorized Version "besieged places," is *matzohr*, used in Isaiah for Mitzraim, Egypt, with a play upon the word, the first meaning of which is "straitened," and so "fenced," "fortified." So the one word speaks of both the country and its military strength; quite unavailing in the mind of the Assyrian.

God's dealings with mankind, in the which all the victories of evil are only working out His "plan" (ver. 26) that has been formed very long ago, even from before the creation of the world.

There never has been, there is not today, a greater source of perplexity to thoughtful men than to harmonize the permission of evil, nay, its long-continued triumph,

> "Truth forever on the scaffold,
> Wrong forever on the throne,"

with an almighty and beneficent Governor!   How is it possible that Love and Power combined can permit such conditions?   But as the victories of the Assyrian had their predetermined limit, so have the apparent triumphs of wrong; we shall learn that a third attribute, Wisdom, governed all, and only carried out God's eternal plan, so that all those apparent triumphs are being over-ruled for the truest good of His beloved people.   Well may we with suffering Job, "faint with longing for that day" (Job 19: 27, true reading).

We have had some intensely interesting opportunities of applying these words of the Lord to our own day.   Look at Christendom, how unavailing are all policies!   How the nations are being driven as dried leaves in the blast!   Yet all things are working out that plan.   Little may America and Great Britain, France and Italy, Turkey and Russia think that there is an almighty Hand upon the helm; and that it is *His* counsels that are being so unconsciously carried out; but "whoso is wise and will observe these things, even they shall understand the loving-kindness of the Lord" for His own redeemed (Ps 107: 43).   This may well account for the Turk being cast out of Palestine, and thus laying it open for the Jew; for this is demanded, as we know, by God's plan.

One other point is of the deepest significance: on the surface it was poor Israel that the Assyrian struck at; but beneath the surface, and behind Israel, it was Jehovah against whom his rage mounted up.   And if there thus was a spiritual Power—even Jehovah—behind Israel, it becomes almost impossible not to discern behind the Assyrian, a spiritual power, even Jehovah's adversary, caring comparatively little for the mere human object of his attack, but ever aiming behind that object, at God Himself, and at that Throne that he was set to guard, and that he would fain fill himself.

The address now turns to Hezekiah and Israel:

> 30: Let this be thy sign:
> This year thou shalt eat
> That which springs of itself;
> Then in the next year
> Naught but its sproutings.
> But in the third year,
> Sow ye and reap; plant vineyards, and eat
> Of the fruitage thus freely produced.
> 31: For again shall the remnant of Judah
> Strike its roots deep into the ground,
> Whilst its branches spring upward above,
> All bearing their burden of fruit.
> 32: For from fair Salem shall go forth a remnant,
> And those who've escaped from Mount Zion.
> The zeal of Jehovah of Hosts
> Bringeth this into effect.

> 33: Therefore thus speaketh Jehovah,
> Concerning Assyria's king;
> He shall not come into this city,
> Nor shall he shoot arrow against it,
> He shall not assault it with shield,
> Nor cast up against it a mound.
> 34: By the way that he came:
> By the same shall he go;
> And into this city shall not come,
> Jehovah proclaimeth!
> 35: For I will defend this city and save it
> Both for My own, and for the sake of
> David, My servant.

Hard times lay ahead for the people of God. This year they would have to live on what the enemy left, since it was too late to sow anything; and next year the fare would be still more meagre, and only what might spring up automatically from some live root, or from some overlooked seed; but on the third, all fear would be gone, and they would be able to enjoy the fruits of what they had sown or planted.

Thus, in the *wisdom* of God (which we are apt to overlook, arguing only from His love and power), the very trial that might have shaken faith becomes a sign to strengthen and confirm it. Supposing our Bibles had foretold nothing but steady growth of love and holiness wherever the Name of the Lord was professed, and that the gospel should thus win constant victories, each hamlet, town, city and country, as they received it, becoming a very "garden of the Lord," till the whole earth should be precisely as was the Church in Acts 4; how should we feel after 2,000 years when we see "wars and carnage, craft and madness, lust and spite," raging within that very sphere? Should we not feel like throwing those Bibles away, and abandoning ourselves to despair? Surely we should. Then when we are plainly told to expect just the reverse, how those very conditions, sorrowful and humbling as they are, yet become a "sign" to us and confirm our faith. Let things, as in our text, get worse and worse; let the leaven of Papal superstition pervade one section of the professing Church, while the opposite leaven of infidel Modernism permeates the other, and the two threaten to sweep away every vestige of the basic truths of the gospel; let earthquakes convulse the material world, and wars and revolutions the political; let millions be forced to idleness, and depression cloud the nations— all shall prove a sign to faith, for so has it been foretold. And difficult as it may become to get wholesome spiritual sustenance for the two years, His poor people shall not be entirely unnourished,* the third year shall come, and the joyful in-gatherings of the harvest-home shall justify the anticipations of faith, based on that Word which, though heaven and earth pass away, shall *never pass away*.

As to Israel, Jehovah has not forgotten David; and for his sake, and for the sake of His own Name—not yet fully told out as it has since been—He will defend that city with which David's name has been so closely identified. Who can help saying: "If He will do this for that poor erring king, what will He not do for His beloved Son, with whom even I (poor sinner as I am by

---

*The Good Samaritan left two pence, the equivalent of two days' need and wages (Matt. 20: 2), to last till he came again. And if his return was delayed, yet the rescued one must not lack.

nature) am identified by the life He has given me; to whom I am joined by the Holy Spirit; and on whom I am depending?" Reader, let us ask ourselves *that*.

That night 185,000 Assyrian soldiers lay down never to rise again in this life!  O strong Hand of God, who can defy Thee with impunity!  But most careful must we be not to introduce any thought of an eternal penalty being involved in this temporal one.  This judgment was not on the individuals slain, any more than on those who suffer in any universal divine chastening.  As in the days of the deluge, many a child must have gone to be with the Lord; nor is there anything to forbid the hope that many a penitent, even after the door of the Ark was shut, and there was no hope of being saved from the flood, found mercy for *eternity*, although not in time.  In the divine government of the earth, we see a type of His eternal government; and those who now reject offered mercy and the love of the truth, will as inevitably suffer in and for eternity, as did the Assyrian 185,000 in and for time.  "Just and true are Thy ways, Thou King of nations: who shall not fear Thee, O Lord, and glorify Thy name?"

The curtain in this first Act of the world drama falls as we see Sennacherib, with the remnant of the Assyrian army, going with utmost speed back to his own land.  His place as a world-power is now taken by Babylon, as the remaining portion of this short division intimates.

# CHAPTER THIRTY-EIGHT

**Hezekiah's Sickness and Recovery**

A LTHOUGH the chapter begins with the words, "In those days," the event of which it tells did not occur in chronological sequence to the deliverance of Jerusalem by the destruction of the Assyrian army, for that is here promised and must therefore have been still in the future.

Hezekiah reigned twenty-nine years (2 Kings 18: 2), and it was fifteen years prior to his decease that he was dangerously ill, as here told. That would bring the sickness back to the fourteenth year of his reign: *the very year in which he was in such deep distress from the Assyrian,* as chap. 36: 1 has already told us. We can well believe that the poor king must have uttered the proverbial sigh that few of the children of men have not breathed: "Misfortunes never come singly." In this light, the sickness, with the tender grace of God in the recovery, must have strengthened the faith of the king for the trial with the Assyrian that Jehovah foresaw was coming on him—*that* is ever His way with His people. He knows what awaits us and strengthens us for it, and nothing so strengthens for trial as trial gone through with Him.

This second Act, then, opens with a sick room, in which the king lies prostrated by a malignant ulcer. To him there comes the prophet of the book, Isaiah, who, as we are reminded, was the son of Amoz,* and tells him to put his house in order, to make his last will and testament, for he is about to die.

This sentence of death was a terrible message for the poor

---

*God's messengers by their very names tell of His ability to carry out His purposes whatever they may be. Gabriel is distinctively the "messenger angel," and his name means, "God is mighty," or, "the strength of God." So we are here reminded that Isaiah is the one born of Amoz, which also means "strength," and we who can throw the light of the New Testament on to the Old feel perfectly justified in seeing that it is "strong faith" that results in "the salvation of the Lord."

king, who turned his face to the wall (what a human touch is that!) that he might, as far as possible, shut out all the distracting objects about him, and be alone with Jehovah. Then he pleads for his life. He does not despair. He may have argued: Would God have thus warned me had there not been a possibility, indeed a purpose of mercy, and that by His servant, whose very name speaks of "salvation?" It is at least His blessed way. Again and again He would stir us up to greater exercise by what would seem on the surface to make all exercise unavailing. "Sleep on now and take your rest" (Matt. 26: 45)—did the Lord really mean that they were then and there to sleep? Surely not, as the very next words show. "Let Me alone that I may destroy them" (Deut. 9: 14); was that God's real desire? Far from it. "Yet forty days and Nineveh shall be destroyed" (Jonah 3: 4). *Was* it? "He that is filthy, let him be filthy still" (Rev. 22: 11). Is *that* His desire for any? No, no; they that have any knowledge of God will draw different conclusions as did the stricken king, as did Jacob and Moses before him, as may we. It often needs, not a mere acquaintance with words, but a true knowledge of God to arrive at what He means by the words.

With his face to the wall, we hear the king speak, and he begins with a word of lowly supplication, "O Jehovah, I beseech Thee." You see it was a very dreadful thing for a Jewish king to die at thirty-nine, in the very prime of life, with no heir to follow. And what light had he on conditions after death? Death in such a case was terribly suggestive of penalty for sin. These Old Testament saints—saints indeed, as they were—may have had in some cases brief twilight glimpses of His "day," and rejoiced even in that far-off sight, but the mass did not have as much light as Abraham. They knew nothing of One, who is the dearest object of His Father's heart, having loved them, and the efficacy of whose precious Blood shed for their sins remains forever. What a stupendous difference, not only in Hezekiah's prayer, but even in the gracious answer to it, and the knowledge that the Christian has in this day. Then, "fifteen years" was added to a life that was still all through these years filled with danger and sorrow. Now in Christ we have a life that is eternal and shall "never see death" (John 8: 51).

The basis of his plea is that of an upright Israelite under the government of God, "I have loved Thy Word, am not conscious of a divided heart, and have had tokens of Thine approval; do, I beseech Thee, remember all this," and he wept aloud. He is thinking of his own faithfulness, no wonder that he weeps! You and I, reader, are like Hezekiah in this, we never sing when we are thus occupied with ourselves. His *song* speaks a different language, has quite a different accompaniment than begging God to remember *his* faithfulness, and there are no tears when we too are speaking of God's faithfulness and patient love. David himself learned that secret when he sang his 77th Psalm.

The answer was not grudgingly given, it was practically instantaneous; for Isaiah had not gone far before he is told to return with quite a different message, and well may we believe that this would make his step much lighter in accord with a lighter heart, for a good man loves to proclaim good tidings. But note that in that gracious answer there is not much reference to Hezekiah's "perfect heart," but what is Jehovah remembering? "David thy father," and surely we may discern behind that David, the true David, through, by, and for whom God overflows with all tender mercy to those whose confidence is in *Him*.

Fifteen years are to be added to the king's life, as long again as he has already reigned, but the answer goes beyond the petition; He does, according to His wont, more than Hezekiah has asked, for not only shall he recover, but the threatened city shall not be captured. That must have afforded solid ground on which Hezekiah's faith could rest later. Further, Jehovah gives him the sign for which he had asked, the significance of which we must now seek (in dependence on the Lord) to discern.

It will be well to look at the text carefully; for it has more than one possible rendering: Verse 8 reads literally: *"Behold, I will cause the shadow of the steps to return, which is gone down on the steps of Ahaz with the sun, backward ten steps. And the sun returned ten steps by the steps which it had gone down."* The most difficult word is that rendered "steps." The prime meaning of the root, is *"to go up,"* hence a "means of ascent," hence a "step," as in its first occurrence (Exod. 20: 26), "Neither shalt thou go up by *steps* unto Mine altar," and would there clearly speak of dependence on one's own conduct, or, as so frequently termed in the New Testament, *walk,* in approaching God. In the titles of Psalms 120-126 and 131-134, the same word is rendered *"degrees,"* and there refers to those *"goings up"* to the House of the Lord at Jerusalem three times in the year, at the feasts in which the Lord gathered His people about Himself.

But here we are compelled to see in these literal "steps" a form of sun-dial. Hence the word is rendered "the *sun-dial* of Ahaz."

We can now transport ourselves in spirit to Hezekiah's palace, and into his chamber. There lies the king, still prone on his couch, but with face no longer turned to the wall, but joy and hope brightening his eye as he looks out of the window to the gardens, in the midst of which, and in full view, stands an obelisk, or column, with a series of steps leading up to it, and at least ten of these are lying in the column's shadow; for the sun has gone so far down as to throw that shadow over that number of steps. But look again, the once darkened steps are now in clearest sunlight—'tis the sign for which the king had asked! What wonder that he sings!

Commentators have written copiously discussing as to how this recession of the shadow was effected, but vain and unsatisfactory it all is; nor may we further darken counsel by words without knowledge by entering the discussion. Of three things, however, we are quite sure: first, it was a supernatural intervention of God, controlling His own laws as being above them: next it was a "sign" which necessitated Hezekiah being able to see what had taken place, for unless a sign appeals in some way to the senses, it would be rather an extra strain on faith than the aid that it was intended to be, so that the sun-dial must have been visible from the sick-chamber. In the third place, it was not a *meaningless* sign—as if anything that came first could be taken at random—but in accord with the divine wisdom that selected it, must have had in itself deep significance, as have the bread and the wine of the Lord's Supper, for instance, and indeed *all* His works. The sign then must not be severed from the deeper truth that it signified.

Well may we be assured that the king would ponder the meaning of the light being on those steps that had lain in the shadow; and his meditations might lead him to remember the "steps" in which that Ahaz of whom the dial spoke, had walked. *His steps were ever in the dark,* a mistrust that, as we are definitely told, "wearied" God (Isa. 7: 13), and led him to a confidence in, and alliance with, the Assyrian. *That* was "shady" enough surely; his "steps" were not in the light.

Now the conditions are absolutely reversed; here the Assyrian is not threatening a son of Ahaz, but a son of *David* (verse 5), who is marked as such by *his* "steps" being in the light of the God of David's grace—like those re-lit steps, the House of David is walking in the light. The same divine power, the same sovereign grace, that brought back the shadow, had made and kept his heart true, as he had pleaded that it was (verse 3). The sign would teach him this. May it teach you and me the same, that all our steps in the light are due to the same divine power.

As the "sign" had, we believe, a deeper than a superficial meaning, so had the healing by the fig-plaister; but that we will reserve for the place in which it is found.

The chapter again clearly divides into *three* parts—the third being the outward manifestation of the other two:

1. Verses 1 to 8: The divine counsels, and authoritative announcement of *salvation.*
2. Verses 9 to 20: The responsive human song of *salvation.*
3. Verses 21, 22: The invariable double evidence or manifestation of *salvation*: (*a*) God, in Christ, in the healing; (*b*) Man, in the light, in the sign.

Let us now turn to the second part and listen to Hezekiah's song, for thus far all has been prose:

10: I said in the noon of my days,
    I shall go to the portals of Hades—
    Of my remnant of days I'm deprivèd.
11: I said, I shall never see JAH,
    JAH in the land of the living.
    When I too am dwelling
    With all who've ceased living,
    Nevermore shall I look upon man!

12:My house* is all broken, and carried
        As the tent of a shepherd, afar.
        I have rolled up my life as a weaver his work,
        And me from the thrum† He hath severed.
        From day unto night Thou art bringing
        My life to its (sorrowful) ending.
13: I patiently waited till morning;
        Like to a lion, so doth He crunch
        Every bone in my body.
        From day unto night Thou art bringing
        My life to its (sorrowful) ending.
14: Like a swallow or crane, so I twittered,
        Or mournfully cooed as a dove,
        Mine eyes with their up-look are failing.
        O Lord, I am greatly oppressed,
        Undertake (I beseech Thee), for me!


Now the air changes:


15: What shall I say?  He hath spoken—brought it Himself
            to completion,
        Softly and solemnly‡ shall I now walk, all the years of
            my life-time,
        Because of the bitterness (even to death) wherein my soul
            has been suff'ring.
16: O my Adonai, by these things men live, and in all is the
            life of my spirit.
        Thou hast recovered me, made me return to the land of
            the living.
17: Bitter, O bitter!  But 'twas for my peace, and Thou hast
            tenderly loved my
        Soul from the pit of corruption, my sins all behind Thy
            back casting.
18: For out of Hades no praise comes to Thee: Death hath
            no song for Thy glory.
        Nor can Thy truth be the hope of the dead who to the
            tomb are consignèd.

---

*Through all time the body has been recognized as only the
tabernacle-house of the person within it.

†Thrum, the thread that still may connect the fabric with the
weaver's beam.

‡The word applies to a solemn walk, suitable to a going to the
temple.

19: The living, the living, shall praise Thee, even as I do this
(glad) day
(Now) shall the father to children make known Thy truth
never failing.
20: Jehovah was ready to save me!  Well may we then touch
the harp-strings,*
And sing to those chords all the days of our life in the
house of Jehovah.

It is a delightful song.  Evidently as the sickness hung like
a heavy cloud over poor Hezekiah, and to his suffering spirit
witnessed that God's Hand was upon him in chastening; so, the
sickness gone, not merely bodily ease resulted, but his spirit rejoiced in the sunshine of that love that he had lost awhile.  How
can he help singing?  Have *you* no fellowship with him?

Verses 10 to 14 are retrospective in a mournful minor key,
and require little comment.  "I had received my sentence," the
king says; "in the prime of my life I was ordered to the portal
of Hades, and the remainder of my years were to be forfeited.
Never again was I to go to Jehovah's house to see Jah,† and even
my fellow-man I was to look upon nevermore.  My tabernacle-
house was to be taken down, broken up, and carried away as
some shepherd's tent by a strong wind.  I was to consider all
my life-work ended, and to roll it up as a weaver does his finished fabric.  It was He who would give the finishing stroke and
cut me off from that work, as does the weaver the thread that
links his work with the loom; nor would that take Him long;
one day would be enough, from day to night, and it was all over
with me!

"But the night passed, and I put a curb on all my emotions
—quieted myself till the morning, but its light brought no relief,
only a repetition of yesterday's sufferings awaited me.  He
crunched my bones as a lion his prey, and I could only repeat
that my end must surely come today!  Thus I twittered as a
swallow or crane, or mourned like the dove, and all the time I

---

*Neginothi n'nagen, lit., "my stringed instruments we will
strike," for nahgan is "to strike strings," and so "to play on a
stringed instrument."

†The word "Jah" eliminates from the longer "Jehovah" the idea
of relationship with men, and speaks of what He is essentially in
Himself.

was looking upward till my very eyes ached, and my heart was crying out, 'O Lord, see the oppression under which I groan— take Thou up my case into Thy Hand, as does one who has gone surety for another and so has to look after him.' "

Beautifully set off by the foil of the dark cloud in the preceding elegy, verses 15 to 20 are like the sunshine that seems to chase away the retreating storm, for the king goes on, "What can I say?   How can I worthily celebrate His praise whose anger is so slow to rise, so ready to abate?   He spoke, and He did! He promised and He fulfilled!   Yet my affliction must not be resultless—the years added: how shall I best use them?   They are few and therefore valuable and not an hour should be wasted. I will walk them humbly and penitently, as one who has needed such chastening, for now I see the benefit of the affliction.   Now I see that it is by such sorrows that men truly live; and I do confess that the life of my spirit has been revived by the very griefs that threatened to overwhelm me.   I suffered, indeed, I did; but the end in view was my peace, and from the very portals of the pit He has drawn my poor soul by the cords of His love, and (oh, joy unspeakable!) my *sins are gone,* He sees them no more, they are not before His Face but behind His Back.   How far better for me not to have to plead a *supposedly* faithful life —which is more than problematical—but to know that transgressions are all forgiven and sins covered!   But had I gone to the pit!   Thine ears would have heard no praises.   Shall my salvation from it make no difference?   I will *sing,* for I *live!* Every day of the fifteen years I will renew my song with the accompaniment of harp-strings* to Jehovah."

---

*If everything in the worship of Jehovah in both Tabernacle and Temple was a type, we may be quite sure that these varying instruments of music are not exceptions, but have also their counterparts in this day.   But not in material trumpets and harps shall we find them, but in the gentle action of the Spirit on our spirits may the wind-instruments be seen, awakening the silences of nature into music.   And so the harp, amid the stringed instruments, may tell us of that Touch of a Master Hand that can make our dull, dormant affections to thrill with joy.   Well may we cry, "Awake, O north wind, and come, thou south" (Cant. 4: 16), but also pray, "Strike, Lord, those stringed instruments till every quivering motion makes melody to Thy praise."

Verses 21 and 22 are again retrospective, telling of the sign and the application of bruised figs. We have already considered the former; but we must not ignore the significance of the latter.

The prophet, acting on behalf of Jehovah, directs a poultice of bruised figs be laid on the ulcer that is here called a "boil," but from its extremely dangerous character, there can be little doubt that it went far beyond the comparatively innocuous, though painful, malady we know under that name.

It was, from the very word used, an ulcer highly inflamed, bringing a burning fever to the patient, and so sapping the vitality of the whole system, that would surely suggest a carbuncle rather than a simple boil.* But leaving this, as comparatively unimportant, the fig thus applied was a well-known mollifying agent to promote the discharge of the offensive matter from the sore, and so the recovery of the patient.

But we ask, Is then God Himself dependent on natural remedies? Was that why He directed this application? Most surely not. We may look for a deeper significance than merely the physical benefit derived from the application of the figs.

The vine, olive and fig were the three symbolic trees that stood for mankind, and especially for the representative of the race, Israel, and in their respective services, for what God desired to find in man according to his tripartite nature. Thus man was to correspond with the *vine* in giving Him *joy* and thus

---

*The word *shechin* is from a root "to be hot." We find it as one of the plagues of Egypt, hence it is called "the *botch* of Egypt" (Deut. 28:27). Leviticus tells us that its presence was very favorable for the outgrowth of leprosy, although this did not necessarily follow. By this means Satan was permitted to afflict Job. It was the result of a disordered internal condition; and, in the symbolic way that all these things are used in the Old Testament, it was an evidence of the "ills that flesh is heir to," but "heir to" solely because of the moral disorder that has been passed down from our first parent to all his race. Thus Hezekiah in this narrative undoubtedly stands for that representative nation of Israel, and this sickness illustrated and evidenced the deep moral disorder of the nation, and their consequent sufferings under the hand of God. Psalm 118 (and especially verses 17-19) is the nation's song of recovery after the chastening, and corresponds with this of Hezekiah.

glorifying Him. "Should I leave my wine that *cheereth God and man?*" (Judges 9: 13). Man was to correspond with the *"olive"* in being a *light*, a true witness for Him in the earth. Of what then does the "fig" speak? It was the tree yielding *food* for the body. It was when the Lord was physically *hungered* that He saw a "fig tree afar off," and since it made claims to vitality in its leafage, He came to it expecting to find *food* in its fruit (Mark 11: 13), symbolically.

Thus the three trees symbolically expressed what God looked for from every part of man's tripartite being: the "fig" told him that he must glorify or satisfy God in his body; the vine that he, as a wise son, must make a *glad* father, and thus glorify God in the sphere of the *soul;* and the olive that he must glorify God by being a true and faithful witness, and thus giving light by his *spirit*.

He has failed from beginning to end in every particular. He is that vine that only produces "stinking" *grapes*, as we have seen in chapter 5; he has never been a true and faithful *witness*, and is indeed a "very naughty fig" (Jer. 24: 2). But we have all *heard of*, and some of us *know* One who is all these: the "true Vine" (John 15), "The faithful and true Witness" (Rev. 3: 14), and the very good "Fig" that satisfies God altogether. So in our narrative, this "fig" applied to that death-bearing sore is the good "Fig," Christ, but not as living, but *"bruised"* (for a fig unbruised could not make a poultice), as He has indeed been, and *so*, thus bruised, applied to the fatal sore. He, and He only, can and does heal poor man's death-bearing sickness, even that burning ulcer, *sin*, that inevitably ends in the second death, the lake of fire. So, reader, you and I, with all mankind, must owe all our recovery from that deadly disease to Him, and to Him alone, and that alone as bruised, or we too must perish.

Now, this is why, I venture to suggest, this word as to the "bruised fig" is placed in the *third* division of the narrative in this book whose very title speaks of "the salvation of Jehovah." It may be, of course, as commentators say, that "some later person, with the feeling that there was a disturbing gap, thought that he would supply it from the second book of Kings, or, as another, that "it was omitted from its place at the close of verse 6 by an oversight, and then added by the same pen." But the numerical structure assures us that even if it were thus due to human frailty, God overruled that frailty for His own deeper purposes; and in that "bruised fig" *manifested Himself*, in healing and salvation, as indeed He did, and as the *third* place witnesses here. And where has He, the Saviour-God, been so manifested as in Him who was *bruised* for our iniquities, by whose stripes we are healed?

# CHAPTER THIRTY-NINE

**The embassage from Babylon and its consequences.**

WE again drop poetry and return to prose, which certainly appears more harmonious with the contents of our short chapter, recording the failure in the testimony of a true saint, followed by the announcement of divine chastening on the nation.

The beloved Hezekiah, whose sincere intention was to "walk softly," has a more dangerous trial to undergo than the threatening of an open and powerful enemy, or the suffering from an internal disorder; and, what neither of these could effect, Babylon, coming in the guise of friendship, accomplished!

Both history and experience combine to tell us that the hour of peculiar blessing is the very hour of greatest danger. The natural tendency (unconscious, as it mostly is) to *presume* at such a time leads to a fall, as poor Peter found; for hardly had he heard the words, "Blessed art thou, Simon Barjona," before they are followed by, "Get thee behind Me, Satan;" while, to go back to an earlier day, that faithful "man of God, out of Judah," who had passed a day of faithful testimony, succumbs to the wile of an old "prophet," and never again shall he witness at all, for the setting sun throws its rays upon his dead body! (1 Ki.13). Perhaps we too may know something of the same kind of failure and sorrow.

The history of that hour is not without its interest. Babylon was then only rising, and struggling to overthrow the dominant power, Assyria. She made but slow progress. Defeat after defeat did Babylon suffer, till her cause must have seemed hopeless. (How slow does God's work in the affairs of the world appear to us creatures whose life is so short!) Yet those repeated defeats were but as "waves" that gave a misleading testimony as to the trend of the "tide," which was really rising; and although this Merodach suffered many disasters after this, as did his son, eventually Nebuchadnezzar gained the coveted

throne over the whole prophetic earth, and Babylon replaced
Assyria, and thus we are introduced to that strange city that
has so sinister a relation to our own race.

It was unquestionably a community of interests that led to
the external amity between Babylon and Judah, that the chapter
records. A common antagonism will bring the most heterogeneous
elements to a unity, but such an accord has the gravest danger
for that party to it who is the Lord's. Thus if a Christian today
finds himself or herself working beside, and yoked with one or
many, to whom the Lord Jesus is not truly "all," the common
object before each being looked upon as in a sense sanctifying
the otherwise unhallowed association—let him or her beware.
How frequently we see such associations for the purifying of
politics, or bettering the world in its distance from God; objects
that have a superficial appearance of goodness, yet all on the
world-side of the Cross, and therefore "wood, hay and stubble,"
that must eventuate in loss to the Christian in the future and
often leading to the vexing his righteous soul here. This religious Delilah-world loves to weave the Nazarite locks of the true
saint with her fair-looking but Christless work; it adds to her
respectability, eventuates in his loss of the power that is due to
separation and dependence, till he finds that, as in this matter
of the Babylonian ambassadors, and as all history confirms, this
world's politeness but too often hides Satan's policy.

We are not told the name of the king of Babylon, Merodach-
Baladan, without some purpose for our profit. The first part of
this compound word seems quite clear in its meaning: the con-
sonants that form the root, *m, r, d,* make the root-verb *marad,*
"to rebel," and the derived substantive is "the rebel." The
suffix *ach* (really only one letter, *k*) may be either the
possessive "thy"; or, as Gesenius takes it, simply formative, that
is, not affecting the meaning of the word, and so, not to be
translated. Our thoughts go back to the founder of Babylon or
Babel, *Nimrod,* a name made up of the same root letters, *m, r, d,*
the prefixed *n* being again only formative. "Merodach" then
is only *"Nimrod"* reproduced. The last part, "Baladan," itself
is a compound, *bal,* the negative "not," and *adahn,* "Lord;" so
that the whole name of "Merodach-Baladan" to Jewish ears would

give the divinely intended meaning, "A rebel, not Lord;" which, thus applied, is surely suggestive enough!

But at once we say, What parent would give such an opprobrious name, or indeed any part of it to his own child, especially a proud dweller in Babel?     That is certainly a very natural question; but the point for us is primarily not what the parent might mean by the word, or such a dweller in that city might understand from it, but what would the sound of it convey to the ears of the people of God in those days?     And that seems quite clear as above.     No doubt there are alternative meanings, and to a Babylonian they would convey quite an opposite sense in accord with these, as is by no means unusual in such terms.     To *him* "Merodach" would stand for, and recall, Babel's supreme deity (as it is written, *"Merodach* is broken in pieces," Jer. 1:2), who corresponded with Bel, or Baal, or the Greek Zeus, or Jupiter, the prince of all the false deities, and the scriptural "prince of the demons," the Devil!     Thus, behind "Merodach" the Jew might be reminded of Babel's founder, Nimrod; and behind Nimrod the Christian may discern the *founder* of all the "confusion" that has come into this distracted scene, that mighty creature, now called Satan or Devil, who would fain be "Lord," "as the Most High" (Isa. 14; Ezek. 28); but who, in this very name, is reminded that he is now but *Merodach,* a rebel; and *Baladan,* not the Lord—that supreme dignity which he, by robbery, would grasp (contrast Phil. 2: 6).*     But it was thus the Babylon-

---

*To illustrate the double meanings that so many of these words have, take the very word "Babel" itself.     God Himself gives us its true sense, "Confusion" (Gen. 11: 9, *marg.*), a word that would for all time express its moral condition, under whatever aspect it might exist, whether civil or religious, city or church.     But would Nimrod have so slurred his capital city?     Surely not; and to him Bab-el would have the other meaning: "The Gate of, or to God"; precisely as the modern representative of that ancient city proclaims herself, even to this day.     Does not the Roman Church insist that there can be no salvation save through her?     She, and she only, is the "Gate of, or to God."     She may pretend to modify this in some countries as a matter of expediency, but let the mask be dropped, and the proud face accords with the lips that make the same unchanged claim of being Bab-el, the "'Gate to God," whilst

ians deified their founder, made him a god, and the devil secured their worship, according to 1 Cor. 10: 20. That condition has not passed away. Still is he *"the god of the world,"* and still men, called Christian, unconsciously worship him behind their mad coveting for this world's name and fame, its wealth and possessions.

Hezekiah was evidently flattered by such attention from a people who had come from so far. He "was glad," and apparently of his own initiative exposed to them all his precious things. This vain-glorious display is made the basis for the announcement of captivity, not to frowning Assyria, but to smiling Babel, not to the threatening, but the flattering Power, not to the dominant, but to the State still to be defeated, and defeated, and again defeated. How utterly improbable must it have appeared, how far away!

We do not get the true force of this exposure if we stop at the mere externals. Of course, *that* was all those ambassadors of Babel would see or care for; but Israel's wealth was not only the token of divine goodness, it always symbolized truer riches that are not so evanescent as those of earth. Let us accompany Hezekiah and the messengers through the house, and seek to look with anointed eye on the treasures thus exposed. They evidently are in three pairs, of which the first mentioned comprises the precious metals, *"Silver and Gold."* These were just what the Christian apostle lacked altogether; silver and gold had he none (Acts 3). But they are symbols of God's own love-gifts *to us,* the "silver" speaking always of atonement (Exod. 30), the price at which we have been purchased, the precious Blood of Christ; and the "gold" speaking of that *divine* nature communicated in the new birth. The "silver" telling of the work *for,* the "gold"

---

she is really Babel, the author of "Confusion." For her proud boast is that she is always the same, everywhere and at all times, Then her canon-law is in full force today, and "he that acknowledges not himself to be under the Bishop of Rome and that the Bishop of Rome is ordained of God to have primacy over all the world, is a heretic and cannot be saved, is not of the flock of Christ." Again, "He is no manslayer who slayeth a man that is excommunicate." Which do these proclaim her to be—"the gate to God," or moral "Confusion"?

of the work *in* every saint. These are very precious treasures. The next pair, *"spices and precious ointment,"* both speak of the work of God, not *for,* nor *in,* but *on* every believer. And as the atonement, of "silver," is peculiarly the work of the *Son;* and the "gold," or regeneration, may be peculiarly attributed to God as *Father;* so these "spices" and "ointment" speak equally clearly of the work of the *Spirit* who puts the fragrance of Christ on all the Lord's people (Exod. 30).    Thus in these two pairs we have the "precious things" with which the divine Trinity endows every member of Christ.

In the third and last place Hezekiah shows, "All the house of his armour, and all that was found in his treasures."  This seems to be added to indicate, first, that Hezekiah appropriated all the divine gifts as if they had been intended for his own glory: and, next, showing the completeness of the exposure of all his personal possessions, whether as provision against external aggression, or indicative of the internal prosperity of his house; as though he would thus say: "See how rich and increased with goods I am, and have need of nothing." Our Lord has blessed us also with "precious things," along these two lines of armor and treasure.   May we not see the former in Ephesians 6:11-18; and the latter in the same Epistle (4:10-18)? A little faith will find wonderful treasures too in chapter 1: 3-14, a casket filled with spiritual wealth.

But what could those visitors from Babel know of the real worth of these treasures?   They were indeed, in the point of view in which we have considered them, "pearls;" but in that same point of view the men were but "swine," who should in a future day turn and rend their possessors.   But for that we must see Isaiah again coming to the king, and we will listen to the ensuing colloquy:

Isaiah:      "What have these men said? And whence came they?"
Hezekiah:  "They are come from a far country unto me—from Babylon."
Isaiah:      "What have they seen in thy house?"
Hezekiah:  "All that is in *my* house have they seen: there is nothing among *my* treasures that I have not showed them."

Isaiah:     "Hear the word of Jehovah Tzebaoth: Behold the
            days come, that all that is in thy house, and all that
            thy fathers have laid up unto this day, will be carried
            away to Babylon: nothing will be left, saith Jehovah.
            And of thy sons that issue from thee, whom thou shalt
            beget, shall they take away, and they shall be eunuchs
            in the palace of the king of Babylon."

Hezekiah:   "Good is the word of Jehovah which thou hast spoken.
            For there shall be peace and stability in my days."

History tells us of the fulfilment of this prophecy, and the
prophet Daniel writes of that part of it that refers to the children
of the king. That punishment was not simply a penalty for the
display of wealth by Hezekiah; had it been so, it would have
fallen on him alone, but *personally* he escapes. The *nation* was
corrupt, the whole community was honeycombed with pride and
apostasy under a fair exterior, and the incident narrated in this
chapter afforded the occasion for the judgment pronounced upon
the people as a whole. Again Hezekiah's word has become true,
"Jehovah hath spoken, and hath brought it to pass," for after
its capture by Nebuchadnezzar, *nevermore to this day has Jerusalem been free*—she has been down-trodden of the Gentiles and
will so continue till the times of the Gentiles are fulfilled.

This captivity to Babylon then is really the beginning of that
series of four monarchies that have followed one another; God
overturning and overturning, replacing Babylon with Medo-
Persia; that by Greece; that in turn by Rome; and this last has
still to be revived, although, as I now believe, not at all according to its *geographical* boundaries, as many of us have thought,
but rather by *spiritual* limits, in accord with the character of this
day. We are standing at the verge of that revival, for it is clearly shadowed in the League of Nations; almost impotent as that
attempted Confederacy appears as yet to be.

But has not this sad history repeated itself? Has there
not been something analogous to Hezekiah's error among us today? Have we not received many precious things in the way of
"truth"? Have we not looked upon it as *ours,* to glorify ourselves therewith? Have *we* not in heart said, "I am rich and
increased with goods?"

Have we not personally too often spread it out and made it common, before the eyes of those who care nothing for it save only as a means of self-exaltation? So the condition of Laodicea—proud and lukewarm—has been, and is being, formed, and we, too, have become captive to the falsely-friendly Babylonian spirit that governs the day, as Samson to the Philistine through the wiles of Delilah. Oh, who can estimate the danger of dealing with God's gifts, whether the precious things of old, or the more precious truth of today, without penitence, without fear, but in order to display *our* wealth, or to gain the esteem of the religious Babylonian world. As that led to the captivity of Israel, so shall this to the Lord's spewing the professing Church out of His mouth; nor, if I err not, is that even as far off as the reviving of the fourth world-empire, which is surely near.

Hezekiah—dear man of God, as he really was—shows his divine birth by bowing submissively to the Word of the Lord, which he owns to be "good." It is just that genuinely lowly spirit that ever characterizes all that is truly of God in this world, through all dispensations, and will evidence the remnant of faith to this very day. He recognizes, too, the great mercy that has promised to keep him out of that time of temptation or trial. Both of the members of this final verse we can surely make our own. We, too, own the coming judgment on the faithless witness, the Church (in which we have our part, as did the Jewish king in the failure of his day), to be just and good; and we, too, may be humbly but sincerely thankful for that sure and sweet promise to be kept, "out of that hour," and to be "forever with the Lord" before it comes.

Thus, with human failure met by divine grace, this second part of our book (so like our own lives in this) is brought to its close.

# The Manifestation of God in His Ways with Israel

**This third part an integral portion of the book and the writing of the same author, not a Deutero-Isaiah. The divine and human authorship both attested by the same mark of "three" impressed upon it.**

ONE cannot approach this last part of our book that speaks so clearly and directly of our Lord, both as to His sufferings and the glory that shall follow, without fear lest he should fail to discern the intent of the Spirit in moving this holy man of God thus to speak; or, on the other hand, to deduce what is not in accord with that intent: that is, to err either in omission or commission. We know well that we are about to enter an apartment of the divine Word in which are treasures of gold, silver, and precious stones of truth, but without the light given by the same Spirit, who is the real Author of the book, we shall fail to find them. May the Lord deign to anoint our eyes with that eyesalve that shall cleanse them from all film, and enable us to see "wondrous things" in this holy Word.

With this in view, I cannot esteem necessary any lengthy attempt to show the unity of the whole book in the single authorship of its threefold parts. For 2,000 years and more there was not a whisper of a "Second Isaiah," or (since no one has ever discovered to whom these marvellous pages could be attributed), "The Great Unknown."

In the eighteenth century there arose a school of theologians, mostly residing in Germany, comprising names that have since become notorious, rather than famous, among all who love and reverence the Bible, as Eichorn, Paulus, Hitzig, Nobel and others, whom we can but class with those keen-witted false prophets that our enemy constantly sends out into the world to offset the grace of God. For just before the time of their appearing, Wesley,

Whitefield, Watts, Doddridge, Venn, and a host of kindred-spirited evangelists had been commissioned to go over all the earth with the gospel of Christ. Then later the modern "Tubingen School" (as it is called, since most of its adherents were connected with the university of that name) sent out its poison marked with that sure evidence of its Satanic source by claiming superior insight, a higher degree of candor and knowledge, generally, enwrapped in the appropriated name of "Higher Criticism."

But it must not be thought that it is because investigation as to the genuineness of this part of the book is feared or shirked that it is not taken up.  Christian scholars, certainly not *less* entitled to respect, both on account of their ability and of their integrity, than those with German names as given above (and indeed, including many from that country, as Keil, Delitzsch, Hengstenberg and many others) have followed patiently all the arguments of these opponents of truth, have analyzed them, and torn them to shreds.*

For us the clear testimony of the prophets, apostles and inspired writers of the New Testament will be all that we need. John Baptist testified of himself as "the voice of one crying in the wilderness, as said the prophet Esaias." That is, not "The Great Unknown," but the well-known Isaiah wrote the words in chapter 40.  This is followed by Luke (4: 17-21), the Lord Jesus Himself distinctly confirming the genuineness of chapter 61. Then comes Matthew (8: 17) and John (12: 37-41).  As to Acts 8: 26-40, Birks writes:

"If these verses which the eunuch was reading are not Isaiah's, and do not really predict the sufferings of the Lord Jesus, but are a doubtful guess at the sufferings of Israel by a nameless writer

---

*As an illustration of this Birks notes, "Forty words, even under the first letter of the alphabet alone, in which the later resemble the earlier prophecies of Isaiah, and which do not appear at all, with one or two slight exceptions, in the writings which are known to belong to the time of the exile, or the return from Babylon. . . . The verbal argument, on which the modern theory has relied in the teeth of all external evidence, when once fairly and inductively examined, is a powerful refutation of the hypothesis of a Deutero-Isaiah."

in the days of Cyrus—what conclusion will follow?  The eunuch would have been deceived and taught a double falsehood by a conspiracy of no less than three parties, the evangelist Philip, an angel of the Lord, and the Holy Spirit of God!  This grand religious fraud would then have been the first step in the conversion of Ethiopia to the Christian faith!"

Paul adds his voice to the sure truth in his letter to the Romans (10: 16-21).  One feels that to pursue the theme further would be an unjustifiable waste of time.

The root of the attack really lies in the determination of the human will to eliminate God from His creation altogether.  Admit that God is, and can be active in the affairs of men, and all such difficulties disappear.  Take the simplest and clearest "proofs" of the impossibility of Isaiah having written this part of the book that has borne his name.  How could Isaiah speak as if he himself were one of the captives in Babylon, whereas when he wrote Israel was not there at all?  Our opponents say: "It is a first principle that the historical horizon of a prophet belongs to his own time.  He takes his stand in his own generation and looks onward from it," which is a piece of reasoning quite worthy of self-styled Rationalism; for putting this into plain English it means that *being a prophet he cannot see beyond the horizon of his own times!*  For, if he can, where is the limitation of his Vision?

But we are even told the very name of the man who should decree the building of the city and the house, long before he came into existence!  Marvelous beyond credence, is it not? that God, who could call all worlds into being, whose every attribute is without limit, should be able to foreknow what lay two hundred years in the future for His people Israel, and by His Spirit actually communicate the name that a man should bear before he was born!  That is far too great a strain on the credulity of, and is detected at once as evidence of fraud by, the keen intellect of Rationalism!

But even as to this name of Cyrus, hear what Josephus, the Jewish historian, writes: "Now Cyrus learned this (as to building the House) by reading the book that Isaiah had left of his own prophecies 210 years before. . . . These things Isaiah foretold 140 years before the temple was destroyed. When Cyrus therefore had read them, and had admired their divine character, an impulse and emulation seized him to do what was written."

With this the first verses of Ezra come into line: "Thus saith Cyrus, king of Persia, the Lord God of heaven hath given me all the kingdoms of the earth, and *hath charged me to build Him a house at Jerusalem.*"

It is therefore certain that whoever wrote that prophecy wrote it before, and long before, Cyrus was born, or the fraud would have been transparent; but who but God could possibly be the Author of such a prophecy, let the human hand be whose it may? How well Delitzsch writes of this blatant, self-styled Rationalism: "Modern criticism visits all who dare assert that Isaiah was indeed the human writer with the double ban of want of science and want of conscience. No prophecies find any favor in its eyes save such as can be naturally explained. It knows exactly how far a prophet can see, and where he must stand in order to see so far. But we are not tempted at all to purchase such omniscience at the price of the supernatural."

We will then leave this question of authorship, and if the learned rationalists of our day prefer to call him "The Great Unknown," we shall adopt the words of the Holy Ghost used in another connection, and say, "Whom ye thus ignorantly name has been declared to us as *Isaiah.*" For that is the only name among men that by its very significance fits the contents of this "third part of the book." Does it not mean "The salvation of Jehovah?" And might not these chapters from 40 to 66 be so entitled, and to have as its author, one whose significant name expresses it? In these "the salvation of Jehovah" is more clearly set forth than in any other of the Old Testament pages.

Further, there is peculiar and inimitable beauty in the numerical structure of this third part that, apart from all other proof (and this abounds), bears on it evidence of its perfect unity with the parts that have preceded it. It is not too much to say that the *three* subdivisions of this *third* division are divinely marked out for us. Twice we get the words, "There is no peace, saith my God to the wicked," marking the termination of the first and second parts by the inerrant Finger of God.

This imprint of the number of divine manifestation, "three," is even more marked in this later part than anywhere else. I have already noted that Delitzsch* gives a testimony as to this that is of peculiar value, since he draws no deductions from it, and is *apparently* unaware of the striking value of what he finds, so that none can say with regard to these writers that they have first put in what they afterwards take out, for they apparently did not discern what was in.

Three! Why, here we have not only one three, but this raised again and again to ever higher powers: *three* main divisions of this third division, and each one of this three itself divided into *three*—and these again similarly subdivided into *three*.

I am not unaware that this will be met with a shrug, and perhaps with a pitying smile by many; but they might as well assume to pity those who with gladness discern the beauties of His works impressed on all nature, and the closer studied, the more clearly discerned—from those constellations that pursue their march through the heavens, down to the invisible diatom; the aid of the telescope on the one side and the microscope on the other only revealing perfections of His unrivalled Fingerprints, not discernible to nature's vision. That same bond of perfection that binds in unity all nature, also binds together the parts of our book, although it may, and does need, more than nature's powers to discern them.

Let me then repeat that God Himself has put His Fingerprint on this part of the book in the divisions. It is composed of 27 chapters divided into three threes each, thus:

1: Chapters 40 to 48, closed by the words, *"No peace to the wicked."*
2: Chapters 49 to 57, closed by the words, *"No peace to the wicked."*
3: Chapters 58 to 66, closed by the same finality of *"No peace to the wicked"* in Gehenna.

---

*And with him this scheme is adopted by Havernick, Hahn, Ruckert, and, among our more modern English writers, Darby, Kelly, and very many more.

The subdivisions of the first are:

1: Chapters 40 to 43: 13.
2: Chapters 43: 14 to 45: 25.
3: Chapters 46 to 48.

But once again, take the first of these subdivisions, and we find three sub-sections there:

1: Chapter 40.
2: Chapter 41.
3: Chapters 42 to 43: 13.

Let the reader consider for himself chapter 40, and can he fail to discern again three divisions?

1: Verses  1-11: The God of all comfort speaks to Israel.
2: Verses 12-26: Contrast with vain idols.
3: Verses 27-31: Divine strength manifested in weakness.

Yet even once again note the clear threefold division in verses 1 to 11, marked by three voices:

1: Verses 1, 2: The "voice" of comfort from Jehovah.
2: Verses 3-8: The "voice" in the wilderness, telling of contrast; frail man and the eternal Word.
3: Verses 9-11: The voice of Jerusalem, *"Behold your God."*

Surely so marvellous a structure, such a succession of trinities, can no more be attributed to chance or mere coincidence than the structure of a flower or of a butterfly's wing. The true Author is neither a first nor second Isaiah, but God.

# CHAPTER FORTY

**Jerusalem comforted. The expiation of national sins. The three voices. The incomparable grandeur of Jehovah. The blessedness of waiting on Him.**

THE marvellous structure of this chapter may merely provoke wonder without attracting the heart; let us then consider its lovely contents, taking the three parts in order.

The prophet is transported into another scene altogether than that in which he corporeally was. Precisely as the New Testament prophet, John, "became in Spirit in the Lord's day," and Patmos, with all man's injustice, disappears; he is where, by the very word "*Lord's* Day" in contrast with "man's day" (1 Cor. 4: 3, *marg.*), he sees the Lord exercising just judgment in the midst of the golden candlesticks. In that atmosphere, so clear, so free of earth's obscurations, John sees far into the future, and in that future the rise again of Babylon in another form, the dominance of hostile powers over the Church of God, and its deliverance. For the plan of that book runs along in two strata, the upper occupied with the Church, and the lower with Israel on earth. So the stream of prophecy flows on through the pen of the New Testament Seer as it does through that of the Old, only the former closes by placing our feet, not on the borders of a millennium as does Isaiah, but on the shore of an eternity of bliss; but both end with a reminder of the inflexible righteousness of the government and the stern severity of God against all creature pride, all defiant wickedness.

In all this John is, in a large degree, the counterpart of Isaiah, nor is it one whit more marvelous that the Spirit should transport the Old Testament Seer into scenes still future, than that the same Spirit should do precisely the same with the Seer of the New Testament. Nor do the names of these chosen vessels tell anything but a harmonious story. Little difference is there between "Isaiah," "The salvation of Jehovah," and "John"

(shortened from "Jehohanan"), "The grace of Jehovah." Are
they not practically the same? Let us then listen to the three
announcements.

> 1: Comfort ye, O comfort ye My people, saith your God!
> 2: Speak ye words of tenderness* even to Jerusalem,
> And cry to her aloud that her trouble† is all ended,
> That her sin is expiated,
> For double from Jehovah's hand
> Hath she for sins received.

The repetition of that first word "Comfort ye" is in itself
eloquent of the emotion behind the cold print. It is far from being a cold argument that is being worked out, it is the very Heart
of Jehovah that is speaking, and the repeated "Comfort ye" tells
of the intensity of the emotion under which the words are
spoken. It is, as we sometimes speak, a "heart-to-heart" word:
Jehovah's Heart speaks to that of Israel. For now again He
calls them *ammi* ("My people") who have been *lo-ammi* ("not
My people") so long.

What limitless significance is there in that one word, *ammi*,
"My people." He cannot possibly leave those whom He thus
owns as His in the power of an enemy, whether that enemy be
Egypt, Babylon, Greece, Persia, Rome, Antichrist, Devil, Death
or Hades; for He is their God at last, their Satisfier, their All.
Not the gifts, but the very Giver of all gifts is theirs now. But
He is not the God of the dead, but of the living, and that neces-
sitates the resurrection of Israel as a nation as it does the per-

---

*Lit., "to the heart." The word always has in it the sense of
great tenderness.

†The word I have rendered "trouble," in A. V. and R. V. "warfare," is *tzebah*, and we have become familiar with it in "*tzebaoth*,"
"hosts." The prime meaning of the root is "to go forth as a
soldier," hence "an army," or "host," then "warfare," used figuratively for a miserable condition which is for an appointed time,
as in Job 7: 1: "Is there not an *appointed time* for man upon the
earth?" Again: Job 14: 14: "All the days of my *appointed time*
will I wait till my change come." So here a certain time of trouble
that is limited in its duration.

sonal resurrection of their fathers, Abraham, Isaac and Jacob, and that of everyone who has died through all the ages of time.

The second verse then must be interpreted in direct accord with this key-note; hence nothing that is not of the most tender nature can be admitted. To that city, so long down-trodden of the Gentiles, does Jehovah now speak, and tells her that her appointed time of trouble has at last come to its end, that her sufferings have been accepted as expiation for her guilt, and that she has in them received of the Lord's hand double that which her sin merited.

Thus this threefold "comfort" is all in one line. It is not a Judge who speaks, but rather One who is as a mother comforting her weeping child. It must not be looked upon then as a logical, precise, *judicial* estimate; but cold reason is bidden to stand aside, and Love is allowed to utter its heart, according to its own blessed illogical reasoning. Just as any mother who has been severely punishing her child, and a malicious neighbor, standing near, insists that the child should be chastised still more. "No," says the mother, as she takes the penitent little one on to her lap; "no, I know the seriousness of his fault, I do not belittle that, but I know too the severity of the punishment that he has suffered, and, *in the estimation of my love,* he has been punished double that which his naughtiness demanded."

This is not a fancy picture that has no Scripture to justify it. In that malignant neighbor it is surely not difficult to discern one who as the accuser ever opposes the forgiveness and blessing of erring mankind; and there is but One who can rebuke *him!*

This throws its light on the second member of the verse, "Her sin is expiated," and shows that that expiation is not by the sufferings of a substitute, but by "Jerusalem's" own. This will awaken astonishment and, indeed, questioning; but Jehovah's dealings with Jerusalem (the city standing for the whole nation) are but a picture of His dealings with mankind, where the issues are not for the earth, or in relation to its government, but for eternity, not with nations, but individuals. In His government of the earth, where the inhabitants are divided into nations, the wrong-doing of the nation is expiated, and can only be expiated, by that nation's sufferings *as a nation* on the earth. Nations, as such, are not rewarded in heaven, nor punished in Gehenna, for they do not exist there as nations.* But earth affords pictures of heaven, the seen helps us to grasp the unseen, and God's ways in truth, divinely recorded for us, give clarifying illustrations of eternal verities. It is thus that we see shadowed in our verse, God's estimate of the atoning sufferings of our Lord.

How filled with divine beauty then do these words, "She hath received of the Lord's hand double for all her sins," become in that light. You and I, believing reader, have also "received of the Lord's hand double for all our sins." It is not, as some greatly err (Oh, how greatly!) in saying that redemption is merely a strictly mercantile transaction, and the sin of the first Adam has been met with an exact "corresponding price" (as they love to put it) by the Last Adam. No, no; a thousand times no! Beneath that "thick darkness over all the land from the sixth to the ninth hour," we can hear One saying to us—even to us— that we there, and there only, have "received of the Lord's hand double for all our sins." What strength of humble, brokenhearted, yet joyous confidence withal, that gives! *That* is Love's estimate—nay, more, that is the strict estimate of Righteousness —of those infinite sufferings of the Sinless One. Worthy of all worship is He! Of the value of *those* sufferings, the estimate of Israel's as here told is but a faint, faint shadow!

The second announcement in three parts follows:

3: Hark!  A voice in the wilderness crying,
   Clear ye a way for Jehovah!
   Prepare in the desert a road for our God!
4: Every valley shall be lifted,
   Every mount and hill brought low,
   The crooked shall be straightened,
   And the rough made smooth.
5: And the glory of the Lord shall be seen;
   All flesh shall see together, the salvation of our God.

*In Ps. 9: 17 the word "hell" may give a false idea; it is *sh'ohl*, the then unknown place of the dead, where they all go.  The verse simply tells of the earth being swept clear of the wicked.

6: A voice saith, Cry!
   What shall I cry?
   All flesh is grass,
   And all its loveliness is like
   The flower of the field.
7: Withered is the grass!   Faded is the flower!
   For the wind of Jehovah upon it hath blown:
   Surely, most surely, the people is but grass!
8: Withereth the grass, fadeth the flower,
   But the Word of our God forever shall stand!

In this second section we hear *two* voices, nor have we the slightest difficulty in identifying the first that is heard crying in the wilderness, for the Gospels have told us of one who when asked, "Who art thou then?" replied in the very words of our prophet that it was *he,* John the Baptist, who was neither Christ nor Elias, nor "that prophet," but only "a voice crying in the wilderness."

That is plain and unequivocal; but equally plain and unequivocal, and infinitely sweeter is it to discern in Him whose way John prepared, none other than Jehovah.   The voice cries, "Clear the way for Jehovah!"   Then if John is the voice, Jesus must be Jehovah!

With what divine skill is the essential deity of our Lord, His co-equality with God in oneness of life and nature, maintained in the Scriptures.   Not only by such plain, simple, clear statements as, "In the beginning was the Word, and the Word was with God, and the Word was God;" or "Christ, who is over all, God blessed forever," and many others (man's carnal mind at enmity with God may throw doubts and slurs on the genuineness of these didactic statements, irrefutable as they are), but so interwoven is that truth into the very warp and woof of the Scriptures that they must be torn to shreds and rejected *in toto* before that most fundamental truth can be annulled.

It was a very "cunning workman" that wove the literal veil of the Tabernacle, with its cherubic glories of blue, purple, scarlet, gold and fine-twined linen; but an infinitely more "Cunning Workman" wove the record of that inscrutable Person, the Antitype to that veil.   None can withdraw one single thread of those answering glories that the Spirit has revealed in Him; they shall bear their witness to the divine glory of His Person, the limitless value of His atoning work, untouched and unaffected by all the vain attacks of demon or man, from age to age, forever and forever!

"Clear the way for Jehovah," the first voice cries; fill up the valleys, lower the mountains, bring all to one dead level (or level of death), for only thus shall the figure express the truth that there is no difference in the poor sinful race to which He comes. Let all be buried in baptism, thus owning the justice of the sentence of death on the race (Rom. 5: 12), and with all hope in flesh thus buried let them take the place of repentance, there to await—Whom? Jehovah? Aye; but shrink not, tremble not; it is indeed Jehovah who comes, but He is to be found in Jesus, as *Saviour* from the sins confessed, both their penalty and power!

Let us not overlook another accompaniment of that preparation of the way of Jehovah; not only must it be levelled but straightened. All that is "crooked," Jacob-like, guileful, not "straight," must be abandoned. For baptism there must not be a claim to saintship, but a confession of sins—a much-forgotten truth.

One more piece of work must yet be done on that road. It is level and straight, but still it is rough, and must be made smooth. Those hard rocks, stones, and clods are not mountains, but they must be broken up; so must all hardness of heart by the conviction of guilt in the sight of Jehovah. The mountain may speak of pride, the rough ridges in the road tell of its accompaniment in "the hard and impenitent heart" that refuses the salvation.

Verse 5 shows that in that salvation shall be such an outshining of glory, that all flesh shall see it together. It shall focus the rapt attention of all mankind as if it had but one eye, and that eye *could* look nowhere else.

Surely that was not the case when the young Child lay in Bethlehem's manger. The "glory" was there, indeed, but so veiled that *no* flesh saw it, or at least "all flesh" did *not* "see it altogether." Only a very few could pierce that veil of humiliation, and discern "the glory as of an only-begotten with a Father, full of grace and truth." But suppose for a moment, that today, suddenly, One visibly came from heaven, with radiant hosts attendant, could people look anywhere else? By modern inventions, space and the formation of the earth have been practically eliminated. A voice in one center is heard to the most extreme bound. So much for the ear, but will not the eye become equally far-seeing by perfected television so that at His revelation, "Every eye shall see Him" (Rev. 1: 7)? Would not that out-rival every other object? Most assuredly it would. It is not merely a truthful man who tells us that this shall be. On no angelic word does its accomplishment hang; but on the very words of that same Jehovah, who Himself said: "Heaven and earth shall pass away, but My words shall not pass away." It is the true saying of God.

In verse 6 we hear the second voice, with that authority that bespeaks divinity, directing the first to "cry;" and then telling him what the burden of his cry must be—the frailty, the transitoriness of all mankind. Poor man! Each coming into the world with no volition of his own; bringing with him from his parents a crooked, perverse nature that leads him in forbidden paths, and yet with a strange inherent consciousness of being intended for something higher and better. The poet expresses a measure and phase of truth in his lines:

"Not in entire forgetfulness,
And not in utter nakedness,
But trailing clouds of glory do we come
From God, who is our home:
Heaven lies about us in our infancy!"*

Man seeks all through the brief days of his vanity for something that shall satisfy and fill that ever-hungering heart, and finds it in nothing under the sun, till he departs with an awful cloud over the future that he cannot see through. Poor man! The grass is his fitting emblem. When at his best, he is but as the herb at *its* best; *i.e.*, when in flower. But that very zenith is a

* From "Intimations of Immortality," *Wordsworth*.

certain prophecy of its decline; from that moment it fades and falls, and so does all flesh.

"O why should the spirit of mortal be proud?"

That truth of the fleeting transitoriness of human life can but give sobriety to every thoughtful mind. Every day a sermon is preached to an opened ear; the morning speaking of the hope of youth, but in the evening,

> "The clouds that gather round the setting sun
> Do take a sober coloring from an eye
> That hath kept watch o'er man's mortality."*

But sweet the harp of prophecy with its hopeful contrast, "The Word of our God forever abides;" and still more precious is the Apostle's comment that we—even you and I—are vitally linked with that never-dying Word. It is the very gospel of Christ which we have received, so that we, in our spirits (not in our bodies yet, for He is away) partake of that everlasting character, *we have eternal life!*

Let, then, grass wither, let its flower fade, let this mortal evidence its mortality, yet with life in Christ, the youngest, poorest, feeblest of us *"shall never see death"*† (John 8: 51), for we have been begotten of that Word that abideth forever.

Well has Mr. Kelly written that "as the end draws nearer we do greatly need simplicity to rest upon God's Word. There may be difficulties to such as we are, and the Word seem a weak thing to confide in for eternity, but in truth it is more stable than heaven or earth." More and more is this becoming the one basic conflict: Have we in the Scriptures the only divine revelation of the Heart and Mind of God to a rebel race?

This brings us to the third and last part of this section, verses 9 to 11, in which the third voice is heard, and again in strict conformity with the significance of the number three, we find in it "the revelation of God."

---

*From "Intimations of Immortality," *Wordsworth.*

†That is, "death indeed," the opposite to "life indeed," as 1 Tim. 6: 19 should read—"that they may lay hold of life indeed," or, that which is truly life.

9: Up to the loftiest mountain, O Zion!
    Thou - bringer - of - sweetest - evangel!*
    Shout out thy tidings with loudest acclaim,
    Thou - bringer - of - sweetest - evangel!
        O Jerusalem!†
    Lift the voice fearlessly;
    Cry to the cities of Judah,
        Behold — your — God!
10: Behold, the Adonai Jehovah is coming,
    A mighty One He, His arm for Him ruling!
    And with Him He's bringing reward for His people,
    A work retributive before Him doth lie.
11: E'en as a shepherd His flock is He tending,
    Gathers the little lambs up in His arms.
    Tenderly carries them safe in His bosom;
    Gently He leads the nursing ewes on.

Zion is here personified as one of those women who announce victory, as in Psalm 68: 11, R. V., "The Lord giveth the word: the women that publish the tidings are a great host," and so wonderfully good are these tidings that no hill can be too high for a vantage ground whence to cry; nor can she lift up her voice too loudly in her shout of joy to all the other cities of Judah, "Behold your God!"

What glorious tidings are these! Jehovah comes; not as once in utter weakness, but with a strong Arm to establish a rule that shall right all earth's wrongs, heal all her wounds, and bring to her peace forever. For this He must sweep away all the vain expedients: the tyranny of the one, and the equal tyranny of the many; of autocrat, democrat, socialist, communist, bolshevik and every other futile nostrum by which the Gentile has tried to govern the earth since his foot was placed on Jerusalem in Nebuchad-

---

*This whole line is the equivalent of the one Hebrew word which Delitzsch renders, "Evangelistess."

†There is some question as to whether Zion is to announce the good news or it is to be announced to her; but both the actual order of the words as written, and when glad tidings are unquestionably to be announced to Zion (as in chap. 52: 7), the preposition "to" is clearly inserted, have led me to adopt the former alternative.

nezzar's day. All must go, for He is bringing reward with Him for that faithful remnant of Israel, and that means retribution for their enemies.

But the stern side of His glorious appearing is not here to be made prominent; in conformity with the key of "Comfort ye," all tenderness must rule towards them, so the prophecy leaves the note of penalty and plays still on the one string of love. How entrancingly lovely is the picture! Here is "the Mighty God," with power irresistible, and with Arm brandished against the foe, turning to His poor people with a tenderness illustrated by no hireling but only by One who is the Good Shepherd. That mighty Arm now takes up, and carries within the folds of His dress, the new-born lambs, and patiently waits on the nursing mothers, gently leading them along, lest, as Jacob said, they should perish by overdriving. Oh, the gentleness of the mighty God!

All this is to be made good to that nation, so dearly beloved for the fathers' sake, in a day soon to come; but surely we too can enter into these lovely intimacies. Do you not remember how careful He was with you in your spiritual infancy, my fellow-believer? How quickly then were your prayers answered! How little you knew then of what has since tried your faith so severely! And those who in their turn tend the little ones of the flock, does He not care for them and identify Himself with the slow-walking of those who thus love them? The mother-sheep will not forsake her lamb, and although the whole flock may be made to linger a bit in consideration for that one, the lamb is as precious to Him as the sheep, and not one single one must be pressed beyond its powers. Precious lesson! Would that we could learn it! We are all too apt to be impatient if the younger ones of the flock do not apprehend in an hour what may have taken us many years to acquire. And who can estimate the shame and sorrow caused by pressing people to go beyond their powers of faith? Oh, that all who assume the blessed ministry of shepherding the flock, might so abide in the Good Shepherd as to be filled both with His tenderness and His wisdom!

This closes the first part of the chapter with "three" so strongly marked upon it, i. e., with God so wonderfully manifested in the three parts, the three announcements and the three voices.

The *second* part of the chapter, verses 12 to 26, like so many "seconds" in Scripture, deals with contrasts. There are *two*, and, in this case, in opposition; but One indignantly declines rivalry, and claims supreme, unshared authority in every sphere. Who is it? It is that same tender Shepherd of whose gentleness we have just been reading. "Fine flour" ever was and is He; no one glory, beauty or dignity overweighted another. His gentleness may indeed make us great, and attract to reverent intimacy (may we ever know more of it!), but we must beware of unhallowed familiarity. Hear what follows:

12: Who hath measured waters in th' hollow of His hand?
Who hath meted out the heavens with a span?
Who hath comprehended in a measure all earth's dust?
Weighed in scales the mountains? In balances the hills?

13: The Spirit of Jehovah who hath governed?
Or as counsellor hath given Him instruction?

14: With whom did He take counsel?
Who made Him understand?
And who hath trainèd* Him
To walk in righteous paths?
Yes, trained Him to go in the way of understanding?
And who the way of prudence hath caused Him to know?

15: Behold (all) the nations—a drop on a bucket!—
Reckoned as the fine dust that settles on the scales!
See, the isles He lifteth, as though they were an atom!

16: Nor could the trees of Lebanon, or all its beasts suffice
Burnt offering to make [worthy Him].

17: All nations are as nothing before Him;
Nullity and vanity He reckons them to be.

18: To whom then will ye liken God?
With what likeness Him compare?

19: The craftsman moulds the idol,
The goldsmith plates with gold,
And casteth for it chains (made of) silver.

---

*"Trained," the prime meaning of the root is to "chastise," hence "to discipline," "to teach," or "train" as a child.

20: The man who is too poor for so costly an oblation
Selects a tree (of hardwood) that will not rot;
Then searches for himself a cunning craftsman,
To fashion him an image that will not totter.

21: Do ye not know?
Do ye not hear?
Is't not proclaimed to you from the beginning?
The foundings of earth,
Have ye not understood them?

22: 'Tis He who sits enthroned above the vault of earth,
To whom its petty dwellers as locusts do appear!
Who stretcheth out the heavens even as a curtain,
And like a tent to dwell in doth spread them all abroad.

23: 'Tis He who bringeth princes even down to nothingness,
And makes the judges of the earth to be a desolation.*

24: Hardly are they planted,
Hardly are they sown,
Than He blows upon them, and lo, they do wither!
And He whirleth them away
As the whirlwind doth the stubble!

25: To whom then will ye liken Me?
To whom would make Me equal?
Saith the Holy One.

26: Lift your eyes on high and see:
Who brought them into being?
Who, numb'ring, marshals all their host?
Who summons them by name?
Through the greatness of His might,
And His resistless power,
Not one of them is missing.

This section fully introduces us into the subject that goes on to, and only ends with the close of chapter 48. It is Jehovah's expostulation with Israel on account of idolatry, that Satanic device for securing the adoration of mankind that was introduced among them after the flood, and from which Abraham was called by the God of glory.

Thus the section opens with the majesty of Jehovah; who shall rival Him? There lies, too, the same indignation in the series of questions as is enwrapped in the archangel's name "Michael," "Who is as God?" To Him all the seas of earth are but a single

---

*Heb., *tohu*, the confusion of chaos (Gen. 1: 2).

drop. Let a man stretch his hand to its fullest, he can but cover a few inches, a span which is but too true an expression of his own short transitory life, as the psalmist confesses, "Thou hast made my days as a handbreadth" (Ps. 39: 5). But Jehovah's span goes beyond both horizons from east to west without limitation. All earth's dust can be comprehended in one small measure. His scales are not for the petty articles of men's commerce, but mountains are weighed on His steel-beam, and hills thrown into the balances.

To whom does He owe aught as to knowledge? His Spirit moved upon the waters of chaos, and brought beauty and order out of the dark scene of confusion; did anyone aid Him with counsel? Did any instruct Him in the path of right? Did the Creator of all need the training of a child?

Closer still now comes the word, even to the affairs of men. The nations, so mighty in their own eyes, Babylon, Persia, Greece, Rome—are all but as that drop that hangs for a time and then falls from the bucket as it comes from the well! Or as that fleck of dust that does not affect by its weight the poise of the scales on which it lies. The isles, not the smaller pieces of land surrounded by water, but the great continents that rise from and are bordered by oceans, He lifts them as if they were one tiny atom!

How can such an One be approached in worship? Forest-clad Lebanon has not wood enough to burn, nor in its coverts could beasts enough be found for one burnt-offering. Aye, to Him all nations are but nullity and emptiness. Nothing could more strongly express the divine estimate of all man's boasted powers.

So comes the direct challenge: "To whom then will ye liken God?" To such *things* as these? A rich man gives an order for an idol, so the craftsman pours the melted metal into a prepared mold, then another coats it with a plating of gold; and lest it should be stolen, silver chains must attach it to its place!

Since the poor cannot afford such costly "spiritual privileges" as that, they must be content with something far inferior; but something they must have, no one can exist without a decent degree of religion. So the poorer man goes to the woods, selects thence a hardwood tree, and by a skillful carpenter fashions it into a form that he can worship; but it must have sufficient base, that it does not totter!

Here there is a pause, a silence like that silence in heaven for the space of half-an-hour (Rev. 8: 1), in which we can almost hear Jehovah breathing heavily with indignation till, again like the trumpet-blasts that follow, He bursts out in questions that burn with indignation:  Can ye not reason?  Can ye not hear?  Can ye not see?  Do ye not discern?  Is not all creation proclaiming truth to you, and telling of His mighty Hand that wrought the whole fabric of creation?  It is He who sits above that vault that encircles the earth.*  By what has come down to you traditionally, by the witness of geology, do not the very foundations of the earth tell out His eternal power and Godhead? And if the earth itself is but a grain of sand, what can its inhabitants be?  They are like little insects that hop.  What folly is their pride, how hollow their pretension!  Take the highest of them, those potent, grave and reverend signors (for indeed these very ideas are in the word rendered "princes"), they too are as the herbs, for they began hopefully enough, but scarcely were they planted and began to root, than—a puff, and lo, where are they?  They have been whirled away as the chaff!

To whom then dare ye liken ME?

Let the heavens declare the glory of God; let the firmament show His handiwork!  Let the day utter its speech, let the night teach you knowledge.  Look up and see how "martialled on the nightly plain, the glittering hosts bestud the sky."  Number them if you can; the stronger the vision, the more the mighty worlds that come within its range.†  How did they come forth thus?

---

*Note it is not the horizon, but the limitless vault of space that here forms His Throne. Link this with Job 26: 7, "He stretcheth out the north over the empty space, hangeth the earth upon nothing;" or as Taylor-Lewis renders:

"High o'er the Void He stretcheth out the North,
And over nothing hangs the world in space."

†As far as the strongest telescopes witness, space is infinite. Although latest science that is Christian (not the mis-named

Whence and from whom that perfect order?  Who can have
maintained that Cosmos, so that not a planet shall swerve a hair's
breadth from its appointed orbit?  Let human pseudo-science attempt an answer, and in its mutually destructive guesses learn its
own futility.  Then bow thy proud head, O little man, and confess
that One and only One—Himself illimitable in all His powers—
could thus create, control, maintain these worlds, summon them
each by the name He gives them, make them tread with incalculable speed their appointed course, and numbering them, discern at once if one be missing.  Oh, the greatness of His might!
Oh, the strength of His power!  At that awful roll-call, not one
fails to respond with "Here!"

Let us ask with trembling reverence: Where shall we find that
One of such illimitable powers?  Where can He be found?  Let
us listen whilst He Himself shall by His Spirit answer: "By Him
all things subsist" (Col. 1: 17).  And who is that "Him" who
holds the universe in order and keeps it in existence?  It is Jesus,
the Man who hung on the cross of Calvary!!  What but silent
awe and spirit-worship befit such a revelation?

In the third section of the chapter, verses 27 to 31, Jehovah
turns again to Jacob, who is now Israel, too, for the nation's thigh
has been touched in that great tribulation, and now, hanging
helplessly on Him who smote, the nation follows in the prophetic
path of its sire, and is a "prince with God," or Israel.

27:  Why sayest thou, O Jacob; why speakest, Israel:
     Hidden is my way from my Lord;
     Aye, from my God my judgment is departed?
28:  Is it not known to thee?  Hast thou not heard
     That God, the Eternal, Jehovah, Creator,
     Fainteth not; never is weary?
     His wisdom passeth all searching.

---

"Christian Science") finds in space not a vast nothingness but
infinity of power: "Outspreading into the trinity of directions,
length, breadth and height, and is that by which Divine Power
translates itself into a physical universe of energy and motion,"
and thus witnesses to the unity and trinity of its Creator. ("The
Secret of the Universe," *Dr. N. Wood.*)

29: 'Tis He who gives power to those who are fainting,
    And to the helpless, strength addeth to strength.
30: Even the youths shall be fainting and weary,
    Young men be weakened—aye, weakened shall be.*
31: But who on Jehovah dependently waits
    Shall new strength ever be gaining;
    Aloft they wing as eagles fly;
    Running, they never shall weary;
    Walking, they never shall faint.

The chapter closes with a tender, yet slightly reproachful, appeal; as, when certain poor children of "Jacob," were crying amid a storm, "Carest Thou not that we perish?" He answered, "O ye of little faith." So here: Why art thou saying that He who calls each one of that illimitable host of stars above thee by its name, knows the path that it takes under His command, yet takes no interest in, takes no note of thine? Is He less interested in those for whom He died than in mere matter? Whilst He is quite able to guide Arcturus and Orion, are the problems of thy life beyond His ability? Are afflictions raining upon thee both from providences and from injustices? Does He not only leave thee to suffer, but even adds to these sufferings the desolate feeling of loneliness, of being forgotten?

Nay, His silence does but test thy confidence! Then, still hang, O thou thigh-broken child of Jacob, on Him who hath conquered thee by His love, and whom thou mayest conquer by thy helplessness. Never forget that weary as thou mayest be, He, at least, is never weary; the ages of eternity do not sap His ability, nor the weight of all the worlds strain His strength. Creation itself may grow old and be rolled away, but He remaineth from everlasting to everlasting; and since the remotest heavens own His creative skill and maintaining power, and that skill and power are equally expressed in the tiniest creature that the microscope alone brings into thy vision, canst thou reasonably think that *thy* path is beyond either His wisdom, power, or His interest?

---

*So Alexander. Heb., *kashohl yikashel*. The reader will see the repetition.

In the last three verses the chapter closes with its final trilogy:

Verse 29: The Source of all true strength.
Verse 30: The failure of nature.
Verse 31: The strength of God made perfect in weakness.

Even the youths in the freshness of their morning powers succumb to weariness sooner or later, and eventually fall in utter weakness.   But there are those who, while the strong are falling, still keep on their way without losing heart; or if at times their step, too, flags, lo, it is again renewed, and as though gifted with eagles' pinions, go on, their faith the wing that lifts them ever upward.   Who are these thus blessed?   They are those who wait on the Lord, owning their weakness, and drawing ever on the Lord Jesus, that limitless Source, for all that they lack, run without weariness, walk without fainting.   May we each prove the truth of this in our journey through our one little life!

T HE significant "three" is clearly impressed on this chapter. Jehovah challenges the idolatrous Gentiles, next turns to His beloved Israel, and then there is again a return to the vain idols of the Gentiles. Thus we have the following divisions:

1. Verses 1 to 7: Jehovah, not the idol deities, has overruled the politics of earth, and challenges opposition.
2. Verses 8 to 20: Jehovah encourages His servant, Israel.
3. Verses 21 to 29: He exposes the vanity of idols.

1: Keep silence before Me, O islands;
    Their strength let the peoples renew;
    Let them draw near and speak then;
    Let us come into judgment together.

Human affairs are fast heading up to just this climax. There is a constant, unceasing conflict between faith and infidelity, a conflict that can never have truce till one or the other prevails. About sixty years ago a far-sighted writer penned these words:

"Never in the history of man, has so terrific a calamity befallen the race, as that which all who look, may now behold, advancing as a deluge, black with destruction, resistless in might, uprooting our most cherished hope, engulfing our most precious creed, and burying our highest life in mindless desolation."*

The writer is not anticipating the great war of 1914-18, but the deeper conflict between faith and infidelity that has continued and intensified exceedingly since those words of foresight were

---

*Quoted by F. W. Grant in an article, "The Future of Infidelity," 1880.

written. And which of these has advanced most in that interval
—Faith or Infidelity? It has seen Deism recovering fast from
the blow that it received in Wesley's day, and taking a prominent, if not a dominant place in "Christian" (?) pulpits; doubts
at first cunningly diffused developing into open attacks on all
that is supernatural, till the blatant and bloody Anti-theism of
the Bolshevik has taken a rooted place in the earth. It is Infidelity that has flourished; whilst in the mass Faith has become so
feeble that the question of the Lord, spoken as with a sigh, has
fresh significance: "When the Son of Man cometh shall He find
faith upon the earth?" But God lets this conflict go to the end.
He bids the clamor of the "isles" (that is really, the sea-washed
continents) to cease, and invites them to a trial in which they
will need all their strength, so it had better be renewed.

2: Who hath raised up one from the sunrise,
   Righteousness* called to attend him,
   Given him nations before him,
   Made kings to submit to his rule,
   Gave them as dust to his sword,
   To his bow as wind-driven stubble?
3: He chased them, passed over in safety
   By a way that his feet had not trodden.†
4: Who is it hath wrought this, hath done it?
   'Tis He who calls into existence
   Generations from the beginning.
   I, Jehovah, the First, with the last,
   I, and I only, am HE!
5: The islands have seen it, and trembled;
   The ends of the earth, and they shuddered
   As they approached and drew near.
6: Then everyone helped his neighbor,
   And to his brother cried, Courage!
7: The smith‡ encouraged the founder,
   And he who smoothed with the hammer
   Gave cheer to him who smote anvil,

---

*Not the "righteous man," but the quality of righteousness that
needs an executor.

†That is, "making no retrograde step."

‡"Smith" is the word applied to one who works either in wood,
metal or stone, and may thus be either a carpenter, smith or
mason.

Declaring the soldering good;
Then fastened it safely with nails,
So that it should not be shaken.

The challenge is in the form of a question:  Who called that
conquering hero from the sunrise?  "Called him!"  Can we not
hear a scoffer of that day saying, "Why, there is not a hint of
any such conqueror coming at all.  Year after year Babylon remains in her security, the Jews remain in their captivity, where
is the promise of this coming one?  It is nothing but the chimera
of fanaticism."  Let us wait and see.

Cyrus, although still unnamed, comes within the vision of the
prophet; and although his coming is still in the future, yet so
sure is it, as determined by the divine counsels, that it is spoken
of as if it were a past event, as is the Hebrew way of expressing
certainty.  Who then could have brought him onto the stage of
the world's history, and laid out for him that path of unbroken
victories, so that nations are broken up before his sword as if
they were dust?  Who, behind that human actor, has both in-
itiated and carried out the plan?  The answer is again that
majestic: "I, Jehovah, without beginning, ever The First, before
there was any creature, visible or invisible; and, since that creation shall never pass away but always exist, I am *with* the last."
The nations see that approaching danger from afar, and take
counsel to resist it.  They are not prepared; their "confidences"
have even to be made, and with haste they cheer one another
to the utmost activity in manufacturing what shall save them!
And, in verses 6 and 7, again we have an ironic description of
the making, not of a *personal* god, as in the previous chapter, but
of a *national* idol; and the poor "god" has to be nailed down lest
he fall!  But might it not be said, as indeed it *is* said, by the
Popish imitators of these ancient idolators, that those who made
these idols knew well that they were in themselves nothing but
metal, stone or wood, and it was not these that they really worshipped, but the Power behind them.  The visible images merely
served as an aid to faith.  Nay, more, would not 1 Cor. 10: 20,
"The things which the heathen sacrifice, they sacrifice to demons
and not to God," fully justify that, although in a very bad sense?
If so, in what consists the point of this ironic description?  Surely

in this: The image is a perfect representation of what it images, differing in this from a type, or shadow (Heb. 10: 1); thus these avowed images justly express, when opposed to the true God, the spirit-powers themselves; and in their utter helpless vanity are excellent representatives of the wicked spirits behind them, as are the images of popery—they amount to *nothing*.

But there is One who is indeed the "image of the invisible God" (Col. 1: 15), for He is the "brightness of His glory, and the exact expression of His substance" (Heb. 1: 3), and He did indeed perfectly express God in every word and work. Any confidence that rivals Him is as vain as the idols of old, or the modern substitute for them, the wealth that we now esteem the safest reliance. O fellow-Christian, may we have grace to cast away every other confidence, but never that in Him, which has "great recompense of reward" (Heb. 10: 35).

8: But, Israel, thou art My servant,
　　Jacob whom I have chosen,
　　Seed of Abraham My friend.
9: Thou whom I've led by the hand,
　　E'en from the ends of the earth,
　　Aye, from its corners* have called thee,
　　Have said to thee, Thou art My servant;
　　Thee have I chosen, nor cast thee away.
10: Fear not, for *I* will be with thee;
　　Be not dismayed, for *I* am thy God;
　　Strong will I make thee,
　　Indeed† I will help thee,
　　Indeed† I'll uphold thee
　　With My righteous right hand.
11: See, wrathful ones raging against thee!
　　They shall all be ashamed and confounded,
　　They shall be as though they were nothing—
　　The men of thy word-feuds must perish;
12: Thou shalt even seek but not find them.
　　The men of thy strivings, where are they?
　　The men of the warfare against thee
　　Shall be as though they were not!
　　As a thing that has no existence!

———

*"Corners" is the literal rendering, and speaks of extremities.

†The Heb. *aph* is clearly intended to give strong emphasis to the promise, but it has too the force of "also." "Language is too contracted to hold all the fulness of divine love" (*Delitzsch*).

13: For I, Jehovah thy God,
    Firmly will hold thy right hand,
    He who saith to thee, Fear not;
    For I, even I, am thy helper.
14: Fear not!   O thou worm Jacob,
    Ye who are Israel's few men,*
    'Tis I who will help thee, Jehovah proclaimeth,
    The Holy One of Isràel!
15: Behold, I will make thee a sharp threshing implement;
    A new form of thresher, with teeth in two rows.
    Thou shalt thresh mountains, beat them to powder;
    Hills shalt thou make like the chaff.
16: Them shalt thou winnow, and the winds scatter,
    Them shall the tempest disperse all abroad;
    And thou shalt rejoice in Jehovah.
    'Tis He who shall be thy sole boast,
    The Holy One of Isràel!
17: The poor and the needy, when seeking for water,
    Their tongue parched with thirst because there is none,
    I, even I, Jehovah, will hear them,
    The God of Israel will never forsake.
18: Streams will I open, e'en on the bare mountains,
    And springs in the midst of the valleys shall flow;
    The desert for them will I turn to a basin,
    Aye, fountains of waters the dry lands shall be.
19: I'll plant in the desert the cedar, the shittim,
    The myrtle, the oil-tree.   I'll place in the steppes
    The cypress, the plane, and box-tree together.
20: That thus they may see, that thus they may know,
    Lay it to heart, understand it together,
    That the hand of Jehovah hath wrought it.
    'Tis He alone hath created—
    The Holy One of Isràel!

My reader will note that the three minor sections are clearly
divinely marked by the recurrence of the term, "The Holy One
of Israel," which comes as the closing word of verses 14, 16 and
20.

The first section (vers. 8-14) opens with *three* words (as if
giving that divine mark to them), used to express ever-inten-
sifying affection, "My servant," "My chosen," "My friend."
How precious to us as well as to Israel is that possessive

---

*The word embodies that idea.

pronoun "My!" Is it not of infinite comfort that we each can say: "I belong to Him; I have cost Him dearly; so I am His property, and He will never fail to take care of that!" What is true of Israel, let me again say, is true of us each as in Christ. We each can say, as in Christ, "I am His servant; even I am a vessel unto honor," His chosen, for did He not say to those representative disciples, "I have chosen you" (John 15: 16)? And in that same discourse did He not say, "I have loved you (oh, how dearly), as My friends?" But when a word, warm with divine Love, comes into this chilling world it is ever apt to lose its gracious heat, as this word "friend" has done, and we have to say, alas, that the word "friend" has lost its first love. It is here the climax of affection, appealing for unlimited trust amid the vicissitudes of life. So the derived word *philema*, translated "kiss," is anything that expresses that affection, as the grasp of the hand will do.

Here then we are introduced to the word that gives character to this part of the book. First, Cyrus is the "servant," then (verse 8) Israel is so owned; but eventually we shall find that Christ is the final Servant of Jehovah carrying out perfectly the "will" that none but He could, as Heb. 10 plainly tells us. But here it is Israel that has that servant place, and is assured in the precise words taken up by the apostle that God has not "cast away" this beloved people.

It is no little comfort to note that it is here "Jacob" who is "chosen," and not "Israel," the "prince with God;" for in our low estate we have a very close relationship with poor Jacob. With all his crookedness and deceitful ways, and thus dependence on divine electing mercy, he is our very brother. How gloriously that unfailing mercy is shown in all that follows here! Is it not a good thing that we are actually "commanded" not to fear, for this is based on the threefold promise of "strengthening, helping, upholding," in verse 10.

But conflict still lies ahead for the remnant here addressed as "Jacob." This also takes three constantly intensifying terms; first, the men of word-fighting, a kind of legal combat, which next comes to *blows*, and finally literal warfare. Thus this little section has three promises meeting the three threatenings of men, so that it is strongly marked with the number "three."

In verses 15-20 we may again note the strong contrast between the character of the final blessing of the earthly and the heavenly people. Both are blessed and both on the same principle of grace, but in how different a way! The former are to "thresh" the nations; the latter are to minister grace, for they are linked with that tree of life, the leaves of which are for "the *healing* of the nations." Little might we be attracted by the prospect of pursuing fleeing hosts—that is not our calling; that is not the manner of spirit that we are of; but it will perfectly suit Israel as a nation, which will be the exponent of divine government on the earth.*

Mountains are of course figures, and must be so understood, as here picturing the proud of earth. It is only by the aid of such clear Old Testament figures that we are able to interpret the same figures in the New Testament book of prophecy, without going into those extravagancies and absurdities that are so rife today. Let the light then of this figure of mountains (as used for the lofty) be thrown on that one word which has been almost universally misunderstood as referring to some spot on the earth, "Har-mageddon," and how clear and simple does the word, otherwise so mysterious, become. *There is no spot on this earth that is called Har-mageddon.* It does not exist at all, and so will be searched for in vain. It is true that many seem to think that it is quite permissible to drop and ignore the first part of the word altogether, *Har,* and assume that the reference is to Megiddo. But the word *"Har"* in "the Hebrew tongue" (and we are plainly told that *this* is the key to the interpretation) means "mountain," which in the symbolism of prophecy stands, as a most appropriate figure, for the lofty or proud of the earth, and thus the whole word rendered from the Hebrew tongue tells us of the "gathering

---

*It is true that in the Lord's promise to the overcomer in the Church in Laodicea, there are two parts, the first that such shall share with his Lord in the judgment of the proud hosts that are in open warfare with Him. But, as if He knew that "breaking in pieces" was not in itself attractive to the Christian's present "spirit," He adds the gentler, sweeter word: "I will give him the morning star." And in its fulfilment this must come before the other, for not till His people are with Him as the Morning Star are they fitted to be with Him in judging.

together of the troops of the proud." Not only is there no mountain of Megiddo on the earth, but every reference to Megiddo itself always speaks of its lowly position, and so warns us against
the popular interpretation. We are compelled to recognize the
*Har* as a sign-word for human pride, and not intended to be literal. Nor is there such a term anywhere in Scripture as the
*"battle* of Armageddon." Such diversions from what is actually
written have led, I believe, to complete misunderstanding of the
term. The word "Har-mageddon" tells of the gathering together
of a people united by pride, and is in contrast to another company
who will mourn at "the mourning of Hadadrimmon in the valley
of Megiddon" (Zech. 12: 11).

Lovely is the picture we have in verses 17 to 20. His people
are parched with thirst as they journey through a dry and thirsty
land to their home. Blessed it is to thirst when there is a
fountain of sweet water nearby to quench that thirst. How
blessed to have been truly thirsty when our Lord "stood and
cried, saying, If any man thirst, let him come unto Me and
drink." It was desert there, even though it was "the great day"
of Israel's happiest feast; but *He* was there, the very Fountain of
living waters, and amid those throngs those only were the truly
blessed ones who were utterly dissatisfied with all the empty
religion, and still thirsted. Nor surely is it less blessed even this
day, when we have such promises as, "I will give to him that is
athirst of the water of life freely" (Rev. 21: 6); for today, when
this dispensation has drawn near its end, as had that, we are surrounded by dry, hollow, heartless "religion;" but how little that
satisfies the new nature of the true child of God. These thirst,
and evidence their divine birth by that thirsting. It is the cool,
self-complacent indifference that is filled with danger, for it will
have a terrible awakening. But here the picture changes in a
moment. Rivers are flowing on the hills, the upper springs pour
forth waters, the lower gush refreshment, and fountains are everywhere. What causes such a change? *"I, the Lord, will hear;* the
God of Israel will not forsake." Has He never thus refreshed
*you* in a moment?

Of course the primary application of this prophecy is to Israel,
and it is an error, leading to others, to take it away from that

nation; but equally sure the same grace that shall make these
lovely trees grow to beautify their land, or the desert around it,
is active in making the spiritual beauties that correspond with
them to grow in another sphere, even in those heavenlies in which
are all our blessings in Christ.  Were we more skilled in such interpretations, we should enjoy the detailed correspondences of
the spiritual with the natural, and find the typical counterpart
everywhere; but human ingenuity must not take the place of the
teaching of the Holy Spirit, and in our poverty we can only mark
what lies on the surface.

Note, then, first the emphatic, "*I* will plant"—these trees do
not grow apart from the direct planting of God.  Nor is it any
more natural for such trees to grow in the desert than for a proud,
overbearing, violent man, as Saul of Tarsus tells us he was, to
become lowly, gentle, and to esteem others more highly than himself, for *that* too speaks of God's planting.  So sang the poet
Cowper:

> "I want the grace that springs from Thee,
>    That quickens all things where it flows;
>  That makes a wretched thorn like me,
>    Bloom as the myrtle or the rose."

Many of us will utter a hearty Amen to that desire.

There are seven different kinds of trees, and as that number,
we have learned, is significant of the perfection or completeness
that ever characterizes the work of God, the seven here include
*all* forms of arboreal beauty.  That seven is divided, as it constantly is, into 4 + 3; nor is there any question but that the
four speak of what is *external,* and carry the beauties of Christ
into the world, as did the four sweet spices of the holy ointment;
while the three deal with what is more hidden, and for God's
eye, as did the three spices that formed the sweet incense.
As to the symbolic meaning of the trees in verse 19, whilst their
identity is not altogether certain, there can be no question that
each tells of some spiritual loveliness.  The cedar speaks of
*majesty, dignity;* shittim (of which the ark was in part made)
tells of *incorruptibility,* and, from its use in the prophet Zechariah, the myrtle tells of the *lowliness* that ever characterizes
the true people of God.  These may all be said to be blended to-

gether by the "oil-tree," a clear figure of the Spirit of God. Nor
does this make a literal interpretation impossible. All these inter-
weavings of the Word of God are full of interest to His children
who rejoice to discern such marks of His Authorship. Beautiful
as is this garden of trees, this quiet paradise, wherein every tree
in its whispering leaves, when stirred by the Breath of the Spirit,
tells of the Love of God in Christ our Lord, we must go on to
the last section of the chapter, verse 21 to the end, in which the
utter vanity of idols is exposed.

21: Bring hither your cause, saith Jehovah;
    Bring out your proofs, saith Jacob's great King.
22: Bring them forward and show us what shall be,
    (Or) let them first show the beginnings,
    And we will lay it to heart;
    Thus may we learn of its issue,
    Or tell us of what is to come.
23: Make known what is to come later,
    Then shall we know ye are gods.
    Do at least *something,* or evil or good,
    That we may be dumb with amaze
    As we behold it together.

         (A pause, followed by this indignant outburst)

24: Behold! Ye are but a portion of nothing*
    And your work a part of naught!
    Abhorred shall he be who makes you his choice!
25: One comes from the north, I have raised him;
    From the sunrise he calls on My name.
    He treadeth on princes as though they were mire,
    As the potter who kneadeth the clay.
26: Who hath declared this from the beginning,
    That we might know it?
    Who hath foretold it from far away back?
    That we may say to him: Right!
    Indeed, there was no one declared it!
    Indeed, there was no one announced it!
    Indeed, none hath heard you utter a word.
27: I was The First who cried unto Zion,
    Behold! O behold them!
    And to Salem I'll give you one bringing good tidings.

---

*Lit., "of nothing," but that means, "ye are only a part of
nothing, not the whole."

28: I looked all around—there was not a man;
   And of these* not one that gave counsel,
   Or when I demanded could answer a word!
29: Look at them all—they are Vanity!
   Their very doings—nothing at all!
   Their images—wind and confusion!

Note here again how each of the subdivisions of this section is marked out for us by a closing comment on the utter vanity of the idols. Verse 24 (I quote now from the A. V.), "Ye are of nothing;" verse 26, "None heareth your words;" verse 29, which is itself a *threefold* summing up, "They are all vanity: their works nothing: their molten images wind and confusion." May we not confidently say that a divine Finger has imprinted that number three again on the chapter?

The section opens with a challenge by Jehovah to His rivals, who are but the creatures of *His* creatures, to enter the lists with Him, and attempt a forecast of things that shall be; but first let them make good their claim to prophetic powers by accounting for the things that *are,* and tell how they came; then if that bring conviction of its truth, we shall be able to place corresponding confidence in the prophecies of what lies in the future, should they attempt them.

These things were not written for that far-off age alone, but for us on whom the end of the ages has come, and this is a challenge well-adapted to the false science that has taken possession of the masses of Christendom. So we repeat the challenge: Tell us how things began; tell us how this orderly Cosmos came into being in its present beauty; tell us how the worlds were formed; tell us whence came intangible moral qualities, and the reasoning powers of man, and if this is convincing, we will, as in our prophecy, certainly say, "Right!" and then trust you further.

But let our scientists speak. We hear this: "Since there are evident similarities, and gradations in the external forms of all creatures: similarities that can be traced by slight changes back from the anthropoid ape, that bears a very striking external re-

---

*"These," *i. e.,* the idols, simply pointing to them as not worth naming.

semblance to man; then to the lower vertebrates; then to the invertebrates; then to the molluscs, and so down to the primordial protoplasmic atom or electron, from which all have been evolved during millions of years, we hold this to be proof enough that everything has come into its present condition by Evolution."

Well, we "set our heart" on it. It leaves us full of questions. It gives no light on the beginnings. It makes matter to be eternal, and, although itself without intelligence, to produce everything that speaks aloud of infinite intelligence! Nor does it account for the introduction of that basic principle, *Life,* and we ask, What *is* Life? Was that "primordial protoplasm" alive? Whence did that Life come? We pause for an answer, and as it was in Isaiah's day, the challenge is met, as it was then, by absolute silence, for "indeed there is no one who utters a comprehensible or reasonable word" to this simple but vital question.

If these "Scientists," falsely so-called, are compelled to confess to ignorance to start with, surely we must lose confidence in them as teachers of anything beyond that. But we invite them on our part to "set *their heart*" to this account: "In the beginning God created the heavens and the earth." That has undeniably the marks of Authority, Dignity, Profundity, Simplicity, and Harmony with truest Reason; in one word, of Divinity. It introduces us to a personal, eternal, omnipotent God, as First Cause, in perfect harmony with subsequent explicit revelation of a Unity in Trinity; to a God far above our reasoning powers to comprehend, which the truest reason confesses to be most reasonable. Yet this very day this contemptible figment of evolution is sweeping away the mass of professing Christians into an apostasy which itself confirms the truth of what it would overthrow, for God has foretold it.

Again, our prophet, as the mouthpiece of Jehovah, speaks as if encouraging the idols to attempt a forecast, and awaits response. But not a word—there is still silence.

Then again He speaks: At least do *something,* even if it be a bad thing; that were better than nothing. After a pause for an answer, there is another indignant outburst of withering contempt, not merely of the idols themselves, but of any sane man who can make choice of such nullities, as there may well be of any foolish enough to put confidence in a false science, that denies experience, reason, and revelation.

Jehovah Himself now will foretell of the coming of one from the north (Media) and from the sunrise (Persia); and, since he comes "calling on the name of Jehovah," he surely cannot be an adversary to Jehovah's people, but their deliverer, a type of their own Messiah whose coming shall effect their final salvation.

Ever is the "sunrise" the quarter of cheerful hope for the earth, and particularly for Israel with whose fortunes those of the earth are so closely intertwined. It is to the Jew that He shall arise as the "Sun of Righteousness with healing in His wings;" whilst we, as having a heavenly destiny, look for Him in the character of the Sun's forerunner, the "Bright and Morning Star," whose light may cheer the watcher but leave the sleeping world still in darkness. So too it is *that* people who, when that Sun shall rise upon them, shall be "set on high above all the nations of the earth," "of whom all the nations of the earth shall be afraid;" for they shall be the "head," and "above only" (Deut. 28), and are therefore termed in Rev. 16: 12, "the kings of the rising again of the sun;"* nor could a people with such an exalted destiny have a better symbolic name.

Jehovah speaks, in verses 27 to 29, under that Name so filled with significance and claim to essential deity: I am "The First," for there were none before Me; self-existent and eternal, wherever I am seen I must ever be "First." And Jesus comes, and ever is He, too, First; whether in the Virgin's womb, or on the foal of an ass; or in the tomb, or to rise from it, none must precede Him; He must be, even in His earthly path, "The First." When that same One speaks in the book of Revelation, three times He calls Himself *"The First,"*† In the Old Testament Jehovah is "The First." In the New Testament, Jesus is "The

---

*The true interpretation of this scripture, I believe, has been hidden by the translation of the two Greek words *anatoloon heeliou* by the one word "east." In a book filled with symbols as Revelation, a word so significant as "Sun" should not have been thus omitted altogether; the interpretation depends on it.

†As chaps. 1: 17; 2: 8; 22: 13. The editiors are against its occurrence in chap. 1: 11 being genuine.

First." Jesus is Jehovah, for there cannot in this same sense be two "firsts."

But what does Jehovah say? To Jerusalem He speaks, and cries: "Look! Behold them! There it is," referring to the fast-approaching salvation; and then He gives to Jerusalem those who repeat that joyful news. What can the foolish confidence that men themselves make do in comparison with *that?* What has all that men today are substituting for the Cross of Christ, to *give?* What salvation? What hope? What comfort in sorrow? What light in darkness? What hope in death?

They are all vanity indeed; as empty and dark as chaos before God said, "Let there be light."

# CHAPTER FORTY-TWO

A S in the Epistle to the Hebrews dignity after dignity is brought into prominence, only to wane and disappear like the stars at sunrise when our Lord Jesus is seen, so here. We have looked at Cyrus as the servant of Jehovah, but now he disappears, for brighter rays than any that could shine from that honored man have eclipsed him. Even Israel, the people that Jehovah constantly owns among the nations of the earth as His servant, is lost sight of here in beams too bright to emanate from any mere nation of earth. No; we must remember a closing injunction in that same Epistle to the Hebrews, and "look away" from all others to One and only One, who alone can, in any true way, answer to these words:

> 1: Consider My Servant, whom I uphold,
> Mine Elect, whom My soul doth delight in;
> On Him My Spirit have I outpoured;
> Judgment He'll bring to the Gentiles.
> 2: He'll not cry aloud, nor will He lift up
> His voice to be heard in the highways.
> 3: The reed that is splintered He never will crush,
> Nor blow out a wick dimly burning.
> Judgment He'll bring, and that truthful.
> 4: Not dimly He'll burn, nor will He be crushed
> Till judgment on earth is firm-rooted;
> And th' isles for His law are all waiting.

Let us obey the first word, and "behold" the perfect Servant, for that sight will not only refresh us, but enable us to discern, in a day of much pretension, those who are the true followers of that Servant. We are given *three marks* that are true of both. First, *Godward*: the Spirit of God is on Him. Not until His service lay before Him, and He came up from the waters of Jordan at John's baptism, did the Spirit of God come upon Him as a dove.

Next, the mark *selfward* is that He seeks no notoriety or prominence. He neither cries nor lifts up His voice in the streets. So His truest servants may be distinguished by their endeavors to put their feet in these self-effacing footprints. The "spirit" that governs the first man, leads in quite the opposite direction, a thirst for prominence. How frequently trouble is introduced into a company of Christians by those who, like Diotrephes, love to have the preeminence (3 John 9). Where all seek the lowest place there is great peace.

Finally the *manward* mark. How gently does He deal with penitents who are like splintered reeds in the confession of their sin. Does He finish them altogether? Their faith is as feeble as a glimmering wick about to expire; does He utterly extinguish it? Far from it. He heals the bruise of the reed, and fans the wick to flame. Aye, does not the tender way He deals with such "reeds" and "glimmering wicks," make us long to be nearer to Him, to love and serve Him better? His truest followers have imbibed that same spirit, and know how to "lift up hands hanging down, and to strengthen feeble knees" (Heb. 12: 12).

Our Lord is by no means undiscriminative. If gentle to penitence, He is stern to pride; and thus He puts everything "to rights," as we say, on the earth, and this He does in a right way, or "according to truth." Nor in that work shall anything discourage Him. As He will not quench nor break, so His own zeal will not be quenched nor broken, till He has enthroned Justice on a firm basis, and the "Isles," or Gentiles, place their submissive confidence in Him.

> 5: Thus saith the Mighty One, even the Lord,
> Creator, Out-stretcher of heavens,
> Who spreads out the earth and what comes therefrom,
> Gives breath to the people upon it,
> And spirit to them that walk on it:
> 6: In righteousness I, Jehovah, have called,
> Holding Thy hand I will keep Thee,
> A cov'nant unto the people Thou'lt be,
> A light to lighten the Gentiles;
> 7: To open blind eyes, the pris'ners to loose,
> And from their dark dungeon to bring out
> Those in its gloom who're confinèd.

8: I am Jehovah—that is My Name;
   My glory I'll not share with any,
   Nor suffer My praise to be given
   To images out of stone graven.
9: The former things that I have foretold,
   See, they are come to fulfilment!
   So of the new things that now I proclaim,
   I tell you before they are springing.

Most solemnly here Jehovah calls us to consider His creative dignities. 'Tis He who stretched the heavens out, and spangled them with the starry host. 'Tis He who clothed the earth with verdure, and gave, not only the *breath* shared by the beasts, but the *spirit* that distinguishes man from them. 'Tis He who has called One who alone is able to carry out successfully that mighty commission of establishing all things in heaven and in earth on a righteous basis, leading out from captivity, not from shackles of literal iron, but from dominating passions of lust and cruelty; and, as He leads the poor prisoners into holy liberty, He gives them eyes to see, and joy in the seeing truth in Himself, and beauty in that truth.

Who can do this? One who can permit no rivalry, and who again demands an unrivalled place since He foretells what is to come centuries later. It is the dawning of that bright day in the prophet's pages, the meridian of which we shall enjoy (if it please God) in the 53rd chapter. But as in nature the day dawns gradually, not as in one thunderclap, but softly, so Cyrus may indeed be accounted as a streak of light in the east, foretelling in *his* deliverance of captives, the coming Sun; but a far brighter Herald than Cyrus shall foretell for us the coming Day, even "The bright Morning-Star;" for that day cannot come till He introduces it, and for that we must come with Him.

Note in verse 6 the distinction between the Jew and the Gentile; the "covenant" is for the Jew, "the people," and that, in these prophetic books, when thus in the singular is always Israel; whilst for the poor Gentiles on whom divine light has not shone—He supplies that need to them, but they have no "covenant."

Every generation has had to echo the words of Joshua: "Not one good thing hath failed" (Josh. 23: 14): so this very day, as we stand and look back upon foretellings fulfilled, may we rest with quiet assurance on the certainty of the fulfilment of what has yet to come to pass.

> 10:  Sing to Jehovah a song never heard;
>        Sing out His praise from earth's borders,
>        Ye that sail sea, all creatures therein,
>        Ye islands afar and their dwellers.
> 11:  Let desert and all of its cities strike up,
>        The villages Kedar doth dwell in;
>        Let the rock-dwellers sing out their joy,
>        From tops of the hills shout their gladness.
> 12:  Let them give to Jehovah the glory, His due,
>        Declaring His praise to the islands!
> 13:  Jehovah goes forth as a strong man of war,
>        Stirs up His zeal as a hero,
>        A war-cry He shouts—a terrible cry,
>        And over His foes is the Victor.

What a joyous burst of praise! And it comes from that people who heard Paul speaking from the steps of the tower, till he reached the word that told him to go far away to the Gentiles; then the blow to their national pride was too heavy, and dust, stones, and shouts of hatred filled the air (Acts 22). Here is that Jew so feeling his own incompetence to give adequate expression to his praise that he begs the Gentile to help him swell the anthem!

Will anyone be bold enough to suggest that this whole joyous scene is not strictly an earthly one? Will our friends who insist that "God has no more use for Israel" point to any moment in the past in which they were thus in such intense happiness? Or since all these promises must be spiritualized and taken into heaven, is Kedar there? Are sailors to be invoked in heaven? And will they maintain that there are sea-washed shores where "there is no more sea?"

This is not what we today term the "gospel," for Jehovah comes forth as a warrior uttering His war-shout, and with that terrifying cry He plunges into the battle. That is not quite the same as, "Come unto Me, all ye that labor and are heavy-laden, and I will give you rest." No; here Jehovah is intervening in the politics of earth. This is the *"new thing"* that is here foretold, never has such song been heard, and well may we note the faith-compelling harmony between the two Testaments, the Old supplying much light on the emotions that accompany the Lord's return to reign, but in this fully in accord with the New, for where will you find a louder doxology than comes from the heavenly "elders" when "The kingdoms of this world are become the kingdom of our Lord and of His Christ" (Rev. 11: 15)?

Again Jehovah speaks by the mouth of the prophet:

14: Long have I held My peace, been silent long;.
    Long have I held Me restrainèd;
    Now will I cry, as a woman travails,
    At one time both gasping and panting.
15: Mountains and hills will I make bare,
    Will dry up all of their herbage;
    Rivers to islands will I transform,
    Water-pools thoroughly dry up.
16: The blind will I lead in a way all unknown,
    In paths that they know not conduct them;
    For them I will turn the darkness to light,
    And roads that are crooked will straighten.
    These things will I do, nor forsake them.
17: But ye who to idols say, Ye are our gods,
    Shall all be turned backward, confounded.

Jehovah has during that long weary time of His people's oppression kept silence, but it has been with great difficulty; now He can restrain no longer, but using the common figure of intensity, child-birth, He pants and gasps in violent breathings, which at length burst forth in such scorching wrath that mountains lose their verdure, rivers dry up and lakes evaporate under its heat.

It is a marvellously strong figure! So desirous is Jehovah for the time to come that shall be the day of His own deliverance from all self-restraint, that the intervening period seems like an eternity to Him—for that is the word rendered "long time" in A.V. Then as the hour approaches, do His exercises increase, till the deliverance from this strange child-birth is a burst of fiery wrath against the oppressors of His people. Shall we pass from this without throwing its light on this present time? Has our Lord Jesus less longing for His redeemed for heaven than as Jehovah He has here for His beloved Israel? Has He no bursting longing desire for that hour to come when He can gather His heavenly redeemed around Himself and introduce them to the Father's House? Indeed He has; and the whole creation is groaning and travailing awaiting the manifestation of the sons of God.

Jehovah now turns to His beloved Israel, and taking them by the hand leads them, blind as they are, in the right way, and that is always one of complete dependence upon Himself, for it is a way that they know not. Set a blind man in a familiar place and he feels about till he touches some object that is familiar, and goes on confidently; but let him touch nothing that he can recognize, then where to step next he knows not. So these poor Israelites (and we, too, even now) can find in all the past no precedent that shall serve to direct them, but Jehovah (our Lord Jesus) takes their hand (and ours) and as they abandon themselves trustfully to His guidance, not one step goes astray. But all who trust to other confidence are covered with shame! These divine principles of dependence and clinging confidence, run unchanged through all dispensations.

Thus these verses deal with one of the greatest perplexities of life; not confined to Israel, nor to any one age, but wherever man is, there is this enigma of not merely the existence, but the apparent victory of evil and all forms of wrong. In the divinely recorded history of Israel, we feel that we have our hand in that Hand that is alone a safe Guide; for that history is given us to throw its light on the invisible.

The foes of Israel are but types of ours. They had Babylon and Assyria; we have the wicked spirits; behind both these, Satan and his hosts. But it is just here, in the very mention of these powers of darkness, that light begins to shine. The existence of that arch-foe goes far to solve the perplexities of the scene through which we are passing, and they who deny it are logically on the road to the fogs of infidelity, and the blackness and darkness of perdition following.

God has long held His peace! That silence has filled the infidel, whether in the pulpit or in the ghetto, with scoff and argument. "Would you permit your dear child to be at the mercy of injustice, oppression, calamity, accident, death, if you had the power to help and save him from these? Yet these are the conditions that obtain on all sides; and you dare to claim that your God is Almighty; that there is no limit to His power, and that He is all-beneficent, with no limit to His love—it is incredible! Every disaster denies it; every untimely bereavement denies it; every calamity, that draws tears, if not blood, from the poor race, denies it—it is incredible!"

Reader, have you never heard something like that? Have you never felt its cutting force? But how splendid the answer that God has given us! True, we say, it is a riddle that God Himself alone can solve; and here is that solution in a word—the Cross! Come then to Calvary; see that central cross there. Regard not him on the right hand nor the left; we know not the names of either; but concentrate thy gaze on the One in the midst. Behold Him! That is the very Son of God, His only-begotten One in whom He delighteth ever, and there He hangs between earth and sky, cast out by earth; by heaven, too, cast out! But now a dense veil is drawn over the awful scene, till an exceeding bitter cry pierces the unnatural darkness, and I know—*know* (mark that)—*my* sins are on that sacred Head, and that He is there being dealt with as those sins of mine merited; nay more, as the *Sin* that I am. It is God both Almighty and All-beneficent, who has loved us; so tenderly, so strongly loved us, that He has given that dearest Treasure of His Heart, and spared Him not one blow that we merited even in the hour of His heart-broken cry! *This* mystery solves *that*, for listen still.

The blackness of darkness passes. The sun again shines, and now in calm peace, as Himself a Conqueror, that Sufferer dismisses His spirit. But the grave cannot hold that incorruptible Body. He is risen! This very hour He sits on high, and has sent us that other Comforter, His Spirit, who brings in some feeble way to my heart as I write, and to yours as you read, the realization of these profound verities, so drawing us out of this evil world, and leading us home through a way that we know not. It is through the darkness of the night, with all its mysteries, that we walk, leaving the earth, for the time, to that usurper the devil, *who fills it with evidences of his wrongful reign.* Every untimely bereavement, every calamity, every catastrophe, every groan of the oppressed, every injustice, every crime—all witness aloud that the earth's true King is rejected, and he whose throne is here, is on that throne wrongfully; is that not a true witness? Would anything else be true? Only those who know the depth of their own guilt and something of the Love that shines so awfully, and yet so sweetly, in the Cross of Christ, can pass through this tangled scene and not be stumbled by the silence of God! That silence is a test to faith; but that faith when thus tested, and by the very test proved true and genuine, is to God more precious than gold is to man (1 Pet. 1: 7). Faith's foot does not stand on air, nor on the morass of vain speculation, but on the solid rock of the Person, the death and resurrection of the Lord Jesus Christ!

But we must return from this excursus to consider other strange anomalies.

18: Hear, ye deaf; ye blind, look up,
    That thus ye may have a clear vision.
19: My Servant!   Who is so blind as is He?
    Or deaf as He sent with My message?
    Who blind as the one on whom I put trust?*
    Yes, blind as Jehovah's own servant?
20: Much hast thou seen, thou hast kept naught;
    His ears are unstopped, but he hears not.

---

*The interpretation given to this difficult verse rests largely on the meaning given to the word *m'shullam*, which I have rendered "put trust." The first meaning of the root is "to be whole" or "perfect," as our A. V.: "Who is blind as he that is perfect?" And, if this be the only meaning possible, we are apparently compelled to see the only One who could be so called, Messiah. But there is another and also not uncommon derivative based still on the idea of completeness: "to make peace;" so, "*to be in close intimacy,*" and so the R. V. reads, "*As he that is at peace with Me;*" Darby, "As he whom I have trusted;" Delitzsch, "As the confidant;" and so the rendering I have adopted, "On whom I put trust."

21: Jehovah's well-pleased for His righteousness' sake;
       His law shall be great and be honored.
22: Yet 'tis a people robbed and despoiled,
       They're all snared in caves, and are hidden
       In houses that are to them nothing but jails.*
       With none to deliver, they're booty,
       They're spoiled, and none says, Restore!
23: Who that are 'mong you will hearken to this,
       Give ear, and list to what's coming?
24: Who was it gave up Jacob for spoil?
       And Israel gave to the robbers?
       Did not Jehovah, 'gainst whom we have sinned?
       To walk in His ways they're not willing,
       Nor to His law would they hearken.
25: Then He poured on them the heat of His wrath,
       The strength of the fury of battle.
       This set him on fire all round about,
       Yet from it has he been taught nothing;
       Burning within him, his heart was untouched!

Verse 18 calls upon some who are truly deaf and blind (little
as they would admit such a charge) to both hear and see. It is
the representatives of the nation who are thus addressed, who, in
the Lord's day, cried: "Are we blind also?"

This gives the key for the right understanding of the next
verse, 19, in which someone, called Jehovah's servant, is not only
deaf and blind, but pre-eminently so; and this pre-eminence in
dullness of apprehension must be due to the bright light that has
shone on this servant, that others have not enjoyed.

Here I quote Delitzsch, who gives a valuable suggestion on
these verses: "It is impossible to read, 'My messenger, whom I
send,' without thinking of the first verse of this chapter, where
the servant of Jehovah is represented as a messenger to the Gentiles. With this similarity, both in name and calling, there must
be a connection between the 'servant' mentioned here and the
servant referred to there. Now the 'servant of Jehovah' is always
Israel. But as Israel might be regarded according to the over-

---

*"The whole nation is confined in prisons of all kinds"—an alle-
gorizing picture of the homelessness and servitude of exile
(*Delitzsch*).

whelming majority of its members (the mass or the many) who had forgotten their calling; or according to the character of those living members who had remained true to their calling (the Remnant) or as concentrated in that one Person (Messiah), who is the essence of Israel in the fullest truth and highest potency—statements of the most opposite kind could be made with respect to this one same-named subject. In the first verse it is the one Person who is referred to—the centre of the inner circle of Israel. In this 19th verse the idea is carried back again from the highest (Messiah), to its lowest basis (the mass), and the servant of Jehovah is blamed and reproved for the contrast between its divine calling and its actual conduct."

This is well worth pondering; nor should it be necessary to point out how such a view of Israel would conform to the corresponding truth of the Church. Just as here we have quick changes from intense approbation to utter reprobation, so the Church at one time is seen as taken into never-to-be-broken favor in the Beloved, and then again is to be "spewed out" of the Lord's mouth in nauseated repulsion, as either the *inner* circle of its living members, or the lukewarm *professing* mass is in view. The correspondence is still more striking, for in one scripture Christ Himself (the "essence," as Delitzsch speaks) is so closely identified with His Church as to be called by the same name: "For as the Body is one, and hath many members, and all the members of that one Body, being many, are one Body; *so also is the Christ*" (1 Cor. 12: 12). That surely is a remarkable expression. The Christ is that mystic Man, *"Head and Body."* Now throw the clear ray of light thus obtained on this verse, for on the surface it looks as if the servant of Jehovah must be the Lord Jesus, as Messiah; but who would not shrink from speaking of our Lord as not only deaf and blind, but that in a preeminent degree, so that none could compare with Him? When did the Lord Jesus open blind eyes, *whilst He Himself was blind?* The blindness must be, one would think, of the same character in both members. But that difficulty does not exist at all with regard to the nation of Israel. All light and truth has come to the Gentiles by the way of Israel. Light that that nation itself rejected, truth that it did not itself believe, has enlightened the Gentile. Look forward a little and you will hear that very people (then seen in the inner circle or remnant, as *Delitzsch* speaks) bewailing their own blindness, in the words, "Who hath believed *our* report?" It was *ours,* and yet we would not have it; we were blind to its beauty, and it was those who had been blind, the Gentiles, who received it. So that here in these verses we are taking the first step that shall eventually lead to Chapter 53.

Verse 22 tells of the condition of Israel—not seen in the inner circle of the remnant, nor in the innermost essence, Christ, but in the outer mass. To it was given the Law, holy and good. They had voluntarily accepted it and placed themselves under the principle of blessing and acceptance dependent on legal obedience (Ex. 19: 18)—what does the righteous government of Jehovah demand? We shall soon hear of its *pleasing* the Lord to bruise One in atonement, for the sins of many individuals: so here, apart from that atonement that cannot be applied to nations as such, He is even pleased to magnify the law and make it to be honored, by giving up the disobedient nation (to which alone the law had been given) to robbery and spoliation, as it is written: "You only have I known of all the families of the earth; therefore will I punish you for all your iniquities" (Amos 3: 2).

Precisely in the same way the apostle to us Gentiles speaks in Rom. 3: 31: "Do we then make void the law through faith? Nay, we establish the law." In the Old Testament the penalty of the broken law falls upon impenitent Israel, and so the majesty of the law is maintained. In the New Testament the penalty of the broken law falls upon the beloved Son, who thus makes a propitiation efficacious for all penitent faith. Thus is the majesty of the law established.

This then is the divine explanation here told as a prophecy of things to come. They have had the law; they have not obeyed that law; Jehovah will make that law to be honored, and for *that,* this people, to whom it has been given, must be spoiled and robbed. Many centuries must pass before any Hebrew could "take joyfully the spoiling of their goods;" they must know their Messiah to have come; they must have seen Him "cut off;" learned that His death alone atoned for their sins, and knowing that He had ascended to the right Hand of God, also know that there in Him they had "a better and an enduring substance." Is there not a harmony that can be no less than divine, in these Scriptures? But whilst the chapter thus closes, the subject does not, and we must eliminate the artificial division of the chapters in this case, would we be intelligent, and go on to the next.

# CHAPTER FORTY-THREE

**Jehovah-Jesus never leaves His people in times of suffering. He is with them in floods and flames, although not to sight as in olden days. When, why and how are nations made to ransom Israel.**

S O swift, so striking, is the change from the last verse of the previous chapter that a separation was made here; but the address continues unbroken to verse 13, with only such rapid changes as are necessitated by either the apostate mass, or the penitent remnant coming into view.

If the miserable condition of verse 25 of the last chapter referred to Israel, the literal nation on earth, then the words of comfort here must also be so applied. The Church being quite hidden from Isaiah, Israel—the literal nation—has the first title to both the sorrow and the solace. That does not nullify the truth that God's dealings with that elect nation are typical of His dealings with His people as individuals today, nor that these exceeding great and precious promises are not "Yea and Amen in Christ Jesus," and so for all who are in Him. So our chapter opens with Jehovah gladly leaving His strange work of punishment and returning to what is far more congenial to Him. As another well puts it, "So the love that has been hidden behind the wrath returns to its prerogative again."

1: But now, saith Jehovah, Creator am I
   Of Jacob, and Israel's Former.
   Fear not, O fear not, for thee I've redeemed;
   Thou art Mine; by thy name have I called thee.
2: When through the waters I cause thee to pass,
   E'en then will I surely be with thee.
   When through the floods, they shall not overflow;
   Or when through the fire thou art walking,
   Harmless the flame, thou shalt not be burnt,
   Nor shall it e'en kindle upon thee.
3: For I am Jehovah, thine Elohim; I,
   Israel's Saviour, most Holy.
   Egypt as ransom for thee did I give,
   Seba and Cush I gave for thee.

4: Since in My sight thus dear thou hast been,
    Greatly hast thou been honored,
    And I have tenderly loved thee.
    Therefore I'll give up men in thy stead,
    For thy life, too, will I give peoples.
5: Fear not, oh, fear not, for I am with thee;
    Thy seed from the east will I bring back,
    I'll gather them too from out of the west,
6: Commanding the north to release them.
    To the south will I order, Hold them not back!
    Bring back My sons from afar off,
    From the ends of the earth bring My daughters.
7: Yea, leave none behind who're called by My name,
    Whom I, for My glory, created,
    Have fashioned, yea, finished completely.

How unspeakably precious are these gracious words! We too
have some knowledge of what it means to pass through deep
waters, so swift and deep that oftentimes faith finds no footing
and has to float on these promises, and we know too something
(all too little, for some are "of little faith" in the hour of trial)
of His being with us in those trials as He was with the three
Hebrew youths in the furnace heated to seven times its usual
intensity. But Israel has the first claim on these promises. On
what ground then is Israel to be saved through that time of trial?
Is it superior holiness that has demanded, as it were, this discrimination? Surely not, but the submissive will, the heartfelt
confession of utter worthlessness, that alone permits the Heart of
God to have its way unhindered; and He cries from that Heart:
"I have created—I have redeemed—I have called thee by thy
name—*thou art Mine!*"

Precious beyond all thought, again I say, is this trinity of
tender words! First "created"—we certainly had nothing to do
with that—then "redeemed—and that too was His work entirely
—and then, old enough to hear Him speak, we hear Him telling
us that we belong to Him. He will surely take care of His own
property.

In verses 3 and 4 we find a perplexity: "I have given Egypt
for thy ransom, Ethiopia (or Cush), and Seba for thee," and
again, "I give men in thy stead, and peoples in place of thy life."

How are we to understand that? Notwithstanding that "none can give to God a ransom" for his brother (Ps. 49: 7), can nations do what is thus impossible to individuals? The word for "ransom" is from the same root and has precisely the same force as that constantly used for "making atonement," as for instance in Exod. 30: 10, 12, speaking of the atonement half-shekel of silver: "They shall give every man a *ransom*," and "Aaron shall make an *atonement.*" Is then the suffering of one nation an atonement for the sins of another? That at least would seem impossible. It would deny, rather than evidence, the justice of God's government. Nor is there any specific word as to sins being atoned for at all. The earth, and the earth alone is in view, not heaven, nor eternal issues. But the earth affords types of heavenly truth, and for that, the righteousness of the divine government must be evidenced *on the earth, among the nations.* All these are evil, nor is Israel, although elect, less so. Indeed God says, "You only have I known of all the families of the earth, therefore I will punish you for all your iniquities" (Amos 3: 2). But at the standpoint of our chapter Israel has been severely punished, her sufferings have been extreme. Her city has long been trodden down of the Gentiles, who have been in the ascendant. It would *look* as if all of these were guiltless, and poor Jacob alone guilty. That unrighteousness must be set right; for it not only gives a false witness to God's government, but also to the work of Israel's Messiah. Israel is His "peculiar treasure" (Exod. 19: 5), and He has bought the field in which that treasure is now hidden. It is being kept for this day of manifestation. *Then* the judgment of God shall pass to the Nations (here represented by Egypt, Cush and Seba) instead of Israel. It is a graphic way of putting before us what is clearly thus brought out later: "Behold, I have taken out of thine hand the cup of trembling . . . and will put it into the hand of them that afflict thee" (Isa. 51: 17, 23).

The judgment of God is over *all* the nations of the earth: Israel has already felt the force of that judgment; but at this time of which our prophet speaks, the oppressing Gentiles must *take the place of, stand in the stead of,* are *substituted for,* and *so, and only so, are a ransom for oppressed Israel* (comp. 2

Thess. 1: 6, 7). There are two scriptures that tend to confirm this
interpretation. Prov. 21: 18 reads: "The wicked shall be a ransom for the righteous." That is very close to what we have been
considering, especially as we know that the only "righteous"
amongst men are those who from their hearts confess the truth
that they are *un*righteous; that is the only possible evidence of
righteousness that any sinful son of Adam can give. But when
is that the case? We turn to another proverb: "The righteous
is delivered out of trouble and the wicked cometh in his stead"
(Prov. 11: 8). The time is certainly drawing near when a penitent Israel, seen in her remnant, righteous in her repentance,
shall be "mourning as one mourneth for his only son" (Zech.
12: 10-14). There we see the *"righteous people,"* and the other
proud, impenitent nations must "ransom" her by *taking her place*
and drinking of her cup.

But we will go a little further. The intrusion of evil into
God's creation has not been permitted apart from a profound
and worthy purpose, whether we can discern it or not. *Even the
wicked shall be made to serve that purpose.* But how can that
be? Thus, they shall serve to manifest that side of God's nature,
Light, His inflexible justice in the infliction of retribution against
obdurate impenitence. How could God be fully known were that
not shown? Thus all shall serve, as it is written: "God hath
made all things for Himself, even the wicked for the day of evil"
(Prov. 16: 4). The devil, his angels, impenitent men, shall all
eventually be seen as "vessels," or servants, but vessels to dishonor, and not to honor. Solemn truth!

How far from evidencing the righteousness of divine government is the earth today! There is no just discrimination whatever. Not only do sorrow, suffering and death come alike to all,
but oppression, wrong, sin, meet with no equivalent retribution
here; on the contrary, these seem often to have the easiest path.
Can that condition be eternal? Most surely not. This prophecy
tells of a day in which all these abnormal conditions shall be
righted, and the activity of judgment on the impenitent shall as
fully express the righteous government of God, as shall the perfect acceptance of the penitent; or, in the words we are considering, Egypt, Ethiopia and Seba shall then take the place of suffer-

ing Israel, and in this sense alone be a ransom. The righteousness of God's government of the earth must make discrimination between impenitence and penitence; in this sense the former shall be a ransom for the latter.

Of course this awakens further questions, as it is intended to do—questions which only find a perfectly satisfactory answer in that Cross where the "righteousness of God is manifested" in the infliction of full penalty on the most holy, but willing Substitute. The Cross of Christ alone meets all such difficulties. Well may we thank God that they are so met.

In verses 5 to 7 we see our Lord Jesus, having come in great glory, taking His place at Jerusalem, and with infinite majesty commanding every point of the compass to send back His long-scattered people to their homeland. East, West, North and South hear the summons; and not as fugitives flying from a Russian pogrom, or from a Nazi persecution, but as the elect of Jehovah they are conveyed with all honor as acceptable gifts to their God. We must never permit this joyous ending of all their wanderings and sorrows to be identified with the present return in unbelief. How firm the foundation that the perfect harmony of the word of prophecy gives us! Let the reader see how perfectly the Lord's words in Matt. 24: 31 accord with those of the prophet.

We are once more taken back to hear Jehovah's challenge thus:

8: Cause to come forth the blind people with eyes,
    And deaf to whom ears are not lacking.
9: Let all the nations be gathered as one,
    And let the peoples assemble.
    Who of them all this can declare,
    Give us of former things tidings?
    And that they may be fully approved
    Let them bring witnesses with them,
    Who, hearing, shall say: That is true!
10: Ye are My witnesses—so saith the Lord,
    And My servant whom I have chosen,
    That ye may know, and in Me believe,
    I am He, thus clearly discerning!
    Before Me no God ever was formed;
    Nor after Me shall there be any.

11: I, even I, am Jehovah alone,
    And beside Me there is not a Saviour!
12: 'Tis I who've proclaimed, 'tis I who have saved,
    'Tis I who have causèd to hearken,
    When no strange god was among you.
    Ye are My witnesses that I am God
    (And none other), proclaimeth Jehovah.
13: Aye, from this very day, I AM HE!
    And none from My hand can deliver;
    'Tis I who will work—who shall hinder?

We have here another challenge to the idolatrous nations of the earth to gather and put the powers of the deities they confide in to the test. And that they may be publicly justified let them bring their witnesses with them, who will publicly announce how they shall answer to it. Israel has been through sore sorrows; were those sorrows foreseen and foretold by these prophets of false deities? Did they faithfully deal with her sin and warn of its certain retribution? Nay; was not all their prophesying ever of smooth things, and giving the assurance of ever-increasing prosperity? They were lies. Jehovah alone announced the sorrows that lay in the future; and by the very sufferings through which they passed, they can bear witness to that truth.

So has it ever been; so is it today. And so shall falsehood ever prophesy a pleasant future as long as the devil is unchained and can deceive the nations of the earth. How unanimous were those four hundred prophets in assuring King Ahab who hired them that God would deliver Ramoth-Gilead into the king's hand (2 Chron. 18: 5), but smooth as were the words, you will remember that the end of that way was exceedingly rough for Ahab. Truth at the close of a dispensation is not always with majority of preachers.

So even to this day (and indeed I speak with much sorrow) false prophets have the same characteristic of preaching peace and prosperity to an impenitent Church. The New Testament shows us behind the little pulpit-pawns on the human chessboard the rebel-spirits that move them, for these are the real adversaries of our God and His Christ. But Jehovah has ever had a very efficient, if unwilling, witness to His truth in poor Israel; her whole history is an involuntary testimony to the one true God. When she no longer rejects her Messiah, she herself also shall recognize that that very Messiah has this divine mark; He too, as Jehovah Himself speaks here, is *"The First and the Last,"* for so He proclaims Himself in Rev. 1: 18.

Very precious to some of us is that short eleventh verse in which Jehovah cries, "Beside Me there is no Saviour." See, a human Babe rests upon a maiden's breast, and God Himself directs that He be called Jesus, or "Saviour" (Luke 1: 31); and what is that but pronouncing that Babe to be very God of very God? Aye, that very Name means that in Him we have Immanuel, "God with us." As that far-off trial on Carmel in Elijah's time ended with the shout of the witnesses: "Jehovah, He is God! Jehovah, He is God!" we too cry, "Jesus is God over all, blessed forever!"

In verse 12 Jehovah insists that every movement in salvation comes—not from man Godward, but from Himself, even to the ability of listening in faith. Thus a wretched nation of unbelief shall express the goodness of and be the "witness" to Jehovah, by becoming a nation of penitents.

Stern are the words of verse 13, for we must remember that Israel's place, hopes and salvation are all, as a nation, upon the earth, and that salvation can only be brought about by a strong hand on her oppressors. This is here the "work" that none can hinder. The text is often applied to the power of the present gospel of His grace, but true as that is, its primary application is assuredly to the government of the earth. This verse closes a subdivision of our prophecy, as similar words did in chapter 14: 27.

With verse 14 we begin to trace another footstep of the Lord's gracious ways with His elect, Israel, here leading up to a time of outpouring of the Spirit—can we fail to be interested in such a theme?

14: Thus saith Jehovah,
      Your Kinsman-Redeemer,
      The Holy One of Isràel;

>       For your sake I sent unto Babel—
>       All of them brought down in flight,
>       Even the Casidim,
>       Whose song of rejoicing*
>       Has been in their ships.
> 15:   I am Jehovah!
>       I am your Holy One!
>       Creator of Isr'el!
>       I am your King!

Clearly to understand verse 14 we too must become Jews, as it were, and throw ourselves back to the time of the prophecy. We have been told to forget the past revealings, for Jehovah is about to foretell another deliverance that is still in the future. Dim indeed may it be to us, but not to Him.  His eye needs no mechanical aid to see clearly events that will not actually transpire till many generations of men have come and gone.  As we listen, what we hear causes us blank astonishment, for the Babylon of our day, is but a very petty State, and quite friendly; yet the prophecy begins with a clear intimation that Babylon is not only to be our foe, but our conqueror; for Jehovah now tells us that it is for our sakes He intervenes in its affairs, and makes those who shall then hold us in captivity themselves to be fugitives, the ships which have been their boast, their song, they will have to use for their flight.  The reference to the ships that have fostered Babylon's wealth reminds us of Rev. 18, where Babylon in another form is suffering under the Hand of God (see verses 11, 17).

In verse 15 again we hear a thrice-repeated claim of absolute and unlimited supremacy: "I am Jehovah," the one unchanging, ever-existing, covenant-keeping God of Israel; that is His personal Name, as we may say.  Next, He is the Holy One, with infinite abhorrence of all that is contrary to His own divine standard of holiness.  Then He owns Himself as the Creator of Israel; and as such, Israel must be under the protection of His throne, and that forbids that she remain captive to Babylon.

---

* The word *rinnah* which I have rendered, "song of rejoicing," is a cry of deep emotion.  Not once does Isaiah use it except as expressing a joyous sentiment; thus, here, a boast.

How blessedly suggestive is this of the impossibility of one single redeemed individual from the race of mankind remaining captive either to sin, or its penalty, death. As sure as we are redeemed by the Blood of Christ, so sure is it that "Sin shall not have dominion over us;" that death has already lost all power or claim over our spirits, although, till the Lord comes, our bodies are still under its sentence; and that, as to those who have already passed away to be with Christ, as yet imperfect, disembodied, they shall again stand up as men; spirit, soul and body evidencing in that perfect condition, the perfect efficacy of the Cross of Christ.

16: Thus saith Jehovah, who maketh a roadway
      E'en through the sea;
      And through mighty billows a footpath;
17: He who the chariot and horses outbringeth;
      Army and hero,
      They lie down together, rise nevermore!
      They are extinguished, as tow are they quenched!
18: Remember no longer events of the old time,
      Neither consider the things that are past;
19: Behold, I do work entirely a new thing—
      Now shall it sprout, and shall ye not know it?
      Aye, through the wilderness I'll make a road,
      And streams in the desert!
20: The beasts of the field shall then give Me glory,
      Dogs of the prairie and ostriches too.*
      For in the wilderness I will give waters,
      And streams in the desert,
      To give drink to My people, even My chosen.
21: The people that I have formed for Myself,
      My praise they shall tell out.

In verses 16-18 the reference is clearly to the past deliverance from Egypt, since it forms a figure of a deliverance still in the future. The "sea," of verse 16, is the Red Sea, through which a pathway was made by that violent east wind that blew in that dark night. The chariots and horses, "the army and soldiers," are the pursuing Egyptians. Then, as if that were a work

---

*Literally, "monsters and daughters of a cry." See notes on chap. 13.

no longer worthy of holding in memory in comparison with what lies still in the future, Forget, He cries, remember no longer, in view of what lies before you, all those long past events.

Of course, that is not a literal command.  Israel could never forget that "night much to be observed," but another intervention is promised her that, in its glory, will eclipse that of the past.  His mercies are never exhausted.  His powers are not enfeebled by centuries; nor does He ever thus repeat Himself, as if the past evidenced the limit of either His power or grace.  He always adds some "better thing."  The same mighty Worker will always do a new thing; and even now if His people will look closely at the present conditions they may discern that new thing beginning to sprout, even as a gardener discerns the ripe and perfected fruit in the bud, for in the present revival of the *national* spirit among the Jews may we not see the "fig-tree" giving sure promise of a coming summer?

Literal was the rock struck in the desert, literal was the man and literal was the rod that struck it, and literal was the water that flowed; but all these literal earthly things were to provide types of the most profound heavenly truths.  The bodily revival that the Israelites received by drinking that water was a type of the reviving of our spirits by the "word of Christ," itself vivified by the Spirit of God.  What a key to many a difficulty is that basic truth that all of earth has been formed as it has been to give figures of heavenly and eternal verities.

Now we must listen to a reproach so tender, so replete with affection, that it becomes itself as sweet as these waters of which we have been speaking.

22:  But thou hast not called upon Me, O Jacob!
    Yes, even of Me thou hast wearied, Isràel!
23:  Thou hast not brought Me lambs for burnt-offerings,
    Nor with thy sacrifice given Me glory.
    I have not burdened thee, demanding oblation;
    Nor have I wearied thee, incense requiring.
24:  Thou hast bought for Me no sweet cane with silver,
    Neither refreshed Me with fat of thy gifts.
    'Tis Me thou hast made to serve with thy sins,
    'Tis Me thou hast wearied with all thy transgressions.

25: I, and I only, am He that doth blot out
    For My own sake thy many revoltings,
    And will remember thy sins nevermore.
26: Let us then come into judgment together,
    And plead what thou canst for thy justification!
27: Even the first of thy forefathers sinned,
    Thy teachers* revolted against Me;
28: Then I profaned the sanctified princes;†
    To curses gave Jacob; to scoffs, Israèl.

Jacob's wanderings are over, Israel is fully restored, and here the restored nation is led to look back to the way it has been led to that restoration. It can but remind one of that analogous counsel given us: "Wherefore remember that ye being in times past Gentiles in the flesh," etc. (Eph. 2: 11). Both Israel, as a nation, and each individual Christian will own, and gladly own, that salvation is due solely to free grace that bore with all waywardness so patiently. How delightful it will be to look back from the joy and security of the Father's house to the long path by which we have been led there! I can but think that here Jehovah tells His beloved Israel that He has been listening at the closed door of their heart, and mourns that it has been so silent toward Him.

In times of acute distress there are always those cries of which Elihu speaks: "By reason of the multitude of oppressions, they make the oppressed to cry" (Job 35: 9); but the crisis past, silence once more reigns, showing that the heart had not been affected—it was but stricken nature's enforced cry. That will not satisfy Him who longs for filial confidence. Israel has been weary of God! Not that there was not "the form of godliness"—plenty of it—but it was a mere external form, as that of which Jehovah complains in the first chapter, and which He abhors. If the reference is merely to the daily sacrifices and the accompany-

---

*The prime meaning of the word is "to stammer," "to speak barbarously." Then as coming between the barbarous speaker and his hearers, "interpreter," as in Job 33: 23, and thus may be rendered here, "teachers."

†See 1 Chron. 24: 5, rendered "governors of the sanctuary," evidently referring to those who have rule in holy things, as in contrast with civil authorities. These princes are priests too.

ing incense, then the Lord surely received what He desired, for all was in order as far as that went then. Have we not already heard: "I am full of the burnt offering of rams?" Surely He could not be both "full" and yet complain that His people had given *none!* No, it is the heart's love, the heart's confidence, that He values more than men value gold; but a dead "religiousness" from those dead in sin is *nothing* to Him.

So Israel, His dear Israel, has pressed Him with iniquity on iniquity, till He is weary under the load. Israel is not morally better than Egypt. But if all are equally evil, what causes the difference? Verse 25 gives the answer, thrilling in its terseness, of just three words: "I—I—He!" All the motive for the Love of God to man must be found—not in its poor object, man, but in Him who exercises it.* Jehovah, and He alone, is the One who blots out all the rebellions of His people, and remembers them no more, and that for His own sake. Humbling, yet precious truth! It is thus that His blessing "addeth no sorrow with it;" for whilst indeed enwrapping us with a love from which none in heaven, earth, or under-world, can sever, yet it hides from us that pride that has been ever, and still is, the very cause of the sorrow.

Verse 26 is a gracious parallel to Chap. 1: 18: "Come now, and let us reason together." Jehovah says, as it were, "I will take no advantage of My infinite superiority as God over thee, My poor sinful creature. Come into court with Me, call to remembrance everything in thy favor, and see if it be possible to stand there maintained by thine own righteousness."

It is impossible! Trace back thy lineage to thy first father, and you will find a poor erring man. Do you make your boast in being children of Abraham? Well, was he chosen because of his holiness? Nay, for what "hath Abraham our father as pertaining to the flesh found?" Grace, and nothing but grace from first to last, suited him; he too simply "believed God and it was

---

*And do we not see Him, the same divine One, in John 13, serving His needy people even because of their proneness to the defilement of the way? Can we ever get low enough when God's beloved Son deigns even to be our *Servant!*

counted to him for righteousness" (Rom. 4). And so all down the line of those who have taken the place of interpreting God and His ways, each and all of them have been but self-confessed erring men; all tell out, in one way or another, human sin, human frailty, human error. Even the high priests who have a place of rule—"princes," thus as they are—He has been compelled to expose as the reverse of holy. They are "holy" as to their position, but "profane" as to their condition. They may have an external holiness, but within—Matt. 23: 25! So Jacob must be given up to the curse, and Israel to the revilings of the Gentiles.

It is well to bear in mind that there is ever an *external* sanctification that God Himself recognizes as that, quite distinct from personal holiness, a position of external acceptance in which there is "much advantage every way;" very precious privileges with corresponding responsibilities resulting from them, as in the days past, in Judaism; and so now in the Christian sphere on the earth, as 1 Cor. 7: 10-14 evidences. Alas, it is greatly to be feared that very many who are thus sanctified as to position will be found even in perdition—that "sorer punishment" than that which befell him who despised Moses' law and died without mercy (Heb. 10: 36). With deep grief do we hear from many so-called Christian pulpits teachings which count the "blood of the covenant wherewith they are sanctified an unholy thing," nor can we think of the end without trembling. "It is a fearful thing [thus] to fall into the hands of the living God."

# CHAPTER FORTY-FOUR

**Continued expostulation as to the folly of idolatry. Meaning and application of the word Jeshurun. The making of an idol described with divine irony.**

WE must again ignore the division caused by the interposition of a new chapter, for although it is true that there is a striking change in the *tone* of the address, it is in the same line as the preceding. Jehovah having portrayed Israel's sins as a dark cloud, now uses that cloud as a foil to set off the bright light of His grace.

1: Hearken, O Jacob, My servant art thou;
   Israel, whom I have chosen;
2: Thus doth Jehovah, thy Maker, speak;
   From the womb of thy mother who formed thee,
   And forming, most surely will help thee.
   Fear not, O Jacob, My servant art thou,
   Jeshurun, whom I have chosen.
3: For I will pour waters on him who's athirst,
   And floods will I pour on the dry land.
   My Spirit upon thy seed will I pour,
   And on thine offspring My blessing.
4: They shall spring up amid the green grass,
   As willows spring up by the brook-sides.
5: This one shall say: I belong to the Lord,
   And another shall call himself Jacob,
   This one subscribe by his hand to the Lord,
   Take the name, Isràel, as an honor.*

Well may Jacob hearken! Well may Israel listen to words so sweet, so tender, so full of perfect knowledge of the way already trodden, which, rough as it has been been, has led at last Home! And well may each of us discern an intended application to ourselves personally as in Christ; for it is to Him all these

---

*This gives the correct idea of the Hebrew word *kahnah*: "to call by an honorable appellation."

promises are given and we participate in them only as being in Him. It is very precious to see in Israel's blessings a picture of our own without robbing that beloved nation! So in that delightful double view, let us cheerily go on.

How can He who has been the very Former of Israel as a nation, when it was cast into the sea of nations like a new-born babe with no maternal hand but His to cherish it, no heart to care for its feebleness but His—how can He then ever forsake His people? Is it not certain that He will complete the good work thus begun? Oh, fear not, Jacob; thou hast been an unprofitable servant, indeed, but He owns thee for His servant still. He has purposes that demand thy preservation, for He has destined thee to show His praise on earth. Oh, fear not, Jeshurun,* for He has chosen thee, and after all thy wanderings, He will treat thee as the heavens respond to the parched earth, sending on it gracious dew and rain; so shall His Spirit, of which these are but shadows, fall upon thee, and renew thy national life. Then, as water causes herb and tree to grow, so the effect of that outpouring of the Spirit shall be a corresponding prosperity and vitality. As the very course of a river may be traced by the luxuriant herbage that grows on its banks, so may the presence of the (ungrieved) Spirit be discerned by the lovely fruits of love, joy and peace— yea, of all that the Holy Ghost brings forth wherever He is permitted to govern.

With conscious, yet lowly, dignity will the poor Jew then say that he belongs to Jehovah, nor shall he then, as once, shrink from confessing his name to be Jacob (see Gen. 32); nay, he will make that permanent by writing, and adopt, as the noblest of titles, "Israel!"

---

*"Jeshurun." In verse 1 the nation is first called "Jacob," and then "Israel," so in the next, it is again addressed as Jacob, but here Jeshurun takes the place of Israel. From this it is clear that the word "Jeshurun" bears the same relation to Jacob as does the word Israel. Jacob is the name that brings to the mind all the "crookedness" of him who bore it, so Jeshurun gives the opposite idea, for its meaning is "The upright"—an antithesis of Jacob. Jacob and Israel, Jacob and Jeshurun, are terms that express the man according to both nature and grace.

6: Thus saith Jehovah, Israel's King,
Jehovah of Hosts, his Redeemer;
I am the First and I am the Last;
There is never a God beside Me.

7: And who, as I, shall the future proclaim?
Then let him speak and declare it,
Form it, and put it in order for Me,
Since I appointed the people,
The people abiding for ever.*
The things that are now coming on,
And what is so nearly approaching,
Let them declare them to all.

8: Be not in terror! Oh, be not afraid!
Have I not long ago told thee?
Declared to thee what did portend?
Of this ye're My witnesses ever.
Speak! Is there ever a God beside Me?
No! Indeed, no; for I know none.

9: The makers of idols are all in despair,†
Their delectable things do not profit.
And these are the things that their witnesses are.
Nothing they see, nothing they know!
Well may they then be ashamed!

10: Who will admit that he formed a god,
A graven image hath molten,
That is so utterly worthless?

11: Lo, his co-workers shall all be ashamed;
The workmen, they all come from Adam.‡
Let them assemble; let them stand up,
Be alarmed, and confounded together.

---

*Heb., *ohlam*. A word of frequent use and various shades of meaning. Its root meaning is "what is hidden," and so "hidden time." From that the transition is easy to an indefinite time, till it gets to be "eternity." Here, as applied to the Jews, it carries with it the idea of permanency, so the rendering "abiding for ever" is justified.

†*Tohu*, "without form" (Gen. 1: 2), "utter confusion," and so "despair."

‡*Lit.*, "And the workmen they are from Adam:" that is those who make the image have their own source no higher than that "man of low degree" made of the dust; what can be expected of such?

The many and varied readings of verse 7 show what difficulty commentators have found in it, but this at least is sure, that once again Jehovah, who identifies Himself with Israel as its King and Redeemer, the First, the Last, and alone God, challenges all rivalry. Has any proclaimed as has He, regarding that nation, which, since in relation to Himself, as owing its very being to Him, has an endless existence; if so, let the rivals begin even from this time to look forward, and foretell what is still in the future and is approaching.

The terrifying judgments that will befall the nations of the earth, will but strengthen and confirm the faith of Israel's believing remnant, as the present distressing conditions of Christendom do but strengthen the faith of the Lord's people today, for those very conditions have been foretold long ago. It is of great value to note that Jehovah of the Old Testament and Jesus of the New speak precisely the same language, for it is our Lord who said: "Now I have told you before it come to pass, that, when it is come to pass, ye might believe"—wonderful provision of grace, making what might otherwise shake faith to its foundations, to confirm it—that is a divine mark.

There is no other God on whom we poor feeble creatures can lean, no other Rock that, amid all the shifting sands of human apostasy, can provide an immovable standing-place for our feet, than He who speaks in both Old and New Testaments, and whose knowledge is infinite; so that when He says: "I know of none," surely no lower powers can find any.

Note the strong contrasts, drawn in verses 8 and 9, between the two companies of witnesses. Jehovah speaks to Israel, there identified solely with the Remnant, and says: Ye are My witnesses, and I have told you what is coming, so that ye do see, hear, and know. Ye are not in the dark, that that day should overtake you as a thief in the night. The false deities have also *their* witnesses, who are now in the same complete confusion as the earth was when "without form and void"—suitable witnesses are they for the idols that have their confidence. But we have only to look forward a little and, in the light of what God has told us, the day is coming when none will boast of having had any hand in making so vain and despicable a god. The majority is now on their side, but let them choose their ground, take as firm a stand as possible, yet in a moment shame shall overwhelm them as it did those many prophets of Baal at Carmel.

A graphic and intensely ironic description of the making of an idol, first by a worker in metal, and then by one in wood, now follows:

12:  The smith doth make a chisel sharp,
      And 'mid the coals doth labor;
      He fashions it by hammer-blows,
      And works it with his strong arm;
      But, hungry, see his strength doth fail,
      And, thirsty, he is fainting!

13:  The carpenter doth mete with rule,
      The wood-block marks with pencil;
      These lines he follows with his planes,
      Then fashions it by compass.
      So makes a figure of a man,
      With human form and beauty:
      And thus 'tis fitted to remain
      Within the maker's dwelling.

14:  He heweth down the cedar-trees,
      Takes the oak and cypress,
      And strengthens one amid the trees
      Of the forest growing;
      Or he plants a mountain-ash,
      Which the rain doth nourish.

15:  This may serve to make a fire,
      He takes thereof to warm him.
      Yea, with part he maketh fire,
      And bread with that he baketh;
      Yea, with part he makes a god,
      And prostrate falls before it!
      A graven image doth he make,
      Falls down to that—adoring!

16:  With part he makes a fire for warmth,
      With part a fire for eating;
      He satisfies himself with roast,
      Yea, warms himself, and crieth:
      I'm (comfortably) warm, Ha! Ha!
      For I sit by the fireside.

17:  A god he of the remnant makes,
      And fashions it an idol;
      To this he prostrates and adores,
      To this he prays, beseeching,
      Thou art my god, O save me!

The worker in iron (as it literally reads) makes the hard metal to be plastic in the fire, then hammers it into the shape he requires, for "the smith, a mighty man is he," but even he gets hungry, and then his strength vanishes, and he—the maker of a god—faints!   But this idol-making is mostly the work of the carpenter, so his work is described in more detail. He first selects his block of wood, and with a measuring line defines the length and breadth of the image that is in his mind; then, having fixed these broad limitations, he marks out the outline, and cuts away all outside these lines.   Then, to get a more exact representation, he uses a compass, by which he measures the various parts of the human frame, and makes his image to conform thereto; thus it finally emerges from his hands the "likeness of an image of corruptible man" (Rom. 1: 23); and expressing in its form the beauty of the human body, is thus made fit to take its place in the home.

That block of wood, from which the image of a man is made, is traced back to its source.   We are told of a forest of noble trees all coming under the one term "cedars;" as "if one should say in order to have apples to eat, I plant an orchard.    The meaning there would be—not that the orchard consisted only of apple-trees, but that term covers all."* So "cedars," in verse 14, covers the cypress and oak that come  nearer to suit his purpose.   But he passes over these, and the description goes back another step, to the planting of a mountain-ash which depends on the rain for its growth.   When this has come to maturity, he cuts it down, and divides it up for various purposes.   With a part he makes a fire, and with the other an idol.   One half is his servant —the other his god!   Could anything exceed the contemptuous irony?

There appears to be no thought here of any *spirits* behind the images, but that was always in the minds of the heathen.   It was a *"goddess* Diana" that was represented by the image that fell down from Jupiter.   The ignorant mass overlook this, and, darkened with superstition, consider the image itself as the god, but the more thoughtful could not possibly conceive of the mere wood

---

*Nagelsbach in Lange.

itself being a spirit-deity; and 1 Cor. 10 clearly assures us that evil spirits were worshipped behind the image. Nor does there need such an idol for the grossest idolatry. The poor papist (and his misnamed "Protestant" imitator) worships a piece of bread, before which all prostrate themselves at the sound of what they term the "sacring-bell"—could idolatry be grosser? Nor indeed is *any* object needed, for the light of later revelation shining into every heart finds there a never-ending hunger, and calls even that longing *"covetousness,* which is idolatry!" Who can claim freedom from it? If we are not satisfied with God in Christ, we too are idolators.

Verses 15 to 17 need little exposition. The contemptuous irony speaks clearly for itself. A block of wood is divided into two parts, and over one of these parts the man cries, "Ha! Ha! It warms me!" and to the other he falls down and cries, "O save me!"

The prophecy goes on in exposing the follies of idolatry thus:

18: Naught do they know, naught understand;
For their eyes, lest they see, hath He plastered,*
And shut up their hearts from true knowledge.
19: There is not a man that doth lay it to heart,
Hath knowledge or sense thus to reason,†
Part of the wood I've burned in the fire,
Have even baked bread on its embers;
Flesh too I've roasted, of that roast did eat;
Can I make of the remnant an idol?
A mere block of wood can I worship?

In verse 18 there is a strong insistence on divine sovereignty. But does that mean that God arbitrarily closes the eyes that would otherwise have seen? Far from it; for He who was the exact expression of God's substance (Heb. 1: 2) did precisely this very thing. He plastered a poor man's eyes with clay mixed with spittle (all graphically speaking of Himself in utter humiliation

---

*"Plastered" is quite literal.

†Literally, "to say;" but the verb has in it the idea of thinking, reasoning, as in Ps. 14: 1: "The fool hath said in his heart."

and contempt), and smeared it on blind eyes. *If those eyes had made any pretension to seeing,* that would have sufficed to make them blind!   Siloam's waters wash away all blindness, and in that humbled Man the once-blind one sees the Son of God (John 9).   But the religious self-complacent Pharisees, who confessed to no blindness, were indeed eye-plastered by the lowly grace of Him who healed the blind!

There is surely nothing new under the sun.   As it was then, so it is today.   At the same moment that the best established truth is rejected, a silly lie is accepted.   When the heart is at enmity with God the most stupid fables will be accepted by the hardest-headed business man.   Not merely the ignorant mass, but the educated and refined, without shame accept the follies of Romish superstition, the contradiction of the plainest facts by "Christian Science," and the anti-Christian pseudo-scientific hypothesis that is sweeping over Christendom, Evolution, which, by repeating the guesses of the heathen of ages long passed, at least disproves its own claim to have made any advance whatever.

Those idolators of whom Isaiah wrote were not incapacitated by mental affliction, and so worthy of compassion rather than blame; with all the natural powers of moral discernment, they made no use of those powers.   It is one of the many evidences of the near approach of the Day, that men so easily believe a lie, for it shows us how soon that "strong delusion" of the near-future shall sweep over truth-rejecting Christendom.

20: Feasting on ashes, his heart has misled;
      His soul he cannot deliver.
      Nor can he say: I am grasping a lie,
      And holding it fast in my right hand.
21: These things, O Jacob, recall to thy mind,
      And Israel who art My servant.
      Thee have I formed, My servant art thou,
      Israel, never forgotten!
22: All thy revoltings, as a dense cloud,
      Have I (forever) out-blotted;
      As a thick cloud I've blotted thy sins.
      Return unto Me; I've redeemed thee.

Man's appetite is depraved. He craves after what, were he normal, he too would discern to be as disappointing and valueless as ashes, ever leaving him more hungry than before.

With that undercurrent of evangelic tenderness that so often shows itself coming up to the surface of our book, Jehovah turns to His true Israel, whom He has Himself formed to be His servant to carry out His purposes, and express His praise on the earth. With what attractive affection does He speak: "I have never forgotten thee, through all thy wanderings, thy sins, thy sorrows!" Nor is it less true, nor less attractive to us poor straying ones, as we so often are; for we too have learned something of His sufficiency and faithful love, as one of our poets sings:

> "Through life, death, through sorrow, aye, through sinning,
> Christ shall suffice me, yea, He hath sufficed;
> Christ is the end, as Christ was the beginning,
> Christ the beginning, and the end is—Christ."

"As the clouds have their rising from the swamps of earth, and hide the blue of heaven, so have thy revoltings veiled the light of My love," says the Lord here, and then (Oh, the blessedness of it!) He cries: "I have now blotted them all out: the clouds are dispelled, the mists are gone, for I have redeemed thee. Oh, then return from all thy wanderings to Me!" Do we not say: Who could resist such tenderness? Who could turn away from such love? Not the restored nation, true Israel of the future, for hearken to her song:

> 23: Sing, O ye heavens, for Jehovah hath done it!
> Triumphantly shout, ye depths of the earth!
> Break joyously forth, ye mountains exultant!
> Sing, O thou forest, and all trees therein!
> For 'tis Jehovah, Redeemer of Jacob,
> Who by Isràel doth show forth His praises!

What irrepressible joy is in this verse! Like a song-bird that almost bursts its throat in its singing, so this singer feels his inability to give adequate expression to his joy, and calls on all the universe to aid by its music. It is joy *unspeakable,* and so requiring aid in order to be told. "Ye heavens above, O help my praise!  Let sun, moon, and glittering firmanent be melodious in harmony with my new-found joy!  Ye deep places of the earth, be ye too in accord, so that one full strain of praise may ascend to Jehovah, for He hath redeemed Jacob—shown all His glory in His grace to Israel!"  It is magnificent!

With this joyous note this section worthily closes.

The words, "Thus saith Jehovah," indicate clearly enough a new beginning here.  It may be a human hand that holds the pen; it may be human lips that are used in the speech, the very lips that confessed to uncleanness at the beginning of the book, but now those lips are used to speak Jehovah's words, and the prophecy goes in a kind of stately march to its present culmination in Cyrus.

24: Thus saith Jehovah, thy Kinsman-Redeemer,
       He who hath formed thee, e'en from the womb,
       I am Jehovah, the Maker of all things,
       Who stretched out the heavens by My power alone,
       And spread forth the earth all by Myself;
25: Frustrating the signs of the boasters,
       Diviners exposing as fools,
       Making the wise to walk backward,
       Exposing their science as folly,
26: Confirming the word of His servant,
       Performing His messengers' counsel,
       Who saith to Jerusalem, Thou shalt be dwelt in;
       To the cities of Judah, Ye shall be built;
       And their waste-places I will restore.
27: Who saith to the deep: Be thou dry,
       And I will dry up thy rivers;
28: Who saith unto Cyrus, Thou art My shepherd,
       And all of My pleasure he shall perform;
       To Jerusalem saying, Thou shalt be built,
       And to the temple, Be founded!

In verse 24 Jehovah owns to being Israel's nearest of kin, and therefore his Redeemer.  Most assuredly that could only be true when the nation has acknowledged its true Messiah, and is seen as identified with Him.  But He is also the Maker of all things.  It was He alone who stretched out the starry heavens, commissioning them ever to give their silent but powerful witness

to His eternal power and Godhead.   That is the first step in this
march.

But then His foot falls to earth, and that too must bear the
same witness in its lovely surface, so marvellously adapted to its
dwellers that evidently none other than the same mighty Worker
has spread it out as a park, with forest, mountain, valley and
stream.   And is there one elect nation amid the inhabitants of
these fair scenes that shall be the centre of His ways there?   Yes,
Israel, the nation that He has formed from its very beginning,
and not only created but redeemed.

But where is this beloved Israel?   Far forward pierces the
Seer's eye, and he tells of Israel captive in that home of earth's
proud sophistries, Babylon.   Here the false prophets foretell a
glowing future.   He covers them with ridicule and shame, bringing all their forecasts to naught, so that they appear rather as
madmen than divinely inspired prophets.   Thus all the wisdom
of the world is exposed; its boasted science is shown as foolishness, and its progress as really retrogression.   If that be really
*true*, if this be really a divine word, what a light it throws on
the unparalleled boasting of this day—boasting that certainly has
a very distinct kind of basis.   Was ever such progress?   Were
ever, in all the past ages, such wondrous discoveries and inventions? If one who lived even fifty years ago could return to earth
he would hardly know it.   When he heard a voice that was
familiar to him yet speaking from a city a thousand miles away!
Millions of listeners can in their own homes listen to speech, lec-
ture or song from a spot on the other side of the world from any
of them, with no more apparent channel of communication between them than the atmosphere or ether!   Is not *that* progress?
Is not *that* true science?

The answer surely depends on what is the goal to which the
unsatisfied heart of man would attain.   What is that "good thing
for the sons of men, which they should do under the heaven all
the days of their life?" (Eccl. 2: 3).   What shall fill that empty
longing heart and satisfy it permanently and perfectly?   Do all
these marvels have that desired effect?   Are men more content,
more completely satisfied with electricity than with gas?   With
gas than with candles?   Has that wandering, restless heart found

its home and sunk to rest with a sigh of satisfaction on Radium? Alas, discontent has kept equal pace with progress. Deeper spiritual darkness, denser perplexity, has come with this increased "wisdom" and "science," till discontent is giving birth to its children in varying spirits of revolution, looming in almost every land. Surely then, the boasted progress has again been *backward!*

On the other hand, God ever confirms the word of His own servants, for they have but passed on what they have themselves received from Him. When one remembers the day in which the ending of this chapter was written, that Jerusalem was still a great and prosperous city, that the cities of Judah needed no rebuilding, that Babylon was but a struggling petty power, that no potentate of the name of Cyrus was known to exist; there cannot be the least surprise that modern rationalism has to make the prophecy to date after the event. Since no miracles are possible; since the Creator of all has been, always "reverently," expelled from His own universe; and since this would be as wonderful a miracle as any that could be conceived, then to them it follows that Isaiah did *not* write this prophecy; it came from the pen of "The Great Unknown." Since they *know* that God is unable to foresee and foretell, their claims certainly approach to omniscience, for who but one omniscient could tell us of the Divine limitations?

But this verse is of peculiar interest to us, since it has been accepted in some quarters as giving the starting-point of the great prophecy of the "seventy weeks" of Daniel 9, a prophecy that never fails to claim and to command the most absorbed attention of the Christian. We reserve detailed comment on it to its more specific reference in the next chapter.

# CHAPTER FORTY-FIVE

**Continuation of the prophecy as to Cyrus.  How can God be the Author of evil?**

THE introduction of a new chapter again mars the unity of this part of our prophecy, which begins with verse 24 of the preceding chapter, and consists of five strophes, each being introduced by the words, "Thus saith Jehovah." Thus verses 1 to 10 form the second strophe, and speak directly to, as the preceding one spoke of, Cyrus.

1: Thus saith Jehovah to His anointed,
   To Cyrus whose right hand I've strengthened,
   To bring down the nations before him,
   And ungird the loins of kings,
   To open before him the two-leaved doors,
   And the gates that shall not be shut.
2: Before thee I'll go, rough places make plain,
   Will break into pieces the portals of brass,
   The bars of strong iron cut asunder.
3: And to thee have I given
   The treasures of darkness,
   The wealth that is hidden in secret,
   That thou should'st know that I am Jehovah
   And He who hath called thee by name,
   The God of Isràel.
4: 'Tis for the sake of Jacob My servant,
   Israel, whom I have chosen,
   That I have called thee by name,
   Given thee titles of honor,
   E'en when thou knewest Me not.
5: I am Jehovah—there is none other!
   For beside Me there is not a God.
   'Tis I who've equipped thee,
   Though thou hast not known Me:
6: That they may know from rising of sun
   E'en to its going a-down,
   That besides Me, there is not a God.
   I am Jehovah—there is none else!

7: Former of light!   Creator of darkness!
   Founder of peace!   Creator of evil!
   I am Jehovah who worketh all this!

8: Distil, O ye heavens, distil from above!
   Ye skies, pour righteousness down!
   Open, thou earth, and bloom with salvation,
   And righteousness blossom therewith.
   I, even I, Jehovah created it!

9: O woe be to him who strives with his Maker—
   A potsherd 'mid potsherds of earth—
   Shall the clay say to him who doth fashion it,
   Why hast thou formèd me thus?
   And shall thy work say: He hath no hands?
10: Woe unto him that doth say to his father,
   What is it that thou hast begotten?
   And to the woman, What bringest thou forth?

Cyrus is here given a title of transcendent dignity and significance, for he is called "Messiah" or "Anointed;" doubtless because in the deliverance of Israel from Babylon he was to be a shadow of the true Messiah, and of His eternal salvation. All obstacles are to give way. Babel's hundred brazen gates with their bars of iron shall prove no hindrance to him, and the immense wealth that has been placed in secret places for safety shall all be his. And we too know of One who, having spoiled principalities and powers, has both distributed gifts to men, and even to His God has given that which is more precious than "gold that perisheth," the love and confidence of the heart of man, restored to its true and only rest.

But here we have a contrast: Cyrus is chosen long before he knew the Lord, but our Cyrus ever knew that He "came from and went to God," who had loved Him from "before the foundation of the world" (John 17: 24).

Did we say that Israel was the centre of God's purposes as to the earth? True; but they do not stop with Israel; for, far as the sun can shine, and as there is "nothing hid from the heat thereof," so the warmth and light of God's love in Christ shall compass the whole earth. O happy earth when in such case!

As God, and He only, is "God over all, blessed forever," so both light and darkness are within His control, so that He is here said not only to "form light," but to "create darkness." Not that darkness comes *from* Him who is Light, any more than night is due to the presence of the sun; but that even the darkness would not be, save that He had a worthy purpose in permitting it. A prisoner ordered into a dark cell for a punishment knows that the cell has been made by the Government for that very purpose. So here, the contrasted word to "evil" is not "good," but "peace." The origin of moral evil is by no means affirmed as being of God, which would be the worst form of blasphemy.

There is no sorrow of bereavement, no distress due to losses, no pain or sickness, that is not by *His* permissive will, who, overruling all, works by it good for penitent faith. The wisest of all men with no light but that afforded by his natural intelligence found himself quite unable to solve the contradictory mysteries of what is termed Providence. He saw the race not to the swift, the battle not going in favor of the strong, neither bread to the wise, nor yet riches to men of understanding, nor yet favor to men of skill; *but time and chance happening to them all* (Eccl. 9: 11). Verse 7 refutes this entirely, and *we* have a still further revelation, for all such contradictions are in His Hand by whom they work in perfect accord for the truest good to all who respond to His Love by the confidence of responsive love through all the maze of life. Was not Job right in attributing both the giving and the taking away of his all to the Lord, even though Satan was the active intermediary?

In verse 8 we have a foreshadowing of the very heart of the Gospel. Cyrus, Israel, Babylon, may be at first in the foreground, but soon they all fade, and their place is taken by our Lord Christ and His eternal salvation. How lovely it is to see here Righteousness and Salvation—two plants that, although both very beautiful, appear to our afflicted consciences impossible to bring into harmony—both springing up from, and blossoming from one root! It is inexpressibly precious to us poor guilty sons of earth, to see that not one whit of the demands of strict righteousness is diminished and yet that very Righteousness results in salvation! Before that "Root" is found that can bear such contrasted glories seven hundred years must pass, then shall Law and Prophets look on with complacence while "the righteousness of God which is by faith of Jesus Christ is unto all and upon all them that believe," protecting instead of condemning, for that Righteousness has seen the unmitigated penalty paid in full by the Holy One of God. The Plant that can bear on one stalk both Righteousness and Salvation must surely be the true *"heart's ease"* for us poor weary men.

Verses 9 and 10 are parenthetical, and a very different tune is played upon them. It reminds us of the epistle to the Romans. After the oft-read chapter 8 we come to the neglected chapter 9. After sweet words of grace, we listen to the protest, "Why then doth He yet find fault, for who hath resisted His will?" (Rom. 9: 19). And there too we read a similar rejoinder: "Nay, but, O man, who art thou that repliest against God? Shall the thing formed say to him that formed it: Why hast thou made me thus?"

How the proud spirit of man rises up in resentment and says, "If I were nothing but earth nothing could I say; but my very *speech* puts me in another class altogether to a 'potsherd,' and that destroys the parallel."

Not as regards the one point that it was intended to figure. Who gave thee that faculty of speech or reason? Canst thou reason? Then use that reason, and own that thou hast not an ability for which thou dost not owe as much to thy Maker as the vessel its existence to the potter. As well might a lovely vase use its very beauties to insult its maker with, *"Thou* hast no hands of power," as for thee to use thy natural endowments in rebellion. Surely, the reasonable way to use reason is to say that my very being speaks of His precious thoughts that are ever to usward. My very body is fearfully and wonderfully made, and its marvelous adaptations to its environment speak of a Maker as beneficent as He is wise. Ah, it is the lowest rung of a ladder that leads us to that Cross where the thoughts, the wondrous thoughts, of God to usward are told out in full. This brings us to the third strophe.

11: Thus saith Jehovah, Isràel's Most Holy,
    And He who hath formed him,
    Ask what I purpose far in the future
    Concerning My sons, and the work of My hands.
12: I, and I only, have formed the earth,
    And man have created that he may dwell on it;
    My hands alone have stretched out the heavens,
    Commanded their hosts to come forth.
13: 'Tis I who have raised him up in My justice,
    And all of his way will I straighten before him;
    My city he'll build, releasing My captives,
    Not for a price, and not for reward,
    Saith Jehovah Tzebaoth!

With what gracious condescension Jehovah actually commands His people to enquire of Him what His purposes are in the future, that they may know that He is ever leading to the one end of manifesting Himself in all His Love and Light for their everlasting blessing. Are *we* to be deaf to this encouragement? Have *we* no need of cheer—after nearly two thousand years of unfulfilled hope for the return of our Lord—to sustain that hope? May we not then ask Him of things to come? Nay, did He not send to His people the Comforter *for that very purpose?* (John 16: 13.)

This absolute control of all the events of earth, irrespective of their character, has its witness in the physical creation. See the perfect order of the worlds in space, ever telling of one unrivalled Arm of limitless power maintaining that order. Consider the earth and note the beautiful inter-adaptations on all sides, ever telling of one Mind of infinite wisdom, filled with thoughts of interest and affection for man. Shall He, who called into being and maintains all things visible, not have a worthy purpose in this well-ordered creation and ability also to carry out that purpose to finality? It is true that there are both in nature and providence contradictory testimonies that lead us to ask, Can His righteousness permit the present condition of the earth to be permanent? It is *man's* earth. Formed in all its intricacies for him, the very atmosphere is composed of such a balancing of gases exactly demanded by the human lungs, and so carefully proportioned that if one single constituent element be increased or diminished, discomfort, unconsciousness and death follow. Both earth and heaven witness that it is man's earth, would it be then simply righteous to leave it as it is today in Satan's sway, for him to use these contradictory providences for our perplexity forever? No! And as the deliverance of the earth shall be through the one people Israel it follows that the same righteousness demands that One be raised up for the deliverance of that people.

The one directly referred to is, of course, Cyrus, but Cyrus only as foreshadowing a greater Deliverer who shall build again the tabernacle of David which is fallen down, and bring back all the banished of Israel (Acts 15: 16).

Here is foretold *directly,* not what our Lord has done, or will do, but what Cyrus will do, and (must we not assume?) has done. It is plainly foretold that it is he who will say to Jerusalem, "Thou shalt be built," as well as to the temple, "Thy foundation shall be laid."

Yet both human chronology (which might easily be dismissed as lacking all authority to the believer, were it unsupported by Scripture) and Scripture itself tells us that it was not Cyrus who gave commandment for the rebuilding of the *city,* but of the *"house"* only, for so reads Ezra 1: "Now in the first year of Cyrus, king of Persia, that the word of the Lord by the mouth of Jeremiah might be fulfilled, the Lord stirred up the spirit of Cyrus, king of Persia, that he made a proclamation throughout all his kingdom, and put it in writing: Thus saith Cyrus, king of Persia, The Lord God of heaven hath given me all the kingdoms of the earth; and He hath charged me to build Him an *house* at Jerusalem."

And so all through the book, without one single clear exception, it is the *house,* and not the *city* that is the subject of Cyrus' proclamation.

The special interest that attaches to this for students of prophecy is that on the strength of this one word in Isaiah, the starting-point of the "70 weeks" of Dan. 9 has been taken to be, by some, the proclamation of Cyrus in B.C. 536. Yet this date would not accord with the full limit of the 490 years that should bring Daniel's prophecy to its completion, or the 483 to Messiah

the Prince (Dan. 9: 9). Further, Ezra says nothing of the prophecy given by Isaiah but distinctly tells us it was that "the
word of the Lord by the mouth of Jeremiah" should be fulfilled,
and this simply spoke of the restoration of the people back to
their land in 70 years from the date of their servitude and de-
portation. That in itself perfectly accords with the uninspired
chronology. Jerusalem was captured by Nebuchadnezzar B. C.
606, and 70 years would bring the decree of Cyrus to the very
date given, B. C. 536. But on their arrival at Jerusalem the first
care of the return refugees was the building of the *house*. This
was interrupted by a letter to Artaxerxes sent by "the adversaries
of Judah and Benjamin" (Ezra 4), in which they make the false
charge that the Jews were "building the rebellious and bad *city*."
This falsehood sufficed to make "the work of the *house* of God to
cease till the second year of Darius." Just at that precise date
Haggai comes in with his divinely-sent expostulation, referring
exclusively to the *house;* and under this incentive the work is
again begun and carried to its conclusion in five years. But when
we come to the civil writer, Nehemiah, we find, appropriately
enough, that the *city* with its walls and gates is *his* care, and no
longer the *house* which had been completed long before—"A gor-
geous shrine in the midst of a ruined city" (*Anderson*). It follows that it was Artaxerxes, and not directly Cyrus, who gave
"the commandment to restore and rebuild Jerusalem;" and it is
*his* decree, in the 20th year of his reign (B.C. 445), that is the
starting-point of that prophecy of "70 weeks." This is confirmed
beyond question by the Lord presenting Himself in lowly majesty,
as "Prince," on the *very day* of the completion of the 69th week*
(Luke 19: 37-42). What then of this distinct prophecy? Does
it fail in this particular? We must not say that. But the fulfilment of a prophecy is often progressive, and the first step in
that fulfilment, although in itself it does not go to completion, is
recognized as fulfilling what it only initiates.† May not this

---

*See "The Coming Prince," Sir Robert Anderson.

†Readers familiar with Sir Robt. Anderson's "The Coming
Prince" will remember how this principle of progressive fulfilment
is shown in the "servitude," "captivity" and "desolations" of
Israel.

*apparent* failure on the part of Cyrus, have been permitted to loosen our thoughts from him, and fix them on Christ who indeed builds the City that hath foundations, as well as the House, and of whom Cyrus was but a figure?

Verses 14 to 17 may be thus illustrated: A wealthy nobleman has invited a large number of guests to partake of a feast. The chair of state, in which he himself will sit, is placed at one end of a long table covered with every evidence of wealth and refinement. Each guest, as he enters, takes the place to which, he assumes, he is entitled, some pressing to the seats of greatest honor, nearest that of the host, whilst others, who have a more lowly estimate of their claims, are satisfied to occupy a lower position at the table. Then, when all are thus seated in the places which show their own estimation of themselves the host enters, and has his chair moved to the other end of the table! At once the highest become the lowest, and the lowest are the highest! So here in the fourth strophe of the chapter, the proudest are bending to the humblest:

> 14: Thus saith Jehovah:
> The labor of Egypt,
> The traffic of Cush,
> And the Sabeans,
> Men of tall stature,
> To thee shall all come,
> And they shall be thine:
> After thee shall they walk,
> In chains shall they come;
> To thee shall they bow
> And supplicate thus to thee:
> Indeed, God is in thee;
> Than Him there's no other,
> Nay, no other God.

> 15: (But verily, (verily,)
> Thou art a God
> Who hidest Thyself,
> O Elohim, Israel's Saviour!)

> 16: They are ashamed, they are confounded;
> Together they go to confusion,
> Those who are makers of idols.

> 17: But by Jehovah is Israel saved,
>     With an eternal salvation;
>     Ye shall neither be shamed nor confounded;
>     No, not forever—forever and aye.*

The oppressing enemies of Israel shall in the end confess their dependence upon her, and own that with her is their deepest need, God.

In our New Testament prophecy our Lord takes up and applies precisely the same figure to the Church, only the "synagogue of Satan" takes the place of the lofty Sabeans, Cushites and Egyptians: "Behold, I will make them of the synagogue of Satan who say they are Jews and are not, but do lie; behold, I will make them to come and worship before thy feet, and to know that I have loved thee" (Rev. 3: 9). So the apostle Paul surely had this word of Isaiah in mind when he wrote to the Corinthians that the unbeliever would, on seeing their order, "report that God was in them of a truth" (1 Cor. 14: 25). True confidence in our Lord brings the forced respect even of the unbelieving world.

Verse 15 is the adoring cry of the prophet at the marvellous way in which God works out His purposes amid the nations of the earth, just as Cowper has beautifully written:

> "Deep in unfathomable mines
>     Of never-failing skill,
> He treasures up His bright designs,
>     And works His sovereign will."

And to a far higher burst of adoring praise was the apostle led when, considering the same profound theme, he cried: "O the depth of the riches both of the wisdom and knowledge of God! How unsearchable are His judgments, and His ways past finding out!" (Rom. 11: 33).

The last lines of verse 17 again forbid our looking in past history for any true fulfilment, for no one can say that up to this time Israel has been saved with an everlasting salvation.

---

*A difficult idea to put into English. It is a threefold expression of perpetuity.

Even the return from Babylon in the days of Ezra and Nehemiah was but a very partial deliverance, if it can be so called at all, for still they confessed themselves to be servants. That poor nation has but exchanged one Master for another; still to this day Jerusalem is in a sense "trodden down of the Gentiles;" but who can question that those "times" are rapidly drawing to a close? This brings us to a deeply interesting subject:

18: For thus saith Jehovah, Creator of heaven,
    The God who Himself formed the earth,
    Finished and founded it firmly,
    Not as a chaos did He create it,
    But fashioned it so that it might be indwelt:
    I am Jehovah, and there is none other!
19: Nor have I whispered in secret
    In some darkened spot of the earth;
    Nor have I cried to the children of Jacob,
    Seek ye My face, without purpose.
    I am Jehovah, righteousness speaking,
    Proclaiming the things that are right.

We must consider verse 18 a little carefully, for not only does it awaken the deepest interest, but forces a series of questions as to the beginning of the earth and indeed much more than that, that only the inspired volume as a whole can answer. In reading Genesis 1: 1, 2 for the first time who would not inevitably conclude that God created the earth a chaos, "without form (*tohu*) and void"—waste and desolate, and out of that chaos fashioned it in six "days" (irrespective of the length of those days) to be a fitting dwelling-place for man?  So apparently speaks Genesis, but verse 18 absolutely denies it! Moses seems to say that it was created "without form," or (to use the same Hebrew word) *tohu*, while Isaiah tells us that it was *not* created *tohu*.  Is there not then a glaring contradiction between them here?  But anyone in the least thoughtful would say, "God surely does not create ruins."  Would chaos express His creative power and wisdom?  Is there not perfection attached to all His creative acts?  Does even a human mechanic—such as a watchmaker—express his skill by a confused jumble of wheels?  Surely not!  Apart from other Scripture, a thoughtful

Jew reading those two verses would say that some stupendous and tragic cataclysm must have occurred to bring the primal perfect creation of the first verse to the ruined or *tohu* condition of the second.

But centuries pass, and again we see the earth a ruin. Again the restless waters of the great deep cover it. Again there is *tohu* everywhere, save where a little ark floats, bearing within it a family on which all earth's hopes depend. But in this case we know that it was the creature's wickedness, the violence and corruption which filled the earth, that caused the ruin. Inevitably we are led to ask if a similar cause had not intervened between the two first verses of the Bible? But what creature could it be whose wickedness wrought the ruin? Again must centuries pass, generations come and go whilst a divine revelation is gradually unfolding, and when that is completed all uncertainties as to Genesis 1: 1, 2 are removed, and we find that indefinite hiatus between these verses to have been filled with a tragedy indeed —a mighty revolt of a pre-Adamite race, headed by one sinister figure now called Satan or Devil, whose mighty crime was his claim to be equal with God his Creator (chap. 14: 13). Here then we find the cause of that *tohu* condition. As in Adam's sin we find the cause of "the creature being made subject to vanity" (Rom. 8: 20)—which we may justly call the *tohu* condition of this creation—so in that mighty creature's rebellion we find the reason for the condition of our earth in Genesis 1: 2. Not alone did Lucifer (his first name) then fall, but he brought down with him the whole creation of which he was the head in one cataclysmic crash and ruin! From that we learn this basic truth: the work of the head brings its consequence on all whom, as head, he represents before God. That in its turn leads us to our Lord as the Last Adam who, by *His* work of righteousness on the cross, brings the infinite benefits of that work on all vitally linked with Him. And as God made this earth a fitting dwelling-place for man as our verse tells us, so has He prepared a dwelling-place for all His people that shall never become *tohu v'bohu*, waste and desolate, but is incorruptible, undefiled, and its beauties fade never.

After the ruin of that creation God did not abandon it, but *formed* it for another race to inhabit. He who did not create this earth aimlessly has not spoken aimlessly, we learn from verse 19, when He invites the sons of Jacob to seek His Face. He does not whisper the glad tidings of His love, nor retire to some dark spot where few can find Him; but all abroad with a shout of longing tenderness He cries in Old Testament language, "Ho, everyone that thirsteth," and in the New, "Come unto Me," and in both cases the gracious call is to the sons of erring, wandering Jacob of whom we too are true sons. There is not the slightest taint of unrighteousness in these calls, for the Cross itself makes such invitations to be righteous. In perfect harmony with this Old Testament music is the string that the apostle touches in the New; for in the Gospel, God proclaims things that are not simply merciful (though infinite mercy is the basis of all) but *right;* for the righteousness of God is shown plainly to the universe, not in condemning but in justifying the poor sinner who has already suffered for his sins in Him who loved and gave Himself for him. Could any man invent that plan of salvation?

Now the call sounds out afar in wider sweep and louder note, for the Gentiles are addressed:

20: Gather together, and come;
    Draw near, ye escaped of the nations:
    No knowledge have they who carry the wood
    Of their images graven,
    And pray to a god helpless to save!
21: Sound it abroad and let them draw near;
    Let them take counsel together.
    Who hath caused this to be heard
    E'en from a time that is long past?—
    Declared it from the beginning?
    Who but I, Jehovah, hath done it?
    For there is no God beside Me,
    A God, both just yet a Saviour—
    There is no other beside Me!
22: Look unto Me and be saved,
    All ye ends of the earth!
    I am the Mighty One—there is no other!

23: By Myself have I sworn,
    Gone has the word from My mouth,
    And, since righteous, shall ne'er be recalled:
    To Me shall ev'ry knee bow!
    To Me shall ev'ry tongue swear!
24: In Jehovah alone, shall it be said,
    Righteousness have I and strength.
    To Him shall men come; and they shall be shamed
    Who've burned in their anger against Him.
25: 'Tis in Jehovah that Israel's seed
    Shall be righteous, and so in Him glory.

With stately march, step by step, the prophecy advances to its goal, the blessing of all, both Jew and Gentile. The standpoint of time from which the prophet speaks is after Israel's deliverance, the salvation of Israel has come out of Zion; and the nations are bid to look at those who have placed their hopes and confidence in the gods that they themselves had to carry after fashioning them from wood; where are they now? Again Jehovah appeals (if that word may be used consistently with His divine dignity) to His foretelling from very far back, even from the beginning of the Purpose that lay close to His Heart, "that He might have mercy upon all" (Rom. 11: 32). From that earliest dawn of history, when poor man lay prostrate, the victim of the great foe, even then our God had told of the reversal 'of that conflict by another Man (Gen. 3: 15); and every inferior deliverance, as that of Israel from Egypt or from Babylon, was only a foreshadowing of the final and decisive victory in which God has power to save the worst, without a shade of stain that even the keenest eye in the universe can detect upon His righteousness. Well then may He cry, Turn thy face to Me, and look, all ye ends of the earth! Wherever there is a human dwelling, wherever there is a weary heart, wherever there is a burdened conscience, oh, look! It is all that is needed; ye need not cross a sea, ye need do no toilsome labor, ye have but to look; and as sure as the serpent-bitten dying Israelite sprang to new life at a look at that serpent hanging upon the pole, so one glance of simple confidence at Him who was made sin shall meet with a better salvation, for it is everlasting!

Now we listen to the strongest oath ever uttered in all the universe. God actually swears by Himself, for there is no greater by whom He can swear, and the oath comes from Lips that never speak in vain, and what He thus speaks is in itself nothing but strictly Right! That is a threefold cord not soon broken —indeed, it is not. But what is it that is thus so surely certain? That every knee shall bow and every tongue shall confess—what? That "Jesus Christ is Lord to the glory of God the Father," for so the Spirit of God makes use of this prophecy in Phil. 2: 11. O blessed certainty! Is it not surpassingly wonderful that of this very One we each can say in the words provided for us by the loved Bride in the Song: "My Beloved is mine, and I am His." Perhaps the idea of the glory does not so much attract some of us, but the Love that is not satisfied save in giving that glory is precious indeed, for have we not a divinely just claim?—poor erring ones as we are at the best. By faith we too are "Abraham's seed," or as here (ver. 25), the seed of Israel; and as such we have learned in some measure to make our boast alone in Him who is Preeminent Lord of all!

# CHAPTER FORTY-SIX

### Divine Judgment on Babylon's False Deities

THE three chapters that now follow form another of those significant trilogies that we have learned to be a characteristic feature of this prophet:

1: Chapter 46: Judgment on Babylon's false Deities.
2: Chapter 47: On Babylon herself.
3: Chapter 48: Restoration of Israel.

This short chapter also clearly divides into three parts, thus:

1: Verses 1, 2: Babylon's idols go into captivity.
2: Verses   3 to 11: The contrast with Israel's Jehovah, with warning to the apostate mass.
3: Verses 12, 13: Salvation revealed.

The Seer now speaks of Babylon's gods:

1: Bel sinketh down, Nebo collapses,
   Their idols are carried by beasts and by cattle.
   The things that ye carried are now made a load,
   And weary the beasts are that drag them.

2: They stooped, aye, they sank down together;
   Nor could they deliver the burden;
   But they themselves go into bondage.

Here once more we see Dagon, under another name, falling prone before Jehovah. How impossible it is to stop at these dumb senseless idols! Who can question but that on the stage of this comparatively little planet, the earth, we are shown that which is invisible. An awful drama is being enacted, in which the human actors are the visible figures of the spirit-powers behind them. Scripture gives us the clearest proof of this. Even today, when Bel is unknown, and Nebo a strange unintelligible word to most Christians, we hear the beloved disciple telling us that all the multitudinous false prophets of this age are really only "mediums" for the spirits behind them. "Try the *spirits*," he says, "because many *false prophets* are gone out into the world" (1 John 4: 1), thus identifying the false prophets with the evil spirits. So it is here. Bel! Who is Bel? What do we care about a piece of stone to which they may have attached the name "Bel." But behind that "Bel" is he who was created the fairest of all the principalities and powers, to whom was given the name that he has long lost, "Shining one, star of the morning" (chap. 14), and who is our living adversary today. Knowing this, our interest in the whole scene becomes intense at once. The conflict of the ages, between Jehovah and "Bel" is still going on, not now on earth, but in the heavenlies (Eph. 6), and *we*—even you and I—wrestle not against human Babylonian or Assyrian potentates, but against Bel, Nebo, and all their lords, the spirit-powers that were behind those earthly empires, and who still resist our enjoyment of our own portion in Christ (Eph. 6: 9). Here are our foes. This is our battle-field. From this point of view it is good indeed to see *Bel bowing down and Nebo stooping;* the collapse of these vain images is a prophecy of the day when that "strong angel" shall bind with a chain the "old serpent which is the Devil and Satan," and shall consign him to the bottomless pit, to leave this poor earth untouched by his foul presence for a "thousand years" (Rev. 20: 2, 3).

It is a pleasant sight. See, the images once carried in processions are on the ground; they must be lifted up and loaded on the beasts that bear the heavy weight with difficulty; and the "gods" they represent cannot deliver that helpless burden; but must, in their utter impotence, accompany those images into the bondage to which they are now being ignominiously carried. It is the climax of absurdity, gods being carried away as booty to grace the triumph of their conquerors!

How can we avoid thinking of Him who, by the paradox of being overcome, overcame principalities and powers, stripping them of all honor, and made a show of them openly? (Col. 2: 15). Then not only "Bel" and "Nebo" were opposing, but holy Michael and Gabriel were powerless to accomplish what His death so perfectly effected—the putting away of sins forever. O helpless Bel! O impotent Nebo! Nay, more, for we hear the elect angels joining with us in self-obliterating ascription of worthiness to the Lamb "to receive power, and riches, and wisdom, and strength, and honor, and glory, and blessing" (Rev. 5: 12), for He has done what they could not.

"Bel" is an abbreviation of the familiar "Baal," meaning "lord"—"*Beel-zebub*" of the Gospels, where he is called "the prince of the demons." "Nebo" means "prophet" or "speaker." Thus the heathen of Lycaonia thought the more silent Barnabas to be "Bel," or Jupiter, the Greek prince of the demons, and Paul to be "Nebo," or the Greek Mercury, as being the chief speaker.

But now for the contrast:

3: Listen to Me, O ye household of Jacob,
   And ye, the whole remnant of Israel's house,
   Ye who've been borne by Me from the womb,
   Ye whom I've carried from lap* of (your) mother.
4: E'en to old age I am He!
   And to the day of grey head
   'Tis I who will carry you.
   'Tis I who have made, 'tis I who will bear,
   'Tis I who will carry and will deliver.†
5: To whom can ye then liken Me,
   Place side by side and compare,
   That we should be equal?
6: They who pour gold from a bag,
   And weigh out the silver with balance;
   These hire a goldsmith to make it a god,
   Prostrate themselves, and so worship!
7: They lift it high on their shoulder,
   And thus do they carry it off;
   Then set it down in its place,
   Nor can it thence ever remove.
   Men pray—but there is never an answer,
   Nor can it save any from trouble!

---

*So Delitzsch, nor is it unjustifiable, for the Hebrew word has always the idea of maternal tenderness well expressed by our "lap."

†The fivefold reiteration of "I" is emphatic.

8: Call this to mind, quit you as men,
　　Take it to heart, ye apostates.
9: Remember (your nation's) beginnings,
　　Even from days that are far back.
　　For I am God—there is no other!
　　God—and like Me there's none!
10: Foretelling the end from beginning;
　　From times that are far-off, the future,*
　　Saying My counsel shall stand,
　　And I will do all of My pleasure.
11: Calling from sun-rise a ravenous bird;
　　From a land afar-off, the man of My counsel.
　　I've not only spoken, but will bring it to pass;
　　I've not only purposed, but also will do it.


How tenderly the Lord here speaks to the poor "House of Jacob, the remnant of Israel," and so to all new-created in Christ Jesus, for are not all the promises of God Yea and Amen in Him? His gracious ways with Israel, as a nation, so tender, so faithful, are but pictures of the same gracious ways with individuals in Christ now. As surely as Israel will never be cast away as a nation, so never will be the feeblest who have put their hearts' trust in Jesus the Lord. In sharpest contrast with the impotence of those idols, whose beginnings go only as far back as the money-bags of the wealthy, and that have themselves to be carried, He Himself creates Israel and begins the good work with His people. He carries them from the beginning of their existence, nor will He ever cease to care for them even to old age, and when the weakening effect of the years is shown in gray hair. While this applies directly to the nation of Israel, yet what a comfort it is to those who have come to the time when they are "such as the aged," and feel the increasing infirmities that accompany the passing of time, but sometimes question whether the grace of our Lord may be counted on to offset these. To the end He loves, to the end He deigns to serve. We then may grasp that threefold promise, based on His work of new creation: He will bear, He will carry, He will deliver! The picture is of a helpless weeping infant, lying on the ground; the

* Lit., "What not done."

mother takes it up, then carries it in her arms, and soothes its cry, till the ever-less-frequent sobs tell of troubles departing.

Did not our Lord use a very similar figure when He pictured Himself as a Shepherd finding His poor lost sheep? He lifts it up from the brambles and the mire, then lays it on His shoulders, and not till He gets it safely home does He lay it down!

How varied to the end is Christian experience! As a rule, old age in the Christian is a time of calm meditation on all the way that he has been led through the wilderness of this life; and many a tear of sorrow bedews his eyes as he remembers opportunities lost that never were repeated, many a sad fall, many a shameful wandering of heart; but the same eye overflows with tears of thankfulness at the tender patience with which God in Christ has dealt with him, forgiving his errors, and healing all his backslidings. Such an old age is like the evening of a calm summer day. But not always is the evening sky cloudless. At times a poor believer's sun goes down behind a cloud. We recently heard of one suffering from senile decay, and—as sometimes occurs in such cases—had lost all hope of his soul's salvation. Well may we be assured that in all such physical frailties no change whatever is in His Heart who "knoweth our frame, and remembereth that we are dust" (Ps. 103:14); nor will He ever leave nor forsake the soul that has ever leaned upon the Lord Jesus for repose. Never! How could He? We are all "in Christ" by new birth, and we might as well speak of God again forsaking His Beloved One, as to forsake any thus in Him. No! To old age and to gray hairs, He will carry till He has us all Home. If *death* cannot separate us from His love in Christ, we may be sure the involuntary frailties of age or mental disease cannot do so.

Well may God challenge any comparison of rivals with Himself, as in verse 5; and well may we respond: "Whom have I in heaven but Thee? and there is none upon earth that I desire in comparison with Thee" (Ps. 73: 25).

Now once more we have the beginnings of a "god." Rich men give the gold and silver, hire a goldsmith, and the metal, when formed, becomes the object of worship. But it has to be carried to its place, and there it stands immovable, deaf, blind, silent, helpless! Will ye, cries Jehovah with indignation, will ye compare *such* with ME?

Oh, the power of gold! Was there ever a day when it was more worshipped than today? Was there ever a day in which it had more power? The wealthy of earth pour out their gold to obtain superior "spiritual privileges." They can afford the very best; let the poor take the leavings! The brightest intelligences, the keenest scholar, the most eloquent orator is ever sought by the wealthy! And if wealth seeks them, the hirelings seek the wealth. Colleges are endowed with the rich man's gold, and to show to whom that gold has been really dedicated, they respond, alas, by pouring out a broad and ever-broadening stream of youth well-based in—infidelity! Infidelity, the product of gold! Beloved fellow-believer, is *that* God's way? Or is it still that really "to the *poor* the Gospel is preached," and, as of old, preached *by* the poor.

But is there not a failure in the correspondence between the impotent idol and our mighty dollar? Can that dollar do nothing? Does it not secure deference, pleasure, ease and comfort? Who can deny it? Yet place these to the credit of money, there are a few weighty items to go to the debit side of the account. Mark that disappointed heart that expected full satisfaction to come with wealth. Empty and hungry still, it cries with him who was the wealthiest of men: "Vanity of vanity—all is vanity!" No peace, no rest, no joy waits here on wealth. It is as impotent as those idols to respond to the hunger of the poor heart of man.* And how often it brings discord and moral ruin to those that inherit it!

In the Church, too, who does not know the large proportion of trouble among the true people of God that lies at the door of "money" and the love of it? Eliminate every discord that is directly or indirectly due to money, and comparatively few would remain.

---

*Even as I write, I read in "The New York Times" of a man who commits suicide and leaves fifteen million dollars behind him.

Shall we, then, compare the living God, *our God and Father*, with gold and silver? Our hearts confess their shame that even such a question should be asked, and utter their cry: Oh, so to know Him that we too may esteem all things but loss for the excellency of that knowledge and in every dark and gloomy day of trial wait alone on Him with hope and confidence!

Verse 8 is somewhat ambiguous as to who is addressed, for the first line seems an encouragement to the true, the second a warning to the false. But the former is probably the Spirit's counsel to the wavering who were tending to idolatry, and merges into the threatening tone to the apostate mass. Let this contrast make you firm, lay it well to heart, ye whose hearts are even now departing from the living God.

We have in the next verses the one strong evidence of true Deity. Who can foretell what still lies in the future save He who so controls the events of earth as to bring to pass what His counsel had predetermined to be done (Acts 4: 28). So here: "Look back," He says, "look back to the very beginning of your nation. Its whole history has been plain before Me; and now I foretell to you that an executor of my judgments on Babylon, your oppressor, is on the way. Will that not strengthen you to quit you like men?"

Is this a cup of cheer from which we are forbidden to drink? Can we not look back at fulfilled prophecy that shall give life to our nerveless faith? Surely we can. Did He not foretell that the mustard-seed should become so great that the birds of the air should rest in its branches? Has that not been fulfilled beyond all controversy, in the growth of that which was but a grain of mustard-seed in that upper room in Jerusalem, until now a popular and nearly apostate Christianity shelters the very spirits of evil, pictured by those "birds" that can only destroy the good seed sown? (Matt. 13: 4, 19).

Did He not foretell, even at the very beginning, when there was not the faintest hint of anything but an immediate collapse of all His claims, that in the sphere of professed faith in Himself there would be introduced such man-exalting, pride-feeding doctrine till that "kingdom of Heaven" should become completely leavened with the evils that are today all about us?

Did He not say that this degeneracy should go on till *all* was leavened?—a contingency that involves in itself, the taking out of that sphere the only hindrance to that complete leavening, the living members of His Body. Consider His own words to the seven Churches; has not the course of the professing Church, as there foretold, been so fully fulfilled that for the little while left we may not cast away our confidence that has great recompense of reward, but quit us like men in our confidence of His coming for us? Aye, and here what a blessed contrast! No bird of prey, no judgment-bringing "eagle," do we now look for; but still, as long ago, we are waiting for the Son from heaven who shall come as Saviour. How loudly does the whole condition of the prophetic earth cry for that coming!

12: Hearken to Me, ye strong-hearted,
    From righteousness ye that are far off,
13: Near is My righteousness, and not afar,
    Nor doth My salvation delay:
    Salvation will I to Zion accord,
    To Israel will I give glory!

The stout-hearted are those who in obstinacy wilfully resist all such evidences as "that a notable miracle hath been wrought, we cannot deny; but, that it spread no further, let us straitly threaten" (Acts 4: 4). Those men were surely very far from righteousness, although they, and all like them, always claim to be the only ones who *are* righteous. It is the Christless religious who are the "stout-hearted," for are they not well-intrenched? Who can convince the "religious" man that *he* needs salvation? Is he not spending a fair proportion of his life in careful and respectable religious observances? Who so constant in attendance at Church, at least to a sufficient degree? Who so decently liberal in contributions? Is he not doing his best, and what more can any man do? Ah, poor man! He is quite ignorant of the righteousness of God, that righteousness in which God must ever deal with sinful man, which meets its perfect satisfaction in "Christ as the end of the law for righteousness to everyone who believeth." It is thus that God's righteousness is very near indeed to the confessedly guilty; and well it is for us that it is so, for it was when we were without *any* strength that Christ died for the ungodly.

So our chapter closes with the constantly repeated promise of God's salvation being found in Zion, His glory given to Israel. Nor do they err who press that Zion stands as a symbol of grace as in contrast with Sinai—it surely does for believers now, as Heb. 12: 22 explicitly states—but when they tell us that the prophet himself meant the Church, of which he knew absolutely nothing, and not the nation to which he had been directly commissioned to go, in *that,* we are compelled to say, they greatly err.

Do you find it weary waiting for the Lord's coming unto salvation? How long have you known Him as your own Saviour? Think then, beloved, think; and suppose He had come *one day before that, where would you have been?* There are others today of His poor wandering children who will be thankful that He waited till *they* were safe in Him. It is ever a "very little while, and He that shall come will come, and will not tarry." No reader of the Scriptures in any generation could find discouragement in reading that as it will be many centuries before He comes, they might settle down in the world, for any present hope is bound to be in vain. No; every reader has been compelled to read, and, when that reading is mixed with faith, to be cheered and strengthened by the renewed hope in the words: "For yet a very, very little while, and He that shall come will come, and will not tarry" (Heb. 20: 36, 37).

# CHAPTER FORTY-SEVEN

### "Babylon is fallen—is fallen."

LITTLE would it interest those living over three thousand years after the event, if the fall of Babylon, foretold in this chapter, had no bearing whatever on our own time, or guidance for us as individuals, each through his one short life. Babylon has gone—gone long ago! The sands of the desert have long covered the palaces of her princes and the hovels of her peasants; the howls of the wild beasts have replaced the songs of her festivals. Nor does our interest in Babylon depend on the mooted question whether that same city is to be rebuilt, and take her place once more as a metropolitan city of the earth. Apart from all such questions, which may justly be the subjects of discussion, there cannot be one shade of doubt that the ancient literal Babylon shall have a successor in the closing days of this age, not of a material, but of a spiritual and religious character in harmony with the character of the present testimony of God upon the earth; and in the fate of the material we may read the doom of the spiritual, till the refrain that we have already heard in our twenty-first chapter: *"Babylon is fallen!—is fallen!"* shall be heard again as that fast-coming representative of man's spiritual pride is brought to her end, and the strong angel of Rev. 14 shall announce that *"Babylon is fallen—is fallen!"* (Rev. 14: 8); and still once more in the Scriptures, the cry comes to us, like a clear strong echo: *"Babylon the Great is fallen!—is fallen!"* (Rev. 18: 2). Most assuredly the very repetitions are intended to impress upon us the importance of the event in the awful drama of the ages.

Have we then no interest in Babylon? Surely we have. The unification of men politically, welding the present nations of Christendom into one universal State, which is clearly foretold (Dan., chaps. 7, 9; Rev. 17, etc.), has a corresponding unification of men in the same sphere, *religiously*, in a universal Church, which is equally clearly foretold (Rev., chaps. 17, 18). Both are being strongly urged today, and are the twin goals of statesmen and clergymen alike. If we look carefully through the divinely provided telescope that brings these events very near, we shall even be able to read on the forehead of that one Church, composed as it will be, of the spiritually lifeless members of the present-day Denominations, with Rome at their head: "Babylon the Great, the mother of harlots, and abominations of the earth."

What child of God, who loves his Bible, and is wise enough to observe these things, but must be deeply interested, and anticipate with joy the hour when the foul dishonor that is everywhere being done to his Lord in the very religion of the day shall come to its end, with the cry: *"Babylon is fallen!—is fallen!"*

I take it then, as Isaiah was anticipating the fall of the material Babylon, which, when he wrote was only beginning to form her glory and greatness, so do we, by the same spirit of faith, stand at the same place, and even *before* the spiritual "Babylon the Great" has been fully developed or reached *her* glory, we can see her final doom. Thus we can address ourselves to our chapter with the attention that comes from having a personal interest in what we are reading. Aye, and more; shall we forget that He, to whom we owe everything, has an infinitely deeper interest in those events that must still precede His own reign over the earth? So let us listen to Jehovah's command to Babylon, first noting the now familiar mark in the three divisions.

    1: Verses 1-4: A Voice tells Babylon of her doom, and the Remnant recognize it.
    2: Verses 5-11: Contrasted conditions of Babylon dominant and Babylon fallen.
    3: Verses 12-15: Ironic counsel to Babylon to appeal to the spirit-powers for aid.

    1: Down! Down!  Sit in the dust,
        Thou virgin-daughter of Babel.
        Take thy seat on the ground!
        Never a throne shall be thine,
        O thou Chaldean's daughter!
        Nevermore shalt thou be called,
        The Tender One and the Delicate!

2: Take the mill!   Grind the meal!
    Doff the veil!   Lift the train!
    Bare the thigh!   Wade the streams!*
3: Let thy nakedness be bared,
    Yea, e'en expose thy shame!
    'Tis I who will meet thee, and not a mere man.†

(A pause, due to astonishment; then a shout)

4: Our Redeemer!
    Jehovah Tzebaoth His name!
    The Holy One of Isràel!

One does not marvel at unregenerate men insisting that this must have been written by someone who lived long after Isaiah, for Babylon was then but in its infancy as a kingdom, and here is its end clearly foretold. The Bible is either divine or—what I will not soil my page by expressing. In that case, the future is just as plain to its Author, God the Holy Spirit, as the present or past, and there is no difficulty whatever.  But one has to make up one's mind as to that most fundamental of all questions, the divine inspiration of the Scriptures.

The city of Babylon is addressed as a virgin, since she has not yet been dishonored by capture, and what a striking picture she makes—the dust must be her seat, the ground her throne! A queen over a mighty empire is in a moment a slave, and she who was most delicate is so treated.  Into captivity she must go. She is not merely compelled to abandon all royal honor, but she must put off with those dignities even what is only consistent with womanly self-respect. Rivers have to be crossed, yesterday slaves would have carried her in her palanquin over them; today she must wade them on foot as best she can, with such exposure as

---

*"Isaiah's artistic style may be readily perceived both in the three clauses of verse 1 that are comparable to a long trumpet-blast, and also in the short rugged involuntary excited clauses that follow."—*Delitzsch*.

†A very doubtful line, as the many vastly different readings evidence.  That which I have eventually adopted corresponds with the A. V., and many Hebraists, and seems to accord with the context.  The word for "man" being Adam justifies the "mere."

could only express the deepest humiliation.   But there are spectators to the scene, and after a moment of dumbfounded silence, a shout rends the air, a kind of response to Jehovah's word, "No mere man meets thee," and they burst out with a recognition of who has effected this, "Our Redeemer!   The Lord of Hosts, the Holy One of Israel!   He hath borne long, but interposed at last."

But now the triumph-shout dies down and again that mighty Voice of command is heard, continuing the stern command to Babylon:

5: Sit thee in silence!   Creep to the dark,
   O thou Chaldea's daughter!
   For never again shalt thou be called,
   The queenly lady of kingdoms!
6: I was indeed wroth with My people,
   My heritage I have profaned,
   And given them into thy hand;
   Thou hast shown them no mercy,
   Thy yoke thou hast heavily pressed
   E'en on the aged.
7: And thou hast said:
   I shall be lady forever,
   Nor didst thou take to thine heart,
   Nor remember the end that awaits
   All thy cruel oppression.

8: Now hearken, thou lover of pleasure,
   Dwelling at ease so securely,
   Thou who hast said in thy heart:
   I am, and none other beside me;
   I never shall droop as a widow,
   Or be bereaved of my children.
9: But both of these evils shall 'fall thee
   Suddenly all in a day:
   Bereaved of thy children and widowed.
   These in full measure befall thee,
   In spite of thy sorceries many,
   In spite of thy witchcrafts abundant.
10: For thou did'st trust in thy sin,
   Saying, There's no one can see me;
   Thy wisdom, thy pride-feeding knowledge,
   Have turned thee aside and misled thee;
   So that thou said'st in thy heart,
   I am, and none other beside me.

11: Therefore shall evil befall thee,
  Nor can'st thou charm it away.*
  Mischief shall surely befall thee
  Which naught shall avail to ward off thee;
  Ruin comes suddenly on thee,
  Of which thou had'st no apprehension.

This needs but brief comment, but it is deeply interesting to note the cause of Jehovah's wrath with proud Babylon. He indeed had cause for chastening His people, and made use of Babylon for that purpose. Far too eagerly she had done that work, and *over*done it; forgetting, if she ever knew, that Jehovah's love for His people never waned, although His *expression* of it might be forbidden by their naughtiness. If sweet to the ear of Jehovah was the plea of a Moses to spare the sinful nation, if Phineas is rewarded with an everlasting priesthood for turning away His wrath from His sinning people, then Babylon's opposite conduct of merciless oppression, using Israel's sorrow for her own exaltation, is to Him a most grievous abomination, and brings its inevitable penalty on the oppressor.

Note how perfectly this exponent of human pride assumes the very claim that God alone can justly make to being unrivaled: *"I am, and beside me there is none!"* Is it possible not to discern, even behind Babylon, another dreadful personage, the highest of created Intelligencies, whose great wisdom and knowledge are all marshalled against us; and who leads his captives in his own path till his own man, the man of sin, shall come, who shall "sit in the temple of God, and show himself that he *is* God" (2 Thess. 2: 4). 'Tis he who instils this, his own crime, into man's but too receptive heart.

Now listen—not to the *lip*, but to Babel's proud *heart*, speaking: "I am a Lady forever, and sit a Queen enthroned! *I* a widow! *I* bereaved! The very thought is impossible!" Aye, there is indeed but One who can abase thy pride, and now He

---

*The R. V. reads in the text, "Thou shalt not know the dawning thereof," but in the margin, "How to charm it away," and this I have finally adopted, since it is in accord with the parallels that follow.

speaks: "Both these evils shall come upon thee suddenly. In one day thou shalt become as desolate as a widow who has lost her protector, and her children too. Nor shall all thy dealings with the invisible powers of darkness save thee: none of them can ward off thy doom, for the very deeds that thou esteemest to be *good,* and in which thy trust is placed, are thine evil deeds, and thy religion is really the cause of thy reprobation, as they were of thy father Cain, who was wrathful because the best he could do was rejected as evil. So the stern word continues:

12: Stand with thy sorceries many,
    Stand with thy witchcrafts abundant,
    Wherein thou hast toiled from thy youth;
    It may possibly be of some use,
    It may possibly serve to alarm.*
13: Thou art wearied in all thy consultings.
    Let the astrologers come,
    Let the star-gazers approach,
    Let them that foretell month by month,
    Stand up and endeavor to save thee
    From that which is coming upon thee!
14: Behold, they themselves are as stubble.
    The fire shall even consume them.
    Nor shall they deliver themselves
    From the force of the scorching flame.
    For 'tis no glowing coal one may warm at,
    Nor (comforting) hearth-fire to sit by.
15: Such shall they be to thee,
    Those with whom thou hast labored,
    Thy partners in trade from thy youth.
    They wander each on his home way—
    Not one of them all is thy saviour!

Very clearly this third part goes on to the wicked dealings of Babel with the unseen spirit-powers, and with terrible irony Jehovah counsels her to call all these powers to her aid, for she will need them sorely. Let her King Belshazzar "cry aloud for his astrologers, Chaldeans and soothsayers," and see if they may not profit him by both reading the mystic writing and turning

---

*This is the true sense of the word, and is constantly so used, as in Deut. 1: 29, "dread," Joshua 1: 9, "be not afraid."

aside the threatened doom it foretells by terrifying the agents of it.  From Babylon's very youth she had toiled in the black art, and her wise ones had day and night consulted the heavens, divided the stars into constellations, and issued their monthly bulletins as to what their combinations portended, as in the day of Esther (chap. 3: 7).  Then let them now stand between her and her doom!  Save her!  There is not one of them that can save himself from this flame of divine wrath, which is no gentle fire serviceable for warmth and comfort, but a raging conflagration that devours everything in its path.  And that shall be the end of all her traffic with the powers of darkness.  As for the human merchants* that have enriched themselves by their dealings with thee, their profit gone, they wander, each to his own way, and none can save doomed Babylon!

Babylon, on the Euphrates, has long since passed away, but her history and end is a divinely given prophecy of what still lies before another Babylon still to come.  We see, even today, a Satanic religion, calling itself "Christianity," everywhere dominant as a "queen," a religion that as it, by rapid steps, leaves the basic truths of man's fall and ruin, goes either to superstition on the one hand or infidelity on the other.

Beloved, our day is very dark and very difficult!  May grace be granted to both writer and reader to be occupied with our Lord Jesus Christ, till He becomes so real, so precious, to us as to be the load-star and magnet of our lives, attracting us out of every association where He is dishonored, and making us in very deed—not merely in word—"strangers and pilgrims upon earth."

---

*It would seem impossible that those who shall be consumed as in ver. 14, can be the same as those who wander away to their own place in ver. 15; compare with Rev. 18: 11.

# CHAPTER FORTY-EIGHT

**Final pleading with Israel as to idolatry. The mass not refined as silver, whilst the remnant is.**

LET me remind my readers that the whole of this third main division of our book, from chapter 40 to chapter 66, is remarkable as being a threefold three, God in this way calling our attention to the complete display of Himself that is to be found in it. The present chapter brings the first of these trilogies to its well-defined close in the words which, like a divine sigh—as indeed they really are—tell of "no peace to the wicked." Similarly, at the close of all God's ways with mankind at large, we not only hear the hallelujahs of the penitent, but also, alas, the sorrowful note of restlessness of proud rejectors of grace, for "they have no rest day nor night who worship the Beast and his image" (Rev. 14: 11).

The chapter opens with a call to Israel as a whole; but before the close there is a very distinct severance between the apostate mass and the penitent remnant of faith, and in verse 12 these latter alone are addressed. These too must first be stripped of all claim to deliverance from Babylon on account of their own righteousness; but, when thus stripped, there is poured out to them, without check or hindrance, all the fulness of love in the Heart of their God. How like to His blessed ways with us individually that surely is!

I again attempt a paraphrastic rendering, first noting the divisions as they seem to me, in a double "three" thus:

1: Verses   1-11: Pleading with the mass and the remnant manifested.
2: Verses 12-22: Pleading with the remnant and the mass manifested.

1: Verses  1, 2: The call to the mass to hear.
2: Verses   3-8: Reproach for the neglect of prophecy.
3: Verses  9-11: Remnant manifested in chastening.

1: Verses 12-16: The call to the remnant to hear.
2: Verses 17-21: Tender reproach of the remnant.
3: Verse     22: The apostate mass manifested in penal suffering.

1: Hearken to this, ye household of Jacob,
   Ye who are called by the name, Israèl,
   Who from the waters of Judah have flowed,
   And by the Name of Jehovah do swear,
   By lip e'er confessing* the God of Israel,
   But that not in truth, nor in righteous sincerity.
2: They claim to belong to the city all-holy,
   And on the God of Israèl stay—
   Jehovah Tzebaoth His Name!

The divine address here turns from Babylon to those who are called Jews, and are that outwardly. They are of the house of Jacob, even called by that name of honor conferred on their father in the night of his wrestling, Israel. Nay, more; as a river is not severed from its source, so these are linked, in an external formal way, with the royal tribe of Judah. But coming still closer, they claim citizenship in the holy city, Jerusalem. And all this is quite true—these are the undoubted privileges of those addressed. But there is no privilege that does not cover corresponding responsibility, and how have they answered that? They have truth beyond that of all other peoples; how have they used it? Alas, they have held it in unrighteousness.

In all this they form but too clear a picture of Christendom. Amid those called "Israel," only a very few were entitled to that name in its full significance. So does the apostle Paul speak, "For they are not all Israel which are of Israel" (Rom. 9: 6), which he himself explains, not as de-nationalizing any Jew, but by showing the sovereignty of God in electing Isaac in the place of Ishmael, and Jacob in the place of Esau; so that the line of promise was not dependent on the accident of primogeniture, but on the sovereignty of God's electing grace. It does not mean

---

*Lit., "Make mention," or "remember," but this is equivalent to a profession of faith in the one true God. Delitzsch renders it: "Extol the God of Israel;" Lowth, "publicly acknowledge."

that anyone who is by natural birth a Jew, is *not* a Jew. Ishmael could only be Abraham's son, though not in the line of promise, and so not in the profound sense attached to the word "Abraham's seed." Esau was quite as much the son of Isaac as was Jacob, nor could he be anything else, but he was not in that line of life. It is the sovereignty of God on which the apostle is here insisting, and is sweeping away the pretensions of the leaders of his nation, who depended on mere fortuitous privileges due to natural birth. The very word, "not in *righteousness*," says that there was no confession of sin, and like the "way of Cain" maintained the false claims of the flesh.

The passage in Rev. 3: 9, "Who say they are Jews, and are not," does not mean that one who is born a Jew is not of that people; but the Lord is not considering at all anything outside of the professing Church, and *within that sphere* there were and still are those called Christian, who by the place they take that belongs exclusively to the Jew, do thus say they are Jews. For example, all who put themselves under that law which was given to no people but the Jews at Sinai, do in the most emphatic way insist that they are themselves Jews and are not. The Christian is indeed enlawed to Christ to whom he gives the willing obedience of a responsive love (1 Cor. 9: 21). But it is a serious error to distort such texts into the denial of the national recovery of Israel, as our chapter is enough to prove.

Today by far the numerical majority of mankind is enveloped in utter heathen darkness. A bright light of truth has shone on about a third; but in that third, how few are genuinely penitent believers in the Lord Jesus! All take that Name which is above every name, and whether of the Roman, Greek or various Protestant Denominations—all are "Christian." Yes, there is truth, Christian truth, everywhere in this sphere, truth that this poor world lacked for over 4,000 years; yet now who values it, save a few poor simple souls who make no noise, and have little place in the tumult of the world? The correspondence is only too strikingly clear.

Now the prophet is thrown forward in spirit to a point where he looks upon the fulfilment of what he has foretold.

3: The former events I've declared long ago,
   Yea, from My mouth have they gone forth.
   These have I caused to be heard;
   Suddenly carried them out;
   Thus have they been brought to pass.
4: Well did I know that thy heart was so hardened,
   That thy neck was as stiff as a sinew of iron,
   Thy brow was as brass!
5: Therefore I told it thee long, long ago,
   Made thee to hear it before it took place,
   Lest thou should'st say, 'Tis my idol hath done them,
   My images-graven have ordered them all.
6: Thou surely hast heard!    Then consider it all,
   And wilt thou not make thy confession?
   From this time I'll make thee to hear what's still new,
   Things that are secret, thou never hast known.
7: Now they're created, and not long ago,
   Nor till this day hast thou heard them;
   Lest thou should'st say, Lo, I knew them!
8: Yea, thou hast heard not!
   Yea, thou hast known not!
   Yea, in the past thine ear was not ope'd;
   For well did I know thy treach'rous heart,
   And that from the womb thou'st been called a transgressor!

Here, if I err not, as with John in Patmos, the Spirit of
God raptures the spirit of the Seer, and places him at a point
not yet actually reached.  The "former things" must include all
the dealings of Jehovah with Israel down to the very time of
Cyrus (who had not yet been born); but as events come to pass,
so must the conviction that He who could, and had foretold them,
had them all under His control, and events yet to come which are
now to be foretold must be under the same control, and surely will
come to pass in due time.  This is not uncommon in prophetic
discourse.  The eye is so divinely enlightened that time ceases to
obscure the sight, or indeed to intervene at all.  Thus our Lord
anticipating what had not, and has not even yet, actually taken
place, said: "I saw Satan as lightning fall from heaven" (*cf.* Rev.
12).  So in that infinitely clear and pure atmosphere of the book
of Revelation we have statements that apart from this would
have exceedingly perplexed us, such as, "Behold, I come *quickly,*"
spoken nearly 2,000 years ago, and our Lord has not come even

yet.  The prophetic eye, cleared of all the films of earth, sees the far off as being close at hand, and so the prophet speaks.  It is surely neither incredible nor unworthy that God should so speak, who sees the very end of all our checkered history from its beginning.  Here, then, He anticipates and announces the deliverance of Israel by Cyrus, so that they may not attribute that deliverance to any such false agency as their idol-deities.

But in verse 6 Jehovah ceases to look back at events that have already occurred (from His present standpoint), and looks forward to something of which He had never spoken at all, something absolutely new; and still it is that the treacherous heart of poor sinful man may not attribute the event when it comes to pass to some false deity.

What a strong confidence the fulfilment of prophecies in the past gives for the fulfilment of those that, even for us, still lie in the future.  Our Lord's coming, rejection, death, resurrection and ascension to the right hand of God, are all clearly foretold, and have already taken place.  But *the same word* speaks of His coming for all His redeemed people, and with them returning in great glory to reign over the earth.  Does not the past in itself justify our cleaving to that hope?—and the more strongly as we see the avalanche of apostasy that is sweeping the great mass of professing Christians away, of which we have also been forewarned (1 Tim. 4: 1).

> 9:  'Tis for My name's sake My wrath I defer,
>     And for My own praise, from thee refrain,
>     Lest I destroy thee.
> 10:  Lo, I've refined thee, but 'tis not as silver,
>     In the furnace of suffering have I elected thee.
> 11:  'Tis for My own sake—yea, for My own sake—
>     That I will do it:
>     (For how hath My name been polluted!)
>     And My glory I give not another.

In these verses Jehovah strongly emphasizes the motive that leads to His intervention on behalf of His people.  It is not because of their goodness that He defers His anger, and in its place brings salvation to them.  So in that day of old when Israel made the golden calf, and the anger of Jehovah waxed hot against them, Moses' plea was: "Wherefore should the Egyptians say: For mischief did He bring them out to slay them in the mountains?" (Exod. 32: 12). And again when the spies returned and discouraged the people so that unbelieving Israel desired to return again to Egypt, Jehovah's wrath waxed very hot, but was deferred by Moses' plea: "Then the Egyptians shall hear it" (Num. 14: 13).

What do we (you and I) not owe to that Name of *"Jesus!"* Could He rightly be called that, if He did not "save to the uttermost those who come unto God by Him?" If only one poor erring believer in Him were finally lost, then, may we plead, would not Satan hear of it? And what shouts of derision would ring through the ranks of the fallen principalities and powers: "He could not bring that one to God! He failed to bring that one home! He could not save that one—that was beyond His power; was too great a strain on His love; He is falsely called Jesus, for He could *not* save that erring one that trusts in Him."

The glory of that Name is at stake in the eternal salvation of the feeblest of His poor people who puts his heart-confidence in Him.

> "The soul that on Jesus hath leaned for repose
> He will not, He *cannot*, forsake to its foes."

Verse 10 apparently contradicts such scriptures as Zech. 12: 9, which reads, "He will refine them as silver is refined," whilst here it is the very opposite, "I have refined thee, but not as silver." Only one must carefully note that in Zechariah and other similar scriptures, it is "the *third part*" of which the prophet spoke, whilst here it is Israel as a nation, or mass, led back to their land without any such remnant yet manifested. The people are refined, not as being silver yet, but the "furnace of affliction"—the "great tribulation" does this service. It manifests those who are faithful, and then those thus manifested *are* refined as silver, and the dross that still clings to them is purged away by that same affliction.

Now we turn to that beloved "remnant" whose history is a foreshadowing of our own.

12: List to Me, Jacob, and Isr'el, My called:
   I am the One!  The First and The Last!
13: 'Tis My hand hath laid the earth's strong foundations,
   My right hand hath spanned the heavens above;
   When I do summon they stand up together.
14: Gather together, and listen (then) all of you;
   Who, midst them all, hath this thing proclaimed:
   That he whom Jehovah loveth will do
   His will upon Babel,
   And on the Chaldeans his arm shall alight?
15: I—none but I—have spoken and called him,
   Caused him to come, and will prosper his way.
16: Come near (then) and hearken, for 'tis not in secret
   That from the beginning I have foretold it—
   Before its existence, I have decreed it,
   And now hath Jehovah Adohnai forth sent Me,
   And with Me His Spirit.

The Creator of all that is visible here speaks.  "Look," He
says, "at earth and heavens."  Mark the stability of the rock-
foundations of the former; then look up at the latter, and reckon
if you can the number, weight and distances of those worlds
above, and know that one word of Mine brought them into being,
and, obedient to My summons, they stand up.  By that same
word they still exist and tread unwaveringly their prescribed
orbits.

If the Spirit of God does not make exactly the same claim
for our Lord Jesus Christ in Col. 1: 16,17, then words have ceased
to have meaning: "All things were created by Him, and for Him;
and He is before all things, and by Him all things subsist."
Jesus *is Jehovah!*

Now in the last words of verse 16, another voice is heard.  It
comes from One who is sent forth by Jehovah, the Spirit with
Him.\* Who can that be but Jesus our Lord, and Israel's Messiah?
Nor can I do better than again quote Delitzsch:

"Since the prophet has not spoken in his own person before;
whereas, on the other hand, these words are followed in the next

---

\*Thus in the last clause of verse 16 we have a clear forecast of
the truth fully told out in Matt. 28: 19—the three Persons of the
Godhead.

chapter by an address concerning Himself from that servant of
Jehovah who announces Himself as the restorer of Israel and
light of the Gentiles, and who cannot be therefore either Israel,
as a nation, or the author of these prophecies; nothing is more
natural than that the words, 'And now hath the Lord,' etc., form
a prelude to the words of the one unequalled Servant of Jehovah
concerning Himself, which occur in chapter 49. The surprisingly
mysterious way in which the words of Jehovah suddenly pass into
those of His messenger, can only be explained in this manner."

Nor do I see any possibility of questioning this. Of the Lord
Jesus has it been written: "For God giveth not the Spirit by
measure" (John 3: 34); that is, it was not with the Lord Jesus
as it was with the prophets of old, a partial communication of
the Mind of God, a fleeting glimpse of His Heart; or, as to
Moses, His "back-parts;" but with Christ, there was no such
limit. The Spirit who came with Him revealed in and by Him,
the very wisdom, the very Heart, of God to man with all its
infinitude of Love. The two scriptures thus have a very precious
correspondence.

17: Thus saith Jehovah, He who redeems thee,
      The Holy One of Isràel,
      I am Jehovah thy God,
      Teaching thee ever to profit,
      Guiding thee too in the way
      In which thou should'st go.
18: Oh, that thou hadst hearkened unto My commandments,
      Then had thy peace been as a river,
      Thy righteousness been as the waves of the sea.
19: Then too thy seed had been as the sand,
      The sons of thy body had been as its grains,
      Nor cut off, nor perished, its name from before Me.
20: Go out of Babylon! Flee from the Casidim!
      With the voice of sweet singing declare this report;
      Let it go forth to the earth's furthest bounds:
      Jehovah (frail) Jacob, His servant, hath saved!
21: Tell how they thirsted not,
      Though He led them through droughts.
      Streams from the rock He caused to flow for them;
      The rock He did cleave, and the waters gushed forth!
22: Peace, never peace to the wicked shall be,
      So saith Jehovah!

Jehovah speaks to Israel. He has only desired the submission of their will, the confidence of their heart, and He would have still borne them, as He did from Egypt, on eagles' wings. Had they continued in trustful dependence, unbroken as the flow of a river had been their peace; and the righteous requirements of the law would have been fulfilled, not by legal effort, but by spontaneous response to His grace. That grace will still preserve the nation, in a remnant that shall not be destroyed. Their self-chosen path has led to captivity and shame. But the Lord will never leave His poor people in such case, and so the next words (verses 20, 21) call to the captives to leave Babylon with the speed, but not with the terror, of the flight from Egypt, for no songs were heard all through that dark night, but now they leave their place of captivity with songs of joy.

No rock was cleft to provide those humble fugitives, who returned with Ezra, with water; surely then this prophecy must refer to some other deliverance than *that*. That is so undeniable that most of our commentators apply all this in a spiritual way to the Church, and such application is perfectly justified when confined to the individual believer in Christ, for none would deny that we are passing through a "dry and thirsty land where no water is;" and for our refreshing, life-giving waters do flow from the stricken Rock, Christ—there is surely a correspondence.

Does this then finally and perfectly fulfil this prophecy? If it did, then Israel's deliverances are forever passed, and God *hath* "cast away His people whom He foreknew" (Rom. 11: 1, 2). No promises are theirs, for all such are appropriated by the Church. But that is absolutely opposed to the whole tenor of Scripture. Israel, the literal Israel, the Jew, as we speak, is yet to blossom and fill the whole earth with fruit, for the blessing of the earth itself awaits the recovery of Israel from her national death. Still another captivity awaits that devoted people to another Babylon. The day approaches when those Jews that we see now returning to Palestine shall, having founded an independent State, make a treaty with the revived fourth empire of Daniel's prophecies—the "Beast;" and this means, for the true Jewish saints, a captivity to that "Babylon the Great" who sits upon that Beast, or interpreting the prophetic form of speech, the universal apostate

"Christian" Church that shall then be entirely *supported by* the civil power. Then again shall that call to separation be heard, that is really ever sounding in this mixed scene: "Come out of her, My people, that ye be not partakers of her sins" (Rev. 17: 4). But Babylon is the first of the evil triumvirate of those last days to be destroyed, not by the direct Hand of God but by those on whom she has depended (Rev. 18: 16). This synchronizes precisely with the fulfilment of Dan. 9: 27: "And in the midst of the week he shall cause sacrifice and oblation to cease;" the destruction of the falsely professing Church, excluding God from *Christendom;* the stopping of sacrifices, ending the recognition of God among the *Jews.* But this manifests the Remnant, who shall be tried "as silver," and those who escape the persecution in Jerusalem (Rev. 12 and 13) go forth and preach the gospel of the coming Kingdom to the nations of the earth (Matt. 24: 14). Even that is not the final deliverance, for still the devil rules over our poor devoted earth, and this demands the return of Israel's long-rejected Messiah, and earth's rightful King. When that comes to pass, "to Pul and Lud, and to the nations afar off" (Isa. 66) do joyous and willing missionaries go, with feet beautiful, to tell of what God hath done for the final deliverance of His people, the children of Jacob.

The prophecy does not end without that last word in which sternness and sadness, justice and sorrow, are strangely blended: *"No peace, saith Jehovah, to the wicked!"* The very word used for "the wicked" denies the possibility of their peace. Its first meaning is "to make a tumult," "to be disturbed," and is thus applied to those whose inward moral nature is in that state of chaotic confusion that is due to being "without God." Most careful must we be not to confine it to the debased or profane; it may cover the most moral and indeed religious—*all* who have not come to Christ for the rest He only gives. There can never be true rest or peace apart from Him.

## CHAPTER FORTY-NINE

**We approach the heart of the book: the holiest of all. The Gentiles called to listen to the Lord Jesus speaking. His ministry. Rejected by Israel, God gives Him a wider sphere. Zion mourns, Jehovah comforts. Application to both the earthly and heavenly seed.**

THIS brings us to the very heart of this book of Isaiah, to the very heart of "the Salvation of God," nor surely do we need to be told whom we may expect to find there! For the very "heart of the heart" is the 53rd chapter with which we are all familiar, and yet of which we never weary. Hitherto, we may say, we have trodden the "court," now we shall enter the "Holy Place," and soon we shall be conducted into the "Holy of Holies!" If seraphs veil their faces in that Presence, well may we—poor, sinful creatures as we are—seek to be hidden altogether. That, thank God, is perfectly effected by the Cross, for by it we are not only hidden, but exist no longer before God— we have died with Christ. In dependence then may the Spirit of God exalt Him before us as we walk these holy paths with their varied scenery of sunshine and cloud, till we eventually see the darkest of all storm-clouds bursting, with divinely concentrated force, on the Head of One standing in our place to receive it!

The chapter marks clearly its own threefold division by its three speakers, thus:

1: The ideal Servant speaks in verses 1-6.
2: Jehovah speaks in verses 7-13.
3: Zion speaks in verses 14-26.

Just as Peter, James and John listened to Him as they walked the roads of Palestine, or sat together with Him on the hill-side, so in these verses do we hear the very Voice that then spoke to them. Can we listen too reverently or intently?

1: Listen, O isles, unto Me;
   Give ear, ye peoples afar:
   Jehovah called Me from the womb;
   E'en from the breast of My mother
   Hath He announcèd My name.
2: My mouth hath He made a sharp sword;
   In the shade of His hand hath He hid Me;
   He hath made Me a bright polished shaft;
   In His quiver hath He concealed Me;
3: Hath said to Me, Thou art My Servant,
   Isràel, in whom I'll be honored.

Here we may boldly say that this Speaker is none other than our Lord Jesus calling on the nations outside of Israel to give ear, for Jehovah hath called Him, the virgin's Son, and made His Name to sound forth even from the first moment of His incarnation in those songs of that little company of Israelites that we hear in the opening chapters of Luke's Gospel. His mouth—that is, of course, the words that come from it—has been made so sharp a sword that none, Pharisee or Sadducee, Ritualist or Rationalist, could ever stand against it. Yet for a time, as a spear may be laid up in an armory, or an arrow be left in the quiver ready for service when needed, so was He hidden in His lowly home at Nazareth for thirty years.

As the "Salvation of God" is now to be announced, and as that is equally needed by Gentile as well as Jew, so must it go far afield to the "isles," which we have already learned to be a term applied to those Gentiles.

What harmony, what unity binds together in one volume the whole Word of God! Not one single discordant note is heard to this foundation truth, that the blessing of every individual of Adam's race, Jew or Gentile, rests alone on Him we know as our Lord Jesus Christ. In the Old Testament He is the very life-germ of the nation of Israel itself, and still maintains that buried people in being, as He does all men, living or dead, by their spirit, and by a still stronger tie in His redeemed, by that same spirit being quickened by the Spirit of God; so that it is as impossible for death to hold them permanently, as it is for the Jew to be forever entombed amid the nations of the earth, for He stands as the Representative of Israel in verse 3.  Can Israel then be lost forever?  But now this Speaker mourns:

> 4: And I—I have said I have labored in vain,
> My strength for naught and for vanity spent.
> But with Jehovah My judgment still rests,
> My work remains with My God!
> 5: And now, saith Jehovah who formed Me,
> E'en from the womb, for His Servant,
> That I should bring Jacob back to Him.
> Though Isr'el be not brought to Him,*
> Yet honored I'll be in the eyes of Jehovah,
> And My God shall be ever My strength!
> 6: And He saith to Me: 'Tis but a light thing
> That Thou should'st be for My Servant,
> To raise up the tribes of (My) Jacob
> And Israel's saved ones to bring back:
> I'll give Thee a Light to the Gentiles,
> My salvation to earth's furthest bounds!

The beloved Servant is saddened by the failure of His work. He has wearied Himself, but apparently fruitlessly; yet His confidence in Jehovah is unshaken, for He well knows that He is destined to be glorious in His eyes, and that God will ever be His strength.  If we would listen to the Heart of the Lord Jesus we should surely hear it uttering these words in Matt. 11: 20-30; although rejected by Israel, still He says, "I thank Thee, O Father."  To this confidence the next verse is the answer.  Let Him be rejected in one sphere, He shall be exalted in a far wider!  Let Him be compelled to mourn over the failure of one mission; another, far more glorious, shall be given Him.  Let one door be closed, a far wider one is opened at once.  Let Israel for a time refuse, and Jacob long turn away; then for that long interval a world-wide call is heard: "Come unto Me, *all* ye that labor and are heavy-laden, and I will give you rest."  He, the rejected of one people, becomes Jehovah's salvation—the veritable "Isaiah" unto earth's furthest bounds!

———

*The *"keri"* (*i.e.*, what Jewish commentators thought should be read, altering the *"kethib,"* or written text) reads as R.V. in text, "And that Israel be gathered;" but I fear the motive that may have led to the alteration and retain the original.

Do you not join with me, believing reader, in joyful praise as we listen to that invitation? Like the bells on the High Priest's garment every letter rings with joyous music. When it comes to a weary spirit there is no distinction between Jew and Gentile. A burdened conscience is as heavy a weight for one as the other. Wherever there is sin with its handmaids, suffering and sorrow, there is He to be proclaimed as Jehovah's *salvation*. Will you not aid my feeble note of praise with your stronger one, dear fellow-believer?

But now we continue to listen, for Jehovah is about to speak:

```
7: Thus saith Jehovah,
      Israel's Redeemer, most Holy One—
   To Him, the despised of man's soul,
   To Him whom the nation abhorreth,
   To Him, the servant of rulers;
   Kings shall see and rise up!
   Princes shall fall and adore!
   For Jehovah is faithful (forever).
   Israel's Holy One, He—
   And His Elected One, Thou!
8: Thus saith Jehovah:
   In a time of acceptance I've heard Thee,
   In a day of salvation I've helped Thee,
   Safely will I preserve Thee,
   To the people as cov'nant give Thee,
   The ruined land to restore;
   That they may once more inherit
   The desolate homesteads.
9: To prisoners saying, Go free!
   To those in the darkness,
   Come ye to the light!
   The roads that they walk on shall feed them,
   The hills that are bare supply pasture.
10: They shall not hunger nor thirst,
   No mirage* deceive, no sun smite them;
   He who doth pity them shall be their leader,
   By fountains of water shall guide them.
11: My mountains I'll make to be pathways,
   My highways shall all be up-raisèd.
```

---

*The word "shar⌐  ' is "to be hot," and in the shimmering heat the dry sand ⌐'        appears like water and is termed "mirage."

12: Lo!   These shall come from afar!
Lo!   These from the north and the west!
And these from the land of the Sinese!*
13: Shout, ye heavens!   Be joyous, ye earth!
Break forth into singing, ye mountains!
For Jehovah doth comfort His people,
Hath compassion upon His afflicted!

Now the Servant is silent, and Jehovah addresses Him. He is despised of man from his very soul to this very hour; the nation, as such, abhors Him, and its rulers oppress Him; but kings shall rise from their thrones in reverence, and princes prostrate themselves in adoration.

The apostle Paul quotes verse 8 in 2 Cor. 6, and directly applies it to this present time, as he speaks of himself standing in the place of an ambassador for Christ. Here, the address is directly to the Servant. It is for *Him* the acceptable time, for *Him* the day of salvation. The apostle uses the words as a warning to those to whom that salvation may be announced, not to presume on its being without limit—that day, as all others, shall come to its close. So "we beseech that ye receive not the grace of God in vain." Thus all these gracious promises, although given directly to Christ, yet are ours as having life *in* Him, for our blessing is alone on that same ground of grace. But they do greatly err who, because this is true, would deprive the elect nation of that covenant which is ever made primarily with it. Thus in this journey homeward of Israel's banished, every footfall, marked by divine solicitude, has its correspondence in spiritual journeying mercies on our way homeward to our Father's House. By refreshing springs He leads; mountains become easy paths, and through defiling marsh and moorland, exalted causeways give clean and solid footing; it is not difficult to discover the spiritual correspondences with these terms. From every quarter the happy pilgrims flock to the one centre, and as they approach we hear such an irrepressible burst of joy, as demands that all nature, both heavens and earth, must be in accord with,

*The Heb. word *"Sinim"* is now almost universally accepted as referring to the Chinese.

and aid them in uttering His praise to whom that joy is due.* And in those heavens that are thus invoked, we may have our part, for at that time the sons of God shall be manifested, and all creation awaits that for its perfect restoration (Rom. 8: 19). But let us listen to Zion before her song begins:

14: But Zion hath said, Jehovah forsakes me,
    My Lord doth surely forget me.

15: Can mother forget the child at her breast?
    Have no compassion on son of her womb?
    Yes, even these may forget,
    But never will I forget *thee!*
16: Behold the palms of My hands,
    For there thou art deeply engraven;
    Thy walls stand ever before Me.

The answer to the plaint is inimitable. God has made one earthly relationship more irrefragable than any; for it is quite independent of any responsive affection. The mother holds to her breast her new-born babe, so dependent on her as it is for everything that shall sustain life, this affects every maternal emotion. With a tenderness no words can depict she yearns over that frail little creature, unconscious as it is of all her tendernesses. Can she actually forget it? Is it not a law of nature, for her at least, though none other care for her infant? It is *hers*, and she can think of little else.

Nor does Jehovah here compare His thoughtful love to that of some callous debased woman of earth, who may forget, and indeed has all too frequently forgotten and forsaken her infant. No; that we altogether refuse. It would be little for His love to exceed such callousness. It is mother-love at its purest, its strongest, and its best. It is far more possible for even that irrefragable tie to be broken, and the most tender mother that the earth has ever seen to abandon her infant, than for Jehovah to forget Zion, or for our God in Christ to forget, leave, or forsake

*If the reader delights in these appeals to all nature for aid to praise, let him turn to "Paradise Lost," Book 5, lines 192-205.

the feeblest of those who have derived their true life from His love.

For see that mighty Hand is fast closed over something, as if it held a treasure too precious to be exposed; but here He opens it for us, that we may see what that treasure is. As it unclasps, no fragment of paper with our names written flutters to the ground; no parchment similarly inscribed drops; nor do we see our names cut into wood or even stone, but they are actually *cut into His own Hands!* Oh, consider it, who can pluck us thence? Who can erase *that* engraving?

It is true that in our prophet He is directly speaking to "Zion," nor will we deprive the Jew of the primary and direct application of this word to His own holy city, but as surely as that Zion speaks of grace in contrast with Sinai that thunders out the law, so have we come to that lovely mount by faith, and partake most assuredly of the grace of which it speaks (Heb. 12: 18-22). Have we not too even clearer basis for this assurance? Do we not remember Him who said, "My sheep hear My voice, and I know them, and they follow Me; and I give unto them eternal life, and they shall never perish and *none can pluck them out of My hand.* My Father who gave them Me is greater than all, and *none can pluck them out of My Father's hand;* I and My Father are one" (John 10: 27-29). Oh, strengthen our shamefully feeble faith in Thy love, our Father-God!

> 17: Thy children are hast'ning to thee,
> Thy destroyers and wasters depart!
> 18: Oh, look on all sides around thee;
> 'Tis to thee that all these do gather,
> To thee (to thee), do they come!
> Thou shalt put them all on as adornment,
> Bedeck thee with them as for bridal.
> 19: For thy waste and desolate places,
> Thy land of ruins so full,
> E'en now is too strait for its dwellers,
> When they that brought it to ruin
> Are far (far) away.
> 20: Thy children of whom thou wast 'reft
> Shall speak again in thine ears:
> The place is too narrow by far;
> Make room that I may have dwelling.

21: Then shalt thou say in thine heart:
Who hath begotten me these?
For I've been robbed of my children,
Barren, banished and homeless.
Who then hath nourished these up?
Behold, I was left all alone;
But these—where were they then?

22: Thus saith Adohnai Jehovah:
Behold, to the Gentiles I'll lift up Mine hand,
To the peoples I'll raise up My banner,
Thy sons they shall bring in their bosom,
Their shoulders shall carry thy daughters.
23: Kings for thy fostering-fathers,
Princesses thy nurses shall be!
Face to the earth shall bow to thee,
The dust of thy feet they shall lick,
And (then) shalt thou know that *I* am Jehovah;
Those waiting on Me shall ne'er be ashamed.

By the light of these verses we can see a vast host of Jews
returning to the land of their patrimony; but not as they are
going back now, in unbelief of the Lord Jesus being their true
Messiah, and consequently to sorrow and suffering, but with
assured faith and joy. The city of Zion standing for the whole
country, and so for its people, is personified as a widow who has
long been desolate and forlorn. With astonishment she sees returning to her those whom, at the first surprise, she dare hardly
recognize as really her own children. For she cries: Who has
begotten them? I am a widow! Who has brought them up?
And in the long years of my banishment where were they?

Jehovah answers the questions, and tells her that He will
signal to the Gentiles, and they shall place every facility within
their power at the service of the Jews who are still scattered, and
with such solicitude as can only be likened to a woman carrying
her infant in her bosom. The ensign that is thus lifted up may
well be the Lord Jesus Himself, who has returned for the relief
of His earthly people, as we have already read: "In that day
there shall be a root of Jesse *which shall stand for an ensign to
the peoples;* to it shall the Gentiles seek, and his rest shall be
glorious" (Chap. 11: 10).

Kings shall foster the new-born State. Their princes shall count it an honor to nourish it; and all the nations, lately so hostile, shall bow down to lick the very dust whereon the one recently so desolate, now walks.

But mark, reader, the connection between earth and Heaven, between Israel and the Church of God, for by turning to Rev. 3: 9 we listen to almost identical words, only now applied to the Church living in Philadelphia, or "brotherly love," and there it is not the Gentiles who worship, but "them of the synagogue of Satan, who say they are Jews, and are not, but do lie." That refers to nominal Christians who, wilfully ignorant of all that the Cross of Christ means, still assume the place given to the Jew, as if that Cross had not done away with the legal trial of man, and thus, not by words, but by *acts* say they are *Jews*. There is a vast difference between the "synagogue of Satan" and the Gentiles, who are specifically referred to here, and yet Israel on earth ever foreshadows in her history, the Church in the heavenlies; and the earthly enemies of the former symbolize the spiritual foes of the latter.

But some may say, By your putting the fulfilment of all these prophecies in the future, do you not rob the present portentous events of all their significance for us? By no means. For we are seeing this very day, with our own eyes, a shadowy fulfilment of Rev. 16: 12-16, in the drying up of the Euphrates—that symbolic river that ever stands for the people who issue from it, as shown us in Isaiah 8: 7. But *now* that people is the Turk; and in his enforced recession from Palestine, where his place is taken by the Jew, we can see a very striking foreshadowing of the final and future complete fulfilment—but it is only a "shadow."

We must not pass over without pondering those last few words: *"Those waiting on Me shall ne'er be ashamed."* It is not easy to "wait;" the pressure is often so intense that we feel we must have immediate relief, and yet it comes not, we cry in vain, and have still to *wait!* Thus is our knowledge of God in Christ tested, and, alas, how many of us fail under that test! A king once lost his entire realm because he did not wait a few minutes more. Saul waited up to the beginning of the appointed seven days, but not to their close. Philistines were pressing him, his army was being constantly lessened by desertions, and he failed! Aye, it is by no means easy to wait. But *no one who has waited has ever been disappointed or brought to shame by His failing them,* never!

Now let us listen to the closing words:

24: Shall the prey from the mighty be wrested?
    Or those rightfully captive escape?*
25: For thus saith Jehovah:
    Free from the mighty the captives are wrested,
    The prey from the terrible ones shall escape;
    And with thy contender Myself will contend,
    To thy children will bring My salvation.
26: They that oppress thee, I'll feed with their flesh,
    And with their own blood make them drunken,
    As though it were with new wine.
    So all flesh shall know that I am Jehovah,
    Thy Saviour, Redeemer—the Mighty of Jacob!

Jehovah, stronger than the strongest, espouses the cause of His earthly people. Their foes, He counts to be His; their friends are His. Who can deliver that feeble little remnant who have the whole military power of the world against them? One, and only One.

Who can deliver from the power of Satan's yoke?—stronger he than Babylon or Rome. One, and only One.

---

*There is such difficulty in this line that I have felt it impossible to determine with any strong assurance whether it speaks of the captives being righteous, and so to be delivered on that ground, or that notwithstanding that they are rightfully captive, they shall be delivered. This has seemed more in line with the context, and so I have adopted it.

Since writing the above an incident recorded of Miss Henrietta Soltau has strikingly confirmed this decision, as to the correctness of our A. V. On her way to an interview with a poor prodigal, a "down and out," in that simplicity of faith that characterized her, she asked for a promise to take hold of by faith. As she went, the word was given. It was this verse 24, as in the A. V. I might add that that "captive" was fully delivered. If the Lord thus used the verse we cannot make a great mistake in accepting it.

Who can deliver from that last dread foe, Death? One, and only One.

In all these conditions we are powerless, yet in all we can sing: "I thank God through Jesus Christ our Lord."

In Him Satan's power is broken. In Him sin's yoke is off our necks. In Him that mighty foe Death shall hold His saints not one moment longer than shall accord with His purposes: His promise of return is sure—*wait!*

# CHAPTER FIFTY

THREE divisions are again very clearly marked in this little chapter, which, although short, is of entrancing interest. Even before considering the details, we may again discern three different Speakers; and in these are suggestions—by no means obscure—of the Persons of the Divine Trinity, although in different relations with men, and so under names differing from Father, Son and Holy Ghost. In these hidden ways has divine wisdom interwoven these vital truths in the very warp and woof of Scripture, whence they cannot be torn without destroying its texture altogether. My readers will discern the divisions without any difficulty, thus:

1: Verses 1-3: Jehovah speaks, recognizing the breach in His relationship with His people, represented by Israel, and accounting for it.
2: Verses 4-9: The Servant speaks. He has learned the path He must take to redeem His people.
3: Verses 10, 11: The Spirit's counsel to those who are of the day: the doom of those who are of the night.

1: Thus saith Jehovah:
Where is the bill of your mother's divorcement,
With which I did put her away?
Or 'mid My creditors, to which of them is it
To whom I have sold you?
For your iniquities, lo, ye've been sold.
For your transgressions your mother is cast off.
2: Why when I came was there no man to welcome?
Why when I called was there none to respond?
Is My hand shortened it cannot redeem?
Or have I no power My own to deliver?
Behold, at My word I dry up the sea!
The rivers I turn into desert;
Putrid their fish, without water,
Of thirst do they perish!

3: 'Tis I clothe the heavens with mourning!
'Tis I do make sackcloth their cov'ring!

Here Jehovah Himself speaks to Israel. Has He put them away with that too easy method that evidenced the hardness of their hearts (Matt. 19: 8) by giving a bill of divorcement? If so, let them show that bill. They cannot do it. Very lightly were such "bills" given by heartless men. Little was enough to justify severing the sacred bond. Has Jehovah so acted to that nation to which He stands in the relation of a husband? Is His heart equally hard? Will trifles account for its miserable condition?

Or again, He says: "Have I sold you as, at times, a man's children had to be sold to meet his legal obligations?" (Matt. 18: 25). Pitiless was the law, but how hard pressed any father, worthy of that name, before he would allow his children to be sold. Only utter inability to prevent it could account for such an unnatural separation. Is that the case here? Has Jehovah become so impoverished, and has some creditor pressed a legal claim which He cannot meet, so that He has to sell His people to satisfy it? Let that creditor step forth. There is none!

What then can account for Israel's misery? Never let them attribute it to Jehovah's will, but to their own iniquities. But was there any specific evil that can be told? Yes, when *He —Jehovah—came to them, there was no welcome for Him!* That lies at the base of all their sorrows!

But when did Jehovah thus come directly, not by prophets but Himself, to Israel and look for such a welcome? Once and only once—for Isaiah looks far forward. It was not when He descended on Sinai to give them the law. He looked for no welcome then, but bade them keep at a distance, nor dare even to touch the mount on which He stood. But He came again in other guise, filled with grace and truth, but none welcomed Him then: *"He came unto His own, and His own received Him not"* (John 1: 11). In that rejection lies the cause of all their sorrows. It is this, and this alone that accounts for their being forsaken—it is the climax of their iniquities! Lowly He came, and in utter gentleness, yet mighty to save. For it was *His* word by which Egypt's sea had been made dry, and the rivers (as Jordan) turned into dry land. It was He who had visited them, in a gentleness that would have made them great, as a poor and lowly man, but who could put the heavens into mourning, clothing them with sackcloth—and they would have none of *Him!*

Not only did He thus come, but He *called* to them, announcing the kingdom that He came to set up, but their heart being turned away, they heard not that Voice, nor responded to that call.

For the ear has a strange faculty; sounds may be quite audible, but with the attention elsewhere, they are not really heard at all. Our very hearing, although all the delicate mechanism of the ear is in perfect order, depends still upon our *will*. In a room full of people, many of whom may be speaking at the same time, we have the power of directing our ear to one particular speaker, and be practically deaf to all the rest. Thus today, a hundred voices in this world are crying, but amid them all is One who says: *"If any man hear My voice I will come in to him, and will sup with him and he with Me."* Alas, how few are *hearing* that Voice! The call of business with its gain is heard. The cry of worldliness and its pleasures is listened to, but *His* is unheard, for it speaks an unwelcome truth, telling the present witness on the earth, the Church, that it is, with all its boasting, "wretched, and miserable, and poor, and blind, and naked"—no one *wills* to hear that! Indeed, Israel's sad history is repeating itself this very day.

Jehovah closes by recalling the past evidences of His power, and asks them to remember that although He does not now make seas dry or turn rivers to desert as once, yet still it is He who clothes the heavens with mournful clouds and covers the earth with depression. Do they then suppose that He is not equal to dispelling those clouds and bringing the cheer of sunlight in their place? Has Time shortened the reach of His arm, or enfeebled its power?

But now the Servant speaks:

4: Jehovah Adohnai hath given to Me
   The tongue of those who are taught,

> That I might know how a word of good cheer
> To speak to him who is weary.
> Morning by morning He wakeneth,
> Mine ear He awakens to list,
> As those who are truly disciples.
> 5: Adohnai Jehovah hath opened Mine ear,
> Nor was I rebellious, nor turned away backward;
> 6: Nay, to the smiters I gave up My back,
> My cheeks unto them that plucked off the hair;
> I hid not My face from shame nor from spitting.
> 7: For Jehovah Adohnai will help Me,
> So shall I not be confounded:
> Therefore I set My face like a flint,
> For I know I shall not be ashamed.
> 8: Near to me—near—is He that doth justify,
> Who then is he that contendeth?
> Let us stand up face to face.
> Who's My opponent?  Let him draw near.
> 9: Behold, Jehovah Adohnai defends Me,
> Who can he be that condemns?
> Lo, as a garment they all shall wax olden,
> Eaten up by the moth shall they be.

Here we note the constant repetition of the divine appellation, *Jehovah Adohnai;* nor is this without its appropriateness in the mouth of the perfect Servant.  Jehovah is to Him indeed *Adohn,* a word that carries with it the idea of the most supreme authority and ownership.  It is only used when the utmost reverence is desired to be expressed, and here the very Lord of glory, taking the place of the perfect Servant, calls Jehovah, *"Adohnai"* —"My Lord and Master."

See then that perfect Servant reading, pondering, meditating upon the Word of God.  Morning by morning from the slumbers of the night He awakes, and as a *disciple,* as all who are really taught of God, He listens to the living Voice that may be heard in those inspired pages.

"God manifest in the flesh" is He; "The Lord of Glory" is He; "Lord of all" is He; yet see Him, bending over those very Scriptures that are in our hands today, and by them growing in wisdom (Luke 2: 52), as perfect as a dear human Child, as He is as a mature Man; just as a rosebud is as perfect in its place as the beauteous flower in its prime!

For as He reads He learns the path that that Word pledges Him to take. The "evil" that lies before Him, and which He refuses, is the smile and favor of a world at enmity with His Adohn-Lord. The "good" that awaits Him and which He chooses is rejection and persecution, yet He willingly addresses Himself to that path, surrendering His back to smiters, His face to spitting.*

He shrinks not from suffering, rejection and shame, for no adverse will has ever closed that ear. Long, long ago, in the past, when His happy abode was in the Father's bosom, as the ineffective sacrifices smoked on Israel's altars, and He saw that they gave no pleasure to the God who longed to embrace penitent men, even then were His ears opened, and He cried with the spontaneous willingness of love: "Lo, I come to do Thy will, O God."

And that will He has done! That lonely path, "uncheered by earthly smiles, led only to the cross," where our sins (oh, let us join in acknowledging this) were upon Him, and because of that, God Himself was the Smiter! No blows does that almighty Arm strike as feeble as those of the Roman soldiery! *They* indeed ploughed deep into His holy flesh, quivering and sensitive as that was, but *these* pierce and cut into His very soul. *They* could awaken no cry; *these*, the exceeding bitter, *"Eli, Eli, lama sabachthani"* (verse 7). Mark, too, that through all He maintains His confidence in the final intervention of His God—Adohnai Jehovah. He knows well that His soul shall not be left in hades nor His body see corruption. In one dark hour indeed, when the Powers of darkness clustered thick around Him in Gethsemane and pressed Him sore, He did cry, with tears, that, were it possible, the cup might pass from Him. It might well have done so, if God had cared less for us poor sinful men, and left us to perish forever. How He must have loved *us* that He, even for our sake, put that cup of suffering into the hand of Him He loved infinitely!

And, although He drank the cup, still He was "heard," and that because of the very fear that evidenced His perfect holiness.

---

*Note carefully the holy light this throws back on chap. 7: 15.

For it was not the fear of physical death, the fear that Satan would take away His life before He reached the cross, as some so wrongly teach; but of being made sin, and so of God's forsaking Him, and that forsaking being endless! He was about to be made judicially in the sight of God what you and I really are; that is, sin—to Him the most awful of horrors! Is *that* to be endless? Is there to be no relief from that? Nay, He was *heard*, and His salvation "out of death," in resurrection, is the answer to that cry, for thus is He justified, as our verse 8 speaks. He was not saved *from* death, but was saved *"out of"* it.

In resurrection-acceptance He challenges some opponent to condemn Him, and who can that be save that keen-eyed "serpent" who is ever the great accuser of mankind. Let him find, if he can, one film of injustice upon the throne of God by that justification! But still clearer light is thrown upon this word in our New Testament, for there we find that it is we who are fully identified with Him in that cloudless atmosphere of perfect acceptance, so that the weakest, feeblest, youngest—aye, the very chief of sinners—may, as being one with Him, take up that challenge, and looking at our adversary, cry: *"It is God that justifieth. Who is he that condemneth? It is Christ who died, nay, rather, who is risen again, who is even at the right hand of God, who also maketh intercession for us"* (Rom. 8: 31-39).

In very truth He is rightly named "Wonderful," for in the first part of this little chapter He is identified as one with Jehovah; and here, in the last, He is identified with His people whom He has redeemed. He thus lays His hand on both, and is the "Daysman" that Job, and not he alone, sorely needed and longed for!

How altogether incomprehensible to finite minds is His infinite Person! The one single Personality, having all the unlimited attributes of God, yet all the dependencies of man; omnipotence and weakness, infinities and limitations, thus combined in One! What folly to think of comprehending Him! What wickedness to attempt to analyze Him! He loves us and we worship Him, and there we rest!

But what of those who venture to come into conflict with Him? The last clause of verse 9 tells us. They are like a tattered garment ruined by being moth-eaten, a "terrible figure" of slow but certain destruction, as another has said.

Well might we linger here, nor can I leave it without one practical word, which I address to myself first: must I not, too, follow my Lord in that morning-by-morning meditation over the Word? And if I do, surely, it will point out the same path to me as to Him, a path made sunny with the approval of God, but dark indeed as far as the smile and favor of this world goes. The "good" is for us, as for Him, in rejection, reproach, and it must be in some degree of actual persecution; whilst the "evil" too is for us, as for Him, in the friendship of the world with all its wealth, honor, and even its religion.

This introduction of the Servant leads to the sharpest severance among those who are professedly the Lord's people, and this third part gives us the revelation of the righteous judgment of God in the consolation the Spirit gives to the persecuted Remnant, and the doom announced to the persecuting mass.

10: Who is among you who feareth Jehovah,
    Obeying the voice of His Servant,
    Walking in darkness, having no light?
    Let him still trust in the name of Jehovah,
    Let him still stay himself on his God!

11: Behold, then, all ye who do kindle a fire,
    Who compass yourselves with its sparks,
    Walk ye along in the light of your fire,
    Let the sparks ye have kindled enlighten.
    This shall ye have of My hand:
    In sorrow shall ye lie *down*.*

The two verses speak of companies so different that we may well adopt the very language of Scripture, and speak of them as two "generations." Verse 10 is the "generation of His children" (as Psalm 73), whilst in verse 11 we discern that evil generation of whom the Lord said: "Ye are of your father the devil" (John

---

*The last word in the chapter is *tishkahboon*, with a strong emphasis on the last syllable. One can easily detect how this would make it sound as a knell; announcing the sorrow foretold in the *tolling* sound of *"boon"* forcefully and solemnly uttered.

8: 66).  Strange, yet alas, but too evident a truth!  From the same parents have ever come most divergent offspring, as represented by the two brothers, Cain and Abel.  Nor does what men call "religion" give us the dividing line, for Cain equally went to "a place of worship," as did Abel.  Man cannot live without some form of religion; but Christ, and the relation they bear to Him, marks the distinction.  It is the penitent confession of sin, with heart-confidence and delight in Christ on the one hand; and complacency, whether it be in the fruit and flowers of Cain in the past, the Christless church-membership of the present, or the man-made "sparks" of the future, on the other.

To review the chapter in a few words: the first three verses are the goal to which what follows leads.  For Jehovah has visited His people in the person of the Servant, but found none to welcome Him; nay, the path of that Servant is one of suffering and shame, yet He walks in it firmly, for He knows that Jehovah will finally justify Him in resurrection; and He utters a cry challenging any to condemn Him who has even been made sin under the cloud of the cross!  It is this that leads to the sharpest severance, distinguishing a remnant from an apostate mass, till He comes with retribution for each.

The terms "darkness" and "light" are evidently used metaphorically, the one for adversity, the other for prosperity.  Thus, in verse 10, we see the beloved remnant of faith passing through the "darkness" of the great tribulation, and in verse 11, the apostates are told to go on walking in the light that they themselves have kindled—that is, in whatever prosperity they may have thought to have gained in their treaty with the Prince of the revived world-empire.  As far as my present light goes this is the whole of what is now called Christendom, including the two Americas, North and South, the boundaries being religious or spiritual, and not geographical.

When Jehovah does intervene, the company of the persecuted shall have rest, while the persecutors shall lie *down,* in torment; as seen in 2 Thess. 1: 6, 7: "Seeing it is a righteous thing with God to recompense tribulation to them that trouble you; and to you who are troubled rest with us, when the Lord Jesus shall be revealed from heaven."

It would never do to shut out the believer of the present day from the encouragement of verse 10, or the merely "religious" from the warning of verse 11. While our peace really rests on "God's thoughts of His own Son;" yet, alas, we know practically, as to our condition, that there are seasons of spiritual darkness, to which some temperaments are much more liable than others. We remember Rutherford's lines:

> "But flowers need night's cool darkness,
>   The moonlight and the dew,
> So Christ from one who loved it,
>   His shining oft withdrew."

In such times the counsel of the same blessed Spirit is surely quite applicable. Let us still trust in the Name of our Lord Jesus, and stay ourselves on our God, so graciously, so righteously revealed in His beloved Son. But let us never think for a moment that there are really clouds between God and that beloved One; nor is the *position,* or standing, of all who are in Christ altered at all by the darkness of the *condition.* We are ever in the light of that love from which nothing can really sever us. In Him, the very least of us whose confidence is alone *in Christ,* is in everlasting light and unbroken acceptance.

# CHAPTER FIFTY-ONE

**A threefold call to listen directed to Israel; first, as a nation following after righteousness; second, as in relation to the Gentiles; third, as in relation to Jehovah. The cry from the Remnant to the Arm of the Lord to awake, answered by Jehovah's cry to Jerusalem to awake.**

AGAIN the three divisions that experience has led us to expect are clearly marked in the first section, verses 1-8. As in the preceding chapter there were three *speakers*, here we have a threefold call to *listen*. This repetition is, I doubt not, intended to impress us with the importance of what is said.

Whilst there is but one Speaker, three different companies of one people are addressed.

    1: Verses 1-3: A personal word to Israel as following after righteousness.
    2: Verses 4-6: To Israel in her relation to the Gentiles.
    3: Verses 7, 8: To Israel in her relation to Jehovah.

This is again, "selfward," "manward," and "Godward;" nor are these divine fingerprints to be ignored without loss.

    1: Ye that pursue after righteousness, hearken!
       Ye who are seeking Jehovah,
       Attentively look at the rock whence ye came,
       At the pit's hollow whence ye were digged.
    2: Carefully look at your father, Abraham;
       And to Sarah, the mother who bare you;
       For he was but one when I called him, and blessed him,
       And multiplied him into many.
    3: For Jehovah hath comforted Zion,
       Comforted all her waste places,
       Made her desert (to blossom) as Eden,
       Her steppe as the garden of Jah!
       Joy and great gladness are now dwelling in her,
       Thanksgiving and melody's voice!

It is not altogether easy to distinguish with precision who the speaker here really is. Is it Jehovah, as some claim? Or is it the Servant, as others? One word from the clear light of the New Testament spoken by that Servant solves the difficulty: "I and My Father are one." It is then Immanuel, God in Christ, and thus we can approve the very ambiguity, discerning beauty in what we otherwise might esteem blemish.

The first section evidently addresses the whole nation of the literal Israel. A nation which was distinguished, as Romans 10 tells us, by "a zeal of God, but not according to knowledge, for they, being ignorant of God righteousness, and going about to *establish their own righteousness,* have not submitted themselves unto the righteousness of God," that is, they follow after a righteousness of their own. Very evidently both the prophet and the apostle speak of the same people, Israel, and what has characterized them in contrast with the Gentile. These latter have not "followed after righteousness" (Rom. 10: 30) as has the Jew, who is here addressed.

It is then, not the Church, as some insist (how could it be since it was quite hidden from Isaiah? Rom. 16: 25), but the literal people of Israel who are here exhorted to consider how small their beginning. Abraham was their father and Sarah their mother; what hope could there be of their very existence if it depended on parents who had long given up hope of progeny? Abraham was alone, in hopeless solitude as far as a legitimate heir went. Sarah was dead as far as child-bearing went—what hope from such? Yet Jehovah called, blessed, and multiplied that solitary man and barren woman till the vain boastful name of Abram, "highly exalted father," became by the addition of one humbling letter,* Abra*h*am, "the father of many nations," as the word is divinely interpreted for us. It is thus He humbles that He may bless without adding sorrow in the blessing.

So from their beginning, let the downtrodden nation learn, first, that it is as dependent for its recovery on the intervention

---

*The added "h" is the Hebrew numeral 5, the number that speaks of *"man* the creature in connection with God, his Ruler yet his Helper" (F. W. Grant).

of Jehovah as was its father for its existence; but secondly, that He *will* interpose, and as He comforted Abraham by promise and fulfilment, so will He comfort Zion; and her present barrenness shall also be turned into the fruitfulness of that garden of which Jehovah Himself was the Husbandman; and where He placed the first solitary man—the father of the whole race. No silent city then shall Zion be, for silence does not honor Him, far less do groans or sighs speak His praise, although they well suit the present reign of the usurper. King Theebaw of Burmah erected a torture-house near to his palace that he might hear the groans of the sufferers; thus he was an excellent representative of his master who is indifferent to the sufferings of the race beloved of God. But our God loves a very different tune, and Zion must be filled with unforced spontaneous melody from joy-filled hearts. How that speaks of our God who so loved us as not to spare Himself the sacrifice of His Son! Who would willingly be away from Him?

Now the address turns to Israel in their relation to the nations:

4: Hearken attentively,* O ye My people;
   My nation, give ear unto Me;
   For from Me there shall go forth a law,
   My judgment will I establish,
   To be a light to the Gentiles.
5: Near is My righteousness,
   Gone forth My salvation,
   My arm, it shall judge all the Gentiles.
   The isles shall wait upon Me,
   Expectantly wait on My arm!
6: Lift up your eyes to the heavens,
   Then cast them on earth at your feet;
   For the heavens shall roll off as smoke,
   The earth as a vestment be frayed.
   E'en thus shall its dwellers all die,
   But forever shall be My salvation,
   My righteousness ne'er be abolished.

---

*The word is stronger than that used in verse 1. Here it is "Hearken attentively."

Note in what close amity are the two words "righteousness" and "salvation." In view of a world of sinners one would assume that they must be opposed to each other, but here they go hand in hand in closest accord. But this accord forbids our seeing the "law" that went from Sinai in what is here said to proceed from Zion: *that* never went further than to Israel; this goes far afield to the Gentiles; there was no salvation proclaimed then, as there is here. Thus the law here must be that instruction as to the ways and will of Jehovah with which the second chapter of our book has made us familiar. Zion is the literal mountain that shall speak to Israel of the grace that recovered her in the earth, as it speaks to us of the grace that gives us a heavenly place and blessing still nearer to the heart of God in Christ. The scene here is millennial, and the righteousness of God, that shall then be in accord with salvation of sinful men, settles in the metropolis of that renewed earth, Zion, whence it radiates on all sides, a light for the farthest nations and bringing holy joy everywhere.

Let God's earthly people regard the heavens above them (verse 6). How majestic the unwavering march of these mighty worlds—so sure, so unchanging, that men can compute with absolute certainty when their paths shall cross each other! The earth, too, with its "everlasting mountains," which, as far as human experience goes, voiced by its wisest, "abideth forever" (Eccl. 1: 4). But both heaven and earth are transient. The time shall come when human eyes shall look up and see those heavens rolling away as smoke, and the earth shrivelling like a moth-eaten garment, when earth-dwellers, in that evil sense that we have it in the book of Revelation, shall perish with the earth, their dwelling. But amid that wreck of worlds, the "righteous salvation" shall remain unaffected, and those who have embraced it, and by whom it is embraced, shall also remain forever, for they have a life not of earth.

We have one more call to hearken:

7: Hearken to Me, ye who know right,
   The people whose heart hides My law,
   Fear not the reproach of frail mortals,
   Nor be afraid of their scoffings;

8: For as a garment the moth shall devour them,
   Yea, as if woolen, the worm shall devour them.*
   My righteousness ever shall be,
   My salvation shall ever remain,
   To the age embracing all ages.

Here the true Israel of God is addressed, and by that term we do
not understand the Church (of which mystery these prophets
knew nothing, Rom. 16: 25, 26), nor the Servant, nor the nation
as a whole, but the beloved Remnant of faith, with whom our
present position and condition have so much in common, that
although not identified, we are very closely related by a common
dependence on the same grace, based on the same mighty sacrifice. That remnant has learned the secret of God's righteousness,
and grace has written His law in their hearts. They are indeed
as sheep in the midst of wolves, but let them not shrink from the
reviling that faith has ever met in this devil-ruled world; for
after all these wolves are but frail mortals, over whom there
hangs penalty—not merely of a death that is common to all, but
into that first death they depart, in the gloom of divine displeas-
ure, to a second death also that is unending! But *they*, the sheep
begotten to a new life by that Word in which salvation accords
with absolute righteousness, shall abide, with that life, forever.

So lovely a prospect has been brought before the eye of those
addressed in the section we have just considered, that it awakens
a passion of longing that breaks out in a cry, whose intensity is
beautifully expressed by the repeated word:

9: Awake, awake, and clothe thee with strength,
   O thou arm of Jehovah!
   Awake again, as in days of long past,
   The ages that now lie afar back.
   Art thou not it that Rahab hath hewed,
   And wounded the (terrible) dragon?

---

*In these two lines we have another evident play on words as
anyone can detect: *Kabeged yoklem ash* (as a moth devours a
garment), *katzemer yoklem sas* (as a worm devours wool). "The
*sas* is brother to the *ash*" (The worm is brother to the moth)—
Jewish proverb.

10: Art thou not it that hath dried up the sea,
      Even the flood of the great deep?
      Art thou not it that hath turned the sea-depths
      To a path for thy ransomed to cross by?
      [A pause.]
11: Aye, the redeemed of the Lord shall return,
      Come unto Zion with singing:
      Crowned with a joy that never shall end,
      Gladness and joy overtaken, sorrow and mourning take
      flight.*

The Remnant last addressed now respond; and yet the spokes-man must be found in Him who, as the one Mediator, at one time represents feeble man; at another, the mighty God. We have heard Him called "Wonderful," and as we trace His glories through these pages, we own the truth of that title—He is indeed Wonderful! For here He is both Servant and Lord, both the One who calls, and the One who, in another relation, responds. Thus He gives expression to the longing cry of His people: Dost Thou hold out such entrancing anticipations before us, and yet Thyself put forward no activity for their attainment? O awake, awake, thou mighty Arm: clothe Thee once more with Thine ancient strength! Thy silence is interpreted as Thine impotency. Repeat the deeds of old, and silence Thy traducers. Was it not Thy might that forced proud Rahab (Egypt) to surrender us? Then, when the seas shut us in, was it not *Thou* that didst turn the sea itself into a dry pathway? Worthy of Thyself are the ways of escape Thou makest for Thy people.

As we thus meditate on the past, we are filled with confidence as to the future. As this vision passes before the eyes of our faith, we see Thee moving once again, and lo, there are the re-deemed of the Lord, returning to their long-lost inheritance! Aye, our ears can even hear the songs they sing. Their heads are garlanded with joy and gladness which they have vainly pursued hitherto, but have overtaken at last, whilst the storm through which they have passed rolls off like a thick cloud, taking with it all their sighs and tears!

---

*This is strictly literal. They have pursued joy and gladness long, and at last have overtaken them.

Nothing but unpardonable violence to Romans 11, as well as
to a great part of the Old Testament can account for the denial
of the restoration of the Jews to their land, and eventually to the
favor of their Jehovah. But whilst this must be maintained, in
a very true sense we too can utter the same questions as to hew-
ing Rahab and wounding the dragon. "Is it not Thou?" we can
cry to Him who is Himself the mighty Arm of our God, our Lord
Jesus—"Is it not Thou who, in the day of our captivity to sin
and death, proved Thyself stronger than that strong armed man
who held us, overcame him, the dragon that he is; gave us deliverance through the Red Sea of judgment, and thus through
death destroyed him who had the power of death? In the clear
atmosphere of Thy resurrection, we too have found joy and gladness, pursued in other ways but never overtaken; and although
it may here be not unmixed with tears at times, 'through manifold temptations,' is yet unending, for it shall be carried on in
the holy merriment of the Father's House forever."

Now gently, like the soft dawning of a clear day after a
night of storm, the answer to that cry of "Awake, awake!" comes,
and these next verses are, as it were, the twilight of dawn before
the sun itself rises:

13: Thou hast forgotten thy Maker, the Lord,
    Stretcher of heavens, earth's Founder,
    And hast feared constantly, day after day,
    Before the oppressor's hot fury,
    As he makes ready thee to destroy.*
    And where's the oppressor's hot fury?
14: He that's bowed down 'neath the weight of his chains
    Speedily shall be delivered,
    Nor shall he die, nor go to the pit,
    Nor shall his sustenance fail him.
15: For I am thy God who stilleth the sea,†
    E'en when its surges are roaring:
    Jehovah Tzebaoth His name!

---

*See Ps. 11: 2: "They made ready their arrow." Israel is terri-
fied as he sees the oppressor getting ready to assault him.

†The word "*roga*" is primarily "to frighten," and then "to restrain by fright," and so "to make still." But it is still a question
whether here it should be rendered, "stir up," or "make the sea
quiet," or, "divide it," as Job 26: 12.

16: Mine are the words I've put in thy mouth:
In sheltering hand have I hid thee,
The heavens to plant, the earth to found,
And say unto Zion, My people!

Jehovah places a strong emphasis on its being Himself who will intervene. The *law* may be given by the disposition of angels, but He will depute no one to *redeem*—it is Himself from beginning to end. Thus He cries here, "I, even I, and no other; no archangel, principality, or power of heaven will I permit to comfort Zion." His eye has watched those trembling saints--trembling, yet maintaining a true witness against the pretensions of "Beast" and "False Prophet," for both combine in hot fury against all who will not worship that image. "Fury!" says Jehovah, "I look forward a little, and where has that fury gone? One little breath, and lo, it cannot be found" (2 Thess. 2: 8). Captivity ceases, chains are cast off, and the tomb no longer awaits the poor chain-bowed prisoner. God now comforts those thus cast down, God, whose command the truculent waves obey: Jehovah Tzebaoth His Name.

Up to verse 16 the address has been to Zion, but now it is diverted to the Servant, for into no other mouth have Jehovah's words been put, so that what *He* speaks, Jehovah speaks. Taking a backward look, it was His word by which the heavens have been planted; as one plants a garden with its beauties, so has He garnished the heavens with the glittering host. It was His word too that called the earth into being. But here we have not a backward, but a forward look, and therefore it is not the old creation that is in view, for as to that, both heaven and earth shall pass away, but what follows? Then again that same Voice shall be heard, as it cries: "Behold, I make all things new!" The new heavens shall be garnished with new plantings, a new earth be strongly founded. Afar off that may still be. A millennium may interpose before that final accomplishment, yet may we in very truth hear that grand solemn word "DONE" that, like the single stroke of a bell, announces to the whole universe that all God's counsels have at length been carried out, and both heaven and earth are now and forever, in full accord in their glad submission to His Throne, and so, immovable.

Now let us hear a still more direct call from Jehovah, echoing back to Zion her own cry:

17: Awaken, awaken, and stand up, O Salem!
    Thou who hast drunk from the hand of the Lord
    The cup of His hot, burning fury,
    Drunken the dregs of that cup that brings reeling,
    Yea, drunk to the very last drop.
18: Not one, 'mid the sons she had borne, who could guide her!
    Not one, 'mid the sons she had brought up, could lead
        her!*
19: These twain have befallen thee:
    (And who sorrows for thee?)
    Desolation—destruction!
    The famine—the sword!
    By whom shall I comfort thee?
20: Thy children have fainted!
    Prostrate at all the street-corners they're lying,
    Like to an antelope caught in a net.†
    Filled with the wrath of Jehovah!
    Filled with rebuke of thy God!
21: So listen to this, O thou sorrowing one,
    Thou drunken, but not from wine-bibbing.
22: Thus saith Jehovah, who is thy Lord,
    Thy God who defendeth His people:
    Behold, I am taking out of thy hand
    The cup (of My wrath) causing reeling,
    My fury wherein is the dregs,
    Thou shalt drink it again nevermore!
23: But into the hand of them that tormented thee,
    Who have said to thy soul, Bow thee down
    That we may walk over thee,
    Into that hand will I put it.
    Thy back hast thou made like the ground,
    For a passenger's pathway.

In that return to Israel of her cry, "Awake, awake," there is deep significance.  Jehovah says, "It is *thou* who must awaken.

*"What elegaic music we have here in the deep cadences,
    *mikkol-banim yaladah,*
    *mikkol-banim giddelah*" (*Delitzsch*).

†This beautiful figure is changed (although not improved) in the Septuagint to "*like a half-baked turnip.*"

*Thou* art benumbed by the sorrows that have befallen thee. Thou art stupefied by the cup of which thou hast drunken so deeply. Thou art altogether as one asleep to the reserve of love that thy Lord has for thee. Thou thinkest that He has naught but chastening blows. O awake, awake to the Love that is behind every blow! It is indeed a cup that causeth reeling that I have pressed into thy hands, but this is not the end of My ways with thee, but only the means to that end."

Note the meditative tone in verse 18, as if Jehovah Himself were weighing fully the sorrows of His afflicted people. Zion has borne many sons, but she has none that can guide her in her perplexity now, not one to lead her by the hand. These two things have befallen her: to the land, desolation; to its dwellers, famine; and those dwellers lie at every street corner, dull and motionless, as when a wild antelope taken in a net, exhausted with vain struggles, at last lies still! "Listen, O thou stupefied sufferer, I will take that cup of reeling out of thine hand, and thy oppressors shall drain it: the pitiless who have made their pathway over thy prostrate body, *they* shall now drink of this cup!"

Have we no sympathy for Israel in the sorrows that she must still pass through? Have *we* never been stupefied by the chastening strokes of our God? Has never a blow, or a series of blows, befallen us, and the heavens were brass, the while the very moan of petition died upon our lips, and, in silent misery, we lay like that netted deer? Then, as the storm passed, we became awake to a Love that had directed all these sufferings for our truest good; and as a chastened child with the tears still on his cheeks, climbs his father's knee and lays down his head on the shoulder, so we have awakened to a Love that we thought we knew well, but now feel how shallow that knowledge has been.

If there should be one who reads these lines, who has recently wept under affliction, Awake, awake, my beloved brother or sister. Be not so stupefied as to forget that chastening is not the *end*, but only the *way* to peace and most tender comforting. That is the mark of a true-born child. The whole race suffers from the consequences of sin. Bereavement, loss and pain are not the sole heritage of faith. An infidel or atheist can weep quite as much

as a Christian, but the one proves his illegitimacy by resenting
the providences that have afflicted him; the other evidences his
legitimacy by self-judgment, and drawing nearer to the Heart
whose love he knows and from which he may have wandered.

## CHAPTER FIFTY-TWO

### Verses 1 to 12

**A further call for Zion to awake.  Feet speed that are well shod. The Lord, neither in the Old Testament nor New, uses unclean vessels.  A greatly misunderstood text.**

IT is scarcely necessary to say that the introduction of a new chapter here is an intrusion that mars the beauty of the divine arrangement.  This portion is clearly unified by the cry, "Awake, Awake!" *three* times repeated; nor is there much difficulty in discerning the same number again imprinted on this final section, thus:

1: Verses  1-6: Jehovah's Name demands the deliverance of
                   His redeemed.
2: Verses  7-10: The announcement of that deliverance.
3: Verses 11, 12: The deliverance pictured.

1: Awake, awake, O Zion,
   And clothe thyself with thy strength:
   Clothe thyself with thy garments of beauty,
   O Salem, city most holy!
   For nevermore shall there enter in thee
   Th' uncircumcised or unclean.
2: Shake thyself free of the dust,
   Arise and be thronèd, O Salem!
   Loose thyself free from the bands of thy neck,
   O captive daughter of Zion!
3: For this doth Jehovah say:
   For naught were ye sold (into bondage),
   And for your redemption therefrom
   There shall (no silver) be paid.
4: For thus saith Jehovah Adohnai,
   My people went down into Egypt,
   In the beginning as guests,*
   The Assyrian then did oppress them,
   And that without provocation.

---

*This is quite the force of the word *goor*.

5: And now, saith Jehovah,
   What part have I here?
   For My people is taken for naught;
   They that rule over them make them to wail,*

   And My name is ever derided,†
   And that without ceasing day after day!
   Proclaimeth Jehovah.
6: Therefore My people shall learn of My name,
   And so shall they know in that day
   That I am Jehovah who promised:
   And lo!   Here I am!‡

Once again Jehovah's voice rings out in Zion's ears, returning to her cry that she has uttered.   It is true that she lies captive, prostrate in the dust, all her strength gone, all her glory fled;
but let her listen: "Awake, awake; it is *thou* who art sleeping,
unconscious of My tender affection for, or of My deep interest
in thee, and of the strength that is really thine in this.   Awake, O
awake, put on that strength; shake off that humiliating dust;
array thee in those garments of royal beauty that I have provided for thee: for among all the cities of the earth thou, and
thou only, art indeed the holy one, since I have separated thee
to Myself.   Away then with those tatters, they ill befit the
bride of the King.   Away with that band of slavery that is about
thy neck; it tells a very false story now; for thou art *Mine,* and
Mine must ever be free!   Exchange that seat in the dust for the
throne for which I have destined thee; for never again shall they
tread thy streets, whose very footfall defiles.   Further, since I
received nothing to compensate Me for my loss of thee, so shall
they, who have gratuitously made thee their slave, receive nothing.   The Egyptians invited Jacob to come as a guest, and then
how were his children treated?   The Assyrian then took a hand,

---

*Delitzsch renders: "Their oppressors shriek," adding, in com-
ment, "proud and haughty bluster," but this I am unable to adopt.
The word ever speaks of distress, not triumph.

†"Derided" is the root-meaning of the word.

‡This is Lowth's rendering, conforming so perfectly with the
subject that I have adopted it, admitting that it is a free rendering.

with no more ground for cruelty than had Egypt, so neither the one nor the other shall be the richer for losing thee. What then am I waiting for? Where is My glory in such a condition of things? How does My people's captivity, how do their sorrows, how do their wailings, how does the insolent cruelty of their captors speak of *Me?* What is My portion in it all? I used to hear the joyful songs of praise that ever awaited Me in Zion (Ps.65: 1); and now groans, sighs and wails alone meet Mine ears. That is not music in which I take any pleasure; that is no true witness to Me! Nay, My Name, that in itself tells of My power to save, is brought into contempt by such a testimony. Unclean, rebellious spirits ridicule My apparent impotence to save such sinners. I will endure this no longer. My people shall have no question as to the deep significance of My name: they shall learn that I am indeed *Jehovah;* the eternal, ever-present, unchanging, faithful God, who hath promised to appear for their relief; and, as My Name is Jehovah, so I am here in accord with that promise and that Name!"

Precious beyond thought must such gracious words be; but to whom then are they addressed? Who may without presumption appropriate them? Who can "Zion" stand for save that remnant of Israel that are preserved by the grace of which Zion speaks, to form the nucleus of the new nation that shall fill the earth with fruit? Surely it was the literal Jacob who went down into a literal Egypt to sojourn. It was a literal Israel that was oppressed by a literal Assyria. It was a literal Israel, although then seen in the two tribes, that was taken captive to a literal Babylon; although in the verses we are considering only Egypt and Assyria are named, and Babylon, not at all. But Assyria, as the World-power of the time in which the prophecy was written, represents, as we have seen, all the four empires that succeeded it. It will surely be a literal Israel that, in a time of unparalleled distress will be the direct heir to these promises: their covenant-keeping Jehovah hath not cast them forever away.

Yet we are by no means debarred from listening to the message these ancient prophecies would speak even to us. If we are still servants of sin, that is a very false witness to the name of Jesus.

Look at the condition of things in the professing Church today. What glory does *that* give to our God? What part has He in such an appalling condition? Is not the Name of our Lord Jesus blasphemed by it? Does not that condition cry aloud for His intervention? Can it go on everlastingly?

But of all the expressions of human wickedness that have brought that Name, which by divine decree is above every name, into the lowest contempt, let that word expressive of extreme subtlety have the preeminence. What must God the Father think of the name "Jesus" being the basis of "Jesuit," a word that has become a synonym for subtlety whereby the very principles of morality have been subverted, evil declared good, and good evil! Not only have the Jesuits been again and again expelled from every State in Europe, but even Pope Clement XIV, by his "Bull" of July 21, 1773, *"extinguished and suppressed them"* (he died in 1774 of poison*). Yet today they are more numerous, more active, more influential than ever! It is of the spirit behind them of which this speaks.

So to go still deeper, leave man, and apply the words to that "last enemy" of our race, that takes the place of Israel's last enemy, the Assyrian, "Death." What has God in such a state? Does disseminated dust speak His praise? That, the serpent could effect. Is it to the glory of the redeeming work of His Son that His redeemed should be in that marred condition, neither angels nor men? Surely God and the Lamb have no part in such a condition: every unclothed spirit must, by its very state, cry aloud, like those "souls under the altar" (Rev. 6: 9), "How long?" before the inevitable intervention of God in power shall clothe them with their eternal "house which is out of heaven?" (2 Cor. 5: 2).

Then look at those last lines: "I am the unchanging One who promised, and lo, here I am." Has He, that same unchanging One, only now under the name of Jesus, promised to be with two or three gathered to that Name, which in itself means that they are attracted by what that Name speaks of power and will to meet their deepest felt needs, and will He not, does He not, fulfil that promise? Has He promised, and shall we not, in His gather-

*From "Schaff-Herzog Encycl."

ing shout, hear Him saying: "Here I am." To this the next words
may be applied.

7: How beautiful upon the mountains
   Are the feet of those bringing
   Good news, peace proclaiming!
   Of those who are bringing
   Evangel of blessing!
   To Zion proclaiming,
   Thy God is now reigning!

8: Hark!
   Thy watchmen are calling;
   In unison raising
   Their voices in song.
   'Tis because they are seeing
   Jehovah returning,
   (Returning) to Zion!
9: Burst forth into singing,
   In sweet accord singing,
   Ye ruins of Salem!
   For Jehovah doth comfort His people,
   Jerusalem He hath redeemed!
10: Jehovah hath made bare His arm,
    His arm that *is* indeed holy,
    In th' eyes of all of the nations;
    And all of the ends of the earth
    Have seen the salvation of God!

In these musical verses we can, without a great stretch of
imagination, see a company dancing joyously before, and heralding that salvation that is now approaching. The very feet of those
who thus foretell it, springing over the intervening mountains
(Song 2: 17) with the energy of unselfish joy, are beautiful to
those awaiting the good news.

It is the shoe that beautifies the foot. "How beautiful are
thy feet with shoes," sings Solomon (Song 7: 1); and very beautiful are these messengers, shod with the very message that they
bring, the message that adorns the messenger. In the cry that
these watchmen unitedly lift up, we note again that significant and
comprehensive number "three." In itself, it is "good;" towards
His people on earth, it is "salvation:" and rising ever higher

"Godward" it announces that He is reigning.  Oh, the joy that the very thought brings!  What must the reality afford?

We cannot leave this refreshing theme without a reference, at least, to our own beautiful shoes.  In exhorting us to put on the whole armor of God, the Spirit tells us that divine love has provided what shall cover us from head to foot; and our feet are to be shod with "the preparation of the gospel of peace."  Strange armor!  Peace itself a defensive part of it!  But the armor must be adapted to resist the foe, and since our great enemy and all the wicked spirits in the heavenlies are opposed to our peace, this becomes a very suitable piece of our panoply to resist them (Eph. 6: 15).

Nor does the "preparation" mean a kind of composition of which the shoes are made, but the preparedness, the being always "ready" at any time, under any circumstances, our "peace" witnessing to our gospel, and not overthrown by whatever may befall.  We must have the peace that comes from knowing that God loves us with an unbroken tenderness, irrespective of the providences that our great foe is permitted so largely to control, and which so often, by terrifying and bewildering storms seem to deny that love.  The cross alone, unchanged amid all life's storms, provides a "footing" that changes not.

How strikingly beautiful is verse 9!  Look at those ruins which witness to the Lord's words of the complete devastation of Jerusalem.  For the centuries of Gentile rule those huge stones have only echoed the wails of that poor nation whose condition they so aptly symbolize.  But now those wails must cease, and as their God approaches, these "very stones cry out" His praise with a joy that is inimitable.

Let us ever bear in mind that God's dealings with Israel form types of His dealing with each of His people personally, but not with the professing "Historic Church" as a unit; that unfaithful witness is to be utterly reprobated and "spewed out of His mouth" (Rev. 3: 16).

11: Depart ye!  Depart ye!  Go ye out from thence,
    And touch not the thing that is unclean.
    Go ye from the midst of her, and see that ye be clean,
    Ye that are the bearers of the vessels of the Lord.

12:  For not in haste or tumult shall ye now go forth,
     And not as though in flight shall ye go;
     For Jehovah is your vanguard, going on before you,
     And your rear is safely guarded by the God of Israèl.

The whole context points to this being a final deliverance, never to be repeated, and therefore cannot have been fulfilled in the return of a few captives from Babylon in the day of Ezra, although that was a foreshadowing of what still lies in the future. To what place can the words "from thence" (verse 11), apply but to Babylon? From Egypt they certainly did go out "with haste" (Deut. 16: 3), and laden with gold and silver which they are here warned not to touch as being unclean. In calm dignity are they to march, with van and rear protected by the power of Jehovah.

For as Assyria in these later prophecies of Isaiah stands for whatever political power may dominate the earth at any time, so Babylon would stand for whatever religious power may share that dominance.   This at least gives clear direction to the urgent call:: "Come out of her, My people" (Rev. 18: 4); nor can that call be limited to one dispensation.   In the day of literalness, it was the literal city on the Euphrates that was to be left in obedience to the cry: "Depart ye! Depart ye!"   Today it must be discerned in whatever bears the mark of that woman, Jezebel; that is, any Christ-dishonoring system such as is headed up in the Papacy on the one hand or Unitarianism on the other.   In the day to come the call will apply to all the "religion" of the earth, in open apostasy from God.   So that the cry: "Come out of her, My people, and touch not the unclean thing," is always applicable, yesterday, today, and as long as there is a Christ-dishonoring religion upon earth.

This life is in itself so valuable and yet so brief, that we cannot close this section without a word on, "Be ye clean, that bear the vessels of the Lord;" because the corresponding New Testament scripture is not only so little understood, but I believe seriously, however innocently, distorted from its purpose, and the consequences of that distortion have been literally tragic.

"In a great house there are not only vessels of gold and silver, but also of wood and earth, and some to honor and some to dishonor. If any one therefore purge himself from these, he shall be a vessel to honor, sanctified, and meet for the Master's use, prepared unto every good work."

I will not question that you, whose eyes are scanning these lines, are not a mere worldly professor, but a true child of God. Then let me press on you that God has by that very fact, made you "a vessel unto honor;" and, continuing the pictorial character of the illustration, you are *of gold and silver."* For gold, when thus used, invariably speaks of what is purely divine, and thus here is a symbol of that divine life and nature communicated in new birth. Silver, the medium of all barter in the East, speaks of the *cost* of redemption (Ex. 30: 15), the precious Blood of the Lamb; the divine work both *in* and *for* being thus pictorially expressed. So let us seek to grasp this as a certainty that you and I are, as in Christ, *vessels to honor!* God be thanked!

Does it follow necessarily that we are meet for the Master's use? Not at all. Does a good housewife use vessels covered with dirt, irrespective of the material that composes them? She would be ashamed to be herself so unclean. Nor does the infinitely holy Lord use vessels that are so covered. Hence the promise of being useful to the Lord depends on our *purging ourselves from "these."* But, mark carefully, the "purging" does not *make* a vessel—that is nonsense. God alone can, or does, make "vessels to honor" (*cf.* Rom. 9: 21-23); that is effected by the internal work of regeneration (gold) and the external of redemption (silver), and our acceptance of that redemption by faith. But then comes human responsibility in the "purging;" and this is followed, as surely as effect follows cause, by being "sanctified," "set apart," and *that* equally surely by being fit for the Master's use, and ready for any good work in which He may wish to use these vessels.

Can then anything be of greater importance than to know what is meant by the "these," since the usefulness of our lives depends on it? According to our English idiom, the simple and direct antecedent of the pronoun must be "vessels to dishonor," made of wood and earth, which must in that case represent not only unregenerate and unredeemed people, but those who evidence that condition by their wicked conduct, and so who are termed elsewhere, *wicked* (1 Cor. 5: 12).   Any wilful association with such *in the Church of God,* necessarily defiles, and although the usual plea for remaining in such association is for the sake of usefulness, that end is far more likely to be attained by obedience to the Word of God.

But it may at least be questioned if separation from any other *persons* is here in view at all.  I believe not.  This so easily, so quickly, degenerates into the most hateful of all evils, Phariseeism (a separation from other fellow-believers, which, far from resulting in usefulness, destroys it) that we are compelled to look for an antecedent, the purging ourselves from which, shall inevitably, assuredly, result in our divine Master being able to make use of us.  Consider again that homely illustration.  Does a housewife cleanse her soiled vessels by simply placing them at some distance from other soiled vessels?  Of what use would that be?  No; she first cleanses each one from all the dirt on the vessel itself that defiles, and then sets it aside, apart from those still soiled,* for that use to which it is now fitted.

Now, whilst as born of God and redeemed by blood, we are "gold and silver," yet as born of Adam there is still that old nature in us all; that is pictured by wood and earth, and it is from "these"—whatever is of wood or earth, whatever is the product of that old nature, proud, self-confident and opposed to the cross—it is from "these" that we must purge ourselves. This, then, is not a call to discern evil in *others,* but to judge *ourselves,* to put aside as worthless all that is of the flesh, to have no confidence in it!

Does not this commend itself to your conscience in the sight of God?  It is the one essential for happy and profitable service that shall save our brief lives from being wasted.  Did you ever know of anyone, anywhere, at any time, who had "no confidence in the flesh"—that is, in himself as born of Adam (wood and earth), but trusted alone in all that there is in Christ, who was *not* used of the Master?  Most surely he who "purges" himself

---

*But a soiled vessel is not necessarily "a vessel to dishonor"— that is determined by the material of which it is made, wood and earth.  Such are not fitted for the same honorable uses as gold and silver.

from *these* (the wood and earth of the old man), who has no confidence in the flesh, can never lead a useless life: and here in Isaiah all in the Lord's service must be clean.

The scene closes. The dancing measure stops. We see the returning ones marching in calm dignity, expressive in itself of that security and honor that attends them. There is not one tremor in all their ranks, not a shade of anxiety on any face, for Jehovah, the Irresistible, is their Vanguard, and He too secures their rear. Compassed thus with love that has no limitation of power, directed by boundless wisdom, the feeblest may pass on to their rest with a peace that passes all understanding. Oh, that we (if one may speak for others) knew more of it! Oh, that it were not simply as a very pleasant song, but a joyous experience, that our hearts were thus unbrokenly garrisoned! For we ought not come behind Israel in our testimony to Him who is the Spring of all our greater privileges.

**The construction of the Heart of the Book: its significance. Correspondences with the Pentateuch of Moses. Exposition of this Pentateuch.**

W E are now standing on the very threshold of the Holy of Holies of our book, and we do well to fear lest a carnal touch should make its defiling mark on this sanctuary, the walls of which are surely whiter than any fuller on earth could whiten them. Is there not at least *one* of my readers who will join with me in supplication that the Spirit, whose holiness alone accords with that of this scripture, will guard us from error, lead us into truth, and so take of the things of Christ and show them to us, as to attract our wandering hearts to Him, and bind them there forever. Amen.

The section is the very heart of Isaiah, and we must bear in mind the meaning of that name, and say the very heart of *"the Salvation of Jehovah"*—the very Bosom of our God here lies exposed to reverent faith and responsive affection, and whom should we expect to find there but Him whose abode has ever been in that Bosom, and who came forth from it to express its tender grace to sinful man? (John 1: 18).

Before entering, let us go round about our scripture a little, tell the towers thereof, mark well its bulwarks, consider its palaces, enjoy both the beauty and strength of its very structure, and this shall introduce us to its subject, our Lord Himself!

We can all discern one soiling human finger-print in the division between the chapters, for it evidently breaks into the construction in a way that damages and obscures its significance.

But remembering that the division of the verses in Hebrew poetry is as much by divine inspiration as the text itself, we note that there are just fifteen verses, which a little pondering will show to be divided into five threes. But, as we have already seen, "three" and "five," when in this relation to one another,

tell out in themselves the vital union of God (3) and man (5).
But at once we ask of whom must such a union speak if not of
that "Word who in the beginning was *God*" (John 1: 1), and yet
who was "made *flesh,* and dwelt among us" (John 1: 14). *That*
can speak of no other than of Immanuel, which being interpreted
is "God with us;" or to give that same name, Immanuel, another
form, JESUS, which, being interpreted, means "Saviour," and
therefore equally means both Man and God over all, blessed
forever, for it is God who says, "Beside Me there is *no* Saviour"
(Jesus).

Here, then, in these five sections we have again a Pentateuch,
whose parts have a striking correspondence with the first Pentateuch of the Bible; and thus the first three verses form what is
the *Genesis* of this prophecy, for it has in it, as has that first
book of our Bible, the seed of all that follows.

But as we go round about our Scripture and mark the impregnable bulwarks it presents to all forms of infidelity—the
towers with which it defends our faith—we see another tower,
stern and rough indeed, yet those very features are its beauty to
us, for they and they alone are in full accord with the solemn
theme.   "There are only two passages in which the language becomes more harsh, turbid and ponderous, namely, chapters 53
and 57.   In the former it is the emotion of sorrow that throws
its shadow upon it; in the latter the emotion of wrath"
(*Delitzsch*).  If that be the case, we must not expect to find here
that smooth joyous musical note that we have recently heard, and
which lends itself to a metrical rendering with little change. Here
it is, and must remain, uneven and rugged, even as the subject of
which it speaks.

13: Behold My Servant, He shall act wisely,
    Raised shall He be,
    Extolled shall He be,
    High shall He be; yea, the Highest!
14: As there were many astonished at Thee,
    (So marred was His visage,
    More than that of a man,
    More marred was His form
    Than of all Adam's sons).

15: So shall He make with astonishment start*
     Many peoples!
     E'en kings shall be awed into silence;
     For there shall they see what had never been told them,
     Then shall perceive what had never been heard.

The Speaker giving this command is evidently God, the very God who in the opening words of Genesis appears as the Creator of the heavens and the earth. It is He who here tells us to "behold," that is, to consider with deepest, most concentrated attention One whom He terms His Servant.

Who then can that Servant be? Where shall we find Him that we may consider Him? In this prophecy that word "servant" (as we have seen in chap. 42) has three different applications: first, to the mass of Israel, then to the Remnant of faith, and finally to Messiah. To which of these is it to be applied here? The mass of the Jewish people, scattered in its sorrow as it is, have always insisted that that afflicted nation itself must be

---

*The rendering here given to this line demands some explanation. The word "sprinkle" in our A. V. has been a veritable battleground among commentators, and whilst seeking to weigh all that has been urged for the different renderings, I can only give briefly the reason for that conclusion to which I have come. The prime meaning of the root is "to leap, as exulting with joy," hence as applied to liquids, "to spurt," and as here used, "to cause to spurt," and so, "to sprinkle," and it is so rendered in all other places of its use in Scripture, which of course tells weightily for that rendering here. But on the other hand—and now I quote Delitzsch—"The word is never construed with the accusative of the person or thing sprinkled." As for instance, to give one out of many, "He sprinkled thereof upon the altar." It is *whatever is sprinkled* that is connected with the verb. So here this would necessitate the many nations being sprinkled, and so many do render it "scatter many nations," which must be refused. As Delitzsch justly says, "There would be something very abrupt in this sudden representation of the servant as a priest sprinkling." Thus it would appear certain that its use here differs from all the others. But in the tongue closely kindred to the Hebrew, Arabic, the word is used of persons in its primal sense of leaping up as impelled by some deep emotion, and as this makes a perfect antithesis to the first line of verse 14 I have felt clear in adopting, "make start with astonishment."

seen as the object of the prophecy, and we must understand Israel to be referred to as the Servant all through. Let us test that by so applying one or two sentences. "The Lord hath laid on that people the iniquity of us all;" "That people was taken from prison and from judgment, and who shall declare its generation?" "They appointed the grave of that people with wicked men and with the rich man in its death." Do we need to go further? It is not worthy of refutation—it refutes itself.*

The lowly "remnant" would never even make the claim, so that we are forced to the simple clear truth that it is none other than Jesus of Nazareth, the true Messiah of Israel, our own Redeemer, of whom we here read. Indeed, so clear, so simple, so marvellous are the correspondences in every detail, that the strange thing is that anyone who has the normal power of thought should raise one single question as to its application. There can be no explanation of any man gifted with the faculty of reason, refusing all reason, except in that strange enmity of the carnal mind to all that is of God, and which is under the control of a more powerful and malignant enemy.

The very first words reveal to us that it has been this same One who has been in the Mind of the Spirit in these later chapters that have led up to this as a climax. It was He whose ears had been opened morning by morning; it was He who had thus been taught the path of suffering and shame that lay before Him, and who submissively addressed Himself to it. It was He who had been taught to refuse the evil and choose the good, who now is seen here acting very wisely even in making that choice; and walking in that clear light of the volume of the book that pointed Him to the Cross and the glory following it.

———

*"Christian scholars," says the Jew, Abravanel, "interpret this prophecy as referring to that man who was crucified in Jerusalem about the end of the second temple, and who according to their view was the Son of God, who became man in the womb of the virgin. But Jonathan ben Uzziel explains it as referring to the Messiah who has yet to come; and this is the opinion of the ancients in many of their midrashim" (commentaries). Well, that at least shows that the ancient Jews knew that the subject of the prophecy was Messiah!

He ever acted so wisely as to insure success, hence the very word rendered "act wisely" comes to mean, as in the Authorized Version, to "prosper," and both meanings may well be seen in it here: His wisdom and its prospering are united in the one word. His wisdom led Him to infinite suffering, and by that suffering His purpose was attained. This first line then takes us to that "wise" path of suffering only terminated by the Cross.

Then in the next three lines we have the three steps resulting from that wise-doing. First, He is raised up from the depths of humiliation, to which that path had led Him, the tomb: then still higher does He rise, as from Olivet His feet leave this earth, and the cloud hides Him from sight; till finally to Him is given the highest place in all the universe, or, as a very literal rendering of these last words would be, *"High, Very."* Thus are we told in these few words the whole path of the Messiah, till He reaches, as Man, the Throne He had left as the divine Son. Is it not the Genesis of this Pentateuch?

Verse 14 now goes back to the depths of His humiliation: "As many were astonished at Thee;" and then intervenes a parenthetical "aside," telling the cause of the astonishment. *"His visage was more marred than that of any man, either of high or low degree."* But here we must definitely part company with many a commentator (and among them Delitzsch), for they refer this marring to our Lord in His life; as if His appearance was so distorted as to be "no longer really human." Such an application is to be rejected with horror. Little children, whose simple intuition is unerring, in their willing approach, and resting on His knee, or nestling in His breast, tell another story, for they were *attracted,* not repulsed by His visage, or appearance. How could it, then, at that time, be so distorted as to be no longer human?

Yet the words point beyond all question to some unparalleled depth of suffering, and its effect on that blessed Face and Form. Up to the stroke of noon on that fatal day in April, A. D. 32,* the thieves on either side of Him may have equally suffered, or with only such difference as was due to the greater sensitiveness

---

*By Sir Robert Anderson's chronology, which seems strongly assured.

of the perfect human organism of His body. But then for three hours, and for three hours only, did He so suffer "more than any of the sons of men," as to mar His visage more than any. It is quite true that God drew a veil over those sufferings, thus telling, in a most solemn symbol, that none could really "see," or enter into their profundities; but here the holy silence of the Gospels is supplemented by the inspired words in our prophet; and in that unequalled agony, God, who is here the Speaker, tells us what *He* saw in that great darkness. Oh, the suffering *to Himself* that this tells, for that Sufferer was His beloved Son!

For note carefully His visage has been *marred;* that is, it is not as it was *by birth*. Something has occurred to disfigure that face, so gracious, so winsome to little children, and to penitent sinners always. It would not seem just to limit the scope of the first line, and make those who were astonished to be solely the wretched men who were blind to His divine dignity; for angels who desire to look into these sacred mysteries would not be absent from that awful scene, and these might well be struck with deepest marvel that He—their own Creator—should voluntarily endure such vicarious agony.

Verse 15 takes up the conclusion of the first line of verse 14: "As many were astonished at Thee" (because of that unparalleled humiliation of One so perfect) "so shall He cause many to spring up with astonishment." Even kings shall be struck dumb at such a report as utterly transcends anything that they have ever heard.

Our first, or Genesis, section has closed with the prophecy of a report going out to those who had never seen or heard of such a marvel, and that must be the Gentiles, to whom no revelation—no oracles of God—had been given as to Israel. Now the second, or *Exodus,* section begins with the prophet taking his place among his own people, and musing sorrowfully and penitently over their blind unbelief with which he identifies himself in his lowly confession. Thus this section has the clearest correspondence with both the Exodus of the Old Testament and that of the New, called The Acts of the Apostles, for in both, as here, a salvation is announced to Israel, and in both there is the same rejection of it, as it is written: "This Moses whom they refused, saying, Who made thee a ruler and a judge, the same did God send to be a ruler and deliverer." "Ye stiff-necked and uncircumcised in heart and ears, ye do always resist the Holy Ghost; as your fathers did, so do ye" (Acts 7: 35, 51). Thus history ever repeats itself. But now we see the prophet himself standing like that publican with bowed head, or like that other beloved man, Daniel, identifying himself with his people in confessing their sin and mourning thus:

1:   Who hath believed the report* that is ours?
       To whom is the Arm of Jehovah revealed?
2:   For as a *suckling* He grew up before Him;
       And as a root sprouting up from dry ground.
       No lovely form, nor beauty had He:
       We saw Him; but naught in that sight drew us to Him.
3:   Despisèd He was, and of men was rejected:
       A man of deep sorrows†; with grief well acquainted;
       We hid, as it were, our faces from Him;
       He was despised—we esteemèd Him not!

We must retain the close connection this first section has with the last of the preceding chapter, to get the force of the confession. There, Gentiles and their kings received with amazement some report; but that report was, says the prophet of Israel, *ours* first. It was intended for us, it was sent to us, and yet, alas, who among us believed it? The Arm is the member of the body by which work requiring strength is accomplished. It carries out the dictates of the will. Could any figure be more fitting for Him who was indeed Jehovah's Arm? And who, as that Arm, delighted to do His Will, in work so mighty that though heaven, earth, and the infernal regions be searched, not one single individual could be found who could do it (*cf.* Rev. 5: 3). Yet to whom was that Arm revealed? Who discerned in that lowly Man the mighty Arm of Jehovah? Israel has cried and repeated the cry of, "Awake, awake, O arm of the Lord!" but when that Arm

---

*"Report," that which was heard, not what we spoke. See 2 Sam. 4: 4, where the same word is rendered "tidings."

†The word "sorrow" is in the plural, thus giving the idea of intensity, or of more forms of sorrow than one.

came who recognized It? Can He—that son of the carpenter (as supposed)—can *He* be the Arm of Jehovah? Can He, who dwells hidden, unknown in that humble home in despised Galilee, can He be the Arm of Jehovah? Never a good thing comes out of Nazareth (John 1: 46), can the Arm of Jehovah come thence? And when He did come forth from that home He was rejected by all up to whom we had looked as being the respectable, the wise, the reputable, the religious of our nation. Is it possible that He, despised of all these, can be the very Arm of Jehovah?

We expected quite a different sight! Our vain gaze was in quite a different direction. We were looking for one who should come with,

> "Royal banner, and all quality,
> Pride, pomp, and circumstance of glorious war,"

and thus leading Israel's host, as did that Captain of the Lord's Host in the days of old (Josh. 5: 14), deliver us from the Roman yoke by victory after victory. Great beauty would such have had in our eyes! Joyously would we have gathered about such an One! But with such expectations, with our eyes thus lifted upward, what beauty could we see in One whom we could but overlook entirely at our feet, as it were, in His lowly estate, weeping with those who wept, a Man of many sorrows, and of few short moments of rejoicing with those who rejoiced.

But the veil is falling from the eyes of our hearts, and we remember that our paschal lamb is never marked out and set apart until the tenth day of the month. For the first ten days of our year, that lamb is before Jehovah alone, and His Eye alone rests upon it with delight, but no other knows it! So with our Messiah, He too was hidden, and not marked out as God's Lamb till thirty years had passed. Thus did He *"grow up before Him"* only.

But the royal House of David has long been as a tree cut down, and centuries have passed since a son of David sat upon his throne; but here, from the roots of that felled tree, has sprung a living sprout which thrives whilst all about it is sere, dry and dead.

Thus He grew, a lovelier human flower than either God or

man had ever seen on earth before, and yet when He did come forth, and went about His gracious ministry of doing good, sharing, as well as relieving, the sorrows of mankind, our leaders despised Him, and alas, even we, who now mourn our unbelief, esteemed Him not.  We were like men who turn away from an object in which they have no interest.

History, man's sad history, is repeating itself this very day. We are standing on the verge of His coming again, and once more the respectable, the learned, the merely religious, are turning away from Him who is alone the "Power of God unto salvation"—the true Arm of the Lord.

But as a few in that day, with a sense of their deep need clave to Him, so in this too, is history repeating itself.  There are a comparative few whom the sense of sin and need has pressed to His feet; and to such He is indeed beautiful, and precious beyond all earth's jewelry.  We only mourn that our intimacy with Him is so slight, and (may I speak for others?) it is the thirst of our parched hearts to know Him better, for to Him alone will we owe all our salvation, past, present and future, for He to us is the only "Arm of the Lord."

This brings us to the third section of this prophecy, corresponding to the third book of the Pentateuch, *Leviticus;* and as that took us into the Sanctuary, with the many offerings connected with it, so here we have the one Offering that has displaced all these shadows, and by which we have access even into the Holiest.  Thus the next three verses reveal the secret of those sufferings; and well will it be for us if we listen, not coldly, but with some degree of affection stirred by that revelation, for we each have the deepest personal interest in what is here written.

4:  Surely the griefs that He bore were our own;
    The sorrows were *ours* that He carried:
    Yet we did count Him as stricken,*
    As smitten of God and afflicted.

---

*Heb. *nahga,* "*to strike heavily.*"  It is the word used for the plague of leprosy as in 2 Chron. 26: 20.  Comp. "The hand of God hath *touched* me" (Job 19: 21).

5: But *ours* the transgressions for which He was pierced,
   Ours the iniquities for which He was crushed;
   Ours is the peace—His the chastisement;
   Ours is the healing—His were the wounds.
6: All we, like sheep, have gone far astray,
   Each one to his own way hath turnèd,
   And Jehovah hath caused to meet upon Him
   Th' iniquity done by us all.

How clear, as well as deeply affecting, are the rays of sanctuary-light that these words throw on those sufferings that were hidden from every human eye by the three hours of darkness on Calvary; so clear that it is difficult to realize that the words were written more than seven hundred years before the fulfilment.

The first word of verse 4 is the "Amen," adopted in the New Testament, and which was so often on the Lips of our Lord Himself. It expresses the strongest affirmation. None must have the slightest question as to the true cause of those sufferings that had no parallel, and most surely that cause could not have existed during that lovely life, which was all spent in the sunshine of His Father's delight. No; one must go to the very last three hours on the cross for what we are here told.

No rod that ploughs His flesh, no thorn that tears His brow, no nail that pierces His hands and feet, can wring from Him one groan:

> It needs still deeper agony,
> E'en than these, to wake the cry,
> "Eli lama sabachthani."

What could inflict that agony?

At the meridian hour man's gibes cease; and then the cloudless sun refuses to send down its light on that most solemn scene, whilst *my* sins (Will you not join with me, with bowed head, and eye not undimmed?) are on Him, and God, even His own God and Father, forsakes Him therefor, and stripes from *His* Rod—compared with which, the Roman rods were but as a caressing—are falling on Him. It was from this, and this alone, that His holy soul shrank, so that even in anticipation His sweat was as it were great drops of blood; and yet there too, in that garden, it was but the shadow. *What, oh, what, must the substance have been?* Surely if we realized this in any slight measure, our hearts would not be as divided as they are: our lives would not be so wasted as, alas, they so largely are, in self-seeking. May I again speak for others in adopting the words of one greatly beloved in the far-off past: "We have heard of Thee with the hearing of the ear, but now our eyes see Thee, wherefore we abhor ourselves and repent in dust and ashes"—if that sight does not produce self-abhorrence and repentance, nothing can.

We shrink from turning from these affecting meditations to consider a strange and erroneous deduction that has been drawn from these words, but it cannot be passed over without any notice: The first Gospel in the New Testament quotes (chapter 8: 16, 17) the closing words of this verse thus:

"And when even was come they brought unto Him many that were possessed with devils and He cast out the spirits with a word, and healed all that were sick: that it might be fulfilled which was spoken by Isaiah the prophet, saying, Himself took our infirmities and bare our sicknesses."

From this it has been deduced that the Lord, then and there, bore in His life the sicknesses that He took from others, and therefore His people should never be sick! But, in the first place, He certainly did not *become* sick or infirm. He did not bear them in that sense. If He healed a man with a withered arm, no corresponding effect followed on Himself. His holy Body was ever free from any of those afflictions that our "flesh is heir to;" but heir to only because of the introduction of sin. Of all *sinless* infirmities, as hunger, thirst, weariness, He, in grace, partook, but not one single thing that was the consequence of sin. He was tempted (tried) in all points like as we are—*sin apart* (Heb. 4: 15).

Why then does Matthew write that He took "our infirmities and bare our sicknesses?" It could not be by merely sympathizing with the sufferers. He sees on all sides the sorrowful consequences of sin: demon-possession, disease, pain, deformities, tears, and He removes them all. But He who had the power and authority on earth (Mark 2: 10) to remove the *effect,* or penalty, thus *made Himself responsible for the cause.* And who could do that save He who was to bear the sin that caused those sufferings, in His own body on the tree? He could not remove one single twinge of pain without, in due season, bearing the sin that caused the pain. And just as the feeblest groan, or a single teardrop is a testimony to the presence of sin, so the hushing the groan, the drying the tear is in the same way a testimony *to the sin being atoned for;* and for that, nothing in the whole universe would avail, but those sufferings during the last three hours upon the cross; and as Matthew tells us, He did remove them *so that* the prophecy of Isaiah might be fulfilled; and fulfilled, as in a shadow then,* but for the final true fulfilment we must look alone to the Cross.

But if the cause has been thus removed, why has not the effect ceased?—at least in those who, in penitent faith, have availed of the propitiation. Why do believers still suffer sickness, disease and death? Because all God's ways with men are governed by the place occupied by His beloved One. *He* is still rejected, and not here on His own Throne; and whilst His atoning work is absolutely perfect and finished, Godward, so that, "He is the propitiation for our sins, and not for ours only, but for [the sins of] the whole world," *its application to our bodies* remains yet to be accomplished, and in those bodies sin is still present, or why are we told to "mortify the deeds of the body" (Rom. 8: 13)? We still await the adoption (that is, God owning and revealing us publicly as His beloved sons), to wit, the redemption of our body (Rom. 8: 23). The Lord Jesus is still rejected, and the Spirit of God is here on earth, the blessing of God therefore does not consist in the physical healing of those bodies still under the power of death (Rom. 8: 10), but "in all *spiritual blessings in the heavenlies*" (Eph. 1: 3), to conform with Christ's present place, and that of the Spirit of God.

Sinless, spotless, not bearing our sins during His life, not bearing them up to, but alone *on,* the tree, passing His life in

---

*In the same way as His baptism in Jordan was a fulfilling of all righteousness in a shadow or figure.

the sunlight of God's delight, He, as the spotless Lamb, offered up Himself, bearing our sins on the cross, and there alone.

In verse 5 the light of God breaks in on those sufferings, and it reveals (and how affecting the revelation!) that *ours* was the transgression, *His* the stroke for it. *Ours* was the iniquity, *His* the wound for it. *Ours* was the sin, *His* the death, its wages and due! But here we must let our words be few, and even pause in a silence more expressive than speech, for behind the stroke, the wound, the death, we must apprehend something of the LOVE that was to usward!

Here we look at what the highest of created Intelligences consider with profound amazement; and they ever desire to fathom those unfathomable depths still further. That God, the very God from whom every one of us has wandered afar, although in different directions, should Himself cause the iniquities of us all to meet, as myriads of foul black sewers might meet, and in one awful, rushing, roaring, filthy, malodorous flood empty themselves at one spot—on *Him,* the dearest Object of His own heart! Can any keep away from such a God as that? When it is known that not merely bread, but an embrace; not a servant's place, but the Father's breast; nor a hired-servants's clothing but the best robe await—what prodigal would not hasten to return? I would take the hand of my reader, and say, Join with me in the cry to that same God: "Let, O Father, the remainder of my few days here be Thine, for Thou hast truly bought them at a great cost. O God, my Father, let the love, that even for poor worthless me, did not spare Thy beloved One, bind this heart, alas, still so prone to wander as it is, to Thyself forever. Indeed, not only in unregenerate days did I wander afar, but even since I have known something of Thy love. My soul is bowed with shame, and cries, Oh, let the time past suffice for such wandering. Frail beyond words as I am, Lord Jesus, I am still Thy poor sheep, and Thou art alone my Shepherd who hast even laid down Thy life for me. Keep me near Thee, I beseech Thee, till I am with Thee forever!"

We have been in the sanctuary, considering the Godward side of our Lord's sufferings. We must now turn back, as it were, as in the first Pentateuch of the Bible, for after Leviticus, the

Book of the *Sanctuary*, we have the Book of Numbers, the "Book of the *Desert*," as it is called in the Hebrew Bible, in which the pilgrim-path of Israel is told with all its desert-testings, and their constant failures under those testings. Here too we come to just that aspect of the Saviour's sufferings, as testings from man, and His perfect bearing under them—He failed never.

> 7: Hard was He pressed, and deeply afflicted,
>     But He opened not His mouth.
>     As a lamb to the slaughter is led,
>     As a sheep 'fore her shearers is dumb,
>     So He openèd not His mouth.
> 8: Hurried was He from prison and judgment;*
>     His posterity who shall declare?†
>     For He was cut off from the land of the living,
>     For My people's transgressions was stricken.
> 9: His grave was appointed to be with the wicked,
>     But with the rich man after His death,
>     For never a violent deed had He done,
>     Never deceit had come from His mouth.

We are listening to the retrospective meditation on sufferings that are past, and what here strikes those who are thus penitently meditating is the meek self-surrender of the Sufferer. That strange acceptance of unjust sufferings, without a whisper of a protest, is as attractive as it is compelling to responsive affection, and it is an important, a vital, basic element in the whole plan of atone-

---

*The idea in the word translated "taken," in A. V., is not that of "translation" as Enoch, but of being *hurried away*.

†This line is one of acknowledged difficulty, as the divergent renderings show. For instance, the word rendered "declare" is primarily "to bring forth;" if this be applied to words, then it is "to declare or speak;" if to thoughts, it becomes to "meditate," as many insist it should be here. If those thoughts are happy, then the idea of "singing" is introduced (Ps. 45: 5); if sad, it becomes "to complain" (Job 7: 11). So too the prime meaning of *"dohr"* (generation) is "to go round in a circle," then from this, "an age" or "generation," as being the circuit of the years of life. Then, into this, a moral element is introduced, and it becomes a race of men, distinguished by some *moral* trait, as Deut. 22: 15, and Matt. 23: 36. Nor is the idea of "posterity" excluded, as Num. 9: 10 ("If any man of you, of your posterity") shows.

ment, for had there been one whisper of protest, that would have denied *the voluntariness* of His offering, and who can measure the consequence? The charge of injustice in punishing the innocent for the guilty, would have had some basis. You will remember that it was this that struck Pilate with astonishment. Instead of the noisy vociferations of innocence, with which his office had made him so familiar, there stood before him a Man, with that terrifying death threatening Him, yet calm and silent, a Man whose very presence spoke with convincing eloquence, whilst His Lips uttered never a word! Never was there such eloquence in silence! Never did a closed Mouth express such depths of truth! Had He spoken a word of sorrow or protest on the one hand, or of cheerfulness in prospect of sin-bearing on the other, how fatally marred His personal perfections!—how ruined His work of atonement! What mind could conceive, what human hand could depict, such divinely perfect balancings? Never, I say again, was silence so eloquent!

God has evidently made every creature on the earth to aid us in apprehending unseen divine verities; and thus the majestic, the beautiful, the gentle, amongst the animals, tell us of the moral attractions of His Son. The lion speaks His dignity, the ox His patient ministry; shall the lamb be silent? Or if so, shall not that very silence in view of death tell us of the Love that upbore Him to "endure the cross, despise the shame," in order that His God might have the power to save, and *He* the joy of saving poor sinful men, and share with them those pleasures at the right Hand of God that He might Himself ever have had alone without the suffering?

So in that common hall where they disrobed Him, and in mockery clad Him in the imperial purple, no reviling answered the mockery of the rough Roman soldiery. Then to Golgotha, but ever with that submissive silence that was foretold over 700 years before, and which is here meditated upon by us, thousands of years after the endurance—and shall be the theme of our meditation for all eternity!

Verse 8 takes us further along this *Via Dolorosa,* and the prophet sees the Sufferer hurried away from bonds and from the parody of a trial, to death. Adam's generations have been de-

clared to us in Gen. 5; who shall declare *His?*  Where is the
progeny that shall carry along His line, and with it, His claims
to the throne of David, His father "after the flesh?"  It expires
with Him.  That claim is His alone, and falls to the ground with
His death.  All the nation's hopes appear to be quenched, and
sorrowful indeed were those poor disciples during that dark three
days, for they "trusted that it had been He who should have redeemed Israel" (Luke 24: 21), and their hope lies dead and
buried in Joseph's tomb.  Then adopting the alternative meaning
of these words: Who by meditation discerns the true, the real
inner significance, of these sufferings, of that short life, so soon
cut off?  Who discerns that it was not for His own, but the
transgression of God's people He was stricken?  And that stroke
was really inflicted, not by man, but by God!  Ah, who discerned the *real* secret of those sufferings?  But now the sorrow ceases;
the shame is forever past.  From the time that His death was
evidenced by the Roman's spear, not one single mark of indignity
shall be permitted, but,

> Henceforth Love alone shall pour
> On His feet her richest store!

As far as the intent and purpose of those who had accomplished His death went, they would have had Him buried with the
thieves among whom He had been numbered, but although *that*
death of shame had been permitted as fulfilling the determinate
counsel and foreknowledge of God, there the waves of man's
wickedness are stayed—thus far may they go, but no farther.  No
hand save that of reverent affection may touch that holy Body,
and no tomb which any corruptible body has defiled shall be
permitted to receive that "Holy Thing" for, as has been said, He
who came from a virgin-womb can only be laid in a virgin-tomb.
So a rich man comes, and his own tomb shall have this dignity
of receiving the Body of the Lord of Glory, and wherever this
gospel is preached, shall the name of this rich man be told.  Nor
can I, when treading such holy ground, believe that we are told
that name without its meaning having deep significance: "Joseph
of Arimathea."

"Joseph," with its hopeful, cheering meaning of "He shall add," was the name given by Rachel to her own firstborn, for, says the happy mother, shall this precious gift be the last token of God's grace? No, indeed; "The Lord *shall add* (that is, 'Joseph') to me another son," and He did. So we may ask, Is that cross, is that tomb, the very end? Is nothing to be *added?* Is there to be no Benjamin, no "son of my right hand?" Let that name, "Joseph," answer, for wherever we find it propheti- cally used it tells the story of a recovery, as for example (Ps. 81: 5), the trumpet's joyful sound is "appointed in *Joseph* for a testi- mony;" and tells to an opened ear that as Israel was recovered from Egypt, this shall be *added,* Israel shall be recovered from the dust of the earth (Dan. 12: 2). Just so, there is yet the infinitely mighty work to be *added* to that burial, a "Joseph" must, however unconsciously, bring his name to tell of it. But what is that mighty work? Let the city whence he comes answer; for he is "of Arimathea," the meaning of which may be found in Chapter 52: 13 in "lifted up,"* and this is what is "added." The tomb, even though it be undefiled, shall not hold Him, He shall be "lifted up" out of it; and that most precious of all truths, the name and city of that timid but true disciple, that honorable counsellor, that rich man, Joseph of Arimathea, shall speak, and it may still be heard where ears are not too heavy.

The perfection of the Saviour's spotless holiness, with neither deceit nor violence, could not meet its due recognition simply in His being laid in an unstained tomb—that would be vain indeed. Monuments, inscribed with the assumed goodness of him whose mouldering bones beneath them are telling a different story, may suit all other sons of Adam, but His perfections can only be evidenced by resurrection, and He who in the days of His flesh offered up strong cries and tears, was "heard for His piety," or "holy fear." That very "fear" that caused Him to shrink with submissive anguish from being made what *we* are, itself evidenced the perfection of His holiness; and *resurrection* evidenced that He had been heard for that piety (Heb. 5). So that even here, in this apparent obscurity of two names, we find hidden, as a

---

*It is the word rendered "exalted" in chap. 52: 13 of A. V., the first movement in the path of victory.

sweet violet under its leaves that announces its presence only by its fragrance, one of those scriptures that the Spirit appeals to as proving His resurrection, for He was raised the third day "according to the Scriptures." "Joseph of Arimathea" tells us that *resurrection* must be *added* to the cross. It is a lovely spot—the more welcome after the storm that bowed that blessed Head, a storm that is hushed forever. But still may its black cloud be seen as it rolls away nevermore to return on Him, and we, standing in the clear sunshine of perfect and eternal acceptance, may and will from time to time, till He come, look back and remember Him in the breaking of the bread, in the drinking of the cup, that tell of His cross and the spear-thrust, the judgment and death, that He bore for *us*.

Still must we linger here a little longer, for we are not told that the tomb was in a *garden* without divine purpose. Let us in spirit then visit that first garden planted in Eden by the Hand of the Lord God Himself. Fair as it is, an atmosphere of gloom pervades it, for it has heard the sentence of death passed upon the sinning progenitor of our race, who has passed down that sentence, with the sinful nature that was its cause, to all his posterity (Rom. 5: 12). Now let us go to Joseph's garden: it is early in April, A. D. 32,* and, as the women come to it "very early in the morning" (Mark 16:1), the birds are awaking to song, and on every side, in budding fruit and flower, are tokens of nature's resurrection from the death of winter. All tell the gospel that the gloom of Eden has been dispelled. Death has been made of none effect,† life and incorruptibility have been brought to light (2 Tim. 1: 10). Look within that tomb! It is empty save that linen clothes are still there to bear their double testimony, first to the supernatural Power by which that tomb was emptied, for no hasty "body-snatcher" would wait to disrobe a body, and arrange so perfectly the cerements that they should tell exactly where the Body lay; and then, in the being thus left behind that He would (in contrast with poor Lazarus, who brought his out with him) never need them more.

---

*I have adopted Sir. Robt. Anderson's careful chronology.

†This the is strict meaning of the word rendered "abolished" in A. V.

Further, as a brother in Christ‡ reminds me, no tree of knowledge of good and evil appears in the last garden that we may see in Rev. 22. The Tree of Life, however, is there as in the first garden; but now, quite unguarded by Seraph's flaming sword, it lies open to all who, in distrust of their best, wash their robes, thus symbolized, in the Blood of the Lamb that has quenched its fire forever.

The last clause, "For never a violent deed had He done, never deceit had come from His mouth," is another guard thrown about His Holy Person, but at the same time it necessitates another agent for the burial than for the death. It was the work of wicked men to appoint Him a place with transgressors in death, and that was permitted, nor had they any other purpose than that His grave should evidence the same association. But *they* had not the final disposal of that holy Body, and the very tomb must evidence that not one touch of either of those two elements of evil, "violence and corruption," could be attributed to Him! Let the rejecters of Christ point their finger at His inconsistent followers, and vainly seek to justify their own choice of eternal perdition by that inconsistency; not one film of shade will they find on *Him*. Because of that, a far higher Will than that of Chief-priest or Ruler, of Scribe or Pharisee, makes His sepulchre bear its testimony to His perfection, and that it was not for Himself that that bitter cry had rung out: "Eli, Eli, lama sabachthani." Reader, you and I know for whom that was.

We come to the last and Deuteronomic section of this Pentateuch; and, as Deuteronomy is a summing up of God's ways with Israel, when, with their desert journeys past, they stand on the borders of their inheritance, and see their own fair land across the interposing river, so here, the path of the Servant is reviewed. His wilderness journey is over, and we may see Him standing here looking forward to that long life that is before Him, even length of days forever and ever. But little would even that satisfy the gracious love of His heart; He must have sharers in that unending day to satisfy Him, as we now see.

---

‡Mr. C. H. Burchell, of Birmingham, England.

10: Yet it hath pleased Jehovah to bruise Him,*
    To put Him to grief:
    When His soul has been made
    An offering for sin,
    His seed He shall see,
    His days shall prolong,
    And Jehovah's good pleasure
    In His hand shall go forward,
    In triumph unceasing.
11: Of the fruit of His soul's bitter travail
    Shall He see, and be well satisfied.
    By His knowledge,† My Servant, the Righteous,
    Shall make many righteous,
    Their iniquities bearing.
12: Therefore I'll give Him a portion in many,
    And He, with the mighty, the spoil shall divide;‡
    Because unto death His soul He hath poured out,
    And with the transgressors was Himself numbered;
    Yea, He Himself bare the sin of the many,
    And for transgressors He made intercession.

Of all the words ever written or spoken, surely none can equal, in their amazing depth, their most affecting significance, and the awe-compelling truth they contain, these: "*It pleased Jehovah to bruise Him.*"

With genuine fear and trembling at even touching this holy word, we must yet consider every expression in it. Who then was thus bruised? It was none but He whose pleasure it was to do the will of that very One who here is "pleased to bruise *Him!*"

If then He was so submissively obedient, why did Jehovah bruise Him—nay more, was actually *pleased* to bruise Him?

Was He moved to anger by some grievous fall in that beloved Servant? Nay; He Himself could testify that He always

---

*This word is a very strong one, as Ps. 90: 3 shows: "Thou turnest man to crushing." The word for "bruise" in Gen. 3: 15 is quite different (here *daka*, there *suph*), nor must it be permitted that Satan had any part whatever in this atoning bruising—*that* was from Jehovah only.

†The sense of the word is a divinely acquired knowledge.

‡Lit., "I will allot Him a portion in many, and with strong ones He shall allot the spoil."

did those things that pleased Him (John 8: 29); and none could convict Him of the slightest frailty, far less of sin.  Indeed, no; for the very floor of heaven must break and break again under the weight of Jehovah's delight in that one sinless, blemishless, spotless human life, and those words at His baptism and on the holy mount witness to a pleasure that was never marred.  But still is it written: *"Yet it pleased Jehovah to bruise Him!"*

What motive could have moved that almighty Arm to strike with blows that brought "grief" indeed to that beloved One? What could have induced Jehovah to inflict such suffering on Himself as a father would have in causing suffering to a son who was dear to him?

*His love for poor sinful man was such, that for him He spared not His own beloved Son.*  Measure that love then, if you can! Is there a trouble or sorrow that life or death can bring us, that we cannot go through rejoicingly if we but take *that* in?

But what as to the *"pleasure"* in bruising Him?  As that Son *delighted* to do His will, and yet that will led to such anguish that, even as only its shadow fell upon His soul, He prayed with strong cries and tears that if possible that cup might pass from Him; thus, and only thus, did it please Jehovah to bruise Him, a bruising from which His love shrank from inflicting even as did the beloved Son from suffering, but which His love for us poor sinners led Him to inflict and His Son to endure.

Let us note that it is His *soul* that is made an offering for sin: the soul that is physically represented by the blood; the soul that is the intermediate link between the spirit above and the body below, putting a hand on both; the soul that, as another has said, "seems to bear the same relation to the spirit as the woman to the man, the one predominant in emotional, as the other in mental activity, each the complement of the other; and as the sin began with *Eve's* being deceived, so it is the *soul* that is made the offering for sin."

But what is the result?  "He shall see His seed."  The corn of wheat has died and now bears much fruit in resurrection. He has suffered, even as the creature in giving birth, and these atoning measureless sufferings are the birth-pangs whence the seed springs.   None could declare His generation, for He had no seed according to nature, but spiritually how many. The Psalmist joins his voice with our prophet when he cries, "A seed shall serve Him" (Ps. 22: 30).

*"He shall prolong His days."*   "Long life shall be His, even length of days forever and ever" (Ps. 21: 4); as having that life from Him, His seed too are in a scene where death is not, and not one of them with that "life indeed," shall ever see "death indeed" (John 8: 51).

"The pleasure of Jehovah shall prosper in His hand."   These words are like a ray of sunshine on a storm-cloud, throwing a bow of promise across it.   From that dark scene on Golgotha, where it was Jehovah's pleasure to bruise Him, we see that pleasure carried on, enwrapping in an embrace from which nothing in all creation can sever, such poor guilty, sinful, erring creatures as we are!   What a joy that must be to God, since, although naught but the bruising of His beloved Son would permit His having it, He spared Him not!   That pleasure shall go on, nor cease till He has made all things new.

And what of Him who suffered?   *"He shall see His seed,"* *and in seeing them shall be "satisfied."*   How deep the Love of which those few words tell!   He might at any moment during His life have gone back to the Bosom whence He came; but He would not have returned there satisfied.   He might have been spared the shame and anguish of the cross; but still He would not have been satisfied.   He might have been raised from the dead, and gone alone back to the right hand of God where there are pleasures forevermore; but even there amid even those pleasures He would have been forever *dissatisfied*.   But see those myriads, not one of whom has not known sin and its consequences of sorrow and suffering, not one that was not an heir of wrath, and now not one before whom does not stretch an eternity of joy, all owed to Him—it is these that He sees with Himself, and He *is satisfied*.   Oh, to know the love that indeed passeth knowledge!

"By His knowledge" is not the knowledge that His people may acquire of Him, for the Spirit of God here is focussing our hearts on the Lord alone, and this word attributing knowledge to

Him links the last series with the first. For as there it was predicated of that Servant that He would "act prudently," so here it is by that knowledge or prudence acquired "morning by morning" that He learns of the path laid out for Him, culminating in justifying many by bearing their iniquities.

The ordinary reading of verse 12 is, at least, questionable, even though supported by the Revision. It seems an anomaly that as a recompense for those humiliations and sufferings that can have no rivalry, the Sufferer should *only* share among, and on a level with others who had and could have no part in them. So strongly does the Spirit resent any creature having such a place, that, if the Hebrew words used will justly permit the avoidance of this rivalry, apparently so unseemly, we are strongly attracted to such a rendering, whilst keeping a curb on the slightest deviation from plain Scripture which never needs defence. Now there is precisely the same construction in Job 39: 17: "Neither hath He imparted to her understanding." Let us put the two passages side by side and they would read literally thus:

| Job 39: 17 | Isaiah 53: 12 |
|---|---|
| "He hath not given her a lot in understanding." | "I will give him a lot in many." |

Here there would appear no ambiguity; but just as God has *not* imparted "understanding" to the ostrich, He *has* imparted these "many" to His Servant. The ostrich does not divide *with* understanding—that would be meaningless—but just so our Lord does not divide *with* the many. The many are not those who share with this unrivaled Servant, but are themselves the objects apportioned to Him, and here the reference would appear to be to the Gentiles.*

As to the second clause, "He shall divide the spoil with (*eth*)†

---

*Many Hebraists have adopted this; for instance, the Septuagint reads: "Therefore He shall inherit many;" Luther: "I will give Him a great multitude for booty;" Birks: "I divide Him a portion from the many."

†The *beth*, meaning "in," as in the previous clause, is in this turned to *eth*, meaning "with," which makes the difference, as in text.

the strong," it is by no means as certain that we should follow those who, as Luther, render, "And He shall have the strong for spoil," for the preposition changes, and as we again have a close parallel in another scripture, this must at least have its weight with us.   Prov. 16: 19 is a construction that closely corresponds, and reads, "Than to divide the spoil with (*eth*) the proud," and in this light I have felt compelled to translate as above.   But who then are these "strong ones?"   They must be His "willing people," who, like their ancestors, the Maccabees, "out of weakness were made strong" (Heb. 11: 34), and who shall also "do exploits" (Dan. 11: 32).   He, as once before, identifies Himself with, and takes His place at the head of, that people, with whom He will divide the spoil of His and their enemies: "When I have bent Judah for Me, filled the bow with Ephraim, and raised up thy sons, O Zion, against thy sons, O Greece, and made thee as the sword of a mighty man" (Zech. 9: 13).   Of this too we have a God-given illustration in him who was so strong a type of Messiah, David, as we see him dividing the spoil with Israel (1 Sam. 30: 26-31).   If then I am correct, the earlier allusion would be to the hostile *Gentile*, the later to the penitent *Israel*, the believing remnant.   The former become His spoil which He divides with the latter.

Once again the text leads us to ask, "Why this exaltation?" and again the answer comes in four reasons:

1. He hath poured out His soul unto death;
2. He was numbered with the transgressors;
3. He bare the sin of many;
4. He made intercession for the transgressors.

How thoroughly Deuteronomic is this in its character of a comprehensive review of all that has been said.   Oh, the depth of the love of God to poor mankind!   He exalts His Son *because* of that death that permits Him to pour blessings on the lost race!   Every display of Christ's love to man calls out fresh love from His Father's heart.   *"Therefore doth My Father love Me, because I lay down My life that I might take it again"* (John 10: 7).   Have we not gathered some delight from that? Was there ever a moment when the Father did *not* love the Son with infinite tenderness?  Yet He, that Son, here says that all other love is, as it were, eclipsed in this, that He laid down His life for the sheep, that He might take it again in resurrection, so as to communicate a life free from all condemnation to His poor people!  *Therefore* His Father loves Him.  I say again, who can measure the love of God the Father to poor men—aye to us! aye to me!  This is the divine motive for true holiness.

Let us not then for one moment do Him the dishonor of thinking that the "intercession for transgressors" is to win for them the favor of a stern, austere God.  Not the intercession of Blastus with "highly displeased" Herod (Acts 12) affords the divine illustration to *His* intercession; rather turn to Queen Esther, who in her own personal beauty, and adorned with her royal splendors, moved the affections of the king, so that when the golden sceptre was held out to her, every single one of her countrymen was as safe as she herself (Esther 5).  But what is the poor shadow to the Substance?  What can figure the delight of God in His Son, as He returns to Him after pouring out His soul to death, being numbered with transgressors, and bearing the sins of many?  Does that beloved Son need to bend the knee and appeal with such earnest supplication as shall even change the attitude of an unwilling God?  Far, far from that.  Those atoning marks of His beauty that permit longing love to come forth to the poorest of His people, themselves make such an intercession to Him that there is no obstruction to the free-flowing of that love.  If there be any such barrier it must be found in cold, suspicious human hearts.

Thus, as we see Him ascending from Olivet with His hands raised in blessing, so do we part with Him here, still interceding for those whose sins He bore; and he who tells us all this is the prophet who is speaking for Israel, "mourning in bitter sorrow, the lateness of its love."

# CHAPTER FIFTY-FOUR

**The joy that ever follows faith in the atoning sufferings of Christ. The harmony between heaven and earth. The one city composed of street and wall. The old limits of Jerusalem must be extended. The everlasting strength and tenderness of Jehovah's love for Israel.**

HOW fitting it is that the very first word that we hear, whether it be in the original Hebrew or in our translation of it, is "Sing." Dispensations may change, a heavenly calling may replace an earthly, but wherever the gospel is heard and in heart accepted, there is, and ever will be, "great joy in that city" (Acts 8: 8), and joy finds its expression in song.

1: Sing, O thou barren, thou who didst bear not!
   Break forth into singing, with joy cry aloud,
   O thou who with child didst not travail!
   For more are the children of her who was widowed,
   Than of her who was married, Jehovah doth say.

2: Enlarge the place of thy tent!
   The curtains that make up thy dwelling
   Let them outstretch!
   Hinder it not!
   Lengthen thy cords!
   Strengthen thy stakes!

3: For thou shalt break forth on right hand and left,
   Thy seed, of the Gentiles, shall take full possession,
   And cause to be filled with their dwellers
   Desolate cities.

4: Fear not, O fear not; thou shalt not be ashamed;
   Set reproach at defiance, for ne'er shalt thou blush!
   The shame of thy youth thou shalt no more remember,
   Reproach of thy widowhood shalt thou forget.

5: Thy Maker's thy husband,
   Jehovah His name, Jehovah of Hosts,
   Thy Kinsman-Redeemer,
   The Holy One of Israel,
   The God of the whole of the earth
   Shall He be called!

6: For as a wife who has been forsaken,
   Her spirit burdened with sorrow,
   So Jehovah hath called thee;
   Aye, as a wife in youth wedded,
   Yet who has since been despised,
   Saith thy God!
7: Short has the moment been that I've forsaken thee,
   Great the compassions in which I'll regather thee.
8: In quick burst of anger My face I hid from thee,
   With kindness unending shall mercy be on thee,
   Saith thy Redeemer, Jehovah!
9: For this is to Me as the waters of Noah!
   For as I have sworn that the waters of Noah
   Shall nevermore cover the earth,
   So have I sworn that I nevermore
   Will be angry with thee,
   Never again will rebuke thee!
10: For mountains may go, and hills be removed,
    But My lovingkindness from thee shall go—never!
    Nor shall My cov'nant of peace be removed,
    So saith Jehovah who loves thee!

How fitting, let me say again, is that first word "Sing!" coming directly after the atoning work of the Lord Jesus, for joy in this scene of sorrow is one of the very best testimonies to the efficacy of that work. Here then, that efficacy is first applied to Jerusalem, the city that is destined to be the joy of the whole earth (Ps. 48: 2), but no one can communicate joy who is not himself filled with it, so Jerusalem must begin the psalmody. This earth is here the sphere of this singing, not anywhere above or below it, for there are surely no "nations" as such, anywhere else than on the earth. Neither national nor sectarian distinctions can exist in heaven. Its very atmosphere slays separation, cherishes unity. But whilst this is undeniable, it would appear equally so that this singing on earth is in full harmony with similar singing in heaven, and that there is such accord between the saints on earth and those in heaven, that their notes at this time make one perfect melody. Are we not distinctly told *that?* Does not the book of Revelation (chap. 14) reveal to us a scene in heaven in which twenty-four elders offer the prayers of the saints on earth (Rev. 5: 8), and later we see "harpers," and hear

them "harping with their harps?" But that is not all; the song
that they sing is learned and sung by 144,000—that mystic number that stands for the remnant of Israel's tribes on the earth;
and on earth none but that 144,000 can sing that heavenly song,
for none but they have gone through the experiences that alone
give it birth. So the song begins in heaven; but on Mount Zion,
which is on earth, another part of that one orchestra stands, as it
swells even the melody of heaven. So here in our prophet, it is
Jerusalem on the earth that is bidden to sing; but so closely
identified is the heavenly Jerusalem with that on earth during
that millennial day, of which this speaks, that together they make
up one city; and thus the same Spirit who spoke through Isaiah,
spoke through Paul, and applies these very words to the saints
of the present day, or "Jerusalem which is above" (Gal. 4: 21-
31).

We must not press this so far as to take the whole prophecy
away from the Jew altogether, and apply it solely to the Church,
leaving Israel cast away permanently—*that* all Scripture clearly
forbids. Nor, indeed, can this whole prophecy be applied to the
Church; for, *as in Christ,* God *never* hides His face from her "in
a little wrath;"* nor is the figure of a married wife applied to the
Church, but that of a "chaste virgin" (2 Cor. 11: 2); so that the
whole scope of Scripture demands that this address be seen as
directed *primarily* to the penitent remnant, representing the redeemed nation.

Here we have a widespread difficulty: how is it that the
apostle—and, we may say, God the Holy Spirit—applies this verse
in Gal. 4 to the heavenly Jerusalem? We have thought that the
Old Testament prophets knew nothing of that. How then could
it be so applied? This has not only perplexed many, but has
been misused to obliterate all distinction between the calling of
Israel to blessings on the earth and that of the Church to blessings in the heavens. In all such difficulties it is vitally important

---

*The Hebrew again has the rhyming so characteristic of Isaiah,
*b'shetzeph quetzeph,* which together signify a burst of wrath like
a thunderclap, but of short duration. Compare, "His anger is but
for a moment" (Ps. 30: 5).

to consider the peculiar needs and dangers of those who are addressed. The Galatians were being attracted away, by certain false brethren, from "the grace of Christ," to "works of the law" as the basis of acceptance with God. The question then is as to which of the two covenants that had been made with Israel. Promise or Law, Grace or Legality, were they to be attached? Will they adopt the bondwoman Hagar to be their mother, or the free-woman Sarah? The former represented the Jerusalem that "now is" (note, it is not said "on earth," for there is still to be one on earth, of the free-woman), and is in bondage with all her children. The latter represents Jerusalem above which is as free as was Abraham's wife. It is the great conflict of all the ages; on which principle are we accepted—by law or grace? In that respect, there is literal unity between the Jerusalem that shall be the metropolis of the millennial earth and the Jerusalem above. As far as the basis of their eternal blessedness is concerned, they are a unit, and both may and will "sing" of perfect acceptance on one and the same principle of free grace; that free grace is far more productive of fruit to God than the marriage with law.

Verse 2 shows that the old limits of the city shall be so extended as to be figured by lengthening of the cords that hold a tent with the forcing of the stakes down deeper. Nor must she, Jerusalem, hinder the workman in doing this, as if it were unnecessary, for on all sides shall she grow.

But will there not linger, as a sad memory, all her past sorrow and shame? Will not the thought of Babylon, and the shame of her captivity there, bring a blush to her cheek? Never! For her God bids her forget it all, or only think of it as a cause of fresh joy and singing at the contrast with her present condition. Just as a poor sinful one today may well remember the shameful past, but as a stimulus to, and not a check on his present joy; not to throw the shadow of a question on the value of the Blood of Christ, nor of his own perfect and never-to-be-broken acceptance with God, as based on that value.

Rationalistic criticism delights to speak of Jehovah as the "tribal deity of the Jews." How different is the grand claim of verse 5! He is indeed the Redeemer of Israel, but of all "hosts" is He Lord whether in heaven or earth, and a God whose claims, as far as this earth is concerned, are only limited by its bounds.

What a delightful term is that by which He next speaks of His people, "A wife of youth," when affections are freshest, and most tender; and though there has intervened a long period of apparent estrangement, Jehovah's first love has never cooled, and now He calls her to His heart again, compassionating her desolation, even though it be due to her own sin.

Yes, He was compelled to forsake *her,* in the day of her forsaking *Him;* but now that penitent tears well from her eyes, His arms are wide-stretched, and as a father gathers to his bosom the child he has been compelled to chastise, with a joy that far exceeds that of the one thus restored, so does Jehovah as He cries: "It is meet that we make merry and be glad, for it was but in a temporary burst of anger in which I hid My Face, for a moment, but with never-ending lovingkindness will I cherish My beloved earthly people."   This surely applies no less to His poor people in Christ, who have nothing on earth to rival Him. It is a lovingkindness, He assures us, which is as eternal as that covenant of which the bow in the cloud was, and is: the token that never again should waters destroy the earth, so never again shall waters of sorrow overwhelm Israel: more sure is this than the stability of the everlasting mountains.

In the second part of this section, we hear, as in so many *seconds* of Scripture, of a foe to God's people, Israel, and in view of that opponent, their representative city, Jerusalem, is addressed, as being their mother.

11: O thou afflicted, storm-tossed and comfortless,
        Fair are the colors I'll place in thy stones;
        Thy very foundations I'll make to be sapphires;
12: Thy minarets all, with rubies shall shine,
        Thy gates with glistening jewelry;
        Lovely the stones that shall mark out thy borders.
13: Thy children shall all be taught of the Lord:
        Yes, perfect the peace of thy children!
14: In righteousness shall thy foundations be sunken:
        From anxiety far, naught shalt thou fear!
        From terror removed, it shall not come a-nigh thee!
15: Lo, armies are leaguing, 'tis not of My will,
        Who leagues against thee, by thee shall they fall.

16: Behold, it is I who've created the smith,
    Who blows up the coals into fire,
    And by his skill formeth a weapon.
    'Tis I who've created the one who destroys,*
    That he should go forth and lay waste.
17: But never a weapon that's formed against thee,
    Shall ever have aught of success:
    And every tongue that riseth 'gainst thee
    In judgment thou shalt condemn.
    This is their lot, Jehovah who serve,
    And their righteousness cometh from Me,
    Saith Jehovah.

Jehovah has not been ignorant of Jerusalem's sorrows—not a tear has escaped His attention; not a sigh that He has not heard; and now that she is fully restored, He will let His affection be told by the beauties that He puts on her. The very cement used in her walls shall be itself a beauty. But there must be a worthier and deeper reason than a mere literal reading can give in the recital of this adornment of Jerusalem with precious stones. For instance, her foundations are to be sapphires, and to press this into literalness would be to destroy the intent of the Scripture, for the foundation of a city is not even visible. But the deep spiritual truth told by that stone is nothing less than divine, as we may see.

Take the garments of the High Priest. We know well that the breastplate which glistened in the Light of God, told out, in the varied beauties of its stones, the glories of that Light which was itself invisible. For God is Light; and Him no man hath seen nor can see, nor could any single stone possibly express all the loveliness that dwells in Him; but all have been told out by that only begotten Son, who is "in the bosom of the Father, and hath declared Him" (John 1: 18).

As we know, light itself is a trinity, and every flame may be distinguished into three parts; the invisible in the centre; then the visible or light-giving, and that in its turn is surrounded by an invisible bordering of chemical or actinic rays, which effect

---

*I have been tempted to render this by the Greek *Apollyon,* for that is found in the Septuagint, and it takes our thoughts to the greatest of destroyers.

actual changes in that to which they are applied.  Apply the simple parable.* *God, in His essential Deity, is the invisible Centre of all; and is only declared by the visible Light-giving Son; but this revelation is only made effective to men by the operation of the unseen Spirit, corresponding with that part of the flame that tells of changes wrought by the divine Spirit in those subject to His leading, changes far beyond all earthly chemistry.

Thus too we all know that there are three primary colors: Yellow (or Golden), Red and Blue, again telling precisely the same truth as to the divine Trinity.  The Golden speaks of His *essential Deity;* the human color, Red, expresses the second Person who became *Man;* whilst the Blue speaks eloquently enough of that *heavenly* Spirit, who is leading us, His people, back to the heaven whence He came.

But further: What makes our sky to be blue?  Take a balloon and ascend some miles, and all the blue disappears; we have only starlit darkness above us.  Nor is such an ascent needed.  Let the sun sink from sight and almost at once the blue has gone and the canopy over us is black.  Again, how precious is this parable of nature!  It is the sun's rays, coming down to our atmosphere, that make the heavens to be blue.  So it is Christ coming from God—the very brightness of His glory—into this earth, who gives us to discern the grace, mercy, and peace, of which the "blue" ever speaks, in God as our Father.

Let us then return to the city's foundations, "sapphires." Their color speaks of what we should learn.  God has painted the ceiling of man's dwelling, this earth, with this lovely tint, which, whenever he looks upward shall speak to him of the *grace* that no storm that sweeps across life's sky can forever hide.  Clouds may veil the "blue" for a time, but the clouds are swept away, and there is still the sapphire-blue unchanged and unaffected. Precious truth! Well it is for us to remember that as Jerusalem's foundations are in sapphires, so are we to be rooted and grounded in that unchanging *love* whereof the sapphire speaks.

The word rendered in the Authorized Version "agates," which,

---

*The tri-unities of the universe are elaborated in "The Secret of the Universe," by Dr. Nathan Wood—a remarkable book.

with the Revised Version, I have translated by "rubies," is still
somewhat uncertain; but there can at least be no question as to
its being such a jewel as made every minaret, pinnacle, and bat-
tlement sparkle as with the flashing of rubies; and with this the
gates are in accord with their "stones as of fire" telling out her
royal glories in all directions.

So much for the externals; but what of the internal condition?
Every single dweller therein (ver. 13) shall be in very truth
a child of God.  No longer are they the children of Hagar, the
bondwoman, but of Sarah, the free.  Abraham is himself a figure
of faith, and when human faith is united with divine grace, the
result is children that are the source of joy to God, as the name
Isaac (laughter) surely implies.

We will not be envious of our brethren on the earth in that
future day, but rejoice that our God shall have there one people
that shall ever be delightful to Him, and give Him the laughter
of Isaac.  But neither will we refrain from extracting some delight from these precious stones being even put upon us.  For
if we are walking in the Spirit, then a string of jewels (Gal. 5:
22, 23) adorns us, and Jerusalem will never show greater glories,
when seen in a divine light, than may we.  We must not be
occupied with that, however, for it led to that crashing downfall
of Lucifer, whose "heart was lifted up because of his beauty"
(Ezek. 28:17).  No; the Spirit of God never occupies us with our
own spiritual graces, or beauty, but with that of our Lord; and
in occupation with Him alone are we changed into the same image
from glory to glory (2 Cor. 3:18). It is this sorrowful self-occupation that makes that change so very slow in some of us; but when
actually in the glory of heaven, we shall be delivered from that
altogether, as was the "man in Christ" who was caught up to "the
third heaven" (2 Cor. 12); so free was he from self-intrusion
there, that he actually did not know whether he was in the
body or out of it!  So, dear fellow-learner in the school of God,
do we grow up from "little children," through the grade of
"young men," till that gracious, patient Teacher brings us to the
last grade here of "fathers," which is attained when we really
"know Him that is from the beginning."  We can never get
beyond *that*.  There is no advance from the knowledge of Christ,

and great is the peace of all those who have experimentally learned that they have come to their end in the Cross, and Christ—the living, risen, all-satisfying Christ—is their ALL.  Do we not re-echo that cry: "O that I may know Him!"  It is this that gives peace, perfect peace, and by it the Lord's words are carried out: "Take My yoke upon you, and learn of Me: for I am meek and lowly in heart, and ye shall find rest unto your souls" (Matt. 11: 29).

But to return: That much-besieged city may again have gatherings against it, but let her not think that it is a repetition of the day when the armies of Babylon encompassed her.  The past was for *her* chastening; the future shall be for *their* destruction.  Neither at that day nor in the one that even then shall be far in the future (Rev. 20: 9) must they think that their Lord has any part in such hostility.  Far from that, He then shall be not against, but for her, and if her enemies dash against her, it shall be for them as when an earthen pitcher strikes a rock.  Can we too not say, "If God be for us, who can be against us?"

In the last two verses Jehovah says: "Do not think of your adversaries, however powerful they may be, as being beyond My control.  For as the smith makes a weapon, and another takes that weapon and uses it, it is I who am behind the smith, and I never lose My control of the weapon he makes.  So remember that it is I who have created the destroyer, whoever he may be; whether hostile man or still more hostile spirit, he is but a creature; I am his Creator, and hold him ever in leash."

Who can fail to discern here an allusion, and by no means an obscure one, to the great "destroyer" (Abaddon or Apollyon) of our race?  If there should be any question of this, look at the next verse, 17.  We too have foes innumerable, armed with weapons that they know well how best to use, sometimes throwing a fiery dart, and again seeking our overthrow with subtle wile.  Let us appropriate the comfort here given to the earthly people, for we, who are through grace in Christ, surely have title to these exceeding great and precious promises, and no weapon, whether dart or wile, formed against the feeblest in Christ shall ever be permitted to destroy them.  Nay, more; the picture changes from a battlefield to a court of justice; and there is

Apollyon again in other guise. Now, in apparent zeal for the righteousness of God's Throne, that he was, as the cherub appointed, to cover, or shield from taint (Ezek. 28), he *accuses* us day and night, nor does he ever accuse of what is false. Those whom he accuses are not innocent people; they are guilty of all that he brings against them. Yet it is *he*, and *not they* who shall be justly condemned in that High Court of Divine Justice!

Marvellous secret! But, God be praised, we have learned it, for it is our accuser who is found guilty of denying the unassailable righteousness that has taken full note of all our sins—aye, of the very nature that is sin—that has not winked at the slightest lapse, but has exacted a full penalty, without any modification. Since that penalty has been fully paid, it is *righteousness* itself that now demands our complete justification, and *unrighteousness* that would deny it. Something very striking follows from this: when one accuses another falsely, the accuser becomes as guilty as the accused would have been, had the accusation been justified. Nor is it difficult to see the justice of this. If, for instance, I accuse a man of murder, the penalty of which is death, then do I aim at *his death,* and if there be no just ground for the accusation, I become the murderer. That is the principle here. So perfectly freed are the redeemed, so thoroughly is justice satisfied by the full penalty having been borne, and not a vestige of guilt left, that the accuser, ignoring this, is himself guilty. To use a legal phrase, his case is thrown out of court; and we may go still further, and see *him* thrown out too! (Rev. 12).

This freedom from all condemnation is the inheritance of all who, deriving their life from, also share the lot of that Servant, and so are themselves, as here, servants. Putting this truth into New Testament language, they are "heirs of God and joint-heirs with Christ." As such, they may all take up the triumph-cry: "Who shall lay anything to the charge of God's elect? It is God who justifieth" by having wrought such a perfect righteousness for them that they can look even that keen-eyed enemy in the face as they ask, "Who is he that condemneth?"

# CHAPTER FIFTY-FIVE

**The third of a triad of chapters, in which the glad tidings goes to the Gentiles. The only prerequisite is thirst. What are the sure mercies of David? No man that ever lived capable of inventing the gospel of God, it must be therefore divine. A parable of nature. All nature called to assist in praise.**

THESE three chapters, 53, 54 and 55, form in themselves one of those significant triads that characterize our book. The first—chapter 53—gives the groundwork in the sufferings of the Cross; then, in chapter 54, the efficacy of those sufferings announced to Israel; and now in chapter 55 we come to their world-wide proclamation to all men.

> 1: Ho! Every thirsty one, come ye to the waters;
> And he that hath no silver, come ye, buy and eat!
> Come, both milk and honey buy, without a price or pay-
> ment.
> 2: Why weigh out your silver for that which is not bread?
> Why spend the fruit of all your toil for what gives no
> content?
> Listen then, O list to Me,* and eat ye what is good,
> So let your soul luxuriate in fatness.
> 3: Incline your ear and come to Me;
> Hear, and your soul shall live.
> A cov'nant I'll make with you that shall be everlasting:
> E'en that on which do safely rest the mercies sure of
> David.
> 4: Behold, I have appointed Him a witness to the peoples,
> A leader and commander of the peoples He shall be.
> 5: Behold, then thou shalt call to a nation that thou knowest
> not,
> And nations shall run unto thee to whom thou wert
> unknown!
> And that because Jehovah, Israel's Most Holy One,
> [Jehovah] thine own Elohim hath covered thee with glory.

Now the Spirit of God lifts up voice loudly, for this is no whispering word of prophecy, but a call as from a silver trumpet.

---

*It is very emphatic: "listening, listen," justifying the repetition.

It begins with a cry of a "Ho!" for now the glad tidings of what those sufferings have effected must go to the furthest bounds of human dwelling, and wherever there is a burdened, a sorrowing, a dissatisfied heart, there this silvery invitation is welcomed.

Is it not beautifully appropriate that such a call should be broadcast with trumpet-strength that it may reach afar to all, awaken the attention of all? Thus the "Ho" must not be overlooked. Nor is it less appropriate that the intimate communications of prophecy should be, as it were, whispered, that only those that are near the divine Speaker can hear them—*they* are not meant for the careless at all.

Let us listen then, as if we had never heard the melody of this tender and gracious invitation before. Who are the guests here invited? *All who thirst!* All that is needed to be welcome then, is—not to *need* (for that is true of all)—but to *want* what is offered. Am I utterly dissatisfied with myself? I thirst! Am I dissatisfied with all the world can offer me, and of which I have tasted? I thirst! Is my spirit altogether dissatisfied with all the formalism of religion; then do I thirst! Blessed thirst! It is the only prerequisite to enjoyment! Let us then delight ourselves, not only in the freedom, but in the gracious insistency seen here in the threefold cry of "Come!" "Come!" "Come!" First for "water," of which there is such an abundance that the word must be in the dual. No one can live long without water; it is really man's life; and so symbolizes the Spirit as Life-Giver, for He alone gives and maintains it, and that by the Word of God, which is therefore included in the symbol. Water thus comes first, as the first need is to infuse our spirits with divine *life*. Then "wine" for the soul, to fill it with joy; for wine* is itself the very symbol of joy. Finally, come for "milk," for we must not forget that we need constantly that "milk of the Word, that we may grow thereby." All three are quite free now, for all have been paid for by Him who holds them out to us for our acceptance. Do you not recognize the voice of the Speaker as His who cried: "If any man thirst let him come unto Me and

*Here the word for wine is *yayin*, which many insist is always the pernicious kind of wine; could it be that here?

drink" (John 7: 37). We are like those water-pots in Cana, quite empty, but let us be filled with the "water" of life, and instantly this becomes through His divine alchemy, the "wine" of joy.

What gracious, what convincing reasoning! You are spending all the labor of your one short life, and for what? For wealth, pleasure, name and fame? Why, that is not "bread"— these will not satisfy. Do we not all know it?

We have within us what nothing of that kind will ever satisfy. Then wherefore toil for such? When this one short span of life is passed, and there is nothing to show for the pursuits in which we have passed it, but the soul departs, still hungering and, alas, to hunger forever, is it not a reasonable question: "Why weigh ye out your silver for that which is not bread? Why spend the fruit of all your toil in what gives no content?"

In contrast with this vain spending, just listen—do nothing but listen; and if the heart takes in what the ear hears, then shall it be drinking of the very waters of life. How quick the God of all grace is to respond even to the inclination of the ear!

So incline your ear to Me, saith the Lord. Shut out all the vain babble of the world; listen not to its promises, have you not proved them false? Heed not its threats nor its contempt! Lend *Me* your ears, and listen; for more than your natural life depends upon it.

Have you never heard an address being given, but without awakening any special interest, till a subject is touched that instantly controls the attention of every listener? A strange hush comes over the audience, not a foot moves, not a rustle of a garment breaks the spell, so that one "may hear a pin drop." Just so, this Speaker has that to tell which none in the universe but He can tell—secrets of the very Bosom of God in which He has dwelt from all eternity, and whence He comes to tell them—shall we not listen, spellbound?

What then does He say? "I will make an everlasting covenant with you, even the sure mercies of David!" Are you disappointed? Did you expect something simpler than that? That is to prove whether we are really thirsty, and want the water, are really hungry, and long for the milk: if so, we shall not go away offended, but stop and ponder the words.

Let us then turn to 2 Samuel 7: 1-6. David is ashamed to
be living in a house of cedar whilst the Ark is dwelling in curtains. The Lord sees and interprets according to His grace the
desire of that faithful heart; but forbids the building, since
David's hands have shed much blood, and well-established Peace
is the only ground on which the House of God can be built, and
David's son, whose very name, Solomon, means Peace, shall
build that house.

But how often do we see the near-by fulfilment of a prophecy
pass away as a shadow, and leave the true definitive fulfilment
still to come. So was it with Solomon. The throne that he
passed on to his sons was overturned; the house that he built was
soon in ruins; *he* was but the shadow, the Substance was still to
come.

And in due time He comes, presents Himself to Israel as their
true Messiah, Jesus, David's Son, but also David's Lord. He is
rejected, slain, and Israel's hopes seem forever buried in that
tomb of Joseph of Arimathea. Where now is that "everlasting
covenant ordered in all things and sure?" Where now are the
"sure mercies of David?"

Let us go to Antioch of Pisidia and listen to a preacher in
the Jewish synagogue. He says: "We declare unto you glad tidings, how that the promise which was made unto the fathers, God
hath fulfilled the same unto us their children, in that He hath
hath raised up* Jesus; as it is also written in the second psalm,
Thou art My Son, this day have I begotten Thee. And as concerning that He raised Him up from the dead, no more to return to corruption, He said on this wise, I will give you the sure
mercies of David" (Acts 13: 32-34).

Do we not see that no "mercy" could be made "sure" for
poor sinning Jews, still less such poor sinners of the Gentiles
as you and I are, my fellow-sinner—my fellow-saint—except in
our sins being forever put away in sternest justice; and they
have—*they have!* "He was delivered for our offences, and was
raised for our justification:" and high above principalities and
powers, He sits, whose sacred Head was weighted with our sins;

---

*"Again" should be omitted. See R. V.

the sins are gone forever, and "mercies" are so founded on justice that they are forever "sure." No justice is marred; no stain is on the Throne of God in embracing in an everlasting clasp such creatures as we! Verses 4 and 5 tell us that those mercies go far beyond Israel, for "He is not the God of the Jews only, but of the Gentiles also," and those Gentiles are thirsty and hungry to know the disposition of their God towards them. Neither the beauties of nature nor the marvels of Providence can afford a satisfactory testimony as to that. But here is One who has been given to be just the needed Witness, and eagerly does every awakened conscience run to Him, who alone meets their deepest needs.

6: Seek ye Jehovah while He may be found,
   Call ye upon Him while He is near:
7: Let the wicked man forsake his evil way;
   Let the man unrighteous turn from his evil thoughts;
   And let him thus return to Jehovah.
   Who will (surely, most surely) meet him with His mercy;
   Let him to our God return, who will freely much forgive.
8: For My thoughts are not as your thoughts,
   Nor My ways like unto yours, saith Jehovah.
9: For high as are the heavens stretched above the earth,
   So higher are My ways far above your own,
   And My thoughts soar high above all your thinking.
10: As the rain and the snow come from out the heavens
    And ne'er do they return till they've watered all the earth,
    And thus have fertilized it, made its vegetation spring,
    Affording seed to sower, and bread to him who eats,
11: So never shall My word that goeth from My mouth,
    Return to Me without its bearing fruit;
    But surely shall accomplish that which I desire,
    And surely shall it prosper in that for which I sent it.

There are those who object to the use of these words as a gospel-call on the ground that God seeks man, and not man God. But God seeks men by leading them to seek Him, as John 6: 37: "All that the Father giveth Me shall come to Me, and him that cometh to Me I will in no wise cast out." And again, "Every man that hath heard and learned of the Father cometh unto Me" (verse 45). Human responsibility has its place; human will has its power in the gospel. It is not only God quickening dead souls, but men hearing God's voice, believing and acting on that belief, "By grace are ye saved *through faith;*" yet is it impossible to place these in any order of time.   When God is seen coming in Christ in such unparalleled grace, not to judge, condemn, strike, curse, or damn; but to bless, save, at awful cost, and love everlastingly, then men will as inevitably seek Him as a hungry babe flies to its mother's breast.

Beloved reader, we may boldly assert that no man of all the myriads that have lived—let him be the wisest, as Solomon, the very best, as Job—not one could have possibly invented from his own "thoughts" this gospel.   It is thus that our apostle challenges refutation when he cries: "But I certify you, brethren, that the gospel which was preached of me, is not after man" (Gal. 1: 11). That means that it was absolutely impossible for such a plan of salvation ever to have been devised by man's thoughts.   It is utterly at variance with those thoughts.   It is infinitely too intricate in all its marvellous adaptations to all the involved problems that have to be met, so that no careless, thoughtless one could ever have conceived it.   He would cease to be careless!   But that eliminates the greater part of mankind; for, alas, are not the majority careless?   But could a proud man, let him be never so thoughtful and intelligent, have invented it?   Most assuredly not, for it humbles him to nothing, telling him that he is ungodly and without strength and only as in heart confessing this can he be saved.   Must he not have ceased to be proud in order to have conceived that, to have been its author?

That certainly shuts out a large number of those left.   There only remains the poor in spirit, the conscious confessed sinner. Could such have *invented* the idea that the Creator of all, glorious in holiness, fearful in praises, doing wonders, that so High, so Holy a One should give up His dearest Treasure to bear the sins of one like himself, so conscious as he is of his utter unworthiness? Would it be "after" a humble mind to invent such a plan?   How proud—how blasphemously proud—would such an one be!   He must have ceased to be humble to have invented it!   Then it remains proved that since no man—careless or thoughtful, proud or humble, bad or good—could have conceived it, it *must* have been a divine revelation, the result of God's thoughts and not man's.  And from our hearts we own that His thoughts are not as our thoughts; His ways are not as ours!  Indeed, they are not.

Verses 10 and 11 present another parable of nature, and how surrounded we are by these preachers of the gospel!  Evangelists are they, that speak truly in parables, but parables that are intended to be understood, and so to preach.  In that magnificent call for all creation to join in one melodious diapason of praise in Psalm 148, we read: "Fire and hail, snow and vapour, stormy wind fulfilling His word."  And do they not do that in a very profound sense?  Let us consider the rain that is called to witness here.  It descends from heaven, which is, we may say, its source: so the word that God speaks comes from Him—*He* is its Source.  The rain falls on the thirsty earth, so the Word falls on man's dry and thirsty spirit. Rain falls indifferently on mountain and on valley, but the hard, lofty mountain casts it off, and the valleys receive and profit by it.  So the Word of God is for all; but lofty pride casts it off, and lowly penitence takes it in.  The rain softens the clods, and this permits the seed to suck its nourishment from the earth, and thus the earth is rendered—what it could not be at all, but for the rain—fertile, and so is covered with every form of vegetable life, grass, herb and tree.  So where the Word is received the fruit of love, joy, and peace abounds.  Then the harvest provides for a future reproduction as well as for the present nourishment of men.  So the Word of God wherever it falls and sinks in, not only produces a corresponding harvest, and there is bread for the hungry, but there is, too, seed for further sowing.  No one truly receives the gospel without wanting to propagate it.  It must flow on, it cannot stagnate.  Finally, the rain is drawn back to the heavens, and so the Word of the Gospel goes back to God, accompanied as it were, by the singing joy of those who have partaken of its blessing.  Thus the last verses go on:

12: With joy shall ye go forth; in peace shall ye be led;
    Before you shall the mountains and hills burst forth in
       song;
    The very trees that stud the field with joy shall clap their
       hands.

13: In the place where grew the thorn, shall then spring up the
   cypress;
 In the place where grew the brier shall then spring up the
   myrtle;
 For the name and the fame of Jehovah this shall be,
 For an everlasting sign that shall ne'er be swept away.

Truly a refreshing picture, telling in the highest style of
poetry, the effect of an inward change on external scenes. In
grief even the twinkling of the stars is sad and ghastly, and the
rippling of the brooks loses all its cheeriness, its laughter sounds
as mockery, for the heart within is not attuned, and would fain
have the sights and sounds of nature to accord with its own
misery. But let strong emotion fill the heart with delight, the
witchery of that joy changes all the external scene into harmony
with itself. I expect some of my readers can remember how all
nature appeared to share their joy when the Lord revealed Himself to them in His love; did not everything sing?

With no haste, as if in flight, with no fighting, as if opposed,
but in festal joy, those who were but now in the lowest depths of
distress, leave the gloom and come forth with such melody of
heart, such hand-clapping of the spirit, that it overflows all their
own being, and the surrounding woods and hills share the joy and
its expression.

This is of course poetry, yet well may we feel sure that this
poor earth, in one spot at least, will be in perfect harmony with
the redeemed Israel of that day. The evidences of the curse, the
frown of God—thorn and brier—shall disappear, and trees that
in their dignity and beauty tell of God's smile, take their place.
The nations of the earth mark the mighty change, and it becomes
a "Name," that is, expressing what Jehovah really is—it tells
Him out as does a name, and becomes a permanent Sign, forever
bearing its witness to Jehovah from age to age, just as today,
sorrow, sighing, pain, suffering, disaster, injustice and oppression
rightly express the reign of a usurper upon the throne of this
earth.

In the place of the noxious thorn springs up a tree that has
found a place in that Temple in which "every whit of it uttereth
His glory" (Ps. 29: 9, *marg.*). In the place of that pride-express-

ing brier that would reign over the trees (Judges 9: 8-15) there
shall spring up the lowly myrtle which ever speaks of the penitence that characterizes all that is of God among men, whether in
the Gentile or, more directly, in the beloved Remnant of Israel.
This "myrtle" spirit is what alone, even this day, makes any of
us "meet for the Master's use," and beyond all question it is
alone the spirit He does ever use.   Let His poor servant lie helpless upon a bed of sickness, still he may be a very useful servant,
by whom the Lord expresses the power of His grace; and *that* is
for a "Name" to our Lord Jesus; the very best evidence that He
is risen, and that the servant is abiding in Him.   Not always is it
the most active who is the most useful.

## CHAPTER FIFTY-SIX

The Sabbath linked with the Covenant. True Rest linked with the Cross. The institution of the Sabbath and our present relation to it considered. Israel's watchmen so torpid that the nations are invited to spoil. Our present day "dumb dogs."

O N the surface we now appear to be led back rather than forward, to law-keeping and strict Sabbath observance as the ground for acceptance and blessing. But, as we know this is impossible, we must not be satisfied with the surface, but must most carefully consider what is written, and "the Lord giving understanding" we shall see that we are not being led back to Sinai, but still onward in those morally clean paths that have ever marked the footsteps of the flock.

We have had the ground and cost of our redemption by the blood of Christ in Chapter 53; we have listened to the gracious call to poor Israel, as to a wife long forsaken, but ever loved (54); then to a wider call to the nations afar (55); and now what is looked for to follow all this grace? What path must be taken to reach full, perfectly enjoyed blessing, for this has not yet come, although brought near? A clean path, a path of practical holiness, shall alone evidence that all this grace has not been received in vain, so only can we have the realized companionship of our Lord (John 13).

We are not here led back to Sinai and its legal covenant, but onward to that covenant of grace that God will make with Israel in a day to come, and on the principle of which, being grace, we too are alone blessed now. But it is with Israel that the prophet primarily deals, and it is Israel that now under that new covenant whereby God's laws are written in their hearts (Heb. 8: 19) can really keep that Sabbath which is the "sign" that everything is "very good."

1: Thus saith Jehovah: Keep judgment, do right,
　　For My salvation is nearing,
　　My righteousness nears revelation.

2: Blessèd the frail man* who doeth this,
   And the son of man who doth grasp it.
   Blessed is he who My sabbath doth keep
   From pollution; his hand from all evil.
3: Nor let the son of the stranger e'er say,
   Who to Jehovah hath joined him,
   Jehovah hath severed me quite from His saints;
   Nor eunuch mourn, Lo, I'm a dry tree!
4: For thus e'en to eunuchs doth the Lord speak,
   To those who My sabbaths are keeping,
   Taking their pleasure in what pleaseth Me,
   My covenant faithfully holding,
5: To them will I give a place in My house,
   Within its fair walls, far surpassing
   A name carried on by daughters and sons:
   I will give them a name everlasting,
   That nevermore shall be cut off!
6: The sons of the stranger that cleave to the Lord
   To serve Him, Jehovah's name loving,
   Thankful His faithful servants to be;
   Yea, all that do keep from pollution
   His sabbath, and covenant hold fast:
7: Them will I bring to My holy mount,
   Glad in My prayer-house will make them.
   Their offerings burnt, their sacrifice slain,
   I'll accept when laid on My altar;
   For My house a house of prayer shall be called,
   And that shall it be for all peoples.
8: This doth Jehovah Adohnai proclaim,
   Who gath'reth Israel's outcasts,
   Others there are whom to him I'll restore,
   In addition to those I have gathered.

The prophet is standing on the verge of that reign of Christ termed the Millennium. It has not yet come, but, as in the day of John the Baptist, it is near; and little did either Isaiah or John conceive of a period of nearly two thousand years that should intervene between the sufferings of Christ and His manifested glory—a period in which the God of all grace would not be otiose, but active in carrying out purposes that were in His own Mind, though hidden until the Holy Ghost came and revealed

---

*Heb., *enosh*, the word for "man" in his frailty and mortality.

them to His holy apostles and prophets, and particularly to our apostle Paul (Eph. 3). But let us note this striking difference: in our prophet, God's redeemed people are led to His house on earth, placed on His holy mountain, but we to our *Father's House on high;* this is a characteristic distinction between the two dispensations.

When Jacob was told to go up to Bethel and dwell there, instantly he commanded his household to prepare for that, by putting away everything inconsistent with such a place (Gen. 35) So when John cried the Kingdom of Heaven is at hand, he too added: "Bring forth therefore fruits worthy of repentance" (Luke 3). So here; because Jehovah's salvation was nigh, the Spirit of Christ in the prophet cries, "Keep judgment; do right;" and to-day, with a hundred signs telling us that we are standing on the verge of the return of our long-rejected Lord, does it not become each of us to see to it that our lamps are well-trimmed, and that nothing of this world, or the flesh, be allowed inconsistent with our welcome of His shout that calls us to be with Him forever?

But you will also have noted the place given the Sabbath, and its close link with "keeping the hand from doing any evil." I find it difficult to express the importance of this divinely formed union between the Sabbath and holy living. It means this: If there be a Sabbath—no evil doings. If there are any evil-doings —no Sabbath! But let us not judge what is "evil" by our natural standards of morality. The natural conscience can pass judgment on murder or adultery, confining all its attention to what is called the second table of the law, and ignoring the first altogether. As the blood of Abel speaks, so let us permit Cain to speak to us for a minute. Look at him as he is building his altar and offering upon it the very best of his own labor. Do you think that he had the slightest idea that those very works in God's searching light were not good but evil? Would his neighbors say as they saw him thus piously engaged, "What a wicked man!" or rather, "What a good, religious man Cain is!" And yet it is those very deeds that the Spirit of God brands as "evil!" The murder of Abel was surely evil enough, yet it is not that that is so termed in 1 John 3: 12, but what preceded and led up to the murder, as it is written: "Wherefore slew he him? Because his own works were evil and his brother's righteous." The cause must come before its result. What, then, were Abel's righteous deeds? Nothing but his offering "by which he obtained witness that he was righteous" (Heb. 11: 4). What were Cain's *evil* deeds? Nothing *but his religious offering.* We can easily apply this without further aid. But with Cain's offering there can never be a Sabbath, for that was an evil deed. There can be no rest based on our religious works.

The Sabbath was to be the sign that there was no evil, of any character. If there had been any evil in Eden, aye, if one feeble groan could have been heard, would—aye, *could,* God have rested till He had hushed that groan? Will He, *can* He rest, or keep Sabbath till all again is very good? "My Father worketh hitherto and I work," said the Lord, and work is surely the opposite of rest, which the very word "sabbath" means.

That ever was, and is still, the battlefield between God and religious men, for it was not till the Lord presumed to work on the Sabbath that His enemies "took counsel together to destroy Him" (Matt. 12: 1-4). Thus the first step to the Cross was Love working on the Sabbath!

But with what divine strength is the keeping of the Sabbath here insisted upon, a strength that must not be diluted in the slightest, nor on the other hand must we close our eyes to all that the Scriptures teach with regard to it. In Eden, not till *all* was "very good" was there a sabbath. Redeemed from Egypt it was first given as a privilege expressive of Jehovah's gracious care, and not law; but some poor foolish people heed it not, and Jehovah grieves that they refuse to keep "His commandments and His laws" (Ex. 16: 27, 28); not those from Sinai surely, for that had not yet been reached, but the commands of grace of a Father to His children. *Then,* embodied in the very heart of the decalogue, with responsibilities Godward on one side, and manward on the other, is the Sabbath. What then was God's purpose in giving the decalogue? "It was added because of (for the sake of) transgressions" (Gal. 3: 19), nor does that mean to restrain transgression, for there was none at all before the law—*sin* was in the world indeed, but no trangression, for "where no law is there is no transgression" (Rom. 4: 15). The law turned sin into transgression and so worked wrath (Rom. 4: 5). In a word, the law was given to shut man's mouth entirely (Rom. 3: 19). What part then had the Sabbath in that purpose? It was given as a "sign." "Verily, My sabbaths ye shall keep, for it is *a sign* between Me and you throughout your generations, that ye may know that I am the Lord that doth sanctify you" (Ex. 31: 13), and again this is reiterated in verse 17. "Wherefore the children of Israel shall keep the sabbath, to observe the sabbath throughout their generations, for a perpetual covenant. It is a *sign* between Me and the children of Israel for ever, for in six days the Lord made heaven and earth, and on the seventh day He rested and was refreshed." Again, retrospectively: "I gave them My sabbaths to be a *sign* between Me and them, that they might know that I am the Lord that sanctify them" (Ezek. 20: 12). And again similarly in the 20th verse. This then is clearly and unequivocally the signification of the sabbath, it was a *sign*. If God could rest, as He did on the first seventh day, and Israel could rest with Him, then it became a sign that all was again "very good." But if God could *not* rest, but work, because of sin and its sad consequences, then this gracious working of God became in itself a sign that all was out of order, and there was no sabbath at all. His Love would not permit "rest" in such conditions. The impossibility of God's resting became the *sign* of a broken law, of poor man being in a pit, like that sheep of Matt. 12: 11, from which none could lift him but God. *God then has never had one sabbath from Eden to this very day,* and we, even we, do pollute the sabbath *if we make any claim to keeping it,* apart from perfect observance of the whole decalogue. And who can stand there? It was by not walking in Jehovah's statutes and despising His judgments that Israel polluted His sabbaths of old. For if they claimed it, whilst even one of these commandments was broken, they came with unclean hands and defiled that sabbath that they touched. Can we then pretend to, or claim a sabbath? One only is its Lord, for One alone has not forfeited His title to it. But our "memorial"—the day of which we would remind our God and Father, and on which we would enjoy rest with Him—is not the old creation rest based on a finished work of *creation;* but the new creation based on the finished work of *redemption,* and thus we enjoy a sabbath of rest of conscience and heart with Him, for in Christ all things are new, and all things are of God, and so all things there are indeed "very good"—blessed be His Name!   In our prophet it is a forward look, not to the present time, of which he knew nothing, but to that millennial day when the Jew will be the centre of God's ways, and when God's laws being written on their hearts they shall keep the sabbath in truth. *Now* our place in spirit is with our Lord Christ in *heaven*, and there are no "weeks" there—angels surely do not keep any sabbath day.

But greatly as these truths need pressing when men are still claiming that they can keep a sabbath with God, we must leave it, not without reluctance, and go on with our prophet.

Those who have no hope of posterity to continue their name, are promised, conditioned on basing all hopes on the new covenant of grace, a new name, better than that posterity might give to them.   No bar will there be to the stranger, but He will welcome all who, by their new nature, desire to please Him.

Verse 8 reminds us strongly of John 10: 16:   "Other sheep I have which are not of this fold, them also I must bring, and they shall hear My voice, and there shall be one flock and one Shepherd."   But in this the reference is to the present day, and we hear nothing of walls, of cities, or of holy mountains, but in Isaiah the reference is to the millennial reign of Christ over the earth.

Now under the figure of wild-beasts, the nations of the earth are invited to attack Israel, ill-guarded as she is:

> 9: Come, all ye beasts of the field,
>    Come and devour!
>    Come, all ye beasts in the forest!
> 10: Blind are his watchmen,
>    Ignorant all of them!
>    Dumb dogs are they all,
>    That cannot e'en bark!
>    Dreaming, they lie,
>    And love thus to slumber!
> 11: Greedy the dogs are,
>    Never are satisfied.
>    And these are the shepherds
>    That have no understanding.

Yea, for the whole of them
Are seeking their own gain,
E'en to the last of them!*
[And thus they speak.]
12: Come, [Come,] and I will bring wine to you,
And with strong drink will we be filled:
Then as today, so will tomorrow be,
Only [in pleasure] still more abundant!

These verses clearly show that whilst the salvation of God
as regards Israel may be near, it has not yet actually come, for
here again we see that unbelieving mass, so careless that the
hostile nations, under the figure of beasts of field and forest, are
invited to come and devour them. The picture is of a flock of
sheep. There are the watch-dogs whose duty it is to guard that
flock, but they are all sound asleep; the beasts of field or forest
need have no fear of such, they are too stupid even to bark!
They are wakeful enough when it comes to seeking their own;
but as to the flock, they cannot even discern the dangers that
threaten, they dream that all is well, and still are recumbent. So
fared it with Israel; and, alas, how history repeats itself! Is
this picture quite unlike what we see about us today? Even
weeping, must we own the sad correspondence with this, our own
time.

The beasts of the field are the surrounding nations hostile to
Israel. Come, then, we might echo, Come, ye beasts, Saracen and
Turk! No, the time for such chastening is over now. They were
used in the past centuries; but now there are others of another
character, beasts of the forest. Come, then, all ye darkness-loving
evil spirits, for few are the watchmen that are awake; the mass
of them are, as Milton termed them in his day, "blind mouths!"

Verse 12 is such an invitation as the god of this world is
ever holding out to his votaries, of pleasures unending, only that
each day shall give a still greater satisfaction. Alas, to what an
awful awakening do such invitations ever lead. "Vanity of vanities!" is the heart-cry here, and endless weeping beyond!

---

*The word rendered in A. V. "from his quarter" literally means,
"from his utmost extremity;" in other words, "throughout the
length and breadth of his own circle" (*Delitzsch*).

# CHAPTER FIFTY-SEVEN

**The Final cleavage between the Penitent and Impenitent.**

WE are now looking at the closing scenes on this earth, just prior to the revelation of its true King. The preceding chapter has given a picture of the profusion, luxury, and sensuous pleasure in which the mass are living, and now, in the strongest contrast with this, we have another smaller company who have for their portion, prison and death.

> 1: The righteous man perishes; none lays it to heart!
> The pious\* are taken, and no one considers
> That 'tis from the evil impending
> The righteous is taken away.†
> 2: He goes into peace,
> They rest on their beds,
> Each one who walketh uprightly.

We know well that sorrow will always grasp at every crumb of comfort, but that these two verses are being fulfilled today in the death of every Christian, can scarcely be esteemed satisfactory. For what discrimination is there in this respect between the pious and the profane, between the believer and the infidel? Death is a very indiscriminating executioner; he takes away all equally. It follows that what is true of the one is equally true of all, so far as impending evil on this earth goes. If the righteous are saved from it by decease, then so are the unrighteous.

The prophecy must therefore refer to some specific hour, when there is a peculiar call for light on the death of the pious alone, who are being taken away, whilst the ungodly are in ease, luxury

---

\*"Pious." Hebrew, "men of piety." The word meaning "gracious," both Godward and manward.

†The Hebrew word *"asaph"* has in it contrasted ideas, both "swept away," as in Ezek. 34: 29, and "gathered home," as Gen. 25: 8. Note how fitting these contrasted ideas are here; the righteous is slain by men, but gathered by God.

and profligacy, as in the closing verses of the preceding chapter. It is not the common lot of mankind that is in view here at all, but bitter persecution of the pious, and their slaughter under that persecution.

Today the bereaved have solid comfort in such words as that it is "far better" for those they have lost awhile, and they look forward with cheerful hope for that hour, ever drawing nearer, when the Lord shall descend from heaven with a shout, and the dead in Christ shall rise first, and *together* we shall be caught up to meet our Lord in the air. But suppose that hour to have passed; suppose the Jews back in their land with a government of their own; the mass, with Antichrist at their head, have erected an image to the "Beast," and death is the portion of all who will not worship that image (Rev. 13: 15). Think of what *that* would mean for their friends. They stand between the two "hopes;" that of being "caught up" is behind them; that of sharing in their Messiah's glorious return has not yet come; so they have apparently lost both. And, lo, they are "taken away!" Would it not need some special word? Surely it would! And they get it! It is but as a whisper here, but it rises into a strong divine voice in Revelation 14. It is precisely such an hour as we have assumed is to come; and the pious Jews are the saints who are supplying their quota of martyrs' blood to the river that has run, since the first trickle from Abel's wounds. This is the comfort given *them*: "Blessed are the dead who die in the Lord from henceforth: Yea, saith the Spirit, that they may rest from their labors, and their works do follow them."

Note the words, "from henceforth." They mark one special moment, and should not be appropriated by any of us now. It is the harmony in the interpretation of prophecy that assures us of its correctness, and both Isaiah and John, both the Old Testament and the New, refer to that "hour of trial" between the coming of the Lord for His present heavenly people and His revelation on behalf of Israel. Those slain during that interval have a heavenly place and blessing, and it is *they* whose resurrection completes that which is called the "first."

Peace was not their portion here, but to that peace they go; they have forever left the scene in which the wicked trouble, and peace unbroken lies before them now. Look at that tomb! It is blood-stained.   True; but look again through the medium of those spectacles called Faith, and lo, it is on their beds they are lying.   Hear the shouts of hatred as Stephen falls beneath the shower of stones, but let Faith hearken, and the martyr is quietly "falling on sleep."   It is the normal path and end of all who walk with their Lord through a world in which His foe is reigning.

Now the address changes from the persecuted to the persecutors:

3:   As for you, ye sons of the sorceress,
     Ye seed of th'adulterer and of the whore,
     Come, draw ye nearer!
4:   Over whom do ye make yourselves merry?
     At whom do ye stretch your mouth wide,
     And thrust out the tongue?
     Are ye not brood of rebellion?
     Are ye not seed of a lie?
5:   Enflaming yourselves with your idols,
     Beneath ev'ry tree that is green,
     Slaying even the children
     In valleys under the rock-cliffs?*
6:   Among the smooth [stones] of the torrent,
     There, there is thy portion,†
     They, they are thy lot.
     Even to them thou hast poured a libation,
     And laid a meat-offering on them!
     Can these be pleasing to Me?
7:   High on a mountain lofty, exalted,
     There hast thou spread out thy bed,
     Even there thou didst climb,
     To sacrifice there thy slain off'ring.
8:   Behind the door and the post,
     Thou hast hid thy Reminder,
     What time thou uncoveredst thyself
     To another rather than Me:
     Thou didst go up,

---

*The picture is of a valley flanked by high rocks—dark and forbidding, a suitable setting for the horrid rites that are described.

†Another play on the words, for both "smooth" and "portion" are "chehleq." That is, those stones are thy gods, as Ps. 119: 57 in the opposite sense.

Made thy bed broad,
With them made agreement,
Lovèd their bed,
Saw their nakedness.*
9: Thou hast gone to the king with [thine] ointment.
Unstintedly measured thy spices;
Didst send thy messengers far,
And degraded thyself down to Sh'ohl!
10: So long was the road, thou didst weary,
Yet said not: Attainment is hopeless.
Thou didst find a revival of strength,
Therefore thou wast not exhausted.
11: And of whom hast thou been so afraid?
And of whom so stricken with terror
That thou becamest a liar?
And hast not been mindful of ME,
Nor laid to thy heart what must follow?†
Have I not long held My peace?
And thou didst give Me no rev'rence!
12: Thy righteousness [vain] I'll expose,
And thy works shall yield thee no profit.
13: When thou dost cry let thy rabble deliver thee;
A wind shall disperse them, a breath take them off;
But he that takes Me for his trust,
Even he shall inherit the land,
And possess My mountain most holy.
14: Then shall a cry be heard:
Cast up!  Cast up!
Take from the path of My people
Everything that might stumble!

Jehovah here brings an indictment against His witness upon earth, Israel, under the most scathing terms. They are commanded to draw near, and that part of the nation that is in downright apostasy is first addressed. Jehovah has marked their persecution, even though it might only consist in putting out the tongue in ridicule of the true-born penitent children of faith,

---

*A difficult line as the many varying renderings evidence. I have adopted the translation of Delitzsch, who is followed by Darby, always a conservative. There is a natural shrinking from what is so repellent, but Scripture often uses very plain language for these secret abominations.

†Too free as a translation, but giving the sense.

whilst their character—the nature that must show itself in some form of evil activity—evidences them as the offspring of rebellion and falsehood. They follow in the path of that ancestry, violence keeping equal step with corruption, as witness those sacrifices even of little ones in the gloomy valleys under the shadow of the rock cliffs. Stones smoothed by the brook, such as once slung by the hand of faith killed the threatening giant, are themselves worshipped as gods,* everything once used is now worshipped. Can Jehovah look on such scenes with complacency?

Even worse remains. The figures become more repulsive. Jehovah's witness, Israel, in the mass, is likened to an adulteress, who, first putting that Memorial that she was ever to keep in a prominent place, out of sight—behind the door instead of on it,† —abandons herself to the vilest impurity, not even ashamed of her shame, but exposing her lewdness on a lofty mountain, requiring toil and energy to climb, enlarging there her bed, inviting her lovers, and loving their unhallowed company.

Under such repellent terms is simple departure of heart from the Lord pictured. Oh, how little is thought of that among men! No laws are aimed at it; no court takes notice of it; Society is very lenient to such violators; but well may we be sure, and lay it to heart, that the same unfaithfulness on the part of our God's present "witness," the professing Church, is not looked at with any greater complacency this very day; as it is written: "Thou hast there them that hold the doctrine of Balaam, who taught Balak to cast a stumbling-block before the children of Israel, to eat things sacrificed to idols, and to commit fornication" (Rev. 2: 14-20).

Let us not think for a moment that "our God," who is also "a consuming fire," can endure complacently in Christendom what He so abhorred in Israel, nor that greater privilege diminishes responsibility; it vastly enhances it.

---

*Small stones were actually worshipped in the New Hebrides prior to the reception of Christianity, as Mr. J. G. Paton tells us.

†"And these words which I command thee this day shall be in thy heart...and thou shalt write them on the posts of thy house and on thy gates" (Deut. 6: 8, 9, 11, 20).

Verse 9 is of deep interest. Israel, in insatiable lust, cares not how far she has to send her go-betweens; and all self-respect stifled, she so lowers herself that her abasement is likened to a descent to sh'ohl, the lowest depths. The representative of that "sh'ohl" is here called "the king," and again we have that agreement that in chapter 28 is termed "the covenant with death, and agreement with sh'ohl," which speaks of some alliance that has in it a voluntary connection with evil powers. But this leads up to a question the answer to which will govern our understanding of other prophetic Scriptures; who is that *"king"* to whom apostate Israel goes with her present of ointment?

Whilst there may be a pattern of this in the past, yet for the definitive fulfilment we must surely look to that "time of the end," when all the powers of evil are being headed up, and the devil, cast out of heaven, has his only sphere of activity here (Rev. 12). Many excellent commentators insist that this "king" will be found in him who is the Jewish Antichrist. Thus Mr. W. Kelly writes:

"This will be the climax of their heartless desertion of Jehovah and rejection of Messiah. They received not Him who came in His Father's name, they will receive another who will come in his own name. The spirit of this has been often verified, doubtless; but it awaits its full signature (*sic*) in the Antichrist of the last days"—"The king will be in the land and city destined for Messiah"—"The Beast and the false prophet, or 'the king,' perish together."*

Thus the writer identifies this "king" of verse 9 with the Antichrist, who is also the false prophet and Beast from the land, of Revelation 13. But we ask, How can that possibly be? Those that are here addressed are, beyond all controversy (nor does Mr. Kelly differ), the apostate mass of Israel; and it is equally certain that the Antichrist, or False Prophet (for we are in full accord with Mr. Kelly, that these are different names for the same person) will be at the head of this last Jewish apostasy. But then it would·follow that the apostate mass *make an agreement with their own king!* Surely no people need to make agree-

---

*From "Exposition of Isaiah," p. 439, by Mr. Wm. Kelly.

ment with their own self-chosen leader.*  Even if this be granted
as a possibility, why should they send messengers "far off;" for,
as Mr. Kelly very justly says, the false prophet (whom he identifies with this "king") will be "in the land and city destined for
Messiah."  He will surely be in the land, and in the city too,
when it is captured (Zech. 14: 9); then why send messengers *far
off?*  That in itself would appear enough to condemn the interpretation we are examining; nor has it, as far as I am aware, any
support in any other Scripture—it must surely be abandoned.

But assume that "the king" here is the head of the revived
Empire, not the Beast from the land of Rev. 13: 11, but from the
sea (ver. 1), "the party of the first part" in that covenant of
which Daniel 9: 27 speaks; "And he ('the prince who shall come,'
of the previous verse) shall confirm a covenant with many, for
one week."

That is, the Roman prince, the prince of the people who destroyed the city Jerusalem, and who at that time had not come,
makes a covenant with the mass of the apostate Jews, who are
addressed as seeking that alliance in our prophecy.  For that purpose *they* might send their messengers afar, bearing with them
presents.  That surely is as reasonable, as it is in accord with
all Scripture.  We have a pattern of this covenant in the history
of Israel: "Ahaz sent messengers to Tiglath-pileser, the king of
Assyria, to say to him, I am thy servant; and Ahaz took the
silver and the gold that was found in the house of the Lord, and
in the treasures of the king's house, and sent it for a present to
the *king of Assyria*" (2 Kings 16: 7, 8).  Ahaz was a fitting representative of the foretold leader of a revolted mass of Jews in
the future.  Nor is the Gentile Assyrian king a less fitting representative and type of him who shall hold precisely the same
political position in the future, the "coming prince" of a future
world-empire.  That covenant between the Jew and the Gentile
our prophet tells us in the words, "Thou wentest to the king with
ointment," shall be repeated in the future.

---

*For we are looking forward to the day figured by "iron and
clay," and thus the God-defying democratic principle of the authorities being elected by an apostate people will have a large
place.

This "king" then, in this case, I take it, is not the false prophet, the "Beast from the land," the Jewish Antichrist, but "the Beast from the sea," the *Gentile* world-ruler of the last days, who, since he becomes completely possessed and energized by the devil, whose own place is the "bottomless pit," is "the Beast that ascendeth thence" (Rev. 17: 8); and thus that covenant is, as chapter 28 tells us, "with death and sh'ohl," terms expressive of the lowest source. This, again I say, accords with all Scripture and throws its light on other texts that have, for the lack of it, been misunderstood; but on such subjects, dogmatism does not become us, for we are all only disciples, or elementary learners, in the school of prophecy.*

In verse 10 appears a slight change to pity, even for the wanderer, as Jehovah says: " 'Tis a weary road thou art travelling, meeting constant disappointments, yet never despairing of finding something that will satisfy thy ever-hungry heart; with every novelty, thinking that in *it* at last thou hast a panacea for all thy troubles; and so, with that reviving of a false hope, never taking the place of being sick and thus needing a physician." How perfectly that applies to poor man at all times! Those Pharisees to whom the Lord spoke, really needed Him as Physician as much as the veriest publican and sinner, but resenting such a thing they perished in their pride.

Jehovah continues (ver. 11): "I know there is a fear overhanging thee, and this has led to that covenant with death and agreement with sh'ohl; but thus in making a Lie thy refuge, thou hast shewn thyself to be a liar; and because I have held My peace, and not interposed in wrath, thou hast not feared Me." Note the reverential fear of God is the best possible antidote to any other fear.

Verse 12 is strongly ironic: "I will tell abroad thy boasted righteousness, and expose its hollowness; and when I am dealing with thee according to its real value, then, in thy trouble, let that rabble in whom thou hast placed thy confidence, save thee! *They* be of help! Why, a breath disposes of them, a puff of wind blows them away! But he who makes Me his trust shall possess

---

*This is examined in greater detail in the earlier chapters.

the land, and have his place in My holy mountain. And not only that, but a causeway shall be cast up and make a clear and clean road, and never, in any dispensation, will I permit without penalty, an offence to those who are returning to Me. Better far that a millstone were hanged about his neck and he cast into the sea, than that he should offend one of the least of the little ones who believe in Me" (Matt. 18: 6).

This brings us to these last few verses of our chapter:

15: For thus doth He speak, the High and Exalted,
    Even the One in eternity dwelling,
    Whose name is ever The Holy:
    I have, for My dwelling, the high and the holy,
    Yet 'tis with him who is contrite and lowly,
    To revive the lowly one's spirit,
    To revive the heart of the contrite.
16: For not everlastingly will I contend,
    Neither be angry forever;
    For then would the spirit before Me wax faint,
    The breathing I've causèd would cease.
17: For the iniquity of his self-seeking
    Have I been angry and smote him:
    But still he went on ever turning
    In the way of his own evil heart.
18: His ways I have seen and will heal him:
    Will lead him, and will restore
    Lost comforts to him and to his,
    To all of them who do mourn.
19: 'Tis I who create the fruit of the lips:
    Peace, peace to him who's afar,
    And to him who is near, saith Jehovah,
    And I'll make him perfectly whole.
20: But as to the wicked—they are as the sea,
    Storm-tossed, nor able to rest,
    But its waters are ever upheaving,
    Upheaving the mire and the dirt!
21: No peace can there ever be,
    So saith my God,
    Unto the wicked!

With what solemn grandeur is this part introduced! ·It becomes in itself a challenge to every opponent of the Scriptures; for we are bold to say that it could not have been conceived by the man who held the recording pen, had he not been himself moved by the Spirit of God. To claim to be the very mouthpiece of God without any justification, is only possible to one insanely fanatical, or inconceivably debased, with conscience so seared that he does not shrink from being a false witness of God—the very climax of wickedness, short only of assuming *to be* God. Yet being that, the prophet has given such a conception of the one true God as, in its blending of majesty and condescension, cannot be found in all human literature.

Note how the dwelling and the Dweller correspond, as they ever will. God has His own place, high and exalted is He, high and exalted His place, and as He is ever the Holy, so can He only dwell *in* the holy.

The verse divides into two parts: Jehovah first introduces Himself as "high," that is what He is in Himself alone, then "exalted," as in relation to all creation. Alone in unrivalled supremacy, there is not one on the same level as Himself. It would be "robbery" for the highest archangel to claim equality with Him! Take the wings of light and speed high, high and ever higher, and still higher till the finite mind can conceive no more, and still is He infinitely far above that feeble conception! Nor does His nature ever vary—He is ever The Holy, and that burning seraphic holiness is also infinite.

Well may we veil our faces, put hand over lip as we ask, as two of old, "Lord, where dwellest Thou?" "I dwell in Eternity"— a word far beyond our finite powers to compass; but using our own lives as a stepping-stone, we may at least approach its meaning. Man is said to inhabit threescore years and ten. Call on him during that time, and you may perhaps find him, as we may say, at home; but soon after that, man leaves his dwelling, and the place that has known him, knows him no more. But He, God, His dwelling is from everlasting to everlasting, and thus is ever the "I AM," and ever "Holy" is His Name.

But He, the infinitely high, infinitely exalted, infinitely holy, chooses one other dwelling-place. What other dwelling can by its grandeur be suitable for Him? This—*the contrite and lowly spirit!* And what is the effect of this exalted One thus coming to dwell? Is it a shrinking fear, a terror, a blasting and withering of all life, as when a conqueror overwhelms a feeble opponent? Nay; it is always the revival of true life with its hallowed accompaniments of love, joy and peace.

How thoroughly this breaks down all barriers of social caste, all national, and all mere ecclesiastical distinctions! Jew and Gentile, King and Peasant, Romanist and Puritan, with all the sub-divisions that man has made, all go to the common dust, and penitence, contrition, confession of sin, and a low estimate of self form the only discriminating boundary. 'Tis with such He dwells, and the spirit (the highest, or reasoning, part of man's being) and the heart (the seat of emotion and feeling) are both revived by that indwelling.

There is not one word as to ecclesiastical position being correct or the reverse, not a whisper of any discrimination because of clear intelligence in the Scriptures. The religious, the reputable, and the moral are not selected; there is solely a distinction that will make a strange severance in all our ecclesiastical companies. Many a self-satisfied heart, in the most perfectly scriptural outward position, will have no such Visitant. Many a lowly and contrite heart, although it may be in a very unscriptural church-association, will (and is today) entertaining that high and exalted Guest. Does my reader ask: "How can I, even I, prepare a chamber that shall attract so wondrous a Dweller?" Shall we seek an answer together? Let us not then look within to see if we can discover any lowliness there; for, even should we assume that we have found it, it will turn instantly to pride because of that very assumption. But let us not be discouraged, but turn our eyes to the Cross, take a long, long look there, and as we discern *Who* is upon it, and *why*, we shall see,

> "How vile our low estate,
> *Since our ransom was so great.*"

We shall again take our place with penitent Job, and say: "I see Thee with the eye and I abhor myself and repent in dust and ashes," and thus shall we "pour contempt on all our pride." Nor shall we esteem this an act of piety, *assuming* to accept a lowly place, because we know that it is the right thing to do, but simply owning what is the bare fact, save indeed that we can never be contrite enough, or as low as is our true place.

We may, if grace permit, go a little further.  Another has used this same language, and One with whom we poor sinners of the Gentiles have had some common intimacy, for He said: "If a man love Me, he will keep My words, and My Father will love him, and We will come and make Our abode with him" (John 14: 20).

What a divine ray this scripture throws on the other! Isaiah is again seeing the glory of Jesus, and speaking here of *Him* (John 12: 41).  It is He who thinks it no robbery to be equal with God, the High and Exalted One, who inhabiteth eternity: it is He who, by His Spirit, with His Father dwells in the contrite heart that knows something of His love and would respond by submissive obedience.

But Jehovah's address continues: "Were I to be forever angry with My frail creature, man, not one of them could endure it. The spirit indeed could not cease to exist, but it would faint or fail, and that breath whereby man became a living soul would cease."

This verse has been much used in the interests of annihilation of the impenitent; but it gives no footing whatever for such an insistence.  The prophet gives no revelation here of heaven, paradise, or the lake of fire, but deals solely with the earth and its government, which indeed provides a pattern of eternal things. Here the object is the humble and contrite, and for *such* there is a limit to their affliction under the chastening Hand of God; but no such limitation is predicated where there is no contrition. *Eternity of penalty rests on eternity of character,* and if Scripture gives no hope of any change after this life, then equally is there no hope of limitation of penalty—varied however as this is by the measure of privilege enjoyed.

This hungering heart of man *must* seek satisfaction, and if Christ, in whom is all the fulness of the Godhead, does not satisfy, it will, by the law of its own fallen nature, seek that satisfaction somewhere else.  Nor will chastening apart from accompanying grace serve to countervail that law, but when He heals, recalls us from all our foolish wanderings, sheds once more the sunlight of His love on our spirit, heals, guides, and restores, then mourning ceases, and comforts once more abound.  The "fruit of the lips" is a poetical form for the noblest use to which the lips can be put. So from God manward, it is that gospel that comes both to those nigh (Jew) and those far off (Gentile), while from man Godward, it is "praise continually" (Heb. 13: 15).

Note the last words of verse 18: "To all of them who do mourn," to all who show that mark of true relationship with the true Israel of God, by mourning over the defection. Mourning in a day of apostasy is a very sure and prominent mark of the true child of God; and the mocking cry of "Pessimist" only completes the picture according to this scripture. It is sorrowful that the Scriptures never end with universal peace and responsive praise. So in verses 20, 21 the prophecy closes with the rejecters of grace. Such, not merely the profligate, profane and morally debased, are here in view as wicked. In reality, the publican in the temple was righteous, the Pharisee was wicked. The penitent prodigal was righteous, the proud elder brother was wicked. The self-judged penitent is always the righteous: the self-complacent religious one, ever the wicked.

The ocean may as soon refuse to respond to the gales that blow upon it, and remain calm as a mirror while the storm-blasts tear over its surface, as the restless heart of man find rest apart from Christ!

## CHAPTER FIFTY-EIGHT

**Jehovah's salvation again fully manifested. A renewed insistence on the observance of the Sabbath, as it shall be by Israel in the future.**

WE now come to the third and last subdivision of the third and last part of Isaiah, and both name and number again remind us that we have *"The salvation of Jehovah fully manifested."* Here the book begins again, as it were, since we have in these closing addresses a reiteration of the exposure of sins, the pleadings of love, the warnings of danger, the divine discrimination between pride and penitence as at first, and in all we may discern graphic pictures of what affects us to-day. The Word of God, like its Author, never becomes aged, but bears the vitality of youth through centuries and millenniums. Yes; thousands of years may intervene, generations, as we count them, may come and go, yet these are all linked vitally together, and so unified by a common nature that they are morally one generation—a truth that throws its light on Matt. 23: 36 and 24: 30. That generation repeats its sad history constantly; Christendom is only heathendom veneered with a form of godliness. So our chapter begins with the wrestling of the Spirit of God with us, poor foolish Jacob-like men, who ever seek to maintain our "standing" in the flesh before Him, and in verse after verse of convicting power He touches the hollow of the thigh, till we again hang helpless, dependent and therefore happy, upon Him who thus overcomes that He may bless, without any sorrow accompanying the blessing.

1: Cry aloud!  Spare not!  Lift up thy voice!
   Yea, lift it up as a bugle!*
   Show to the house of Jacob its sins,
   Their rebellion unto My people.
2: Day after day do they seek after Me,
   Take delight in My ways to be learning,
   As though 'twere a nation that always did right,
   Nor the judgment of God had forsaken;

---

*The word involves a sharp, clear awakening sound.

> They call upon Me for the judgment of right,
> In approaching to God they take pleasure.*

The prophet must not whisper, but cry aloud so unpalatable a truth, bringing home to them as constituting God's witness on earth, what is its true condition. It is in rebellion! They would never have recognized it, nor owned to it, apart from this Voice thus lifted up. If a reasonable degree of "religion" be maintained, a sleepy conscience readily acquits of so heinous a crime as rebellion. Is it then to be wondered at that the gift of prophecy is by no means popular? People do not love unpalatable truths, and when they have the alternative of listening to soothing assurances, moving eloquence, pleasing illustrations, and entertaining anecdotes, they not unnaturally avoid and withdraw as far as they can from the scathing rebukes of the prophet, and so prophecy is despised (1 Thess. 5: 20). *They* rebellious! What steady attendants they are in the Temple, or Synagogue, or as we should say, "How consistently we 'go to Church,' or attend some 'Meeting!' What more can we do?" So confident are those here addressed, that they call on God to intervene in the most thorough judicial investigation, which they are assured can but issue in their justification. Do they not take pleasure in Temple ritual? Do we not enjoy the Church-services? There *is* a Prophet who is lifting up His Voice aloud this very day. Have you heard It, reader? (Rev. 3: 14-23). There is great blessing attached to hearing that Voice, incalculable loss in being deaf to it. Here they actually indict Jehovah for lack of response to their religious fidelity:

> 3: Why do we fast?  Thou dost not see!
> Why humble our souls?  Naught Thou carest!

and He answers:

> Lo, in your fasts, 'tis your pleasure ye find,
> Exact a full tale from your labor.
> 4: Lo, ye do fast with wrangling and strife,
> And smite with the fist closed in anger.
> Your fasting today doth not avail
> To make your voice heard in the heavens.

---

*Delitzsch renders: "They desire the drawing near of God." I have hesitated long before adopting the alternative as in the text, but Matt. 15: 8 seems decisive.

5: Is it such fast as *this* that I choose?
   A day for a man's soul's affliction?
   Is it to bow his head as a rush?
   To spread sackcloth and ashes beneath him?
   Wilt thou indeed call *this* a true fast,
   A day of delight to Jehovah?
6: Is not this rather the fast that I choose,
   T'unfasten the fetters of falsehood?
   That ye loosen the bands of the yoke
   And let the oppressed go in freedom,
   Break every yoke into pieces?
7: That thou divide with the hungry thy food,
   And bring to thy home the poor outcasts?
   When seeing the naked, thou provide him with clothes,
   And from thine own flesh never hide thee?
8: Then shall thy light break forth as the dawn,
   And thy health shall speedily spring up;
   Then shall thy righteousness march in thy van,
   Jehovah's full glory thy rear-guard.
9: Then shalt thou call, and Jehovah respond;
   Thou shalt cry. *Here I am,* shall He answer.
   If thou dost banish the yoke from thy midst,
   Cease pointing the finger; stop slander;
10: If to the hungry thou draw out thy soul;
    Comfort the soul of the mourner;
    Then shall thy light stream out of the gloom,
    Thy darkness be as the noonday!
11: Then shall Jehovah constantly guide,
    Thy soul in dry seasons replenish,
    Infuse with new vigor thy wearying bones,
    Thou shalt be as a well-watered garden:
    As a fountain whose waters fail never.
12: The ruins of ages thy children shall build,
    Thou shalt raise up again the foundations.
    So shalt thou be called, Repairer of breach,
    Restorer of streets for man's dwelling.

13: If thou shalt turn from the sabbath thy foot,
    My holy day using for pleasure,
    But shalt call the sabbath a day of delight,
    The holy day of Jehovah;
    Owning that He hath honored that day,
    For thus shalt thou give Him full honor;
    Walking no longer in thine own ways,
    Nor seeking to do thine own pleasure,
    Nor speaking the words that are idle;

14: Then shalt thou have thy joy in the Lord,
    Shalt ride upon earth's highest places;
    I'll feed thee the lot of Jacob, thy sire:
    For the mouth of Jehovah hath said it.

Here we have Jehovah's probe going deep into the wound that sin has made. Here we see the contrast between religious man's idea of fasting and Jehovah's. As to man, self and self-interest being the center of all his thoughts, even while he himself religiously fasts, he seeks his own profit by making others work for him. Further, the very fasting, the very abstinence from food, results in an increased irritability that leads to wrangling, and even smiting with clenched fist.* Is *that*, says Jehovah, the conception you have of your God? Does *that* show that you have any true knowledge of Him? What pleasure can He take in seeing a man merely put on sackcloth, sit on ashes, and bow down his head as a bulrush! Prayers from such self-centering can never rise higher than the petitioner's own head. The very fasting fills you up full with pride! The very humbling is a source of boasting!

But this is what delights Him—to see unloosened the bonds of sin wherewith all men are shackled, those works of the devil; that the burdened conscience be relieved; the hungry fed; that thou take to thine own house the homeless, and clothe the naked, finding thy "neighbor" wherever there is *need* among *men*. Remember that thou sharest their flesh; withdraw not thyself then from any in suffering, sorrow or need.

Long had He to wait before He saw that which perfectly answered these desires in any on earth. At length One comes, who goes about doing good, healing all oppressed by the devil, feeding the hungry in thousands, clothing the naked, till they sit in their right mind at His feet. On Him, the Spirit of God as a dove that had long sought a resting-place as He hovered over this sea of humanity, at last found a congenial home. So He went on, never hiding Himself from His own flesh—that is, from any man. Let the publican, Matthew, make Him a feast, He de-

---

*Possibly this may have been the reason the Papacy permits a full meal on fish and calls it fasting!

spises not the company of publicans and sinners. Let the Pharisee invite Him to dine, and He refuses not the cold invitation. Till at length that "path uncheered by earthly smiles," led Him to the Cross, and there, the very spear that pierced His side —the spear at the point of which all man's hate may be said to have been focussed, became the point at which all God's love was also focussed, for it drew forth the Blood to save.

Yes; One, and One only, ever thus gave to God perfect delight; but here is a very precious secret: *as we abide in conscious helplessness in Him even we too please God, and in no other way.* He, Christ, is the Fountain whence flows perennial floods of all goodness. We are but leaky vessels, yet abiding under the flow of that Fountain, we, even we, may be channels of those living waters (John 7: 37). In the few days that may be left to us may their flow be not hindered by our own self-sufficiency or unbelief!

Note the lovely circle of blessing that verses 6 to 12 puts before us. Grace leads to self-forgetful holiness, and this receives such tokens of approving love as He told of in John 14: 21-23. Does one speak for any beside oneself in mourning the rare enjoyment of these tokens? Then let us not indict His truth, but draw nearer to Him in assured confidence that it is not due to any change in *His* love, for He longs to make us each a channel of that goodness that actually needs human channels for its outflow.

The address is indeed to Israel on earth, but we are dull indeed if we cannot hear under it a word for ourselves. The gloom of Israel's sorrows shall all pass away; the gracious light of His love shall shine upon her in her remnant, not at first with that noonday brilliancy that would blind under present conditions (for we need to be ourselves like Him to endure that, 1 John 3), but in the lovely rose of dawn. Then, by a second figure, sickness shall give place to perfect health, and Israel (and we) shall be led in triumph, as He here speaks: "Then shall thy righteousness march in the van, and the glory of Jehovah be thy rear-guard"— a triumphant procession of safety, certainty, and enjoyment; for Jehovah here puts Himself as listening for the very first appeal or cry, and at once answering, "Here am I." Think of that, my fellow-believers, think of the "high and exalted One who inhabits eternity" waiting on such poor creatures as we, and instantly responding to our cry with "Here am I!"

But there may still be some obscurity as to the precise force of "Thy righteousness shall go before thee." Might we not say, "*My* righteousness, Lord! Why, what righteousness have I, when it is, at its best, only filthy rags, and does not all Scripture confirm this verdict? Both Old and New Testament concur in crying: 'There is none righteous; no, not one.' What righteousness then have I?"

But both Old and New Testament also concur in this, that there is another righteousness that is still ours: "Not having my own righteousness which is of the law, but that which is through the faith of Christ, even the righteousness which is of God by faith" (Phil. 3: 9). And with this our prophet is in perfect harmony: "And their righteousness is of Me, saith the Lord" (chap. 54: 17) and again, another prophet writes (Jer. 23: 6): "The Lord our righteousness," *Jehovah Tzidkehnu.*

The promise cannot refer to our own works, of whatever character they are; it is Christ our Lord who of God is made unto us *"righteousness"* (1 Cor. 1: 30), and who, thus preceding, is indeed our Guide and Protector. We are on our way to God: Apollyon bestrides the way and by constant accusation opposes our advance. Let *our Righteousness* answer him, and this what we hear: "Who shall lay anything to the charge of God's elect? It is God that justifieth. Who is he that condemneth? It is Christ that died, yea rather, that is risen again" (Rom. 8: 33, 34). Can he answer *that?* No, indeed; he flees from "our Righteousness," and our van is secure.

Well may "the glory of Jehovah," the perfect outshining of His highest divine excellencies, bring up the rear, for there are always some weak stragglers, who cannot, for one cause or another, keep up with the main body. Shall these be cut off by the flying squadrons of the foe? How much the "glory of God" would suffer! It is secured by gathering up* those poor, feeble,

---

* The very word rendered "rearward" is *asaph,* which means "to gather," and so, "bring up the rear."

halting ones with whom some of us have much sympathy. God be thanked for both vanguard and rearguard.

In verse 9 we have *three* present evils that prevent the expressions of the Lord's love; first oppression (or the yoke) of those over whom some social or financial advantage may give that power. Then scoffing (pointing the finger) at those on the same social level; and, lastly, feigning friendliness publicly, yet speaking evil (or vanity) of those in some superior position to ourselves. These are the muddy waters from the cesspool of the first Adam, and not the clear crystal spring that flows from Christ who "is the Fountain, the clear sweet spring of love;" and apart from whom all human love is but a shadow of what flows from His gracious heart.

Self-forgetful solicitude for others in distress will never lack tokens of our Father's approval (see John 14: 23). Nor does this good Shepherd leave His poor sheep to find their way by themselves. He so leads them by the waters of quietness, that let the drought be ever so prolonged, they shall not be affected. Nay, more; they themselves shall not be as a mirage that deceives the thirsting traveller, but their ministry shall be refreshing to all. And those old foundations, that have been covered up with earth for many generations, shall be again built upon, till far and wide shall Israel's fame spread, and the very name of "Breach-repairer" shall be given her (ver. 12).

This reference to the dirt-covered foundations being again used, has its first application to the cities of Palestine; but who can fail to see the striking spiritual corespondence in the history of the Church of God? We know well that at the Reformation there was a marvellous uncovering of the "foundation" of justification by faith; and that uncovering has gone on ever since, till within comparatively recent years the Lord's return as a present hope has been "uncovered," and given great joy to myriads.

The chapter closes with another strong reference to the sabbath, which shall be in the millennial day the "sign" of Israel's complete restoration. Man by nature loves his own way, and ever looks after his own interests. The legal sabbath, calling him from this, is, and ever will be anything but a delight, for it severs him from what *is* that; so that if his pursuit for gain be prevented by long-established custom, he will turn what is thought to be the sabbath to an opportunity for his pleasure, as the crowds of pleasure-seekers do on Sunday. If then he can genuinely and sincerely find his truest joy in cessation from everything that is for his own profit or fleshly pleasure, it evidences a new birth, and then indeed restored Jacob's portion shall be his.

Does this mark out *our* path as to the sabbath? Must the Christian if he would please God (and there can be no true Christian to whom this is not the first desire) observe, by absolute rest, the seventh day of the week? For let tradition say what it will, Scripture at least knows no substitution of the first day for the seventh. Nay, he lives in a sphere where, as far as true rest goes, of conscience and of heart, his sabbath is perpetual; and he neither knows nor looks for a sabbath beyond this, save that future rest of God—that sabbath-keeping that remains still for the people of God (Heb. 4: 9) and to enter into which he now "labors." Rest and labor are antithetical, and can never synchronize.

As to any day being observed as a religious obligation, that is, from a scriptural point of view, impossible. The Christian does indeed delight in the law of God after the "inward man;" and what Scripture calls "the righteous requirements of the law"* are indeed fulfilled in him as he walks after the Spirit. But the sabbath, as given to the Jew, and, in the decalogue never to any but the Jew, although its primary institution was for man *as man*, he soon lost all claim to it, which became lodged alone in the "Son of Man" (Matt. 12: 8). The observance of the sabbath is never pressed in the New Testament as one of those "righteous requirements," but rather is the believer warned against any who would judge him "in respect of a sabbath," for to him even that is but a shadow, the *substance* of which he has in Christ (Col. 2: 16).

Here the addressed are the children of Jacob; a word that with peculiar force attaches the mind to that people whose path nationally has reduplicated that of their father Jacob in its wandering from their home, in its long toiling service, in its sure

---

*A strictly literal rendering of the Greek *dikaioma* in Rom. 8: 4 (See Revised Version, *margin*).

restoration to its land, in its there passing through that time called "Jacob's trouble" (the night of the wrestling), and finally in
its complete restoration to Bethel.

The sabbath must be considered in the light of the present
place of our Lord Jesus Christ, the Son of God, in the heavenlies, above the sun, and therefore above all those divisions of time
that result from the earth's revolutions around it. He now is not
resting only on the seventh day; nor do angelic Principalities
and Powers observe the sabbath. In the world we have tribulation, whether on the seventh or any other day; but in Christ, and
in Christ alone, have we rest and peace. The very observance
of days, months, times and years (apart from that love which
would not stumble any) is in itself a practical denial of the
Christian's position (Gal. 4: 10).

# CHAPTER FIFTY-NINE

**The cause of severance between God and man. This confessed and broken down forever.**

THIS chapter forms the second section of this division of our book, and like so many "seconds," has in it both the idea of the work of an enemy and the salvation of God from that enemy. Here the personality of the enemy is not yet revealed; but his work is, and his dupe, man, is seen having to bear the full responsibility of the rebellion into which that enemy has seduced him.

Most clear are the *three* divisions of the chapter:

1: Verses  1-8.  Conviction.
2: Verses  9-15.  Confession.
3: Verses 16-21.  Salvation.

In the first part the Holy Spirit has supplied Himself with words that He uses in Romans 3: 15-17, to bring conviction of guilt to us all, as it is written: "That every mouth might be stopped, and all the world may become guilty before God."

Let us listen to this indictment of One who knows us well, and, knowing the worst, still loves:

1: Behold, the hand of Jehovah
   Is not too shortened to save,
   Nor His ear too heavy to hear.
2: Your iniquities are the dividers
   That sever 'tween you and your God.
   Your sins have hid His face from you
   So that He doth not attend.
3: Your hands with blood are defiled,
   Your fingers iniquity stains,
   Your lips have been speakers of lies,
   Your tongue doth murmur perverseness.
4: Not one of you crieth for justice;
   In faithfulness none of you plead.

In nothingness* trusting, in vanity speaking,
    Profitless toil† men conceive,
    Iniquity do they bring forth:
5: Eggs of the adder they're hatching,
    And webs of the spider they're weaving;
    Who eats of their eggs surely dieth;
    If crushed, then a viper springs forth.
6: Their webs shall be useless for clothing,
    No covering shall their works yield;
    Their works are works of corruption,
    And violence the deed of their hand!
7: Their feet run ever to evil,
    Swift to shed innocent blood!
    Their thoughts are iniquitous thoughts:
    By waste and by ruin their pathways are marked.
8: Nothing they know of the pathway of peace,
    And nothing is right in their goings.
    Crooked the paths they have made them;
    Who treads them shall never know peace.

The prophet speaks on the part of Jehovah. How different are the days to those early ones of Israel's history! Then the answers to cries were prompt; His interventions on behalf of His people frequent. What a difference now! They pray, but there is no answer. No ear seems to listen. Sorrows not only take their course unchecked, but fresh blows come upon them; what can be the reason? How can such silence be accounted for? Has He changed? Has He forgotten to be gracious? Indeed, no! He changes never. His power to save is not lessened. His ear has not become dull as with age; it is as keen as ever to hear a wordless sigh, or the first whisper of penitent faith. The cause of the silence is precisely the same as in the day when those two brothers brought their different offerings. He respected not the persons of either; but Cain's sin still lay as a barrier between him and God, unremoved by his fruits and flowers (Gen. 4: 7). So with us, sins must be removed, or never can we see that Face that

---

*The word is *tohu*, "waste," "empty," as in Gen. 1: 2. That is, their confidence has no real foundation.

†The very word *ahmal* has in it the idea of wearisome toil, that profitless "labor" from which the Lord calls us in Matt. 11: 28: "Come unto Me, all ye that labor" with no results.

"diffuses light when it unveils itself, and leaves darkness when it is veiled; the sight of which is blessedness, and not to see which is damnation."*

Does Jacob ask, What sins? These. Your hands are blood-stained; your fingers defile all they touch; your lips are false; your tongue untrue. In your midst on all sides are injustice and untruth. Men's trust is in what shall prove as empty as the desolations of chaos. But that quick active brain has its conceptions, and what does it bring forth? Profitless weary toil! Gain is ever its object, money its attraction, and to attain it, "they disquiet themselves in vain" (Ps. 39: 6). Weary and ever unsatisfied are they, and all they produce is as those eggs which when hatched bring forth a brood of poisonous adders. Such doings shall prove as ineffective for their clothing as would the web of a spider. Let any feed on what they minister, they must die; and when what they minister is opposed, examined, and refuted, or crushed, then is it seen in its true Satanic character, for forth there springs a viper! Their feet are ever on murderous errands bent! Their thoughts are evil, only evil, all the day and every day (Gen. 6: 5). Of the true way of peace they know nothing, and, as long as they thus walk, never can.

"What baseless extravagance! What gross exaggeration! What self-confuting absurdities!" Does someone so speak? Then that evidences you are not well acquainted with your own heart, or you would know that, although dormant, there is latent in it just such a brood of vipers. Still and quiet they may be now; but let suitable occasion arise, and you will see them raise their heads, dart their fiery tongues, and show their poison-laden fangs. God does not look at the surface—how innocent we can make that! The greatest rogue is often the most honest-looking; the biggest liar may speak the most speciously, and even the murderer can be intensely sanctimonious. God looks deep down beneath the surface, and tells us what He sees in the heart, just as if our eyes could see under the surface of our beautiful lawns, so soft and green in the cool days of spring, but let the burning heat of July come, and roots and seeds of all kinds of noxious

---

*Delitzsch.

weeds germinate.  Let us never forget that though we may have
been Christians for a century, we still bear within us that old
Adamic nature, and apart from a present abiding in our risen
Head, this will express itself as it ever has done.  The principle
on which the new life begins, of repentance Godward and dependence on the Lord Jesus Christ for all power for holy living,
with the Blood of the Lamb for our confidence, continues to the
end.  Let us not deny the divine verdict; far wiser and truer is
the confession that follows:

    9:  That is the reason that judgment's far from us,
          And righteousness cannot o'ertake us.
        We hope for the light, but lo, a dense darkness!
          For the brightness of dawn, and we walk in thick gloom!
    10:  We grope by the wall as the blind do,
          Aye, grope as those who are eyeless.
        In the clear light of the noonday
          We stumble as though it were night.
        In the midst of the lusty and flourishing*
          We move as though we were dead.
    11:  We all of us growl as the bears;
          And mourn—yea, mourn as the doves.
        We hope for the right, but it comes not;
          For salvation, it stayeth afar.
    12:  For our transgressions are many before Thee;
          Our sins bear their witness against us.
        For our transgressions remain ever with us,
          And our misdeeds, we know them full well!
    13:  Rebelling against and denying Jehovah;
          Departing away from our God;
        E'en from the heart conceiving and uttering
          (Nothing but) words of base falsehood.
    14:  And judgment is turned away backward,
          And justice standeth afar.
        For truth in the street lieth prostrate,
          And honesty finds no admission.

---

*The *Hebrew* word, *ashmanneem*, is somewhat uncertain, not
occurring elsewhere in that form.  Both Gesenius and Delitzsch
believe it to be identical with the word for "fat," *shahman*, as in
Judges 3: 29, "lusty."  It evidently is in strong antithesis to the
word "dead."  I have given the fuller meaning by using two ad-
jectives.

15: Aye, truth is utterly lost;
    And he who departeth from evil
    Exposeth himself to be plundered.
    And the Lord saw—'twas ill in His eyes—
    That of judgment there was none at all.

These pathetic verses give the true Israel's confession of the truth of the indictment in the first verses. Personifying that pious remnant as one man, we may see him standing afar off, and without lifting up so much as his eyes to heaven, saying: It is true; and it is this that accounts for the apparent indifference of our God. He has given us light, the sun of His revelation is shining, and yet we stumble as though we were in the night. Aye, we are blind, and grope our way by feeling along a wall, while among our careless neighbours who are merry and flourishing, we move in sadness as though we were the very shades of the dead. Our distress is heard in our groanings, our sorrow in our sighs; for although we have hoped long for the intervention of Jehovah to put things right, it is still apparently very far off! The truth that used to have power over men, and which they at least outwardly reverenced, seems now to have failed altogether; for if anyone does leave the broad road of evil, if one refuses to worship the image of the Beast, and to receive his mark, he becomes, in another way, a marked man, as being a fair victim for spoliation, for he is not permitted to buy nor sell (Rev. 13: 14-17). Jehovah has surely seen all this, and evil—very evil—must such a sight have been to Him who will have all things right, but now sees all things wrong!

A lesson lies for us in these words of lowly self-judgment, which yet are nothing but the bare truth. There is not one particle of merit in them, except that they admit what is absolutely true. Fellow-believer, we too stand at the end of our day; and this is the weighty truth that these words, preserved for over 2,600 years, press upon us: *They only are the true children of God, and not bastards, who sincerely confess their part in the common sin.* Let Daniel, being dead, yet speak to us as he does in his ninth chapter. Those heart-broken sighs are but an example of what we have just been considering. Let the many confirmations we have had in our prophet assure us that he only who confesses his sins and the sins of his people can hear the sweetest of all words that ever fell as balm on a troubled heart: "O man greatly beloved!"

The last words of verse 15 form so close a link with the third and last section that they may be repeated:

> And Jehovah saw—it was ill in His eyes—
> That of judgment there was none at all.
> 16: And He saw that there was not a man;
> Marvelled that none could be found
> Able to make intercession.
> Therefore His own arm brought Him salvation,
> His righteousness was His support.
> 17: So He armed Him with justice as with a breastplate,
> A helm of salvation He put on His head,
> Clothed Him with garments of vengeance as armor,
> Covered Himself with His zeal,
> As though 'twere a blood-red war-cloak.*
> 18: A recompense fitting will He repay;
> To His enemies, fury, to His foes, recompense.
> The islands afar, He'll repay with chastisement.
> 19: So shall men fear the name of Jehovah,
> E'en from the West where the sun goeth down,
> So shall His glory bring reverent fear,
> E'en from the East where it riseth.
> For when the foe shall invade as a flood,
> The Spirit of Jah lifts banner against him,†
> 20: And a Redeemer shall come unto Zion,
> To those who in Jacob do turn from revolting,
> Proclaimeth Jehovah!
> 21: This is My covenant that I make with them;
> The Spirit which is upon thee,
> And the words I have put in thy mouth,

---

*"Zeal," from a root, "to be a deep red." His fiery zeal becomes His blood-red mantle.

†A much disputed passage. Delitzsch, Nagelsbach, Lowth and many others read it quite differently: "When he shall come as a river straitened in its course, which a strong wind driveth away;" that is: "Jehovah will come as a stream hemmed in, which a strong tempestuous wind sweeps away." All things considered, I see no reason to abandon the received version, which is retained in the margin of the Revised, and by Darby, Kelly, and many other conservative commentators.

> Shall never depart from thy mouth,
> Nor from the mouth of thy seed,
> Nor from the mouth of the seed of thy seed,
> From now till eternity ends.

Jehovah sees, Jehovah speaks. The case is desperate. Earth, nay, the universe, fails to supply a single individual who can meet it. God is amazed that there is not a single intercessor or mediator between God and men, in heaven or earth, to save poor man from his conquering foe. What then is to be done? There is nothing for it but He Himself must do what none else can do. He cannot—His love will not allow Him—leave poor Israel captive to his conqueror (Zech. 14: 1, 2) or poor sinful man alone in his misery. That would so lacerate His own Heart that He Himself needs salvation from such a condition! Does not the father who sees his only son in danger of being lost to him forever, need salvation from such impending grief? The mother who is agonized by the thought of losing forever her daughter—does she not need salvation from such a condition? Can God lose man without suffering?

Marvel of marvels! God Himself says here, in words that it is impossible to misunderstand, however much they may astonish us, that He, even He, must find salvation for Himself from the suffering of losing forever His rebellious, sinful, yet dearly-loved creature—man! And since there is none other, His own Arm, His own strength of infinite Love combined with infinite Wisdom, must "bring salvation unto Him." But His righteousness, His inability to save unjustly, upholds Him on that path of infinite suffering (ver. 16).

Must we not have erred in interpreting the text? No; nothing else is possible, nor does that interpretation lack the strongest and clearest confirmation in Him who was "the brightness of His glory; the express image of His Person" (Heb. 1: 3), and who, as being just that, said: "I have a baptism to be baptized with; and how am I straitened till it be accomplished!" (Luke 12: 50). He too needed to be "saved" from the distress of infinite love that was hindered from saving its object. What is salvation for His beloved, is salvation for Himself. So Paul, following Christ as none other of His people, accounted that even his *death*, if Christ were glorified thereby, was itself his salvation (Phil. 1: 19, 20), "For I know that this shall turn to my salvation . . . acording to my earnest expectation and my hope that . . . Christ shall be magnified in my body, whether by life or by death."

It is a mighty work; and keen is the mighty foe that ever opposes mercy to mankind, so He must put on armor for the conflict. But where shall God Himself find a panoply? No creature surely can clothe Him with armor. God is Light; and, being Himself Light, He covers Himself with light as with a garment (Ps. 104: 2), and thus He draws upon His own nature for His investiture. First, then, Righteousness must be His breastplate. None must be able to impugn the justice of one single step that He takes in the salvation of His people. Then, as that salvation is ever the aim and goal of all He conceives, He places it on His Head as a helmet. But the salvation of His people involves judgment on their oppressors, and so vengeance and zeal must clothe Him for the war, for since we now know that heaven itself is not broad enough to hold both the accuser and the accused (Rev. 12: 7) so earth—that mirror of heaven in a sense—must give as here a pattern of that coming conflict in the heavenlies by retribution on the foes of Israel.

Once more we hear this humbling truth—let grace be shown, it will leave the wicked only the harder of heart. Let judgments be abroad in the earth, and its inhabitants will learn righteousness (chap. 26: 9), and that along the whole line of the sun's daily path. But here the order is reversed, the evening precedes the morning, as in Gen. 1 where the evening and the morning form one day; for here too the evening of these judgments will introduce a morning of glory without clouds, as clear shining after rain. His ways never end in night but morning.

The last clause of verse 19 gives a kind of meditative comment, and the common reading seems quite in accord with the context. Israel's foe has come in like a flood, captures the city, and the little remnant are at their last gasp (Zech. 14); then Jehovah comes with uplifted standard, and His "willing people," the dew of His youth, as Ps. 110 speaks, flock to that standard, and the foe is put to flight. With us, how often has this scripture cheered, for in the successive attacks on the foundations of our faith, our only confidence, our only hope, is in the Spirit of the Lord lifting up a standard against him.

The two concluding verses tell of a Kinsman-Redeemer who comes to and delivers Zion, as was the basal intent even when first He came, although then Israel was not gathered, for the Redeemer was rejected; but in that future coming all transgressing shall be turned away from Jacob.

The covenant is always and alone with Israel in her faithful remnant which becomes the nation, and while Jehovah in speaking of this nation, uses the plural, "those who turn," yet the covenant is made with the nation in the singular ("thee") as a unit.    The redeemed nation is to be from this time forth the mouthpiece of Jehovah to the nations of the earth, from generation to generation.

My readers will perhaps notice a slight difference in the apostle Paul's quotation (Rom. 11: 26) from verse 20.  He says the Deliverer shall come *"out of* Sion," whilst our prophet pictures Him as coming *"to"* Sion.  The reason may be found in the evident aim of the Spirit of God in Rom. 11 to bring down the loftiness of us Gentiles.  The Septuagint gives: *"For the sake of* Sion the Deliverer comes," the needed link.  Poor Jacob!  It is to deliver him that the Messiah shall then come, as He once delivered Jacob himself from the wrath of his brother Esau.

# CHAPTER SIXTY

THIS being the *third* section of this division of our book, the significance of that number is strikingly imprinted upon it; for "God is fully manifested" in His government of the earth by the glory that falls upon Zion, and which makes her in her reflection of it the glory of the earth.   There is no clearly marked division throughout the chapter, but the one number "three" is evidently marked on the whole of it.   The very words have a lilt that tell of the joy that the manifestation of God ever brings to His people.   It is an everlasting gospel.

1: Arise! Shine! For thy light is come,
   And the glory of the Lord is risen upon thee.
2: For gross is the darkness that covers the earth,
   And dense is the gloom that enshroudeth the nations,
   But upon thee Jehovah doth rise,
   His glory doth shine forth upon thee;*
3: And the Gentiles are drawn to thy light,
   And kings to thy clear-shining dawning.
4: Lift up thine eyes round about thee—
   See how they all crowd together!
   To thee they are coming!
   Thy sons from afar come unto thee,
   And thy daughters are borne on the hip.†
5: Then shalt thou see, and 'twill cheer thee,‡
   Thy throbbing heart shall enlarge;
   For the sea's riches to thee shall be turned,
   The wealth of the Gentiles come to thee!
6: Great are the herds of the camels that cover thee,
   Camels from Midian, camels from Ephah,
   They come all together, from Sheba they come;

---

*That is, Jehovah's glory not only shines upon Zion, but radiates for all to see.

†As women often carry their children in the East.

‡There are two roots to the word here used, the first has been adopted by the translators of A.V. "to flow together," the other, "to shine," hence "to be glad," and this is, I believe, the sense here.

> Gold and sweet incense they're bringing,
> And joyfully publish the praises of Jah.
> 7: All Kedar's flocks shall be gathered to thee,
> The rams of Nebaioth shall serve thee,
> They shall come to My altar accepted;
> And glory shall fill the house of My glory.*

The previous chapter has given us those preliminary dealings with Israel that necessarily precede blessing; for never till the mouth is stopped can God pour out His unchecked love on man. But the last section of chapter fifty-nine shows how effectively that has been done, and now Isaiah the *prophet* is hidden altogether, but Isaiah the *sign* (chap. 8), Isaiah, the *salvation of Jehovah,* shines forth in exceeding brilliancy. For it is still night, the earth's dwellers have not been won to the gospel of grace; the "Sun" has not yet risen, although there must have been the harbinger of that sunrise in the bright Morning Star, and the heavenly redeemed have gone; but on that very account the shades hang thicker than ever over the earth. Like the little daughter of Jairus, Israel (whom she typifies) sleeps still. But the same Voice that awakened that sleeping damsel is heard, and in the first word of this chapter it utters precisely the same word, *"Cumi,"* "Arise," and again, with the word, as in that chamber of grief, power for obedience comes with the command, and Israel, long in the sleep of death, awakes and rises!

What gracious intertwinings there are between the Old and New Testaments in these ways of God's dealings with men! In the Old, we have the earth alone in view, focussed and represented by one people; and that people focussed and represented by one city, Jerusalem, which shall express His ways of government. In the New, nations disappear, and the heavenly Church takes the place of Jerusalem. Thus the earth becomes a pattern of the invisible; and in Israel's awakening we may see that of many a poor sinner of the Gentiles, of many an unwatchful saint, as Eph. 5: 14 shows.

Let us throw our vision forward, it will not need to be far, and look on the scene as depicted in these first verses. The gos-

---

*The word for "glory" here has in it the idea of beauty. The line might be rendered, "Beauty shall fill the house of My beauty."

pel has been preached for 2,000 years with more or less clearness and fidelity; but that light of truth has been turned into a dense darkness that enshrouds the whole race of man, darkness the more dense because of the light rejected. Yet see that harbinger, the Star, has not given a false testimony, a dawn is breaking over Jerusalem—it is Jehovah-Jesus who is rising upon her, with that healing in His wings of which another prophet speaks (Mal. 4:2).

That light is from no withering, blasting fire; it is a gracious beam that attracts, for the chastened nations with their kings are drawn thereto as steel by a magnet. It is a strange picture! All the governments of earth wait upon Zion, and govern their conduct by her decrees! Not only are the Gentiles attracted, Jerusalem's own sons, who are still scattered, come from far, and her feebler daughters are pictured as children carried by their mothers on the hip.

When Zion, the personified, representative city of the nation, sees all this, a smile replaces the downcast look; her heart, filled with emotion, throbs, and her affections, no longer self-centered, give that delightful evidence of the work of God in all dispensations, for they are enlarged with unselfish joy to sing: "Let the peoples praise Thee, O God; yea, let all the peoples praise Thee!" (Ps. 67: 3).

In that millennial day earth's metropolis will lack no temple, nor that temple lack an altar, nor that altar lack offerings. Ezekiel gives details of the ritual (chaps. 40-44), whilst Isaiah tells us that Kedar and Nebaioth shall send their flocks to provide these offerings; and they shall be accepted.

But will, then, animal sacrifices be renewed? Delitzsch says "No," and writes:

"The sacrifice of animals has been abolished once for all by the self-sacrifice of the Servant of Jehovah, and by the spiritual revolution that Christianity has produced. . . . The meaning is that Jehovah will graciously accept the sacrifices which the church offers from the gifts of the Nabateans, etc."

Fair as this may look on the surface, it leads us into dense fogs, and worse. Delitzsch seems to allow that Jerusalem here refers to the literal city on earth, representing restored Israel;

that the ships that bring them back to that literal land must also be literal, that wherever Tarshish and the isles may be found, they certainly are not in heaven, but *on earth;* that the flocks of Kedar could be nothing else than literal—all this is necessarily admitted. But as soon as it comes to making a worthy use of those flocks, then instantly Jerusalem on earth becomes the Church of the heavenly calling! Others carry this to the extreme till Israel is actually "exterminated" as a nation forever; and there is substituted for that people, ever beloved for the fathers' sake (Rom. 11: 28), the Church, and these Jewish prophets are supposed to speak of a mystery which we are divinely told was completely hidden from them! (Rom. 16: 25; Eph. 3: 4; Col. 1: 26).

The New Testament tells us all that we can know of the Church; and where is there the faintest hint of that Church offering sacrifices *from the gifts of Kedar or Nebaioth?* Her ministers, far from this, took "nothing from the Gentiles" (3 John 7).

On the other hand, no Christian will admit for a moment that any animal sacrifice can ever rival, and still less replace, that one Offering, the efficacy of which has abolished them in that sense of rivalry forever. That is surely true. But that must not be allowed to evaporate all meaning from what is here so clearly stated, that in a coming day Israel's sacrifices shall be accepted. Christians have the Lord's Supper, and in it they show the Lord's death with perfect acceptance. But we do not permit any sacrificial efficacy to be attached to that memorial; that error we leave to Jezebel-Rome (and alas, she wills not to repent). Nor will the enlightened Israelite (and they will all be thus enlightened) in the future permit any atoning efficacy to be attached to those sacrifices; they will also be memorials, and only memorials, of that same all-sufficient offering of Christ crucified. In this light there is no lack of harmony between the literal understanding of this prophecy and the basic word in Heb. 10. The entire absence of the veil in that future Temple will be evidence enough of the sacrifices being memorials and not propitiations. One can but have the fullest sympathy with the zeal for that one Sacrifice never to be repeated, but we also need zeal for the integrity of the Word, which is too clear to permit any other interpretation.

How beauteous the light that last line throws on our own abode, the Father's House. The word rendered "glory" is not the common one, but has at its base the idea of *beauty*, as in verse 13, and that, in its turn, of what meets and delights that æsthetic faculty of enjoyment that distinguishes man from all the creation below him. No blinding beam will that "glory" be, but of fair and holy attractions, so suited to the new nature that they shall thrill with such praiseful delight as can only find relief in worship. If He will thus beautify His House on earth, we can well leave it to His Love to make His House in heaven not less entrancing.

8: Who are these that fly as a cloud,
    As doves wing their way to the dovecotes?
9: The isles are waiting for Me,
    And the ships of Tarshish come first,*
    To bring thy children from far,
    And with them their silver and gold,
    To the name of Jehovah thy God,
    To the Holy One of Isràel:
    For He hath greatly adorned thee.
10: The sons of the stranger shall build up thy walls,
    Their kings shall be at thy service.
    For in My wrath I did smite thee with strokes,
    But in My favor have had mercy on thee.
11: Thy gates shall ever stand ope,
    Nor by night, nor by day shall be closed,
    To bring into thee the wealth of the nations,
    And their kings as though led in triumph.†

---

*As to the exact place that is here meant by "Tarshish," when Young tells us that this means "Tartessus" in Spain, or Carthage in Africa, or Ceylon in India; that the original Tarshish, son of Javan, settled in Italy, and there was a Tarshish on the Red Sea; whilst Knobel places it in Tuscany, and Josephus in Cilicia—we are disposed to gather that the word is to be applied to no specific country, but to the sea itself, and to those maritime nations that bordered it, being thus a parallel with "isles," in the first line. In the Septuagint (Isaiah 2: 16) the word "tarshish" is rendered by "sea;" which confirms the suggestion.

†Delitzsch and others translate the word to denote the kings being literally led as captured forces. It is not impossible, but seems hardly in line with the willing offerings of the Gentiles, nor does the word necessitate it.

12: For the nation and kingdom that will not serve thee,
    Shall itself be brought to destruction:
    The nations that will not freely serve thee
    Shall themselves be utterly dried up.*
13: Lebanon's glory shall come unto thee,
    Cypress and pine and box-tree together,
    The place of My sanctu'ry thus to adorn,
    My footstool thus to make splendid.
14: The sons of oppressors that once oppressed thee,
    Shall approach with lowly obeisance,
    And all who contemned thee shall themselves be ashamed,
    To the soles of thy feet shall be humbled.
    Jehovah's own city, thou shalt be called,
    Zion, the city of Him,
    The Holy One of Isràel.

Zion is pictured as a woman looking seaward; a cloud appears on the horizon, which, as it draws near, resolves itself into a fleet of ships whose white sails are like a flock of homing pigeons flying to their cotes. Then she looks upward as inquiring, and Jehovah explains the marvel. The nations of the earth, He says, are all now waiting submissively upon Him and placing their ships at His disposal; and prominent amongst them are those sea-bordering nations (Tarshish) whose navies and merchant-ships have covered the seas.

No longer do thy people come back in unbelief as in those years of the twentieth century; but as those whose very coming will enrich thee, for they bring with them their gold and silver. Thy walls must be built; but thine own hands shall not labor; the sons of those very strangers who a short time ago were pulverizing those walls with their artillery, shall build them up. Even kings become thy servants; for when My face was turned away from thee because of thy crooked ways, then the nations carried out My purposes in chastening thee; but now, when I smile upon thee, even thy former enemies must give cheerful submission to thee and to thy King.

But should any refuse, they must perish, for it shall not then be as in that long day of unmixed grace; but perfect divine gov-

---

*The prime meaning of the word is "to be dried up," denoting the loss of water, as in Gen. 8: 13. The verse throws its light on Rev. 16: 12.

ernment shall then be in full exercise, with righteousness reigning all open rebellion will promptly be put down.

Every beauteous tree shall adorn that holy place where thy God touches, as it were, the earth, and shall make that "place of His Feet" glorious, so that from the beauty of the footstool men may gather what the beauty of the palace must be!

Thy former oppressors have been swept away, but their children shall come, and would have thee place thy feet on their prostrate bodies, so low would they make their obeisance, and they will salute thee with the cry: "O City of Jehovah! O Zion of the Holy One of Israel!"

This very word is repeated almost literally in that letter that our Lord sends to those who are living in "brotherly love" (for we may well insist that this promise is not addressed to any who are not living in Philadelphia, or brotherly love, in truth): "Behold, I will make them of the synagogue of Satan, who say they are Jews and are not, but do lie; behold, I will make them come and worship before thy feet, and to know that I have loved thee" (Rev. 3: 9).

Who can deny the correspondence in the words used? But those words cannot refer to literal Jews surely. Israel was not, and is not, and will not be in Philadelphia, but in Palestine. And while there are striking correspondences, there are striking differences too, quite enough to save us from that double mistake, first, of taking the earthly promises away from the Jew, and then of putting the Christian in his place, as if he were a literal Jew. We see how sternly those are rebuked who, by act (not lip) taking their place under the law never given to them, say they are Jews. That is precisely what is being done all about us. Nothing in the Lord's letter is said about previous wrath or smiting; but enemies there are, nor are these the literal Philistine or Ammonite, Assyrian or Babylonian, but what answer to these in the spirit-world, various forms of superstition and rationalism, of legality and worldliness, the proud exponents of religious formality and error.

O sweetest promise! We ask not that others should thus abase themselves to our feet that do but too often wander, but no music could be so entrancing to us, as to hear one whisper from Him that should tell us of the "breadth and length and depth and height" of His own patient, tender love to such poor creatures as we.   But must we not deduce, that if we are *not* despised now, if we are sharing in the honors of the world now, if we are *not* sharing in His reproach and  suffering  with Him now, how can we hope to have any part in this promise?   O Lord Jesus, so draw the eyes of our heart to Thee that in these days of lukewarmness  we may be  whole-hearted and with no divided affection!

15: Whereas thou wast left alone, utterly hated,
     And no one walked through thy desolate streets,
     I will make of thee a splendor eternal,
     Source of delight from age unto age!
16: Thou shalt suck too of the milk of the Gentiles;
     From the breasts of their kings shalt thou nourishment
          draw,
     Thus shalt thou learn I'm Jehovah thy Saviour,
     Thy Kinsman-Redeemer, of Jacob the Strength.
17: Instead of the copper, I'll bring to thee gold;
     Instead of the iron, I'll bring to thee silver;
     Instead of the wood, I'll bring to thee copper;
     Instead of the stone, I'll bring to thee iron.
     I'll make peace itself fill the place of thy judges,
     And righteousness be all the police-force required.*
18: Injustice shall no more be heard in thy land,
     Nor waste nor destruction within all thy borders,
     But thou shalt call Salvation thy ramparts,
     Thy gates in their joyousness shall be called Praise.†
19: The sun shall light on thee by day nevermore;
     Neither for brightness the moon shine upon thee;
     But Jehovah shall be to thee light everlasting,
     And thy God shall Himself be thy glory!
20: Thy sun—it shall nevermore set;
     Thy moon—it shall nevermore wane;
     But Jehovah shall be to thee light everlasting,
     The days of thy sorrow forever be past!

---

*"The meaning is that righteousness is to Jerusalem what the whole body of civil officers are" to a city (*Delitzsch*).

†Much too free as a translation, but giving the idea in the words literally rendered, "And thy gates praise."

21: As for thy people, they all shall be righteous,
   And the land shall be theirs evermore:
   A sprout of My planting,
   A work of My hands,
   That shall be for My glory!
22: The smallest one of them shall grow to a thousand,
   The least shall become a strong nation.
   I, even I, Jehovah, will speed it,
   Will bring it to pass in due time.

Our prophet foresees a day in which Jerusalem shall be as glorious as she has been contemptible, as attractive as she has been repulsive. What a striking picture she is, in both respects, of us individually. She has long been in a figure, dead and buried, for as Abraham so pathetically said, the dead must ever be buried out of our sight; we cannot look on the progressive repulsiveness of dissolution in those forms that we have loved so tenderly. But this prophecy of Jerusalem's joyous recovery is a prophecy of the recovery of all who are "in Christ," and the glories that are here portrayed of that representative city, shall have their more exceeding beauteous counterparts in the bodies of glory like unto our Lord's and be as attractive as the dead were repulsive!

All the nations of the regenerate earth shall bring their riches to that city, and the very kings shall act as its foster-parents. When we read this chapter of Isaiah we have some difficulty in remembering that we are not reading the later chapters of Revelation. This in itself tends to confirm the conviction that there is a real identity between the heavenly and earthly Jerusalem, the former being the subject of the New Testament, and the latter of the Old, these unified in the Millennium, as all Heaven and all earth shall be in eternity (Rev. 21: 3).

As in Solomon's day "silver was nothing accounted of," so what had been valued loses its place, and everything, except the four metals that figured the four world-empires in Nebuchadnezzar's vision, is put aside. This should not be pressed into strict literalness, so as to exclude even those beautiful woods that we have just been told shall adorn the Sanctuary; nor, on the other hand, does it justify a spiritualizing of everything so as to eliminate all reference to Israel, and the appropriation of all for the Church. It speaks of vast wealth in prophetic language, but it does not follow that we can insist that it is solely spiritual gold, silver, brass and iron adorning a *spiritual* "Zion," or Church. It is precisely that against which we are warned, for it has made us, Gentiles, wise in our own conceits (Rom. 11: 25), since we ignore entirely the purposes that God still has for Israel. How far different from this beautiful picture is the condition of the professing Church of these last days. Alas, the ignored poverty, wretchedness blindness, and misery of Laodicea give a far truer representation than this splendor.     By verse 19 we learn by what means Zion is to shine, and as we know not what we shall be in resurrection (1 John 3: 2), so there are indefinable glories here.     For who can speak of them? The heavenly Jerusalem is seen in the Apocalypse coming down from heaven, enlightened by no natural sun or moon, but the glory of God enlightens it and the Lamb is its light. It descends, and still majestically descends, till above the earthly city, now filled with its own corresponding beauty, it stays. Thus it shares its glory with that city on earth over which it forms a canopy (chap. 4: 5, last clause), and the whole earth is enlightened by their unified beams which are still purely the outshining of God's glory. Here then, in that one spot during that millennial reign there is a "new heaven and a new earth" in this twofold Jerusalem, but not outside its limit. That *universal* new heaven and earth must still await another and eternal day, at the close of the Millennium, when again that mighty Voice shall cry "Done," for, "Behold, I make all things new."

All the dwellers in that favored land shall not be merely relatively, but absolutely righteous: not only born again, and thus still having two divergent natures, the one evil and the other good, for that would still leave a further work to be done, as in Christians now; but all of them without exception shall be "Jehovah's planting, the work of His Hands," and so perfectly expressive of what He can do, so then there shall be no death there.

The last verse gives an intensely interesting suggestion: *there shall still be growth.* Even perfection does not forbid growth, as indeed we have seen in one lovely instance (see Luke 2: 52).     So on earth the little one becomes a thousand, and if there be one less esteemed than his neighbors, he shall become a strong nation. Let that pattern of earth throw its light on heaven; and we shall see that there too there is no banal limitation in which, having reached all that is possible in one burst, the redeemed have nothing before them for all eternity than to contemplate that with which they have already become familiar. No; there too, since the sphere of our contemplation is itself without any limit but infinite, since it is God as revealed in Christ, there must necessarily be constant and endless growth as here patterned for us in the earthly Israel. We do not enter heaven with nothing more to be discerned, with nothing to be hoped, with nothing to be attained beyond what flashes upon us in that twinkling of an eye. There is growth, aye, even without these limitations of earth, for the element in which we grow is boundless, for it is "the fulness of God."

# CHAPTER SIXTY-ONE

**The Man of Nazareth. His ministry: its result in the millennial day. He leads the praises of His people.**

OUR chapter is not a long one, but it will be found filled with interest and refreshment if we can trace in it the path of our Lord Jesus Christ from His early home in Nazareth, till in a day, yet future, He finds a dwelling with His beloved Israel in a land itself resting under His beams as the Sun of Righteousness.

Again the division is so clearly a threefold one that it could not be mistaken, thus:

1: Verses 1-3: The threefold ministry of the Lord; first in grace; this rejected, in judgment; then finally in healing.
2: Verses 4-9: Israel in millennial blessedness.
3: Verses 10, 11: Messiah rejoices with His rejoicing people.

We will seek to enjoy and profit by each in order:

1: Adohnai Jehovah—His Spirit's on Me,
   For I am Jehovah's Anointed.
   To preach the glad tidings to penitent poor,*
   To heal the heart-broken He sent Me;
   To cry to the captives: Ye are free! Ye are free!
   Prison doors ope to the fettered!
2: To cry, 'Tis the year of Jehovah's good will,
   The day of our God's just avenging,
   And all who are mourning to comfort,
3: The mourners in Zion with raiment to clothe,
   To give to them beauty for ashes;†
   The oil of rejoicing in place of lament,
   The garment of praise for sad spirit.

---

*The one word in Hebrew covers this double idea of lowliness and penitence.

†In the words, "beauty for ashes," we have a peculiarly interesting Isaiahan play on words. The roots of the Hebrew words rendered "beauty" and "ashes" are composed of the same letters,

That strong trees of righteousness they might be called,
Oaks of Jehovah's own planting,
That ever should be for His glory!

This chapter should surely be of supreme interest to us, for 1900 years ago, a mechanic, about thirty years of age, might have been seen standing up amid a Jewish congregation in a simple place of worship, in a village of a despised district in a despised country, as though He were desirous of addressing those present. We are told nothing of His personal appearance, but evidently He is not of any exalted social standing. His clothing must have been that of an ordinary artisan, for He was but a carpenter, and the son of a carpenter, or at least so thought to be, and the villagers among whom He had grown up assumed that they were thoroughly acquainted with Him and all His relatives.

Esteemed and respected indeed He was, or they would not have handed Him the roll of Scriptures from which to read; and as He stands there, He unrolls the book, not carelessly, taking the first page that comes, or the first text that strikes His eye, as being providentially intended; but He "finds the place where it is written: The Spirit of the Lord is upon Me," and having read a few words only, He resumes His seat. There is a pause while the eyes of all the congregation are expectantly fastened on Him, to hear His comment on the text He has selected.

Now mark the astonishment that comes over every face as He—the carpenter, the son of Joseph (as they think)— says, "This day is this scripture fulfilled in your ears," and then quietly assumes the place of being *Himself* the very One who was the Speaker in the prophecy of Isaiah! Can we not picture the scene? And as He goes on taking every sentence and applying it to Himself, amazement sweeps over the congregation; and had we been there, should we not have shared that amazement? He, our neighbor who has gone about among us for over thirty years; He the One who now claims to have been divinely anointed

---

but *transposed*, and thus telling in itself of the exchange of beauty (*par*) for ash (*apr*). Moffatt transfers this into English thus, "To give them coronals for coronachs," as the mournful dirges of the Celts are called.

To preach the glad tidings to penitent poor,
To heal the heart-broken:
To cry to the slaves: Ye are free!
Prison door ope to the fettered:
To cry: 'Tis the year of Jehovah's good will.

Can you not see the agitated assembly? And yet they are most gracious words: they bear in them nothing but beneficence. Between two general proclamations of "preaching the gospel" on the one side, and "the acceptable year" on the other, are three specific forms of grace; first, the "heart-broken," those who no longer stout-heartedly insist that they have "done their best," but, finding tender love where they expected a curse, are filled with self-abhorrence—these must be healed. Next, and along the same line, men have but dark and false views of God—"I," says this speaker, "am going to give them light as to that, and proclaim Him by a Name that shall draw their heart's confidence to Him in joyous liberty and make them free indeed" (John 8: 36). In a word it is the year of jubilee, when the sound of the silver trumpet sweeps over the hills and vales of Palestine, and as those notes reach the ear of every bondman, he springs up free, and hastens to resume the patrimonial inheritance that he had forfeited. Oh, 'tis a picture too beautiful to be spoiled by human comment! For it tells of poor man's place in the very Heart of God, forfeited indeed; but in, and by that Speaker regained, and more than regained, for it is with eternal acceptance never again to be lost.

But here the Reader stops. Not that the next sentence "the day of vengeance" does not in itself mean "the acceptable year" *for Israel;* it most surely does. The only way of deliverance for the Jew on this earth will be by retributive justice on the oppressing nations. That vengeance was by the Spirit in the mind of the Old Testament prophet, Isaiah, who made no pause whatever, for to him the two things, "acceptable year" and "day of vengeance," were indissolubly linked together, they were one and the same thing. The farther-seeing Prophet of Luke 4, foreseeing and foretelling that He would be rejected by "His own" (and the hill of Nazareth soon witnessed that rejection, foreshadowing

Calvary), also foresaw and foretold that these eternal spiritual blessings should go forth to "every creature under heaven," and His stopping in the middle of the verse leaves room for the heavenly calling of the Church.

Have you not been struck with God's appreciation of mourners? The very beatitudes seem to affix blessing to what the worldly Christianity of our day ridicules as "pessimism." *"Blessed are the poor," "Blessed are they that mourn," "Blessed are ye that weep now!"* Is *that* the language of the present day? "Laugh and the world laughs with you; weep and you weep alone," is this world's way. "But," you say, "that was altogether Jewish, and we are told to rejoice in the Lord alway," which seems rather to forbid, than to approve of mourning.

True, but there are strange paradoxes in the life of a Christian. One of them wrote, and he not the least of the apostles, that he himself was "sorrowful, yet always rejoicing" (2 Cor. 6: 10); and today, as long as the Holy Spirit is with us to take of the things of Christ and show them to us, we can but rejoice in all we have in Him. But yet that same Spirit would undoubtedly lead to sincere mourning at the appalling condition of Christendom, and the wave of apostasy that is sweeping over it. Bochim ("the place of weepers") is not at all an inappropriate spot for us to frequent, for the "Angel of the Lord" is still there (Judges 2). Let us not shrink from the taunt of "pessimism," but confess ourselves to be pessimists indeed as to all that depends on the "first man," but optimists without limit as to all that depends on "The Second Man," for He ever doeth all things well.

But in our prophet we have to do with the Jew, who is today going back to his land, an undistinguishable mass of unbelief in the true Messiah, Jesus. Soon a sharp dividing line will be drawn, and on one side of that line will be some who mourn, "as the mourning of Hadadrimmon in the valley of Megiddo" (Zech. 12: 11); and on the other, a mass of impenitent, who are morally gathered at Har Mageddon which is in the English tongue, "The gathering-place of the lofty."

4: The wastes of the ages they shall rebuild,
   Old ruins restore to new beauty;
   Cities all wasted they shall repair,
   Desolations from long-past abandoned.
5: Strangers shall stand and shepherd your flocks,
   Your ploughmen and vinemen be foreign.
6: But ye shall be called the priests of the Lord,
   The servants of God shall be namèd.
   The wealth of the Gentiles shall then be your food,
   And ye shall make boast in their glory.
7: Ye shall have double in place of your shame,
   For insults they joy in their portion;*
   Double shall be their lot in their land,
   Their joy shall be everlasting.
8: For I—e'en Jehovah—take pleasure in right,
   Hate theft with iniquity added,
   Them will I recompense in very truth,
   A covenant will I make with them,
   That shall indeed be unending.
9: Amid all the Gentiles their seed shall be known,
   And their offspring among all the peoples;
   All who shall see them shall own them to be
   The seed that Jehovah hath blessèd!

It has become increasingly clear that the prophecies of this book have a double application. First, they were addressed through a Jew to the nation of the Jews, and therefore their scope is earth and not heaven: the penalty threatened is reprobation on, and from the earth. But it is equally clear that the first words of this chapter must have a wider and more spiritual application to the present day—a day that was unknown to the Old Testament prophet.

But as we come to verses 4-9 it becomes increasingly difficult to apply such words to the Church. I do not say that the professing Church, as left to man's responsibility, is not in a ruin that corresponds with Israel. It is, and there are indeed many "waste places;" but the end of that faithless witness is not for those waste places to be restored, or the ruins rebuilt, but (the true having been caught up to be forever with the Lord) absolute

---

*Here there is a change in the construction—it becomes declaration.

reprobation as a vile thing to be "spewed out of the Lord's mouth"—no longer owned as His witness at all. *That* is not a rebuilding as is promised here, nor any form of restoration.

Apply the prophecy to the literal nation of Israel, and how simple it all is. Its cities shall be rebuilt; its wastes covered with fertile beauty, and its desolations throbbing with life. Foreigners shall do the rough servile work, while Israel's own people shall be known as having peculiar access to God, and so a nation of priests. The very wealth of the nations shall be the glory of Israel (how could such a word apply to the Church?—although the harlot of Rome does carry it out consistently enough, and in so doing becomes the synagogue of Satan) and their joy shall flow perennially in unbroken song.

Jehovah's own character is ever the basis of His dealings with men. He loves righteousness. Every act of His, then, must be in strict accord with it; but robbery, the assumption of that to which the pretender has no right, is in view here as when the Devil would be as the Most High, or man, his dupe, would claim to be God (2 Thess. 2), that is robbery of such a transcendent character that it is called "robbery with iniquity" and it is hateful indeed to Him.

There was One to whom even such a claim was no robbery. It was He whose mind was to go to the lowest place on earth, and that is the Mind His Spirit works in His people (Phil. 2).

In that day, no longer shall the word "Jew" cover a reproach, but as in chap. 25: 8, every Israelite shall be honored as one of a people peculiarly blessed.

10: Greatly will I rejoice in the Lord:
    In My God shall My soul sing, exultant!
    'Tis He who hath clothed Me in salvation's robe,
    In the garment of Justice enwrapped Me,
    As bride decks herself with her jewels.
11: For just as the earth her sproutings sends forth,
    And a garden makes sowings to spring up,
    So shall Adohnai Jehovah effect:
    Righteousness causing to spring forth,
    And praise before all of the nations.

Here we listen to the song of Messiah as He identifies Himself with His beloved Israel: He leads their joyful singing; His joy is one with theirs; nor surely less so with ours. Here we see the fulfilment of the word: "In the midst of the congregation will I praise Thee" (Ps. 22: 22). On the feeblest of us, too, are the garments of salvation, and the very righteousness of God covers us, for it is "on all those who believe" (Rom. 3: 22). Let us be very careful that we go into the presence of God with no other! It is to the nations of the earth that Israel is the vehicle of the display of this glory, while it is "unto principalities and powers in heavenly places that is made known *by the Church* the manifold wisdom of God" (Eph. 3).

Again, what a beautiful figure, not as a lightning-flash, gone as soon as seen, but as a garden sprouts with what is to be long enjoyed; and in *this* case forever. Righteousness is used here in the most comprehensive way: First, God's righteousness, His very character, as on a throne of inflexible justice, has become actually (Blessed be His Name!) the safeguard, protection and clothing of His redeemed, and then the knowledge of this consumes legality, exterminates rebellion, wins the heart, changes the bent of the will, and so practical righteousness springs up, and thus the Jew is no longer despised, but is the object of praise of all nations, as flowers cover a garden.

So is it ever, through all dispensations; it is the knowledge of love to us poor, wrath-deserving sinners, that results in practical holiness. Not legal endeavor, but finding that love has provided for all our helplessness in the beloved Son; and now the Spirit's law is that our true life, with all its powers, is alone in Christ Jesus, and the righteousness of the law is fulfilled in us "who walk not after the flesh but after the Spirit" (Rom. 8: 4). So may it be with us all!

# CHAPTER SIXTY-TWO

**Jerusalem, the metropolitan city of the millennial earth: the center of light, the focus of all that is beautiful. Her new name.**

SOUL-entrancing have been the visions that have passed before the eye of the prophet, but it is now the Spirit of Christ *in* the prophet (1 Pet. 1: 11) who speaks, and as He in resurrection-joy leads the singing of His people, so here He directs their longings. That same Spirit, indwelling us, directs our desires, and gives expression to them in "groanings that cannot be uttered" (Rom. 8: 26).

1: For the sake of mount Zion, I'll ne'er hold my peace,
   For the sake of Jerusalem will I rest, never,
   Till her righteousness beams as the brightness of morn,
   Her salvation shines forth as a night-torch that's blazing!
2: Then shall the Gentiles thy righteousness see,
   All the kings of the earth see thy glory;
   And thou shalt be called by a name that is new,
   Which the mouth of Jehovah determines.
3: A coronet glorious then shalt thou be,
   Held in the hand of Jehovah;
   A diadem royal then shalt thou be,
   Held in the palm of thy God!
4: Azùbah* shalt thou be called nevermore,
   Nor thy land be called Shemàmah,
   But Hephzibah shalt thou henceforth be called,
   And thy land shall be callèd Beùlah.
   The delight of Jehovah shall then be in thee,
   And thy land shall be loved as if married.
5: A young man marries a virgin,
   Thy children shall thus marry thee!
   The bridegroom joys o'er the bride,
   Thy God shall joy over thee!

We have heard the gospel preached to Israel; shall it be "mixed with faith" in the hearers? If it be, then it will awaken

---

*The words should either all be in Hebrew, or all translated—they mean in the order given: "Forsaken," "Desolate," "My delight in her," and "Married."

the keenest longings for the actual fulfilment of the promises as to Zion's glory. The very purpose of the visions has been to awaken such thirsting as only their fulfilment can satisfy. It is thus—on the same principle—that God ever works in men. Glorious things were spoken of that land that flowed with abundance; its hills and vales, its fountains and rills, its stones of iron and brass-filled mounts—all were made to pass before the people brought out of bondage. Would they spring eagerly to grasp the prize? Alas, it was not mixed with faith in them that heard, and two only of all the mass of adults ever saw that fair scene! (Heb. 4: 2).

Look at poor Job; a dark, gloomy, dense cloud overhangs him. But a beam of light surprises him and, for a time at least, he sees God, not *against* but *for* him, and in that clear light he looks afar into the future when his Redeemer shall stand—the Last—upon the earth and from his flesh he shall see God (Job 19). That vision closes with: "My reins faint with longing for that day."*

Hearken again, and give closer attention, for we are personally interested here: "And God shall wipe away all tears from their eyes: and there shall be no more death, neither sorrow, nor crying, neither shall there be any more pain: for the former things are passed away. And He that sat on the throne said, Behold, I make all things new...These words are true and faithful." Do we believe them? Do we mix them with faith? Then shall we thirst for their fulfilment, and thirsting, we may hear this word: "I will give to him that is athirst of the water of life freely." Thirst, longing, desire is the necessary prerequisite of salvation, not only in its beginnings, but to the very end!

So here the Spirit of Christ says, O rest not content till what we have seen in vision becomes an actuality, and all the nations of the earth shall see in Jerusalem's glory that she is now at last counted righteous by her God; for here the very word "righteousness" is parallel and equivalent to "salvation," as indeed it often is in the Old Testament; the righteousness shines as the *day*light, the salvation as a *night* illumination. How beautiful

---

*As the last clause of verse 27 should read.

shall Jerusalem be then! Jehovah holds her in his hand as a king may admire the crown that he takes in his hand for that purpose, and that beauty and glory must surely have another name than "Forsaken" or "Desolate"—these must be changed to "Delightful," and "Married," for she has a Protector now who loves her with an everlasting love. There is no "as" at the beginning of verse 5, but the force of the simile is strengthened rather than not by the omission; a young man's affection forces him to its object, equally naturally thy children will be drawn to thee with a love, to which nothing can compare save the first fresh love of a young man for his bride. And it is well to note that it is only the tender affection of that bridal love that is in view; for this alone would be fitting in the words, "Thy children shall marry thee." The young bridegroom has gained, and joys in, the beauty of his bride. Thy children shall gain their beloved city and rejoice in its beauty.

6: O Salem, I've placed a watch on thy walls,
Nor by day nor by night to be silent.
O ye reminders who wait on the Lord,
Be ceaseless in your intercession;
7: Nor give Him to rest till Salem He make
The object of earth's jubilation.
8: By His right hand, Jehovah hath sworn,
And by His arm that is mighty,
Ne'er will I give thy wheat to thy foes,
Nor thy wine, for which thou hast labored,
To be drunk by the sons of the stranger:
9: But they who have toiled in reaping the wheat,
Shall themselves eat the bread, the Lord praising;
They who have gathered, shall drink of the wine
In the courts of My Sanctuàry.

Again Israel's Messiah speaks, and so identified are His desires with the full accomplishment of Jerusalem's glory that He appoints watchmen on her walls, not only to oversee and guard the beloved city, but neither to rest themselves nor, by their importunate appealings, to give Jehovah rest till He brings the word of the prophetic vision to its perfect fulfilment. Jerusalem is restored to Jehovah's favor; her walls are again rebuilt, but still she has not reached the perfection of her destiny, nor until she has, must she rest, nor (and this is surely a marvellous expression to be suggested in the inspired Word) *permit her Lord to rest!*

He loves such importunity that, when assured of His mind, will not accept "no" for an answer, nor take silence as a refusal.

Does this then mean that if we only pray long enough, we may obtain *anything* that we may desire? Most people would probably refuse this; and say surely it must have the limitation of being in accord with His will, not our fickle desire. But even granting this, must we not guard it still further? For this would make *us* to be real beneficent distributors of blessings whether for ourselves or for others, and God so hard to move that only the utmost importunity, the most strenuous pressure of our petitions could change His attitude. *He* does not long to bless, it is *we* who are the real source of good. It only needs to be thus stated to be instantly rejected by every true child of God. We feel that it is nothing less than blasphemy, and yet is it not the way that the matter is commonly put? Does not this scripture, "Give Him no rest," teach it? And would not the parable of the unjust judge favor such a thought? Alas, people press that parable till they actually make it teach that God is Himself the unjust judge, or has the same callous disposition manward. I have read that one mighty in prayer used to argue it out syllogistically thus: "I desire the eternal salvation of an individual. I am told in the Scripture that God 'will have all men to be saved' (1 Tim. 2: 4), therefore He would have *that* man to be saved, so I know that I am desiring what *He* wills; and, 'If we ask anything according to His will He heareth us: and if we know that He heareth us whatsoever we ask, we know that we have the petitions that we desired of Him' (1 John 5: 14, 15), so I *know* that my prayer will result eventually in the salvation of that individual, even if I have to pray fifty years for it, as in some cases I have." That sounds perfectly logical, and yet who does not feel somewhat uneasy even in reading it? For we say: "Why limit your prayers to *one,* or even a few? The Scripture says "all men." Why not then pray persistently and feel sure that all men will be eventually saved, and not one of all mankind ever be lost, since you have been told that that is the will of God? And are you not seriously at fault if you do not grasp and plead thus confidently for all men?"

It is really, while apparently logical, a distortion of the Scripture, however innocently and even piously done. The word in Timothy simply tells us of the *disposition* of God to man— what is His wish. It does not speak of His eternal purpose, or His counsels, which must be irresistibly carried out, but of His beneficent attitude manward.

Has God then purposed and willed men to be lost? How carefully that is negatived, not only here but by 2 Peter 3: 9: "The Lord is not slack concerning His promise, as some men count slackness; but is longsuffering to us-ward, not willing* that any should perish, but that all should come to repentance." The apparently logical argument mentioned leaves out a most important factor, *the human will;* this Scripture never does. Was it because our Lord was not *willing* to give life, that those Jews lacked it? Nay. "Ye *will not* come to Me that ye might have life" (John 5: 40) is His faithful and true word. Is one saved? It is entirely of God's grace. Is one lost? It is entirely of his own will. The human will must ever be taken into account, and never must we place the God of all grace, whose very name is Love, in the position of being the unwilling One, and *we* the willing.

Here God has distinctly made it clear that His purpose is to bring Jerusalem to the place of metropolitan glory; then, cries Messiah, let us place the foot of our faith on that sure promise, and beseech Him to do what He has told us it is His purpose to do; for thus He admits us men into a partnership with Himself in the work of blessing. Our Lord (the Express Image of His Person as He is) said: "Pray ye therefore the lord of the harvest that he would send forth laborers into his harvest" (Luke 10: 2), as if the gathering in of the sheaves were not the very strongest desire of the farmer himself, and he needed to be importuned—"given no rest"—to *save his own crops!* It is nothing

---

*The word here is *boulomai,* which is stronger than the *thelo* of 1 Tim. 2: 3.

but God's gracious thoughtfulness and love for man, as if He said: "I want your companionship, your partnership, in this happy work; and there is not one of you that cannot ask Me to send out laborers into the world-harvest field. That is not a matter of gift or discriminative ability, but open to all, but when I hear one asking that, I shall know whom to send." Let us be careful not so to distort prayer that we, however unintentionally, make the salvation of sinners to depend on our winning over to mercy an unwilling or indifferent God, and ignore entirely the power of the human will.

Verses 7 to 9 are too clear to need comment.

10: Go forth!   Go forth through the wide-opened gates!
    Make the road clear for the people!
    Raise up!   Raise up the way for their feet,
    Clear it from stones that might stumble!
    A banner lift up o'er the nations.
11: Jehovah hath caused this word to resound
    Afar to th' earth's furthest borders:
    Announce to the daughter of Zion the news,
    Behold, thy salvation approaches;
    Behold, His reward with Him He doth bring,
    His retributive work lies before Him.
12: They shall be called a nation of saints,
    Those whom the Lord hath redeemèd;
    Derooshah* the name that thou shalt be called,
    A city that is not forsaken.

Here again we have an illustration of that basic truth that earth ever provides symbols of heaven, the seen being pictures of the unseen.   In this way Israel, the elect nation of God on the earth, provides pictures of the heavenly people.   Thus in the repeated, "Go forth!   Go forth through the gates," it is literal Babylon whose gates open to let the captive Israelites go free. Then their return to their own city is made easy by that "highway" that shall make the journey homeward a path of triumph. Literal as all this is, it still affords the picture that affects us.

---

*This word means, "Sought out," but as it is a title, and we have adopted the Hebrew in verse 4, it seems only consistent to do so here.

Quite as surely as Israel was subject to Babylon, so we, even this very day, are in subjection to that "Confusion" of which the very name Babylon speaks. Is there no confusion in Christendom? Out of that confusion the Lord is ever calling His people, although their complete deliverance will await that gathering shout of 1 Thess. 4: 16, when indeed a very *high-way* will be ours, for the clouds of heaven shall be our chariots to take us to His Presence.

If we agree with those who hear in these stirring words a call to the captives in Babylon to flee from that literal city, yet reason revolts from being satisfied with the escape of about 40,000, under Ezra and Nehemiah, definitely fulfilling such a series of glorious prophecies as in these few verses.

All this divinely recorded history has its deeper meaning beneath the surface, and the ancient literal Babylon, and the deliverance from it, become a foreshadowing of eternal verities, both for us on whom the ends of the ages are come, and for Israel.

It also foreshadows another earthly fulfilment when the restored Jerusalem shall attract her children from earth's remotest bounds; and the Gentiles shall at length own that that is indeed the favored nation, the one that is truly "holy," amid all those on earth. Once again, too, here we have that figure of a banner raised aloft so that all eyes are turned to it; for what, of all the events of history, could so win the rapt attention of earth's inhabitants as Jesus the Lord enthroned in Jerusalem, and His Jewish people flocking to Him, the nations owning that this is as life from the dead for Israel, and for the earth itself, its *"regeneration."* But let no one think that this prophecy is being fulfilled today; for unbelief cannot attract this tender delight of God.

# CHAPTER SIXTY-THREE

**The antiphonal character of the opening verses links them with Psalm 24. The strange misapplication by the "fathers" which has been almost universally followed. The "winepress" judgment always refers to the Jew, as the "harvest" to the Gentile. Meditation, confession, vehement desire, in natural sequence.**

THE first six verses of this chapter are clearly to be taken by themselves, and form the third and closing section of this minor division of our book. The structure is antiphonal, at once reminding us of Psalm 24, the closing verses of which give question and answer in the same way. This unique correspondence of structure leads us to question if there are not other links between our verses and that psalm. Let us see!

Both Psalm 24 and these verses occupy a third place, and even by that position both speak of the *revelation* of the same majestic Divine Personage. The first of this trilogy of psalms (Ps. 22) speaks also of a winepress, in which He on whom we are looking in Isaiah, was Himself not the Treader but the Trodden, so that the Blood that there flowed was indeed His own, and of unspeakable preciousness to us, for it was that of atonement—it is the Blood of the Cross. This is followed by Ps. 23, the few verses of which tell of a wilderness journey, through which every need is supplied by the same One who is here the Shepherd; and the psalm ends (and this we need to mark carefully) not with an introduction to our *Father's* House, but to the House of *Jehovah*. That Name fixes the *primary* application of the psalm to Israel, yet quite as evidently it makes that ending to be a type or shadow of the end of *our* wilderness journey in *our* unending dwelling in our Father's House. But we must not put aside Israel as the prime object, for the following psalm (Ps. 24) closes with the triumphant entry of her Messiah into the city whose gates are commanded to admit the Sufferer of Ps. 22 and the Shepherd of Ps. 23, but in a third character as the King of Glory. Here He is assumed to be unknown, in order that He may be introduced in the most graphic way. Let us listen then to the question, "Who is this King of Glory?" to which this answer comes: "The Lord, strong and mighty; the Lord mighty in battle." This awakens a universal shout: "Lift up your heads, O ye gates; and be ye lifted up, ye everlasting doors, and the King of Glory shall come in." But the question is repeated, as if the announcement were too stupendous to be taken in quickly: "Who is this King of Glory?" to which we hear the final word: "The Lord of Hosts, He is the King of Glory."

We must recur to this later, but it is surely intensely dramatic; nor is *this* less so:

> 1: Who is this who cometh from Edom,
> Comes with stained garments from Bozrah?
> This One so splendid in His apparel,
> Marching so proudly in fulness of strength?
>
> 'Tis I who speak in righteousness,
> And mighty am to save.
>
> 2: Why is there red upon Thine apparel,
> Thy garments like his who treads a winepress?
>
> 3: The winepress I've trodden, and trodden alone,
> Not a man of the peoples was with Me!
> For I have trodden them down in My wrath,
> And trampled them down in My fury;
> Their life-sap* upon My clothing did spurt,†
> And all of My raiment was stainèd.
> 4: For the day of avenging has been in My heart,
> And the year for redeeming My people is come.
> 5: I looked all around—there was none who could help!
> That none could uphold made Me marvel!
> Then 'twas My arm that brought Me salvation,
> Then did My fury become My support!
> 6: And down I trod nations in My just wrath,
> Made them drunk with the cup of My fury—
> Thus made their life-sap* to flow to the earth.

---

*"Life-sap," literally, the juice of the grapes; it is not the usual word for "blood."

†"Spurt," the same word we have rendered "start" in Chap. 52: 15.

The scene opens with One advancing from Edom, and more specifically from Bozrah. We shall not reach the mind of the Spirit if we take these as merely geographical localities. This in itself is not free from difficulty, for whilst this glorious Personage is evidently marching from some victory, the context makes it clear that the reference is to the last judgment upon apostates, both Jew and Gentile, at that crisis of all crises in human affairs—the Day in which our Lord comes in glory to assume His Throne over the earth. Joel (chap. 3: 12) tells us that that last judgment takes place in the "valley of Jehoshaphat" (a name that itself means "The judgment of Jehovah"), which lay to the east of Jerusalem, separating the city from the Mount of Olives. "Thither cause Thy mighty ones to come down," is the way the Spirit invokes the Lord in that prophet. In accord with this Zechariah (chap. 14) tells us that His Feet shall stand at that day on the Mount of Olives, which is also on the eastern side of the valley of Jehoshaphat.

This seems clearly enough to determine the site of that last battlefield ( although in the light of Rev. 6: 15, 16 it is too one-sided to be called a battle) to be in the vicinity of Jerusalem; but here we learn that it is in the land of Edom and near the city of Bozrah. But that does not necessarily involve any discord; for such a revelation of divine Majesty would at once cause a flight, and the pursuit may be carried on from Olivet, till the confused rout crosses the Jordan, the last stand being made in Edom, whence the divine-human Conqueror is seen returning with the evidences of His victory upon His apparel!* But even admitting this as a possible interpretation, the whole character of our book would lead us to discern a deeper than a mere geographical significance in these names. "Edom" is but another form of Adam, and may thus well stand for Adam's race, governed by that carnal mind that is enmity against God, just as Edom was ever in hostility to Israel.

---

*This does away absolutely with any possibility of Megiddo in the north being the Har Mageddon of Rev. 16: 16. Edom is not there.

In perfect harmony with this, too, is Bozrah, from *bazar* "to cut off," and applied to the gathering of grapes in the vintage (See Lev. 25: 5). Thus, in these very names we get a key to what follows; a double infliction—Edom standing for "man" as such, in a broad sense, or the Gentiles; and Bozrah for the vine of the earth, or Jew.\* Nor is it without interest to note the differences between the picture here and that which closely corresponds with it in Revelation 19, for it is the same moment. Here in Isaiah, the Conqueror is seen marching with infinite dignity; "swinging his body from the hips,"† as Delitzsch says; and coming *from* the infliction of judgment. In Revelation, however, while coming *to* that judgment (there called the "Supper of the great God"), yet even there His vesture is already seen as "dipped in blood." This forbids a literal interpretation, for His raiment could not have been dipped in what we know as blood in *heaven* whence He then comes; but it is a perfect *symbolic* picture of a judgment that has already been inflicted in the heavenlies upon rebellious principalities and powers as in Rev. 12: 7-9. This is clearly confirmed in our book, for punishment has to fall on "the host of the high ones on high," as well as "on the kings of the earth upon the earth" (chap. 24).

Let us then endeavor to recast the scene. We are standing in Palestine, and looking eastward from Jerusalem. From afar we discern One advancing. Nearer He comes till we note that His apparel, splendid as it is, is deeply blood-stained. To question One who here comes in such splendor, such awe-inspiring Majesty, as when transfigured on the Holy Mount, would be too familiar, and so we ask—not addressing anyone directly, but looking about as if to find anyone who can tell us—who this can be. He Himself must reply, for His Name no one knows

---

\*This spiritual significance of the words Edom and Bozrah is confirmed by the twofold reaping in Rev. 14. The time is the same, and there we can see "Edom" in the widespread harvest of the *earth* (verses 14-16), and "Bozrah" in the localized harvest of the *vine;* the Gentile in the former, the Jew in the latter.

† This is the meaning given to the word rendered in A.V. "travelling" (ver. 1), or as in text, "marching so proudly."

but Himself (Rev. 19: 12). That reply is stern and terse, again uniting those two apparently opposing terms, "righteousness"' and "salvation," for He speaks in righteousness and yet is "mighty to save." His very righteousness makes Him mighty to save those who are oppressed. Emboldened by His condescension in thus answering, we ask Him directly: "How is it that Thine apparel is thus stained as one that treads the winepress?" He takes up that word and says: "It is indeed the winepress that I have trodden, and that alone, for of the peoples, the Gentiles, there was none with Me. In this winepress guilty men have taken the place of the grapes; and it is *their* blood that has thus stained My raiment."

Here we must tread carefully, for in no passage in our book has the error that has come down to us from the so-called "fathers," of forcing Christian truth into Jewish Scriptures, been more evidenced than here. They taught that the blood that stained His garments was His own. But the mere superficial reading of the verses should be enough to dispel such a distorted application in a moment. Some of the "fathers" taught it, "Rome" adopted it, and what she calls "the Church" accepted it through the centuries. This certainly provides a loud call to accept nothing that has only tradition to justify its existence. Well may we test, by the Word of God, *everything* that we have accepted.

This blood is that of Israel's oppressors, and yet, if I mistake not, it is not the Gentiles who are, at least primarily, in view in this terrible picture of the trodden winepress. For we must ever remember that in that last day of the revelation of the Lord in righteous judgment—the heavenly redeemed having been taken Home—there will be four distinct parties left upon the stage. First, the Gentiles, confederated under one federal head, forming that clearly foretold event, a revival of the fourth empire of Daniel's second chapter. In close alliance with these, both politically and in Satanic apostasy, will be the mass of the Jews, back in their land, to which our own eyes see them now going. Then in the third place there will be a large number of penitent Gentiles whom we see in the latter part of chapter 7 of Revelation. Finally, a fourth company will be composed of the penitent remnant of Jews, who will repeat the opposition to the future Antichrist, as the Maccabees made to the past Antiochus, and these will seize the citadel of Jerusalem, stand siege there by the combined forces of apostasy, both Jew and Gentile, suffer defeat (Zech. 14), and, when at their last gasp, will be relieved by the revelation of that glorious Person of whom our chapter speaks, and who will inflict judgment on both Jew and Gentile apostates.

But even in this there is some discrimination between them. The Lord here says, "Of the peoples (and in that plural form it always means the Gentiles) there was none with Me;" but if the Gentiles were themselves the object of the infliction, it would be incongruous to expect their assistance or association in inflicting it. So I conclude that the "winepress" refers to judgment on the apostate mass of the Jews (as also in Rev. 14: 18), who are fully as hostile to the pious remnant of their brethren as the Gentiles, and who are here seen in the winepress.

The emphasis on "Of the *peoples* (or Gentiles) there was none with Me," seems rather to imply that the Lord places Himself at the head of those Jewish youths who, as the psalmist says, shine like morning dew in the rays of the Sun of Righteousness. They are at this time His "willing people" (Ps. 110), and, when we turn the light of other Scriptures on the scene, have the honor of sharing in that dreadful day of avenging, as speaks Ps. 58: 10: "The righteous shall rejoice when he seeth the vengeance, he shall wash his feet in the blood of the wicked." And again: "To execute upon them the judgment written: this honor have all His saints" (Ps 149: 9),

Returning now to the scene in Isaiah, let us draw nearer but without joining in the "vengeance," for which we have little desire. The most one-sided of all battles is over. The Victorious Commander (chap. 55: 4) is returning, heading His little band of "willing people." We will join it and accompany it, as it re-crosses Jordan, and goes on its way to Jerusalem. Would that, think you, be a silent journey? How far from it! Every possible ascription of praise would fill the air, and all might be focussed in the term, "King of Glory." As we approach the city,

we are met by another company from it, and they take up the
word asking: "Who is this King of Glory?" Can we not hear
the shout, as all hands point to the Leader: "Jehovah Tzebaoth!
He is the King of glory!" Then comes the command of the
Zionists: "Lift up your heads, O ye gates, and be ye lifted up,
ye everlasting doors, and the King of Glory shall come in!" So
Salem welcomes the King she crucified. It is with joy and sorrow
mingling; the joy we see here, the sorrow in Zech. 12. Thus
would the two antiphones meet, and the psalm take its place of
sequence after Isaiah.

A change now comes over the spirit of the prophecy—a striking change from the vision of the Victor triumphantly marching
from Edom. Gently and meditatively it begins, but the retrospect warms the heart, the words increase in strength, till they
close in a perfect storm of confession and longing desire, which is
carried into the next chapter.

This is the first of the last sub-section, and again has marked
upon it the significant "three."

1: Verses 7-14: Retrospective and meditative.
2: Verses 15-19a: Confession and Petition.
3: Verses 19b-Ch. 64: 12: Vehement desire.

As Israel always provides patterns for us (1 Cor. 10), her
condition just prior to the intervention of her Lord will be of
peculiar value, as telling us what shall be our condition as the
responsible witness for God on the earth, just prior to our Lord's
intervention on our behalf, and gives us the one sure mark that
shall evidence those who are true amid a mass of dead and
luke-warm profession—*that* surely must command our interest.

7: The mercies of Jehovah will I now remember,
   The praises of Jehovah will I now recall,
   According unto all that Jehovah hath bestowed on us;
   The goodness so great He hath shown to Isr'el's house,
   The which He hath given them in His lovingkindnesses,
   According to His many, very many, mercies.

8: He hath said to Himself: Surely they're My people,
Children that will never turn to lie:
So He was to them a Saviour, and that in very deed.
9: In all their distresses distressed too was He,
By the angel of His presence did He save them!
In His love and compassion He redeemed them,
Took them up and carried them all the days of old.
10: But they did rebel, and grieve His holy Spirit;
Then He turned against them and became their foe!
Aye, He did indeed even war against them!
11: Then His people called to mind* the days that were gone by,
E'en the days of Moses; and they cried, Oh, where is He
Who raisèd them from out of the sea's dark depths,
By the shepherd of His flock?
Oh, where is He who put His holy Spirit in him?†
12: The arm so majestic that did lead them,—
Led them by the right hand of Moses,
Before them split the waters, to make Himself a name,
A name that should remain forevermore!
13: Who led them through the deeps, like a horse in a pasture,‡
So that they did not even stumble?
14: Like domestic cattle that go down to the valley,
The Spirit of Jehovah brought them to their rest.
Thus didst Thou lead Thy people in the past,
To make Thyself a Name of excellent renown.

When Isaiah wrote this chapter, Israel certainly had not reached the low condition it describes. Not yet was the sanctuary in Jerusalem trodden down; not yet had Jehovah fought against them; not yet was the House of David set aside. On the contrary the most gracious promise that the Word contains is in a communication to the worst of the kings, Ahaz (chap.

---

*There is much question as to the subject of the verb "called to mind." The A. V. and Revised in the text, with many others, make it read as Jehovah asking, "Where is he?" but I have eventually adopted the marginal reading of the Revised that the word "people" is the subject, for it brings the whole passage into direct accord with all Scripture that tells of the result of chastening. When it leads to exercise it awakens memories of a better time, and thus a longing for the recovery of it.

†That is, in Moses.

‡"As a horse gallops over the plain" (*Delitzsch*).

7), while, as we have seen, the message that the "sun-dial" brought to Hezekiah was full of grace. But in these verses the Spirit of Christ transports the spirit of the prophet far into the future; and then he speaks from that standpoint, telling what he sees *there*. This foresight is, and must be, the very essence of divine prophecy, and the clearest proof that, in the Book that records these prophecies, we have to do with God. This was the very ground of Jehovah's challenge to the false deities, and it will still serve today as a test of what is called "spiritualism;" for we too can take up that challenge and say, "Let them show us what shall happen." Wicked spirits may, through their human mediums, tell where a lost article may be found, or the physical condition of another who is far away, and a hundred other wonders, but not one of them can foretell with any certainty the future. But with Jehovah, so certain is the accomplishment of what He foretells that He speaks of it as already accomplished and past.

In our book of *Christian* prophecy with its significant title "Revelation," it is revealed to us how the human spirit is thrown forward into future scenes; for there the human writer, John, is transported by the Spirit of God into what is termed "The Lord's Day" as being in direct contrast with *man's* day (1 Cor. 4: 3, where the marginal reading is the correct one). John's body was in *man's* day, suffering from the injustice of man's judgment. John's spirit became in the Lord's day, and so he sees the Lord Jesus standing in judgment, not of the world but in the midst of the churches (Rev. 1: 10).

Thus in the first six verses of this chapter of Isaiah, the prophet becomes in Spirit in *the day of the Lord* (not the Lord's Day), and sees His triumphant intervention for His afflicted earthly people. But in what follows we are led back to those exercises in the remnant of His people that justified that intervention.

Keeping in mind that in Israel we have a pattern for ourselves, and that what led to Jehovah's intervention for her will lead to our Lord Jesus intervening for us, we note that the first step is in remembering the past. Strange paradox in the ways

of God with His people, for is it not written: "Forgetting the
things that are behind" (Phil. 3: 13)?   Yes, but it also written:
"Remember what ye were in times past" (Eph. 2: 11).  We have
both to forget and to remember; to forget, that is, not to dwell
on, any past attainment that would hinder our race to our goal,
Christ in glory; but still to remember what we were in the
bondage of sin, and the love that delivered us from that bondage,
for that too shall quicken our steps on our homeward way.

In verse 8 is a sentence that demands some comment: "For
He said, Surely they are My people, children that will never turn
to falsehood."  The prophet appears to attribute to Jehovah an
expectation that proves baseless, as if He did not know what was
in man, and here sighs His disappointment.  This has led some
to translate, "Children must not lie;" that is, it is a prohibition.
But apart altogether from any deeper consideration, this is such
a very tame, weak, and flat rendering, so entirely inconsistent
with the lively force and beauty of the prophet's style, that we
reject it.  We must remember too that this is not a direct word
from Jehovah Himself, but a retrospect by one speaking for the
people, and thus he makes his thoughts vividly clear by this human way of speaking.  Jehovah has done everything that a human father could do for his children, and had every reason for
expecting the filial affection and full confidence of their hearts.
For this is, I believe, the force of the word "lie" here, as in chap.
28:15, "Under falsehood (the same word) have we hid ourselves."
In neither case is it merely a mis-statement of facts, but the heart
turning away from God to idols, from Christ to other confidences,
as in 1 John 2: 22, "Who is the liar but he that denieth that
Jesus is the Christ?"

Is there nothing in this for us?  Can we read coldly and
unmoved of His dealings with Israel and not see the correspondences there are to His dealings with each of us?  We were
in bondage; were we not?  He redeemed us by His own sufferings; did He not?  He has borne with us to this hour; has He
not?  Is He not entitled to our heart's full confidence?  Every
rival to Him then is a *lie*.

In verse 10 the Redeemer, kind and pitiful, is changed in

His governmental dealings with them to be their enemy. But bear in mind this is not Jehovah speaking, but an inspired record of Israel's experience. It does not mean that Jehovah *really* was their foe, but His providences had that appearance, for He gives them up to foe after foe as in the Book of Judges, since they have grieved His holy Spirit. The word "Spirit" is not used here exactly as it is in the New Testament, of the third Person of the Holy Trinity, for that truth was not yet revealed. To a pious Jew the term "Spirit" seems to have referred, when thus used, to the realized presence of God, as in the parallelism of Ps. 39: 7: "Whither shall I go from Thy Spirit? or whither shall I flee from Thy Presence?" It is the felt, realized presence of God who is Spirit, and in our chapter is a parallel idea to "the angel of His Presence."

How blessed is adversity to the true people of God! In itself, it does not distinguish them from the world, but in its effects it does. They are not marked today by freedom from bereavement, loss, or sickness, or death; all these come indifferently to all. It is man, as man, who "is born to trouble as the sparks fly upward" (Job 5: 7). Let verses 11 to 14 show where the distinction begins. On the one hand there is hopeless despairing grief, or an endeavor to drown all memory in worldly excitement, or a bitter arraignment of God's ways; but on the other, there is a remembrance of, and a turning to, Him whose love has been so clearly shown in His ways with them from the beginning. Our memories turn not to the shadows of Moses and the Red Sea, not to the strong east wind and the black night, but to the substance of these in the "storm that bowed His blessed head"—to the sorrows of Gethsemane, and the unseen but deeper sorrows of the Cross. No; neither sorrow nor sickness, pain nor death, are in the least discriminative; but penitent self-judgment, due to memories of the past, and finding our way to His Feet, do mark the child of God, and turn the *suffering* that is common to all into chastening which distinguishes the true-born child from the bastard (Heb. 12: 8).

Here Israel remembers the sea and its depths through which their fathers were led with such a sure foot that it was like a

horse galloping over a pasture, or as cattle quietly leaving the
mountains for the valleys to feed and rest, and after first asking,
"Where is He who led them?" answers it by, "It was Thou who
didst this, to make Thy Name attractive, as Saviour and Lover, to
be remembered forever." This awakens the cry:

> 15: From heaven look down and regard,
>     From where Thy holiness dwells,
>     From where Thy glory inhabits.
>     Oh, where is Thy zeal? The display of Thy strength?
>     Thy yearnings of love to me? All are restrained.
> 16: For Thou art our Father alone:
>     For Abraham knoweth us not,
>     Israel owneth us not;
>     Our Father, Jehovah, art Thou,
>     Our Redeemer Thy name from of old.
> 17: Oh, why, from Thy ways hast Thou made us to stray?
>     And hardened our hearts from Thy fear?
>     Lord, for the sake of Thy servants, return,
>     The tribes that Thou dost inherit!
> 18: How brief is the time that Thine own holy ones
>     Have held it in their own possession.
>     'Tis *Thy* sanctuary our foes have downtrodden.
> 19: We've become as the rest of the nations,
>     Over whom Thou hast never borne rule,
>     Who have not been called by Thy name.

What pathos there is in this affecting appeal! Our printed
page reads coldly, and the living Spirit of God can alone communicate to us the real feeling with which the words were written.
It is not here a little company of Jews who are weeping at the
stones of their ancient city, but these are looking heavenward,
with tears streaming down their cheeks, and they cry: "Look
down once more from that heaven so uncontaminated by human
foe, and regard the conditions on this earth. In heaven Thy holiness and Thy glory still find unrivalled dwelling; but what a
contrast is here! Thy Temple is closed and downtrodden (Dan.
9: 27). Oh, where is Thy zeal, and where Thy strength? Alas,
those yearnings of Thy love are now restrained.

"We sprang from Abraham—he is our father. Israel is our
mother. But both have forsaken us, and will own no relationship.

But is it not written that, 'When my father and my mother forsake me, the Lord will take me up' (Ps. 27: 10). We confess
that we have turned from every expresssion of Thy love, till now
Thou hast hardened our hearts, and we have lost all that we
enjoyed for such a brief space, and are become as those who have
never had Thy rule, or borne Thy name. Could anything exceed
our misery?"

In this pathetic picture of Israel in those last days we may
see our own state today, as our Lord speaks to us in the letter
to the Church in Laodicea (Rev. 3: 14). The boastings that we
hear on all sides are but history repeating itself, as it ever will,
while the comparatively few who are confessing, with many a
secret sigh, the true condition of the Church, take the place of
that "Remnant" of Israel to whose cries we have been listening.
Many a heart is joining with that beloved earthly people in the
cry of the next chapter: "Oh, that Thou wouldst rend the
heavens and come down!" It is indeed *our* hope, as well as
theirs, although ours is to join Him in the air, before He reaches
the earth in judgment.

## CHAPTER SIXTY-FOUR

**Jehovah's intervention irresistible. Jehovah's discrimination in judgment. Confession and appeal.**

THIS chapter is in such close relation with the preceding one that in the Hebrew Bible the first verse of this is placed in the earlier chapter; and since the second verse, as we have it, speaks of the consequences of Jehovah coming down, we see that there cannot be any real separation between them. The "three" parts may again be discerned thus:

1: Verses 1-3: Jehovah's intervention irresistible.
2: Verses 4, 5: Jehovah's discrimination in government.
3: Verses 6-12: Confession and final appeal.

The first of these continues an ardent appeal for Jehovah's intervention and is again clearly divided by the threefold "from before Thee."

    1: Oh, that Thou wouldst the heavens rend,
       Thyself to earth come down;
       So would the very mountains melt
       And trembling pass from 'fore Thee!
    2: As the fire makes brushwood burn,
       As the fire makes water boil,
       So would Thy Name to foes be known
       And nations shake from 'fore Thee!
    3: When Thou didst do those deeds of dread,
       Which we had not expected,
       Thou camest down, and mountains then
       Did trembling pass from 'fore Thee!

Look at the scene! Here is a man, representative of Israel, with streaming eyes and bent knees crying for Jehovah to tear the very heavens apart, come to earth, cause mountains to flow down, and shaking in terror pass away; then, as sure as fire makes brushwood to kindle and water to boil, so would these enemies of Jehovah (for our foes are His too) learn what the Name of

"Jehovah" really means, and would call, but call in vain, for the fleeing mountains to hide them from that burning wrath that once before caused that "mountain" of Egypt to pass away from before His face with trembling terror.

Now if Israel still provides types for us—and who that reads 1 Cor. 10: 11 can admit that to be even a question?—so shall we too, out of the depths of our distress, cease lukewarmly to "hold the doctrine of the Lord's coming," and cry like them, "Oh, tear the heavens apart and come!" Only such aspirations can justly express the heart's longing for the coming of our Lord Jesus.

With that self-centred spirit that remains in us all, we are but too prone to attribute to our prayers themselves, the gifts of divine grace. "Prayer changes things," we say, and true as that is, we must still be careful that in the words we do not transfer our praise from our prayer-hearing God to our own prayers. How frequently God hears the Intercessor who is nearest to Him (His Son) and acts without any prayer at all from His people, for His grace surpasses all that we ask or think. Did the disciples beseech Him to wash their feet? Did the two on the way to Emmaus beg for His company? Were the disciples gathered together on the first day of the week praying that He would come to them, when He appeared in their midst? Not at all; He is ever active in grace. Of this we have a sample in verse 3, as the prophet identifying himself with his people cries: "What Thou didst once, when we did *not* wait on Thee expectant, Thou wilt surely do now that we *do*." There is no setting aside or belittling the value of prayer in this, for the speaker goes on: "With terrifying deeds Thou didst come to our relief in Egypt, when our pain-extorted groan alone appealed to Thee, but now, not those groans alone, but our hearts, cry, Oh, tear open the heavens, and come down, for groans surely cannot end Thy ways with Thy people." Then the speaker goes on:

> 4: For from everlasting none has ever heard,
>    No ear has e'er perceived,
>    No eye has ever seen,
>    A God to be compared with Thee,

Who does such deeds on his behalf
Who waits expectant on Him.*
5: Thou meetest him who doth rejoice
In doing what is right,
And those who bear Thee aye in mind
In all Thy wondrous ways:
Behold, behold, Thou angry wast,
'Twas *we* then who had sinned:
In these is everlastingness
And so we shall be saved.†

The apostle quotes verse 4 very freely in 1 Cor. 2, and adds, "Neither hath it entered into the heart of man." No one has ever discerned a God who interposes so marvelously for those who trust Him, and with a confidence that tells of a heart won, just quietly wait His time for their relief. But in the New Testament Epistle it has quite a different connection, for there is added the significant sentence: "But God hath revealed them to us by His Spirit." There the reference is not to the manifested acts in the past, but to the deep things of God which are even *now* *revealed* to those who are themselves spiritual. None but the Spirit of God can communicate these precious things, for the very capability of a *man* is limited to "the things of a *man*" (1 Cor. 2: 11), and these are far beyond that. But the Spirit of God has not now left the future of eternity in the dark, to be the subject of imagination, speculation, or poetic sentimentality, but to the Christian with whom that divine Teacher is not grieved, these unsearchable wonders are revealed. The basic idea common to both the Old Testament writer and the New is that none can wait upon God in vain, for His delight is to give and bless.

This is emphasized in the fifth verse. Never hast Thou turned Thy back on any one who rejoiced in Thy holy ways; but then

---

*Amid many various renderings I have kept as close as the text will permit to the apostle's free quotation in 1 Cor. 2: 9.

†This line is obscure, and even the R. V. suggests that the text is corrupt. "Few texts have caused interpreters more perplexity than this, and twenty or thirty renderings have been proposed" (Birks). Under such conditions, any translation must be more or less a paraphrase to be intelligible at all; nor is the latent idea as obscure as the words that clothe it.

look at the sad history of our nation; it seems summed up in
"wrath and sin: sin and wrath." Thou changest never in Thy
attitude to sin—it is always wrath; but neither dost Thou change
in Thine attitude to confession and penitence—it is always salvation. Thy ways are ever consistent and unchanging; we can say,
"In them is everlastingness," so on our part we will continue in
the way of penitence and confession, and so shall be saved. We
will therefore confess the simple truth:

> 6: For we are become as a vile filthy thing,
>     Every one of us!
>     As a garment defiled are our righteousnesses,
>     Every one of them!
>     E'en as an autumn leaf do we fade,
>     Every one of us!
>     Our sins as a storm-blast have swept us away!
> 7: There is never a one who calls on Thy name,
>     Stirs himself up to take hold upon Thee;
>     For Thou hast turned Thy face away from us,
>     And given us up to the hand of our sins.*
> 8: But now, O Jehovah, Thou art our Father:
>     We are the clay and Thou art the Potter,
>     And we are the work of Thine hands,
>     Every one of us!
> 9: Oh, be not, Jehovah, wroth to the uttermost,
>     Nor our iniquity aye bear in mind;
>     Behold and consider, oh, we beseech Thee,
>     For we are Thy people, Thy people indeed,
>     Every one of us!
> 10: Thy cities so holy have now become desert,
>      Zion itself has now become desert,
>      Jerusalem now has become desolation.
> 11: The house of our holiness and our adorning,
>      Wherein our fathers adored Thee,
>      Has been utterly burnt up with fire.
>      The things we deemed to be precious
>      Have now been laid utterly waste,
>      Every one of them! †

---

*"Given up" is literally "melted," that is, Jehovah had given
them over (as one pours melted metal) to the power (hand) of
their sins, just as in Rom. 1: 24, 26, 28.

†Note the doubled "three" pressed upon these verses: the "all"
in the A.V., "every one of us" here.

12: Oh wilt Thou, Jehovah, restrain Thee,
   In view of such doings as these,
   And in Thine unlimited silence
   Leave us to unlimited suff'ring?

Is it not pathetic and affecting?  What can we plead before
Thee?  We look at ourselves, there is not one of us but is polluted.  We consider our doings, the very best of them; our
righteousnesses, far from being an honor, are as a filthy rag that
defiles all it touches.  While Godward, our sins have provoked
Thy wrath, and this has swept us away, as the faded leaves of
autumn are scattered by the blasts.

But that does not affect this truth, that Thou art the Source
of our existence as a nation.  We are as fully Thy work as is
the vessel that the potter makes from the clay.  Canst Thou,
then, leave Thy work so defaced?  Canst Thou leave us in such
wretchedness as shall make all creation judge that Thy love,
wisdom, and power are helpless?—that Thy love is so limited
that Thou canst leave us in our shame, Thy wisdom so limited
that Thou canst find no way of restoring us, and Thy power so
limited that Thou canst not carry out that way?

"O Jehovah, look at Thy cities, once so populous!  They
are as silent as the desert now!  Consider Zion itself; it is
desert now.  Jerusalem lies at the mercy of the desolator, and
shows it in her miserable condition.  That very Sanctuary, holy
and beautiful as it was, in which our fathers raised their songs
of adoration, is worse than silent now—it is in ashes!  While
those precious things, laver, lampstand, table, are now all laid
waste!

"But Thou dost love; how hard it must be for Thee then to
restrain those tender affections!  Is it possible that Thou canst
have such self-control as to see the miserable conditions of those
Thou hast loved, without interposing?  Wilt Thou by keeping
limitless silence—for that is all that is needed—leave us to a
suffering limitless?"

So wrote the prophet with eyes so anointed that he saw afar
to a time that even now, to this day, lies in the future, when

a God-fearing remnant of Jews will thus be mourning as they who mourn for their first-born (Zech. 12: 12). The interposition of Jehovah on behalf of the penitent remnant of His people of which Isaiah speaks, is to be final, and cannot possibly be fully exhausted by the return under Nehemiah, for that was only to eventuate in fresh sorrow, whilst in the prophet's eye Jerusalem is to be a new creation, and the voice of weeping is to be heard nevermore in her (chap. 65: 18). That justifies our saying that this prophecy awaits still its fulfilment; for do not Zion's stones still only echo her wailings?

Again we may ask, Is there no correspondence between their condition and ours? Is Israel alone the "clay?" Scripture gives a clear negative, for Rom. 9: 21-24 permits no such limitation. The whole race of men is but "clay" and of this the Jewish people is only a sample. In the picture our prophet gives us we can see our own condition as the present responsible witness of God upon the earth. It is then "we who have sinned." We may have relegated too much to the evangelist the confession, "All our righteousnesses are as filthy garments,"* leaving him to convict by it the careless and profane. Such disposal of it is scarcely permissible, unless we esteem the prophet himself to be an ungodly sinner and not a forgiven saint, for he must be included in the "us." The truth is that to the very end, our very best deeds, even those that have been wrought in us by the Spirit of Christ are ever—let that infinitely searching ray of the Light of God fall on them—so stained by the defiling medium by which they have been done, that they are filthy. The very basis of our title to eat of the Tree of Life is that those "garments" have been washed (Rev. 22: 14), the Blood of the Lamb alone makes them white (Rev. 7: 14), and makes them form those white robes that are the righteousnesses of the saints. This is not what Scripture terms "the best robe"—that is Christ in all the virtue of His atoning work, and that needs no washing at all; let us be very careful not to lack that garment, or the result can

---

*The unjustified word "rags" is apt to divert the mind from the correct meaning of *beged*, "garment."

be foreseen in Matt. 22: 12, 13.   There is that danger, or the Lord would not warn us (Rev. 16: 15).

I beg any fellow-believer who reads these lines to note this mark of the Spirit of God in the last hours of any dispensation: the speaker is ever saying, *"Every one of us."*   No Pharisee is this petitioner, thanking God that he is not as other men.   He identifies himself with all the rest, confesses his own full share in all that has brought dishonor on the Name.   It is by this humble confession, amid a mass of boasting, that the true Israel was, is, and ever shall be manifested.

Surely we have, "every one of us," to use the words of our prophet, a part in that responsible witness, and so we will not say *"they,"* but *"we* have sinned," and thus confess to our place and part in the present Witness upon earth, a Witness that has failed as much beyond all who have gone before as its privileges have exceeded.   But our boast and hope shall be in One sitting at the right hand of the Majesty on high, with whom failure is unknown, and with whom interest and love for His redeemed never chills nor varies!

# CHAPTER SIXTY-FIVE

**Jehovah repudiates the religion of the mass, tenderly appreciates the penitence of the Remnant. The grace of God, if dammed up at one spot, flows with undiminished power in another. The race of men in danger of extermination: what prevents it. Meaning of "dust, the serpent's meat."**

SO portentous is our day, so evidently do we see another day approaching, that every glimmer of light that the Holy Scriptures may afford can only be welcomed with heartfelt gratitude to their Author. The present dispensation is about to come to a close, a close that is filled with judgment from God, a judgment terrible in proportion to the proud boasting of men and of privileges unavailed of. All prophetic Scripture gives one united testimony to the awful failure of the one responsible witness of God upon the earth, and black and threatening indeed is the cloud that overhangs the whole sphere of Christian profession. Can we neglect any light that our Father has given us? Has He not caused Israel's history to be recorded for the very purpose that we on whom the ends of the ages have come (1 Cor. 10: 11) may have that light? With these thoughts to increase our interest let us turn to the first seven verses of this chapter, noting that its *three* divisions may each be sufficiently characterized by one word, thus:

1: Verses  1-7:  Denunciation.
2: Verses  8-16:  Discrimination.
3: Verses 17-25:  New-creation.

1: By those who asked not for Me I'm sought,
   Whilst those who sought not have found Me.
   I said to a nation: Here am I!  Here am I!
   To a nation My name not invoking.
2: But all the day long have I stretched out My hand
   In appeal to a people rebellious,
   To a people that walk in a path that's not good:
   The way that their own thought devises.

3: A people that ever provokes Me to wrath
   To My face without intermission.
   For the place of their sacrifice, gardens they chose;
   On altars of brick burn their incense.
4: Who dwell in the tombs, in dark caverns lodge,
   The flesh of the swine is their eating,
   Abom'nable broth's in their vessels.
5: Who cry, Keep away!   Come not to me near,
   For I am than thou far more holy!
   These are indeed a smoke in My nose,
   A fire continually burning.
6: 'Tis written before Me: no silence I'll keep,
   But pay—yea, pay to their bosom—
7: Your sins and the sins of your fathers combined,
   Who incense have burned on the mountains,
   And brought Me to scorn on the hill-tops.
   'Tis for this I will weigh the reward for their work,
   From the very first,* into their bosom.

Here Isaiah is indeed, as the apostle speaks, "very bold" (Rom. 10: 20), for like those kine that, leaving their calves behind, went lowing to Bethshemesh (1 Sam. 6: 12), so he goes in a way contrary to all his natural and national inclinations, for what Jew would of his own will speak of his nation being set aside in favor of the uncircumcised Gentile?   The tender grace of God to poor man is like a mighty river.   Let human pride, let lukewarm indifference, let self-complacent religion, bar its course, it sweeps away in another direction.   Let Judea make Him weary, Samaria shall give Him refreshment (John 4).   Let the Pharisee exclude, the Publican shall welcome.   Let New York and London turn from Him, then China and Africa shall turn to Him: if barred in one course it sweeps on in another.   But what of those who have turned away from those appealing Hands?   What of those who have rejected that tender grace?   There can be noth-

---

*The precise bearing of the word is rather doubtful. It means either, "the first thing that Jehovah will do," or He will recompense all the former sins, the sins of their fathers, upon them, since they have walked in the same path. I have adopted this latter in accord with Matt. 23: 30-35.

ing but judgment!  And, inflicting that, Jehovah would strike
where their affections were most sensitive, their *"bosom."*

In these seven verses, then, we have three cryptic indictments
brought against the Christ-rejecting Jews and against Christ-
rejecting Christians.

1: They sacrifice in gardens and burn incense on altars of
   brick.
2: They dwell among the tombs and lodge in the darkest
   places.
3: They feed on swine's flesh and their broth is made of
   abominable things.

Further in these three we again discern that all three parts
of man's tripartite being are in view:

1: *God*ward in their sacrifices; in the sphere of the *spirit*.
2: *Earth*ward or *Man*ward in their dwelling among men; a
   relationship of the *soul*.
3: *Self*ward in their food, which clearly speaks of the *body*.

In such minute details as these we discern the inimitable
Fingerprints of our God, binding the whole volume together into
one, of which He alone *can* be the Author, and we have to do
with Him.

As these first verses speak of the Lord turning from Israel to
the Gentiles, the standpoint of the time of the prophecy must
be those earlier chapters of Acts in which we see God still linger-
ing over Israel, for even after the Lord Jesus was taken up to
heaven, for a time His Hands were still stretched out appealingly
to Israel, as Peter speaks: "Repent ye therefore, and be converted, that your sins may be blotted out, that so there may
come seasons of refreshing from the presence of the Lord, and
that He may send Christ, who hath been appointed for you, even
Jesus" (Acts 3: 19, 20, R.V.).

That clearly speaks of the possibility of the Lord's return even
at that time for Israel's blessing, and He would have so returned
had the representative heads of the nation repented, as they will
do when He does come (Zech. 12: 12, 13).  But at last, after the
stoning of Stephen, Paul and Barnabas pronounce the fateful sen-

tence: "Lo, we turn to the Gentiles" (Acts 13: 46). Then Israel's history as a nation, is ended for a time, although only for a time (Hos. 3: 4, 5).

But that being the time of the prophecy it is sure that the Jews did not, at that time, sacrifice in gardens or on altars of brick. Very far from that. They were most punctilious in the observance of every external detail of their religion. That religious man whom we see praying in the temple (Luke 18: 10) was an excellent representative of them all; would he—with his fasting twice in the week, and giving tithes of all he possessed— would *he* have eaten swine's flesh, or done anything that is here charged? It is unthinkable.

But that puts into our hands the needed key. These charges cannot be taken literally; but Jehovah looks at the sacrifices, and tells the worshippers what is *His* estimate of what they were bringing to Him with such self-complacent assurance.

In that light it is not the temple, but their "gardens" in which they are really. They may be externally and corporeally in the temple, it is true, but their spirit is entirely occupied— not with *His* glory of which "every whit" in that temple ever speaks (Ps. 29: 9)—but with their own religious goodness; and so it is in the "gardens" that their own hands have made, that they are really sacrificing. Was not that Pharisee, again I say, who tells God of all his own excellent doings, was he not, while in the temple literally, really sacrificing in his *garden?* Indeed he was. He was following closely in the way of his father Cain, who "brought of the fruit of the ground"—that is, of *his* garden —although in that early day we have only the seed, the full-grown plant of which we have developed later. There was no lamb, no confession of sin, no offering of blood, the need for them is ignored.

Further, look at the altars on which they are burning their incense; they are made of bricks. That sends our thoughts back to Babel and its tower, for there too "they had brick for stone and slime for mortar." Those bricks, like the gardens, then also clearly speak of the work of their own hands; and based on these, as the offering is on the altar, they expected their approach to God to be acceptable. It is the "altar that sanctifies the gift," and can such an altar as defiled and defiling human works sanctify anything?

Are these "gardens" as beautiful in God's sight as in their own? Very far from it. Since they have not come to Him for *life*, who alone can give it, they are not "gardens" that speak of life on all sides, but "tombs" in which they are really dwelling with all the dead for their companions, and in a darkness that is intense, since the very light they claim is itself darkness (Matt. 6: 23).

This brings us to the third and strictly personal mark: they "eat swine's flesh, and the broth of abominable things is in their vessels." This will no more bear a literal interpretation than the others. No Jew of that day, "tithing mint, anise, and cummin," would even think of touching swine's flesh. But while he thus avoided the shadow, he embraced the substance. To get what that substance is, we must throw on it the light of Lev. 11, where Jehovah specifies what His people may eat and what they must avoid among the creatures of earth, air and water. It was not simply because these might be indigestible foods that they were forbidden. We have not arrived at the truth at all, if we thus stay on the surface of such scriptures. If we do, then the profane criticism of our "modernists" is largely justified, and "no person of education or refinement can read Leviticus with either pleasure or profit."*

When our Lord said: "Not that which goeth into the mouth defileth a man, but that which cometh out of the mouth, this defileth a man" (Matt. 15: 11), He surely showed that the real *source* of defilement was not the external eating, but something *within*, and these injunctions were given for the very purpose of showing that, in a figure. This demands a few words more. "Feeding" in the prophetic scriptures evidences what people are; for they hunger for, and eat what is in accord with their own nature. Place hay before a man, and meat before a horse, and

---

*This was actually said in my hearing by one of the leading teachers of that school.

both would turn away with disgust. Reverse the offerings, and both would be received with pleasure. So people show what they are spiritually by what they feed upon spiritually. The Germans have a saying, "*Man ist was er isst,*" "Man is what he eats," and that is true both in the lower and higher sense, for what he eats becomes in both senses a part of himself. If one feeds on any food, that becomes part of one's body. Thus if one feeds on what "swine's flesh" spiritually symbolizes, it evidences that spiritually he is of the same nature. He has selected his food to accord with his own nature. He assimilates it; it suits him, for by nature *he is a swine!* Let us then seek to discern why this swine's flesh was forbidden. Lev. 11:7 reads: "The swine, though he divide the hoof, and be cloven-hoofed, yet he cheweth not the cud." Both these marks, dividing the hoof and chewing the cud, were needed for the animal to be fit food for the people of God. I venture again to say, that if this has no meaning below the surface, it is unworthy of a child's primer, and nothing more puerile can be found in the religious systems of Maories or Hottentots. But reason revolts at such an unreasonable conclusion, and rather says though we may be unable to interpret, that by no means proves that no interpretation is possible.

But is interpretation difficult? Of what would the "hoof" be the simplest symbol? Surely of the *walk;* and that again is but the common word for external conduct. We understand perfectly that what is meant by, "That ye henceforth walk not as other Gentiles walk" (Eph. 4: 17), is that our conduct should be very different from those who have not Christ.

Of what then does a *divided* hoof speak? The root idea of a division would of course be "separation." Every step that the animal took told of separation. But is that always good? Does it always tell the same story?

Just as some creatures that divided the hoof were clean and others unclean—the ox being an example of the former, and the swine of the latter—so may separation be either most excellent or most repulsive. There is a separation to the Lord Jesus, won by discerning His attractions, that has the fullest approval, for it is always marked by low thoughts of self, or no thoughts of it at all.  There is a separation from our fellows, due to our self-appreciation, that meets with the sternest reprobation.  The Nazarite, by the meaning of the very word, spoke of one *separated to* the Lord; the Pharisee by the same meaning was one also *separated,* but it was from those whom he esteemed less holy than himself.  The one found, and still finds all his boast in the Lord, in utter self-distrust; the other in his own assumed superior piety.  This is what is here sternly condemned.

But what of the other mark that was needed to show that the creature was clean, "chewing the cud?"  Let us go into that pasture.  See that ox; it has been moving about, cropping the herbage as it walked; but now it retires to the cool shade of a tree; and, first lying down, it ruminates.  The grass that it has cropped has not done it an atom of good yet, it has only been stored in the *rumen,* or the first stomach, to be regurgitated, chewed betwen the teeth, and finally swallowed and digested.  For that it quietly reposes.

How lovely the very picture!  How far more lovely its clear significance!  Here is one whose time is fully occupied all day; but in the early morning he "crops" a little from the Word of God, then throughout the day his spirit, in repose amid the activities of life, recalls, if even but for a few moments, what he has read, and he ruminates, or chews the cud, between the teeth of his faith, so that it becomes a part of himself.  We may well say that Paul counselled Timothy to "chew the cud" when he said: "Consider what I say; and the Lord give thee understanding in all things" (2 Tim. 2: 7).

Now see that swine.  It is moving about with divided hoof; but little does it care for the sweet living herb, it is seeking for unclean things on which to feed, nor in that feeding does it chew the cud at all.  So much for the symbol, and now again for what it symbolizes.  Here is one who is externally moral and religious.  He is not at all like "this publican;" he severs himself from such, and thus divides the hoof.  Every footstep, everything he does, leaves marks of that self-satisfied separation, but he does not ruminate; he does not chew the cud; has no self-obliterating communion with God over His Word.  His own unclean works are his delight. Christ is not his joy and boast; he is, in spite of that separation—nay, even by it—a leper, utterly unclean.

This gives divine light on the few remaining words: "Broth of abominations is in their vessels." Jehovah is still looking on what gives these religious ones such satisfaction that it is their *food,* they feed upon it, and here He tells them what is *His* estimate of it—it is abominable! This "broth" then symbolizes something "highly esteemed among men, but is an abomination in the sight of God." But while this is what Jehovah through Isaiah tells us, we have quoted the very words of the Lord Jesus Himself as recorded in Luke 16:15. To whom was He referring? Was it to the publican, the profane, the debased and the harlot? Not at all, for, say what you will, neither these, nor their doings, are highly esteemed among men, nor even by themselves. It was the most *religious men of that day that were then* before Him, precisely as in the Old Testament prophet!

It is "religion," without penitence and confession, against which the sternest words that ever fell from those gracious Lips were levelled: "Woe unto you, scribes and Pharisees, hypocrites ...serpents, generation of vipers, how can ye escape the damnation of hell?" (Matt. 23: 33). Was He not saying to them exactly what He had said in our prophet: "The broth of abominable things is in your vessels?"

That "generation" is by no means extinct. It has its representatives in every age. We see that same abhorrence in those deeds and doctrines of the Nicolaitanes, which specifically too He hates (Rev. 2: 6). Then He finds in the self-satisfied condition of the last Church to which He writes, Laodicea, so clearly representing our own day, the same "abominable broth" that brings the same utter reprobation. Consider it, reader, and you will surely conclude that there is nothing—literally *nothing*—so loathsome to God, as the assumption of religious superiority over others. O Christless Religion! O impenitent, tearless Religion! O self-complacent Religion! What myriads in everlasting perdition will have thee to thank for their damnation, for thou art the broad way that "seemeth right to a man, but the end thereof are the ways of death" (Prov. 14: 12).

The second division of the chapter, verses 8 to 16, is in accord
with the natural significance of the number "two," and speaks
of more than one object being in view.   Here it is discrimination
between two different companies, the remnant of faith and the
apostate mass.   First, then, we have the divine tenderness for the
penitent:

> 8: Thus doth Jehovah speak:
>      As the new wine in the cluster is found,
>      One pleads: O do not destroy it,
>      For in it alone is a blessing,
>      So will I do for My servants' sakes,
>      That I bring them not all to destruction.
> 9: For even from Jacob I'll bring forth a seed,
>      An heir to My mountains from Judah,
>      To this My people elect shall be heir;
>      My servants shall there find their dwelling.
> 10: And Sharon shall be a fold for the flocks,
>      A rest for the herd, Achor's valley,
>      For My people beloved who have sought Me.

What a valuable ray of light this throws on Matt. 24: 22: "Unless those days had been shortened, there would no flesh have
been saved, but for the elect's sake those days shall be shortened."
The figure is of a bunch of grapes, so repulsive that it is about
to be thrown away and destroyed altogether.   But one intervenes,
pointing out that it is not all hopelessly bad; a small part of the
cluster is sound and sweet, and this may become a blessing, in
making that new wine that "cheereth God and man" (Judges
9: 13).

Evidently the moment is most critical, for there is but one
little link between God and the whole world of men; and if that
be broken, or to use the prophetic symbol, if the cluster be
destroyed, nothing can save the whole race!   That link is here
the remnant of Israel; and when Jerusalem is captured (Zech.
14) and this little remnant is about to be exterminated, it looks
as if all were over.   Then the days of sorrow and affliction are
suddenly cut short by the appearing of their long-expected Messiah, and His Feet standing upon the Mount of Olives whence

they had ascended two millenniums before!  Just as ten righteous would have saved Sodom, and have been the new wine in
that cluster, so these few afflicted captive Jews will save the whole
race of men of that day from destruction.   From the west, where
the fertile plain of Sharon stretches along, to the east where lies
that valley that saw the infliction on Achan, all shall speak of
peace and prosperity.  But now the prophecy returns to the
apostate mass.

11: Ye who your God, Jehovah, forsake,
       Forgetting His mountain so holy,
       Preparing a table for that idol, Gad,
       Filling a cup full for Meni,
12: Therefore I'll number you all to the sword;
       Ye all shall bow down to the slaughter.
       For when I called, ye gave no reply,
       When I spoke ye did not e'en listen,
       But ill have ye done in My very eyes,
       Have chosen what gave Me no pleasure.
13: Therefore Jehovah Adonai thus speaks:
       Look at My servants, they feed whilst ye famish,
       Look at My servants, they drink whilst ye parch,
       Look at My servants, they boast* whilst ye're blushing.
14: Lo, from heart's joy My servants shall sing,
       The while ye in sorrow are wailing,
       In crushing of spirit are moaning.
15: Your name ye shall leave as the form of a curse,
       'Twill thus be of use for My chosen.
       For thee Adonai Jehovah shall slay,
       And give a new name to His servants.
16: So he that doth bless himself in the land,
       Shall bless by Elohi of Amen,†
       And he who utters an oath in the land,
       Shall swear by Elohi of Amen;†
       For the past sorrows shall all be forgot,
       For from Mine eyes they have vanished.

---

*The first meaning of the word is to "sing with joy"—its con-
trast with "ashamed" permits the rendering "boast" and "blush."

†"The God of Truth," but the written word *Amen,* in view of
Rev. 3: 14, cannot be dropped without loss.

Note the parallelism of the first lines: Person and place are identified. They who forsake Jehovah are those who forget His holy mountain. But surely there is little danger, or indeed possibility *of our* being charged with forgetting a mountain that we have never seen and know nothing about. Exactly seven times in this prophet do we find the term "holy mountain," and this "seven" itself serves to show the importance of the term. What then is the name of this mountain? But one all through the book is named, nor can we err in assuming that must be the mountain meant; and Zion then becomes Jehovah's holy mountain. But why is this mountain selected out of all the many hills of Israel to have attached to it that title of "holy?" The answer is suggested by Heb. 12: 18, 22, for Zion is the mount that represents the whole Heart of God told out in grace, in contrast with that principle of Law with which He ever found fault, for in His dealing with sinful, but ever-beloved men, law shuts up both Heart and Hand. Further, we deduce from the word "holy' that this way of grace is the true way of holiness, and is as far removed from license as it is from law.

Thus to "forget God's holy mountain" today, is to forget the abundant grace of Christ that alone can, and does meet all our poverty, need and helplessness. In short, it is to *"fall from grace"* (Gal. 5: 5).

Little should we profit in the search for Gad and Meni of old. The names are lost to us, but what they signify remains. They stand for the dual form that evil takes, called Violence and Corruption. These become deified, and their devotees seek to propitiate them by their varying forms of "religious duties," or, in the language of prophecy, in "preparing a table for them." After the manner of Isaiah there is a play on the word Meni, in the first line of the next verse, for the word means, "number," and so Jehovah says, "I will *meni*, or number, you to the sword." It is again the principle of God turning sin into penalty, as He does both with men and the devil, as we shall see in verse 25.

Verses 13 to 16 repeat the strong contrasts that the day of revelation shall show between the proud impenitents and those poor and contrite ones whom He owns as His servants. Satiated

shall these be, famished shall those be.  In this present sphere
there is inextricable confusion; or, if there be discrimination, it is
rather the proud who are the favored and the lowly are despised.
Generation follows generation in telling the same story, for we see
it when the perplexed psalmist goes into the sanctuary, and lo,
he sees the ungodly wealthy of earth, as soon as they pass out
of this scene, to be in desolation in a moment, while the poor
penitents are ever with God (Ps. 73). A little later it is seen
in a rich Dives in torment, and a poor Lazarus in bliss; and
still later it shall be seen in those two contrasted companies,
the proud gathered at Har Mageddon (Rev. 16), and the penitent
in the Valley of Megiddo (Zech. 12).

The proud shall leave a name to provide an oath for the
true, as "Jehovah slay thee as He slew them" (*Delitzsch*).  But
far sweeter than that to our hearts are the thoughts we attach
to that Name *Elohi Amen;* for in it we see our Lord, who amid
the disgrace that we have made of our witnessing, is Himself not
only The Faithful and True Witness, but so brings all God's purposes into being, so fulfils all His counsels, that He does not, as
we, *say* "Amen" to them, but *is* that, not only says, "May it so
be," but makes it to be.

Now we pass to the scene of those fulfilled counsels.

17: For behold, I create new heavens, new earth;
    And the former shall not be remembered,
    Nor come evermore into mind.
18: For well may ye joy, and forever exult
    In that which shall then be created;
    Jerusalem I'll create a delight,
    Her people a source of rejoicing!
19: For over Jerusalem I will exult,
    And greatly rejoice o'er My people;
    Nor ever again in her shall be heard
    The sound of weeping or wailing.
20: No more shall there be an infant short-lived,
    An elder whose days are not lived out;
    Should he die aged a hundred they'll call him a child,
    And the sinner thus dying count cursed.*

---

*This is but a paraphrase, but it gives the meaning of the
original: "And the sinner, son of a hundred years, is accursed."

21: They who build houses shall in them dwell,
    And they who plant vineyards enjoy them;
22: They shall not build what another shall use,
    Nor shall they plant fruit for another.
    As the years of a tree My people shall live,
    Enjoying the fruit of their labor.
23: They shall not wearily labor in vain,
    Nor bring forth for sudden disaster;
    For they are the seed of the blest of the Lord,
    And their offspring have part in their blessing.
24: Ere they utter a cry, an answer I'll send;
    Whilst yet they are speaking, will hear them.
25: The wolf and the lamb together shall feed,
    The lion eat straw like the oxen;
    But dust shall still be the serpent's one food.
    None shall hurt nor destroy in My mountain,
    My mountain ever be holy!
    So saith Jehovah.

For Israel, the new heavens and earth commence with her perfect blessing. She is henceforth as secure and as blessed nationally as the heavenly saints will be at their rapture to their heavenly and eternal home. Not, however, that at this moment, all the earth and its heaven is in itself altogether and everywhere altered; but as today it can be written, "If any man be in Christ, he is a new creature, old things are passed away, behold, all things are become new, and all things are of God" (2 Cor. 5: 17), when indeed *nothing* is new except as "in Christ," so Israel now being "in Christ" by a new-creation life, for her too all things in heaven and earth are new, and all things of God; while still outside of Israel and her land, there is very much (as subsequent events, when the Devil is loosed from his prison, evidence) that is not new. We need no other illustration for this than our own experience. Do you remember the morning after Christ was first seen as your own Lord and Saviour—no longer a mere name but a real living Person—was not everything *new* to you then? The skies had another tint; you thought the whole world of people were different, and perhaps wondered that all were not converted. The joy in your heart sent its music through the whole earth. Nor earth alone. How new the heavens were when

you could look up and for the first time say, "My Father!"
That was *your* regeneration; *this*, the earth's.

There is no need to write much of the beauteous scene. It is
better to meditate and thus get the refreshment such lovely and
well-based anticipations must give. We visit in spirit that "holy
mountain" where alone naught defiles, where alone naught doth
hurt. We see the harmony of Eden renewed once more, and
the wild fierce creatures of the jungle graze in the company of
the fearless flocks of the farm. Still we have a hint that the
scene is not one of absolute perfection, for even here we listen
to an echo of that primal sentence on the serpent, for the dust
shall still be his food.

We cannot look upon this as merely telling us literally on what
the serpent family feeds.* Utterly unsatisfactory are all such
explanations as Delitzsch and others give us, when he says: "The
serpent will no longer watch for human life, but content *itself
with the food assigned it in Gen.* 3: 14. It still *continues to
wriggle in the dust*—the words affirm nothing more than this!"
He must permit us to differ. If all we get from this word is that
dust being the serpent's food means that he "wriggles in the dust,"
it would be altogether unworthy of a divine revelation to a race
ruined by that "old serpent." Let all Scripture throw its light
on this, and at once there are profound verities—not "put in,"
as some say, but seen to lie imbedded in these few words:
"Dust shall be the serpent's meat," or food.

Who can help thoughts turning to that scene of sorrow and of
judgment in Eden? There stand our weeping first parents, and
there too is their destroyer, still in the form that he assumed
in order to carry out his work. What has that work been? The
answer to that question is as important as it is simple and clear.

The work of the Lord God had been to "form man (Heb.,
*adam*) of the dust of the ground" (*adamah*, Gen. 2:7), and having
thus formed, to give him a life suitable to that earthly or dust
body and to his dwelling upon the earth, the man and his abode
thus corresponding, for both are dust. The work of the serpent

---

*Moffatt disposes of this by simply omitting the sentence en-
tirely.

had been to bring death to the man, and consequently the return of the body to the dust whence it came. It *was* "dust," the Lord God made it a body; it thus *was* a body, the serpent made it dust—a complete reversal!

We need to bear in mind these two basic principles of divine judgment: first, where people *are* forever, depends not on what they have done, but on what they *are*. We all know that heaven is not attained by "doing," nor is banishment to hell for the same reason. All go "to their own place," a place that is determined by whether "in Christ" by a new creation life, or only in Adam by the old one. The man only in Adam would be as much out of his own place in heaven as the man in Christ would be out of his in hell. But *retribution* in either place is determined strictly by what each has *done*. Thus Isaiah speaks in chap. 3: 10: "The righteous shall *eat of the fruit* of their doings." Again, Wisdom cries: "They shall *eat of the fruit* of their own way" (Prov. 1: 31). The same principle is in the New Testament: "Whatsoever a man soweth that shall he also reap" (Gal. 6: 7), and many other scriptures might be given. Thus every responsible creature goes to *his own place*, but himself works out the *retribution* that he receives there.

Can any then impugn divine justice, since all go to the place to which they are suited, and each "eats of the fruit of his own doings?"

This being the sure teachings of Holy Writ, then the sentence passed upon that responsible creature, that "serpent," must be in accord with that truth; so that the "dust" upon which he is sentenced to feed cannot be simply that in the making of which he had no part, but that to which his "doings" have brought man (as identified with his body), and on *that* he must feed, for that, and that alone, is here "the fruit of his doings."

That must be all his satisfaction, for the feeding can no more be literal than that the serpent was nothing more than a merely literal snake. All through Scripture "feeding" figures absolute satisfaction, as in Deut. 14: 19, "The Levite...shall eat and be satisfied." Again, in Ps. 103: 5, "Who satisfieth thy mouth with good things," and any number of Scriptures might be added to

the same effect. Satan's food, or satisfaction, must be found in
that dust to which his "doings" have brought man's body. But,
and I pray you mark it well, on not one single human *"body"*
shall he ever feed. Never! For hear what the wisest of men
tells us, when speaking of a man's death, "Then shall the dust
return to the earth as it was" (Eccl. 12: 7), just as it was before
it was formed, so it becomes again. It is no longer a body,
but dust.

Is *that* what Satan craved? Is *that* what he hungered for?
Does *that* give him absolute satisfaction? Was *that* his final
object in tempting man? Let me answer these by asking a few
similar questions regarding a scene where the devil's own children
are doing the very works of their father (John 8: 1-11, 44). Did
those Pharisees care a snap of the finger as to the fate of the
poor adulteress? Did they aim at *her?* Would it have satisfied
their hungering longing to have *her* stoned? It is absurd even
to ask such questions. They could have effected that without
any appeal to Him. It was our divine Lord Himself that they
attacked, and it was with the final purpose of himself securing
the Throne of God that their father, the devil, the serpent,
brought back to the dust the dearly-loved man.

That this idea—not of literal feeding, but of the same satisfaction to the inner, as that feeding gives to the outer man—is intended by the use of the word "meat" here, is confirmed by the
Lord's words when His disciples would have Him eat of the food
they had gone to the village to get for Him. *"I have meat to eat
that ye know not of"* (John 4: 32), and that meat was, even in His
case, we may reverently say, the "fruit of His own blessed doings,"
for it consisted in bringing a poor sinning wanderer back to everlasting rest in a love of which till then she had known nothing.
What an absolute contrast there is in the two "meats," that of the
"old serpent" and that of the Lord! The one consisted in bringing man to the dust of death, the other in not merely restoring
the lost life but giving a life eternal. The one set poor man to
the hopeless task of covering himself: the other by His own death
provided the covering. The one severed man's heart from God,
the other restored man's heart to find a Father's love in that

same God.  We can surely well afford to let the devil have the sin-infected and so penalized dust for his food, whilst we in Christ shall be clothed with a New Creation body of glory; for so God ever works.  He never merely offsets the work of the devil, as if in His poverty, He must repeat, since His powers are so limited that He can produce nothing beyond that has been thus marred.  By the universal truth of all Scripture, His works never witness to limitation, but He ever does "much more" (Rom. 5: 15), and always makes "better things," as the Epistle to the Hebrews tells us—always!*  Never one shade of disappointment shall we have; the future will be far beyond all that we can conceive.

But when the body has returned to what it was and to where it belongs, is the unclothed spirit to remain thus naked?  Far from it!  Such a clothing shall be given it as will tell to the universe that these are "the sons of God" (Rom. 8: 19).  So that we can invite the "serpent" to look again, and see how God even makes use of his malevolence and pride to express His own attributes of benevolence and humble him to feeding on dust!

One word more of balancing truth is necessary.  We can never ignore—far less condemn—the use of phenomenal, ordinary, inevitable expressions of human thought.  It ever has its place. As surely as "it doth not yet appear what we shall be" (1 John 3: 2), as surely as it is impossible even to picture to ourselves that body of glory, or, to use the divinely given illustration of 1 Cor. 15: 37, as it is impossible to deduce the beauty of the flower by merely looking at the bare seed, so we are compelled, by the very conditions of our being, to expect the return of all who have "fallen asleep," precisely as they were last known to us, and from the tomb to which we saw them consigned.  As that is inevitable, so is it inevitable to use the ordinary language whereby we speak of things as we see or know them.  But again, when God is the Worker the reality for His people is always "much more" and "better," and expressing His "immensely varied wisdom."

―――――

*See Eph. 3: 10, "the manifold (Gr. *immensely* varied) wisdom of God."

# CHAPTER SIXTY-SIX

**The final scenes both in blessing and judgment.**

OUR final chapter continues rapid changes from threat to comfort, and back again to threat, as either the impenitent or penitent of Israel come into view, till at the close we see a company of the latter going out of the city to look on the evidences of divine judgment on the former in Gehenna (the Valley of Hinnom), beyond its walls. That scene the Lord Himself uses as a symbol of the Lake of Fire of the New Testament; things seen ever providing pictures of the unseen. We must note that the threat and the comfort are quite in the same line; that is, the threat to the one company *is* the comfort to the other.

The divisions of the chapter are not as clearly marked as others, but the "three" has been so strongly imprinted on what we have seen that I keep to it here:

1: Verses 1-4: The Majesty of Jehovah; whom He chooses, and whom He reprobates.
2: Verses 5-16: Israel's blessing in judgment on her foes.
3: Verses 17-24: Final destiny of both.

The first part reads thus:

1: Thus saith Jehovah:
  The heavens above alone are My throne,
  And earth's but a stool for My feet:
  What kind of a dwelling then will ye build Me?
  And what kind of place for My rest?
2: All that exists, 'tis My hand hath made,
  And thus they all came into being,
  So saith Jehovah!
  But this is the one on whom I will look:
  On him who is poor,
  In spirit contrite,
  And trembleth for fear at My word!

3: Who slayeth an ox, killeth a man!
   Who offers a lamb, breaks the neck of a dog!
   Who brings an oblation, 'tis the blood of a swine!
   Who burneth the incense, 'tis the blessing an idol!
   Yea, they have chosen their ways,
   Have delighted in what is abhorrent;
4: So will I choose their delusions,
   And bring their terrors upon them.
   Because when I called none did answer,
   Because when I spoke none did listen,
   But evil they've done in My eyes,
   And chosen what gave Me no pleasure.

The chapter begins with the passage quoted by Stephen as he summed up his charge against the representatives of impenitent religion of his day. Jehovah has the infinite heavens above, tier above tier with no limitation, for His throne, and this expresses that there is no bound to His government. His glory must be announced through all that limitless realm, as we are told later. The earth is but as a footstool for His Feet: will any think that He needs a house built upon that? Will any think that He is wandering restlessly looking for some settled dwelling? There is not any physical thing existing that does not owe that existence to His word. "All these things"—and as He speaks, He points, as it were, with His finger to the visible universe—"are but the work of My hand."

But notwithstanding the infinity of His inscrutable being, His limitless majesty, His glorious splendor, His resistless power, there is one dwelling that He will not despise, one object that will arrest His Eye; well may we ask with deepest interest what that can be.

First we note that that object of delight is not here found amid the principalities and powers of heaven. Neither Michael nor Gabriel, nor any of heaven's glories, stay the search of that Eye. To earth must it come, and when there, it is not on some mighty host or large company. His Eye passes over all, all crowds, all congregations, all assemblies, to rest on one individual!

Let us look at that one very carefully. We shall perhaps

be surprised to note that he is not distinguished by anything that men esteem of value. He is not remarkable for wealth, for power, or social position. No marvel of invention, no feat of daring, no eloquence that thrills, no power in debate, no activity in church-work marks him. Orthodoxy, energy, ability, eloquence —all suffice not to arrest His Eye. It passes over all such, and continues its search till it rests on *one*. Shall we not, I again say, look at him carefully, and learn what is so attractive that the Eye of the Omniscient stays its search and rests *there?*

There are three marks that are approved, and the first is, he is "poor." We may be quite sure that any thought of mere financial poverty must be dismissed, although in Israel's day it might cover that; but the very word used goes deeper. It speaks of such consciousness of deep need as brings to the ground every high thought of self. It goes far beyond mere lip confession, which may be the language that utter indifference may use. No, it is the one who *is*, actually *is*, poor, and is *afflicted* by the sense of that poverty, for the word here used for "poor" carries in it the closely related thoughts of affliction. That man who stood in the temple with bowed head, and eyes cast down, saying simply: "God be merciful to me the sinner," was poor indeed; and God *looked* upon him! Myriads may utter almost the same words: "Lord, have mercy upon us, miserable sinners," but that Eye of God may find little resting-place there—the proudest spirit may utter the lowliest words. Saul of Tarsus is quite wealthy in his own estimate as he journeys to Damascus; but in a moment all his wealth shrivels in the glory of the light that shines, and he too becomes instantly "poor;" yet then that Eye marked him, and sent Ananias for his comfort. To this very day, 'tis with such, and only with such, that the mighty God has His dwelling. There was one spot on earth where He, who was the brightness of God's glory and the exact expression of His substance, ever found His dwelling-place. Again and again we find Him going to Bethany, "The house of the poor."* Is not that in perfect accord with the word of our prophet?

---

*The *"any"* in Bethany is the very word here used for "poor."

The next mark is the outcome of this poverty: he is "of a contrite spirit," precisely the reverse of what is so highly esteemed among men, "a man of spirit," that is, self-assertive and insistent on what he esteems his right.   It does not mean one who is abject, but one whose conviction of his own real poverty, need and sin has stopped his mouth not only from all self-justification, but from all accusation of others.  Perhaps one of the best illustrations that we have of such contrition is in that poor thief who hung by the side of our Lord when he said to his fellow: "Dost thou not fear God, seeing thou art in the same condemnation?   And we indeed justly."   That only is true contrition which stops all accusation of others.

Thus contrite, all self-esteem broken down, all pride abased, the spirit is awake to the voice of Jehovah in His Word, and he listens to it, or reads it, with trembling reverence.  This becomes the third mark.  It is one of the grave dangers of the form of government under which we live—and in so speaking, I have no thought of denying that, although the very antithesis of the divine ideal, it may yet be the best that is practicable under present conditions—it has at least one very grave danger for the child of God, in its tendency to destroy all *reverence*.  To fear anything or anyone is assumed to be a weakness to be condemned, and the irreverence with which our highest magistrates are spoken of is only the thin edge of a wedge that will at last drive asunder all the ties that maintain order among men, and overthrow, temporarily at least, all human authority and order(Rev. 8: 8-12). That spirit, alas, has invaded the Church, and we need to ponder that path of our Lord which led Him from "Godhead's highest glory down to Calvary's depth of woe," for that is the "mind" that is to govern all our conduct here.   But today as reverence for any political authority—be it king or president—is esteemed by many to be a remnant from feudalism, so any reverence for spiritual authority is a remnant of the superstition of the Middle Ages.  Alas, who of us now really "trembles at His Word?"   Forgive me for asking, but do *you*, dear reader?   We are told that this sacred Word is entitled to anything but reverence, that it is filled with errors and outgrown superstitions.   Who then trembles at that Word now? But he who sees anything or its marvels, the eternal issues that it unfolds, the stupendous drama that it reveals, involving another creation than this, its divine marks of majesty, profundity, simplicity, unity, the infinite tender loving-kindness and unfathomable wisdom in the plan of eternal salvation it brings to us poor guilty men, and at such a cost to our God—His very Bosom lying open before us—who can but reverently fear? It is not from slavish terror, but from the sense of responsibility such a possession puts upon us, and our utter inability to measure up to that responsibility. Not then with abject terror do we tremble, but with filial reverence; not because of threats, but even because of the love of which it tells, and our testimony to which our lives may either adorn or mar. Not as Moses quaked before the mount, with its fire, tempest and gloom; but as Paul at Corinth (1 Cor. 2: 3), lest he should not speak as he ought to speak.

Note then again, we have that number "three" that has followed us all through the book; first, what he is *personally*, "poor;" then the next word brings *man* in; and the third shuts up to *God* altogether.

In strong contrast with this appreciative "look," we have next the most startling expressions of disgust that Jehovah directs, not against murder or adultery, but against what people naturally look upon as being irreproachable. It is precisely in line with the preceding chapter, in which we have seen the divine estimate of men's "gardens," etc. There is, He says, no difference, so far as My acceptance of your formalism, between your offering an ox as a burnt-offering and committing murder! I take as much, but no more, pleasure in your sacrifice of a lamb than I would in the death of a dog! That offering, so filled with profound truth as to the Person of Christ, if *that* be not discerned, but the assumed worshipper is occupied with himself and not with My Son, then you might just as well approach Me with swine's blood! While as to the sweet incense, when severed from delight in the perfections of Christ of which it speaks, I no more regard it with pleasure than I should the adoration of an idol!

Startling enough! Could any words be more calculated to awaken attention? It virtually returns to the burden of the first chapter, and thus unifies the book, as the whole sacred volume is unified by Revelation returning to Genesis, with its allusion to Paradise, and the tree and river found in both.

Has our Lord nothing to say to us, even *us*, in all this? Think of telling one who has just soothed his conscience by "going to church," and perhaps "taking the sacrament," that he might just as well have killed a man! But we can recognize the identity of this Speaker with Him who spoke in precisely the same way to the most religious men of His day, telling them that it was the very deeds upon which they rested to give them acceptance with God as being their good deeds, that were their "evil deeds" (John 7: 7). Can you wonder that they hated Him? You may possibly obtain popularity if you thunder against the flagrancies that the natural conscience revolts at, but few will love you greatly if you witness that the heartless church-membership, the cold taking of the sacrament, the formal religious observance, the indifferent breaking of bread, the lukewarm prayer-meeting, are themselves unspeakably abominable to the God and Father of our Lord Jesus Christ. It is not against the murderer or adulterer that the threat of being spewed out of His mouth is directed; but that falls on the *Church*—the literal Church—of which you and I are a part. Is not that worth some reflection?

But never must we permit ourselves to speak thus without genuine sorrow, and knowing something of the deceitfulness of our own hearts, for only so shall we have that "look" of divine approval that rests solely on the poor, the contrite and the trembler at His Word.

The divine address next turns to the penitent remnant of Israel, and since that remnant will be composed of our brethren in the one family of God, we can scarcely help having an interest in their welfare, even if it did not afford a prophecy of our own.

5: Hear ye the word of Jehovah,
   Ye tremblers at His word;
   Your brethren who, filled with their hate,
   For the sake of My name cast you out,
   Have said, Give the glory to Jah:
   But 'tis for your joy He'll appear,*
   'Tis they who will then be ashamed.

In the very terse, crisp, energetic sentences used, we can almost hear what is described:

6: A sound of a tumult—
   It comes from the city!
   A sound from the temple—
   'Tis the sound of Jehovah
   Requiting His foes!

Then the prophecy goes back to speak both of the Child and children, as it did in chapters 7 and 8.

7: Before she travailed
   She was delivered!
   Before her pangs came
   A man-child was born!
8: Who ever heard such a marvel as this?
   Who ever saw such marvels as these?
   Can the earth e'er be made to bring forth in a day?
   Has ever a nation been born in a moment?
   For as soon as she travailed,
   Zion brought forth her sons!
9: Shall I bring to the birth and not cause to bring forth?
   Saith Jehovah.
   Shall I who've begotten restrain from the birth?
   Saith thy God!

---

*Notwithstanding the many excellent authorities who render the Hebrew of this line, "Let Jehovah be glorified that we may see your joy," which is assumed to be ironical, I find it impossible to abandon the far simpler construction above, as more harmonious with the context, and indeed with Scripture at large; nor does it lack the support of many Hebraists, as Lowth, Kelly, the A.V., etc.

10: Oh, joy with Jerusalem,
 Dance with delight,*
 All ye who do love her.
 Rejoice with great joy,
 All ye who mourn o'er her.

11: That ye may suck and be sated
 From the breasts of her comforts,
 That ye may suck and delight
 From the wealth of her glory.

12: For thus saith Jehovah,
 I'll cause to flow to her
 Peace like a river,
 And the glory of nations
 As a torrent o'erflowing.
 At her breasts shall ye suckle,
 On her hip shall be carried,
 On her lap shall be fondled.

13: E'en as a man whom his mother doth comfort,
 So will I bring My comfort to you;
 And in Jerusalem ye shall be comforted.

14: This shall ye see, and your heart shall rejoice,
 And your bones, as the green herb, shall freshen;
 His servants shall learn of the hand of the Lord,
 Whilst His wrath 'gainst His foes shall burn fiercely.

15: For, behold, see Jehovah! In fire doth He come!
 His chariots are as a whirlwind,
 To breathe forth His anger in burning,
 His rebukes in the flamings of fire!

16: For in flamings of fire doth Jehovah rebuke,
 By the sword doth He judge all the peoples,
 And the slain of Jehovah are many!

Neither intermissions of time, however long, nor the intervenings of space, however great, can affect the heart of man. As it was in the day of Cain, as it was in the day of Isaiah, so is it to this day. All forms of persecution are ever done under the cloak of the most pious expressions. "Let the Lord be glorified," cry the religious persecutors in our chapter, even as they cast out their brethren. "Give God the praise" is the echo of this as the most religious men of their day cast out the

---

*This is strictly the sense of the word; its first meaning is, "to go in a circle;" then, "to leap for joy."

poor object of His love and grace in John 9: 24. So, through the centuries of our era, never a turn of the rack in the inquisition, but it was done "to the glory of God!" Never was a martyr's fire lighted, never a holocaust of saints, but it was called an *auto-da-fé,* an act of faith!

Was truer word ever spoken than, "The time cometh that whosoever killeth you will think that he doeth God service" (John 16: 2)?

In verse 6 we have the same time, and the same double evidence of the Lord's intervention as in the pouring out of the last vial (Rev. 16: 17). There, a "great voice comes out of the *temple* from the *throne,*" announcing that the trial of man, both in the spiritual and political spheres, has come to its end, in his rejection as a complete failure.

If we attempted to see the order of events at that critical hour, putting the various scriptures together, we might say that first the Lord's Feet stand upon the Mount of Olives, and that results in the complete scattering of all the military forces that, under "Beast" and "false prophet," have been besieging and at last have captured Jerusalem that has been held by Israel's pious remnant. Then, after pursuing to Bozrah (chap. 63), the Lord returns, and again as in the day of the small cords, cleanses the temple and the whole city, which is here noted by the tumult that comes from them, for it is the Lord rendering recompenses to Israel's enemies whom He counts His own.

That brings us to one of those beauties of Scripture that itself compels conviction of its divine Authorship. Let us note the strange difference between verses 7 and 8. In the former it is *before* Zion travailed she brought forth *a Man-Child,* while in the latter it is "as soon as Zion travailed she brought forth her *children,*" those *"children"* then are the fruit of suffering.

It is quite true that the system of prophetic interpretation so long adopted by Christian expositors has compelled them to see no distinction in these two verses: the Man-Child *is* the nation born at once, and then that "nation" has to become the Christian Church. But this is surely indefensible, both because it evacuates the plain word as it is written, in both members, and also because Israel is never called "the Man-Child;" that is a term applied to Christ when thus used, as in Rev. 12: 5, where the word is "a son, a male."

Consider how entirely it is in accord with what occurred seven centuries later. All was at peace when the shepherds listened to the chant of that angel-choir on Bethlehem's hill. No travail-pangs disturbed the nation then; and so "*before* she travailed," Israel, "of whom as concerning the flesh Christ came" (Rom. 9: 5), has brought forth the Man-Child, and there He lies in the manger at Bethlehem!

Many a long year must pass before the next verse—quite contiguous though it be on the sacred page—is fulfilled; and then Zion must go into those travail-pangs of which the Lord spoke as her "sorrows" (Matt. 24: 8), the very word for the pangs of child-birth. But, as soon as she does—at once—lo, there are her children, in that true God-fearing remnant that are then evidenced, produced to sight, by their refusal to worship the Beast or receive the mark of his number in hand or head.

Looking forward to that day, hitherto there has been no discrimination among the Jews who have returned to Palestine, between the many and the few—all have gone to the renewed morning and evening sacrifice as one company. Zion's true children are not distinguished. But now that sacrifice has been stopped suddenly in the midst of that last "week" of seven years, and in its place "the abomination that maketh desolate" has been set up. It is that which exposes the false and manifests the true; and lo, there in that anguish of birth-pangs, are Zion's children in those refusing to worship. That test reveals the "children" at once.

The siege of Jerusalem, and its capture by the Romans under Titus, will not lend itself as a *final* fulfilment of this prophecy, although it has been almost a universal interpretation of it. For it is written: "*Immediately after the tribulation* of those days shall the sun be darkened, and the moon shall not give her light, and the stars shall fall from heaven, and the powers of heaven shall be shaken, and then shall appear the sign of the Son of Man in heaven: and then shall all the tribes of the earth mourn, and *they shall see the Son of Man coming in the clouds of heaven with power and great glory*" (Matt. 24: 29, 30).   Did anything of that kind take place "immediately" after the capture of Jerusalem?   The tribulation of those days still lies as much in the future as does the coming of the Son of Man.

As the "tribulation" that begins and centers at Jerusalem spreads over the whole earth and becomes that "hour of trial" from which the true Church of God will be kept (Rev. 3: 16), so does the joy that follows that time of unparalleled distress.   No longer does the exclusive spirit of the Pharisee govern that exclusive people, but they long for every nation and tongue to share their exultant joy.   If Jerusalem is nourished by the Gentiles, she, in her turn, nourishes them.   If she is enriched by their temporal wealth, they are over-paid by the spiritual joys that she has to give; for her Messiah, our Lord Christ, is in, and with her!

No doubt the address in verses 10 to 16 is primarily to that pious people, the Jewish remnant; but it is not to be strictly confined to them, for all who love her, and all who have mourned over her sorrows, are invited to join the festal singing.   Peace unhindered, like an unchecked stream, flows through that beloved city; and every expression of nursing care is used, to show her people's nourishment, security and rest in her.

But that must not be taken as if, in every sense, her people were but unreasoning or thoughtless infants, for in the next verse (13) we have a different figure.   Here is a full-grown man whom we see being comforted.   That is much more affecting.   Who is greatly distressed at an infant's cry?   It is its only power of speech.   It has "no language but a cry."   But a grown man's tears mean far more; and here we see a mother clasping the hand of her full-grown son, as she speaks words of comfort to him.

The figure again changes in verse 14, and the nation is likened to an aged man, no longer in his prime, for his bones are dried, like the branches of a tree that are seared.   A new life is made to surge through those branches, and so the "bones" of the nation shall again become life-filled and vigorous.   Pictures from infancy to age are thus brought together to tell of Jehovah's relation and love to Israel.

This very earth is by God's unbroken purpose to be the stage on which His righteous government shall be displayed; and in that display may be seen the same righteous government in the sphere above the earth, in which the conflict is with principalities and powers in the heavenlies. But here it is with "flesh" that He strives—the shadow of the more awful drama going on in the unseen.

The time for the revelation of that righteous government has not even yet come. Even to this day,

> "Right is ever on the scaffold,
> Wrong forever on the throne."

So it must be, as long as the earth's true King has filled earth's scaffold, and is not yet on earth's throne. From this point of view how far from the truth is Browning's popular line:

> "God's in His heaven; all's right with the world."

Far truer would it be to say:

> Its King is rejected; all's *wrong* with the world.

The injustice and reversal of right that have perplexed the excellent of the earth all through its sad history, still goes on, and God intervenes not. It is the "mystery of God" which shall only have its full and satisfactory solution at the sounding of that seventh trumpet that introduces this earth's true King to His rightful Throne.

We now come to the last division of the last chapter of our prophet, and ever filled with solemnity is the *last*, for although it is only the earth that is directly in view here, yet as already said, the events that take place upon it afford pictures of eternity. We are standing as it were upon the shores of the boundless sea of eternity—a solemn place!

Perhaps the most striking feature in that final judgment is in the objects against whom it is directed.  We all approve of penalties against the breakers of the moral law, or on everything that militates against the security, comfort, and well-being of society; but that the wrath of God should be directed against what seems to us in itself admirable, the very religion that commends itself to us because of its respectability and careful moderation, *that* tends to arouse resentment. We are inclined to attach no little merit to those observances by which we still preserve much more than a shred of our native self-complacency.  And people say, although perhaps not audibly, "It is a comfort to think that God could hardly turn to everlasting perdition those who have 'joined the church,' gone through all the forms of religion; have lived (with those little exceptions that still cling to every human being) at least decently in conduct.  No, it is unthinkable that God could finally reject such."

Alas, it is the voice of Cain that thus speaks, and speaks precisely as of old.  A stupendous error, although it is the broad road, and many still travel it!  Not one word is there in it of sincere confession of truth, not one breath of penitence, not one thought of the need of forgiveness, not one whisper of gratitude for the love that does forgive, not one emotion of adoration for the wisdom that permits that forgiveness to be granted without unrighteousness through the precious Blood of Christ.  Most certain it is that there is no peril, even to this day, equal to that of such a religion.

17: They who do set them apart,
    Make themselves clean in the gardens,
    Following one in the midst,*
    Eating the flesh of the swine,
    Abomination and mouse,
    These all together shall perish,
    Proclaimeth Jehovah!

----

*A most obscure line.  The translation above is fairly literal, and probably refers to one "who leads the people in religious worship."

18: And I their works and their thoughts...!
    The time has come for all nations
    And tongues to be gathered together,
    To come and behold My glory.
19: A sign will I set in their midst,
    And send forth those who've escaped,
    To Tarshish, to Pul and to Lud,
    Benders are they of the bow,
    To Tubal and Javan: th' islands afar,
    That never have heard My report,
    That never have seen My glory,
    Among those nations afar.
20: And these shall bring all of your brethren
    Out of all of the nations,
    For an offering unto Jehovah,
    On horses, in coaches, in litters,
    On mules, and in carriages ever swift-rolling.*
    To My holy mountain of Salem,
    Saith Jehovah!
    As the children of Israel bring
    An offering in a clean vessel,
    Unto the house of the Lord.
21: Also of these will I take,
    To be for priests and for Levites,
    Saith Jehovah!
22: For as the heavens anew,
    As the new earth which I make,
    Shall forever stand fast 'fore My face,
    Proclaimeth Jehovah,
    So shall your seed and your name
    Forever stand fast.

---

* "Swift beasts" in A. V., or "dromedaries," but being used nowhere else, the word is uncertain. It is from a root meaning, "to go round in a circle," and has been assumed to refer to the rolling motion of a dromedary, but I am inclined to believe that it is one of those prophetic words, that, without definitely specifying modern inventions, leave room for, and apply to them when invented. Thus in this word, railway-trains, automobiles, and even airplanes might be covered by the Hebrew *karkaroth*, which Richardson renders, "Machines turning round with the swiftness of the clouds." That was written long before airplanes, those successful racers with the swiftest clouds, were thought of. The word *karkaroth* permits this inclusion.

23: And it shall then come to pass,
    That from new moon to new moon,
    From sabbath even to sabbath,
    All flesh shall come and bow down,
    Before My face, saith Jehovah!
24: Then shall they go forth and look
    At the corpses of men, the rebellious,
    For their worm never shall die,
    Their fire shall never be quenched;
    Abhorred shall they be of all flesh.

Verse 17 tells us who are the objects of the judgments of fire
and sword of which we have just heard; they are primarily
directed against the very people that we might assume would
escape them if anyone could, for they sanctify themselves, and
make themselves clean. If *these* are to "perish," must we not
ask with the Lord's first disciples, "Who then can be saved?"
But what is the motive of their sanctifying themselves?  It is
that they may have that external appearance of piety that has
great honor from their fellows; and is in harmony with their external environment, the places that they have chosen for their
worship.  God must meet them in the place of their own choice,
"in their gardens," where, as we have seen, everything speaks
of their own good works.  As all through the book, Jehovah here
sweeps away the outward veneer of a popular religion, and looking underneath the fair garden-show, the external sanctification,
the formal purifying, says, "Your real appetite is for those forbidden unclean creatures, swine and mouse (Lev. 11: 29), with
which your unrenewed nature accords; and since that reveals your
moral identity with them, you must take your place with all the
impenitent, for ye all shall perish together!"  Then, in verse 18,
the emotion under which Jehovah Himself now speaks is told in
the broken ejaculation, as the Apostle Paul, under the power of
the same Spirit, makes us hear his sighs by the fragmentary character of his writings, as in Gal. 5: 7-9.  The only way the line can
be interpreted is in view of the deep emotion under which it was
spoken, for there is no verb.  As if the subject were too shock-
ing to be continued, the Speaker breaks off abruptly.  It is very
much as in Gen. 3: 22, which reads, "And now lest he put forth

his hand, and take also of the tree of life, and eat and live forever," and there He stops, as if it would be unspeakably dreadful
that poor man must necessarily live away from God in his sins
forever!

In verse 19 we see, if I err not, that same "sign" of which
the Lord spoke in Matt. 24: 30: "Then shall appear the sign
of the Son of Man in heaven," but here, consistently with the
spirit of the Old Testament, that Sign has reached the earth, and
the Son of Man is "in the midst of His people." But although
that excellent glory is only in one single spot, it cannot be confined there, and so from that saved remnant, missionaries are sent
with this gospel of the kingdom to the furthest bounds of earth,
to those to whom the present gospel of the grace of God has not
been preached—that "report," the rejection of which our prophet
mourned over in Chapter 53, these have never heard at all.

In the New Testament the angels are seen as being sent forth
to "gather the elect from the four winds." Here the angels are
not seen, but many a warm-hearted Jewish missionary, who has
been through that time of great tribulation, goes to make those out-
lying lands aware of what has taken place in and around Jerusalem and how the Lord has there revealed Himself in His essential glory of absolute Love and Light.

We must carefully note that this excludes those who have
*wilfully* rejected that "report" when they did hear it. 2 Thess.
2: 10-12 must throw its light on this solemn theme, and in that
light we fail to find any hope for those who have, in this day of
grace, *wilfully* rejected "the love of the truth;" for such there
would appear to be nothing but perishing.

In what way is the success of these missionaries evidenced?
Thus: the converted nations hasten to take back to their homeland all the Jews whom they can find. And what a contrast do
we here note to the complete ignoring of the present journeyings
of those Jews who are returning in this day. The Scriptures are
quite silent about it, for at the present time the Gentiles are not
carrying them back in honor and affection at all; but rather
pushing them out as unwelcome guests, and often treating those
who will not go to bloody persecutions. We are told of the very

means of transport to be used, for so interested is Jehovah in what is then occurring, that every vehicle that carries one of His elect is noted by Him!

These missionaries are now preaching "the gospel of the kingdom" as foretold in Matt. 24: 14, and as commanded in Matt. 28: 19; and that, not the kingdom merely as at hand, nor in its present form of "mystery," with the King rejected and away; but with the King revealed and reigning in all the splendor of His manifested glory, and His presumptuous rival chained in the bottomless pit (Rev. 20). We can almost hear that saved remnant singing those psalms that have been composed especially for that very time, as for example:

> "O sing to Jehovah, sing a new song!
> Sing to Jehovah!   Sing all the earth!
> Sing to Jehovah, bless ever His name;
> Shew forth His salvation day after day;
> His glory declare among all the Gentiles,
> His wonders among all the peoples" (Ps. 96: 1-3).

This then shall be the joyous call of Israel to the Gentiles; and, in response, the Gentiles bring the scattered Israel to Jehovah, as the priests of the Sanctuary bring a "gift-offering;"*

---

*There are some who teach that a dispensation shall intervene between the reign of the Lord that we term The Millennium and Eternity. They think that the imperfect conditions that are evidenced during that thousand years, and so sadly and clearly are expressed at its end (Rev. 20), are quite inconsistent with such scriptures as Eph. 1: 10 and Phil. 2: 10, 11. I have not been able, with my present light, to share this conviction. There is so evidently a divinely intended correspondence between the experiences of man and those of his earth, that it would seem as if such a dispensation thus introduced would need a corresponding condition between our present state of regeneration — imperfect enough, alas, as we know it to be—and that eternal condition of perfection into which Scripture assures us that we shall be introduced at once at the coming of the Lord. The personal history of every redeemed child of man may be told in the three conditions: chaotic disorder, regeneration, and being made perfect. So with the earth, it is now in the first, chaotic enough; with Israel, all righteous, it will be regenerated; and then follows the perfection of eternity, with no intermission.

and Jehovah accepts those Gentiles in that way. He even takes some of them for priests and Levites, so that in that millennial day, even in the very temple in Jerusalem, will be found Gentiles serving as priests. That certainly forbids any continuance of the enmity between Jew and Gentile, since they are together in that holy service (verse 21). To restored Israel, eternal conditions are introduced at the very beginning of the reign of her Messiah; and yet, as with all prophetic scripture, this promise must find its place and be in harmony with all others. There shall be in one spot a "new earth," and above it a "new heaven," but that condition will only widen out to embrace the whole earth and the whole heaven at the *end* of the reign of a "thousand years," after the Devil has been loosed from his prison for a little season, and finds the smouldering hostility of many an unregenerate heart only waiting for his incitement to burst out into that last flame of rebellion that is finally met by "fire from heaven" (Rev. 20: 9). Then comes the final judgment of The Great White Throne. The old earth and its attendant heaven flee away, and no place is found for them; the "second death," the "Lake of Fire," receives those impenitent and proud, appointed alone by their own rejection of grace to that everlasting doom, and then, and not till then, do we hear the grand words: "Behold, I make all things new."

It would follow that this new creation is no more universal throughout the millennial reign, than "all things" are literally new even now for those who are in Christ. In the land of Israel, and in the heavens that canopy it, all is literally new and eternal; nor shall there ever be change there. Thus these prophetic Scriptures are seen to be in perfect harmony.

It is a beautiful and restful theme, even to us who are not the literal Israel, and we linger over its messages. For that people, have, as we again must say, ever afforded "types" for the heavenly or spiritual. Their Egypt is our state of nature, away from God and slaves to sin. Their Red Sea and the wild east-wind and the dark night, are our Calvary and the "storm that bowed that blessed Head." Their wilderness journey finds its clear counterpart in our spiritual journey to our Home above, which was their "land." But do the types end there? Israel, in her conflicts, failures, and periodic but short-lived revivals under the Judges, still affords just as clear types as those referred to. Then where shall that service that Israel renders to the heavenly people come to its end? Each age or dispensation is a prophecy of the one that succeeds it. Before our chapter closes we have in the last two verses an earthly scene that our Lord Himself specifically uses as a picture of an eternal one; the literal fire and worm of the one telling of spiritual counterparts in eternity.

Then we ask, Why should not the service of Israel be also a type of the service of the heavenly redeemed for eternity? Then, as the eternal doom of the impenitent is told in the literal fire and worm of lost Israel, so the ministry of the saved is prophetically told in the ministry of saved Israel!

The earthly people are sent to out-lying lands to whom the "report" had not come, to proclaim the glory of which they had not heard. That would then be a type of the ministry of us, His servants, who shall even in eternity serve Him (Rev. 22: 3) by proclaiming His glory, in the atoning work that He has accomplished. But where could that be, save to those star-worlds that have, as far as we know, no limitation in number, and each one having its spirit-ruler: the literal material host of Heaven thus having its counterpart in the heavenly host of spirit-principalities and powers, both being termed in Scripture the Host of Heaven, and in their infinity providing a field for unending ministry.

This is but a deduction, but it is a deduction based, and, it seems to me, firmly based on the Scriptures; for once admit that Israel's history is recorded, whether historically of events past, or prophetically of events future, to be "types for us on whom the ends of the ages are come" (1 Cor. 10), and the suggestion becomes almost, if not altogether, divine certainty. How different the stirring picture this gives of eternal occupation, from the imaginations that endeavor to fill eternity with nothing at all but singing! "At Thy right hand are pleasures for evermore." Note the plural, for there is not one kind of pleasure only, but such changes of unselfish occupations that forbid our thinking of heaven as a scene of unvarying repetition, precisely as made

Solomon utter his groan of "Vanity of vanities!" as he saw generations and constellations, winds and waters, all going in endless
unvarying circles; is that to be our heaven? Are we, as ages
pass, at last even there to cry, "Vanity of vanities?" No. A
thousand times, no. Solomon found no new thing under the sun;
we are to find all things new, and forever and constantly new,
"above the sun!" New scintillations of divine beauty, new visions
of divine Love in Jesus our Saviour, new worlds to which to
announce that glory! The active service of Israel on the earth
is but a picture of similar, although far more widespread, active
service of God's redeemed in the heavenlies; and we are plainly
told of the one that we may, by an inevitable deduction, know
of the other. Surely every little ray of light on our eternal home
and its occupations is to be welcomed with thanksgiving.

So our book closes, as does the whole volume of revelation,
with another scene. Zion is the joy of the whole earth; thither
all the nations go to worship, month by month and week by week,
for moons are still there to wax and wane, and sabbaths are again
to be kept. It is the marriage-time of Israel, and the waterpots
of Cana, those Jewish ordinances that have been so empty of life
because empty of Christ, now yield wine of the very best, for
Christ is seen in everything. The memories that the new moon
brings, awaken worship; not from Israel only, but from all mankind, for Israel's new moon has been "as life from the dead for
the whole world" (Rom. 11: 15). The sabbath is a delight, for
it is full of memories of that One on whom all now truly *rests*,
and in whom everything is "very good."

But there is another side to the picture. Greatly do they err
who conceive that either Israel in the Millennium or the universe
in eternity will show one side of God's nature only. He is not
only Love but Light; and not only His "goodness," but His
"severity"—solemn truth—will be expressed for ever (Rom. 11:
22). Thus none can live in vain. All are made to *serve!* We
may see the visitors to the splendid city, Jerusalem, walking out
of it to the valley of Hinnom, and as they look on the scene there
is no sympathy for those whose corpses are in that awful pyre.
"All flesh" is then and there in full accord with that divine

penalty, as it shall be in a wider sphere in the day of Rev. 20. Not a whisper shall be raised in all the universe challenging the perfect justice of God. All have at last reached their "own place," and even those who have maintained final impenitence, will at least be more in harmony with their environment than they would in the pure light of God's glory in heaven. The whole universe shall proclaim His glories, Love and Light.

Nor can I close without one word of thanksgiving to God for permitting a continuance of life sufficient to complete the task. I trust that it will not be without some blessing to its readers, as it certainly has not to the writer. To our God be humble praise from us both, and from all, through Jesus Christ our Lord, to all ages.   Amen.

# INDEX of SUBJECTS

# INDEX of SCRIPTURES